THE DEVIL AND KARL MARX

THE DEVIL AND KARL MARX

COMMUNISM'S LONG MARCH OF DEATH, DECEPTION, AND INFILTRATION

PAUL KENGOR, PHD

TAN BOOKS

GASTONIA, NORTH CAROLINA

Cover design by Caroline Green

Cover image: Karl Marx by Alevtina_Vyacheslav/Shutterstock

Library of Congress Control Number: 2020936885

ISBN: 978-1-5051-1444-7

Published in the United States by
TAN Books
PO Box 269
Gastonia, NC 28053
www.TANBooks.com

Printed in the United States of America

Take no part in the unfruitful works of darkness, but instead expose them. . . . For we are not contending against flesh and blood, but against the principalities, against the powers, against the world rulers of this present darkness, against the spiritual hosts of wickedness in the heavenly places.

Ephesians 5:11; 6:12

"Thus Heaven I've forfeited,
I know it full well.
My soul, once true to God,
Is chosen for Hell."

—*Karl Marx, "The Pale Maiden," 1837*

"Look now, my blood-dark sword shall stab
Unerringly within thy soul. . . .
The hellish vapors rise and fill the brain,
Till I go mad and my heart is utterly changed.
See the sword—the Prince of Darkness sold it to me.
For he beats the time and gives the signs.
Ever more boldly I play the dance of death."

—*Karl Marx, "The Player," 1841*

CONTENTS

FOREWORD

Ronald Reagan described a communist as one who reads Karl Marx and an anti-communist as one who understands Karl Marx. Pithy and true, at least at the time, but conservatives in the decades since Reagan won the Cold War have begun to forget just what makes Marxism so wrong, and their failure to articulate Marx's fatal flaw has left an entire generation prey to the deadliest ideology in history, imperiling not only minds but also souls.

The majority of young Americans today hold a favorable view of socialism, according to a 2018 Gallup poll. Socialism is on the rise more than three decades after conservatives thought it had died in the rubble of the Berlin Wall. In just the past few years, admitted social-ists have won elected office throughout the country, from the local to the national level. They have succeeded because, while conservatives have blabbered themselves hoarse denouncing the economic effects of socialism, they have ignored the deeper spiritual questions that actually move men's souls. That is why this book could not be pub-lished at a more opportune time.

Karl Marx envisioned a merely material world in which religion is "the opium of the people" and nothing matters but matter. Rather than question this false vision—indeed, our ability to question any-thing at all dispels it—many conservatives have contented themselves to debate Marx on his own materialist terms. "Socialism destroys economies," they observe. Then, "Socialism distorts markets." And finally, "Socialism just doesn't work."

But whether or not a political system "works" depends on what it's working toward. Socialism strives to tear down traditional society.

At that task, socialism has succeeded everywhere it has been tried, at least for a time. The problem with socialism isn't the inefficiency; it's the evil. Marx did not set out to tinker with markets and redistribute some wealth. He sought to radically transform society by changing human nature. He hated religion because he opposed God, the author of human nature. He sided with Satan, as he confessed in letters and ghoulish poetry quoted in these pages. Ex-communists such as Arthur Koestler and Richard Wright came to call Marxism "the god that failed." Karl Marx erred not through mere miscalculation but through sin and heresy.

Unfortunately, the same softening on Marxism that took place in the realm of politics infected the Church as well, at times through misunderstanding and at others through outright infiltration. The Church has condemned Marxism since the mid-nineteenth century. Yet in 2019 the leading Jesuit periodical in the United States published "The Catholic Case for Communism." Around the same time, the Holy Father made common cause with communists, according to the left-wing Italian newspaper *La Repubblica*. "If anything," Pope Francis reportedly told the paper's founder Eugenio Scalfari, "it is the communists who think like Christians." One wonders if Karl Marx could hear the Pope's compliment amid the wailing and gnashing of teeth in Marx's eternal abode.

Still, Pope Francis has refused to count himself among Marx's followers. "Marxist ideology is wrong," he affirmed flatly in 2013. Francis's predecessors spoke even more forcefully against communism in years past. "Religious socialism, Christian socialism, are contradictory terms; no one can be at the same time a good Catholic and a true socialist," declared Pope Pius XI, who considered socialism "irreconcilable with Christianity." His predecessor Pope Leo XIII condemned socialists as "a wicked confederacy," "a pest," a plague," "a hideous monster . . . that threatens civil society with destruction," and "an evil growth" that attempts to "steal the very Gospel itself with a view to deceive more easily the unwary." Bl. Pope Pius IX, writing even before Marx, decried communism and socialism with the same vigor.

Communists read Marx, anti-communists understand Marx, and no one understands Marx better than Paul Kengor. His was the unhappy task of wading through such diabolically inspired drivel, and for that we owe him a debt of gratitude. Kengor knows, like few others writing today, that terms such as "collectivism" and "individualism" only take the debate so far. Quibbles over marginal tax rates have never inspired a soul, least of all Karl Marx. Ultimately the fight comes down to spiritual warfare: good versus evil.

In his most famous Cold War speech, Ronald Reagan, quoting Winston Churchill, warned, "The destiny of man is not measured by material computations. When great forces are on the move in the world, we learn we're spirits, not animals." And spirits must choose a side.

Euphoria at the fall of the Berlin Wall made utopians of otherwise hard-nosed conservatives, who declared "the end of history as such," ironically echoing the grandiose rhetoric and barmy theories of the ideologue they claimed to have defeated. But history did not end. If anything, it has begun to repeat itself, "first as tragedy, then as farce," just as Marx predicted in *The Eighteenth Brumaire of Louis Napoleon*. The Evil Empire collapsed, but evil spirits continue to prowl about the earth seeking the ruin of souls because we contend in the end not against flesh and blood but "against the spirits of wickedness in the high places," which will endure until the end of the world. In the meantime, we must know our enemy. In *The Devil and Karl Marx*, Paul Kengor masterfully helps us to do so.

Michael Knowles
Los Angeles, CA

NOTES ON STYLE

Style guides differ on the usage of upper- or lowercase for the word "communist." Some use exclusively uppercase (a bad choice). This book uses uppercase if describing a person who was a formal member of the Communist Party vs. lowercase for someone who was a communist ideologically but not a party member. The distinction is very important. Everyone throughout the history of the communist movement knows that an uppercase "Communist" is a major distinction from a lowercase "communist." The vast majority of communists ideologically refused to go so far as to join the Communist Party and become uppercase "Communists" because doing so required them to take a formal sworn loyalty oath to Stalin's USSR, to the Kremlin, to the Soviet Comintern, and to Communist Party USA. They were unwilling to do that. Those Communists who did swear the oath took a huge step beyond those communists who refused to take the leap. (Public education pioneer John Dewey, to cite just one example, objected to "Communism, official Communism, spelt with a capital letter." He had been a lowercase communist.) Thus, regardless of what rigid style guidelines might demand, we must be careful to make this crucial distinction. Likewise, this book employs an uppercase P for "Communist Party" (and a lowercase p when "party" is alone).

"THE DANCE OF DEATH"

THE COMMUNIST KILLING MACHINE

The purpose of a preface is to briefly set the table for what is to follow. In a book on the evil that is communism, that is a tall order. The blood banquet that is communist ideology could not be sufficiently laid out in a vast hall of volumes let alone a mere preface. To adequately convey the array of victims of communism is humanly impossible. I will restrict these opening observations to a few pages sketching only generally "the dance of death" (to borrow from Marx's strange poetry) orchestrated by the handmaidens of this killer ideology.

It is important to start with a presentation of the numbers—the estimated number of victims. They speak for themselves—that is, for communism. Any ideology with a trail of rot like this is not of God but of the forces against God. It is not of God's creation but a fallen angel's anti-creation. It is not of the light but of the dark.

No other political ideology has produced as much wretched poverty, rank repression, and sheer violence. In country after country, implemented in varying forms across wide-ranging nationalities, traditions, backgrounds, faiths, and ethnicities, communism coldly and consistently violated the full sweep of most basic human rights, from property to press, from speech to assembly, from conscience to religion. So restrictive was communism in the twentieth century that its implementers routinely refused to allow citizens the right to exit (that is, escape) the destructive systems imposed within their borders.

In some cases, they erected walls to herd and fence in the "masses" they claimed to champion.

That bears repeating: so restrictive was communism that its advocates had to build walls—poured with cement, topped with barbed wire, patrolled 24/7 by secret police with automatic weapons turned on their own citizenry—to keep their people from fleeing. The ultimate symbols of that repression were the Berlin Wall and the frozen people-zoo that was the Soviet Gulag. Even then, those are just two symbols of the repression. We could point to so many more: the killing fields of Cambodia, Romania's Pitesti prison, the NKVD's Lubyanka basement, Fidel's and Che's La Cabana execution house, and modern concentration camps such as North Korea's Camp 22 or China's Laogai. Where to start, where to end?

Communism's most successful form of redistribution was not wealth, which the ridiculous system fails to produce, but government-orchestrated crime. Everything was so nationalized and so centralized that it was as if the government seized crime too. And really, there were few more proficient political gangsters than communist leaders. Al Capone looks like Mister Rogers compared to a Pol Pot or Nicolai Ceausescu. It is no exaggeration to say that a Jeffrey Dahmer or Jack the Ripper could not begin to compare to a Felix Zherzhinsky or serial rapist Lavrenti Beria in sheer scale of victims. Not even close.

Communism committed a "multitude of crimes not only against individual human beings but also against world civilization and national cultures," wrote Stephane Courtois, editor of the classic Harvard University Press work *The Black Book of Communism*. "Communist regimes turned mass crime into a full-blown system of government."[1]

In both theoretical and practical form, communism deprives individuals of their unalienable rights. It is a totalitarian, atheistic ideology. Communism's chief form of redistribution is repression, crime, and murder.

Under communism, there was no profession of self-evident,

inherent "unalienable" rights—that is, absolute rights endowed by the Creator to humans to begin with, and thus protected by a just government. Governments were not "instituted among men" to help secure such rights, as Thomas Jefferson put it. No, communist governments took away those rights, depriving them, robbing them, absconding with them, in the name of a totalitarian system that, at some point, promised to usher in utopia.

"Communist regimes did not just commit criminal acts," observed Martin Malia, a Harvard PhD and professor at the University of California-Berkeley, noting that there have been non-communist states that likewise committed criminal acts, "but they were criminal enterprises in their very essence: on principle, so to speak, they all ruled lawlessly, by violence, and without regard for human life."[2]

The communist culture of death has been prolific. Whether by bullet, by starvation, by exposure to the elements, by war and terror against internal citizens and "enemies" of the state, or by whatever means. How many victims? Truly only God knows.

In 1999, *The Black Book of Communism* endeavored to attempt the impossible task of tabulating a Marxist-Leninist death toll in the twentieth century. It came up with a figure approaching 100 million.[3] Here is the breakdown:

- USSR: 20 million deaths
- China: 65 million deaths
- Vietnam: 1 million deaths
- North Korea: 2 million deaths
- Cambodia: 2 million deaths
- Eastern Europe: 1 million deaths
- Latin America: 150,000 deaths
- Africa: 1.7 million deaths
- Afghanistan: 1.5 million deaths
- The international communist movement and Communist parties not in power: about 10,000 deaths

The Victims of Communism Memorial Foundation, the preeminent US-based center for detailing communist crimes, cites the figure of 100 million deaths.[4] Numerous others agree and could be listed here. Dr. Malia aptly noted that the communist record offers the "most colossal case of political carnage in history."[5]

And even then, here is something still more shocking: These frightening numbers are quite conservative.

Take the figure relating to the Soviet Union, where the *Black Book* recorded *merely* 20 million dead.[6] Alexander Yakovlev, a high-level Soviet official who became one of Mikhail Gorbachev's chief reformers, and who, in the 1990s, was given the official task of trying to add up the victims, estimates that Stalin alone "annihilated . . . sixty to seventy million people." His figures are consistent with those long estimated by the likes of Nobel dissident Alexander Solzhenitsyn, among others.[7]

Most accounts of the overall Soviet death toll (Stalin plus other leaders) exceed 33 million, some twice that. Cold War historian Dr. Lee Edwards, citing the epic work on "democide" by political scientist R. J. Rummel,[8] as well as the research of Solzhenitsyn, of the great Soviet scholar Robert Conquest, and of still others, estimates that Soviet governments were responsible for the death of 61.9 million of their own from 1917 to 1987.[9] And yet, the Bolsheviks would be matched if not outdone by China's Mao Zedong, who, by numerous estimates, was responsible for the deaths of at least 60 million in China, and more likely over 70 million, according to the latest biographical-historical research.[10] And then there were the killing fields of North Korea, Cambodia, Cuba, Ethiopia, Eastern Europe, Africa, and more. Among them, North Korea's pile of body bags unquestionably stack higher than the two million listed in the *Black Book*'s bullet points.[11]

Really, the death generated by communist governments in the twentieth century, and, primarily, in a more concentrated period from roughly 1917 to 1979, is surely closer to 140 million.

This would equate to a rate of multiple thousands dead per day over the course of a century. Even Adolph Hitler got nowhere close to that. In fact, neither did the two deadliest wars in history, World Wars I and II, which need to be combined and doubled to get near communism's butcher's bill. The highest estimates of the death produced during the entirety of the Spanish Inquisition (a period of some sixty years) come nowhere near the level of death in Stalin's military purge or even Lenin's first year in power.[12]

Anonymous wise-guys randomly surfacing and disappearing on the internet (many of them Millennials born after the fall of the Berlin Wall) emerge to dispute or nit-pick these numbers. Fine. Go for it, guys. Again, truly only God knows the real number. The devil might know too. Besides, the devil is in the details.

This much we do know beyond dispute: this was and remains a lethal ideology of boundless destruction and stupidity. One needs to think of viruses, bacteria, plagues, disease, to approximate this level of man-made death. Even then, a malicious modern virus such as COVID-19, which placed a world on lockdown in the year 2020, comes nowhere close to communism's fatality rate. "Mankind has survived all manner of evil diseases and plagues," said Ronald Reagan, "but can it survive Communism?" Reagan called communism a "vicious" "disease." For good measure, he added that "Communism is neither an economic or a political system—it is a form of insanity."[13]

What sort of warped idea could unleash such agony? Conventional explanations simply do not suffice. The fullest answer resides in the realm of the spirit, a spiritual explanation. The dogged, hell-bent pursuit by many of such a perverse ideology—immediately evident as idiotic and unworkable from a cursory skim of the *Communist Manifesto*—is an utter mystery not explainable by mere rational understanding. This was and is, flatly, a diabolical ideology, with an inexplicable attraction to its adherents. It possesses a bizarre seductive quality to its ideological cultists.

And yet—and yet—those same cult-like adherents denounce

religion as the "opiate of the masses." They have denounced it with a passionate hatred.

This book deals with the grim, disturbing, militant atheism and intense anti-religious elements of Marx and other founders and practitioners of communism. It is not a full-blown biography of Karl Marx, though it is partly a spiritual biography of the man (covered at length in parts 1 and 2).[14] It contains many pages on his views on religion and, even, his words on the devil. This book tackles Marx spiritually but ultimately goes well beyond that to the wider matter of his communism and its various manifestations. This book might be better called *The Devil and Communism*; still, the literal manifesto began with Marx (and Engels), and Marx had things to say about the devil—things not pretty. The book starts with Marx, with the other communist disciples following. Many of these men were messing with some nasty stuff. This was not a routine atheism.

For the record, I will state upfront that I have not encountered nor do I present evidence of Karl Marx, say, conducting seances or engaging in black Masses or Satanic rituals, even as other writers on Marx have speculated on that stark possibility.[15] Regardless, there was a fanatically deep hatred of religion and flirtation with the dark side that is undeniable and chilling, especially in Marx's poetry. It also gives pause, as we shall see in these pages, to repeatedly encounter in the life of Marx family members and close friends referring to him with words like "governed by a demon" (his father), "my dear devil" (his son),[16] "monster of ten thousand devils" (Engels), "wicked knave" (his wife), or the striking number of intimates and associates who did not hesitate to compare him to *Faust* or Mephistopheles, or use words like "possessed" to describe his demeanor, and on and on. One friend, journalist Karl Heinzen, was not unique among contemporaries and biographers who observed or recorded Marx shouting or "chanting the words from *Faust*," and described him as "mocking," trying to take under a "spell," and possessing eyes "like a wet goblin." To be sure, this is very much a short list, and some of these were likely in jest or expressed with a weird playfulness, though that is not always entirely clear.[17] The frequency of such observations of and by Marx really is quite bracing and far too frequent to shrug off. Readers will see that there are way too many of these to blithely ignore. And no figure that I have ever studied or pursued in a biography was described in language like this.[18] I am sure that every biographer reading this now (other than those of Marx) will nod in agreement.

"There were times when Marx seemed to be possessed by demons," recorded Robert Payne in his chapter "The Demons," in his groundbreaking, seminal 1968 biography of Marx. A prolific academic biographer of Marx, and a respected scholar and academic not expected to level such a shocking charge lightly, Payne asserted of Marx, "He had the devil's view of the world, and the devil's malignity. Sometimes he seemed to know that he was accomplishing works of evil."[19]

How evil? Well, I certainly have no proof that Karl Marx was a Satanist, nor can I can confirm whether he was possessed. I would not dare hazard such a charge. I can affirm that he was an atheist. That is easy. No one denies that. Marx did not deny that. Some will say that an atheist would not be a Satanist because of an atheist's non-belief in the supernatural. More likely, what some mean to say or would like to say about Marx is that he was an atheist doing the work of the devil, whether he was fully cognizant of it or not. Some would be more inclined to say that Marx was possessed rather than a Satanist, as Payne even speculates. Perhaps. Again, these are things I cannot venture to attempt to authenticate.

And again, what is undeniable is the evil associated with and wrought by Marxist-communist ideology. It is a malignant track record that could only please the denizens of a darker world.

Most sentient human beings have at least a flickering notion of the immense suffering caused by communist ideology in the aftermath of Marx's *Communist Manifesto* penned two centuries ago. Far too many people, however, separate Marx the man from the evils ushered in by Marxism. That is a grave mistake. Not only are the results of

Marxism very much the result of Marx's ideas and his very pen, but Marx himself penned some downright devilish things. Karl Marx wrote not only about the hell that was communism but about hell itself. In some such cases, Marx portrayed himself as chosen for hell, or chose hell for himself; in still other cases, he, in the role of the master of hell, consigned others to it.

"Thus Heaven I've forfeited, I know it full well," wrote Marx in an 1837 poem, one of many explored at length in the pages ahead. "My soul, once true to God, is chosen for Hell." That certainly seemed the perverse destiny for Marx's ideology. That statement also seems at least partly autobiographical, given that Marx, once a believer, once a Christian, had once been true to God. In another poem, Marx wrote, "The hellish vapors rise and fill the brain, Till I go mad and my heart is utterly changed. See the sword—the Prince of Darkness sold it to me." Here, too, seems an ironic metaphor for the bloody sword of communist ideology, surely favored if not wielded by the Prince of Darkness. And it, too, seems partly autobiographical, given how Marx's own heart had been utterly changed.

Alas, this book offers a close, careful look at the genuinely hellacious side of the ideology of Marx, of Engels, of Lenin, of Stalin, of Mao, of Pol Pot, of Fidel Castro—of communism. In part, it is a tragic portrait of a man but, still more broadly so, an ideology, a chilling retrospective on an unclean spirit that should have never been let out of its pit.

We see here in this book a long march of destruction, deceit, manipulation, and infiltration. It does not stop with Karl Marx, who was only the beginning. It merely starts with Marx. He was the launching point for an assault on religion that eventually included a penetration of churches worldwide and possibly even seminaries, including within the Catholic Church, and most certainly within Protestant denominations. That infiltration had terrible success in communist countries, of course, but its tentacles also reached into free nations, including the United States of America.

"You may be interested in knowing that we have preachers, preachers active in churches, who are members of the Communist Party," candidly admitted Earl Browder, general secretary of Communist Party USA, to students at Union Theological Seminary on February 15, 1935.[20] He and his party initiated an aggressive push to create a "united front" led by communists and socialists attracting a broader coalition of liberals and fellow travelers. The goal was to expand the party's support, its membership base, and above all its agenda, which was always an agenda that saw religion as a menace. Nonetheless, communists and socialists would happily accept the support of the gullible religious left, knowing that they had many sympathizers in the mainline Protestant churches in particular, especially among certain clergy. Browder boasted that he and his comrades "could recite a thousand local examples of the successful application of the united front tactic, initiated by the Communist Party," looking for "new recruits" to spread this united front "throughout the country and among all strata of the population."[21]

This included recruitment among the religious and flat-out infiltration of churches. Communists would even seek out Catholics— their hardest nut to crack because of the intense, institutionalized, vehemently anti-communist counterforce of the universal Roman Catholic Church anchored at the Vatican. Browder warmly albeit deceptively offered, "We extend the hand of fellowship to our Catholic brothers."

One of Browder's erstwhile buddies, ex-communist J. B. Matthews, who had spearheaded the "united front" strategy, noted that, consistent with the party's and Moscow's and Lenin's "communist code of ethics," religion was to be exploited for advancement of the revolution, even if that involved blatant deception. "It is not surprising to find the Communist Party in the United States engaged in a systematic effort to lure the churches," averred Matthews, "especially the Catholic Church, into the net of the party's united fronts." And though Matthews here singled out the Catholic Church, the communist efforts were far more vigorous and successful in Protestant churches. The Catholic Church was protected and preserved by leadership in Rome and savvy clergy at home, from the likes of Popes Pius XI and Pius XII to Fulton Sheen and Cardinal Spellman, among so many others. But that does not mean that all was kept pure and untouched and unscathed. The smoke of Satan, to borrow from Pope Paul VI, did manage to seep under cathedral doors. Nonetheless, whatever the level of infiltration, Catholics and Protestants alike were in communist crosshairs, as were Jews, Muslims, Buddhists, and so many other believers. Communists sowed the seeds deep and wide, and the harvest was harsh, with bitter fruits that would grow throughout the remainder of the twentieth century, and continue today. Many of today's naively self-described socialists and "democratic socialists" have no idea of the rancid roots of this poisoned tree.

Drawing on documents that have been archived or shelved for decades, some of them being published or quoted at length here for the first time, what is included in this book will shock readers but also alert them to a destructive force not merely historical and ideological but spiritual and diabolical. Remarks like these from Browder and Matthews and Marx are just the tip of the Siberian iceberg. Many such alarming words will be shared here from Soviet Comintern archives, from Communist Party USA documents, from sworn testimony by ex-communist leaders, from a disquieting assortment of minions and pagans and weirdos and radicals, and still more.

Readers no doubt will be taken aback by the devil in the details.

PART I

THE SPECTER

CHAPTER 1

"A SPECTER IS HAUNTING EUROPE"

THE UNCLEAN SPIRIT OF COMMUNISM

The opening lines of the *Communist Manifesto* could not have been more eerily apt: "A specter is haunting Europe—the specter of communism," wrote Karl Marx and Friedrich Engels in 1848. "All the powers of old Europe have entered into a holy alliance to exorcise this specter: Pope and Tsar, Metternich and Guizot, French Radicals and German police-spies."

Marx and Engels opted for such words: a specter, a *haunting* specter—a specter haunting Europe. Marx and Engels further opted for the word "exorcise"—the process for expunging a demon. Jesus Christ expelled demons. The Roman Catholic Church has long had a Rite of Exorcism for ridding people of demonic infestation. The very first image chosen by Marx and Engels to describe their ideology in the opening line of their book seems quite telling if not chilling. Whether it was serious or sarcastic, perhaps tongue in cheek (Marx had a mordant sense of humor), it was nonetheless fitting, and prophetic. They were on to something, or something was on to them and their ideology. If ever a force could be described as a haunting specter in dire need of exorcism, the phantom unleashed by Karl Marx and Friedrich Engels fit the bill.

The two could not have conjured up a better description of what would play out in the course of history.

Marx and Engels correctly noted that all the powers of Europe were allied against this phantom or, that is, had "entered into a holy alliance to exorcise this spectre." They named great statesmen like Klemens Von Metternich as well as authorities such as German police-spies (who actually had Marx under surveillance). They singled out the pope. They pointed to the Russian czar, one of which three decades earlier had called for a Holy Alliance at the Congress of Vienna. Scarcely could Czar Alexander have foreseen the infernal beast that would devour his beloved Russia a century later. The pope of the day, Pius IX, actually had foreseen it.

And why wouldn't the powers of Europe desire a holy alliance against this specter? They all recognized that an unholy spirit dwelled within their midst. Here in this chapter, we will take our first look at the contours of that specter and of the man who summoned it.

Communist Catechism

Marx and Engels viewed the initial draft of their manifesto as a revolutionary "catechism" for an awaiting world. More than that, they saw it and referred to it, certainly in the initial draft stage, as a literal *Communist Confession of Faith*, before opting for the title that stuck. "Think over the Confession of Faith a bit," Engels wrote to Marx in November 1847. "I believe we had better drop the catechism form and call the thing: *Communist Manifesto*."[22]

Even then, the document was, for these proud atheists, very much a catechetical confession of faith for communists. Their communism became their religion, even as they scoffed at religion as something for superstitious idiots. Truly, their manifesto was and became their catechism—their bible.

At a more material level, one might better accuse communists of fashioning a golden calf than channeling an unclean spirit. What communists effectively bowed down to was just that: a material idol forged and focused on money, property, gold. It was not about the soul. The key to the communist-Marxist utopia would be economics. Solve the economic problem, the communists believed, and you would solve the human problem.

Why such an economic goal was ever perceived by any group as the pinnacle of human development is a darned good question. To most people, economics and class simply are not that monumentally important. Sure, a roof over one's head and food and financial security are obviously important, especially for those lacking basic necessities; no one denies that. Still, for most individuals, economics is not the centerpiece of existence. To communists and many socialists, however, this is the alpha and omega. They speak as if man truly does live by bread alone; if society resolves, say, "economic inequality," levels all incomes to the same dollar number, or more fully redistributes wealth, then something closer to heaven on earth can follow. As Pope Benedict XVI said, the fatal flaw of communists and socialists is that they had their anthropology wrong. They did not adequately understand man. As Augustine said, we all have a *God*-shaped vacuum that God alone can fill; not a dollar-signed vacuum. We crave the divine manna of heaven.

Atheist communists and socialists have always mistakenly felt that the answers to man's miseries are found not in God (the existence of which they deny) but in economic materialism. It is so ironic that communists and socialists blast the wealthy for being allegedly obsessed with money and material things when, in fact, communists and socialists are obsessed with money and material things. But as most rich people learn, money does not buy happiness. Humans desire more than that. How profound that Jesus told Satan that man does not live on bread alone. As the two debated, the Living Bread told the tempter that man lives by every word from the mouth of God. Marx took not the side of Christ on that one. Of course, Marx rejected Christ in total. Communists are atheists after all.

Communists are also, curiously, utopians—*secular* utopians. They sought a heaven on earth—for them, an earth without religion. They did so without realizing that utopia is not only elusive but such a literal self-contradiction that it does not exist. The Greek roots of the word are *ou topos*, or "no place." In other words, there is no utopia, at least not in this world and realm. And yet, communists would pursue this *no place* with religious-like zeal.

In his classic *Private Property and Communism* (1844), Marx grandiosely exclaimed that "Communism is the riddle of history solved, and it knows itself to be this solution."[23] Few ideologies, or ideologues, have been so boastful. In his *German Ideology* (1845), Marx fantasized, "In communist society, where nobody has one exclusive sphere of activity but each can become accomplished in any branch he wishes, society regulates the general production and thus makes it possible for me to do one thing today and another tomorrow, to hunt in the morning, fish in the afternoon, rear cattle in the evening, criticize after dinner, just as I have a mind, without ever becoming hunter, fisherman, herdsman or critic."[24]

That is a picture of utopia. And the *Manifesto* was a utopian treatise. Marx and Engels published their *Communist Manifesto* in 1848 as the official programmatic statement of the Communist Party (or Communist League) outlining exactly what communists believed and planned to pursue. That is what the *Communist Manifesto* really was—namely, a manifesto for the party which, at that point, had lacked a single written statement laying out communist beliefs.

Notably, usage of the word "communism" preceded the *Communist Manifesto*, as Marx and Engels were able to refer to it in the book as something that already existed (though not by long) and was known to certain people. It is possible that they coined the term themselves in Paris a few years before the publication of their *Manifesto*, but pinning that down is elusive; they certainly, however, popularized the term. Quite fittingly, Marx and Engels met in August 1844 in the left-wing looney bin that was and is Paris, where Marx a year earlier had already moved with his wife and begun studying the

French Revolution and various utopian socialists, while attending workers' meetings and engaging in other fanciful leftist functions.[25]

Marx envisioned an apocalyptic revolution leading to the overthrow of capitalism by the impoverished working class, the common people, the masses—the so-called "proletariat." The stage in the revolutionary process immediately following this overthrow would be that of the Dictatorship of the Proletariat. That "dictatorship" would be a waystation on the road to the ultimate utopian goal of a "classless society." The state, in the process, would be abolished; it would die out; it would "wither away." With a classless society, class antagonisms would hence disappear, as would conflict (including armed conflict), as would economic inequality, as would social inequality, and peace and harmony would follow. Society would evolve through dialectical stages: from feudalism to capitalism to socialism to communism.

Note that final transition: from socialism to communism. When asked to define the difference between socialism and communism, Marion Smith, director of the Victims of Communism Memorial Foundation, likes to say that Christians go to heaven, whereas socialists go to communism. That is indeed the transitionary process, and Smith's language is apt, given that the communist views full communism as a sort of New Jerusalem. The atheistic communist, whether realizing it or not, subscribes or aspires to a messianic vision.

Moreover, Marx and Engels insisted, this wondrous socialism would need to sweep the planet in order to work. It had to be worldwide. That was the plan, and that is no small thing. Nonetheless, Marx and Engels, and then Lenin and Stalin and a train of others still to this day, felt it could happen. It was the ultimate utopian pipedream.

And yet, the plan was not so dreamy as to lack any specificity. To the contrary, Marx and Engel had a ten-point plan. Here it is, taken verbatim from their manifesto:

1. Abolition of property in land and application of all rents of

land to public purposes.

2. A heavy progressive or graduated income tax.
3. Abolition of all right of inheritance.
4. Confiscation of all property of emigrants and rebels.
5. Centralization of credit in the hands of the state, by means of a national bank with state capital and an exclusive monopoly.
6. Centralization of the means of communication and transport in the hands of the state.
7. Extension of factories and instruments of production owned by the state; the bringing into cultivation of waste lands, and the improvement of the soil generally in accordance with a common plan.
8. Equal obligation of all to work. . . .
9. . . . gradual abolition of all the distinction between town and country by a more equitable distribution of the population over the country.
10. Free education for all children in public schools.

Marx and Engels demanded that such a ten-point program be implemented not merely in one nation but throughout all nations of the world. Many subsequent socialists, beginning with Vladimir Lenin and his Bolsheviks in 1917, worked from that blueprint.

Of course, Marx and Lenin and the boys knew that terror would be necessary to implement such a truly radical, totalitarian ideology. After all, their philosophy demanded an unequivocal rejection of most basic rights, including property. Stated Marx, "The theory of the Communists may be summed up in the single sentence: Abolition of private property."

Many Marxists and socialists and "democratic socialists" today fuss over the extent to which Marx wanted to remove or limit property, but in the *Manifesto*, he (and Engels) doubled down. "You are horrified at our intending to do away with private property," they wrote. "But in your existing society, private property is already done away with for nine-tenths of the population." And then this: "In one word, you reproach us with intending to do away with your property. Precisely so; that is just what we intend."

That is truly radical, revolutionary. It constitutes nothing less than a fundamental transformation of human nature.

The rejection of such a natural if not sacred right violates the most basic precepts of all peoples, from the cave to the courthouse, from Judeo-Christian thinking to the most innate urges of primitive tribes. God's commandment *Thou shalt not steal* implies a right to property. Marx was not oblivious to just how radical his vision was. He himself acknowledged that his views stood undeniably contrary to the "social and political order of things." Communism, he and Engels wrote in their *Manifesto*, not only seeks to "abolish the present state of things" but represents "the most radical rupture in traditional relations." They knew what they were advocating; this was a revolution, touching on everything from property to the family. "Abolition of the family!" they wrote with an exclamation. "Even the most radical flare up at this infamous proposal of the communists."[26]

Again, look at just a few of the specific policy recommendations in the ten-point plan of the *Manifesto*, which included "abolition of property in land" (point 1), "a heavy progressive or graduated income tax" (point 2), "abolition of all right of inheritance" (point 3), "centralization of credit in the hands of the state, by means of a national bank with state capital and an exclusive monopoly" (point 5), "centralization of the means of communication and transport in the hands of the state" (point 6), and a breathtaking call for "gradual abolition of all the distinction between town and country by a more equitable distribution of the population over the country" (point 9). Chew that one over: Marx and Engels and friends wanted to distribute not only your property but you yourself.

If that is not a ready-made recipe for coercion and despotism, then what is?

Indeed, Marx and Engels willingly conceded that this program would require despotism. They stated of their ten points, "Of course, in the beginning, this cannot be effected except by means of despotic inroads."

Of course, it cannot. Human beings would not give up such fundamental liberties without resistance. Seizing property alone would require a terrible fight, prompting implementers to use their guns and gulags. This is a vision that necessitates prison camps.

Lenin, Trotsky, Stalin, and a long line of implementers candidly admitted that force and violence would be necessary. In the close of the *Manifesto*, Marx said, "The Communists . . . openly declare that their ends can be attained only by the *forcible overthrow* of all existing social conditions" (italics added).

How could it not? How could this not lead to bloodshed, even terror? It would, and with no excuses before, during, or after.

"We have no compassion and we ask no compassion from you," Marx wrote in May 1849. "When our turn comes, we shall not make excuses for the terror." Marx added, "There is only one way in which the murderous death agonies of the old society and the bloody birth throes of the new society can be shortened, simplified and concentrated, and that way is revolutionary terror."[27]

He stated emphatically that "Socialism cannot be brought into existence without revolution."[28]

Pierre-Joseph Proudhon, the French socialist, prophetically saw where Marx and his ideas would lead. He viewed Marx as intellectually merciless, pitiless, as the "exterminator" who was perfectly prepared to let Europe drown in blood if such was what was required for his cherished theories to be vindicated. And true to his personality, Marx would denounce Proudhon as an idiot worthy of towering disdain and of being crushed.[29]

Again, violence would be necessary.

To borrow from Leon Trotsky, communist revolutionaries would not arrive at the kingdom of socialism on a polished floor with white gloves. Blood would need to be spilled. The blood of innocents would consecrate the communist ground.

Vladimir Lenin saw his Bolsheviks as "glorious" Jacobins—the sick, depraved killers who guillotined some forty thousand people in France in one year in the late eighteenth century. He compared his Bolshevik faction of his Russian Social-Democratic Labor Party to Jacobins, or, as Soviet Comintern head Grigori Zinoviev put it, "the most glorious of the Jacobins of the time of the Great French Revolution."[30] Lenin loved the Jacobins. He praised the "great, ineradicable, unforgettable things provided by the Jacobins in the eighteenth century," and claimed that "the Jacobins gave France the best models of a democratic revolution."[31]

Lenin, too, knew implicitly that violence would be necessary. "The truth," explained Lenin, a moral relativist who saw himself as supreme gatekeeper of Marxist doctrine, "is that no revolution can be successful unless the resistance of the exploiters is crushed." A few months later, in November 1918, Lenin warned that "Anglo-French and American imperialism will inevitably strangle the independence and freedom of Russia unless world-wide socialist revolution, unless world-wide Bolshevism, conquers."[32]

As this suggests, Lenin also simultaneously expressed a favorable view of war. "To reject war in principle is un-Marxist," he wrote in July 1914, knowing full well that Marx himself said the same. Averred Lenin, "Who objectively stands to gain from the slogan 'Peace?' In any case, not the revolutionary proletariat." He reaffirmed this one year later, in July 1915: "We cannot support the slogan 'Peace' since it is a totally muddled one and a hindrance to the revolutionary struggle."[33]

I will have much more to say about Lenin and the Bolsheviks later. For now, it should be clearly understood early on that they, in the spirit of Marx, would not make any excuses for the terror they would pursue as they harnessed the specter of communism.

Marx and Hegel

Sticking with communism's launch at this stage in this book, it is helpful to understand Marx's view of the so-called "dialectic" of history, which he took up at the University of Berlin as a student. This was the philosophy of Georg Wilhelm Friedrich Hegel, which taught that history is a series of struggles between opposing forces, with each successive struggle unfolding on a progressively higher plane than the one that preceded it. Ultimately, according to Hegel, human history is a dialectical unfolding of the truth—that is, "Truth" itself. Hegel was a Christian.[34] As one Hegel scholar wrote, this "dialectical unfolding ends in the revelation of God."[35] Marx himself even referred to Hegel as "a theologian."[36]

Hegel envisioned a different plane for the struggle than Marx did—one based on ideas. Hegel's was an "ideational dialectic." Marx's plane was not one based on the battle of ideas—the so-called "ideational plane" of Hegel—but one based on economics and classes and materialism. It was a dialectical materialism.

Though Hegel deeply impacted Marx, unpacking Hegel is not easy. While doing so fully is beyond the scope of this book, it should be noted that there have long existed "Right-Hegelians" and "Left-Hegelians," especially in the German-speaking world. The Hegelians on the right, in the day, defended the Prussian monarchy, Lutheran Christianity, and private property, whereas the Hegelians on the left defended *democracy*, atheism, and socialism.[37] As noted by Grant Havers, philosophy professor at Trinity Western University, the Left-Hegelians have certainly been more successful in defining, if not appropriating, Hegel's name and legacy, to the point that Hegel today is seen by most as a man of the left. His most famous appropriators included Marx, Ludwig Feuerbach, and Bruno Bauer.[38]

Havers notes that Hegel "declares that religion is for all human beings." Or, as another source put it, for Hegel, religion, together with philosophy, was the "highest form" of a person's spiritual life.[39]

The "conservative Hegel," some scholars believe, "insists on the necessity of Christianity because he rejects any 'End of History' narrative that makes religion unnecessary." Some Hegel scholars believe that Hegel's interpretation of the resurrection of Jesus Christ on the final day is the actual conclusion of the march and movement of history that Hegel expected.[40] Such, of course, would constitute the complete opposite of the Marxist view, which removes Christ entirely from the dialectic of history. The Marxist utopia ends not with a Christian Second Coming but a secular, atheistic classless society, a workers' paradise.

By the 1840s, many of these Young Hegelians had become vocal atheists.[41] One of them was Karl Marx, as was his buddy Bruno Bauer.

Marx and Bruno Bauer and Friends

The leading member of this group of Berlin Hegelians was Dr. Bruno Bauer, who had a profound influence on Marx.[42] Marx biographer Jonathan Sperber probably puts it best when he describes the thuggish intellectual Bauer as an "unsavory character," the farthest left and "most radical" of the Young Hegelians, an "open atheist," an anti-Semite, a "nasty individual," and "arrogant and self-centered to boot." And he was Marx's pal, even roommate, during a crucial formative period for Marx in his early twenties. Sperber is spot on when he records that contemporaries saw Marx as Bauer's protégé.[43]

Bauer became a professor of theology at the University of Bonn, where he specialized more in the finer points of atheism than theology.[44] His field of specialty was New Testament criticism, which he embraced with vigor. His treatise, *Criticism of the Synoptic Gospels*, denied the historicity of Christ and portrayed the Gospels as fantasy, as mythical inventions.[45]

Bauer started lecturing at the university in 1834. The radical theologian became Marx's closest friend once Marx got to the University of Bonn.[46] They met during the summer of 1837, when Marx had just turned nineteen years old. Marx became a frequent visitor to the home of Bruno and his brother Edgar. One of only two courses that Marx took at the University of Bonn after abandoning his legal studies was a course that Bauer did on the Hebrew prophet Isaiah.[47]

A buddy of Bauer and Marx was another German theological jester, Ludwig Feuerbach, who in 1841 let loose his magnum opus of heresy, *The Essence of Christianity*. "Then came Feuerbach's *Essence of Christianity*," gushed Engels. "With one blow it pulverized the contradiction, in that without circumlocutions it placed materialism on the throne again. . . . The spell was broken; the 'system' was exploded and cast aside, and the contradiction, shown to exist only in our imagination, was dissolved. One must oneself have experienced the liberating effect of this book to get an idea of it. Enthusiasm was general; we all became at once Feuerbachians."[48]

Here from Feuerbach was another arrogant tome on how man created God rather than vice versa.

One of Marx's close contemporaries, Arnold Ruge, wrote to a friend that Bauer, Feuerbach, Marx, and another associate were forming a dubious band "making atheism their slogan. God, religion, and immortality are cast down from their thrones and man is proclaimed God." Georg Jung, still another contemporary, wrote to Ruge, "If Marx, Bruno Bauer and Feuerbach come together to found a theological-philosophical review, God would do well to surround Himself with all His angels and indulge in self-pity, for these three will certainly drive Him out of His heaven."[49]

Precisely that was in store. In March 1841, Bruno Bauer was planning to start a philosophical journal called *Archives of Atheism*. He planned to do so with no less than the young Karl Marx as co-editor. It never got off the ground because it lacked funding from a wealthy capitalist or two. Apparently, a rich atheist socialist willing to share the wealth was not found. The bitter Bauer moaned that what he really yearned to do "as a professor" was "to preach the system of atheism publicly." Shortly, the professor of Protestant theology was fired from his lectureship in March 1842, thus eagerly framing himself a martyr to the atheist cause.[50]

But Bauer and Marx had more antics up their atheist sleeves. As a parting shot in anger over his dismissal, Bauer enlisted Marx in what biographer Jonathan Sperber called a "public, atheist provocation." For that Easter season 1842, Bruno and Karl went to the nearby village of Godesberg, which was a favorite excursion site from Bonn, rented donkeys, and rode them through the village in what was a direct and deliberate parodying of the entrance of Jesus into Jerusalem. The incident, says Sperber, would be spread by word of mouth in and around Bonn, and would be recalled fondly by Bauer in the years ahead.[51]

No doubt parodying, if not mocking, Christ's entrance into Jerusalem was considered by Karl and pals a hilarious secular hosanna. Their supporters to this day surely get a good chuckle out of the display. It was probably the kind of thing that admiring Marx biographer Francis Wheen had in mind when he wrote with a smile, "In July 1841 Marx went to stay with Bruno Bauer in Bonn, where the two reprobates spent an uproarious summer shocking the local bourgeoisie—getting drunk, laughing in church, galloping through the city streets on donkeys."[52]

What a couple of cards!

Of course, laughing in church and mocking Christ were private gestures by Marx seen only by small gatherings. What Karl really wanted to let rip were some anti-religious screeds for the ages, ultimately to be seen by millions.

Francis Wheen also finds oddly amusing and endearing another perverse episode in Marx's behavior at this time—from another associate who ran in these circles. The journalist Karl Heinzen, a friend of Marx, helped walk Marx home "after several bottles of wine." Heinzen recounted, "As soon as I was in the house, he shut the doors, hid the key and jeered comically at me that I was his prisoner. He asked me to follow him up into his study." The smashed Marx soon forgot that Heinzen was there, but then he came around and began acting very strangely—nay, impishly, with intended deviltry. Literally so. Heinzen recorded:

> He came over to me, gave me to understand that he had me in his power, and, with a malice that recalled an imp rather than the intended devil, he began to attack me with threats and cuffs. I begged him to spare me that sort of thing, because it went against the grain to pay him back in the same coin. When he did not stop I gave him a serious warning that I would deal with him in a way which he would certainly feel and when that too did no good I saw myself compelled to dispatch him into the corner of the room. When he got up I said that I found his personality boring and asked him to open the front door. Now it was his turn to be triumphant. "Go home then, strong man," he mocked, and added a most comical smirk. It was as though he was chanting the words from Faust, "There is one imprisoned inside . . ." At least, the sentiment was similar, although his unsuccessful imitation of Mephistopheles made the situation comic in the extreme. In the end I warned him that if he would not open the door for me, then I would get it open myself and he would have to pay for the damage. Since he only answered with mocking sneers, I went down, tore the front door off its lock and called out to him from the street that he should shut the house up to prevent the entry of thieves. Dumb with amazement that I had escaped from his spell, he leaned out of the window and goggled at me with his small eyes like a wet goblin.[53]

Marx biographer Francis Wheen strangely describes this episode as "attractive," reflective of the jolly Karl's "taste for revelry and rough-housing." Heinzen clearly did not perceive it that way, nor likely would most others.

As we shall see, this is but one written account from someone who knew Marx and witnessed such disturbing behavior. Heinzen used words like "imp," "intended devil," "Faust," "Mephistopheles," "chanting the words from Faust, 'There is one imprisoned inside . . . ,'" "in his power," "mocking sneers," "dumb with amazement that I had escaped from his spell," "small eyes like a wet goblin." (Quite eerily, we shall see that this smacks of Karl Marx's description of the devilish behavior of his character "Oulanem" in his dramatic poem by the same.)

Are we supposed to laugh this off? Shrug it off as *playful*, as *delightfully roguish*? What are we supposed to think when we encounter fiendish (*er, goblinish*) behavior like this from Marx?

This is nothing to laugh at.

There is a coda to the Heinzen story, a sequel that Wheen concedes "is all too predictable." Marx, a mean and vindictive man, years later lashed out at Heinzen as a "loutish philistine," an "untrustworthy egoist."[54] Marx's obsequious puppy Engels jumped in, piling on for Karl, barking that Heinzen was "the most stupid person of the century" (quite a statement coming from the two persons with the most stupid ideas of the century). As for Heinzen, who by this point in late 1860 had immigrated to America, he fired back, describing Marx as a mix between a cat and an ape, a liar with a yellow dirty complexion, and, among other things, a man of small eyes possessed by "a spirit of wicked fire."[55]

No doubt that last description was in keeping with the small-eyed wet goblin whose gaze and spell Heinzen had encountered years before. All common traits of the hovering specter of communism and its keeper.

Marx and Bakunin

Another atheist ally of Karl Marx was Mikhail ("Michael") Bakunin (1814–76), a Russian atheist and revolutionary socialist-anarchist, and every bit the wild man. The two would later split, but they first met in Paris in the early 1840s and hit it off.

"We saw each other often," wrote Bakunin, "for I greatly respected him for his learning and for his passionate and serious devotion to the cause of the proletariat. . . . I eagerly sought his conversation." When he first met Marx, Bakunin said that Marx was "already an atheist, an instructed materialist, and a conscious socialist." Bakunin said that because of their temperaments, there was no "frank intimacy" among them.[56]

They would later become adversaries, as was typical for Marx and just about everyone he eventually could not stand. Marx flung his usual vitriol at Bakunin, and Bakunin rightly denounced "Marx's habitual weapon, a heap of filth." Bile aside, the essence of Marx's intellectual departure from Bakunin was probably valid. Marx surely found it hard to reconcile how one could be a socialist and an anarchist, given that socialism champions the state and anarchy undermines the state. And yet, there are crucial similarities between Marx wanting to ruthlessly criticize everything that exists and Bakunin likewise lashing out at all authority, whether the authority of God, the Church, the factory owner, the state, et cetera. Still, by the time of the First Internationale in the 1870s, decades after they first met, Marx was eviscerating Bakunin as a "buffoon."[57]

Nonetheless, Marx and Bakunin knew each other well. This is not the place to lay out all of Bakunin's thinking, but it is worth taking a few paragraphs to look at some of the halting sections of his best-known work, *God and the State*, published in 1871. The sentiments there very much reflect Marx's thinking about religion.[58]

Bakunin began the book with a very Marxist sentiment: "Yes, the whole history of humanity, intellectual and moral, political and social, is but a reflection of its economic history." Marx would applaud that totally, as he would Bakunin's opiate-like caricature of religion. Maybe Bakunin's worst and most well-known phrase about God and religion is this one from *God and the State*: "If God really existed, it would be necessary to abolish him."

Yes, you heard that right: "If God really existed, it would be necessary to abolish him."

Bakunin had a nasty, angry, cynical view of God and religion, stating that religion enslaves, debases, and corrupts, and that "all religions are cruel, all founded on blood." Curiously, however, he was not so nasty, angry, and cynical toward Satan, who he hailed as "the eternal rebel, the first freethinker and the emancipator of worlds." This glorious rebel view of Satan is not unusual among certain radical socialists; as we shall see later in this book, this was how Saul Alinsky framed Satan as well—namely, as the "very first radical . . . who rebelled against the establishment."[59]

That larger passage in Bakunin's *God and the State* is worth quoting at length for a fuller idea of where this anarchist-socialist friend of Marx stood. Read it carefully, sentence after sentence, and prepare to be shocked:

> Yes, our first ancestors, our Adams and our Eves, were, if not gorillas, very near relatives of gorillas, omnivorous, intelligent and ferocious beasts, endowed in a higher degree than the animals of another species with two precious faculties—*the power to think* and *the desire to rebel*. . . .
>
> The Bible, which is a very interesting and here and there very profound book when considered as one of the oldest surviving manifestations of human wisdom and fancy, expresses this truth very naively in its myth of original sin. Jehovah, who of all the good gods adored by men was certainly the most jealous, the most vain, the most ferocious, the most unjust, the most bloodthirsty, the most despotic, and the most hostile to human dignity and liberty—Jehovah had just created Adam and Eve, to satisfy we know not what caprice; no doubt to while away his time, which must weigh heavy on his hands in his eternal egoistic solitude, or that he might have some new slaves. He generously placed at their disposal the whole earth, with all its fruits and animals, and set but a single limit to this complete

enjoyment. He expressly forbade them from touching the fruit of the tree of knowledge. He wished, therefore, that man, destitute of all understanding of himself, should remain an eternal beast, ever on all-fours before the eternal God, his creator and his master. But here steps in Satan, the eternal rebel, the first freethinker and the emancipator of worlds. He makes man ashamed of his bestial ignorance and obedience; he emancipates him, stamps upon his brow the seal of liberty and humanity, in urging him to disobey and eat of the fruit of knowledge.

Again, here we see Bakunin's *good* Satan, a "freethinker." Such was a high compliment in the late nineteenth century (and into the early twentieth century), as "freethinkers" were in vogue among the progressive left. This *commendable* Satan is the great emancipator. Bakunin continued, decrying the role of the great spoiler: God. He narrates, characterizing the "good God" as, well, not exactly so:

We know what followed. The good God, whose foresight, which is one of the divine faculties, should have warned him [Satan] of what would happen, flew into a terrible and ridiculous rage; he cursed Satan, man, and the world created by himself, striking himself so to speak in his own creation, as children do when they get angry; and, not content with smiting our ancestors themselves, he cursed them in all the generations to come, innocent of the crime committed by their forefathers. Our Catholic and Protestant theologians look upon that as very profound and very just, precisely because it is monstrously iniquitous and absurd. Then, remembering that he was not only a God of vengeance and wrath, but also a God of love, after having tormented the existence of a few milliards of poor human beings and condemned them to an eternal hell, he took pity on the rest, and, to save them and reconcile his eternal and divine love with his eternal and divine anger, always greedy for victims and blood, he sent into the world, as an expiatory victim, his only son, that he might be killed by men. That is called the mystery of the Redemption, the basis of all the Christian religions. Still, if the divine Savior had saved the human world! But no; in the paradise promised by Christ, as we know, such being the formal announcement, the elect will number very few. The rest, the immense majority of the generations present and to come, will burn eternally in hell. In the meantime, to console us, God, ever just, ever good, hands over the earth to the government of the Napoleon Thirds, of the William Firsts, of the Ferdinands of Austria, and of the Alexanders of all the Russias.

Such are the absurd tales that are told and the monstrous doctrines that are taught, in the full light of the nineteenth century, in all the public schools of Europe, at the express command of the government. They call this civilizing the people! Is it not plain that all these governments are systematic poisoners, interested stupefiers of the masses?

This lengthy, appalling passage from Mikhail Bakunin speaks for itself. It requires no commentary, other than to perhaps note that surely Karl Marx grinned an impish grin as he read it. Actually, one more comment seems due: Bakunin better have hoped to all hope that he was right; otherwise, he was destined to face a mighty reckoning someday in the afterlife. That is, as he faced and dealt with (in his words) this most jealous, most vain, most ferocious, most unjust, most bloodthirsty, most despotic, most hostile to human dignity and liberty, eternally egoistic Jehovah.

From there, Bakunin's rant continued, with the anarchist-socialist-atheist revolutionary himself aware of his own ranting:

I have wandered from my subject, because anger gets hold of me whenever I think of the base and criminal means which they employ to keep the nations in perpetual slavery, undoubtedly that they may be the better able to fleece them. Of what consequence are the crimes of all the Tropmanns in the world compared with this crime of treason against humanity committed daily, in broad day, over the whole surface of the civilized world, by those who dare to call themselves the guardians and the fathers of the people? I return to the myth of original sin.

God admitted that Satan was right; he recognized that the devil did not deceive Adam and Eve in promising them knowledge and liberty as a reward for the act of disobedience which he had induced them to commit; for, immediately they had eaten of the forbidden fruit, God himself said (see Bible): "Behold, man is become as of the Gods, knowing both good and evil; prevent him, therefore, from eating of the fruit of eternal life, lest he become immortal like Ourselves."

Let us disregard now the fabulous portion of this myth and consider its true meaning, which is very clear. Man has emancipated himself; he has separated himself from animality and constituted himself a man; he has begun his distinctively human history and development by an act of disobedience and science—that is, by *rebellion* and by *thought*.

Bakunin's *opus* runs on like this with page after page of such prideful bilge. He asserted, "All religions, with their gods, their demigods, and their prophets, their messiahs and their saints, were created by the credulous fancy of men who had not attained the full development and full possession of their faculties." Thus, he insisted "the religious heaven is nothing but a mirage" created by man, "exalted by ignorance and faith." This is fully consistent with Karl Marx's view that "man makes religion."

Again, this was from one of Marx's early admirers. No doubt, Marx's admirers today in the academy will be quick to rush to his defense and remind us that he and Bakunin became foes, or at least Bakunin became a rival in Marx's eyes. Yes, that is correct, but Marx's disapproval of Bakunin was not for any religious reason or disagreement. As for the words of Bakunin quoted here, Marx would have surely extended a warm smile and generous appreciation. Few appreciated a good rant against religion quite like Karl Marx.

Karl's Opium

In thinking about Marx and religion, or Marx and Bakunin, or Marx and Bauer, or Marx and Hegel, one cannot ignore the smoke that pervaded the Marxist living room. Let us address it here at last.

The most infamous of Karl Marx's remarks on religion was his demeaning assessment that religion is the "opiate" or "opium" of the masses. Few, however, are familiar with the wider context of the assessment, the larger passage that is no less reassuring, and that, like much of Marx and his disciples' writings, becomes even more addled and infantile as one tries to unpack it. Here is the section in full, taken from a mind-grunt of Marx scribbled in December 1843–January 1844, four years before the publication of his and Engels's *Manifesto*:

> Man makes religion, religion does not make man. Religion is, indeed, the self-consciousness and self-esteem of man who has either not yet won through to himself, or has already lost himself again. But man is no abstract being squatting outside the world. Man is the world of man—state, society. This state and this society produce religion, which is an inverted consciousness of the world, because they are an inverted world. Religion is the general theory of this world, its encyclopaedic compendium, its logic in popular form, its spiritual point d'honneur, its enthusiasm, its moral sanction, its solemn complement, and its universal basis of consolation and justification. It is the fantastic realization of the human essence since the human essence has not acquired any true reality. The struggle against religion

is, therefore, indirectly the struggle against that world whose spiritual aroma is religion.

Religious suffering is, at one and the same time, the expression of real suffering and a protest against real suffering. Religion is the sigh of the oppressed creature, the heart of a heartless world, and the soul of soulless conditions. It is the opium of the people.

That in itself was negative enough by Marx, depressing enough, cold and heartless enough. As usual, however, Marx was far from finished venting the acrid recesses of his bitter brain:

The abolition of religion as the illusory happiness of the people is the demand for their real happiness. To call on them to give up their illusions about their condition is to call on them to give up a condition that requires illusions. The criticism of religion is, therefore, in embryo, the criticism of that vale of tears of which religion is the halo.

Criticism has plucked the imaginary flowers on the chain not in order that man shall continue to bear that chain without fantasy or consolation, but so that he shall throw off the chain and pluck the living flower. The criticism of religion disillusions man, so that he will think, act, and fashion his reality like a man who has discarded his illusions and regained his senses, so that he will move around himself as his own true Sun. Religion is only the illusory Sun which revolves around man as long as he does not revolve around himself.

It is, therefore, the task of history, once the other-world of truth has vanished, to establish the truth of this world. It is the immediate task of philosophy, which is in the service of history, to unmask self-estrangement in its unholy forms once the holy form of human self-estrangement has been unmasked. Thus, the criticism of Heaven turns into the criticism of Earth, the criticism of religion into the criticism of law, and the criticism of theology into the criticism of politics.[60]

That is a mouthful, and not worth wasting precious moments of our lives trying to decipher the entire passage in all its futility. But a few of the thoughts stand out and are worth underscoring because of their disastrous implications.

Note that Marx began with an emphasis on the "struggle" against religion, which was a rather negative way to frame humanity's relationship with religion. This was a "struggle against religion" that he contended was merely man-made. Like Bakunin, Marx insisted that man badly needs emancipation. Religion is an artifice of man, he surmised, a creation not of God but of man. Man thus makes religion because he pathetically needs religion. This is a man who has already "lost himself" and thus requires "religion." The state and society "produce religion," which is a deformed, "inverted consciousness of the world." This, the struggle against religion, is also a "struggle against that world whose spiritual aroma is religion." This is why people crave religion as a kind of drug, or opiate, or "opium." Marx coldly assessed, "Religion is the sigh of the oppressed creature, the heart of a heartless world, and the soul of soulless conditions. It is the opium of the people."

That, to borrow from modern parlance (and with apologies to Marx), is the money line in the passage. Modern commentators are only familiar with the second sentence on the opium of the people. The preceding line, however, is equally revealing. It sets up the opium assertion. Look at both sentences again, in tandem: "Religion is the sigh of the oppressed creature, the heart of a heartless world, and the soul of soulless conditions. It is the opium of the people."

That complete assessment by Marx is even more spiteful than the commonly abbreviated "opium of the people" snippet. It is damning. Religion is a "sigh" of an oppressed creature, of a heartless world, of soulless conditions. This is a despairing view.

Marx next used three crucial words he would also use in the *Communist Manifesto*: "abolition of religion." Given what he had said in the previous line, he thus said (not surprisingly) that "the abolition of religion" is necessary for people to achieve "real happiness," especially given that their *clinging* to religion (to borrow a description from Barack Obama, who in 2008 spoke sneeringly of Americans "clinging to their God") is a mere "illusory happiness." It was hence critical, said Marx, that the likes of him criticize religion because religion was the "halo" of a "vale of tears." Here, of course, Marx opted for a striking religious metaphor, turning Christian imagery on its head, as he relished doing throughout his writing and throughout his life. (As Catholics know, the prayer "Hail, Holy Queen" includes the line "mourning and weeping in this valley of tears," which some Catholics render as "vale of tears.") For instance, Marx's famous line, "From each according to his ability, to each according to his needs," is another bastardization of Christian language; in that case, Holy Scripture itself.[61]

Man, said Marx, must "throw off the chain" of "imaginary flowers." He must discard "his illusions" and regain "his senses." Why? Marx's answer is pure nonsense—the sappy, self-defeating, self-contradictory moral relativism that has appealed to and ravaged the ruminations of the wider ideological left for centuries—"so that he will move around himself as his own true Sun. Religion is only the illusory Sun which revolves around man as long as he does not revolve around himself."

This, of course, is relativistic pabulum. It is the sophistry that, unfortunately, has evolved into the modern secular-progressive *zeitgeist* that dominates America and the wider West today. It is the childish philosophical silliness that has enabled modern leftists to redefine everything from life to marriage to gender to sexuality to bathrooms.

When man makes himself his own Sun—that is, his own God—then he destroys his world. As ex-communist Whittaker Chambers observed, Marx and his minions were merely echoing the first mistake of man, initiated way back in the Garden of Eden: *ye shall be as gods.*

Note, too, Marx's obsession with criticizing. The word "criticism" is used twenty-nine times in this essay, starting with the opening sentence: "For Germany, the *criticism of religion* has been essentially completed, and the criticism of religion is the prerequisite of all criticism."[62] This is another well-known and oft-quoted Marxist maxim, usually summed up as simply: "The criticism of religion is the beginning of all criticism."[63]

This was Marx's mindset. It was around this same time, in an 1843 letter to Arnold Ruge, that Marx called for "the ruthless criticism of all that exists."[64] For Marx, criticizing religion would be at the beginning, the very foundation, of all criticism.

Marx finished his destructive passage with an exhortation to history, to philosophy, to law, to politics to undertake the secular righteous "task" to "establish the truth of this world." What truth? That truth, alas, was Marx's "truth."

Ye shall be as gods.

Marx's Brave New World

It is crucial to realize that communism, being a totalitarian ideology, endeavored to change human nature itself. This is clear throughout Marx's writings. In *The German Ideology* (1845), Marx and Engels said that in order "for the widespread generation of this communist consciousness, and for the success of the cause, it is necessary that man himself should suffer a massive change." This was a change, they said, that could only come through "a practical movement, a revolution." There must be a literal process of "overthrowing" the old "filthy yoke and . . . founding a new society only in a revolution."[65]

Human nature itself had to be changed. There had to be a fundamental transformation of human nature. A revolution of (or against, really) human nature.

In that framework, religion was viewed as a dangerous and

ubiquitous rival belief system. It was Marxism's chief competitor for the mind of the working class. The Soviet leadership would want Marxism and the state to be central to all citizens' lives. Hence, the words of the *Communist Manifesto* were to be read and learned, drilled and memorized, internalized. Any challenging text, especially an influential one like the Bible, was unwelcome. Religion was perceived as an ever-present, powerful enemy, not to be taken lightly.

Marx was an atheist-utopian who envisioned a "new morality" without God. The path to utopia was a classless albeit godless society. The "classless society"—which would be a "workers' paradise"—would, said Marx, make its "own history! It is a leap from slavery into freedom; from darkness into light."[66]

Marx promised nothing less than the creation of a "new world." His "generation," he portended, "resembles the Jews whom Moses led out of the wilderness. It must not only conquer a new world; it must also perish in order to make room for the people who are fit for a new world."[67] The old world and current generation must perish. It would be the communists who would play the role of sacrificial savior on behalf of a new covenant for the new world.

This kind of utopian idealism is common to the communist left and even much of the wider left, which otherwise proudly touts its cynicism and suspicion, especially of religious people. But when a centralized government looks to corral and herd the collective masses, the hardest left-wing pessimist can morph into the most hopeful idealist. Leftists scoff at the Baptist preacher clinging to his Bible or Catholic grandma clinging to her rosary, but damned if leftists are not equally as faithful when clinging to government as holding the path to salvation. The most doubting and brooding of communists have not been exempt from such full-faith secular idealism.

For that matter, just as Marx was not very impressed with Christians, he also was quite unimpressed with Christianity. And for those modern-day "social justice" Christians who like to invoke communism as somehow consistent with or reflective of Christian social teaching, well, Karl Marx begged to differ. "The social principles of Christianity preach cowardice, self-contempt, abasement, submission, humility," scowled Marx. "The social principles of Christianity are hypocritical. . . . So much for the social principles of Christianity."[68]

Not that Marx himself was any less self-absorbed than this alleged Christianity he condemned. "The more of himself that man gives to God," Marx groaned, "the less he has left in himself."[69] Marx was all about himself, answerable to himself alone.

Georg Jung, a Marx contemporary, a young lawyer, and a member of the Doctors' Club, said that "Marx calls Christianity one of the most immoral religions." Jung viewed Marx not as a political revolutionary but a theological-philosophical revolutionary who was attempting to overthrow the entire social system, not just an economic system.[70]

The preceding tells us much about where Karl Marx ended up on the religion question. But where did he start? Was he always an atheist? And did his sojourn involve a detour or two along some highly troubled paths? When did his writings first reveal this ominous turn?

PART 2

KARL MARX

CHAPTER 2

"MY SOUL IS
CHOSEN FOR HELL"

MARX'S VERSE

Marxism from the outset was a seriously perverse ideology that brooded in misery, wallowed in misery, advanced itself in the name of misery, and ultimately produced misery. It is no surprise that anyone who has studied its roots sees among them numerous pernicious ideas and influences.

Similarly, Marxism's founder was a seriously perverse man who brooded in misery, wallowed in misery, advanced himself in the name of misery, and ultimately produced misery. It is no surprise that anyone who has paused to peer into *his* roots sees there numerous pernicious ideas and influences.

The reality is that one cannot separate Marxism the ideology from Marx the man. Aristotle observed, "Men start revolutionary changes for reasons connected with their private lives."[71] Karl Marx certainly seems one such case. The communist revolution he had in mind was in many ways the consummation of his unpleasant private life, as it was for many of his most revolutionary and deadly followers, particularly Vladimir Lenin, the other half of the Marxist-Leninist flame-thrower that set ablaze an awaiting century.

And when we cast a gaze into the fiery abyss of the life and mind of Karl Marx, we find some disturbing forces integral to understanding him and what his ideology wrought. We have seen some of those thus far in the previous chapter, but here we will dig deeper, look more closely, to discover just what animated the person of Karl Marx.

How deep? How disturbing? How dark? Looking into the mind and man of Marx inevitably takes one to places where even angels fear to tread.

To that end, *Marx & Satan* is the unapologetic title of a decidedly politically incorrect look at the life of Karl Marx by the late Richard Wurmbrand, who spent fourteen years imprisoned behind the Iron Curtain for his opposition to atheistic communism.[72] The Romanian pastor was brutally tortured—with what he described as a literal demonic zeal—so horribly, so unthinkably cruelly, with such diabolical imagination by his Marxist captors, that the good reverend can be forgiven for any hyperbole, and for sensing that the dark spirit of the devil himself seemed to be oozing out of his tormentors.

"All the biblical descriptions of hell and the pains of Dante's *Inferno* are nothing in comparison with the tortures in Communist prisons," stated Wurmbrand in his international bestseller *Tortured for Christ*. He recalled of his captors, "I have seen communists whose faces while torturing believers shone with rapturous joy. They cried out while torturing the Christians, 'We are the devil!'" He remembered one torturer say, "I thank God in whom I don't believe, that I have lived to this hour when I can express all the evil in my heart."

Pause to look closely at those exclamations: "We are the devil!" "I thank God in whom I don't believe, that I have lived to this hour when I can express all the evil in my heart."

If anyone had a legitimate gripe suspecting a nexus between Lucifer and communism, the Rev. Wurmbrand did. He earned it. He experienced it. He witnessed it. And he traced seeds of it to the founder of Marxism.

Wurmbrand's incendiary thesis that Karl Marx himself, let alone Marxism, owed some debt to the flames of the underworld is hard to coolly laugh off as the paranoid rantings of an embittered man.

The fact is that some of Marx's earliest and most passionate written works dealt with and dwelled in the netherworld. Karl Marx, in short, wrote about the devil.

"Hellish Vapors"

Marx's musings about the prince of darkness is a subject avoided like the seven plagues by his aficionados, particularly recent hagiographers. It is not something students can expect to hear from their progressive professor in their Socialism 101 class at Secular U, where all Marx is good Marx. Yet, those writings by Marx exist and are undeniable, even as the few sources who have dealt with them have tended to be largely (but not exclusively) historians on the anti-communist side. Some of these sources knew communism all too well; they lived under it. They include Yuri Maltsev, the economist who served in the Soviet government (in the central planning bureau), notably on the reform team of Mikhail Gorbachev, and today is a professor at Carthage College. Others who have dealt with this side of Marx include the bestselling popular British historian Paul Johnson, the prolific Christian historian Gary North, the free-market historian Mark Skousen, and the renowned Austrian School economist Murray Rothbard.[73] None of those are left-leaning sources. And yet, there have been academic scholars like Bruce Mazlish and Robert Payne who have addressed this aspect of Marx in books published by (among other houses) top university presses such as, respectively, Oxford University Press and New York University Press.[74] Payne did a deep dive into this sordid side of Marx, notably with a chapter titled "The Demons" in his impressive 1968 biography for Simon & Schuster, one among several biographies of Marx he wrote.

In all, then, Marx's sordid interest in that sordid world is not some unfounded and ungrounded assertion put out by some sloppy internet blogger in our current day. It has been clearly documented for many decades, even while ignored by so many on the political left.

Among these, arguably the best and foundational works which produced groundbreaking research into the subject were by Robert Payne, specifically his already mentioned 1968 work *Marx: A Biography* and his 1971 book *The Unknown Karl Marx*, published by New York University Press.[75] Payne, who was absolutely no right-winger, was a respected and thoughtful British professor of English literature and drama, a biographer, and a linguist—in addition to being an expert on Marx who studied and wrote about the man in great depth. Payne's translations of this shadowy side of Marx came from his reading of Marx's early poetry and theatrical dramas, which Richard Wurmbrand, Paul Johnson, and other authors would pick up, expand upon, and introduce to larger audiences in books published by top trade houses such as (in Johnson's case) HarperCollins.[76] Payne's work, too, reached popular audiences (at least one of his Marx biographies), but some of his work was directed to scholars as an academic's compilation of various poetic and theatrical works of Marx.

As Payne correctly noted, Marx had a special love for poetry: "Marx was devoted to poetry. Poetry was in his blood, and he could no more think of living without poetry than living without his vision of a Communist world."[77]

Marx most admired Goethe, from whom he could cite page after page by heart. (Not without irony, the later cultural Marxists that constituted the infamous Frankfurt School were hatched at Germany's Goethe University.) Payne stated of Marx, "He had a retentive memory and could recite long passages of Goethe's *Faust* with gusto, with a special preference for the speeches of Mephistopheles."[78]

That is no casual thing: a special preference for Mephistopheles. He was especially fond of Mephistopheles's line from *Faust*: "Everything that exists deserves to perish."[79] This is no surprise; it reflects the very thinking of the man who in letters called for the "ruthless criticism of all that exists,"[80] who in the *Manifesto* declared that communism seeks to "abolish the present state of things," and who at the close of the *Manifesto* called for "the forcible overthrow of all existing social conditions."

Marx also knew by heart passages from Dante's *The Divine Comedy*, though Marx clearly did not integrate Dante's worldview in the way that a typical Dante admirer would (like C. S. Lewis, for instance).[81] Marx was no doubt drawn to the great Italian poet's imagery in *The Inferno*. It was a window into hell that Marx apparently yearned to open. Perhaps it is apt that Richard Wurmbrand thought of Dante's *Inferno* when his Marxist captors were tormenting him.

The Painful Significance of Marx's Poetry

Biographers who admire Marx and seek to cover for him will want to ignore his poetry among his corpus of writings. They should nonetheless bristle at what they see in Marx's poetry. They will encounter what Paul Johnson discerned: "Savagery is a characteristic note of his verse, together with the intense pessimism of the human condition, hatred, a fascination with corruption and violence, suicide pacts and pacts with the devil."[82]

For a Marx hagiographer, this is reason to downplay or dismiss the poetry altogether. But to do so would be wrong and irresponsible.

As Robert Payne notes and documents—echoing what any careful reader of Marx can see in his letters and writings—Marx fancied himself a poet. He wanted to be a poet. It was a calling, a first love. He expressed that love for poetry in letters to his father and, more so, in love letters and poems to his beloved Jenny, the girl of his dreams who became his wife. But the poems were hardly restricted to love. Marx's poems burned less often with love than with red-hot rage.

"The young Marx was passionately devoted to poetry," wrote Payne, "and took himself very seriously as a poet. . . . Poetry was the love of his life, the safe refuge from all the turmoils of his revolutionary existence." Payne concedes that Marxist scholars have disregarded the poems as youthful indiscretions, not to be taken seriously and read apart from his more "mature" works. To the contrary, notes Payne, correctly, these poems are very closely related to his mature works, and he absolutely did not regard them as indiscretions.[83]

Payne started his examination of the literary life of Marx with two plays that the young Karl wrote as a student. The first was called "The Player," and was taken seriously enough to be published in the Berlin literary magazine *Athenaeum* in January 1841 when Marx was twenty-two years old—seven years before the publication of the *Communist Manifesto*. They were fittingly published by the editors under the title "Savage Songs," which is precisely what they connote: pure savagery, and then some.[84]

As for "The Player," this unnerving poem describes a violinist who in a delirious frenzy summons up the powers of darkness with his furious strings. In this ballad, the violinist, who seems to be Marx himself, plays so frenetically that there can be only one outcome: he destroys himself. When an onlooker asks the violinist why he must perform this way—it is believed that the onlooker was Marx's love interest and future wife, Jenny von Westphalen—a perturbed Marx answers that he cannot help himself and that he will stab her with his "blood-dark sword" before his violin and his heart burst.[85]

Here is Marx:

> The player strikes up on his violin,
> His blond hair falling down.
> He wears a sword at his side,
> And a wide, wrinkled gown.
>
> "O player, why playest thou so wild?
> Why the savage look in thine eyes?
> Why the leaping blood, the soaring waves?
> Why tearest thou thy bow to shreds?"

Those are some stirring questions for this wild man, this savage with a bow, with leaping blood. And Marx answers for himself in the next lines, the answers of which resound within his soul in the depths of hell:

> "I play for the sake of the thundering sea
> Crashing against the walls of the cliffs,
> That my eyes be blinded and my heart burst
> And my soul resound in the depths of Hell."

> "O player, why tearest thou thy heart to shreds
> In mockery? This art was given thee
> By a shining God to elevate the mind
> Into the swelling music of the starry dance."

The player misuses this elegant art, the graceful sound of the violin. He uses it not to elevate the mind as God intended but for something quite the opposite. He denies God's knowledge. He thinks not of bowing a heavenly chord but thrusting a blood-dark sword. And that is not all. Hellish vapors come too. They fill his brain. And the sword, it comes from the prince of darkness:

> "Look now, my blood-dark sword shall stab
> Unerringly within thy soul.
> God neither knows nor honors art.
> The hellish vapors rise and fill the brain,

> Till I go mad and my heart is utterly changed.
> See the sword—the Prince of Darkness sold it to me.
> For he beats the time and gives the signs.
> Ever more boldly I play the dance of death.

> I must play darkly, I must play lightly,
> Until my heart and my violin burst."

> The player strikes up on the violin,
> His blond hair falling down.

> He wears a sword at his side,
> And a wide, wrinkled gown.[86]

He plays not for God and to uplift the mind but for the "dance of death." He plays it "darkly" until he and his violin both burst. Robert Payne interpreted the pact between Marx's violinist—or, that is, Marx the violinist—and the prince of darkness as evocative of the pact between Goethe's *Faust* and Mephistopheles.[87] It surely is just that. It is a Faustian bargain.

Among these passages in "The Player," it is apropos that the founder of communism waxed poetic about "the hellish vapors [that] rise and fill the brain, Till I go mad and my heart is utterly changed. See this sword? The Prince of Darkness sold it to me. For me he beats the time and gives the signs. Ever more boldly I play the dance of death."[88]

Indeed, *"I play the dance of death."* Marx here proved himself a better prophet than poet. The ideas for which he would be famous, the philosophy that he scripted, the international communist symphony for which he composed the score, represented less a play and a poem than a dance of death, a grand dance of death that left over one hundred million people dead in his name, in the ideology that bore his name—by bullet or sword, and perhaps sold by the prince of darkness, or at least in service to the prince of darkness.

Certainly some hellish vapors.

Those interpretations are mine. It is worth sharing the interpretation of Robert Payne—again, a Marx biographer with special expertise in literary criticism.

Payne describes the Marx ballad thusly: "A musician summons up the Prince of Darkness, a lover offers a poison cup to the beloved, and both run headlong to their deaths in a satanic rejection of the world." Payne states that Marx succeeds in conveying "the terror at the heart of terror." Marx, says Payne, "is not playing games," as these poems not only "reek of fire and brimstone" but constitute "real fire and brimstone." Payne observes that Marx "is here celebrating a satanic mystery, for the player is clearly Lucifer or Mephistopheles, and what he is playing with such frenzy is the music which accompanies the end of the world."[89]

More than that, adds Payne, we see in this poem a literal "pact with the devil," one that is "consecrated by the purchase of the blood-dark sword, which kills with unerring aim." The blood violinist is not destroying the world because he hates it, but is doing so in order to spite God, out of derision and mockery against the Creator. He is a rebel, like Satan, the ultimate rebel against God and Heaven. And Payne is absolutely justified in connecting this to the destructive Marx of the *Manifesto*, who seeks to destroy the world as it exists and fashion his own anew: "He was a man with a peculiar faculty for relishing disaster."[90]

Poisoned Cups and Flames of Hell

The second ballad of Marx that appeared in *Athenaeum* was no less distressing. Titled "Nocturnal Love," the lovers end up once again consuming poisoned cups and consumed by the flames, which they sink into as disembodied spirits. Here again, we are assaulted with violence, grief, despair, pale maidens, doomed souls, and fire, fire, fire:

> He pressed her violently to his heart
> And gazed darkly in her eyes:
> "Darling, thou art on fire with grief,
> Thou tremblest beneath my breath."

> "Thou hast drunk of my soul!
> Mine is thy glowing fire!
> Shine, O my jewel,
> Shine, shine, O blood of youth!"

> "Darling, thou lookest so pale,

> Thou speakest so strangely ever.
> See how the heavenly choirs
> Lift up the world to the skies!"
>
> "Dear one, they are all lifted away!
> The stars shine and shine!
> Then let us fly away,
> And our souls be mingled together!"[91]

And what is the destination of these souls mingled together and about to fly away? That is, the soul of he, the dark one, glowing with fire, and she, on fire with grief and trembling beneath his breath and pressed violently against his heart? That is, she, the blood of youth, yet pale, and he, of glowing fire, whose soul she has drunk from? To where are they flying? The answer, as usual with Marx, was terror and death, and flames, flames, flames—*roaring flames*! Marx continued:

> So she spoke in gentle whispers
> While the terror lay around,
> And the light of roaring flames
> Shone on her empty eyes.
>
> "Darling, thou hast drunk of poison,
> And now thou must depart with me.
> Now the night has fallen,
> There is no longer any day."
>
> He pressed her violently to his heart,
> Death on her breath and breast.
> She was pierced by deeper pain,
> And her eyes were closed forever.[92]

Once again, the object of Marx's heart drinks of poison. She dies—death on her breath and breast, pierced by pain, eyes closed forever. They go to the flames. Another climax for Karl!

According to Robert Payne, the poem was evidently addressed

to Marx's love, Jenny, who is the female permitted to speak in the second and fourth verses. "It is an ominous and deeply disturbing poem," concedes Payne, "for a man does not write such things unless he is on the verge of madness or despair."[93]

Here we must pause for a crucial note of foreshadowing: It seems more than ironic that such despair, death, and suicide—specifically through drinking poison—will pervade the grim family life of Karl and Jenny. As we shall see, two of Marx's daughters killed themselves by drinking poison in suicide pacts.

Upon reading outbursts like this, one marvels at how any biographer of Marx could neglect these writings. Actually, the answer is simple: If the biographer favors or esteems Marx and Marxism, is committed to Marx and to defending Marx, and is taking pains to construct a positive profile, then he avoids these poems like a burning building of flames, flames, flames. That is exactly what Marx's hagiographers have done.

The precedent was set long ago, when Franz Mehring, the preeminent original biographer of Marx, first read these writings in horror and returned them to Marx's daughter, Laura, declaring they should remain unpublished in order to protect Marx's reputation. Laura passed them along to her nephew, Jean Longuet, and they soon vanished. They were eventually retrieved only by the due diligence of Marxist scholar David Ryazanov of the Marx-Engels Institute in Moscow. He understood their significance and had the intellectual integrity to track them down and preserve and seek to publish them.[94]

As for Marx's devotees today, one wonders about their intellectual integrity in blithely ignoring these poems. Most surely do so by conveniently convincing themselves that the poems are unimportant and tell us nothing about Karl Marx. Youthful indiscretions, you see. At least Mehring acknowledged that the writings were ugly and, therefore, should be repressed. Marx's favorable biographers today surely lie to and delude themselves, easily manufacturing excuses to not discuss these writings.

And yet, there were many poems by Marx just like this—some even worse.

"Oulanem"

Still more unsettling is a piece by Marx that became one of the main focuses of Robert Payne's analysis and also of Richard Wurmbrand, Paul Johnson, and others for its sheer iniquitous nature.

The play was, quite remarkably—and quite diabolically—titled *Oulanem*, which Payne explained as an anagram for "Manuelo," "Immanuel," "Emmanuel," or "God." As Payne formulated it, "Manuelo=Immanuel=God."[95]

Wurmbrand was blunter. He identified the anagram as a directly Satanist anagram for the name "Emmanuel" (or "Manuelo"), which is the Hebrew biblical name for Jesus, meaning "God is with us."[96] It is, stated Wurmbrand, a sacrilegious inversion of a holy name.

In Sacred Scripture, the Angel Gabriel says to the Virgin Mary that she shall bear a child, and his name shall be Emmanuel, or Jesus. He will be called great and "Son of the Most High." That is the beloved Son of God, of the blessed Trinity. Those are the words of the New Testament. But these were not the words of Karl Marx in his anagram for Emmanuel—and for his "Oulanem."

Wurmbrand published his observation in the 1980s, and Payne wrote about the play in his biographies in the 1960s and 1970s. If you search for the word "Oulanem" today (as I did too many times in writing this book), you will immediately encounter a Wikipedia reference to the play, *Oulanem*, directly attributed to Karl Marx alone. Wikipedia, not exactly a devil's den of right-wingers, described it as a "drama or poetic play written by Karl Marx . . . during his years as a student."[97] A simple Google search easily yields the full text of the play posted verbatim at the historically very reliable (and pro-Marxist) website www.marxists.org.[98] Such a search generates still more. [Warning: Beware that when you do an online search for the term "Oulanem," your computer will immediately pull up repulsive images of satanic figures that reflexively leave the reader with a sickening unease.] "Oulanem" is also recognized today as an anagram for "Manuelo" by some musicians in the world of heavy-metal (actually "black metal") rock n' roll, where it is seen as synonymous with the term "Anti-Christ."[99]

That is the source that young Marx was messing with. Worse, he was invoking it as a force to destroy others—many others. In that vein, Marx's message in *Oulanem*—which is more than a poem; it is, rather, a poetic tragedy, or drama—is much more destructive than the message in "The Player." As Payne observed, the violence in "The Player" is turned inward, as the violinist destroys only himself, whereas the violence in *Oulanem* is turned outward with the destruction of man—namely, the threatened destruction of all mankind by the character that is "Oulanem." Still more disquieting was Marx's personal role in that vision. Payne observes of this particular play: "We enter a world where all the characters are learned in the arts of destruction, caught in the coils of a secret rage for vengeance. Since we are never told why they are so determined to exact retribution on so massive a scale, we may assume that Marx was giving vent to his own destructive rages. *Oulanem* is a revenger's tragedy."[100]

Act 1 of *Oulanem* takes the audience straight into a dialogue between two of Marx's main characters, including the namesake "Oulanem," described as a German traveler, and his trusty companion, "Lucindo," with the action taking place in a mountain town in Italy. Oulanem and Lucindo find no room in the inn, perhaps akin to Mary and Joseph finding no room in the inn to give birth to Emmanuel.

And yet, Oulanem and Lucindo are no Mary and Joseph, even as they are somewhat of a couple (or almost). Both are male, with the young and handsome Lucindo apparently (states Payne) a homosexual love-interest of Oulanem, who seeks to corrupt the boy. With no room in the inn, they accept the invitation of an Italian man named

"Pertini" to stay in his house. Pertini, too, seems to have a homosexual interest in the boy. (Payne observes that this is written by Marx with such considerable skill that "Marx evidently knew a good deal about corrupting boys, or else he had watched the process closely."[101])

As Marx himself stated in his play, "Oulanem, Oulanem. The name rings forth like a death, rings forth until it dies away in a wretched crawl." He penned this disquieting passage:

> Yet I have power within my youthful arms
> To clench and crush you with tempestuous force,
> While for us both the abyss yawns in darkness.
> You will sink down and I shall follow laughing,
> Whispering in your ears, "Descend,
> come with me, friend."

Each insidious scene crawls on like this, increasingly disconcerting and wrathful. Scene 3 is among the most bitter, where Oulanem is seated alone at a table, writing, with papers tossed all around (not unlike Marx himself, oddly enough, who was notorious for writing and working the same way). He suddenly springs up and stands with arms folded and declares:

> All lost! The hour is now expired, and time
> Stands still. This pigmy universe collapses.
> Soon I shall clasp Eternity and howl
> Humanity's giant curse into its ear.
> Eternity! It is eternal pain,
> Death inconceivable, immeasurable!
> An evil artifice contrived to taunt us.

This is the climactic scene, where the time comes for the death of Oulanem. It is here that Marx, rather astoundingly, appears to have himself declare, in the person of his subject, the Creator (God presumably, or some other all-creating, all-powerful source): "I shall howl gigantic curses at mankind."

Shocking as this is, it is nonetheless reflective of a frightening penchant for violence and world destruction that permeated Marx's poetry, a sort of prelude to enunciating his destructive political-economic vision for the world.[102] In a scene that repeatedly shouts "curses" and that "smashes" the world to pieces—"I will smash to pieces with my enduring curses"—Marx continued with the dreary and hopeless narrative. He summed up coldly:

> The worlds, they see it and go rolling on
> And howl the burial song of their own death.
> And we, we Apes of a cold God, still cherish
> With frenzied pain upon our loving breast
> The viper so voluptuously warm,
> That it as Universal Form rears up
> And from its place on high grins down on us!
> And in our ear, till loathing's all consumed,
> The weary wave roars onward, ever onward!
> Now quick, the die is cast, and all is ready;
> Destroy what only poetry's lie contrived,
> A curse shall finish what a curse conceived.

Note the grim morbidity: Apes of a *cold* God vs. the viper so *voluptuously warm*. Destruction. Lies. Curses. Curses. Curses.

A curse will finish what a curse had conceived.

Payne notes that Oulanem sees himself as the agent of destruction, as the judge who condemns and then acts as executioner, confident that he is in possession of the powers of God to annihilate the universe. Men, in that universe, are no more than apes of a cold God. Payne viewed this Marxist vision as directly transferrable to Marx's philosophical vision. He perceived the dialogue between Oulanem and the other characters as assuming the form of a classic Marxist "dialectical struggle" that is "never completely resolved, precisely akin to the Marxist ideological vision of the world.[103]

Payne thus affirmed that the speech of Oulanem is important to understanding Marx's ideas: "Combat or death, bloody struggle or annihilation." He notes that in the *Communist Manifesto*, "we hear the same strident voice calling for a war to the death between the proletariat and the bourgeoisie, a merciless battle with no quarter given by either side. It is important to observe that Marx's philosophy of the destruction of classes has its roots in romantic drama."

It seems still more important, in light of what Marxism actually produced, that after Marx's Oulenem continued to heap curses upon curses on a hopeless and miserable mankind, he sits down at the table, grabs his pen, and writes. As Payne observed, we are not told what Oulanem was writing, "but it may be a suicide note or a formal sentence of death on all creation."[104] In effect, that is the end result of what Marx himself wrote when he sat down to write his larger manifesto.

Alas, Payne discerned, "Oulanem was Marx as judge and executioner."[105] Indeed he was.

It is also telling that at the time of *Oulanem*, Karl Marx was aspiring to nothing less than write the *Faust* of his age. And to repeat, Marx loved the line pronounced by Mephistopheles in *Faust*: "Everything that exists deserves to perish." As Payne notes, Marx's drama *Oulanem* is an extended improvisation of that theme, a line that Marx himself used in other writings, quoting it with relish, for instance, in *The Eighteenth Brumaire*.[106]

But even then, Marx's *Oulanem* is worse than Goethe's *Faust*. As Payne noted, Marx had effectively brought us the archetype of Oulanem before as the crazed violinist of "The Player" who accepted a sword from the prince of darkness, sawing on his violin in a mad frenzy to drive the world to destruction. "He is Mephistopheles," avers Payne, "but not the Mephistopheles of Goethe; he is an altogether lesser creature bereft of dignity, possessing only malice and the desire for vengeance." It is vengeance that dominates Marx's long soliloquy in which Oulanem exalts in his power to shatter the world through his curses, consigning the entire human race to damnation.[107]

Richard Wurmbrand remarked that *Oulanem* may be the only drama in which every character is fully aware of his or her own corruption and yet all flaunt and celebrate it with prideful conviction. All of the characters are irredeemably bad. And this is not done by the playwright with a noble purpose of revealing the dark to herald the light. There is no light. There is no black and white here in Marx, just black. "Here all are servants of darkness," wrote Wurmbrand. "All are Satanic, corrupt, doomed."[108]

Finally, and perhaps what is most significant and chilling, we must note how Marx himself saw his play. He pridefully viewed *Oulanem* as a personal poetic masterpiece, one in which he flatly nailed his objective. He wrote to his father in November 1837, "These last verses are the only ones in which it seemed to me that I had been struck by the magic wand."[109]

Whose wand? Whoever wielded it, Marx wielded the pen, and it was in writing this grotesque drama that Karl felt he had been at his best.

Trembling in Terror and Horror

Perhaps *Oulanem* was not the "only drama" of Marx in which every character is depraved. To assume so would be to underestimate Karl Marx, who, after all, wrote many, many things, and was, after all, the founder of communism.

There were yet more troublesome Marx writings. Here is a likewise scary poem, titled "The Pale Maiden" (Payne does not deal with this one, which is posted at www.marxists.org),[110] a self-described love "ballad" where Marx exclaimed:

> The maiden stands so pale,
> So silent, withdrawn,
> Her sweet angelic soul
> Is misery-torn.

Therein can shine no ray,
The waves tumble over;
There, love and pain both play,
Each cheating the other.

Gentle was she, demure,
Devoted to Heaven,
An image ever pure
The Graces had woven.

Then came a noble knight,
A grand charger he rode;
And in his eyes so bright
A sea of love flowed.

At this point in what could have become a lovely ballad, Marx's scenario characteristically turned morose. That is no surprise, given that Karl Marx was not one for happy endings:

Love smote deep in her breast,
But he galloped away,
For battle-triumph athirst;
Naught made him stay.

All peace of mind is flown,
The Heavens have sunk.
The heart, now sorrow's throne,
Is yearning-drunk.

And when the day is past,
She kneels on the floor,
Before the holy Christ
A-praying once more.

And nigh, here, yet again for Marx, the scene moved away from the holy Christ, from promise to hopelessness, to terror, to horror, to hell itself:

But then upon that form
Another encroaches,
To take her heart by storm,
'Gainst her self reproaches.

"To me your love is given
For Time unending.
To show your soul to Heaven
Is merely pretending."

She trembles in her terror
Icy and stark,
She rushes out in horror,
Into the dark.

She wrings her lily-white hands,
The tear-drops start.
"Thus fire the bosom brands
And longing, the heart.

"Thus Heaven I've forfeited,
I know it full well.
My soul, once true to God,
Is chosen for Hell.

He was so tall, alas,
Of stature divine.
His eyes so fathomless,
So noble, so fine.

"He never bestowed on me
His glances at all;
Lets me pine hopelessly
    Till the end of the Soul."

What had begun as a potential redeeming romantic ballad by Marx turned into a late-night, B-movie horror show, with the sickly pale and lily-white-hands and icy-and-stark maiden rushing out into the murky night, trembling in terror. Here again, the characters forfeit heaven in favor of choosing hell. It was typical Marx.

What to make of this? In fact, one is tempted to literally ask, what the *hell* to make of this? What was Karl Marx saying? What kind of freak-horror show was he offering?

Well, we can discern what he was saying; his bleak messages of despair are fairly evident. It isn't rocket science. But more pointedly, to the question of the poet-philosopher himself, what part was Marx himself playing in this and other poems? From which end of the abyss did he gaze? What was he advocating? Was Marx "chosen for Hell," his soul no longer "true to God?" Was he pining hopelessly till the end of his soul? Or was he in the role of the devil choosing this gloomy fate for these forlorn, pale people?

Taken individually, the stanzas are not always clear, though the larger narrative of Marx's writings and life undeniably place him somewhere digging in the pit.

Wurmbrand went so far as to make the case that Marx himself was a Satanist, one who plunged "into the depths of Satanism."[111] His soul was no longer true to God (Marx indeed had become a committed atheist by this point) but was now true to Lucifer. Admirers of Marx will surely want to dispute that, given their fealty to their beloved founding father, for whom they make excuses for everything. Nonetheless, there is no debating the man's misery and his shaking his fist at God. Those two attitudes reinforced one another in the Marxist project, whether poetical or political.

"There is no support for the view that Marx entertained lofty social ideals about helping mankind," concluded Wurmbrand. "Marx hated any notion of God or gods. He determined to be the man who would kick out God."[112]

Marx's poetry certainly seemed to do that. And Marx's disciples and implementers would certainly kick out God. The devil was in their details.

Historical Context

Modern Marxist oddballs will find reasons to defend this nightmarish trash—in a way, of course, they would never do if, say, a Republican president had penned such pernicious claptrap. They will want to say he was joking, having fun—thus begging the intriguing question of how, exactly, this is humorous or fun—maybe being ironic, perhaps role-playing of some curious sort. The problem with such assertions is that we cannot say any of that with certainty. At the same time, those who dislike or disdain Marx should not go dashing in the opposite direction and chalk this up as a telltale sign of, say, explicit devil worship—of Marx using the same pen to pull out a piece of paper to sign a contract selling his soul to Satan. There is likewise no evidence to assert that.

We should all, however, concede one reality beyond dispute: this is highly disconcerting.

Marx's progressive cheerleaders might also want to write this off as the innocent musings of youth. There are at least two big problems with that: First, typical youth do not write (and publish) verse like this. If Marx's pom-pom boys and girls would like to go that route, then I ask them directly here and now: Did all of you write garbage like this? I bet not. Second, however, is a bigger problem, namely, Karl was not exactly a kid when he scribbled this twaddle. He wrote "The Pale Maiden" in 1837, his nineteenth year of life. He wrote "The Player" in 1841, his twenty-third year. And if Marxists suddenly want to toss out that whole period of Marx for the convenience of ignoring such alarming writings, then they should shelve their recent hagiographic film universally hailed by all of them: "The Young Marx."

Do they want us to celebrate the young Karl or not? Embrace him or ignore him? Do we lionize the young Marx or not? Hero or goat? You ought to be willing to accept the bad with the good. This material, dear comrades, would fall into the bad category.

But more than that, one still cannot shrug off such poems from Marx by simply claiming they were mere youthful musings. After all, this period of 1837–41 (and beyond) is when Marx became Marx. These were his college years, his graduate work years, his dissertation period, the time that he left his Christian faith of his teen years, the period when he launched into his most prolific writing. The 1840s were the peak of his writing, culminating in his writing the *Manifesto* in 1847. Modern Marx biographers coo over his "touching" letters to his father at this time.

If defenders of Marx want to try to make an eternity of the six years between 1841 and 1847, or of the ten between 1837 and 1847, well, we can make that messy for them as well. The timeline is not as long as they would prefer for their purposes of denial. It was the summer of 1837 that Marx first encountered the Young Hegelians, becoming a member of the Doctors' Club. Again, the leading member of the group was Dr. Bruno Bauer, and it was that year, in March 1841, that he and Marx planned to launch their review journal *Archives of Atheism*, with Karl as co-editor. Think about that. Such would reveal the Marx of 1841—that is, the Marx of "The Player"—to be a rather aggressive atheist, and hence not an unlikely candidate to write something as unheavenly as "The Player."

Those are just two examples. Here is a mere partial list of Marx writings and categories of writings from this period, again reflecting someone who was not exactly a kid who had written nothing but a few silly poems about Satan in his notebook. This is a cut and paste from the categories of various Marx writings posted at the Marxist clearinghouse, www.marxists.org:

1837	The Young Marx A Book of Verse Letters
1838	Letters
1839	Notebooks on Epicurean Philosophy Letters
1840	Letters
1841	Marx's Doctoral Thesis Letters
1842	On Freedom of the Press Articles in *Rheinische Zeitung* (Marx and Engels) Letters
1843	Critique of Hegel's Philosophy of Right Letters
1844	Comment on James Mill Deutsche-Französischer Jahrbücher (Marx and Engels) including Introduction to Critique of Philosophy of Right Economic & Philosophic Manuscripts On The Jewish Question Letters
1845	The Holy Family (Marx and Engels) Theses On Feuerbach The German Ideology (Marx and Engels) Letters
1846	Saint Max Letters

1847	The Poverty of Philosophy
	The Communist League
	Wage Labour & Capital
	Wages
	Articles in *Deutsche-Brüsseler Zeitung* (Marx and Engels)
	True Socialism
	The True Socialists
	Letters

As any informed Marxist knows, listed here are just some of the numerous poems, letters, published articles, books, notebooks (on Epicurean philosophy), critiques of Hegel, and many long, serious writings—some of Marx's most important and lasting—between 1837 and 1847. These include his 1841 doctoral thesis, titled *The Difference Between the Democritean and Epicurean Philosophy of Nature*. Again, that was published the same year as his 1841 poem, "The Player." They include his autumn 1843 essay *On The Jewish Question*, his autumn 1843 screed *The Holy Family*, his 1843 "A Contribution to the Critique of Hegel's Philosophy of Right" (where he wrote of religion as the "opium of the people"), his famous 1845–46 work *The German Ideology*, his 1847 book *The Poverty of Philosophy*, and much more.[113] The *Communist Manifesto* immediately followed, published in 1848.

Above all, Marx met Engels during this time, in November 1842, and thereupon began plotting to change the course of history. This Karl Marx is the Karl Marx of history. The man's heart was tormented, governed, as we have seen, by some sordid and disturbing things.

CHAPTER 3

"GOVERNED BY A DEMON?"

MARX'S MISERIES

"**A**nd since that heart is obviously animated and governed by a demon not granted to all men, is that demon heavenly or Faustian?"

So pondered a pensive, perturbed Heinrich Marx, Karl's father, in a letter to his son written March 2, 1837. The heart in question was Karl's. Heinrich was concerned about what was animating and governing his son's heart. The full passage of the letter reads:

> At times my heart delights in thinking of you and your future. And yet at times I cannot rid myself of ideas which arouse in me sad forebodings and fear when I am struck as if by lightning by the thought: is your heart in accord with your head, your talents? Has it room for the earthly but gentler sentiments which in this vale of sorrow are so essentially consoling for a man of feeling? And since that heart is obviously animated and governed by a demon not granted to all men, is that demon heavenly or Faustian? Will you ever—and that is not the least painful doubt of my heart—will you ever be capable of truly human, domestic happiness? Will—and this doubt has no less tortured me recently since I have come to love a certain person like my own child—will you ever be capable of imparting happiness to those immediately around you?[114]

It was at the same time a prophetically sad question, a concession, as well as a premonition by the father. Could Karl ever be happy? What was possessing his heart?

A good question. One that we today are still left pondering.

"Religion Lies at Our Feet"

Karl Marx was born on May 5, 1818, in the city of Trier, one of the loveliest, oldest, most tranquil, most peaceful, most religious, and most deeply Catholic cities in Germany (a population that was 90 percent Roman Catholic).[115]

It was hard to find a more Catholic place. The Christian roots of Trier are remarkable. None other than St. Ambrose, the future bishop of Milan who brought Augustine into the faith, was born in Trier in the year 340. The city boasts the oldest church in Germany, dating to AD 320–330. It is said that St. Helena (AD 246/248–330) herself gave a portion of the land to build the church there. She also gave Christians no less than Constantine, her son, the great Roman emperor and protector of Christians. Among the most sacred relics believed to be held at Trier's grand cathedral is the Seamless Robe of Jesus, also known as the Holy Robe, or Holy Coat, which Christ wore on the way to his crucifixion—the one for which the Roman soldiers had cast lots. According to tradition, St. Helena obtained the robe in the Holy Land around AD 327 and brought it to Germany.

Such is the city of Trier. It is special, long beloved by Christians.

Not surprisingly, Karl Marx's literary idol Goethe disapproved. "The place is burdened, nay oppressed, with churches and chapels and cloisters and colleges and buildings dedicated to chivalrous and religious orders," grumbled Goethe upon a visit in 1793, the year the Jacobin guillotine was dropping incessantly upon necks in Catholic France, "and this is to say nothing about the abbacies, Carthusian convents and other institutions which invest and blockade it."[116]

Only Goethe, and later Marx, could detest Trier.

Karl's father and mother started their family there. Karl had such a world of promise and decency in front of him. Holiness was fully available at practically every corner.

Marx's family was Jewish, on both his father's and mother's sides. They were not only ethnically Jewish but had a healthy family history of devout Judaism. There had been several rabbis in the recent family history, from the nineteenth century back to at least the late seventeenth century.[117] "It would be difficult to find anyone who had a more Jewish ancestry than Karl Marx," writes biographer David McLellan.[118]

Under the social pressures of the day, Marx's father left Judaism and converted to Protestantism at some point in the late 1810s or early 1820s, most likely at the end of 1819.[119] It is particularly intriguing that Heinrich chose Protestantism over Catholicism, the latter being a much more common choice for Jews who left Judaism in Catholic Trier, including his brother Cerf. Marx biographer Jonathan Sperber explains that Heinrich was much more liberal, a product of the Enlightenment, who, tellingly, if not fatefully, had read Voltaire aloud to the young Karl.[120] He knew Voltaire and Rousseau by heart.[121] With the sort of candor and disdainful language his son would use, Heinrich denounced what he called "the Gospels polluted by ignorant priests," in favor of what Sperber described as "a liberal and Enlightened Protestantism, not entirely separate from Deism, that would be Heinrich Marx's Christianity of choice."[122]

Heinrich became Lutheran. It was a choice that allowed him more choices to define his own views. The son would seize upon such choices with wild abandon.

Still, Heinrich at least saw value in believing in God. He advised Karl that "a good support for morality is a simple faith in God. You know that I am the last person to be a fanatic. But sooner or later a man has a real need of this faith, and there are moments in life when even the man who denies God is compelled against his will to pray to the Almighty."[123]

Heinrich's wife, Henrietta, was much more reluctant to convert, and thus delayed not only her own conversion but the baptisms of her children as well. Karl was baptized not as an infant, which would have been just about the time that Heinrich converted, but in 1824, the sixth year of his life.[124]

Karl, too, became Lutheran. He kept the faith—even if he was not always devout or clear or particularly orthodox—until probably his late teens and initial college years.[125] He definitely shed his faith during his college years and was unquestionably an atheist by the time he did his dissertation at age twenty-three in 1841. In his dissertation, he approvingly quoted the first century BC Roman philosopher Lucretius's eulogy for Epicurus, condemning the "burden of oppressive religion," which "with gruesome grotesqueness frightfully threatened mankind." Lucretius exalts, "Religion lies at our feet, completely defeated."[126]

That was the triumph to which Karl Marx thereafter committed himself: religion at our feet. It was a shame, a waste of the richly religious soil he had tread and was raised upon. He would stomp upon that religious bounty rather than feed upon it as nourishment for his troubled soul.

Marx, Luther, and the Reformation

Though this book is not the place to adequately treat the subject, it is noteworthy that Karl Marx seemed to appreciate Martin Luther's rebellion against the Church. In no way is that observation intended to equate Luther with Marx or his goals, and certainly not with the destruction produced by communism. For starters, Luther was, of course, anything but a godless atheist. Whereas Marx liked what Luther did, or, more specifically, liked the byproduct of what Luther did in terms of undermining the authority of the Church of Rome, Luther surely would not have liked what Marx did, nor the results of Marx's ideas or communism's madness.

Marx seems to have appreciated that Luther pulled away from

the authority of the Church, which, for Marx, was a crucial step in the ongoing march of the dialectic of history—that is, of advancing and progressing to the next crucial stage in history, according to Marxist theory. He mightily approved of that step, even if he did not necessarily approve of Luther at a spiritual level. This is stated most emphatically by Marx in the long concluding section of his famous 1843 work "A Contribution to the Critique of Hegel's Philosophy of Right." It was there he described religion as "the opium of the people." Interestingly, there he also credits Luther, who, he says, "overcame bondage," specifically that bondage imposed by Rome. "On the eve of the Reformation," Marx lamented, "official Germany was the most unconditional slave of Rome." Just as Luther made a crucial break from the religion of Rome, now Marx and his fellow philosophers would make a crucial break in their revolutionary "emancipation." Stated Marx, "As the revolution then began in the brain of the *monk*, so now it begins in the brain of the *philosopher*" (emphasis original).

Thus, for Marx, Luther had provided an indispensable service in clearing the path Marx envisioned for history.[127] What the monk began, the philosopher would conclude, although he would extend the path in directions of which Luther never dreamed, even in his worst nightmares.

In an 1854 piece that he wrote for the *New York Tribune*, approvingly titled "The Decay of Religious Authority," Marx wrote that the "Protestant Reformation" allowed "the upper classes in every European nation" (here again, Marx viewed nearly everything through the prism of class) to begin to "unfasten themselves individually from all religious belief, and become so-called free-thinkers." That included statesmen, legalists, and diplomats.. He noted that the Protestant Reformation had this effect not only among Catholic nations but even among those nations that adopted Protestantism. The Protestant Reformation that begat Protestantism allowed them all to think for themselves apart from the authority of the Church,[128] the Church founded by Christ. Again, this was a huge historical breakthrough, one which would serve Marx and the furtherance of his vision and ambitions.

Marx's father liked that Lutheranism allowed him more latitude to think for himself. Karl, too, wanted full freedom for the widest "free-thinking." Thinking completely apart from the Church of Rome could pave the way for him to open the door to philosophical communism. Breaking with Rome was the break he needed to pursue atheistic communism.

Notably, in that same article for the *New York Tribune*, Marx offered an insight into his view on the Crusades. The Crusades, greatly misunderstood and maligned to this day, were pursued by various popes, beginning with the First Crusade at the end of the eleventh century, as efforts to come to the defense of besieged Christians relentlessly attacked in Christian lands by Muslims in their holy war against "infidels." Each Crusade had to meet the requirements of Just War theory. The goal was to rescue those Christians and recover land and sites (such as the Holy Sepulchre) that had been theirs until Muslim invaders seized them violently.[129] Karl Marx reversed this entirely, portraying the Crusades as the period "when Western Europe, as late as the eighteenth century, undertook a 'holy war' against the 'infidel' Turks for the possession of the Holy Sepulchre."[130] This was a complete and outrageous reversal of which side had persecuted which. Of course, Marx's misunderstanding of the Crusades is now the consensus of secular leftists today; what is worse, they are not the only ones who subscribe to that view.

Marx's anti-Catholicism would show up in his writing. He wrote of one political associate, David Urquhart, who, "with his Catholicism, etc. grows more and more disgusting."[131] Curiously, as the *New York Tribune* piece suggests, he seemed to have a favorable opinion of Muslims. He praised certain Muslim Arabs, acknowledging a sympathy for their "hatred against Christians and the hope of an ultimate victory over these infidels."[132] Sure, Muslims believed in God, and that, to Marx, was a bad thing, but at least they were against Christians. They had that redeeming quality.

Yet again viewing everything through class and economics, Marx criticized "the monetary system [as] essentially a Catholic institution," and "the credit system [as] essentially Protestant." He lamented that the credit system "does not emancipate itself from the basis of the monetary system any more than Protestantism has emancipated itself from the foundations of Catholicism."[133]

Like his old man, Marx expressed a negative attitude toward Catholics in his midst. Marx would remember the Catholic pupils in his class as a bunch of "peasant dolts," which Jonathan Sperber says was probably reflective of the opinion of upper-class Protestant classmates.[134] I wouldn't blame them. Karl Marx never needed outside influence to view people as inferior idiots and rabble, or, to borrow one of Marx's handy phrases of derision, as the "lumpenproletariat." It came easy to Karl to see others as slack-jawed morons.

"Giving Birth to Monsters:"
Father, Son, and the Restless Spirit

By winter of 1837, the demons that young Karl wrestled with were increasingly tormenting him. He wrote his father a long, heartfelt, sorrowful letter that began, "When I left you, a new world had opened out before me, the world of love, which began by being a love deprived of all hope and full of frenzied yearnings." In that state of mind, confessed the yearning poet-turned-philosopher to his father, "it was inevitable that lyric poetry should be my chief interest." But sadly, he conceded, poetry "could and must be only a casual companion." When he got to Berlin, where he had broken all previous existing ties to Trier, he began to study jurisprudence and, "above all," felt "an urgent need to wrestle with philosophy."[135]

The unrest reflected in his poetry, along with its associated demons, would be transferred to his philosophy.

Karl finished this letter, dated November 10, 1837, at about four in the morning, as the candle went out and he could no longer see what he had written. Nearing his final thoughts, he wrote, "A deep unrest has mastered me, and I shall not be able to lay the specters that haunt me until I am in your dear presence."[136]

The man who would write about the specter of communism that haunted Europe was writing about the specters haunting him. A deep unrest had mastered him.

One biographer referred to this as a "monumental" letter from the son to the father, which is fair to say (I have quoted only a small portion). It took the father some time to digest it. On December 9, Heinrich Marx vomited out his response in an epic letter oozing with bile. He vented at the boy. What Heinrich wrote is worth quoting at length:

> God's grief!!! Disorderliness, musty excursions into all depart-ments of knowledge, musty brooding under a gloomy oil-lamp; running wild in a scholar's dressing-gown and with unkempt hair instead of running wild over a glass of beer; unsociable withdrawal with neglect of all decorum and even of all con-sideration for the father. . . . I am almost overwhelmed by the feeling that I am hurting you, and already my weakness once again begins to come over me, but in order to help myself, quite literally, I take the real pills prescribed for me and swallow it all down, for I will be hard for once and give vent to all my complaints. I will not become soft-hearted, for I feel that I have been too indulgent, given too little utterance to my grievances, and thus to a certain extent have become your accomplice. I must and will say that you have caused your parents much vex-ation and little or no joy. . . .
>
> On several occasions we were without a letter for months, and the last time was when you knew Eduard was ill, mother suffering and I myself not well, and moreover cholera was

raging in Berlin; and as if that did not even call for an apology, your next letter contained not a single word about it, but merely some badly written lines and an extract from the diary entitled *The Visit*, which I would quite frankly prefer to throw out rather than accept, a crazy botch-work which merely testifies how you squander your talents and spend your nights giving birth to monsters; that you follow in the footsteps of the new immoralists who twist their words until they themselves do not hear them; who christen a flood of words a product of genius because it is devoid of ideas or contains only distorted ideas. . . .

As if we were men of wealth, my Herr Son disposed in one year of almost 700 talers contrary to all agreement, contrary to all usage, whereas the richest spend less than 500. And why? I do him the justice of saying that he is no rake, no squanderer. But how can a man who every week or two discovers a new system and has to tear up old works laboriously arrived at, how can he, I ask, worry about trifles? How can he submit to the pettiness of order? Everyone dips a hand in his pocket, and everyone cheats him, so long as he doesn't disturb him in his studies, and a new money order is soon written again, of course.[137]

The father was incensed not only at the son's selfishness, personally and financially, but that the son squandered his talents and dad's money "giving birth to monsters." He did so as he "every week or two" ripped up old works and discovered new systems. The father continued to fulminate, finishing with a nasty flourish:

True, these poor young fellows sleep quite well, except when they sometimes devote half a night or a whole night to pleasure, whereas my hard-working talented Karl spends wretched nights awake, weakens his mind and body by serious study, denies himself all pleasure, in order in fact to pursue lofty abstract studies, but what he builds today he destroys tomorrow, and in the end he has destroyed his own work and not assimilated the work of others. In the end the body is ailing and the mind confused, whereas the ordinary little people continue to creep forward undisturbed and sometimes reach the goal better and at least more comfortably than those who despise the joys of youth and shatter their health to capture the shadow of erudition, which they would probably have achieved better in an hour's social intercourse with competent people, and with social enjoyment into the bargain!!!

I conclude, for I feel from my more strongly beating pulse that I am near to lapsing into a soft-hearted tone, and today I intend to be merciless.

The old man was being merciless alright. Not that the son had been selfless. Karl was selfish, and Heinrich let him know it, returning again to a theme that would always obsess Karl: money.

I must add, too, the complaints of your brothers and sisters. From your letters, one can hardly see that you have any brothers or sisters; as for the good Sophie, who has suffered so much for you and Jenny and is so lavish in her devotion to you, you do not think of her when you do not need her.

I have paid your money order for 160 talers. I cannot, or can hardly, charge it to the old academic year, for that truly has its full due. And for the future I do not want to expect many of the same kind.

To come here at the present moment would be nonsense! True, I know you care little for lectures, though you probably pay for them, but I will at least observe the decencies. I am certainly no slave to public opinion, but neither do I like gossip at my expense. Come for the Easter vacation—or even two weeks earlier, I am not so pedantic—and in spite of my present epistle you can rest assured that I shall receive you with open arms and the welcoming beat of a father's heart, which is actually ailing only through excessive anxiety.

The old man was at least willing to open his arms to his prodigal son—the son of the restless spirit, the son up late in the dark giving birth to monsters.

In presenting this letter in his biography of Karl Marx, Robert Payne notes that Heinrich finished with a shaking hand, concluding to his son that he could not write anymore. He was incensed.

The father died a few months later, on May 10, 1838, at age fifty-six. "Marx did not attend his father's funeral," recorded Payne. "The journey from Berlin was too long, and he had other things to do."[138]

Marx as Son, Father, and Moocher

With the death of his father, Marx turned to his mother—for money.

Heinrich's death was especially tragic because he was the only influence who seemed to inspire discipline in Karl's life. The mother now faced an uphill battle all to herself. "Let me know when you have received the money," she wrote to her son on October 22, 1838, trying to satisfy his cash demands after his father's death and with graduation looming. Henrietta expressed a heartfelt plea, "May the good God give you happiness in all your undertakings and lead you along the right path."[139]

One must wonder if Karl laughed at that poignant wish from his mom, or shook his fist at her letter. He was not thinking about a good God. Maybe there had already been one too many thoughts, put in writing, in verse, about the one who rebelled against God.

Quite apart from Marx's writings, the devil also seemed to have a role in the daily details of his life in more mundane but likewise troubling ways. Among them, Marx the family man left much to be desired. What follows is a mere glimpse of Marx as a man—that is, as a son, a father, a husband, a partner.[140]

Karl's strained, abusive relationship with family and money got worse when he began his own family.

Marx had viewed his parents parasitically, like a leech drawing blood from its host. He did this not only as a teen and young adult but as he himself became a parent and had children and teenagers. The man refused to work for wages, instead sucking as much income from his parents as possible.

The host in such a relationship eventually has no recourse but to cut off the parasite—to the parasite's writhing displeasure. Marx's parents would need to financially cut him off, enraging Marx in the process. He was draining dry his parents' lifetime savings. His suffering mother expressed the wish that "Karl would accumulate capital instead of just writing about it."[141]

His suffering wife would say the same: "Karl, if you had only spent more time making capital instead of writing about it, we would have been better off."[142]

Karl was too busy devising his self-important theories in his personal office or public library to bother earning an income to provide for his family. He demanded that others provide his income. His parents were the go-to source. Long before there was Minnie the Moocher, there was Marx the Moocher.

It would have been nice if Karl had merely gotten a job. Naturally, those who suffered most from Marx's refusal to secure work was his family, which was destitute from his laziness. His wife and kids lacked money, food, a steady roof over their heads, and even medical attention. He demanded more and more from his parents, until they could no longer give more and insisted on some tough love for their selfish son.

Well, that was enough for Karl. What a dastardly slight that was! He told his parents where to go (a place he knew well from his poetry). Some biographers claim or imply that he ultimately refused to attend his father's funeral out of spite.[143] Perhaps. He no doubt distanced himself from his mother.

Marx would make his first visit to his mother in nearly twenty years for the sake of pressuring her for cash. The guilt-trip and cornering of his mom did not go well, prompting Marx the moocher to write his wife with a complaint about the old woman: "She does not want to hear a word about money but she destroyed the I.O.U.'s that I made out to her; that is the only pleasant result of the two days I spent with her."[144]

Curse the old hag! The forever-prodigal son sauntered back to London whimpering and whining with his tail between his stodgy legs. But at least the old bat tore up the IOUs. At least the momentary reconciliation produced something of value for Karl—the "only pleasant result" of his time with his mother.

But the committed communist was not finished finding a way to hit up the old lady for more subsidies. Karl got himself a lawyer to ensure he raked in a healthy share from the elderly woman once she died in 1863.

He clearly did not care much about her, especially once his dad had departed. "With his father's death he suddenly found himself without a family, for his mother meant nothing to him," sums up one Marx biographer. "When he thought of her at all, it was always cold-bloodedly; she was the woman who prevented him from reaching his full flowering because she controlled the family fortune and refused to part with it. The sullen, smoldering rage against his mother, as it appears in his letters, is not pretty to contemplate."[145]

Unfortunately for Karl, his mother outlived her husband by a good twenty-plus years. Still, this better-late-than-never scheme paid off handsomely for the champion of the proletariat. He would receive about $6,000 in gold and francs compliments of his decaying mother's corpse.

All along, Marx continued badgering other family members, trying to squeeze his uncles for cash. In 1862, he got off his library-bound posterior to go to Holland to angle one of his uncles, who told him to take a hike and get a job, which Karl naturally refused to do. It is not clear from historical accounts if this was the same uncle from whom Marx had already gotten $800 earlier. That money, like the $650 he inherited from his wife's uncle and the $1,050 he bilked from his wife's mother, all quickly disappeared, to the great consternation of his wife.[146]

The laziness in all of this is obvious, but the hypocrisy is especially outrageous. Consider that point 3 in Marx's and Engels's ten-point plan in the *Manifesto* called for "abolition of all right of inheritance." Like so many communist kingpins who would follow, Marx and Engels were exempting themselves from the stringent rules they were writing for the remainder of humanity: other people in the world did not deserve inheritances, but Karl Marx and Friedrich Engels damn well did.

Speaking of Engels, now Marx needed a new host from which to draw financial nutrients. He thus turned to his partner in crime and in cash. Engels, too, suckled from the teat of his parents' inheritance, which was apparently fatter than the Marx family cow.[147] But for Engels, too, Marx's mooching quickly became excessive and obscene. Engels was tossing his parasitical partner as much as $1,825 per year in 1850, which was a lot of money at the time, but Marx found a way to burn through it rapidly.[148]

"Marx was continually begging money from him," writes one biographer. "Day after day, week after week . . . Marx could not hide his envy of Engels's wealth. He was always urgent and uncompromising. He seemed to be holding a pistol to Engels' head and saying that the money must come, or else."[149]

Of course, Marx envied everyone's wealth. Marxism and communism thrive on envy of others' wealth.

Eventually, the gun to Engels's head got to him. He tired of Marx the miser using him for money. And as Engels slowed the spigot, Marx lashed out at him as well, and the moocher's family endured worse hardship.

Engels was particularly offended when the girlfriend he had long shacked up with and refused to marry suddenly died and Marx, rather than extend more than cursory sympathy, asked him to further extend the cash flow. Engels had informed Marx of the tragic news of the death of his love, but Marx responded by lamenting his more important financial situation: "The devil knows there is nothing now but ill luck where we are," moaned Marx. "I simply don't know any more where to turn. My attempts to rake up money in France and Germany have failed, besides the children have no shoes or clothing to go out in." In case the mourning Engels—whose mistress was not even in the grave—did not get the hint, Marx flat-out asked his grieving pal for more money. This prompted a peeved Engels to express his displeasure at Marx's insolence: "All my friends, including bourgeois acquaintances, have shown me on this occasion, which was bound to touch me very closely, more friendship and sympathy than I could expect. You found the moment well chosen to advertise the superiority of your cold philosophy; so be it."[150]

Well, at least Engels understood that the (shared) philosophy was cold. Engels' dead lady-friend, Mary Burns, was barely cold, and Karl Marx was holding out his cold hat for cold coin. Leave it to Engels to play the role of Karl's sucker. He continued to ladle out the silver to the Marx clan.

Marx's insensitivity is so obvious that even his most ardent admirers do not defend it. Biographer Mary Gabriel pauses here to acknowledge that this was one of "many instances" in which Marx showed himself to be a "deeply self-centered man." For two decades, Engels had considered his mistress Mary his unofficial wife of sorts. He grieved to Marx in a letter written the next day that she had died "quite suddenly. Heart failure or apoplectic stroke. . . . I simply can't convey how I feel. The poor girl loved me with all her heart." As Gabriel calculates, the first two lines of Marx's response expressed his surprise and dismay about Mary, followed by thirty-one lines on Marx's financial problems.[151]

Engels was so peeved that he waited a week before responding.

When he did, said Gabriel, "it was in the imperious Prussian tone that terrified his adversaries." Even lousy bourgeois acquaintances had shown him greater sympathy and friendship. But not Karl. "So be it then!" Engels thundered.[152]

This was the one instance in which Engels was so ticked at Marx that their relationship almost came to an end.[153] But not quite. Friedrich would saunter back to continue fulfilling his role as Karl's top sap and sugar daddy.

Boiling Mad

In November 1849, one year after publishing his crowning work, the *Communist Manifesto*, Marx's landlord evicted him and his family because of communism's founding father's revulsion at the idea of an individual providing for himself and his family. Marx would have ached for an all-encompassing, cradle-to-grave, womb-to-tomb, collectivist-welfare state that confiscates revenue from wealthy people and redistributes it to lazy socialist academics and theorists peddling inane ideas from their messy desk piled with papers.

The landlord was also fed up with Marx's resistance to grooming. Karl drank too much, smoked too much, never exercised, and suffered from warts and boils from the lack of washing. He stunk. "Washing, grooming and changing his linens are things he does rarely, and he likes to get drunk," stated a Prussian police-spy report. "He has no fixed times for going to sleep or waking up." As for the family apartment, "everything is broken down," busted, spilled, smashed, falling apart—from toys and chairs and dishes and cups to tables and tobacco pipes and on and on. "In a word," said the report, "everything is topsy-turvy. . . . To sit down becomes a thoroughly dangerous business." Quite literally, the chair you chose to sit upon in the Marx household could collapse.[154]

This was symptomatic not only of Marx's house but himself. Just as the house was dirty and infested and broken down, so was Karl.

Especially gruesome were the boils that plagued his bottom (and everywhere else). He suffered from them for more than twenty years.

"The boils varied in numbers, size and intensity," wrote Paul Johnson, "but at one time or another they appeared on all parts of his body, including his cheeks, the bridge of his nose, his bottom, which meant he could not write, and his penis. . . . They brought on a nervous collapse marked by trembling and huge bursts of rage."[155]

At one point in London in the spring of 1854, Marx had grown a particularly unpleasant boil between his upper lip and nose, hindering his ability to speak. "My face has reached a crisis," he grimaced in a letter to Engels. He fingered a possible culprit for his suffering, a not unreasonable one: "For fourteen days the devil has been hurling shit at my head."[156]

Hmm. Perhaps Marx was joking there. Perhaps. Or is this yet another example where maybe we should take him literally when writing about the devil?

Marx was compelled to wax biblical on some of these occasions, such was his suffering. He told Engels that he was "the object of plagues just like Job, though I am not so God-fearing as he was." Indeed. He said on yet another occasion amid his two-plus decades of boils that he felt like a "real Lazarus," and asked Engels, "Wouldn't it have been more reasonable to send these trials of patience to some good Christian, someone like Silvio Pellico?"[157]

The boils got so bad that at times he could only stand upright or lie on his side on the sofa.[158] The man who said that religion was the opium of the masses ended up taking opium for his boils, as well as doses of arsenic. He and his doctors were perplexed at the cause of the boils, which was not a disease picked up by anyone else in the Marx household. (Marx's obsession with not bathing would seem a rather obvious contributing factor.)

Marx's boils might have been at their worst when he was writing *Das Kapital*, which might explain the sense of oozing pain one feels when reading this blistering piece of work. "Whatever happens," he groaned to Engels, "I hope the bourgeoisie as long as they exist will have cause to remember my carbuncles."[159]

You bet they have. Marx's boils persisted in the lives of that very bourgeoisie. They more than remembered his intellectual boils which fester to this day.

Toss the Bum Out

Marx was, in short, a slob. He was sloppy in his home life, in his desire to earn an income, in his keeping of papers, and even in his research. He avoided the factories and farms for which he devised prodigious plans for their mass nationalization and collectivization. He did his research never from the field but exclusively from the library. He embodied the worst stereotype of isolated academics who never deign to intermingle with the *rubes* they profess to represent. The champagne socialist at Columbia University sees no need to actually sit at a kitchen table in Peoria with some farmer-bumpkin who votes Republican and clings to his God and guns.

Even sympathetic sources underscore Marx's failure to provide for his family. "He and Jenny, his wife, spent the majority of their life together in considerable and frequently miserable poverty, relying on contributions from supportive friends (most reliably Friedrich Engels)," states a writer at the left-wing *Salon*. "If this was hard on Marx, it was surely harder still on Jenny."[160] Jenny herself had been raised as what we today would call a "limousine leftist." (In Jenny's day, perhaps a horse-and-carriage leftist.) Born in Prussia, she was four years older than Karl and was brought up in an aristocratic family. She gave up her life of privilege for a life with Karl.

For the record, Jenny likewise turned against religion. She and Karl had wedded at a Protestant church in the town of Kreuznach in June 1843. Hardly anyone attended. Neither Marx's parents nor anyone from his side of the family came, and the only family member from Jenny's side were her mother and brother Edgar. Whatever religious feelings they had at that point must have been left at the altar. Jenny likewise was not impressed by religious people, once creating a short list of her "aversions"—"knights, priests, soldiers."[161]

Jenny was also averse to Christian religious relics, as was her husband. As she remained in Germany while Karl was in Paris, she wrote to him in lament about the enthusiasm of Catholic pilgrims who had come to town for a special veneration of the Holy Coat at the Trier cathedral, which had drawn in many religious enthusiasts. "People seem to have gone mad," she scoffed in a letter to Karl, knowing he would join her in her condescension toward these superstitious fools. "I suppose all hell is breaking loose with you, too."[162]

In fact, hell already had broken loose with regard to Karl and the Holy Coat. Recall his perverse poem "The Player." For that poetic drama, Marx had not only written words but had arranged the stage furniture and the wardrobe for all his characters in his production. To that end, Marx dressed his satanic violinist in a wrinkled gown that Marx had derived from—yes—the Holy Coat at the grand cathedral in Trier.[163]

Chillingly, if not sacrilegiously, such was the robe of Marx's man as he played out his pact. As he cut loose with his violin and his "blood-dark sword," his soul resounding in the "depths of Hell," with "hellish vapors" filling his brain, boldly playing the "dance of death," he donned the Holy Robe of Jesus Christ.

Nice, Karl. Real nice.

A Pact with the Devil

Not surprisingly, Karl and Jenny had no enthusiasm for passing religious faith on to their children. When Christmas was acknowledged at the Marx household, it was viewed entirely as a secular event. When the children asked Papa Karl about the origins of Christmas, he explained the story of Christ as a tale of a poor carpenter killed by wealthy men.[164] Yet again, Marx shoehorned the message through his prism of wealth, money, and class. Even the life of Christ had to be about economics.

Marx's daughter Eleanor remembered fondly at age five or six being taken to a Roman Catholic church and being stirred by the "beautiful music," and thus "feeling certain religious qualms." Her dad, however, disabused her of these childish sentiments. No matter what she was *feeling*, her father argued that Christianity did not have a rational answer. As Eleanor said, her father stated "many and many a time" that "after all we can forgive Christianity much, because it taught us the worship of a child."[165]

Later, when Marx offered to send his daughters to a boarding school, the girls declined because of the "religious rites." When his daughter Laura got married, it was a civil marriage in London. No church.[166] It sounds like Marx had trained them well.

And while Marx did not want to put the fear of God into his children, he seemed to have few qualms about putting the fear of Satan into them. When he was in London, Marx liked to tell what Robert Payne describes as "an interminable story" to his children during Sunday walks to Hampstead Heath. This was a tale about an imaginary character named Hans Rockle, who kept an enchanted toyshop and who (like Marx) was always in debt. The shop had all sorts of intriguing toys and woodcarvings: little men, kings, queens, dwarves, birds, animals. Rockle was no mere toymaker, however. He was a magician, but his powers were limited because he could never fully meet his obligations to the devil. "He made his pact with the devil," writes Payne, "and there was no escaping from it." And whereas some of Marx's stories about Hans were "wryly humorous," writes Payne, "others made the children's hair stand on end." Eleanor recalls the stories being as frightening as the stories of the Gothic horror novelist of the day E. T. A. Hoffmann.[167]

And yet, here is the crucial moral to this story. In Payne's assessment:

There can be very little doubt that those interminable stories were autobiographical, and that Hans Rockle, who bought and sold wooden men and was always in danger of losing them to the devil, was Karl Marx presiding over the fortunes of economic man. The pact with the devil was the central theme of *Oulanem* and appears in various disguises in many of his early poems. It was a subject on which Marx had brooded frequently, not only in his youth. Goethe's *Faust* was his bible, the one book which he regarded with unreserved admiration, and he liked to roar out the verses of Mephistopheles, just as he liked to sign himself "Old Nick." He had the devil's view of the world, and the devil's malignity. Sometimes he seemed to know that he was accomplishing works of evil.[168]

Among these works, Payne here continued, are certain images that constantly recur in Marx's writing such as death, torture, executioners, mutilation, even ruptured wombs, as well as the ferocious manner in which he blistered his enemies with gutter language and vicious words. Payne is justified in asserting that Marx spent much of his life in a "helpless rage against the world. . . . In letter after letter he roars his disgust at the world and at people, with unbridled malevolence."[169]

Marx even dealt with his allies this way. Friends of many years could quickly find themselves non-persons, the subjects of his derision and vituperation and diatribes. As detailed at length by several biographers, Marx was often dictatorial with his editorial staff and with his Communist League and Party. Payne chronicles what he aptly terms Marx's "purges," a haunting bellwether for how various Communist Parties, from Russia to America to worldwide, would deal ruthlessly with internal dissenters who did not always toe the Party line. "The purges were not invented in Soviet Russia," writes Payne. "They appeared at the very beginning of Marxist communism, and were part of the system."[170]

In all, concludes Payne, "there were times when Marx seemed to be possessed by demons, when rage overflowed in him and became poison, and he seemed to enter into a nightmare." Like in the drama *Oulanem* and other writings and poems, there was a penchant for nihilism and destruction.[171]

And returning to Hans Rockle, remember that this was a favorite story that Marx would share with his children on Sunday walks in London. These were the very Marx children who likewise ended up not only atheists but hopeless atheists—that is, truly people with no hope, to the point (in some cases) of suicide. This was the dark worldview that Marx's daughters inherited and learned from their father.

Karl and Jenny: The Extraordinary Misery of Being a Marx

Prior to London, where Karl and Jenny would spend most of their married life, one of their earliest stops in starting their family and ideological sojourn had been in Brussels, where they moved in February 1845 and had their first child, Laura. They took up residence at the *Bois Sauvage* boardinghouse on the Place St. Gudula. Located in the heart of Brussels, the Marx abode was towered over by the great Cathedral of St. Michael, which, as one Marx biographer notes, almost seemed to be situated above Marx as a "constant reminder of the terrific power of Marx's enemy the Church."[172] That is the very Church whose pope, Leo XIII, composed the prayer to St. Michael to "defend us in battle" against the "wickedness and snares of the Devil" and to "thrust into Hell Satan and all the evil spirits who prowl about the world seeking the ruin of souls."

The young Marxes spent two years in the shadow of St. Michael, as Karl composed the *Communist Manifesto*. It was just the start for Marx in many ways. Here began not only an ideological battle against money but a personal one, which took a terrible toll on his marriage to Jenny. He enlisted her in the battle as well.

The shameless Marx sent his wife begging to relatives. In one case, in August 1850, Jenny crossed the English Channel in a storm and arrived soaking wet at Karl's Dutch relatives' home, unrecognizable. According to one biographer, the uncle told the poor, disheveled, dripping wife that Marx's family had about as much enthusiasm subsidizing godless communism as did that of Engels.[173]

Karl and Jenny hoped that his masterwork, *Das Capital*, might actually earn them some capital. But Marx, who was notorious for not completing assignments, for ignoring word limits, and for missing deadlines, shirked this deadline by sixteen years. The first royalty check from the book arrived sixteen years later still, at which point both Karl and Jenny had died; only their surviving children got some royalties.[174]

Marx had wasted over two decades writing *Das Kapital*, a long, ridiculous tome, a waste of money as well as time. He had initially received a three hundred dollar advance for the book, but extended over twenty-three years of drawn-out writing, it equated to a little over a dozen dollars a year.[175]

Nor did Marx's *Manifesto* against wealth and property help his financial cause. There was not even a paltry sum for the kids in the wretched winter of 1849–50, the year after it was published. That winter the Marx family sought refuge in a dilapidated boardinghouse. (Between 1848 and 1850, the Marx family were like vagabonds, transitioning between Brussels, Paris, Cologne, and London.) There, that bitterly cold season, the family baby, an infant boy named Heinrich Guido (named for Marx's father), succumbed to the elements not long after his first birthday. Really, he arguably perished a victim of his communist father's irresponsibility. Jenny connected the dots. Paul Johnson writes of Marx's wife, "Jenny left a despairing account of these days, from which her spirits, and her affection for Marx, never really recovered."[176]

Marx meanwhile kept up pressure on his mother. In March 1851, he told her that if she did not intervene to cover one of his interminable IOUs—run up with the landlady, with shopkeepers, at the pub where Karl regularly got drunk—that she would let the police arrest him. Henrietta called his bluff on that one. She didn't budge.[177]

Jenny wrote a letter in June 1852 pleading with her husband, "I had firmly decided not to torment you constantly with money problems, and now here I am again. But truly Karl, I no longer have any good course." She explained that the landlady was literally beating at the door. "She has really put me in a state of terror. She has already had our belongings auctioned off. And, in addition, baker, governess, tea grocer, grocer, and the terrible man, the butcher. I am in a state, Karl, I no longer know what to do. For all these people, I am exposed as a liar."[178]

Karl Marx had placed his wife in a state of terror over money and property, just as his writings and ideology would do to countless millions in the centuries ahead.

The nadir for Jenny and Karl during these trials and woes was the death of their eight-year-old son Edgar in 1855. Mary Gabriel, author of a sympathetic biography of the couple, described vividly and painfully how Edgar died of intestinal tuberculosis, "exacerbated by . . . unhealthy living conditions." That loss was heartbreaking. No matter what Karl's numerous transgressions, it is impossible not to feel for him when reading the wrenching accounts of the loss of little Edgar, who suddenly took ill and within a month was dead—in his father's arms. He was a fun, adored child, and Karl apparently loved him immensely. Biographer Jonathan Sperber called Edgar's death "the greatest tragedy in Marx's life."[179]

Mary Gabriel says Mr. and Mrs. Marx's soul-searching for answers about Edgar's death "could have led them to only one conclusion—the revolutionary path they had chosen had killed him." And Edgar was merely the latest victim. As Gabriel notes, by 1851, when Marx had begun writing *Das Capital*, "disease resulting from deprivation had killed two of his [Marx's] children."[180] That deprivation was beyond dispute the fault of Marx. The death of the Marx children would only continue. Edgar was far from the end of the cycle of doom.

Marx knew how this made his wife feel. He later lamented to Friedrich Engels, "Every day my wife says she wishes she and the children were safely in their graves, and I really cannot blame her, for the humiliations, torments and alarums that one has to go through in such a situation are indeed indescribable."[181]

Marx would say of Jenny, "I feel pity for my wife." He conceded that "our situation here is so extraordinarily miserable," and that "my poor wife is . . . completely broken down."[182]

Again, what Karl Marx really longed for was what his socialist-progressive descendants in the West would seek to bequeath: a giant collectivist/nanny state where Big Sister could assume the task of taking care of Karl's family for him.

Karl and Lenchen

The individual who came closest to providing that service for the Marx family was a nanny named Lenchen. There, too, Marx's duties as husband and father left something to be desired. To the devastation of his devoted wife, Marx had a sexual relationship with the family's young nursemaid.[183]

Helene Demuth, known as "Lenchen," had actually worked as a housemaid for Jenny's family, the Westphalen family. She and Jenny had essentially grown up with one another. Jenny's mom sent Lenchen to the young Marx home in Brussels in April 1845 to help out. There, under the eye of St. Michael, Lenchen was dragged into the cabal of communists and socialists brooding and boarding with Karl and Jenny at the boardinghouse.[184]

Actually, it is not quite right to say that Lenchen worked for the Marx family, given that she toiled without pay, almost like an indentured servant for life. One Marx biographer says that Lenchen was Marx's "chattel to be exploited unmercifully." Karl, champion of the proletariat, fulminator against low-paid workers, protester against wage exploitation, never paid Lenchen a penny. The stumpy, frumpy girl gave her everything to the Marx household. She sacrificed her own personal life for the Marx family's life. Still more ironic, given that Marx himself never interacted with or had worked with the proletariat, Lenchen was the only real contact with the working class that Karl ever experienced. And Marx used the poor girl. She gave herself to him fully—mind, spirit, body.[185]

Karl eventually bedded Lenchen behind Jenny's back. Historians have no idea how often or the exact circumstances, including whether it was consensual. "He would take his comfort where he could," wrote one biographer of Marx seeking a sexual receptacle in Lenchen. "That she was virtually his bondslave was a matter of entire indifference to him. It was enough that she was available to serve his sexual needs at a time when Jenny was too ill to satisfy them. We shall probably never know whether he raped or seduced the servant, though the large number of images concerned with rape in his later writings suggest that it was rape rather than seduction. In due course a child was born."[186]

In June 1851, Lenchen gave birth to a baby boy. Karl refused to ever concede that the unfortunate child was his, and naturally refused to provide a penny of child support. The illegitimate son, whose first name was left blank on the birth certificate, was eventually named Henry Frederick, or "Freddy." Marx shirked this moral responsibility too—financially as well as paternally. Engels bailed him out yet again.

"Engels had accepted paternity for Frederick," wrote Marx biographer David McLellan. "The son was immediately sent to foster parents and had no contact at all with the Marx household."[187] Engels was willing to claim responsibility for the pregnancy, though he was not about to raise the child under his own roof, which was always shared with one of the women he was living with and having sex with outside of marriage.

More precisely, what Engels did was agree to say that he was the father of the child. As one Marx biographer put it, "Engels cared not a whit about his reputation, especially with regard to women," with whom he regularly shacked up anyway, never daring to marry.[188] Decades later, on his deathbed, Engels admitted that the child was Karl's and that Engels had intervened to help his friend cover up the truth and to try to save Marx's marriage. The adult Freddy was aware of the truth. He would live well into his late seventies, dying in 1929, outliving all of Karl's legitimate children. Freddy left no descendants.[189]

Of course, Marx's devoted but despairing wife was surely not surprised, albeit heartbroken. What else did she expect from the man she referred to as her "wild black boar" and her "wicked knave?"[190]

Marx and His Daughters

As for the other girls in the family, Marx's relationship with his daughters is more complex and the subject of very different reporting by biographers, often depending in part on the ideological preferences of the biographers. Paul Johnson states that as Marx's daughters grew, he denied them a satisfactory education, if any education at all, and vetoed careers for them entirely. This most adversely affected Eleanor, the youngest Marx girl, who, as Johnson put it, "suffered most from his refusal to allow the girls to pursue careers and his hostility to suitors."[191] As we shall see, this manifested itself in Eleanor's marriage to an utter reprobate, a widely reviled man who seduced and slept with other women and, ultimately, killed her.

This reported rejection of his daughters having independent careers was another irony given the man's stature among a long line of Marxist-feminists, from Alexandra Kollontai and Betty Friedan to Kate Millett and Angela Davis, Communist Party candidate for vice president of the United States, among many others.

But again, views on Marx's treatment of his daughters varies.

Jonathan Sperber shows convincingly that Marx was a kind and loving father—or, in the words of one friend and frequent visitor, "the most tender father." That included his treatment of his daughters. Though perhaps he might have vetoed careers for his daughters (as Paul Johnson stated), Marx was determined to give them lessons expected in those days for raising "proper young ladies" (as Sperber puts it), including learning Italian, French, and receiving lessons in singing, piano, and drawing. And as noted, he and Jenny personally taught them, or at least raised them, to be (as Sperber puts it) "the same outspoken atheists that they were."[192] Marx also may have passed on to his girls his offensive outspokenness regarding members of the black race. In one letter, Marx's daughter Jenny complained to her sister Eleanor, "I drudge like a nigger."[193] As we shall see, that was very much her father's language.

And yet, Sperber also concedes that Marx stated candidly that he preferred male offspring. We have letters revealing this. "My wife, alas, delivered a girl and not a boy," he regretted to Engels of Jenny's deficient birthing abilities.[194] And as for the baby girl delivered by his daughter Jenny, Marx lamented to Jenny, "I congratulate you on the happy delivery. . . . I prefer the 'male' sex among children who will be born at this turning point in history."[195] These Marx opinions ought to receive full-throated condemnation by feminist Marxists and leftists of all stripes, who would not tolerate them if espoused by a prominent conservative thinker.

One highly favorable source, biographer Mary Gabriel, writes that Marx's daughters "adored their father." She asserts that they were born into Marx's "revolutionary household, with all the complications that entailed," and "they relished it." Gabriel likewise adds that the girls were educated, including in "the values of Victorian society—music, art, literature, and languages." They also were taught, she concedes, "a heavy dose of radical politics." And thus, as soon as they were able, they became their father's assistants. But that would come at a political, financial, and moral price. Not until they were women, says Gabriel, did Marx's daughters fully grasp "the high price of being born a Marx." She notes that one daughter lost all three of her young children while devoting herself "to further her father's agenda." Another daughter gave up a cherished life as a journalist for a "miserable marriage" to one of her father's young French followers. And the third daughter became "ensnared by a man whom she believed to be worthy of her father," but who, in the end, drove her to suicide.[196]

So, even a complimentary biographer like Gabriel concedes that Marx's daughters, regardless of his level of affection for them, met tragic ends.

In my mind, those downright calamitous ends should not be separated from the hopeless atheism and despairing atheistic worldview that Marx and his wife passed on. When their daughters hit the depths of despair, they had no God to turn to; their mom and dad had taught them that God did not exist—that religion was false, that it was opium for the masses. Instead of smoking opium, they ingested poison.

In fact, four of Marx's six children died before he did, including his oldest daughter, Jenny. The two daughters who survived him later committed suicide, one of them (Laura) in a suicide pact with her husband, a son-in-law that Marx ridiculed.[197] (Both of the socialist-communist daughters had been financially taken care of by Engels, who left them and their socialist-communist husbands a very healthy sum in his estate.) I will share more details of those horrible fates at the end of this chapter, as we morosely close out the lives of the Marx family.

As for the sons-in-law, that is yet another unhappy tale. Marx detested both of his sons-in-law, whom he viewed as idiots. "May the devil fly away with them!"[198] he exclaimed. Or, as another translation renders his wish, "To hell with both of them!"[199]

No idle matter for a man who waxed poetic about "hellish vapors."

In fact, it is ironic that Marx so disapproved of the girls' suitors given that all were atheist-socialist revolutionaries just like him.

Marx's Un-Christian Racial Views and Anti-Semitism

As we continue this discussion of Marx's family values, we encounter another sordid element of the life of Karl that cannot be avoided and merits pause: his awful statements about blacks and Jews; we see such ugly views by Marx littered throughout his personal and professional writings.

A victim of Marx's racism was his son-in-law, Paul Lafargue, husband of Laura. He came from Cuba, born in Santiago, later home of Marxist revolutionary Fidel Castro. Because Paul was Cuban, Marx viewed him as marred by "Negro" blood in his veins, prompting Marx to denigrate him as "Negrillo" and "The Gorilla."[200] Marx complained to Engels that "Lafargue has the blemish customarily found in the negro tribe—*no sense of shame*, by which I mean shame about making a fool of oneself."[201]

Imagine the rather shameless Marx having the audacity to assess Lafargue and his entirety of "negro tribesmen" as shameless.

Stephen Schwartz, the ex-Marxist and expert on communism, states flatly that Marx effectively "disowned" his daughter for marrying a man of mixed race.[202] At the least, Marx strongly disapproved.

Karl Marx was a racist who cast freely with choice epithets aimed at blacks and even at Jews—ironic given that Marx was an ethnic Jew.

Jonathan Sperber notes that Marx's correspondence is "filled with contemptuous remarks about Jews."[203] Even his admiring biographer Francis Wheen, who habitually defends the worst in Marx, admits that he "sprayed anti-Semitic insults at his enemies with savage glee."[204]

Of one contemporary, Marx blasted his "cynical, oily-obtrusive, phony-Baronial Jew-manners."[205] His fellow German socialist and labor organizer Ferdinand Lassalle, Marx referred to as a "greasy Jew," "the little kike," "water-polack Jew," "Jew Braun," "Yid," "Izzy," "Wily Ephraim," "Baron Itzig," and "the Jewish Nigger." Referring to Lassalle in a July 30, 1862 letter to Engels, Marx discerned with a sense of confident pride, "It is now perfectly clear to me that, as the shape of his head and the growth of his hair indicates, he is descended from the Negroes who joined in Moses' flight from Egypt." Lassalle's "cranial formation," asserted Marx, a strict and proud evolutionist, was the giveaway. Of course, Marx was willing to allow for an exception: "unless his mother or grandmother on the father's side was crossed with a nigger." With a mordant twinkle in his eye, Marx concluded, "This union of Jew and German on a Negro base was bound to produce an extraordinary hybrid." Marx hastened to add, "The fellow's importunity is also niggerlike."[206]

Walter Williams, the economist and well-known black conservative, states unequivocally that "Marx was an out and out racist and anti-Semite."[207]

Marx's single worst written expression of that anti-Semitism was his painful-to-read essay "On the Jewish Question." The essay was written in the fall of 1843 and published in 1844 in the journal *Deutsch-Französische Jahrbucher*. The article was actually a review of two Bruno Bauer books published in 1843, *The Jewish Question* and *The Capacity of Today's Jews and Christians to Become Free*.[208] The essay is classic Marx—meaning that it is long, rambling, meandering, and largely incoherent and incomprehensible. After paragraph upon paragraph and page after page of wasted ink, Marx finally—about three-quarters into yet another interminable screed—gets to something of historical value and personal insight when he cuts loose and lets us know what he really thinks about Jews. Upon reading his words, one wonders how a single Jew could ever speak well of Karl Marx after this, let alone call himself a Marxist.

"What is the worldly cult of the Jew?" asked Marx in "On the Jewish Question." His answer: "Haggling. What is his worldly god? Money. Very well! Emancipation from haggling and money, and thus from practical and real Judaism, would be the self-emancipation of our age."

Ironically, it was Karl Marx himself who treated money as his worldly god—money, economics, class, materialism. This seems a more accurate diagnosis by Marx of himself—that is, autobiographical. Nonetheless, Karl was on a roll. His target here was Jews. He growled, "Money is the jealous god of Israel before whom no other god may exist. . . . The bill of exchange is the actual god of the Jew. His god is only an illusory bill of exchange." Still more from Marx: "What is contained abstractly in the Jewish religion—contempt for theory, for art, for history, for man as an end in himself—is the *actual conscious* standpoint and virtue of the money-man. . . . The woman is haggled away. The chimerical nationality of the Jew is the nationality of the merchant, of the money-man in general. The Jew's unfathomable and unbounded law is only the religious caricature of baseless and bottomless morality and law in general."

Marx repeated those words throughout the essay: *haggling, money, egoism.* The Jew, Marx snarled, was "impossible." The German thus concluded, "The emancipation of the Jews, in the final analysis, is the emancipation of mankind from Judaism."

Damn those money-grubbing Jews! *The world needed emancipation from the Jew.* That was a sentiment that Adolph Hitler certainly shared.

In his seminal edited volume on Karl Marx and religion, Saul Padover sums up Marx's anti-Semitic views: "Marx . . . imbibed the ancient hostility to his people and accepted all the ugly stereotypes of the brutally caricatured Jew then widely prevalent in Europe, and not only among Lutherans. He learned to despise and hate the people from whom he originated. This was an expression of what the Germans call *Selbsthass* (self-hate), a trait which Karl Marx displayed throughout his whole life."[209]

Padover was taken aback by "the extent and virulence of his anti-Semitism." Marx was indeed a self-hating Jew.

Likewise cynical about Jews, and no doubt an influence on Marx, was his Jesus-mocking buddy, Bruno Bauer. Bauer snorted that the Jew "was much too concerned" with "satisfaction of natural needs."

Jewish religious attitudes were "the mere cleverness of sensual egoism," they were "crude and repulsive," they constituted "hypocrisy." In it all, the Jew "is and remains a Jew." To Bauer, Christianity was at least a step toward human emancipation, whereas Judaism was a historical dead end.[210]

Sperber notes that when Karl Marx wrote to Arnold Ruge in 1843 that the "Israelite faith is repulsive to me," he was referring to Bruno Bauer's attitudes. Sperber goes on to credit Bauer as no less than "one of the founders of racial anti-Semitism in central Europe," such was his "vehement" anti-Semitism.[211]

Also impacting Marx in this regard was his friend Moses Hess, one of the original eighteen members of the Communist League (along with Marx, Engels, and even Jenny).[212] Hess had an influence on Marx via an unpublished essay on Jews, money, and capitalism that Marx read before he wrote "On the Jewish Question." How anti-Jewish was Hess? He had written to Arnold Ruge that after the abolition of capitalism and with the creation of a communist society, it would be necessary to guillotine "just a few . . . property owners, stubborn bankers, Jews, capitalists, landowners and landlords."[213]

Yes, guillotine. Chop off the heads of a few Jews, along with other reptiles.

The admiration between Marx and Hess was mutual. Hess described Marx as a combination of Heinrich Heine and several others, calling him "my idol . . . he combines the deepest philosophical seriousness with the most cutting wit; imagine Rousseau, Voltaire, Holbach, Lessing, Heine and Hegel united in one person . . . then you have Dr. Marx."[214] Hess thrilled that "Dr. Marx, as my idol is called, is still a very young man (about 24 years old) and will give medieval religion and politics their last blow."[215]

Who was Heinrich Heine? He was still another anti-Semitic influence and friend of Marx, at once loathsome and infamous for his radical political and religious views. It is Heine who is credited by some for the analogy of religion as the "opium" of the people, with

Marx getting it from him.[216] Heine described Hamburg, Germany, as a "city of hagglers" filled with "baptized and un-baptized Jews (I call all Hamburg's inhabitants Jews)."[217]

Alas, we cannot exclude Engels' influence here. Marx's partner in crime was not much better in matters of race and ethnic tolerance. Engels also was unimpressed with Marx's son-in-law, Paul Lafargue, and likewise for racial reasons. Engels, a fellow Darwinian, endeavored to deduce with scientific accuracy that Paul possessed "one-eighth or one-twelfth nigger blood." In 1887, Lafargue had been a political candidate for a council seat in a Paris district that contained a zoo. In an April 1887 letter to Paul's wife, Laura, Engels cruelly opined, "Being in his quality as a nigger, a degree nearer to the rest of the animal kingdom than the rest of us, he is undoubtedly the most appropriate representative of that district."[218]

Is it any wonder that Marx's son-in-law had such low self-esteem? In fact, one day in November 1911, Paul decided to end it all. He killed himself in a suicide pact with Marx's daughter Laura.

Blessed Is He Who Has No Family

Home was not a happy place for the Marx family. In 1862 Marx wrote a letter to Engels noting that every day his wife expressed a wish to die, such was her misery.[219] In another letter to Engels during one of Marx's many financial crises, Marx asserted to his partner, "Blessed is he who has no family."[220]

That is a curious twisting of the Beatitudes. Jesus seemed to have left out that one.

As for marriage, Marx wrote to Engels, who surely would have nodded in assent, "There is no greater stupidity than for people of general aspirations to marry and surrender themselves to the small miseries of domestic and private life."[221] In a letter to his future son-in-law, Paul Lafargue, Marx asserted, "If I had to live my life over again, . . . I would not marry."[222] (This correspondence was related to the question of Lafargue's prospects for marrying Marx's daughter, and Marx did not approve of Lafargue—that is, "Negrillo." He was happy to do his part to help dissuade "The Gorilla.")

In so many ways, Karl Marx's personal life reinforced his desire for the kind of revolutionary state that he not only wanted but needed; such was also true for Engels and many of the long line of communist revolutionaries, from Lenin to Mao to Castro to Che and on and on. Again, one thinks of the trenchant insight by Aristotle: "Men start revolutionary changes for reasons connected with their private lives."

They do indeed. Marx lived the life of an atheist communist revolutionary and, it may be noted, died the death of one as well. So did his wife.

Jenny died in London on December 2, 1881.[223] She was buried in unconsecrated ground at Highgate Cemetery. Her husband did not attend the funeral. He was apparently too weak to attend, confined to a bedroom and unable to move and, reportedly, forbidden by his doctor to go to the funeral.[224] Engels gave the eulogy, a despairing ode, what one biographer described as an "atheist confession of faith:" "The place where we stand is the best proof that she lived and died in the full conviction of atheist Materialism," averred Engels, soberly staring at a pile of dirt. "She knew that one day she would have to return, body and mind, to the bosom of that nature from which she had sprung. And we, who have now laid her in her last resting-place, let us cherish her memory and try to be like her."[225]

Engels exhorted the atheist faithful to take pride and joy in their shared conviction that the vivacious Jenny was now reduced to mere dust. How thoroughly comforting this must have been to the daughters she and Karl had raised to reject any belief in the supernatural! They could all—the gathered, the secular faithful—aspire to Jenny's memory and try to be like her: a stiff corpse, *rigor mortis*, rotting in a box, food for parasites. What a noble image. What a Marxist image.

As for Jenny's despairing atheist husband, Karl hung on longer, depressed, weak, miserable, before succumbing to an unbreathing nothing two years later. He was buried next to Jenny on March 17, 1883. His coffin bore not a cross but two red wreaths, faithful to the communist religion to the very end. Engels again gave the eulogy, invoking not God but Darwin, whom Marx had admired for dealing such a grand blow for materialism and atheism.[226]

Death Becomes Her—and Her

Engels would not live long enough to deliver the eulogy at the next two Marx funerals. And these were Marxes he had loved and known from their births.

The first to go, in March 1898, was Marx's daughter Eleanor, who poisoned herself upon learning of her husband's (like her father's) infidelity. Here, too, was a sad tale from the family Marx.

Eleanor's husband, Edward Aveling, was a scoundrel. The son of a London Congregational minister, he was a playwright, actor, political activist, seducer of women, and all-around reprobate. And not unlike Eleanor's father, Aveling, a left-wing writer and aspiring politician, was egocentric, had a ferocious temper, and had an uncanny inability to earn money. He was a cad and shameless sponger, who even sought out and bilked Marx's illegitimate son Freddy for cash, which he never repaid.[227] Eleanor had other suitors, including the playwright and notorious dupe of communist causes, George Bernard Shaw, who was said to have been "half in love" with Marx's daughter but found her too strong-willed and neurotic.[228] Another notorious British socialist, eugenicist Havelock Ellis, who carried out an adulterous relationship with Planned Parenthood matron Margaret Sanger (who was married with children), likewise spent time with Eleanor, but he, too, left her to the claws of Aveling.[229]

Eleanor became Aveling's mistress. They openly lived together in London prior to marriage, during which he engaged in a pattern that he would continue throughout their marriage: philandering. Associates described him as a "disreputable dog." All were shocked at the awful manner in which he treated his wife.

Eleanor had tried to kill herself at least once before with an opium overdose that failed. She would try again with urging from Aveling, who convinced her of a joint suicide. The plan was that they would die together in each other's arms. Eleanor consummated her end of the bargain on the evening of March 31, 1898, using a combination of chloroform and prussic acid, suggested by Aveling, who did his research well. As for Aveling himself, a cheat to the end, he did not keep his promise to Eleanor. With Eleanor dead, Aveling retreated to his twenty-two-year-old girlfriend, and inherited all of Eleanor's possessions that had been bequeathed by her father, including his book royalties and a massive collection of papers and documents.[230]

In truth, Aveling had killed her, and yet was never charged with murder, even as many felt he should have been.

Thirteen years later, tragedy struck again, this time striking down the only remaining Marx daughter. It was the next Marx girl's self-arranged date with the grim reaper. Laura and her husband, Paul, entered into their own death pact. Paul Lafargue, Marx's "Gorilla," or "Negrillo," acted as executioner, and (unlike Aveling) kept his half of the bargain. Their joint suicide came the night of November 25–26, 1911. In the role of a future Jack "Dr. Death" Kevorkian, Paul had administered an injection of potassium cyanide into Laura that night, before injecting himself in the morning.

"Healthy in mind and spirit, I kill myself before pitiless old age," wrote Paul in his suicide note. "For many years, I promised myself not to live past seventy years; I picked that year for my departure from this life and I prepared the mode of execution for my resolution: an injection of potassium cyanide."[231]

Recall, of course, that Karl Marx's poetry had included suicide pacts. And such was the path followed by his daughters. One wonders if the very notion had entered the daughters' minds at some point compliments of the warped, destructive thoughts of the father. These were indeed the sins of the father. This is not to say that the father wanted suicide for his daughters. Not at all. But one wonders what grim things the girls might have heard from or had implanted in their imaginations and subconscious by their father at home.

No less a sower of death than Vladimir Lenin himself spoke at the funeral of Laura and Paul. Even Lenin, a man for whom death was an intimate companion, was alarmed at the latest Marx girl's suicide pact. "No, I cannot approve it," Lenin protested to his wife of the Laura-Paul pact. "They could still write, they could still accomplish things, and even if they could no longer work efficiently they could still observe and give good advice." They could still devote themselves to the cause.[232]

Like Lenin, Paul's eternal bride was communism. Likewise faithful to the communist religion to the very end, Paul concluded, "I die with the supreme joy of having the certitude that, in the very near future, the cause for which I have devoted some forty-five years will triumph. Long live Communism! Long live International Socialism."[233]

His death, too, would bequeath a legacy of just that: death. Thus began and ended the family Marx.

CHAPTER 4

"MONSTER OF TEN THOUSAND DEVILS"

ENGELS ENCOUNTERS MARX

As we move ahead in this book, beyond Marx, we should never forget that Marx had an accomplice, a willing partner in this wretched enterprise of constructing a communist-atheist world. His name was Friedrich Engels, and he was every bit Karl Marx's equal and co-author.

There is so much that could be said about Engels biographically in this book. But with the focus here being on the faith aspect of Marx and Marxism, and even how that related to family matters, this chapter will stay within those parameters. Those details alone will be revealing and disturbing enough.

Meeting a Remarkable Monster

We have had several alarming glances at the devil and Karl Marx, particularly as embodied in the poetry of the co-founder of communism. But let us not neglect Marx's co-redeemer of the dystopia. He, too, had something to say about the devilish side of Marx, and also did so via the medium of poetry.

Friedrich Engels's upbringing was, like that of Marx, both interesting and sad. He was raised and for many years remained a committed Christian, much more so than Marx. Marx's Jewish family had converted to the faith of Christ reportedly more out of his father's calculation of cultural necessity in the society they lived in. Such was not Engels's father and family.

Friedrich Engels was born in November 1820 in Barmen, Germany, a town known for its piety. His family was no exception to the community's devoutness. "He did not acquire his revolutionary opinions in the home of his parents," recorded Franz Mehring. "His father was a well-to-do manufacturer of conservative and orthodox views, and religiously Engels had more to overcome than Marx."[234]

Engels would work at his father's "damned business," as he called it. His heart was never in it.[235] Nonetheless, it was a good thing he did, because his future partner, Marx the moocher, would need that hard-earned capital someday so that he and Friedrich could squander it writing about the vagaries of capital and the wonders of forcibly redistributing businessmen's earnings and property.

Though his heart was never in the business, it was in the church. Leaving the faith was much more difficult for Friedrich. Though born in Barmen, he lived in Bremen, which was also a stronghold of German piety. "I pray every day, indeed almost all day, for truth," Engels would write, "and I have done so ever since I began to doubt."[236] Like many youth, he had his questions, and he needed peers who were good men, who would help guide him to right, not to wrong—to truth, not to evil. Unfortunately, men like Karl Marx entered instead.

It was in Bremen that Engels began to really question his faith. One biographer described it as nothing less than a "crisis of faith," exacerbated and intensified by reading the works of the Young Hegelians.[237] He was getting hit from all corners, including by the odious Moses Hess, who convinced him of the *virtues* of communism. Engels's father was so concerned about these subversive influences that he sent Friedrich to Manchester, England, to work with family business partners in order to get him away from his atheist German friends. Engels wryly recorded that his new infatuation with communism had "reawakened all the religious fanaticism of my old man."

The father and other relatives were greatly troubled; this was a matter not only of Friedrich's politics but, with communism, his soul. "You have no clue," he wrote to Marx, "of the malice of the Christian hunt, complete with its beaters, on my soul."[238]

Well, Karl was there to lend a hand. He would enthusiastically pull Friedrich away from God. He was happy to do his dirty work by beating back the Christians.

Men like Marx came and darkened the door to Engels's heart for Christ. And here again, it might not be overstating things to say that Marx felt like a demonic presence to Engels. Or at least that is not an unreasonable interpretation. Engels himself seemed to say as much, if we can take him literally and assume that one particular missive that he wrote about Marx was not in jest.

Like Marx, Engels penned his own verse. In fact, he penned verse about Marx, about encountering Marx and his foreboding presence.

He Hops and Rages Without Rest

Engels wrote of a "hellish song, howling [a] refrain." Like Marx's hellish vapors, they emanated from Marx. He was tormented, apparently, by the encroaching figure of Karl Marx.

Engels had not yet met Marx. He knew of him, but they had not come into contact. But he could nonetheless sense him, feel him.

What Engels wrote can be interpreted in more than one way. As with so much of his writing, like that of Marx, it is often difficult to discern exact meaning and intention, whether serious or satirical or something else altogether. It can be maddening when trying to figure out just what in the world these men were trying to say. Who were they talking about? When? Why? What in the devil's name were they saying on this or that occasion?[239]

On this occasion, Franz Mehring, the definitive early biographer of Marx—who first collected Marx's major writings and posthumous papers (directly from Marx's daughter Laura), and who was a major

German communist, revolutionary socialist, and Social Democrat who knew well Marx's immediate descendants—writes of an Engels poem published in four cantos under the title *A Christian Epic*. I have read all four cantos, variously posted and sourced by others under different titles, and find their overall meaning practically impenetrable—not unlike much of Marx's ludicrous body of writing. They are frustrating in the extreme, bizarre, bewildering. As Mehring interprets this particular poem, Engels was "satirizing the 'triumph of belief' over the 'Arch-Satan' to the great horror and dismay of the latter." Perhaps so. Of special interest, however, is the section dealing with the person, or *figure*, of Marx. Mehring wrote, "The verses in which he [Engels] describes himself and Marx, with whom he had not yet come into personal contact, give us some idea of his manner."[240]

Yes, they certainly do. And it hardly seems satirical, unless this is one very dark, black comedy by Engels. As if prompted by something shady and murky—something that Engels described as "black"—something ominous which his way was coming, Engels was compelled to pen these lines about his future partner (original German followed by English translation):

> Wer jaget hinterdrein mit wildem Ungestum?
> Ein schwarzer Kerl aus Trier, ein markhaft Ungetum.
> Er gehet, hupfet nicht, er springet auf den Hacken
> Und raset voller Wut und gleich als wollt' er packen
> Das weite Himmelszelt und zu der Erde ziehn,
> Streckt er die Arme sein weit in die Lufte hin.
> Geballt die bose Faust, so tobt er sonder Rasten,
> Als wenn ihn bei dem Schopf zenhtausend Teufel fassten.

> Who chases after his tracks [Engels's tracks] with reckless
>   rage?
> A black man from Trier [Marx's hometown], a remarkable
>   monster,

He neither walks nor hops, but springs upon his heels
And stretches high his arms into the air in anger
As though his wrath would seize at once
The mighty canopy of Heaven and tear it to the earth,
With clenched and threatening fist he rages without rest,
As though ten thousand devils had seized him by the
hair.[241]

This, dear comrade, was Friedrich Engels's poem about first meeting Karl Marx, with whom he had not yet come into contact. Was this satirical? A parody? Or was the author dreadfully serious?

Robert Payne, the Marx biographer who so carefully dissected the dark recesses of Marx's poetry, makes no suggestion that this particular poem should be taken as satire. He stated that these lines reflect what "men remembered" about Marx: "his wild temper, his impetuosity, his habit of leaping upon his prey. He would clinch his fist and roar interminably for the remaining forty years of his life."[242] Payne, in fact, translated the original passage this way:

Who comes rushing in, impetuous and wild—
Dark fellow from Trier, in fury raging,
Nor walks nor skips, but leaps upon his prey
In tearing rage, as one who leaps to grasp
Broad spaces of the sky and drag them down to earth,
Stretching his arms wide open to the heavens.
His evil fist is clenched, he roars interminably
As though ten thousand devils had him by the hair.

Payne's translation of this passage is a popular one, and a good one. Note the phrase "ten thousand devils had him by the hair." Here is a Marx with "evil fist" clenched who "roars interminably." It is a frightening image, no matter what the translation. (My translation probably goes easier on Marx.)[243]

This was the Marx that would saunter into Engels's life as Engels struggled to keep the faith, as he sought to "find my way to God, for whom I shall long with my whole heart." The young Engels had written some beautiful Christian poetry, waxing lovingly, longingly, for God. The pre-Marx Engels had earnestly hoped that "I am not lost."[244] Tragically, however, as Engels struggled, Karl Marx entered his life and changed its direction, reversing Engels's ascent to better angels. He needed men of Christ; he instead ran into an anti-Christ.

Marx did chase on Engels's tracks, a man marked by reckless rage. This was the blackened, dark man from Trier—nay, a *remarkable monster*—who neither walked nor hopped but sprung on his heels. This creature stretched his arms high into the air, as if his wrath would immediately seize the mighty canopy of heaven and tear and fling it to the earth. That beast—Karl Marx—would do so with clenched fist, a threatening fist that raged without rest, as if—yes—ten thousand devils had seized him. So wrote Engels.

Again, how serious was this verse by Engels? How are we to interpret it? In its time, and henceforth today? Well, we should not overstate it, nor should we understate it. We should not ignore it.

Whatever might have been the initial intention of his verse, Friedrich Engels, unfortunately, could not resist the Marx, the thing that sprung on its heels. He apparently succumbed to his spell.

By the end of his life, Engels was hopeless. "He was absolutely without God," recalled a friend.[245]

Two hopeless men engaged in a godless cause to ruthlessly undermine the existing order, Karl and Friedrich would join forces, and history would never be the same. Their "specter of communism" was unchained and unleashed. It was as if ten thousand devils were celebrating, and ten thousand million victims (or more) would succumb to the clenched fists of rage that morphed into the hideous Frankenstein monster that was Marxism-Leninism.

It was an ideology governed by a demon far more Faustian than heavenly.

Engels on the Family

Lastly, a parting word on Friedrich Engels and family matters.

For the record, Marx's intellectual partner was no great family man either. Engels refused a family and marriage altogether. He juggled a regular mix of mistresses, including in the 1840s, when he and Karl compiled their magnum opus. These ladies pleaded with Engels to make honest women out of them, to take them to the altar rather than merely to bed. They were asking too much of the co-author of the *Communist Manifesto*.

At one point in the 1850s, Engels seemed to begin referring to one of these girls as his "wife," though he would not officially marry her. When that woman died, he seems to have perhaps married another sexual partner, who happened to be the late woman's sister, but only on her deathbed.[246] That option, after all, entailed less responsibility for the communist.

Like Marx, Engels's ideological preferences were extensions of his personal preferences. In his writings and in his description of his communist paradise, Engels showed his preferences for pre-marital sex, non-committed relationships, and easy divorce.

This was apparent a year after Marx's 1883 death, with the publication of Engels's 1884 book *The Origin of the Family, Private Property and the State*. This book, as Engels noted in the preface, also represented Marx's views on family. In fact, said Engels, Marx himself had eagerly wanted to undertake this crucial work. He said that Marx had produced extensive extracts right up until his death, which Engels had reproduced in the book "as far as possible." Indeed, Professor H. Kent Geiger, in his seminal Harvard University Press book on the subject, notes that "many of the ideas" in *The Origin of the Family* can be found in the first joint work by Marx and Engels, *The German Ideology*, which was not published during their lifetimes. Geiger states that *The Origin of the Family* was really a "joint work" by the two founders of Marxism, based on an "impressive unity and continuity" across four decades of their mutual thoughts.[247]

What sort of thoughts? Engels reiterated a position in the book that both he and Marx had previously advanced—namely, that a mother's housework was yet another private thing that the communist state should seize, to be replaced by collective labor managed by the state. Private housework would be nationalized, with mothers instead being corralled into the fields and factories to do more *meaningful* work. Housework, from cooking to cleaning, would become a government industry, as would childcare, which would become a communal affair. Mothers and wives would thereby be liberated from the chains of traditional family *economic bondage*.[248] "Private housekeeping is transformed into a social industry," Engels envisioned excitedly. "The care and education of the children becomes a public affair; society looks after all children alike, whether they are legitimate or not."[249]

Again, the ironies and hypocrisy here are rich, given Marx's exploitation of the family nursemaid, Lenchen.

In all, Engels and Marx saw this plan as a joyous means to help further their goal of "abolition of the family," expressed in the *Communist Manifesto*. "The single family ceases to be the economic unit of society," hoped Engels.[250]

Of course, in all of this, Engels had his eyes fixed on the figure of the single woman, and how these new-fangled ideas of liberation might personally redound to his own sexual benefit. "This removes all the anxiety about the consequences which today is the most essential social-moral as well as economic factor that prevents a girl from giving herself completely to the man she loves," wrote Engels. "Will not that suffice to bring about the gradual growth of unconstrained sexual intercourse and with it a more tolerant public opinion in regard to a maiden's honor and a woman's shame?"[251]

Friedrich Engels certainly hoped so.

The woman would be freed to give herself more totally (and physically) to the man she "loves," especially as child care, rearing, and education became a public affair, a social industry. For Engels, that "love" meant sex, not marriage. As for child rearing, Professor Geiger notes that Engels and Marx appeared to have "little to say" about the relationships between parents and children beyond the crucial recommendation that "they would not continue to live together, because society was to rear and educate" (Geiger's words). This collective rearing of children by the communist nanny state would bring "real freedom" to all members of the family. Parenting would become the responsibility of the state.[252]

What a perfect statist vision for two men who eschewed fatherhood and the idea of marital fidelity and commitment. Yet again, we see how the theoretical-ideological utterances of the revolution have roots in the personal-private lives of the founders.

And as for the revolution, it would now proceed vigorously and viciously into the twentieth century, no longer by men like Marx and Engels but by remarkable monsters with names like Lenin and Stalin and Mao and Pol Pot and the Kims and Ceausescu and Fidel and Che. These men, too, were hell-bent on a cause that would howl gigantic curses at mankind. It was as if ten thousand devils had them by the hair.

Friedrich Engels, in his verse, was more an unwitting prophet than poet.

PART 3

THE BOLSHEVIK WAR ON RELIGION AND THE CHURCH'S RESISTANCE

CHAPTER 5

"WE DO NOT BELIEVE IN GOD"

LENIN'S NECROPHILIA

"Communism begins where atheism begins," declared Marx.[253] In the *Communist Manifesto*, he and Engels remarked, "Communism abolishes eternal truths, it abolishes all religion, and all morality."[254]

The apostles of Marx and Engels took that to heart. In communist Russia, the Bolsheviks in particular picked up the spear.

"A fight to the death must be declared upon religion," asserted Nikolai Bukharin, founding editor of *Pravda* and one of Lenin's and Stalin's leading lieutenants, adding counsel to "take on religion at the tip of the bayonet."[255]

Bukharin spoke for the Bolsheviks: "Religion and communism are incompatible, both theoretically and practically. . . . Communism is incompatible with religious faith." He also spoke for Marx: "'Religion is the opium of the people,' said Karl Marx. It is the task of the Communist Party to make this truth comprehensible to the widest possible circles of the laboring masses."[256]

The Bolsheviks would do just that. Communists worldwide would do just that. Such was the atheist legacy bequeathed by Marx.

One of the most brutally restricted rights by communist governments was, and remains, the freedom to worship, which communists always and everywhere have attacked with a wild fervor and devotion. In a sense, it is strange that atheistic communists felt so mortally threatened by their people believing in something they insisted did not exist. Yet, communists not only cared about that worship but became utterly obsessed with stopping it. Belief in God stood in the way of the totalitarian desire to transform human nature. God was a competitor to communist control of the body, mind, and spirit of man that Marx and Lenin wanted to redefine in their own image.

In other words, the communists rightly recognized that belief in God was the chief impediment to the imposition of their atheist creed.

"That Religion of Theirs"

Ironically, anyone familiar with or who spent time in the Communist Party will attest that its arrogantly and proudly atheistic members treated communism like a faith.

The writings of Karl Marx and Vladimir Lenin were accorded a sacred status. In the Soviet state and other communist regimes, these writings had effectively replaced the Bible in public life and in the lives of so many communists everywhere. They constituted the new Sacred Scripture. Mikhail Gorbachev denounced the phenomenon. At the July 25–26, 1991 plenary session of the Soviet Central Committee (one of the final such sessions in the soon-moribund USSR), Gorbachev derided what he aptly called "communist fundamentalism," and said that in the Soviet Union the writings of Marxism-Leninism had been turned into "a collection of canonical texts."[257]

In the United States, Arthur Koestler, the renowned ex-communist, spoke of the believer's religious-like conversion to the Marxist faith. He explained in his classic *Darkness at Noon*:

> To say that one had "seen the light" is a poor description of the mental rapture which only the convert knows. . . . The new light seems to pour from all directions across the skull, the whole universe falls into pattern like the stray pieces of a jigsaw puzzle assembled by magic at one stroke. There is now an answer to every question, doubts and conflicts are a matter of the tortured

past. . . . Nothing henceforth can disturb the convert's inner peace and serenity—except the occasional fear of losing faith again, losing thereby what alone makes life worth living, and falling back into the outer darkness.[258]

And with rapturous communism entrancing and absorbing the convert, the party was treated as an infallible authority.

"None of us desires or is able to dispute the will of the Party," stated Leon Trotsky, whose later dissent from and criticisms of Stalin would lead to his excommunication by the Kremlin. "Clearly, the Party is always right. . . . We can only be right with and by the Party, for history has provided no other way of being in the right."[259]

The esteemed diplomat and scholar George F. Kennan described this as the "infallibility of the Kremlin." He noted that communists, like the old "white dog before the phonograph," responded only to "the master's voice." That master was the Kremlin. "Truth is not a constant but is actually created, for all intents and purposes, by the Soviet leaders themselves," wrote Kennan in his classic dispatch "The Sources of Soviet Conduct." "It may vary from week to week, from month to month. It is nothing absolute and immutable—nothing which flows from objective reality." Kennan explained, "The Soviet concept of power requires that the Party leadership remain in theory the sole repository of truth. . . . The leadership of the Communist Party is therefore always right." Since "they alone knew what was good for society"—and since their word was "absolute," "immutable," "infallible," "secure and unchallengeable"—the Soviet leadership was "prepared to recognize no restrictions, either of God or man, on the character of their methods."[260]

Their only guiding force was themselves and their Marxism-Leninism. That was what they answered to.

Ronald Reagan called it "that religion of theirs, which is Marxism-Leninism."[261] He said that communists bowed to "the nativity according to Marx and Lenin," a system in which "Karl Marx is hailed as the messiah."[262]

Lenin on Spiritual Booze and Dope

Thus the hypocrisy and irony of Marx's disciples professing official atheism as they blindly adhered to their philosophy like religious zealots.

And yet, Lenin affirmed Marx's sentiment that communism begins where atheism begins. He considered atheism a natural and inseparable part of Marxism, of the theory and practice of "scientific socialism."[263] "Religion is opium for the people," said Lenin, echoing Marx. "Religion is a sort of spiritual booze."[264]

Lenin saw socialism as incompatible with religious belief, asserting, "Everyone must be absolutely free to . . . be an atheist, which every socialist is, as a rule." Again, Marx said the same, and so did Engels. Marx's son-in-law, the notorious Edward Aveling, who knew Engels well, said of him, "He held, of course, that Christian socialism was a contradiction in terms, and felt very strongly that Christians have no more right to label socialism with the limiting adjective of their shibboleth than we should dream of speaking of atheistic socialism."[265]

Lenin decried "this or that dope by the established church. Complete separation of church and state is what the socialist proletariat demands of the modern state and the modern church." Sounding like a twenty-first-century secular progressive in America, Lenin insisted that "religion must be declared a private affair."[266] Like Bukharin and other Bolsheviks, he demanded an ironclad "separation of church and state."[267]

Lenin wrote that in 1905. Once he and his Bolsheviks took over, they refused to tolerate religion even as a private affair. The party would not accept that. Lenin conceded as much in that 1905 letter: "We demand that religion be held a private affair so far as the state is concerned. But by no means can we consider religion a private affair so far as our Party is concerned." He continued, "We demand complete disestablishment of the Church so as to be able to combat the religious fog. . . . We founded our association, the Russian

Social-Democratic Labor Party, precisely for such a struggle against every religious bamboozling of the workers. And to us the ideological struggle is not a private affair, but the affair of the whole Party, of the whole proletariat."[268]

Lenin summed up, "The revolutionary proletariat will succeed in making religion a really private affair, so far as the state is concerned. And in this political system, cleansed of medieval mildew, the proletariat will wage a broad and open struggle for the elimination of economic slavery, the true source of the religious humbugging of mankind."[269]

That is what religion was to Lenin: a humbug, a medieval mildew; spiritual booze, spiritual dope.

In another dispatch four years later, Lenin again invoked Marx: "Religion is the opium of the people—this dictum by Marx is the cornerstone of the whole Marxist outlook on religion." Here, Lenin was writing in May 1909, and on behalf of fellow "Social Democrats." What he wrote is worth quoting here at length:

> It is the absolute duty of Social-Democrats to make a public statement of their attitude towards religion. Social-Democracy bases its whole world-outlook on scientific socialism, i.e., Marxism. The philosophical basis of Marxism, as Marx and Engels repeatedly declared, is dialectical materialism—a materialism which is absolutely atheistic and positively hostile to all religion. . . . Religion is the opium of the people—this dictum by Marx is the cornerstone of the whole Marxist outlook on religion. Marxism has always regarded all modern religions and churches, and each and every religious organization, as instruments of bourgeois reaction that serve to defend exploitation and to befuddle the working class. . . .
>
> Marxism is materialism. As such, it is as relentlessly hostile to religion. . . . We must combat religion—that is the ABC of *all* materialism, and consequently of Marxism. But Marxism is

not a materialism which has stopped at the ABC. Marxism goes
further. It says: We must *know how* to combat religion, and in
order to do so we must explain the source of faith and religion
among the masses *in a materialist way*. The combating of religion cannot be confined to abstract ideological preaching, and
it must not be reduced to such preaching. It must be linked up
with the concrete practice of the class movement, which aims at
eliminating the social roots of religion.[270]

It is hard to find a more scathing indictment than this. Marxism,
insisted Lenin, is "absolutely atheistic and positively hostile to all religion." It is "relentlessly hostile to religion." Communists thus "must
combat religion," eliminating its very roots. This must be done, said
Lenin, in order to reverse religion's hold on the "backward sections of
the town proletariat"—that is, the town idiots.

Could a priest be a Social Democrat and member of the Communist Party? Of course, but then what kind of priest would want to do
so? And yet even in the year 2019, one hundred years and one hundred million corpses later, the Jesuit-run *America* magazine would
publish a breathtaking piece, at once bizarre and heretical, titled
"The Catholic Case for Communism."[271] Even in Lenin's day, apparently a terribly confused or misled priest or two must have occasionally expressed interest in working with Lenin and his brute atheists.
Lenin considered the absurd thought, answering and explaining:

The question is often brought up whether a priest can be a
member of the Social-Democratic Party or not, and this question is usually answered in an unqualified affirmative, the experience of the European Social-Democratic parties being cited
as evidence. But this experience was the result, not only of
the application of the Marxist doctrine to the workers' movement, but also of the special historical conditions in Western
Europe which are absent in Russia (we will say more about these

conditions later), so that an unqualified affirmative answer in this case is incorrect. It cannot be asserted once and for all that priests cannot be members of the Social-Democratic Party; but neither can the reverse rule be laid down. If a priest comes to us to take part in our common political work and conscientiously performs Party duties, without opposing the program of the Party, he may be allowed to join the ranks of the Social-Democrats; for the contradiction between the spirit and principles of our program and the religious convictions of the priest would in such circumstances be something that concerned him alone, his own private contradiction. . . . But, of course, such a case might be a rare exception even in Western Europe, while in Russia it is altogether improbable. And if, for example, a priest joined the Social-Democratic Party and made it his chief and almost sole work actively to propagate religious views in the Party, it would unquestionably have to expel him from its ranks.[272]

Hence, if a left-wing priest was dimwitted enough to join the ranks of Lenin and friends, well, they would accept the help of the *useful idiot* (Lenin's language) for their revolution.[273] But if the strange priest ever tried to share his faith with the fellas, well, he would be shown the boot and the door.

"Unswervingly Combating Religion"

Lenin spoke often of religion as the opiate of the masses, parroting his materialist idol.[274] This became dogma to the Communist Party both under Lenin and after his death. The program of the Communist International, adopted at the Sixth World Congress in 1928, four years after Lenin's death, stated, "One of the most important tasks of the cultural revolution affecting the wide masses is the task of systematically and unswervingly combating religion—the opium of the people."[275]

Fittingly, given his penchant for vitriolic, over-the-top rhetoric and hate-laced, hatchet prose, Lenin himself said far worse about religion.

"All worship of a divinity is a necrophilia," declared Lenin in a letter to Maxim Gorky, written in November 1913. To Lenin, religion was so odious, so loathsome, that the best analogy was necrophilia: a person aroused at the notion of having sexual intercourse with a stiff human corpse. He scowled that "any religious idea, any idea of any god at all, any flirtation even with a god, is the most inexpressible foulness . . . the most shameful 'infection.'"[276] (According to one Russian scholar and translator, Lenin here was referring to venereal disease.[277])

Lenin seemed torn between whether religion was more like a burning, oozing sexually transmitted disease or something more akin to the vile, unimaginable act of having sexual intercourse with a hardened human corpse. He considered religious belief to be beyond contempt; his only struggle being how best to adequately describe its vileness. Like a cankerous sore, it needed to be stanched. Those who transmitted it must be quarantined, and the houses where they gathered must be shut down or burned down. His views are perhaps best summed up in the following sentence which he wrote to Maxim Gorky: "There can be nothing more abominable than religion."[278]

Lenin boasted that as a teen, he removed the cross that hung from his neck and literally trashed it. "I broke sharply with all questions of religion," he fondly recalled. "I took off my cross and threw it in the rubbish bin."[279] That gesture was a metaphor for how he, his Bolsheviks, and other communists viewed and treated religion. On December 25, 1919, celebrated as Christmas Day in the West, Comrade Lenin issued the following order in his own writing: "To put up with 'Nikola' [the religious holiday] would be stupid—the entire Cheka must be on the alert to see to it that those who do not show up for work because of 'Nikola' are shot."[280]

That was, in effect, what Lenin and his disciples spent the next decades doing to the religious-minded people in the cursed places where they seized power.

In one of his most significant public speeches, made in October 1920 to the Third All-Russia Congress of the Russian Young Communist League, Lenin stated without equivocation, "We do not believe in God."[281] The full context of that Lenin assertion is worth quoting and examining more closely:

> Is there such a thing as communist ethics? Is there such a thing as communist morality? Of course, there is . . .
>
> In what sense do we reject ethics, reject morality?
>
> In the sense given to it by the bourgeoisie, who based ethics on God's commandments. On this point we, of course, say that we do not believe in God. . . . We reject any morality based on extra-human and extra-class concepts.

On what then was communist "morality" based? To what was it subservient? Lenin answers these questions:

> We say that our morality is entirely subordinated to the interests of the proletariat's class struggle. Our morality stems from the interests of the class struggle of the proletariat.
>
> The old society was based on the oppression of all the workers and peasants by the landowners and capitalists. We had to destroy all that, and overthrow them but to do that we had to create unity. That is something that God cannot create. . . .
>
> Our communist morality is also subordinated to that task. We say: morality is what serves to destroy the old exploiting society and to unite all the working people around the proletariat, which is building up a new, communist society.
>
> Communist morality is that which serves this struggle and unites the working people against all exploitation, against all petty private property; for petty property puts into the hands of one person that which has been created by the labor of the whole of society. . . .

When people tell us about morality, we say: to a Communist all morality lies in this united discipline and conscious mass struggle against the exploiters. We do not believe in an eternal morality, and we expose the falseness of all the fables about morality. Morality serves the purpose of helping human society rise to a higher level and rid itself of the exploitation of labor. . . .

Communist morality is based on the struggle for the consolidation and completion of communism.

Such were the depths, or limits, of "communist morality." Such a *morality* was a totally relativistic one directed to the goal of advancing communism. The only *morality* that communists recognized was that which advanced their own interests. To that end, millions would be killed if they slowed or stood against the advancement of those interests. That was *communist morality*. Communists did not believe in an eternal morality. There was no morality outside of themselves.

And what Lenin particularly disliked, and feared, was not a corrupt priest, who was easily countered because of his corruption, but a holy priest who was not so comprised and thus more difficult to vilify before the people. "The Catholic priest corrupting young girls (about whom I have just read by chance in a German newspaper) is much less dangerous," averred Lenin. "For it is easy to expose, condemn and expel the first priest, while the second cannot be expelled so simply; to expose the latter is 1,000 times more difficult."[282]

Lenin preferred his priests unholy. A sacrilegious priest was Lenin's kind of priest. All the better for taking down the churches and religion.

The Militant Godless

For Vladimir Lenin and his comrades, rejecting God was not enough. The Bolsheviks sought to be proactive, undermining belief for generations to come. Lenin and Trotsky launched the League of the Militant Godless, which was tasked with the dissemination of anti-religious propaganda.[283]

Trotsky, too, was a true believer. He believed that God could not save man, but communism sure could. Consider these words from that otherwise cynical man:

> Man will, at last, begin to harmonize himself in earnest. . . . He will want to master first the semi-conscious and then also the unconscious processes of his own organism: breathing, the circulation of blood, digestion, reproduction, and, within the necessary limits, subordinate them to the control of reason and will. . . . The human species, the sluggish *Homo sapiens*, will once again enter the state of radical reconstruction and become in his own hands the object of the most complex methods of artificial selection and psychological training. . . . Man will make it his goal . . . to create a higher sociobiological type, a superman, if you will. . . . Man will become incomparably stronger, wiser, more subtle. His body will become more harmonious, his movements more rhythmic, his voice more melodious. . . . The average human type will rise to the heights of an Aristotle, Goethe, Marx. And beyond this ridge, other peaks will emerge.[284]

We see here how Trotsky, how Lenin, how the Bolsheviks, how communism, sought to make a New Man. Communism held the key to the self, to the universe, to human nature. We see here the full faith in the totalitarian project of fundamental transformation, of fundamentally transforming human nature, of "radical reconstruction." But it would always be without God—or, that is, without the Judeo-Christian God. It would be with the god of Marxism-Leninism, the new faith for the New Man, a superman—*incomparably stronger, wiser, more subtle*. Here was a progressive evolution to a more harmonious and melodious "higher sociobiological type." The communists would harness nature, lassoing it in a way that some phony "God," some ridiculous and cruel "opiate of the masses," could never match.

One could under communism aspire to the greatest of heights—the level of men like Goethe and Marx. So waxed Leon Trotsky, heart filled, tears in eyes, lump in throat. One could glimpse beyond the ridge a new peak, a new height for the New Man to ascend. The political pilgrim might bellow out the "Communist Internationale" as he climbed this secular Mt. Everest. *Forward!*

Trotsky found his gods in Marx and Darwin. "Darwin destroyed the last of my ideological prejudices," he triumphed. He said the "facts" about the world and life and its origins were established for him via this "certain system" of evolutionary theory. "The idea of evolution and determinism," he wrote, "took possession of me completely. Darwin stood for me like a mighty doorkeeper at the entrance to the temple of the universe. I was intoxicated with his . . . thought." Trotsky historian Barry Lee Woolley explained, "Trotsky took up the faith of Marx and Darwin. The conversion experience was genuine and thorough."[285] The feeling was mutual for Trotsky's atheist followers, who, as Woolley put it, "adored him as a god."[286]

The overall atmosphere and attitude of communists might have been best captured by ex-communist Whittaker Chambers, who said that Marxist-Leninists repeated man's first mistake in the Garden of Eden, the fatal conceit that "Ye shall be as gods." In so doing, they despised the notion of the one true God. As Alexander Solzhenitsyn recorded in *The Gulag Archipelago*, "Within the philosophical system of Marx and Lenin . . . hatred of God is the principal driving force."[287]

It was indeed, and the tragic consequences of that hate would be the death of millions of innocent people and a dagger at Western civilization itself.

Prosecuting the War

This Bolshevik contempt for God as the driving force in civic life resulted in an arresting change to Russian society. Prior to Trotsky, Lenin, and their cohorts, respect for religious faith in pre-Bolshevik Russia was rich, including among its leaders. It is hard to find a contrast more marked than the view of Christianity by the Bolsheviks compared to that of, say, Czar Alexander I some one hundred years earlier. One can see this in Alexander's 1815 Holy Alliance, an ideal he championed at the historic Congress of Vienna. Alexander dreamed of an agreement that integrated Christian morality and principles into the way that major European nations—particularly, the Quintuple Alliance of Russia, Prussia, Austria, England, and Bourbon France—conducted foreign relations. The Holy Alliance did not achieve his hopes, but it nonetheless stands as a powerful contrast in the attitude of Russia's leaders toward Christianity before and after the October 1917 revolution.[288]

With the Bolsheviks seizing power, a full-throttle war on religion was underway. "As early as the spring of 1918," wrote Soviet official and reformer Alexander Yakovlev, "an open campaign of terror was launched against all religions, and particularly against the Russian Orthodox Church." It was a "policy of terror . . . felt by every religious faith." Yakovlev underscores an incident (not uncommon) in the summer of 1918 in the Yekaterinburg diocese in which forty-seven clergymen were shot, drowned, or axed to death. That was merely one cruel episode in an ongoing campaign, the originator of which, says Yakovlev flatly and correctly, was Lenin: "His actions against religion and the Church are astonishing in their diabolical ferocity and immorality."[289]

To that end, many policies and proclamations were launched to initiate this Bolshevik war, including these steps all started under Lenin by 1918:

All land and buildings owned for centuries by the Russian

Orthodox Church were confiscated by the state, and all schools were taken from the Church. Communists favored nationalization of everything, and the Church and its property fell under that purview. So would faith itself. In a way, civic religion was first nationalized and then co-opted and transmogrified into the Marxist-Leninist faith. Marxism-Leninism replaced the Russian Orthodox Church and all other conventional faiths; it became the new state religion.

The Bolsheviks immediately forbade religious instruction to anyone under eighteen years of age, and children were encouraged to turn in their parents if they taught them about God. The parental/husband-wife relationship was infringed upon in multiple intrusive ways. Marriage was transformed into a strictly civil ceremony; weddings, baptisms, and funerals were converted into bizarre "communist" ceremonies. Soviet officials instead substituted secular ceremonies infused with communist ideology, pejoratively labeled by outsiders as "red weddings," "red baptisms," and "red funerals." In red baptisms, infants were given social "god-parents" who undertook to ensure the child was brought up to become a worthy "builder of communism." The parents of newborns would promise to raise their children "not as slaves for the bourgeoisie, but as fighters against it." Young mothers would declare: "The child belongs to me only physically. For his spiritual upbringing, I entrust him to society."[290] The "spiritual" upbringing would accord only with the new and approved faith of Marxism-Leninism. Moreover, the Russian Orthodox Church's long-standing prohibition against divorce was lifted—a decision which wreaked havoc on the Russian family and led to an explosion in divorce rates.[291]

Particularly ugly, Lenin's cronies ensured that churches were destroyed or reconstituted into communist clubs, workshops, storage houses, offices, and obscene atheistic museums. The Church of the Archangel Michael, a beautiful red-brick edifice crowned with five cupolas, built in 1740 on the southwest edge of Moscow, was used to store grain.[292] The gorgeous Cathedral of Christ the Savior, positioned on the banks of the Moscow River near the Kremlin, Moscow's most ornate church, was dynamited in December 1931 to make room for a new *sacred* "Palace of Soviets" desired by Stalin. Eventually, the ground was found too soft for a skyscraper. Instead, a decidedly less majestic municipal swimming pool was put in its place.

This, tragically, became the norm, the fate of Russia's holy churches. Of the 657 churches that existed in Moscow on the eve of the 1917 revolution, only 100 to 150 remained by 1976, according to official Soviet statistics. Of those, the Moscow Russian Orthodox Patriarchy said only 46 still held services by the mid-1970s.[293] Among those 46, few to none were free to say what they wanted. They were monitored by full-time, state-employed "church watchers," whose job was to report those who came to the church to pray.

The task in this war on religion was immense. The USSR was a huge country that spanned twelve time zones. Within the Orthodox Church alone, there were over 40,000 churches and some 150,000 priests, monks, deans, and bishops.[294] Whereas churches could be reduced to rubble, recalcitrant priests would need to be carted to Siberia, or sometimes simply executed. That was likewise true for stubbornly faithful nuns who were deliberately housed in special sections of the gulag with prostitutes.[295]

Within Russian churches themselves, there were innumerable holy relics, gems, and precious stones, all of special value, whether financial or spiritual. The Bolsheviks saw only a financial value, and thus initiated a forced confiscation of these items.

"The booty is enormous," said Trotsky, salivating over the "fabulous treasures" of the Church that the Bolsheviks greedily eyed up.[296] They demanded the Church's materials. Naturally, this culminated in fierce battles, leading to the Moscow and Petrograd church trials of 1921–22. These were mere predetermined show trials by the state apparatus, employed to make priests and bishops look greedy.[297]

Lenin was furious (not unusual) when the Church would not give him and his cohorts their icons and jewels and whatever else to sell or melt down. He instructed Trotsky and the Politburo to make sure that all churches were "cleansed," to "shoot ringleaders," and to implement "the death penalty for priests." Lenin hoped, "There is a ninety-nine per cent chance of smashing the enemy on the head with complete success and of guaranteeing positions essential for us for many decades to come."[298]

They immediately put on "trial" the Russian Orthodox Church's patriarch and sixteen other Church officials, all of whom were found "guilty" of not cooperating with the state. Of the seventeen defendants, eleven were ordered to be immediately shot. Patriarch Tikhon, who was persecuted with particular viciousness, denounced what he called the "Antichrist in power."[299]

That was a damned good day for Bolshevism, emphasis on *damned*, as was the mass heist from the churches, which by November 1922 included 828,275 pounds of silver, 1,220 pounds of gold, 35,670 diamonds, and much, much more. Lenin rubbed his covetous little hands at the "hundreds of millions" of rubles before him.

Like Karl Marx, these communists who claimed not to care about property and wealth were, in fact, consumed by such material desires.

To the communists, the sheer number of church buildings, material, and people was evidence that the attempt to purge religion had to be an ongoing, aggressive, and proactive process. God and his faithful were intractable foes. The war on religion would not be an easy one, but it was, the Bolsheviks believed, a righteous one that had to be pursued at any cost. They were hell-bent on making it a success.

"Wholesale War on Religion"

There is no debate as to the Bolshevik intention: Russia expert and onetime Librarian of Congress James Billington said that Vladimir Lenin and his Bolsheviks aimed for nothing less than "the extermination of all religious belief."[300] From inside the empire, Soviet historian Eduard Radzinsky said the Bolsheviks had created an "atheistic empire."[301]

Nary a former Soviet official would shrink from this assessment. "Just like religious orders who zealously convert 'heretics' to their own faith, our [Communist] ideologues carried out a wholesale war on religion," wrote none other than Mikhail Gorbachev in his memoirs.[302] He affirmed that the Bolsheviks, even after the civil war ended, during a time of "peace," had "continued to tear down churches, arrest clergymen, and destroy them. This was no longer understandable or justifiable. Atheism took rather savage forms in our country at that time."[303]

The Soviet Union was openly hostile to religion. It was officially *atheist*. That is a key fact: to be officially atheist does not mean that a nation is irreligious or unreligious or takes no position on religion. The USSR had an official position on religion; it was not neutral. The position was that there was no God. Moreover, that atheism translated into a form of anti-religion that included a systematic campaign to try to eliminate religious belief within the USSR and everywhere outside of the Soviet Union where the Bolsheviks worked diligently to advance the frontiers of communism—most especially in Eastern Europe.

The state hostility to religion begun by Lenin was continued through the Stalin era. Believers, in fact, experienced even worse repression under Stalin, especially in the 1930s and during the Great Terror. Stalin blew up churches, jailed and killed priests and bishops and deacons, and nuns, and generally was hell-bent on squashing any and all traces of religion. In 1932, his League of the Militant Godless, started by Trotsky and Lenin, issued a five-year plan to terminate all religion. Issued on May 15, 1932, the "Five Year Plan of Atheism" set forth this goal for May Day 1937: "Not a single house of prayer shall remain in the territory of the USSR, and the very concept of God must be banished from the Soviet Union as a survival of the Middle Ages and an instrument for the oppressions of the working masses!"[304]

That was very much the mindset of Marx and Lenin. This "medieval mildew" must be scraped away.

There is a view by ill-informed outsiders that things got better in the USSR under Nikita Khrushchev, who denounced the "crimes of Stalin" in 1956 after he entered office following Stalin's death. To the contrary, even during the so-called less violent, more open Khrushchev period, the abuse of Christian believers continued as standard procedure. One Soviet pastor remembered:

> I was born into a Christian family in Tara, Siberia. My father was a pastor, and I can remember how we were viewed as spies and enemies of the nation during my childhood. Even my teachers joined in the accusations! It was rare for us to walk home from school without being kicked, or on the receiving end of laughter. In 1961, father was thrown into prison for his ministry to the church. The official charge was that he didn't want to work and was a parasite on society. Our church continued even though the church buildings were confiscated.[305]

One missionary sentenced to twenty-five years in prison in 1959, during the Khrushchev era, when he was routinely tortured, contended that while Khrushchev "disowned" Stalin, he "continued to do the same thing" in regard to religion. After 1959, half of the churches of Soviet Russia that then remained open were reportedly closed.[306]

The religious repression continued unabated throughout the Brezhnev era, which lasted from the mid-1960s until the early 1980s. Not until the Gorbachev era and the literal end of the USSR did the Soviet repression of religion finally cease.

The Universal Communist Assault on Religion

In all of this, the Soviet Union was reflective of the communist world as a whole. The endemic atheism translated into a form of vicious anti-religion that included a systematic, often ruthless campaign to eliminate belief that began at the outset of the Soviet state and still continues in various forms in communist countries to this day, from China to North Korea to Cuba.

This comprehensive, universal armed assault on religious faith was aimed not just at Christians—Protestants, Catholics, Eastern Orthodox—but against Jews, Muslims, Buddhists, and members of other faiths. So many martyrs, so many victims, so many tortured. Where to start? Who all to name?

One particularly painful example of religious persecution by Eastern European communists was the case of Hungarian priest-turned-cardinal Joseph Mindszenty. Born March 1892 in Hungary, Mindszenty was ordained to the priesthood in June 1915 before being consecrated a bishop in 1944, an archbishop in 1945, and ultimately appointed primate of Hungary by Pope Pius XII in October 1945. Only ten months later, on December 26, 1946, the communists celebrated the Christmas season by arresting Cardinal Mindszenty.

That December 26, just after midnight, the communist tormentors arrived at Mindszenty's home in the dark of night. Police cars swarmed in. Police charged inside with guns pointed at the priest and others in the room, including Mindszenty's trembling mother, who had brought cookies and sausage to celebrate Christmas with her son. The priest quietly dressed, grabbed his breviary, and tried to speak some comforting words to his elderly mother.

There were sixteen communist police. They drove the cardinal to the torture house at 60 Andrassy Street. They arrived at three o'clock in the morning. For nearly forty days and nights, Mindszenty was tortured. Interrogators at the inhuman secret police headquarters excelled not only at beatings but brainwashing and drugging. The communist guards poked and prodded and ridiculed him, exhaled smoke in his face, told him dirty jokes, profaned his presence and his faith, as the cardinal sat dressed in what he later described as a "clown suit."

At one stage in this novel form of communist-crucifixion-without-killing, Mindszenty was kept awake for thirty-five hours while peppered and badgered and bludgeoned by his inquisitors. At another point, he was kept awake for eighty-two hours, during which two nuns were brought before him and punched and pounded to a pulp. The priest tried to bring his two hands together to pray for them but could not reconcile the left and the right. When the image of the thrashed sisters did not compel his "confession," two similarly bloodied priests were escorted in, swollen beyond recognition, hair soaked with blood, necks and arms blue, and bloodied feet.

In his cell between beatings, Mindszenty grew weak from eating limited rations of food and drink that he knew was drugged. He recognized the drugging procedure. Mindszenty had forewarned his countrymen that any "confession" he made should be understood as made under severe duress and in an altered state of mind.

During the communist show-trial that followed, sensationally staged the week of February 3, 1949, Mindszenty, framed by a stack of fabricated documents, reportedly "confessed" before his accusers. He was convicted of treason. The triumphant kangaroo court sentenced him to life in prison.

Pope Pius XII had his say: he excommunicated all individuals involved in the conviction.[307]

Mindszenty spent the next eight years in a solitary confinement that nearly killed him. He was released in 1955 because of ill-health but kept under surveillance. During the 1956 Hungarian uprising, he was freed by rebel forces. Rather than flee, he took residency in the US embassy, refusing to leave his country unless the communist government rescinded his conviction, which, under pressure from the Kremlin, it would not do. He offered up his suffering as a living martyr to Christian life under communism—or, as Bishop Fulton Sheen called him in a 1957 TV broadcast, the "Dry Martyr of Hungary."[308] The communists persecuted him for two and a half decades. Mindszenty concluded that communism is "a kind of religion" that "knows no God, no immortal soul."[309]

Mindszenty was hardly alone. For every Cardinal Mindszenty in Hungary, there was a Cardinal Wyszynski or Fr. Jerzy Popieluszko in Poland, a Richard Wurmbrand in Romania, a Natan Sharansky or Walter Ciszek in Russia, a Vasyl Velychkovsky or Severian Baranyk or Zenobius Kovalyk in the Ukraine, a Moaddedi clan in Afghanistan, a Lutheran or Methodist missionary or follower of the Dalai Lama in China, a jailed nun in Cuba, or one of tens of thousands of Buddhist monks forced to renounce his vows in Cambodia in the late 1970s. The communist war on religion wracked Cuba for a half century, a nation not even one hundred miles off America's shore. The battle remains very much alive, obviously, in China, where Christians worship in underground churches, or in jail cells; because China is religiously unfree, one of every five people in the world are spiritually shackled. And the onslaught rages on in the prison-state of North Korea, once known as the "Jerusalem of the East."

Whether the totalitarian leader was Fidel Castro or Pol Pot or Joe Stalin, the sentiment was the same. Wherever they went, from East to West, from Africa to Asia, from Phnom Penh to St. Petersburg, communists shared one goal: the annihilation of religion. Communists quibbled over the details of how to implement Marx's vision, but they were unanimous in one thing: religion was the enemy, a rival to Marxist mind control, and it had to be vanquished regardless of costs and difficulties.[310]

This atheism was integral to the revolution. Even those communists unable to secure political power—and thus lacking the ability to persecute believers—still did their best to persecute the teachings of organized religion and ridicule the idea of the existence of God. In fact, even in America, it was no surprise to stroll by a city newsstand in the mid-twentieth century and catch bold front-page headlines like this in the *Daily Worker*, the communist organ published by CPUSA: "THERE IS NO GOD."[311] Communists were proud of their atheism, always militant and never shy.

The fact that communists devoted so much time and effort to anti-religion reflects that remarkable devotion—again, an almost religious-like devotion—to the goal of eliminating religious faith. It also attested to the communist conviction that religion truly was incompatible with Marxism-Leninism. Nothing else seemed to elicit such howls and hisses from Karl Marx's disciples.

Hell on Earth: the Richard Wurmbrand Experience

Again, so many such examples could be cited. This chapter will conclude with some frightening images from the vicious communist state that was Romania.

Richard Wurmbrand was a pastor who endured fourteen years of hell in a Romanian prison. He detailed some of the unspeakable cruelty he witnessed in testimony before the US Congress and in his widely read *Tortured for Christ*, first published in 1967. "Thousands of believers from churches of all denominations were sent to prison at that time," remembered Wurmbrand. "Not only were clergymen put in jail, but also simple peasants, young boys and girls who witnessed for their faith. The prisons were full, and in Romania, as in all communist countries, to be in prison means to be tortured." He recalled the example of one pastor:

> A pastor by the name of Florescu was tortured with red-hot iron pokers and with knives. He was beaten very badly. Then starving rats were driven into his cell through a large pipe. He could not sleep because he had to defend himself all the time. If he rested a moment, the rats would attack him.
>
> He was forced to stand for two weeks, day and night. . . . Eventually, they brought his fourteen-year-old son to the prison and began to whip the boy in front of his father, saying that they would continue to beat him until the pastor said what they wished him to say. The poor man was half mad. He bore it as long as he could, then he cried to his son, "Alexander, I must

say what they want! I can't bear your beating anymore!" The son answered, "Father, don't do me the injustice of having a traitor as a parent. Withstand! If they kill me, I will die with the words, 'Jesus and my fatherland'." The communists, enraged, fell upon the child and beat him to death, with blood spattered over the walls of the cell. He died praising God. Our dear brother Florescu was never the same after seeing this.[312]

Wurmbrand's captors carved him in a dozen different parts of his body. They burned eighteen holes in him.

"What the communists have done to Christians surpasses . . . human understanding," wrote Wurmbrand. He said that communist torturers often told him, "There is no God, no hereafter, no punishment for evil. We can do what we wish." Wurmbrand described crucifixion at the hands of communists. Christians would be tied to crosses for four days and nights:

> The crosses were placed on the floor and hundreds of prisoners had to fulfill their bodily necessities over the faces and bodies of the crucified ones. Then the crosses were erected again and the communists jeered and mocked: "Look at your Christ! How beautiful he is! What fragrance he brings from heaven!". . . After being driven nearly insane with tortures, a priest was forced to consecrate human excrement and urine and give Holy Communion to Christians in this form. This happened in the Romanian prison of Pitesti. I asked the priest afterward why he did not prefer to die rather than participate in this mockery. He answered, "Don't judge me, please! I have suffered more than Christ!" All the biblical descriptions of hell and the pains of Dante's Inferno are nothing in comparison with the tortures in communist prisons.

> This is only a very small part of what happened on one Sunday and on many other Sundays in the prison of Pitesti. Other

things simply cannot be told. My heart would fail if I should tell them again and again. They are too terrible and obscene to put in writing.

It was not an unusual Sunday at the Pitesti prison, a frightening house of horrors that even the imaginative Dante Alighieri could not have conceived.

The Hell That Was Pitesti

What Wurmbrand described from the prison of Pitesti is just a small, bitter taste of an awful place filled with tales of depravity. The evils that prowled about that political penitentiary and brainwashing/reeducation center in the city of Pitesti, located on the Arges River in Romania, beginning in 1949 and continuing among several years and perhaps thousands of inmates, have been acknowledged in the communist world (and noted by the likes of Alexander Solzhenitsyn) but have not received the attention they should in the West. A website (with English translation) has been created and devoted to the subject, appropriately titled "The Genocide of the Souls—The Pitesti Experiment." The website, an extension of an accompanying film project, is maintained by Romanian filmmakers Sorin Iliesiu and Doru Lucian Iliesiu, partnering with the renowned French scholar Stephane Courtois, editor of the Harvard University Press classic *The Black Book of Communism*.[313]

The site captures some of the truly ghastly testimonies that have been preserved largely in Eastern European literature. Young religious students in particular were tortured, and often in ways that mocked or sought to commit great sacrilege against their Christian faith. Note that the sources below come from book accounts with titles like *The Devil's Mill* and *The Hell of Pitesti*.[314] Readers beware—this is very sick stuff:

"The delirious imagination of Turcanu [the chief torturer at Pitesti] was unleashed above all when he was dealing with students who believed in God and who strove not to renounce their belief. Thus, some were baptized each morning: their heads plunged into a bucket of urine and fecal matter, while the others around chanted the ritual of baptism. This would last until the contents of the bucket started to bubble. When the recalcitrant prisoner was on the point of drowning, he would be pulled up, given a short respite in which to breathe, then submerged once more."[315]

"In the so-called act of depersonalization, the students were forced, under torture, permanent and unimaginable torture, to betray all they held dear: God, their own parents, brothers, sisters and friends. They were constrained to drink urine and to eat feces! The human being was thereby annihilated. Disgusted at his weakness, he would never be able to recover himself before his own conscience. The pain was beyond the power of human endurance."[316]

"Then they undressed me. . . . What followed is indescribable . . . beatings on the head to induce stupefaction; beatings in the face, for disfigurement; thousands of blows to the back, below the ribs, in the plexus, on the soles of the feet. Dozens of faints and then all over again, for hours on end, and the eye at the peep hole always watching, always watching. They shattered my ribs, lungs, liver, kicking my bones, my kidneys with shod feet."[317]

"When the victim was a theology student or a person with a certain religious feeling, he was made to genuflect to the bare bottom of one of the 're-educated,' to call that bottom an icon and to kiss it. He would have to label the Holy Virgin 'the great whore' and Jesus Christ 'the great idiot crucified on the cross.' If it was known that the victim loved his parents, Turcanu would provoke him thus: Tell me, X, how did you sleep with your mother? or, Tell me how you caught your father raping your sister? The victim, after enduring the purgatory of 're-education,' was never abandoned, but was also drawn into the caste of executioners."[318]

"Performances on religious subjects, black masses staged at Easter or Christmas, horrified the detainees. On such occasions, it was the theology students who were to suffer the most, dressed up as 'Christs,' clothed in cassocks smeared with excrement. They were made to take 'communion' with urine and feces, and instead of the Cross, a phallus was fashioned of soap, which all the others were made to kiss. Alongside them hymns were sung with scabrous words, in which the commonplaces were insults against Christ and the Virgin Mary. Sometimes the detainees would be stripped naked."[319]

"Sexual plays also performed at the orders of Turcanu, naturally. On Good Friday, he shared out the roles: the 'ass' is fellated by 'Mary Magdalene,' 'Joseph' sodomizes the 'ass,' which in its turn stands with its muzzle in the lap of the 'Virgin Mary whore,' concomitantly sodomized by 'Jesus.' The re-educated, headed by Turcanu, displayed a diabolical pleasure in mocking the faithful, nicknamed 'mystics.' Such scenes had a terrible effect on the victims, who as a rule found their only solace in faith. However, after participating in the black masses, their entire faith was shaken to its foundations."[320]

"You were made to tug each other's genitals or one of them would put his penis in your mouth; if you soiled yourself during beatings you were made to eat your own feces and to lick the dirtied long-johns or to eat another's feces from your own mess tin, without being allowed to wash it after that; you were made to kiss each other's bottoms; you were made to urinate in each other's mouths; when you begged for water, you would be given urine from the bucket or they would urinate in your mouth, or others would spit in your mouth; you were made to spit in each other's bottoms and then lick it up; they would wipe a stick smeared in feces . . . on your mouth and in your mouth; you were made to stick your finger up your bottom and then suck it."[321]

"With indescribable fury they began to hit him, with fists, cudgels and feet. And to toss him from one to another, until the bloodied wretch fell almost senseless and could no longer rise. After they had given him a few more kicks to the head, two of them picked him up and threw him on the bunk, making him sit with his hands in his pockets and his head bowed, according to the order. Then another followed, then another, as though in a devilish ring dance intended to annihilate the last speck of physical and moral resistance of those who entered into their rabid game."[322]

These descriptions speak for themselves. No macabre screenwriter or slasher-film master would dare go this far.

Betrayal of God was the order of the day, as was sacrilege in the name of Jesus, "the great idiot crucified," and the Blessed Mother, "the great whore." Holy days were special moments for obscenity and blasphemy. And there were black masses. Of course, there were black masses.

Who would say that the devil wasn't present there at Pitesti?

CHAPTER 6

"SATANIC SCOURGE"

THE CHURCH ON ATHEISTIC COMMUNISM

Alexander Yakovlev was Mikhail Gorbachev's chief aide and reformer. He was assigned the grisly task of looking into the subject of communist crimes more closely than any other Kremlin official. After the collapse of the USSR, he was given access to Communist Party archives as head of modern Russia's Presidential Commission for the Rehabilitation of Victims of Political Repression. He was particularly struck by the "merciless mass terror" against the religious—so intense and insidious that Yakovlev, in his book published by Yale University Press, used words like "infernal" and "evil" and even "demonic" to describe the force that had swept through his "sinful land."[323]

As Yakovlev put it, the USSR had followed a Marxist-Leninist social system that "preaches the demonic religion of evil." What Marxism-Leninism had wrought against religious faith was "infinitely vile." This demanded repentance "of our sins and errors" and a collective kneeling "before the graves of the millions of people who were shot or who died of hunger." Communist officials should repent for the "gulag harvest of crosses" produced in this "biggest cemetery on earth" otherwise known as the Soviet Union.[324]

This is not language typical of a leading scholarly academic press, but Yakovlev could not avoid it. It was also not language typical of a onetime top Soviet official. And Alexander Yakovlev, for the record, was not known to have been religious. Nonetheless, free to speak the

135

truth at last, Yakovlev did not hold back. The evil he saw was undeniable, and words like "infernal" and "diabolical" struck him as the
best description of what had transpired in the USSR. Such was the
inescapable conclusion of so many witnesses to communism.

"Dark Design"

The Roman Catholic Church figured prominently among those
leveling precisely such charges against communism. From the very
outset, well before Bolshevism seized Russia, no institution foresaw
the scourge of atheistic communism like the institutional Roman
Catholic Church.

Quite remarkably, the Church's scathing condemnation of communism preceded even the publication of the *Communist Manifesto* in 1848. A preemptive strike was delivered two years earlier by
Pope Pius IX in 1846, as Karl Marx conspired under the shadow
of St. Michael the Archangel in Brussels toiling at his revolutionary
catechism.

In November 1846, Pope Pius IX released *Qui Pluribus*, affirming
that communism is "absolutely contrary to the natural law itself" and
if adopted would "utterly destroy the rights, property, and possessions of all men, and even society itself." If ever it seemed a man had
held a crystal ball . . . Few statements were so unerringly predictive
of what was to come.

Qui Pluribus stated that communism was a "dark design" of "men
in the clothing of sheep, while inwardly ravening wolves." "After
taking their captives gently, they mildly bind them, and then kill
them in secret," this encyclical somehow knew, or foreknew. "They
make men fly in terror from all practice of religion, and they cut
down and dismember the sheep of the Lord." The writings of communists, Pius IX stated, teach "sinning" and "widespread disgusting
infection." They are "filled with deceit and cunning" and "spread
pestilential doctrines everywhere and deprave the minds especially of

the imprudent, occasioning great losses for religion."

Qui Pluribus continued, "As a result of this filthy medley of errors . . . We see . . . morals deteriorated, Christ's most holy religion despised, the majesty of divine worship rejected, the power of this Apostolic See plundered, the authority of the Church attacked and reduced to base slavery, the rights of bishops trampled on, the sanctity of marriage infringed."[325]

Somehow, this pope and his Magisterium had even foreseen that marriage would be infringed upon by communists. Again, this was two years before Marx and Engels published their opus.

In 1849, one year after the *Manifesto* was published, Pius IX issued another encyclical, *Nostis Et Nobiscum*, which referred to both socialism and communism as "wicked theories," "perverted theories," "perverted teachings," and "pernicious fictions." They were linked together throughout the encyclical.

For the Church and its shepherds, this was just the start of a never-ending response to communism and its ugly stepsister, socialism. (In strict Marxist-Leninist theory, socialism is a mere transitionary step on the way to full communism. More on this in a moment.)

On December 28, 1878, Pius IX's successor, Pope Leo XIII, followed with *Quod Apostolici Muneris* (On Socialism), which defined communism as "the fatal plague which insinuates itself into the very marrow of human society only to bring about its ruin." He stated, "We speak of that sect of men who, under various and almost barbarous names, are called socialists, communists, or nihilists, and who, spread over all the world, and bound together by a wicked confederacy, no longer seek the shelter of secret meetings, but, openly and boldly marching forth in the light of day, strive to bring what they have long been planning—the overthrow of all civil society." These men "leave nothing untouched." These men "debase the natural union of man and woman, held sacred even among barbarous peoples; and its bond, by which the family is chiefly held together. . . . Doctrines of socialism strive almost completely to dissolve this union."

More such pronouncements followed from the Magisterium in 1924, 1928, 1930 (particularly the February 1930 statement *The Soviet Campaign Against God*), another in 1931, two in 1932, another in 1933, with the harshest still yet to come in March 1937.

Among these, 1931 saw Pope Pius XI issue his seminal *Quadragesimo Anno*. Few passages in *Quadragesimo Anno* put it as bluntly as this one (section 120): "Religious socialism, Christian socialism, are contradictory terms; no one can be at the same time a good Catholic and a true socialist."

To repeat: one cannot be a true socialist and a good Catholic.

And then came *Divini Redemptoris*. Released in March 1937, during Stalin's Great Terror, this formal Roman Catholic Church encyclical may well be the most damning official declaration ever issued against communism. In this document, Pope Pius XI, who held the chair of St. Peter from February 1922 to February 1939, escalated the papal tradition of opposing communism, a mantle that would be picked up by (and then some) his successor, Eugenio Pacelli, Pope Pius XII, who served from March 1939 to October 1958, and who was such a formidable enemy of Soviet communism that Stalin and his goons labeled him "Hitler's Pope."[326]

Divini Redemptoris called communism "pernicious," "Godless," "by its nature anti-religious," a form of "perversity," a "fury," "poison," an "extreme danger," a "deluge which threatens the world," a "collectivistic terrorism . . . replete with hate," and a "plague" that leads to "catastrophe." It constituted a form of "class-warfare which causes rivers of blood to flow," a "savage barbarity." Marxists were "the powers of darkness," orchestrating a battle against "the very idea of Divinity." Communism was a "satanic scourge" that "conceals in itself a false messianic idea."

"The evil we must combat," said the encyclical, "is at its origin primarily an evil of the spiritual order. From this polluted source the monstrous emanations of the communistic system flow with satanic logic." The encyclical even underscored communism's attack on marriage, family, motherhood, education, parents.

In *Divini Redemptoris*, the Church made clear that the notion of a "Christian Marxist" was an oxymoron. In the dialectical and historical materialism advocated by Marx, "there is no room for the idea of God." The document was unambiguous: communism was a "truly diabolical" instrument of Satan and his "sons of darkness," a false promise, a "convulsion," yet one more "sad legacy" of the fall of man.

1949 Papal Decree Against Communism

Still another striking example of the Church's rejection of communism was Pope Pius XII's historic July 1949 *Decree Against Communism*. Issued from the Holy Office, it dealt explicitly with the matter of excommunication of communists. The decree is very brief and very simple. It presented four basic questions with four clear answers:

1. Is it licit to join or show favor to Communist parties? Response: **No.**

2. Is it licit to publish, distribute, or read publications that support Communist doctrine or activity, or to write for them? Response: **No.**

3. May Christians who knowingly and freely commit the acts in parts 1 and 2 be given the sacraments? Response: **No.**

4. Do Christians who profess, defend or promote materialistic Communist doctrine incur the penalty of excommunication as apostates from the Christian faith, with the penalty reserved so that it may only be lifted by the Holy See? Response: **Yes.**[327]

Yes, the Roman Catholic Church was so against communism, and against its members joining the Communist Party or promoting communist doctrine, that the pope himself stated that Catholics would incur the penalty of excommunication as apostates from the faith if they were to do so.

Vatican II on Christians "Infected" with Communism

Many Catholics rightly suspect that this toughness toward communism softened, at least rhetorically, during Vatican II (1962–65). Still, even Vatican II acknowledged the dangers of and condemned communism, albeit (quite disappointingly) in documents that went unpublished.[328] Reading those statements is worthwhile for discerning the ongoing consistency within the Church in confronting this lethal ideology so threatening to faith and freedom.

There were three documents—technically considered "preparatory schemas"—written and approved by the "General Session" of the Second Vatican Council from February to April 1962. I will here quote only a few sections to provide a sense of the gist of the statements. The documents were poignant philosophical statements on communism, but still more striking for the practical steps they carefully outlined for the Church to take in countering the ideology. As stated by one source who translated the schemas, "These documents represented a plan to launch a global offensive against communism." They clearly did.[329]

The first of the three documents, titled "On the Care of Souls With Regard to Christians Infected With Communism," opened by identifying "atheistic communism" as a "menace" threatening the "doctrine and activity of the Church," with a specific purpose "to radically overturn the social order and to subvert the foundations of Christian civilization." It stated that communism "offers a false kind of redemption," and is pervaded, "in a pseudo-mystical way, with a certain false idea of justice, equality and fraternity for all in the administration of their needs and labors, for the purpose of inflaming the masses by enticing them with deceitful promises, by which they are aroused as if by a virulent contagion." Communism served as "a false religion without God," as it sought to abolish the very notion of an "eternal Divinity and the hope of another life." Atheistic communism sought to "bring about a new political order," an association of men "that expels God from the earth," and yet, "like a new gospel and like a form of salvific redemption, preaches its message to all of humanity."

The language in that opening preamble set the tone for the document, which then went on to make the crucial point that "the Church, as the Mystical Body of Christ," has a moral-spiritual-evangelical duty to oppose communism rather than engage in "merely political or economic anticommunism." This is "a spiritual struggle against atheistic communism," which the document called an "invention so full of errors and delusions."

But what made this document (to repeat, unpublished) so unique from all previous Church statements on communism were the concrete steps—the specific plan of action—that it laid out in thirteen steps, several of them with additional sub-steps. Among them were these notable suggestions:

6. For this purpose, students are to be educated in seminaries and likewise priests in particular courses are to be instructed regarding the doctrines of communism itself, of the truths of the faith it attacks, and of the most apt pastoral method for defending the faith.

7. The bishops in the National Conferences should promote a firm and constant action against the errors of the communists through the use of experts, and likewise should ensure that in each province or nation there should be a specified group of men who, as true experts in communist doctrine, zealously combat the errors of the same doctrine with meticulous care.

8. Because pastoral activity should be addressed to all men, not excluding militant communists, the bishops should ensure that in each province or nation a select group of priests and laity be designated, men who are outstanding in knowledge or reputation, and particularly in the zeal for their apostolate, who strive to win for Christ those who are followers of communism or who are

infected by its erroneous doctrines. . . .

10. There is a need for an influx of workers' guilds and a common association of laborers for the purpose of counteracting or eliminating the influx of atheistic communism among simpler souls, who have a poor understanding of the nature of communism and do not support it strongly, although they might vote in favor of communism for economic reasons.

We will see in the pages ahead that certain priests and bishops took up these charges (most conspicuously, Fulton Sheen). And as to point 6, there was concern that communists had their eyes on seminaries.

Then came these eye-openers, subsets of step 11, recommending that certain Catholics (churchmen among them) be silenced, severely admonished, or even hit with penalties for succumbing to these pernicious "progressive" doctrines:

§ 7. Catholics who, infected by "progressive" doctrines and zealous for revolution, or because of a false so-called "idealism," or a wavering judgment, or an erroneous notion of charity, or because of fear of Soviet power and a foolish shame of the judgment of man, impede action against atheistic communism, should be publicly silenced by ecclesiastical authority. Priests delinquent in this regard are to be severely admonished, and, if the case so merits, inflicted with penalties.

§ 8. Those, however, who, whether they are bishops or priests or laity, act to counter atheistic communism in a healthy way, are to be lauded and assisted and, if it is necessary, defended.

This was in keeping with the late Pius XII's decree on communism. The Church also recommended these two final concrete steps:

12. An international commission of bishops and of lay experts should be instituted, which, under the leadership of the Holy See, has the task of overseeing and supporting all of those who

seek to defend and liberate mankind from the errors of atheism and communism.

13. It will be the principal duty of this international commission to promote and coordinate the studies, works, ordinances, and laws that debilitate communism and shatter its audacity.

Without a doubt, this was bold and daring. The text of the document closed by stating in italics, "*Text definitively approved in the General Session held on the days of February 5-13, 1962.*"

Unfortunately, these documents were not published, very likely in part because they were obstructed and undermined by Church liberals who found them too provocative and too contrary to the new spirit they wanted to fashion from Vatican II. Pope Paul VI, who closed out Vatican II, years later would warn that the "smoke of Satan" had entered the Church. One wonders if the blocking of these documents were early signals of just that. No doubt, these documents remain notable for how they reflected ongoing Church teaching, but it seems equally notable (and lamentable) that the documents went unpublished.

The "Cunning" "Contagion" of Communism

The second Vatican II document "On the Care of Souls and Communism" (title similar to the first document, albeit abbreviated) reiterated much of the first document. Even then, the language is excellent and worth quoting. It started with this:

> There are a large number of people in many nations who, although they were not born into ignoble families and they were even baptized and educated in the Catholic Church, are enticed by communism, enlist in communist organizations, and vote for communists in political and administrative elections. Many of them, indeed, do not adhere to communist philosophical doctrines in their hearts, and the only basis of their

> merely practical support for the communist cause, or at least the principal one, is that they regard it as an effective way to bring about the perfect establishment of social justice, and, in fact, for obtaining a better salary or wage for less work, for receiving an equal part of the division and distribution of wealth and material goods, and for living a more comfortable and easier life. However, those who favor communism only for economic convenience are mistaken.

The document cautioned against the "contagion of communism" employing its "cunning methods for deceiving the incautious." This was a trenchant warning of the timeless problem of dupes, of people (especially on the "social justice" religious left) being suckered by communists operating with slick slogans or various tricks and tools to manipulate the gullible.

And in one of maybe the most farseeing passages in the three Vatican II schemas, this second document warned of communist penetration of the universities: "It is to be strongly recommended that in universities and in other institutions of higher education of the sciences and arts, particular groups or associations be instituted for professors or students to ensure that they may not only give a public and clear testimony regarding the Christian faith by their truly Christian beliefs and manner of life, but also so they might expressly and efficaciously act to frustrate, or at least restrain, the nefarious work that is carried out hotly and bitterly in the aforementioned schools by so-called communist cells."

The third document, titled "On the Apostolate of the Laity in Environments Imbued With Materialism, Particularly Marxism," is the shortest of the three preparatory schemas. Nonetheless, it likewise had sharp words regarding the "open and militant atheism" of "so-called 'Marxism'" and the "exceedingly grave and universal danger" it posed. Marxism constituted "the most grave form of materialism and the one most hostile towards the Christian faith." The document also powerfully noted (in the endnotes) that while communism is an explicitly atheistic ideology that "combats all forms of religions whatsoever," which it declares to be "the opiate of the people," and that "it especially opposes the Roman Catholic Church," the ironic reality is that communism itself "is a pseudo-religion, and indeed an eschatological one." The ideology promotes an end-times/utopian-like vision of heaven on earth.

Communism, concluded Vatican II, had a "messianic mission," by which the glistening new "collectivity" of the blessed "masses" would be the new "redeemer of mankind." And this "religion defends its dogmatic Marxism-Leninism, condemns heretics and excommunicates schismatics."

Clearly, even the new spirit pervading Vatican II could not escape notice of the unclean spirit of communism. Men inside the Church remained fully aware of the evils that needed to be exorcised.

"Body of the Anti-Christ"

Such condemnations of communism would continue in further statements by many Catholic priests, bishops, and popes. From the shores of America, few were as vocal and influential as Fulton Sheen.

Bishop Fulton J. Sheen (1895–1979) was one of the most prominent Americans of the twentieth century. He was extraordinarily popular not just because of his sermons and his writings but through his powerful radio broadcasts and highly watched television show, *Life Is Worth Living*. Sheen could not be missed, and neither could his blistering attacks against communism. (He can still be seen today, particularly on EWTN television, the global Catholic network.)

Sheen noted that whereas Karl Marx called religion "the sigh of the oppressed creature," Sheen saw *communism* as the sigh of the oppressed creature. In a 1936 Lenten sermon at St. Patrick's Cathedral in New York, Sheen asked, "Why can't the modern mind see there is nothing new in communism?" He called it "a groan of despair."[330]

In another Lenten message, Sheen called the USSR "the most anti-Christ nation on the face of the earth." He told the assembled that it was fitting that Soviet communism's emblem was "a rotted corpse, the body of Lenin—a perfect symbol of that to which all communism must lead us all, unto dust, unto dissolution, unto death."[331]

In 1948, Sheen wrote *Communism and the Conscience of West*, a bestseller. "The truth on the subject is that communism and atheism are intrinsically related and that one cannot be a good Communist without being an atheist and every atheist is a potential Communist," said Sheen. He quoted Marx: "Communism begins where atheism begins." And yet, ironically, said Sheen, it was *communism*, rather than religion, that was an opiate of the masses. Soviet communism adhered to the "preaching of Lenin," the "apostles of Marx," and treated Stalin like a god.

In his 1954 book *The Church, Communism and Democracy*, Sheen wrote that communism was inspired not by the spirit of Christ "but by the spirit of the serpent. . . . The Mystical Body of the Anti-Christ." He said, "They have thrown down the gauntlet to the world. The voice is either brotherhood in Christ or comradeship in anti-Christ." Sheen explained, "In order to understand the communists' idea of truth, we have to substitute the philosophy of communism for God; in other words, the ultimate origin of truth is [found] in their party." He added that "Marx was not first a Communist and then an atheist. He was first an atheist, then a Communist. Communism was merely the political expression of his atheism. As he hated God, so would he hate those who would own property."[332]

Sheen contrasted the redemptive suffering of Christ to the non-redemptive suffering of Marx and communist philosophy. "Christianity," writes Sheen, "comes to optimism through pessimism; to a resurrection through a passion, and to a crown of glory through a crown of thorns; to the glory of Easter Sunday through the ignominy of a Good Friday." Tying that to the suffering wrought by Soviet communism, Sheen advised that the Russian people—for whom, he rightly said, "atheism is not natural"—take heart that Christ's tomb is empty, while Lenin's tomb is not.

Sheen said that communists had failed to convince the world that there is no God. Rather, he quipped, they had succeeded only in convincing the world that there *is* a devil.[333]

That was Fulton Sheen, who was steadfast and omnipresent in countering communism. Of course, these statements are a mere snippet of Sheen's admonitions. Truly, this book could be filled with remarks from Sheen. And all along, Sheen had the backing of a universal Church and its popes behind him.

Among popes, numerous formal statements have already been cited here, and so many personal assessments could be quoted from Pope John Paul II alone, the ultimate battler against twentieth-century communism. We could even look to appraisals from popes of the modern day—that is, our own twenty-first century.

Pope Benedict XVI (2005–13), born Joseph Ratzinger in Germany, is one of the great intellects in the Roman Catholic Church and wider Christian church. His writings on topics from Jesus of Nazareth to the crisis of the Western world are insightful and memorable, warning of everything from a "dictatorship of relativism" to the hazards of a society that exalts a "confused ideology of freedom."

But Pope Benedict also had warned his flock about the pitfalls of Marxism. "Together with the victory of the revolution," wrote Benedict in his November 2007 encyclical *Spe Salvi* (*In Hope We Are Saved*), "Marx's fundamental error also became evident. He showed precisely how to overthrow the existing order, but he did not say how matters should proceed thereafter. He simply presumed that with the expropriation of the ruling class, with the fall of political power and the socialization of means of production, the new Jerusalem would be realized."

Once the existed order was overthrown, noted Benedict, Marx figured that "all contradictions would be resolved, man and the world would finally sort themselves out. Then everything would be able to proceed by itself along the right path." Marx, averred Pope Benedict XVI, had neglected to "work out how this new world would be organized—which should, of course, have been unnecessary." It would have been unnecessary to Marx because utopia would have inevitably swept in and massaged all those inconvenient details.

On those details, Marx was silent. He need not talk, or write, about what came next, because it would simply . . . well, come. It would come.

"His silence on this matter follows logically from his chosen approach," Pope Benedict XVI said of Marx. "His error lay deeper. He forgot that man always remains man. He forgot man and he forgot man's freedom. He forgot that freedom always remains also freedom for evil."

That freedom for evil would be exercised by men like Lenin, Trotsky, Stalin, Bukharin, Mao, Pol Pot, the Kims, Che, Castro.

Said Benedict of Marx, "He thought that once the economy had been put right, everything would automatically be put right. His real error is materialism: man, in fact, is not merely the product of economic conditions, and it is not possible to redeem him purely from the outside by creating a favorable economic environment."

In other words, man does not live on bread alone—as Jesus Christ reminded Satan.

And on Lenin, too, Pope Benedict XVI had something to say, seeing in the Bolshevik godfather the same fatal assumption, banking on Marx for something that had never been deposited: "Thus, having accomplished the revolution, Lenin must have realized that the writings of the master gave no indication as to how to proceed. True, Marx had spoken of the interim phase of the dictatorship of the proletariat as a necessity which in time would automatically become redundant. This 'intermediate phase' we know all too well, and we also know how it then developed, not ushering in a perfect world, but leaving behind a trail of appalling destruction."

That it did.

Such was the previous pontiff, Pope Benedict XVI.

And for the record, updating this treatment to today's pontiff, it should be noted that even Pope Francis, often criticized by conservatives as a "Marxist," has stated emphatically, "The Marxist ideology is wrong."[334]

Rejecting Socialism

It is worth pausing to address the question of "socialism." Today, one often hears certain people object, "Well, I'm not a communist; I'm a socialist," or a "I'm a democratic socialist."

Alas, what is socialism? What is *democratic socialism*? How are they different from communism? Many of those rallying to the flag have the same questions.[335] Without getting into a protracted analysis of nuances, a few clarifications are in order and relevant to this discussion and to discourse today.

For starters, Vladimir Lenin and Leon Trotsky and Joseph Stalin and their fellow communist totalitarians established a "Union of Soviet *Socialist* Republics." It was at the Second Congress of the Russian Social-Democratic Labor Party, beginning in Brussels and ending in London, traversing a period of three weeks from July to August 1903, that Lenin changed the name of his and Trotsky's and Stalin's party from the Russian Social-Democratic Labor Party to what would eventually become the Communist Party of the Soviet Union. It was there that Lenin and his cadre became the Bolsheviks (splitting into Bolsheviks and Menshaviks). The Bolsheviks were first social democrats.[336] Here in the United States, leading communists of the day, such as William Z. Foster and Ben Gitlow and Bertram Wolfe, to name just three, were leaders in the American Socialist Party in the first decade of the twentieth century before they helped launch the American Communist Party in the second decade of the twentieth century. Foster and Gitlow will be detailed at length later. Wolfe, it should be noted here, joined them in turning the American

Socialist Party into the American Communist Party, and likewise became a founding delegate of the American Communist Party to the Soviet Comintern in Moscow. Wolfe correctly said of Lenin and social democrats, "Lenin began his career as a Social Democrat."[337]

Gitlow and Wolfe took the natural step in the Marxist evolutionary process, moving from socialism to communism.

Modern self-identified "socialists" in America or Western Europe recoil at any suggested similarity to or sympathy with Soviet socialism—or to Nazi socialism. ("Nazi" is actually an acronym for National *Socialist* German Workers' Party.) They indeed have committed no acts of violence anywhere near approaching those orchestrated by such tyrants. Nonetheless, socialists generally, in America and the wider West, do have in common with the Soviets and the Nazis the general goal of government ownership of the means of production in some form. Socialists all share that objective. The famous Clause IV of the 1918 British Labour Party manifesto/platform (repudiated in 1995 by Labour Party leader Tony Blair) called for "the most equitable distribution" based on "the common ownership of the means of production, distribution, and exchange." That is a central tenet of socialist thought. When curious seekers search for the word at Merriam-Webster.com, they will discover precisely that standard definition. "Socialism," states Merriam-Webster, is "government ownership of the means of production."

Sometimes the best approach to try to define a term is to go directly to the source—that is, to the advocates themselves.

To that end, the World Socialist Party of the United States declares its overriding "object" as this: "The establishment of a system of society based on the common ownership and democratic control of the means and instruments for producing and distributing wealth by and in the interest of society as a whole." More than that, it sees this object as part of a global movement. "The WSP forms part of the world socialist movement," states the group's mission statement. "Our only goal is to educate people to the urgent need we all have of eliminating wage-labor and capital now in favor of communist-based free access and self-determination of needs. We call this 'common ownership,' but other terms we regard as synonymous are communism and socialism."

This explanation comes right from WSP's website and literature. The group's logo depicts the globe wrapped in a banner that declares "UNITE FOR SOCIALISM!" under the famous Marxist phrase "WORKERS OF THE WORLD" and above the Marxist phrase "YOU HAVE NOTHING TO LOSE BUT YOUR CHAINS."

Here we see that these socialists are communists, as they themselves concede. The World Socialist Party regards the two as synonymous. It is not alone in that respect, and never has been. It sees socialism as the crucial final step to communism, which, according to Marxist theory, it is.

In strict Marxist theory, socialism has that very specific purpose and definition; it is a waystation along the path to a full communist *utopia*. History, according to Marxist-dialectic thought, would pass through a series of planes or stages, from feudalism to capitalism to socialism to communism. Each successive plane or stage would be a higher step in the evolutionary process toward a "workers' paradise" or glorious "classless society."

In probably his most revealing work, *The State and Revolution*, Lenin, in his chapter titled "The Transition from Capitalism to Communism," began with a quote from Marx: "Between capitalist and communist society lies the period of the revolutionary transformation of the one into the other. Corresponding to this is also a political transition period in which the state can be nothing but the revolutionary dictatorship of the proletariat."[338] Lenin also quoted Engels: "According to Engels, the bourgeois state does not 'wither away,' but is 'abolished' by the proletariat in the course of the revolution. What withers away after this revolution is the proletarian state or semistate. . . . In speaking of the state 'withering away,' and the even more graphic and colorful 'dying down of itself,' Engels refers quite clearly and definitely to the period after 'the state has taken possession of the means of production in the name of the whole of society,' that is, after the socialist revolution."

The socialist revolution opens the door to the eventual consummation of the communist revolution.

Returning to the timeline and theme of this book, socialism (the blood brother of communism) began pursuing a militantly atheistic agenda from the outset, and the Catholic Church certainly noticed. Let us consider again some of the Catholic Church's significant encyclicals.

As noted earlier, in his 1849 encyclical *Nostis Et Nobiscum*, Pope Pius IX called both socialism and communism "wicked theories," "perverted theories," "perverted teachings," and "pernicious fictions." They were linked together throughout the encyclical. He spoke of a "most iniquitous plot . . . to drive people to overthrow the entire order of human affairs and to draw them over to the wicked theories of this Socialism and Communism, by confusing them with perverted teachings."

In his second encyclical, *Quod Apostolici Muneris* (On Socialism), issued December 28, 1878, Pope Leo XIII correctly lumped socialists and communists together; they formed a "wicked confederacy." He wrote, "We speak of that sect of men who, under various and almost barbarous names, are called socialists, communists, or nihilists, and who, spread over all the world, and bound together by a wicked confederacy, no longer seek the shelter of secret meetings, but, openly and boldly marching forth in the light of day, strive to bring what they have long been planning—the overthrow of all civil society." He said, "They leave nothing untouched." Not only do they attack the right of property, but they "debase the natural union of man and woman, held sacred even among barbarous peoples; and its bond, by which the family is chiefly held together. . . . Doctrines of socialism strive almost completely to dissolve this union."

Quod Apostolici Muneris spoke of the "pest of socialism," the "plague of socialism," the "evil growth of socialism," warned of the "recruits of socialism," and accused socialists of "stealing the very Gospel itself with a view to deceive more easily the unwary." These socialists "distort it [the Gospel] so as to suit their own purposes."

This is just one of many encyclicals in which Leo XIII blasted socialism and communism. They range from the encyclicals *Diuturnum* (June 29, 1881), to *Humanum Genus* (April 20, 1884), *Libertas Praestantissimum* (June 20, 1888), and *Graves de Communi Re* (January 18, 1901). Socialists were "wicked," "seditious," "insidious," and plotted to bring about the "ruin" of society.

Of course, in May 1891 Leo XIII would issue *Rerum Novarum*. This classic is a favorite of many Catholics, but many liberal admirers of it seem to forget its staunch rejection of socialism. Consider this passage (sections 4–5):

> To remedy these wrongs the socialists, working on the poor man's envy of the rich, are striving to do away with private property, and contend that individual possessions should become the common property of all, to be administered by the State or by municipal bodies. They hold that by thus transferring property from private individuals to the community, the present mischievous state of things will be set to rights, inasmuch as each citizen will then get his fair share of whatever there is to enjoy. But their contentions are so clearly powerless to end the controversy that were they carried into effect the working man himself would be among the first to suffer. They are, moreover, emphatically unjust, for they would rob the lawful possessor, distort the functions of the State, and create utter confusion in the community. . . . Socialists, therefore, by endeavoring to transfer the possessions of individuals to the community at large, strike at the interests of every wage-earner, since they would deprive him of the liberty of disposing of his wages, and thereby of all

hope and possibility of increasing his resources and of bettering his condition in life.

Rerum Novarum notes that socialists "strive against nature in vain." They even undermine the family: "The socialists, therefore, in setting aside the parent and setting up a State supervision, act against natural justice, and destroy the structure of the home" (no. 14). *Rerum Novarum* added, "Hence, it is clear that the main tenet of socialism, community of goods, must be utterly rejected, since it only injures those whom it would seem meant to benefit, is directly contrary to the natural rights of mankind, and would introduce confusion and disorder into the commonweal" (no. 15).

Rerum Novarum became the basis for another classic, the encyclical *Quadragesimo Anno*, which was released forty years later, in May 1891.

Recall that section 120 of *Quadragesimo Anno* states bluntly, "Religious socialism, Christian socialism, are contradictory terms; no one can be at the same time a good Catholic and a true socialist."

There are some fifty references to socialism in *Quadragesimo Anno*. Section fifty-five speaks of "the Socialists who hold that whatever serves to produce goods ought to be transferred to the State, or, as they say 'socialized.'" That ambition is "all the more dangerous and the more apt to deceive the unwary. It is an alluring poison which many have eagerly drunk whom open Socialism had not been able to deceive."

Importantly, the encyclical affirmed that the very "characteristic of socialism," including more modern non-communist, non-totalitarian forms that had developed since the time of Leo XIII, was "fundamentally contrary to Christian truth" (no. 111).

The encyclical gave careful thought to this. Sections 113 to 124 of *Quadragesimo Anno* deal with an extended discussion of the "more moderate" form of socialism that some more recent "socialists" had sought to develop as distinct from communism. Some of these socialists, stated the encyclical, might even try to "incline toward" or "approach the truths which Christian tradition has always held sacred." Nonetheless, the Magisterium here recommended that if one is seeking "demands and desire" consistent with Christian truth, these are not unique or "special to Socialism. Those who work solely toward such ends have, therefore, no reason to become socialists" (no. 115). It advised, "Those who want to be apostles among socialists ought to profess Christian truth whole and entire, openly and sincerely, and not connive at error in any way. If they truly wish to be heralds of the Gospel, let them above all strive to show to socialists that socialist claims, so far as they are just, are far more strongly supported by the principles of Christian faith and much more effectively promoted through the power of Christian charity" (no. 116).

The encyclical then proceeded to flatly reject socialism:

> We make this pronouncement: Whether considered as a doctrine, or an historical fact, or a movement, Socialism, if it remains truly Socialism, even after it has yielded to truth and justice on the points which we have mentioned, cannot be reconciled with the teachings of the Catholic Church because its concept of society itself is utterly foreign to Christian truth.
>
> . . . Socialism, on the other hand, wholly ignoring and indifferent to this sublime end of both man and society, affirms that human association has been instituted for the sake of material advantage alone. . . .
>
> If Socialism, like all errors, contains some truth (which, moreover, the Supreme Pontiffs have never denied), it is based nevertheless on a theory of human society peculiar to itself and irreconcilable with true Christianity. Religious socialism, Christian socialism, are contradictory terms; no one can be at the same time a good Catholic and a true socialist. . . .
>
> . . . We have also summoned Communism and Socialism again to judgment and have found all their forms, even the

most modified, to wander far from the precepts of the Gospel. (nos. 117, 118, 120, 128)

That is a clear rejection of socialism, and certainly of any notion of "Christian socialism."

Even more liberal popes, like St. Pope John XXIII, stated, "No Catholic could subscribe even to moderate Socialism."[339] That passage actually quotes Pius XI: "Pope Pius XI further emphasized the fundamental opposition between Communism and Christianity, and made it clear that no Catholic could subscribe even to moderate Socialism. The reason is that Socialism is founded on a doctrine of human society which is bounded by time and takes no account of any objective other than that of material well-being. Since, therefore, it proposes a form of social organization which aims solely at production, it places too severe a restraint on human liberty, at the same time flouting the true notion of social authority."

"Christian socialism" is an oxymoron.

John Paul II on Socialism

Again, so much more could be cited from the Church's teachings on socialism, but I will finish with this verdict, issued near the end of the twentieth century and following the collapse of communism in Eastern Europe.

In May 1991, writing in his classic encyclical *Centesimus Annus*, on the occasion of the hundredth anniversary of *Rerum Novarum*, Pope John Paul II stated that Leo XIII had "arrived at the crux of the problem" when "defining the nature of the socialism of his day as the suppression of private property." He called particular attention to Leo XIII's warning: "To remedy these wrongs (the unjust distribution of wealth and the poverty of the workers), the Socialists encourage the poor man's envy of the rich and strive to do away with private property, contending that individual possessions should become the common property of all."[340]

John Paul II also flagged Leo XIII's admonition that socialists "distort the functions of the State, and create utter confusion in the community." The Polish pontiff connected this to the recent slogan of "real socialism," which had been trumpeted by the USSR in the 1970s and imposed upon its Soviet Bloc states in Eastern Europe and around the world. The very slogan signaled a perennial problem with socialists: their ongoing fatal conceit that they were the awaited ones, the enlightened ones, the anointed ones who would do socialism right. Their socialism was the right, the true, the proper, the *real* socialism. Such is the incessant new claim of every new generation of socialists: simply give them enough power and enough of your freedom, and they will do socialism right, this time. Such were the "evils" endemic to "what would later be called 'Real Socialism,'" said John Paul II.

And then came this crucial point from John Paul II, echoing past popes and presaging the diagnosis of his successor, Pope Benedict XVI: "We have to add that the fundamental error of socialism is anthropological in nature. Socialism considers the individual person simply as an element, a molecule within the social organism, so that the good of the individual is completely subordinated to the functioning of the socio-economic mechanism." Socialism assumes that man's problems can be solved by bread alone—and yet, as Jesus told Satan, man does not live by bread alone. John Paul II stated, "Socialism likewise maintains that the good of the individual can be realized without reference to his free choice. . . . Man is thus reduced to a series of social relationships. . . . From this mistaken conception of the person there arise both a distortion of law, which defines the sphere of the exercise of freedom, and an opposition to private property. A person who is deprived of something he can call 'his own,' and of the possibility of earning a living through his own initiative, comes to depend on the social machine and on those who control it."

The person becomes the ward of the state—the nanny state, Big

Brother. "This makes it much more difficult for him to recognize his dignity as a person," said John Paul II, "and hinders progress towards the building up of an authentic human community." This, said the pope, stands in contrast to the Christian vision of the human person: "According to *Rerum novarum* and the whole social doctrine of the Church, the social nature of man is not completely fulfilled in the State."

From socialism's "mistaken concept of the nature of the person" flows many mistakes and many ills, and "its first cause is atheism. . . . The denial of God deprives the person of his foundation, and consequently leads to a reorganization of the social order without reference to the person's dignity and responsibility." Moreover, "from the same atheistic source, socialism also derives its choice of the means of action condemned in *Rerum novarum,* namely, class struggle."

Socialism, communism—it is the same thing, the same problem. These ideologies fundamentally misunderstand man and what satisfies human beings. They fail to grasp what men and women really want and seek. These ideologies get their anthropology wrong. From that fatal, fundamental mistake follow a long line of destructive failures.

John Paul II favored a better method, known as subsidiarity. It argues that, essentially, local is best, or at least the best starting point. It opposes collectivism and statism. The principle of subsidiarity maintains that nothing should be done by a bigger and more complex organization or level of society that could instead be done by a smaller and simpler one. It looks to localism and decentralization first, whether by individuals, private and religious organizations and charities, or even local government, before looking to a larger federal bureaucracy or welfare state. Those closest to the problem or need can usually deal with it more effectively, more compassionately, and at a more human-personal level.[341]

This better path was raised by John Paul II's successor, Benedict XVI, in his critique of socialism in his encyclical *Deus Caritas Est*

(December 25, 2005). There, Benedict warned against the fatal conceit of "the State which would provide everything, absorbing everything into itself," which "would ultimately become a mere bureaucracy incapable of guaranteeing the very thing which the suffering person—every person—needs: namely, loving personal concern. We do not need a State which regulates and controls everything." Instead, said Benedict, what is needed is a state that operates "in accordance with the principle of subsidiarity," and that does not delude itself into the "mistaken materialist conception" of man who lives "by bread alone."

In sum, we see here a storied track record of a Church that forcefully, courageously, and eloquently stood against socialism and communism, all along earning the enmity of those targets. Moreover, it was a Church that did not merely condemn socialism and communism; it also sought to offer a better way. Above all, that way was *the* Way. It was not the path of atheism.

PART 4

INFILTRATION AND MANIPULATION

CHAPTER 7

"LIQUIDATING RELIGIOUS BELIEFS"

WILLIAM Z. FOSTER AND CPUSA

The communist assault on religion was multifaceted and truly intercontinental, ranging from the fields and factories of Moscow to the streets and skyscrapers of Manhattan. Only in the annals of heaven will the full extent of the affront ever be known. Only Omniscience its very self could possibly know.

This part of the book will serve as an eye-opening snapshot in time—several chapters with testimonies that are chronological: specifically, congressional testimony from the 1930s, 1940s, and 1950s, from William Z. Foster to Louis Budenz, Ben Gitlow, Manning Johnson, and Bella Dodd. These sources, all prominent communists or ex-communists, could intimately testify to their comrades' attack on religion in the United States, where the thrust was mild compared to what lashed believers in places like the USSR, China, Eastern Europe, and elsewhere. Still, it is worthwhile to pause for Americans today to see how American communists in the heyday of their movement sought to take on and take down Christianity, especially the mainline Protestant denominations, as well as the Catholic Church.

It is instructive that this part of the book is the longest. The meticulous efforts at infiltration and manipulation recorded here were at the core of what Marxism was about and what communists did. The sources spoke at length and under oath.

These individuals gave significant testimonies that duly earned headlines in their day. Among them, the testimony in this chapter will feature excerpts from a communist who never left the party, but nonetheless spoke rather candidly (though still somewhat guardedly) about how Communist Party USA and American communists generally viewed religion. That man was William Z. Foster, one of the most important leaders in the history of American communism.

"The Biggest Suckers of Them All:" The Religious Left

But before considering the testimony of Foster and others in the pages ahead, it is crucial to convey an idea of the vital assistance that the religious left provided to American communists—a matter so significant that I wrote about it extensively in my 2010 book *Dupes: How America's Adversaries Have Manipulated Progressives for a Century*. This background brief is helpful because several spots in the testimonies that follow invoke some of the names and organizations I will summarize here in part four.

Though it has been long obvious to sentient human beings that communists hate religion, they nevertheless had an almost preternatural ability to enchant liberal Christians. They cynically, contemptuously targeted the religious left. They knew that progressive Christians shared certain sympathies with them: workers' rights, wealth redistribution, shrinking the income gap, denouncing the rich, fomenting class envy. Communists exploited that trust, often invoking the language of "social justice" to enlist liberals in their petitions, their marches, their campaigns, their objectives.

They had their best success with the mainline Protestant denominations: the Episcopal Church, Presbyterian Church USA, the United Methodist Church. Herbert Romerstein, who had long been one of America's most astute and learned expert ex-communists, stated that communists found progressive pastors to be "the biggest suckers of them all." In fact, Romerstein, to whom I dedicated my book *Dupes*, told me at the start of that research, when I asked generally if there was a particular group that communists had more success with than any other, unhesitatingly gave that exact answer: "the religious left, Paul, they were the biggest suckers of them all."

The word "suckers" is an apt choice. One can see in these testimonies ahead (particularly Bella Dodd's) the use of explicit terms like "dupes," "useful idiots," and "sucker lists." That latter phrase was used by even congressmen during questioning of witnesses.[342] It was used to describe lists of liberal individuals and organizations literally drawn up and targeted by American communists for exploitation. These lists often included progressive professors, teachers, unions, journalists, and especially religious left Christians. Suckers. Lists of suckers. Sucker lists.

In my research for *Dupes*, and numerous times elsewhere before and since, I found repeatedly, dating back a century, beginning with the launch of the Soviet Comintern and Communist Party USA (CPUSA) in 1919, atheistic communists clearly tapping social-justice language not because they believed in Jesus (quite the contrary) but to dupe believers in Jesus, specifically progressive Christians. As I dug into the Soviet Comintern Archives on CPUSA, it took little time to affirm what Romerstein had warned me about: the religious left truly did comprise the biggest suckers of them all. That obvious reality smacks one right upside the face. It is painful to see.

At the time, entire investigations were done strictly on the religious left, particularly the compilations put together by J. B. Matthews, the respected former-communist-turned-government-investigator who served as director of research for the House Committee on Un-American Activities (a committee vilified by liberals today but which for most of its life was led by Democrats). One of the most significant of these compilations is known as the "658/NCC" compilation, which indexed and detailed numerous activities (with dates and titles) of far-left Protestant pastors. The full title of the "658/NCC" compilation was "A Compilation of Public Records of 658 Clergy-men and Laymen connected with the National Council of Churches," published in April 1962, with Matthews the chief investigator. The National Council of Churches was the largest umbrella group of left-wing Protestant ministers in America, notorious for a social-justice gospel that invariably lined up with the Moscow-CPUSA party line. Another such source was the "20.5%/Episcopal" compilation, which had the full title, "A Compilation of Public Records, 20.5%, 1411 Protestant Episcopal Rectors (as of 1955)," published in March 1958.[343] Note the shockingly high number of radical rectors from the Episcopal Church—1,411 of them. These two compilations by Matthews constituted a handy "Who's Who" manual of radical Prot-estant preachers, with names like the notorious Rev. Dr. John How-ard Melish, Walter Russell Bowie, Joseph F. Fletcher, and Episcopal Bishop William Scarlett.[344]

Harry Ward: "Red Dean" of Radical Reverends

Among the most damaging pastors was the Rev. Harry Ward, Meth-odist minister, seminary professor, and founding member of the American Civil Liberties Union (ACLU), which he ran with atheist Roger Baldwin. Baldwin wrote a dreadful 1928 book called *Liberty Under the Soviets.*

You read that correctly. Roger Baldwin, founder of the ACLU, wrote a book titled *Liberty Under the Soviets.*[345]

Ward himself wrote a book called *The Soviet Spirit.* One doubts that it was the Holy Spirit that prompted the right reverend to com-pose this valentine to Lenin and Stalin, which the leading communist organs the *Daily Worker* and *Masses & Mainstream* promoted vigor-ously, offering the book as a gift along with a paid subscription.[346]

So bad had been the ACLU in aiding and abetting American com-munists that various legislative committees, federal and state, consid-ered whether it was a communist front. The 1943 California Senate

Fact-Finding Committee on Un-American Activities reported that the ACLU "may be definitely classed as a communist front." The committee added that "at least 90 percent of its efforts are expended on behalf of communists who come into conflict with the law." That 90 percent figure was consistent with a major report produced by Congress a decade earlier, January 17, 1931. In my research, I found constant approving references to the ACLU in CPUSA's flagship publication, the *Daily Worker*. The *Daily Worker* loved the ACLU.[347]

Baldwin served as the founding director of the ACLU. Ward was founding national chairman, a position he would hold for two decades.

Ward was widely perceived as a staunch progressive and one of the most well-known fellow travelers of the Communist Party among clergymen. He was one of the worst offenders in the entire sordid history of the American religious left. Tellingly, a major congressional report (July 1953) on communist activities in the New York City area featured more references to Ward than any other figure—twice as many as the next most-cited figure, Earl Browder, longtime face of American communism.[348]

Was Ward a dupe or a duper? As we will see in Manning Johnson's testimony, Harry Ward may have been an actual Communist Party member. That would make him a manipulator rather than one of the manipulated, a deceiver rather than one of the deceived.

Documents in the Soviet Comintern Archives on Communist Party USA show how communist officials in Moscow and New York deliberately targeted Ward to help push their propaganda. In one letter from December 1920, Ward is listed by Comintern officials as a source to get their materials on the shelves at the seminary library.

It was not atheistic communism that concerned the Rev. Ward. No, it was *anti*-communism. Writing in *Protestant Digest* in January 1940, long before Senator Joe McCarthy arrived on the scene, Ward admonished the faithful of the perils of "anti-communism," which was being employed "under the leadership of [Congressman Martin]

Dies in a new red hunt," one "more ruthless than that of [former Attorney General] Mitchell Palmer." (Both Dies and Palmer were anti-communist Democrats. Dies was a Texas Democrat who headed the House Committee on Un-American Activities during the FDR era, and Palmer was attorney general to President Woodrow Wilson, who was a leading early progressive.)[349]

Ward supported a particularly awful communist front, one that merits mention here because it will rear its ugly head in the pages ahead: the American Peace Mobilization. The APM spearheaded an egregious communist campaign that enlisted liberal Christians. It was a stunning case of successful communist dupery, an abomination.

The American Peace Mobilization was secretly founded in 1940 through a literal conspiracy between Soviet and American communists, with "social justice" pastors the chief target for exploitation. The group's goal was to keep America out of World War II, to push President Franklin Roosevelt to accommodate Hitler. Why? Because Hitler had signed a non-aggression pact with Stalin in August 1939. This group thus demanded no US Lend-Lease aid to the British, as Brits were being savaged by Hitler. The group took this position because it was Stalin's position—at least until Hitler betrayed Stalin and invaded the USSR in June 1941, at which point the group immediately became pro-war, morphing from doves to hawks. As Congress later noted, this was "one of the most seditious organizations which ever operated in the United States," "one of the most notorious and blatantly Communist fronts ever organized in this country," and an "instrument of the Communist Party line."[350]

In a previous book, I shared the actual declassified Soviet document (published on page 142 of *Dupes*) stating that the American Peace Mobilization was created "on the initiative of our Party [CPUSA] in Chicago" in September 1940. To reiterate: the goal of the American Peace Mobilization was to keep America from fighting and stopping Hitler strictly because Hitler and Stalin were (momentarily) allies. They did so on direct orders from their managers and masters in the Kremlin. These communist Americans saluted their flag—the red flag of Stalin's USSR.

This was a pernicious position. Yet, the "peace" mobilization, which suddenly became pro-war the minute Hitler betrayed Stalin and invaded the USSR—and then brazenly changed its name to the American *People's* Mobilization (yes, no kidding)—had more success with peace-loving, turn-the-other-cheek liberal Christians than any other group, far and away. Progressive Protestant pastors were the primary target.

The New York Times described the American Peace Mobilization not as a communist front but a "group of clergymen." And why not? Of the signers to the mobilization's mass rally in New York in April 1941, a quarter of the names began with "Reverend." It is hard to blame the *Times* for being suckered on this one. The social-justice pastors made it easy.

As for the pastors, if these presumably sincere Christians knew how badly they were used to advance the worst of evils, they would have been on their knees pleading forgiveness. In fact, many came to realize how badly they had been used.

William Z. Foster

All of that background is important for better understanding some of the material denoted in the pages ahead by the likes of William Z. Foster, Ben Gitlow, Louis Budenz, Manning Johnson, Bella Dodd, and others. We will start with Foster, the only one among them to have never repented.

William Z. Foster was, in effect, the first public face as well as chairman of what became known as (and remains to this day) Communist Party USA. Holding that spot from 1929–34, prior to which he had been with the Socialist Party of America, Foster would be succeeded as chair by the equally famous (or infamous) Earl Browder. Foster's testimony is powerful for not only its illumination of the communist contempt for religion but for its plainspoken evidence of how American communists were not dedicated to America. Their loyalty lay in a system of government far from America's shores. That is crucial to understand because it also means that their primary country of loyalty, the USSR, gave them orders, including orders regarding religion and how to treat the religious.

Foster, it should be noted, was a member of Roger Baldwin's and Harry Ward's ACLU before he took the helm at Communist Party USA. Such is perhaps another not-so-subtle indicator of how the ACLU's undermining of religion would be more lasting and damaging than anything that CPUSA ever pulled off.

Chairman Foster, twice Communist Party candidate for president of the United States, openly advocated a "Soviet American Republic" as part of a "world Soviet Union." Foster spoke candidly of American communists' goal of creating a "Soviet America." That was the title of his 1932 book, *Toward Soviet America*.[351]

Members of communist parties around the world, including in the United States, saw themselves as loyal Soviet foot soldiers. It would be Moscow first. These communists served not America but the Soviet Union. As Lincoln Steffens, the popular journalist for *The New Republic*, unforgettably put it, "I am a patriot for Russia; the Future is there; Russia will win out and it will save the world."[352] Emphatically agreeing with Steffens was Langston Hughes, the celebrated African-American poet. "Put one more 'S' in the USA to make it Soviet," thrilled Hughes. "The USA when we take control will be the USSA."[353]

Herb Romerstein repeatedly stressed this loyalty point: "Communist Party members were loyal Soviet patriots. . . . Most were not qualified to be spies, but those who were qualified were recruited through Party channels and made available to Soviet intelligence for classic espionage, agent-of-influence operations, or as couriers." He said that "almost every spy" tapped by the Soviets was a member of the American party.[354] CPUSA was a major recruiting ground for

Soviet espionage, and some of those communists in turn saluted the red flag and consciously collaborated with Moscow. That brings us to the testimony of Chairman Foster.

A telling display of this loyalty to the Soviet Union was a 1930 exchange between him and Congressman Hamilton Fish (R-NY):

> Fish: Now, if I understand you, the workers in this country [America] look upon the Soviet Union as their country; is that right?
>
> Foster: The more advanced workers do.
>
> Fish: Look upon the Soviet Union as their country?
>
> Foster: Yes.
>
> Fish: They look upon the soviet flag as their flag?
>
> Foster: The workers of this country and the workers of every country have only one flag and that is the red flag. That is the flag of the proletarian revolution. . . .
>
> Fish: Well, the workers of this country consider, then, the Soviet Government to be their country. Do they also consider the red flag to be their flag?
>
> Foster: I have answered quite clearly.
>
> Fish: Do you owe allegiance to the American flag; does the Communist Party owe allegiance to the American flag?
>
> Foster: The workers, the revolutionary workers, in all the capitalist countries are an oppressed class who are held in subjection by their respective capitalist governments and their attitude toward these governments is the abolition of these governments and the establishment of soviet governments.
>
> Fish: Well, they do not claim any allegiance, then, to the American flag in this country?
>
> Foster: That is, you mean, the support of capitalism in America—no.

Fish: I mean if they had to choose between the red flag and the American flag, I take it from you that you would choose the red flag; is that correct?

Foster: I have stated my answer.

Fish: I do not want to force you to answer if it embarrasses you, Mr. Foster.

Foster: It does not embarrass me at all. I stated very clearly the red flag is the flag of the revolutionary class, and we are part of the revolutionary class.

Fish: I understood that.

Foster: And all capitalist flags are flags of the capitalist class, and we owe no allegiance to them.

Fish: Well, that answers the question.[355]

It did indeed. William Z. Foster's sentiment and loyalty spoke for itself. And yet, this is just a portion of what he said under oath that day. What Foster expressed candidly in his testimony to the Fish Committee, this formal congressional committee, is worth quoting at length as a sterling affirmation of what members of the American Communist Party had believed from the outset. Hamilton Fish asked and asked, and William Z. Foster answered and answered:

Fish: Would you mind stating to the committee the aims and principles of the Communist Party?

Foster: The aims and principles of the Communist Party, briefly stated, are to organize the workers to defend their interests under the capitalist system and to eventually abolish the capitalist system and to establish a workers' and farmers' government.

Fish: Now, can you tell us more definitely if the principles of the Communist Party, as advocated in this country, or anywhere else, are the same?

Foster: Yes.

Fish: Does the Communist Party advocate the confiscation of all private property?

Foster: The Communist Party advocates the overthrow of the capitalist system and the confiscation of the social necessities of life; that is, the basic industries and other industries for producing the means of livelihood for the people. By the property of individuals, personal belongings, and so on, no; that is, in the sense of their personal property.

It is important to note here that not all communists would agree with this, or be so *generous* as to allow even personal belongings under a communist system. The communists who governed China under Mao, Cambodia under Pol Pot, and North Korea under the Kim family were woeful in their complete confiscation of the most basic personal belongings, from pots and pans to deodorant and toothpaste. And that was hardly a mere Asian phenomenon. Castro's Cuba, for example, not even a hundred miles from Key West, Florida, has likewise been brutal in its limitations on personal property, from private garden plots and fruit trees to fishing poles and boats.

The conversation between Congressman Fish and comrade Foster continued, with the congressman asking about religion and marriage under a communist system. Foster's answer was both unsettling and unsurprising:

Fish: Does your party advocate the abolition and destruction of religious beliefs?

Foster: Our party considers religion to be the opium of the people, as Karl Marx has stated, and we carry on propaganda for the liquidation of these prejudices amongst the workers.

Fish: To be a member of the Communist Party, do you have to be an atheist?

Foster: In order to be—there is no formal requirement to this effect. Many workers join the Communist Party who still have some religious scruples, or religious ideas; but a worker who will join the Communist Party, who understands the elementary principles of the Communist Party, must necessarily be in the process of liquidating his religious beliefs and, if he still has any lingerings when he joins the party, he will soon get rid of them. But irreligion, that is atheism, is not laid down as a formal requirement for membership in the Communist Party.

Fish: Have you been to Russia?

Foster: Yes. Eight or nine times.

Fish: You are familiar, then, with the workings of the Communist Party in Russia?

Foster: Reasonably.

Fish: Well, can members of the Communist in Russia be married in the church and maintain religious beliefs of that nature, and practice them?

Foster: My opinion is that a member of the Communist Party of the Soviet Union who would be married in a church would not be any value to the Communist Party.

Fish: Could he maintain his membership in the party?

Foster: He would not.

Fish: He would be put out of the party?

Foster: Eventually, if not for that specific act.

Fish: Would it not be the same in this country?

Foster: As stated before, workers who would be so imbued with religious superstitions that they would be married in a church would be of no value to the Communist Party.

Fish: And the same thing would happen to them in this country that happens to them in Russia?

Foster: Of course.

Foster's answer shocked people in his day, and probably still shocks today. It should not. This has been the standard communist view of religion since the time of Marx and Lenin. As readers of this book know, Foster's views were positively mild compared to his Marxist-Leninist predecessors.

Congressman Fish then asked Foster about class hatred and world revolution.

Fish: Does your party believe in the promotion of class hatred?

Foster: This is a peculiar question. What do you mean by "class hatred?"

Fish: I mean stirring up and exciting class antagonism and hatred of the working class against the other classes, so called?

Foster: Our party believes in developing the class consciousness of the workers; to educate the workers to an understanding of their class interests and to organize them to defend that class interest which, inevitably, brings them into conflict with the capitalist class in its whole system of ideology.

Fish: Do the Communists in this country advocate world revolution?

Foster: Yes; the Communists in this country realize that America is connected up with the whole world system, and the capitalist system displays the same characteristics everywhere—everywhere it makes for the misery and exploitation of the workers—and it must be abolished, not only on an American scale but on a world scale.

Fish: So that they do advocate world revolution; and do they advocate revolution in this country?

Foster: I have stated that the Communists advocate the abolition of the capitalist system in this country and every other country; that this must develop out of the sharpening of the class struggle and the struggle of the workers for bread and butter.

Of course, communists were all about class hatred. The "world revolution" would be based on the separation of people according to class, with certain classes unquestionably the target of hatred—as Lenin had said and showed repeatedly, as had his henchmen, such as Martin Latsis. "We are exterminating the bourgeoisie as a class," calmly explained Latsis, head of the Cheka, a predecessor to the KGB. "In your investigations don't look for documents and pieces of evidence about what the defendant has done, whether in deed or in speaking or acting against Soviet authority. The first question you should ask him is what class he comes from, what are his roots, his education, his training, and his occupation. These questions define the fate of the accused."[356]

They sure did. Foster's bosses in the USSR, carrying out their Marxist-Leninist world revolution and class struggle, exterminated people on the basis of class. Your class defined your fate. Just as being a Jew could get you exterminated under the Nazi system, being a member of the bourgeoisie could get you exterminated under the Soviet system.

That exchange prompted Congressman Fish to ask Foster about the American republican form of government, and if such was precisely what Foster and his comrades wanted to literally overthrow, on behalf of (and with the go-ahead) of the Communist International (that is, the Comintern). Here was that intriguing exchange:

> Fish: Now, are the Communists in this country opposed to our republican form of government?
>
> Foster: The capitalist democracy—most assuredly. We stand for a workers' and farmers' government; a government of producers, not a government of exploiters. The American capitalist Government is built and controlled in the interests of those who own the industries and we say that the Government must be built and controlled by those who work in the industries and who produce.
>
> Fish: They are opposed to our republican form of government?
>
> Foster: Most assuredly.

Fish: And they desire to overthrow it through revolutionary methods?

Foster: I would like to read from the program of the Communist International at this point. The Communist International program says----

At this point in his remarks, Foster paused to read from page 34 of the Comintern program document that he was holding, which he quoted as stating, "The conquest of power by the proletariat does not mean peaceful capturing of ready-made bourgeois state machinery by means of a parliamentary majority. The bourgeoisie resorts to every means of violence and terror to safeguard and strengthen its predatory property and political domination. Like the feudal nobility of the past, the bourgeoisie cannot abandon its historical position to the new class without a desperate and frantic struggle; hence the violence of the bourgeoisie can only be suppressed by the stern violence of the proletariat."

Congressman Fish sought further clarity on this point, asking Foster, "Just what is the Third International?" Foster responded by pointing to the Communist International, which was one and the same:

Foster: The Communist International is the world party of the Communist movement.

Fish: Is the Communist Party of the United States connected with it?

Foster: It is.

Fish: In what say?

Foster: It is the American section.

Fish: You take your orders from the Third International; do you?

Foster: The question, "Do we take our orders from the Communist International?" is a question which reveals the utter distance of the capitalist conception of organization from that of the worker. The Communist International is a world party, based upon the mass parties in the respective countries. It works out its policy by the mass principles of these parties in all its deliberations. It is a party that conducts the most fundamental examination of all questions that come before it and, when a decision is arrived at in any given instance, this decision the workers, with their customary sense of proletarian discipline, accept and put into effect.

Fish: Then you do take the orders and carry them out, as decided in Moscow by the Third International of the Communist Party?

Foster: I stated it is not a question of taking orders.

Fish: Well, putting them into effect?

Foster: It is a question of working out policies with the Comintern, in the Comintern, as party of this proletarian organization.

Fish: Well, they have to carry out those orders; do they not?

Foster: Carry out the policies?

Fish: Carry out the orders and policies as initiated by the Third International of the Communist Party over in Moscow?

Foster: We carry out the policies in the way I have stated.

Fish: You believe that by advocating the substitution of the soviet system of government for the republican form of government you are operating under the law?

Foster: I, of course, do not say we derived our theories from the Declaration of Independence, but the Declaration of Independence says that when a government demonstrates that it no longer represents the interests of the masses it is not only the right but the duty of these masses to dispose of that government and to establish one that will represent their interests—to abolish that government.

> Fish: That is, what you advocate is a change of our republican form of government and the substituting of the soviet form of government?
>
> Foster: I have stated that a number of times.

Again, this exchange was highly illuminating. And in wrapping up, Foster confirmed that he had previously affirmed "a number of times" that he was in fact advocating replacing the American form of republican government with the "soviet form of government." That "soviet form" (the *s* in "soviet" printed in lowercase by the US government's printing office) was the form of government of the Soviet Comintern and the Soviet Union—the home and headquarters of the red flag that Foster and his American Communist Party and their comrades saluted.

Comrade Browder Takes the Wheel

Foster's successor as head of the American Communist Party was Earl Browder (1891–1973), who was chairman of CPUSA from 1934 to 1945. He, too, did not shirk from expressing where his true loyalties resided. "Above all," Browder stated in his 1934 CPUSA convention report, "we arm ourselves with the political weapons forged by the victorious Communist Party of the Soviet Union, with the mighty sword of Marxism-Leninism, and are strengthened and inspired by the victories of socialist construction won under its Bolshevik leadership headed by Stalin." The pro-Stalin, pro-Soviet patriot continued, "Our World Communist Party, the Communist International, provides us the guarantee not only of our victory in America, but of the victory of the proletariat throughout the world."[357]

The Comintern of the 1930s, during Browder's time, had not backed down from its earlier 1920s triumphant and militaristic pronouncements. In its published "conditions for admission," the Comintern stated that its members—which, of course, included

CPUSA members—"must render every possible assistance to the Soviet Republics in their struggles against counter-revolutionary forces. They should conduct an organized and definite propaganda to induce the workers to refuse to make or handle any kind of military equipment intended for use against the Soviet Republics, and should also carry on, by legal or illegal means, a propaganda among any troops sent against the Workers' Republics."[358]

For members of CPUSA, things remained crystal clear: your first priority was the Soviet Union. Period.

And as for CPUSA, it stated forthrightly, "We want our Party to become like an army, a Bolshevik army, who while understanding the policy behind each decision is prepared to carry it out with military promptness, without any hesitation or question, and further, to carry out the decisions with Bolshevik judgment and maximum effectiveness."[359]

A Bolshevik army inside of America. *Forward!*

"The Enemy of Religion"

Summing up all of Earl Browder's anti-religious statements would take up quite a few pages. For simplicity purposes, this section will focus strictly on his important and revealing 1935 book *Communism in the United States*, which conveniently follows the timeline in our narrative here.

In that book, particularly the final chapter, titled "Religion and Communism," which was based on a February 15, 1935 discussion between Browder and a group of students at the "Christian progressive" Union Theological Seminary in New York, Browder was his usual slippery self. Effusive and elusive when talking about the Communist Party and religion, he tried to toe a line between his dedication to the party and to not posing too much of a threat to American believers and their constitutional freedom of religion—while trying to reel in some new suckers from his religious left audience. Still, comrade Browder unavoidably uncorked a few gems that exposed just where he and his American Communist Party stood on matters of religion. He could not avoid stating the obvious: communism and religion were implacable foes.

"It is quite clear that the Communist Party is the enemy of religion," said Browder honestly, in a candid affirmation of the obvious. "We Communists try to do the opposite of what we hold religion does." He noted, "The Communist Party takes the position that the social function of religion and religious institutions is to act as an opiate to keep the lower classes passive, to make them accept the bad conditions under which they have to live in the hope of a reward after death."[360] Marx and Engels would have nodded.

Browder's communists had a special contempt for organized religion. "Institutionalized religion is the particular enemy," noted Browder, surely thinking of the likes of the Roman Catholic Church in particular.[361]

Conversely, Browder understood that religion, being a matter of spirit, was a natural foe of communism, which rejected the spiritual in favor of the strictly material. "Religion does not fit into a dialectical materialist system of thought," affirmed Browder, reaching for more belligerent, Lenin-like language: "It is the enemy of it."[362]

And yet, Browder did his best to try to not seem too harsh toward American religious believers—because he was looking to continue to grow his party. He was always willing to welcome some new suckers. He said that the Communist Party was now up to 31,000 members, a sharp rise of 14,000 members over the past year and a half. The party was pushing hard for new recruits, whether among labor, farmers, teachers, women, racial minorities—"the majority of the Negroes are influenced by the Communists," said Browder, particularly amid the party's push in the "Black Belt" (the "Negro South")[363]—and perhaps even possibly among the religious.[364]

When asked what the party does with those who are religious but strangely interested in joining the party (no doubt an interest by some of the left-wing UTS students), Browder explained, "When workers come into the Party still actively religious, we accept them, not because we accept their religion, but because we know that the process of discarding religious beliefs, which are in the last analysis reactionary, is a more or less protracted one. We expect religion to be eliminated only in the course of a few generations of the new society, the socialist society."

Recall that Vladimir Lenin had said precisely the same.

Stupid "Christian communists" might be allowed in, but only under the pretext that their stupid Christian beliefs would soon be discarded. And if the discarding was not done soon enough, the comrades would prod, perhaps with a little harassment: "While we do not ask of them that they give up their religion," said a charitable Browder, "we will subject their religious beliefs to a careful and systematic criticism, and we expect that the religious beliefs will not be able to stand up under such criticism." In practice, such criticism took the form of ridicule and haranguing—or, in the USSR, a process of suggest, shove, and shoot. A little goad here, a little gulag there. Moreover, added Browder, they certainly would not place "in the most responsible leading positions of the movement people who had strong religious beliefs." Such people would be considered "dangerous" because of the social influence they could have on "the masses."[365]

So, while this slight tolerance might be accepted for new comrades into the party, a clemency would only be granted so long, until those religious beliefs were purged and self-liquidated. "I would not want to hold out any hopes that the Communists will be converted to religion," Browder told students at Union Theological Seminary. "We would not want to give the slightest indication that there is any prospect of a rapprochement between communism and religion as such."[366]

No question that such was the true spirit of communism. But in the coming days ahead, Comrade Browder would be singing a sweeter tune, as part of an outstretched hand of *peace* and purported rapprochement with the religious. Or, at least, such would be the new tactic.

CHAPTER 8

"OUTSTRETCHED HAND"

EARL BROWDER'S BACKHAND

Far and away, communists had their greatest success pursuing left-wing Protestants. This will be clear in the testimony in the chapters ahead, particularly the witness of Ben Gitlow and Manning Johnson.

Nevertheless, American communists made a hard push for American Catholics, as they did with other target groups—teachers, steelworkers, coalminers, farmers, African Americans, women, professors, journalists, mainline Protestants. This is abundantly evident in their literature and strategizing in the period, both overt and covert. Communists conceded it.

The Venona Secrets, the groundbreaking work by Herbert Romerstein and Eric Breindel, discussed such efforts at length. It detailed the well-known offer in June 1938 by Earl Browder to try to find common ground with Catholics. "We extend the hand of brotherly cooperation to the great mass of democratic Catholics," insisted the CPUSA chairman, in what came to be known as the policy or tactic of the "outstretched hand."[367]

That thinking was explained by communist organizer Louis Budenz, who at a sensitive meeting of the Communist Party Central Committee Plenum in December 1938 noted that "the overwhelming majority of Catholics of all national origins are Democrats." This meant that they were deemed ripe targets "in the building of the democratic front"—a wider popular-front strategy. Communists salivated at the prospect of a wide tent of leftists, drawn from the Communist Party and the Democratic Party, working together on behalf of Marxist-Leninist goals.

Budenz and Browder and their ilk conceded, "We cannot begin to touch the Democratic Party at any point, particularly in the industrial centers and also in its progressive wing, without being confronted with active Catholic leaders." To get Democrats meant getting Catholics, which would not be easy.

Later, after leaving communism and converting to Catholicism, Budenz would confess to his fellow Catholics that communists had employed this "outstretched hand" to manipulate them and infiltrate their ranks.[368]

The saga of this outstretched hand—really, a concealed backhand—is one of the more revelatory episodes in the history of communists seeking to sucker religious groups, notably Catholics. In some quarters, that campaign has never ended, even in the year 2019, when leading Catholic publications like *America* magazine run articles by pro-communist Catholics with titles like "The Catholic Case for Communism."

The story of Earl Browder's long outstretched hand should serve as a cautionary tale for ours and future generations.

Target: Eighteen Million Catholics

A striking document from this period was presented by Romerstein and Breindel in *The Venona Secrets*. Researcher Mary Nicholas procured a copy of it from Romerstein's private papers now archived at the Hoover Institution. Nicholas shared it with me. It is also housed at the Library of Congress in the Soviet Comintern Archives on Communist Party USA.

The 1937 CPUSA document, titled "Confidential report on work in religious and non-religious Catholic organizations," will startle Catholics today, but will not surprise anyone familiar with the webs weaved by communists. The document began:

> Today, with the issue of Spain being in the forefront, a tre-
> mendous organized campaign, world wide in scope, is gaining
> momentum with the purpose of winning the Catholic masses
> for fascism. The two countries wherein this campaign is most
> intense is in Ireland and in the United States.
>
> In the forefront of this campaign, and the directing force of
> it, is the Catholic church as represented by the Vatican. . . .
>
> A real race is on as to which force will win over the Catholic
> people in this country—the forces of reaction and fascism as
> represented by the Catholic church or the forces of progress and
> democracy.

Such was the stark choice posed by communists: Catholic Church "reaction and fascism" vs. enlightened "progress and democracy." The report then noted the recent reelection of FDR as president of the United States, and that "the Vatican, being sensitively attuned to this result, sent to this country, just before the elections, Cardinal Paccelli [spelling incorrect]. As is known, Cardinal Paccelli had an important interview with President Roosevelt."

That Cardinal Pacelli was none other than Cardinal Eugenio Pacelli, the future Pope Pius XII. That conversation between Pacelli and FDR was especially interesting. On November 5, 1936, Pacelli, visiting America as Vatican secretary of state, met with a newly reelected FDR at the president's Hyde Park mansion.[369] It was a friendly get-together, despite what FDR dubbed a "mental sparring contest" with the future pontiff. Pacelli warned FDR of the "great danger" of communism in America, which FDR characteristically dismissed. FDR explained that he was chiefly concerned about America sliding into fascism, not Marxism. Fascism was the fear, not communism. "No," replied Pacelli. "Yes," countered FDR. This went back and forth before a bewildered Pacelli finally said, "Mr.

President, you simply do not understand the terrible importance of the communist movement!"[370] No, he did not.

American communists knew they had a chump in FDR, and they played the president like a violin.[371]

As for Catholics, this 1937 "Confidential report on work in religious and non-religious Catholic organizations" sniffed out an alleged Vatican "anti-communist campaign," as if this was something new and insidious by Rome.[372] The report continued:

> From all known facts there is no doubt that the Vatican has come to a decision to launch a powerful, energetic, anti-communist campaign; and one of the most important focal points of this campaign is and will be the United States which contains approximately 18,000,000 Catholics.
>
> At the last District Convention of the New York District of our Party two things were clearly reveatled [original misspelling] – one, that the Party has within its ranks a pitifully small number of Irish Catholics; and two, that the influence of the Party directly or indirectly through various progressive organizations has very little influence amongst the Irish Catholic people nationally and particularly in New York City which has the greatest number of Irish Catholic people.
>
> Within the territory of Section 18 lies one of the most heavily concentrated areas of Irish Catholics and Catholic churches. Between 110 St. and 59th St. there are approximately eight large Catholic churches and a Catholic population of approximately 80,000.
>
> After the District Convention, it was decided in our Section to do some concentration work amongst the Catholic people and in Catholic religious and non-religious organizations. It was felt that if any results were obtained they would point the direction which the Party should take in its organizational

work, and would also reveal new methods of work that would be of benefit to the Party generally.

The scope of this memorandum will be to report on the steps that we have taken, the results obtained and a few organizational proposals which are felt will further aid and extend our activities. It is trusted also that the report will serve to coordinate the work and give direction to it in other parts of the city.

These were remarkable numbers of Catholics. No wonder communists were salivating like Pavlovian dogs. Imagine: eighteen million Catholics in America, and eighty thousand simply between New York's 110th St. and 59th St. To think that Communist Party USA, even here in the 1930s, its heyday, never exceeded one hundred thousand members nationwide. Eighteen million Catholics crushed one hundred thousand commies. For the reds, if they could pick up even 1 percent of American Catholics, they would explode their membership rolls. It seems pathetic to imagine that they never squeaked out even that.

Page 2 of this 1937 report then laid out in caps this heading: "CATHOLIC ORGANISATIONS IN THE METROPOLITAN AREA—STRUCTURE AND FUNCTION OF SAME," which stated: "In the metropolitan area there are 199 Catholic parishes, parishoners [original misspelling] number an average of 7,000 to each parish. Each parish has within it at least two organizations functioning; that is, a Holy Name Society which is exclusively a men's organization, and a Sacred Heart Society which is exclusively a woman's organization. The average membership of a Holy Name branch within a parish is about 500, and about 700 for the Sacred Heart." The report attempted to profile the work of these organizations. It then made this striking admission, which America's eighteen million Catholics would have ached to know more about in 1937: "Without going into any details as to how certain contacts were made, developed and finally recruited into the Communist Party, we are able to report, as will be seen later, that we now have a small number of Party members in important and strategic posts within these organizations."

This information would have given serious pause to Catholics within these organizations. Very careful not to name names even in an internal confidential report (never knowing if there were saboteurs in the midst), the report stated:

> An example of rendering ineffective many reactionary measures can be cited in the work of our Party comrades in the parish of one of the most important, powerful and strategic churches in New York, which will be un-named in this report. We have a Party comrade who is secretary of the Holy Name branch in this parish, which is one of the largest branches in the city. In addition, this branch is most important because of the fact that it gives leadership and shapes the policies of most of the reactionary and anti-communist campaigns that are now developing in the Catholic world. This comrade is well known in conservative Irish Catholic circles, and the many offices which he holds in various Catholic organizations will be hereinafter described. In addition to this comrade, we have three other loyal and devoted Party comrades who are also members of this important branch. Through careful guidance and skillful work, these comrades have been able to in no small degree render ineffective many reactionary and anti-communist measures which would have been taken on by this branch.
>
> In order to effectively combat the anti-communist campaign originating in these organizations, it is very necessary that as many capable and qualified Party members as is possible become regular functioning members of the various Holy Name societies in the city.
>
> It will be found that admission to these societies is not an easy matter as each applicant is thoroughly investigated, his

background and church affiliations are gone into and he generally must receive the recommendation of his parish priest. This, in turn, will only be forthcoming if the applicant has a fairly substantial record of church affiliations.

It is advisable to set up a leading fraction composed of comrades who are already members of the Holy Name Societies. This fraction would be able to choose those Party members who are best qualified to enter the Holy Name Societies, and the fraction members would also be able to facilitate the admission of Party members into Holy Name Societies by methods and through channels best known to themselves.

Catholics would have been aghast to know the identity of these moles in their ranks. The "Party comrade" is the type that communists used to refer to in those days as a "Judas goat"—that is, a betrayer. In this case, the Judas goat was working for the Communist Party and betraying the Church. (The party comrade, a priest, was identified by Herb Romerstein and Eric Breindel in their book.[373]) The comrades wanted as many Judases as possible working from within Christ's Church.

From there, the report assessed the status of several major Catholic organizations that the comrades had their eyes on. First among these was (again listed in caps), "THE ARCH DIOCESAN UNION." On this group, the 1937 report assessed:

This is composed of elected delegates from Holy Name Societies throughout the State. Invariably the most influential and important leaders of the Holy Name branches are elected to the Arch Diocesan Union, the greater majority of them being priests. This is the highest governing body of the Holy Name Societies and directs the policies and functions and activities of the Holy Name branches. From the New York State Arch Diocesan Union delegates will be elected to a national congress.

It is almost a certainty that our key Party member, secretary of the Holy Name branch described above, will be elected to the Arch Diocesan Union as a delegate of this most important branch. In addition, arrangements are already being made to have one or two other Party members elected as delegates. The importance of this needs no further explanation.

Indeed this needed no further explanation. The smoke of the Communist Party was creeping into the Church.

Next, on page 3 of the single-spaced, wide-margin, nine-page report, Communist Party USA appraised the situation with (again written in caps), "THE EUCHARISTIC LEAGUE." Here it stated:

The crystallization in an organized form of the reactionary and anti-communist campaign being conducted by the Catholic church is in the process of taking shape in the organization of a westside "Eucharistic League". This is being promoted by one of the most outstanding leaders in the anti-communist campaign—a Paulist priest, Father Ward. Father Ward is also the editor of a monthly anti-communist paper entitled "Wisdom".

A meeting of the sponsoring committee of this league was held January 6th in the Paulist church. Difficulties already confront the organization by internal friction. At least one Party member, through our contacts, is sure of appointment to the executive board of the organization.

On January 8 at the Paulist church, the first mass meeting of the Eucharistic League was held. There was an attendance of about 800 Catholics. At this mass meeting about three or four of our Party members were in attendance and became charter members of the organization.

The Party, through the leading fraction suggested above, will also have to carefully select available and qualified comrades to enter the Eucharistic League. Although the Eucharistic League has not definitely announced itself as anti-communist as yet, it must be taken for granted that Father Ward has the objective of using this league to further the anti-communist campaign of the Catholic church.

This section of the report speaks for itself. The comrades were confident that at least one party member was "sure of appointment" to the executive board of the Eucharistic League. Moreover, at the first mass meeting at the Paulist church, three or four party members had managed to hoodwink enough of the attendees to worm their way into being no less than charter members of the organization. That is quite a coup to pull off from within such a staunchly anti-communist organization. From there, these key inside members from the party's "leading faction" would be able to screen out those who did not toe the Moscow line.

Continuing along these lines of infiltration and deceit, the confidential report next noted the communists' successful penetration of a devotedly anti-communist Catholic publication, the aforementioned *Wisdom*:

> "WISDOM"
>
> This is a monthly newspaper publication which has as its masthead the following: "Wisdom - the Challenge to Atheism and Communism". The editor of this paper is the Father Ward referred to above. This publication has a circulation of about 20,000 copies amongst the church parishes, parochial schools, high schools and colleges. It is now also taking on an anti-semitic policy as is evidenced by its last issue. The publication has just started a column which will be a college forum devoted to the crusade against Communism in the colleges. It is developing a staff of college correspondents who will reflect the activities in the various educational institutions.
>
> Through the work of our Party comrades and various

contacts, we are able to report that we have two Party members now on the editorial staff of the publication and who write regularly in the columns of "Wisdom". Attached to this report, you will find issues of "Wisdom" containing the columns of these Party members, the articles are marked off in crayon. It is a most difficult position for them inasmuch as they have to write in such a manner as to be progressive and yet be within bounds so as not to become exposed and dismissed.

This was another magnificent coup by the comrades. They had placed two of their moles, their atheist saboteurs, on the editorial staff of *Wisdom*, this Catholic anti-communist publication. They were even penning columns. They employed a tone allowing them to cloak themselves as progressives rather than communists. The willingness to lie was at once remarkable and shameless.

In the next section of this Communist Party USA confidential report to the Comintern, the dutiful comrades gave their assessment of another Catholic organization they were trying to infiltrate and influence, a group called the Trinity League. The report stated:

THE TRINITY LEAGUE

This organization has its headquarters at 32 West 69th St., and is controlled by such well known reactionaries and red baiters as Father Ward, Martha Byrne and Dr. Schultz. Martha Byrne is a Tammany appointee to the position of County Court Recorder. Dr. Schultz is a weekly commentator on station WLWL every Monday evening at 7 o'clock. The address of Dr. Schultz every Monday evening is strictly anti-communist talk, and is one of the regular anti-communist programs on the radio in this city. Station WLWL is the station owned and controlled by the Paulist Fathers church which has been mentioned herein and will be further described later.

The Trinity League holds public meetings every Monday night, at its headquarters, commencing at 8 o'clock, at which Dr. Schultz officiates, and have an average attendance of 300 people weekly. Both the radio talks and the weekly meetings have been urging the formation of Catholic youth groups.

We have assigned a capable woman comrade to attend the Trinity League meetings, and she will keep the comrades assigned to this work informed of all developments within the league. We strongly urge that a few qualified comrades also enter the Trinity League for carrying on the correct type of work.

One marvels at the audacity of these New York communists. This was not a mere matter of attempting to penetrate a religious left organization within, say, the Episcopal or Methodist denominations, where perhaps "social justice" warriors might be more open and welcoming to the red platform. Quite the contrary, these were Catholic groups and individuals who were diehard and ever-vigilant in opposing Marxism and Moscow. And yet, the comrades did not shy from taking them on and slithering inside.

The confidential report proceeded from there, analyzing still other Catholic entities. Next, it looked at "the Franciscans," which the comrades dismissed as "a violent anti-communist Catholic order." This seemed to be judged a lost cause, with no assessment (at least in this document) of how to try to sneak into the Franciscans.

The same was true for the Knights of Columbus, listed along with the Franciscans on page four of the report, and likewise dismissed as "another Catholic organization, extremely reactionary and anti-communist in policy and set-up." The comrades were impressed by the size of the K of C and its 2,464 councils in the United States and Canada. "Nearly all of the members are members of the petty bourgeoisie," the report sniffed.

In all, the comrades seemed cautiously optimistic, with lines in the report such as, "We already have a number of comrades in the church organizations." The report summed up, "The foregoing facts are evidence that the Party must give immediate attention to this type of work. Within a few months time and after careful attention the above described activities have been developed."

And in addition to the infiltration, the report noted another crucial development: the comrades had slyly created an entirely new front-group, one employing a favored name of choice: *progressives.* The group was called "the American Irish Progressives." This would be of "definite progressive and liberal character on all of the social, economic and cultural matters pertaining to the Irish nationals and Irish Americans." Of course, communists would work from inside the organization, hand in hand with these progressives and liberals, to ensure that they tacitly supported (or at least did not criticize) the CPUSA-Soviet line, all the while denouncing anti-communists for their hysteria—that is, for "attacking Communism rather than organizing and helping the Irish Catholic working people."

Communists clearly were enthusiastic about the prospects for the group. Much could be achieved through "our comrades in the American Irish Progressives." "We have developed an extensive program of activity for the American Irish Progressives," the report concluded. "From the above facts and all the surrounding circumstances, it is believed that the right moment has come for the building of a progressive organization amongst the Irish American Catholics."

Most telling in this report is the sense of assuredness that an organization could be affected and manipulated by only a handful of well-trained Communist Party plants. Communist organizers were consummate sneaks, and grasped far too well the power of having "a small number of Party members in important and strategic posts within these organizations."

Deceitful as this was, one must marvel at the cynical shrewdness at work. Communists understood that just a handful of saboteurs, operating from the inside through carefully calculated dishonesty, could go far in impacting if not redirecting and hijacking an organization.

Alas, it should be noted that, significantly, seminaries are not mentioned here in this confidential report, though active priests were. The general target was Irish Catholics, especially progressive ones who might be manipulated. That included certain priests. Did the comrades expand their scope to include not just the occasional Catholic club or league, or Irish progressives, or the K of C? More specifically, were they so bold as to take aim at Catholic seminaries?

We shall consider that provocative question in a coming chapter.

Catholics Say No

In the meantime, the good news is that Catholics clearly rejected this. In fact, what was confidential in 1937 became somewhat more open in 1938, even if the motives were not stated quite so transparently by the comrades. That year, in May, Earl Browder, who was very open if not downright winsome about desiring to create a wider popular front—including among his outreach and allies no less than Franklin and Eleanor Roosevelt—made a public push for Catholics.

On May 29, 1938, Browder gave an eye-opening public speech—least of all because it was four hours long—in which he extended the Marxist hand to the Catholic Church. "In a speech which has had few parallels in length outside of legislative halls," the *New York Times* rightly reported, "Earl Browder, general secretary of the Communist party in the United States, extended 'the hand of brotherly cooperation' to the Catholics yesterday."[374]

Further revealing the imperative, the Communist Party wasted no time publishing the speech within mere days via a June 1938 booklet by Earl Browder titled *A Message to Catholics*.[375] The book not only reprinted Browder's text but included an introduction by Communist Party USA's National Committee. That introduction noted, importantly, that "early in 1936 the Communist Party of France sent forth a wholehearted appeal for a brotherly alliance and a mutually respectful collaboration between Communist and Catholic workers.

For over two years the important repercussions resulting from this affirmation of our good intentions have strengthened the French People's Front."

This is particularly significant because it underscores the international dimensions of this effort. None of the national communist parties, in America and especially France, did anything without the order and coordination of Moscow.[376] There is no doubt that Moscow would have been in support of this effort, if not directing it and organizing it, and above all approving of it.

As for France giving this a big push, if not the first push, that is hardly a surprise for France, where there was always a huge number of communists (and socialists). By the end of World War II, the two largest political parties in France were run by the communists and the socialists. Prior to even when Marx and Engels first met there, France was fertile ground for communists—and not just from Europe. The likes of Pol Pot and his leading Khmer Rouge cadres from Cambodia got their start in France, where an innocent, non-ideological, non-political Pot first arrived as a foreign student to study "radio-electricity" before being radicalized and returning to his native country in Southeast Asia as a genocidal Marxist maniac. Right through the end of the Cold War, the Kremlin's largest annual subsidies to foreign communist parties went to France and the United States.[377] The Comintern concentrated so heavily on the United States because a victory there could be the grandest of all, albeit elusive. Lenin, as early as 1918, had written his provocative *Letter to American Workers*. The Comintern concentrated on France not only because it, too, would be a grand victory but because it, unlike the United States, seemed a far more likely prospect for Marxist victory.

It was there, in October 1937, that Maurice Thorez, leader of France's Communist Party, made his "outstretched hand" effort to the nation's Catholics. This had been especially fruitful, said Communist Party USA, in the "great trade union movement in France." CPUSA held out hopes that the same might transpire in the United

States, particularly with Catholic workingmen and immigrants in industries from rail and steel to textiles and in groups like the C.I.O. and A.F. of L., where millions of Catholics marched side by side (including in strikes) "with their brothers of all political shades and religious creeds." Perhaps what happened in France could happen in America.[378]

The France example deserves a moment of pause. The key figure in France's popular front—the *front populaire* or *Le Populaire*—was Albert Vassart, who in 1934 coined that expression as a new slogan of French communists. Vassart is a crucial figure in this history, as we will see again in coming pages. He was no less than the French representative to the Comintern, a loyal son—until he broke with Moscow and the party in 1939 because of the Hitler-Stalin Pact.[379]

In France, the Communist Party and Socialist Party had been bitter foes, but suddenly in the spring of 1934 the Comintern began seeking a rapprochement for a *Le Populaire*. Vassart would head the effort. Such an effort would be, he soon learned, his principle task upon being summoned to Moscow in April 1934. The Comintern instructed comrade Vassart that it was imperative to band together the largest number of people in France possible to rally against fascism in a broad united front. "It is as simple as ABC," he was told by Dmitri Manuilsky, one of the top Comintern officials from the time of Lenin to Stalin. "We need a vast rallying together. We cannot stop with Socialists." Stalin himself had made this change to the party line.[380]

The French Socialist Party and Communist Party jostled back and forth but, nonetheless, fairly quickly worked out an agreement. The Socialist Party, Vassart later remembered, was surprised at how "the Communist Party leadership suddenly had become all sugar and honey." Within the next few weeks, by July 13, 1934, they had a deal.[381]

As Vassart would later note, the goal was not only to fight fascism in France. By the end of 1933, the USSR was seeking closer diplomatic ties with the Western democracies. This was being pursued in order to (in Vassart's words) "enable the Communist parties in the respective countries to put pressure on their governments to pursue a pro-Soviet policy."[382]

America was far from excluded from this Soviet effort—quite the contrary. Franklin Roosevelt was lobbied hard, by the Kremlin, by Earl Browder, by communists operating secretly from within his administration, and by duped liberals throughout his administration and within the Democratic Party. FDR ultimately responded positively to this push for formal diplomatic relations with Stalin's totalitarian dictatorship. He became the first president to officially recognize Stalin's USSR, after a long line of previous presidents, from the liberal Woodrow Wilson through three Republican presidents, had all vehemently rejected the Soviet request. They all adamantly opposed it; Roosevelt, however, embraced Stalin with open arms.[383] That warmness by FDR (and his wife) inspired Browder and his band to seek a wider popular front among the broader political left in America. Having had great success coddling Franklin and Eleanor Roosevelt, as well as key White House aides like Harry Hopkins, an emboldened CPUSA made a bid for American Catholics. Given that so many Catholics were Democrats and FDR supporters, including the likes of Cardinal Spellman, it might not have seemed a long shot. Still, given they and their Church's principled anti-communism, it was indeed a long shot.

That brings us back to Browder's May–June 1938 speech and booklet, *A Message to Catholics*. Browder and CPUSA made an appeal to Catholic workingmen and immigrants, especially those in union organizations like the C.I.O. and A.F. of L., insisting that "the Communist Party heartily agrees" with "progressive Catholic sentiments" that stand in solidarity with working people.[384] Browder and the CPUSA National Committee presented their offer to Catholics, appealing to "democracy." "Within the camp of democracy," asserted Browder, "are included the great majority of the members of the Catholic Church. We communists extend the hand of brotherly cooperation to them, and express our pleasure to find ourselves fighting shoulder to shoulder with them for the same economic and social aims."[385]

This claim of shoulder-to-shoulder aims could not have been a more gross misrepresentation. There may have been similar desires for higher employment, more welfare, poverty reduction, a more "equitable" wealth redistribution, a smaller income gap, but a careful read of the *Communist Manifesto* or anything by Lenin and Stalin showed no similarities whatsoever with the language of the Old and New Testaments or the *Catechism of the Catholic Church*. This point deserves a little more elaboration here, because it is based on a surprisingly common assertion by "social justice" and progressive Christians to this day—namely, that communism and socialism have attractive similarities with Christianity, and thus should not be dismissed by Christians. No, no, and no. That is a very foolish and shallow conclusion, one that results from a great ignorance of the actual teachings and texts of communism.

The fact that certain passages of the Old and New Testaments, or certain religious orders, express forms of communalism or sharing or helping the poor or even pooling together of common resources does not, *ipso facto*, mean that those ancient or medieval elements were practicing the nineteenth-century ideology that would become known as "communism." In these cases, from the Acts of the Apostles to, say, the Franciscans, those societies or orders were first and foremost forged on a Christian model; it was religion that served as their anchor, their rudder, their guiding, inspiring, motivating, animating, higher force—the very spiritual force that communism ridicules, rejects, and seeks to abolish. Read any writing by Marx or Engels or Lenin and contrast it with any writing by or about, say, Jesus Christ or the Apostle Paul or St. Francis (sometimes cited by communists and progressive Christians). One will immediately notice that they are completely different in every meaningful respect, irrespective of whether they share a specific commonality such as sharing of resources or giving up property—which, notably, is a fully voluntary choice and endeavor for any Franciscan (for instance) who chooses to join the order, and which is not voluntary for the 100 percent of individuals compelled by the coercive hand of the state in totalitarian communist societies. Moreover, the Bible repeatedly offers vigorous defenses of private property and property rights,[386] as rudimentary as the understanding implicit in the Ten Commandments laid down by the Creator: *thou shalt not steal.* To steal is to take someone's property, which is a sacred and natural right according to both biblical law and natural law. The assertion by Marx and Engels that "the entire communist program may be summed up in the single sentence: abolition of private property" is completely antithetical to the teachings of God. It is a foundational violation of one of the most basic precepts of Judeo-Christian thought and life.

We could go on and on with such examples. In the New Testament, individuals like the Good Samaritan or Zacchaeus or the vineyard owner all voluntarily give their own wealth or earnings as free-will acts of benevolence, not as forced responses to state fiat.

Thus, for communists in the 1930s to try to argue that Catholics or Christians generally should join hands with them because both sides believed in protecting the worker would be to ignore the far more significant and vast differences that permanently separate the two sides. It would be like witches and warlocks trying to reach out to Catholics and Christians because each side, after all, has a spiritual element. It would be like Aztecs trying to reach out to Catholics and Christians because each side, after all, saw certain value in human sacrifice. It would be like Satanists assuring Catholics and Christians that they, too, have a master. And even more relevant to the discussion here in this chapter, it would be like fascists in the 1930s reaching out to Catholics and Christians because, after all, they loved their country just as Franco and Mussolini and even Hitler loved theirs. I choose that particular example because Browder and the Comintern and Moscow all were seeking to reach out to Catholics and Christians in the 1930s precisely in part to help them oppose fascism in Spain and Italy and Germany. That was intrinsic to this effort. (This is clear in reading the full text of the 1937 CPUSA letter, as well as reading Browder's 1938 speech and letter to Catholics.)

Again, the few areas of potential partial agreement between communists and Catholics and Christians could not reconcile or bridge the wider ocean of vast differences, especially given the communist rejection of God and Jesus Christ.

Earl Browder knew that, but he also knew, as he said in his next line, that one-sixth of all Americans were Catholic, and hence to attract even a sliver to the communist cause would have been an enormous coup to CPUSA—ballooning that wider network of allies constituting a "popular front." That was the goal, and thus Browder and the boys did their best to try to claim areas of commonality. One could see Browder practically salivating on his typewriter as he noted that there were "over 20 million Catholics" in the United States. In fact, in a most revealing admission, he wrote, "It must be admitted that they [Catholics] are many and we are few, that as compared with over twenty million Catholics there are less than 10 per cent of that number of Communists and their sympathizers."[387]

Precisely.

Browder continued in his speech and letter, sweetly insisting that "the conflict between Catholics and Communists . . . is not of our choosing at all, and which, insofar as it exists, is founded on misunderstanding and misinformation. We want to clear away all misunderstanding, and refute all misinterpretation, in the interests of brotherly social relationships."[388]

Of course, perhaps a good starting point for easing conflict would be for Browder's international comrades to stop jailing and killing Catholics around the world. No doubt such unfortunate activities, *insofar as they existed*, of course, hindered brotherly love.

Then again, Chairman Browder would have begged to differ, or at least feigned innocence. He betrayed complete shock that anyone could ever suspect communists of disliking religion, let alone the religious. "Communists scrupulously respect all religious beliefs," Browder insisted, "and avoid all offense against them, firmly upholding complete religious freedom and toleration."[389]

This, of course, was a massive whopper. Undeterred, Browder continued weaving all sorts of ludicrously and obviously false claims, such as how communists, like Catholics, were magnificent advocates of the family. "The Communists are staunch upholders of the family," he explained, never bothering to quote infamous lines like that of Marx and Engels in the *Communist Manifesto*: "Abolition of the family! Even the most radical flare up at this infamous proposal of the Communists."[390]

But alas, comrade Browder was not sharing any exhortations from the *Manifesto* in his valentine to Catholics. Such admonitions simply did not seem worth raising at the time. That was not quite the spirit of the moment.

Browder plowed ahead line after line with such bunkum, pivoting from America to Spain to the USSR with fib after fib, no doubt leaving Catholic readers alternately bemused and outraged. When his missive reached Rome, the pope must have fallen off his chair from laughter or from a heart attack. The Chair of St. Peter no doubt saw in Chairman Browder yet another sad son of the Father of Lies. What Browder was revealing was not only his penchant for deceiving Catholics but also his view of them as slack-jawed ignoramuses. Truly no one would swallow this bucket of hogwash. One wonders if even the Right Rev. Harry Ward blushed.

Nonetheless, Earl Browder was deadly serious. He gave it one heck of a shot.

"We extend the hand of brotherly cooperation to the great mass of democratic Catholics," Browder concluded.[391]

Catholics Reject the "Outstretched Hand"

Catholics rejected this bilge shoveled by the outstretched hand of Earl Browder. That is unsurprising given the leadership of their Church on this issue. That Catholic rejection was so clear as to require little need of further proof in these pages. An obvious example are the statements cited in this book from the Vatican and various popes denouncing communism. It harkens back to the Church's encyclicals describing communists as wolves in sheep's clothing. Communists might talk brotherhood and kindness, but meanwhile in secret they bound their victims. Recall the very first encyclical, *Qui Pluribus*, by Pius IX in 1846. Communism, said Pius IX, was a "dark design" of "men in the clothing of sheep, while inwardly ravening wolves." "After taking their captives gently, they mildly bind them, and then kill them in secret." They are "filled with deceit and cunning" and "spread pestilential doctrines everywhere and deprave the minds especially of the imprudent, occasioning great losses for religion."

Had Earl Browder been alive in 1846, the Vatican could have posted his photo next to that passage in the encyclical. In fact, truth be told, Browder was just one example of innumerable swindlers who served the communist cause. William Z. Foster or Gus Hall or any everyday Soviet apparatchik would have done the same. It would all be funny if not for the painful reality that communists did not just lie to people but persecuted them, imprisoned them, tortured them, murdered them.

Many American Catholics, however, did know better and spurned this twisted olive branch. Fulton Sheen and Cardinal Spellman, countless politicians and lay people, knew that their faith and communism were irreconcilable. At the time of Browder's request, the *New York Times* ran a reply to Browder from the New York Chapter of the National Catholic Alumni Federation, which quoted from papal encyclicals to "show the Catholic Church has never been conciliatory toward communism."[392]

Fulton Sheen responded at great length, prompted by a challenge from Louis Budenz. Budenz had written in the *Daily Worker* a lengthy piece posing eight questions to Monsignor Sheen, then a professor of philosophy at the Catholic University of America, and not yet a TV star, albeit well-known for his radio show, his writing, and his lecturing. Sheen was already a force to be reckoned with, which is why Budenz endeavored to take him on. Sheen responded to each question in detail, answering them with communist sources—in other words, taking the words straight from the horse's mouth. Sheen's answers would be published in a small book by the Paulist Press, titled *Communism Answers Questions of a Communist.*[393]

This was an impressive refutation by Sheen, pulling and listing quote after quote from the likes of Lenin to Lenin's widow, from Stalin to Dimitrov, Litvinoff, Radek, and Browder, plus a remarkable gathering of statements printed in *Pravda*, *Izvestia*, and current Soviet publications, all responding to Budenz's claims about communism and the poor, the unemployed, the family,[394] democracy, Spain, modern Russia, fascism, racism, Hitler, the Ku Klux Klan, and on and on.

Among Budenz's challenges was this one to Sheen: "We invite you and the Catholic people to join in a united fight for the preservation of democratic rights and against the black danger of Fascism. Cooperating with those who have ever been in the front ranks in this fight for democracy."[395]

Here was the outstretched hand. In short time, of course, communism would violate this fight against fascism when Stalin joined hands with Hitler—something that Sheen would be among the first to predict shortly before it happened, to the shocked horror of many Jewish American communists.[396] But that aside, Sheen already knew better. He knew that Budenz and others were trotting out the "democracy" canard and (as Sheen put it) "that bogey 'Fascism' again." Sheen stated, "Let us stick to the facts. Thanks for the invitation, but we Catholics and all Americans must decline the invitation to the

'United Front' and why? Simply because it is a front. A front is a camouflage and deceit to be removed when it has served its purpose." Precisely that transpired when Stalin and Hitler signed their pact in August 1939 jointly launching World War II with their mutual invasions of Poland that September.

Sheen continued, "Communism has two faces: one it shows in Russia where it is established, the other it shows to the rest of the world where it hopes to be established. 'United Front,' 'Popular Front' merely mean new tactics are used to present or to disguise the same revolutionary philosophy which has enslaved Russia." Here, too, Sheen quoted Soviet sources, including Dimitrov's work *The Working Class Against Fascism*, which cynically advised that communists in public "suppress the language of revolution, but not revolutionary intentions" and "give the people only as much Communism as they will absorb any given moment." Dimitrov recommended (in Sheen's words) "the drawing of a red herring across the path of the people—namely, Fascism."

Thus, the very real threat of fascism was being used by communists as a tool to try to draw the wider masses to the side of communism and the "democratic rights" it supposedly loved. "The new disguises of the United and Popular Fronts do not mean that Communism has given up any of its revolutionary or atheistic principles," Sheen concluded, "it only means it has camouflaged them." This was a "tactic," merely a "new procedure," to advance the aims of the revolution— and this time aimed at attempting to attract Catholics. Fulton Sheen wasn't buying it.[397]

"No!" said Sheen emphatically. "We Catholics cannot join your United Front because we have found you out. We know the Front is only a front, and we think the less of Communism for insulting our intelligence. . . . [W]e must reject the proposal of those who would betray our liberties with the kiss of Judas." He added, "May we make a suggestion to the Communists? Now that we know your 'new front' is only a front, why not give it up? After all, every disguise becomes ineffective as soon as it is known to be a disguise. Masquerades always fail when one knows who is behind the mask. Why not be honest and assert Communism as it is?" He quoted Soviet documents noting the Comintern's call for a worldwide "civil war" in each nation in order to replace governments like those in America with communist dictatorships.

Sheen finished, "You invite Catholics to join in Communism to 'fight for the preservation of democratic rights and against the black danger of Fascism.' Fascism may be the black danger, but Communism is the red one." Sheen brilliantly suggested that communists change the name of one of their slickest front groups, the League Against War and Fascism, to the "League Against War, Fascism and Communism," and then, he said, "we will join."[398]

The monsignor's evisceration of Dimitrov was classic Fulton Sheen.

The Catholic Worker Steps Up

One striking rebuke of the outstretched hand that will surprise many Catholics today was the swift response by Dorothy Day's *Catholic Worker*. The front page of the September 1938 issue of the *Catholic Worker* featured a long retort by the editors to Earl Browder's offer.[399] It was an extended, thoughtful response, concluding with an emphatic accompanying statement that "Catholics May Not Join C.P."

"Dear Brother Browder," the letter from the *Catholic Worker* began. "As rank and file lay Catholics . . . we welcome your 'Message to Catholics.' We, too, are interested in eliminating falsehood and bitterness between Catholics and Communists. . . . We also understand that many wealthy Catholics side with the reactionary camp in politics." Starting with that olive branch, and a gesture toward a little common ground, the editors then said, "Yet let us place first things first. We cannot subscribe to a philosophy both materialistic and atheistic in essence which finds no room for the divine element in solving the social and economic problem." The editors explained that man is not matter alone but spirit and matter. "Therefore we cannot admit of any putting aside of religious belief, ethics or family morality because they are the essential and natural norms of human conduct—to destroy or to distort these norms is to eliminate the essential standards whereby man can ascertain the validity of his actions."

This latter point would be a focus of the philosophical work of a budding Catholic scholar and future pope named John Paul II, who at this point was a teen in Krakow, Poland. Karol Wojtyla would title his work on this subject *Person and Act*, also variously translated as *The Acting Person*, a central thrust of which is that man chooses his actions, and those actions must be pursued according to standards and ethics prescribed by a divine and loving God.[400] We can ascertain the validity of our actions only through choosing in accordance with the precepts of the Christian faith. The principle problem with communism was its atheism and rejection of any such precepts and, indeed, of the very notion of a Creator and of biblical and natural law.

Digging into questions of determinism versus free will, the editors at the *Catholic Worker* noted to Browder and his cohorts that "history is not merely the interaction of blind economic forces." Then came this sledgehammer from the *Catholic Worker*, which ought to be remembered by friends and foes of Dorothy Day alike: "We Christians love Communists as human beings and potential fellows in Christ's Mystical Body but we hate Communism. Yet, you Communists hate capitalists as well as capitalism. We love men, hate their sins. You hate sinners against the 'Party Line.'"

For these reasons, the editors summed up, "That is why we say that Communism is intrinsically in error and no one who would save civilization may collaborate with it in any undertaking whatsoever. We cannot accept your outstretched hand for these reasons. . . . We believe that this makes it quite definite that no true Catholic can be a member of the Communist Party."

That bears repeating for any (hopefully very rare) pro-communist Catholics today: In the words of Dorothy Day's *Catholic Worker*, "no true Catholic can be a member of the Communist Party."

The letter was signed by Richard L. G. Deverall, editor of the *Christian Front*, and William M. Callahan, managing editor of the *Catholic Worker*. Published on the front page of the newspaper as an "Open Letter To Browder By Editors," it clearly represented the opinion of the editorial staff of the *Catholic Worker*, which no doubt surely included Dorothy Day, the newspaper's founder in 1933 and editor until her death nearly fifty years later.

This elegant, strong response by Day's *Catholic Worker*, widely perceived to this day as left-leaning and soft on communism, is further illustration of the universal, stern rejection of the offer made by Browder and Communist Party USA. In all, it signaled to American communists what they already knew: they would have a devil of a time trying to hoodwink American Catholics to their cause.

That being the case, they doubled down on Protestants. They turned their attention still more vigorously to liberal Protestants, especially in the mainline denominations, particularly Episcopalians and Methodists.

Of course, that does not mean that communists fully abandoned the mission of trying to make inroads with Catholics, and even pursue methods of infiltration.

J. B. Matthews on the Outstretched Hand and United Front

Lastly, one of the single best testimonies to the surreptitious motivations behind this effort was provided by J. B. Matthews in his prodigious work and research. Matthews became one of the leading experts, including for the federal government, on the machinations of the far left in America. Much could be quoted here from Matthews (two of his major reports are cited elsewhere in this book), but our interest lies in a key snapshot from this period: his 1938 memoir *Odyssey of a Fellow Traveler*. This was written at the height of the outstretched hand and united front strategy.[401]

As the title conveys, Dr. Matthews had been a self-described "fellow traveler of the communists"—a socialist who formed a partnership with communists, eventually morphing into some form of the latter. A professor and linguist, with particular expertise in Sanskrit and Asian languages, he was one of the leading organizers for the united front and for creating front groups, such as the American League Against War and Fascism, for which he was the national chairman. He was also an active pacifist and an early ACLU member. In Manhattan, in 1929, he formally joined the Socialist Party, for which he was a prominent, outspoken figure. He worked closely with communists, to the point that fellow socialists thought he was secretly a member of the American Communist Party. He eventually joined the Revolutionary Policy Committee, a group of self-described "revolutionary socialists." He was described warmly as a "comrade" and "conscious Communist sympathizer" by the likes of Jay Lovestone, a leading communist of the day. In 1932, he became a "full-fledged fellow traveler" and organizer for the united front.[402]

Matthews's pro-Soviet bona fides became further evident that year. During that summer of 1932, he capped off his fifth visit to the Soviet Union in five years—making him no ordinary fellow traveler. He was soaking in what the Rev. Harry Ward glowingly called "the Soviet spirit." Matthews traveled up and down the Ukraine that year, where he amazingly denied the very famine before his eyes, and came home rejecting its existence in articles he penned for the *Daily Worker*. Matthews had become a Soviet stooge. He wasn't merely drinking the Kool-Aid; he was guzzling it.

Matthews nonetheless hung his coat in the Socialist Party closet rather than that of CPUSA. He was in demand as a leading socialist thinker and speaker, right up there with the likes of religious left stalwart Reinhold Niebuhr, another radical leftist professor at Union

Theological Seminary (like the Rev. Harry Ward), who, to his credit, later became a prominent progressive theologian who was anti-communist and anti-Soviet. Matthews was second only to Norman Thomas in speeches given around the country for the Socialist Party.

Without digressing too much from our focus here on Matthews, an important note or two is worthwhile on the case of Norman Thomas.

Thomas was arguably the most well-known socialist of the twentieth century, the only competitor being Eugene Debs, from whom Thomas picked up the Socialist Party mantle after Debs's death in 1926. From there, Thomas, who had already run for various elected offices as the Socialist Party candidate in New York, began a run of six Socialist Party nominations for president of the United States, starting in 1928.

Though many today know that Norman Thomas was probably the most famous and successful socialist in American history, few know (and many will be surprised to learn) that Thomas was not merely religious, and a Christian, but was actually an ordained Presbyterian minister. He had graduated from Princeton in 1908 and decided to study for the ministry, following the footsteps of both his father and grandfather. Unfortunately, rather than attending an orthodox Presbyterian seminary, as his father had wanted, he opted instead for the UTS theological crazy house: Union Theological Seminary in New York. It was there that Thomas was seduced by the left's "social gospel." He was so liberal even then that conservatives in the Presbyterian Church tried to introduce heresy charges against him (for, among other reasons, denying the virgin birth of Christ) and prevent him from being ordained. They failed. He was ordained in January 1911. Conservatives merely needed to be more patient, as Thomas eventually and effectively de-ordained himself—from the ministry and the Christian faith altogether. "Although Thomas did not formally demit the ministry until Oct. 5, 1931," writes one scholar, "he made his final break with the Christian church near the end of 1921."[403]

But the main point here is this: Norman Thomas, famous socialist, was once a Presbyterian minister, and yet another dubious product of Union Theological Seminary, a theological looney-bin that did great damage to Protestant Christianity. Atheist socialists and communists alike knew they had plenty of friends at UTS, which was, in essence, like a seminary version of Columbia University—a hotbed for targeting and recruiting and duping.[404]

It was this milieu that J. B. Matthews, as a religious socialist, knew so well in the 1920s.

Matthews ultimately became a Marxist, if not a CPUSA member. "I had become not only a Marxist but a confirmed exponent of the united front," he wrote.[405] That, along with his impeccable Socialist Party credentials, made him ideal for helping to hammer out a "united front" comprised of a wider swath of leftists. He said of himself, "No other person in the United States had such an impressive united front record."[406] Matthews gave all his time, heart, mind, and energy to every silly communist-socialist-"progressive" cause and activity under the sun. Reading them all in his memoirs is painful. One winces at how leftists like Matthews truly devoted their lives and souls to so many insane and ultimately malicious causes.[407]

And yet, J. B. Matthews came to see the light, eventually becoming one of the leading defectors from the far left in America in the 1930s. He was destined to became ex-red persona non grata as he began exposing the comrades and blowing the whistle. His book in 1938, *Odyssey of a Fellow Traveler*, was his most in-depth personal effort.

Matthews began that treatment by illuminating communists' ruse of betraying Christianity with a kiss while subtly infiltrating churches. He quoted Earl Browder conceding to students of Union Theological Seminary on February 15, 1935: "You may be interested in knowing that we have preachers, preachers active in churches, who are members of the Communist Party."[408] Browder had bragged, "We could recite a thousand local examples of the successful application of the united front tactic initiated by the Communist Party."[409] Matthews was not divulging any secrets from behind closed doors. He was quoting directly from Browder's speech to UTS students, which Browder and the Party candidly published in his 1935 manifesto *Communism in the United States.*

As Matthews thus attested, Browder's about-faced out-stretched hand was simply a tactic to hoodwink the gullible. Matthews quoted one of the leading Soviet officials of the Kremlin and its Comintern, Manuilsky: "Tactics, generally, may change, but the general line of the Communist International, the course it is steering for the proletarian revolution . . . remains unchanged. . . . Only downright scoundrels . . . and hopeless idiots can think that by means of the United Front tactics Communism is capitulating to social democracy."[410]

Truly, only an idiot.

The about-face for the outstretched hand was a two-faced tactical maneuver. That, too, reflected communist thinking about *morality,* as defined by Papa Lenin himself. Recall that Lenin had stated that the "only morality" that communists recognize is that which furthers class interests.

Picking up with that Leninist-communist *ethic,* J. B. Matthews noted that, consistent with the party's and Moscow's and Lenin's "communist code of ethics," religion was to be exploited for class gain, even if that involved blatant deception. "It is not surprising to find the Communist Party in the United States engaged in a systematic effort to lure the churches," averred Matthews, "especially the Catholic Church, into the net of the Party's united fronts. Such duplicity transcends the bounds of understanding on the part of those who are not acquainted with the Communist Party's clear pronouncements on the churches and religion." Here Matthews quoted Browder at the tenth annual Communist Party convention: "We extend the hand of fellowship to our Catholic brothers."[411]

Matthews noted how the *Daily Worker* had started the propagandizing a few months earlier, ahead of Browder's big-lie rollout at the big convention. "It is not, and never has been and never will be," insisted the *Worker* with a whopper, "the objective of Communism to wage a religious war against those who believe in God or who hold any other religious faith."[412]

Hmm. Now there was a switch—obviously tactical to anyone but the really, really, really gullible (of which there were too many). Matthews responded by quoting four statements from current communist literature, pamphlets, and books still in bookstores, which the comrades had not bothered to yank from the shelves, replete with timeless gems like these:

> "It is necessary to link the fight against the church and religion with the fight against capitalism and imperialism."[413]

> "The Soviet Union under a workers' and peasants' government is the only country in the world where religion and the churches are being combated with the active cooperation of the government."[414]

> "The unaltering determination of the Communists to do away with religion and the inclusion of this aim [is] one of the chief features of the educational system from one end of the country [the USSR] to the other."[415]

> "The Red Army is one of the most active centers for the dissemination of atheism. Its recruits are given systematic instruction in anti-religious theory just as they are in other Communist doctrines."[416]

The latter two nuggets were produced by longtime Columbia University professor Corliss Lamont, pal of Professor John Dewey, founding father of American public education, and one of the worst "progressive" agitators for the communist cause in American history. Corliss was another fellow traveler to the USSR (if not a formal CPUSA member), from which he returned sporting (among other things) a proud pin and insignia of Trotsky's and Lenin's League of the Militant Godless.[417] Surely when Corliss talked to his religious left friends, however, he sang a different tune when it came to religion—literal hosannas.

As Matthews noted, those four quotes alone ought to have satisfied even the most incredulous into realizing that when Browder and the boys offered the outstretched hand, it was really a backhand. And shame on them if they didn't see the slap behind the greeting.

Matthews further quoted Browder's own words openly published just two years earlier in his book *What Is Communism?* There, Browder had affirmed, "We communists do not distinguish between good and bad religions, because we think they are all bad for the masses." Matthews quoted a telling statement from communists in their cynical rationale for seeking the creation of united front groups with religious organizations: "It is significant that the Communist Party, more than any other labor group, has been able to achieve successful united fronts with church groups on the most important issues of the day. This is not due to any compromise with religion as such, on our part. In fact, by going among the religious masses, we are for the first time able to bring our anti-religious ideas to them."[418]

Note the double intention among the deceivers: In addition to thriving amid a sea of facilitated confusion, to hoodwink the religious to the communists' ultimate anti-religious cause, they might also dupe the religious into eventually becoming anti-religious themselves—confusing them about their own beliefs in God. They could bring to the religious the communists' anti-religious gospel, carefully preaching the ideas not of Christ but of anti-Christ. This could be done by getting all leftists—religious and anti-religious—into one large room (or maybe even church) together. Thus, the united front strategy could pay off handsome double dividends. One can almost picture the devil laughing at the very cunning of it all. And to think that it often worked.

J. B. Matthews noted how the *Daily Worker* marked the following

Christmas 1937 by publishing a warm and fuzzy article heralding the wonderful similarities between communism and Christianity. This prompted for weeks thereafter warm and fuzzy "letters to the editor" from (alleged) readers around the nation impressed by the outstretched hand and its benevolent gesture of goodwill to Catholics. One "writer," someone from Detroit listed with the name "Comrade H. G.," celebrated how the new outstretched hand had helped him draw two new couples into the party—Christmas-time converts. Comrade H. G. further enthused, "And now that the *Daily Worker* has printed the statement from the Pope on accepting the Communist offer of the 'outstretched hand,' it'll be a snap to recruit."[419]

J. B. Matthews hastened to add, "Precisely when the Pope accepted the 'outstretched hand' of the Communist Party, it would take the *Daily Worker*, with its genius for mendacity, to say." Indeed, it would. When had Pope Pius XI done that? Had Comrade H. G. taken a glance at the pope's recently released *Divini Redemptoris* (On Atheistic Communism)—that is, the printed statement describing communism as a "satanic scourge" and its disciples (like the folks at the *Daily Worker*) as the "sons of darkness?" Apparently not. Then again, when did truth ever matter to these marvels of mendacity?

The *Daily Worker* was now describing Jesus as a fellow "real revolutionary" and "proletarian fighter."[420] Alas, a good Jesus—a *communist* Jesus. A political messiah. Precisely what Jesus Christ told Pontius Pilate he was not.

And yet, the sad reality, as Matthews knew, is that too many progressive Christians fell for this nonsense. They were not wise as serpents.

In all, said J. B. Matthews, it would more than surprise many modern politicians, newspaper editors, and public officials to find the sudden existence of so many "Methodist comrades, Baptist comrades, Presbyterian comrades." Nonetheless, he and other fellow travelers and former communists were not surprised at all. They had watched them all in action. They had watched the comrades sow the seed, seed which had taken hold and developed roots in many a Marxist mission field.[421]

Unfortunate future generations, and, yes, many churches and Christian institutions, would reap the harvest and the whirlwind.

CHAPTER 9

"OBLITERATING ALL RELIGION"

LOUIS BUDENZ AND BEN GITLOW SPEAK OUT

As communists sought to enter the churches of Christendom, they simultaneously sought to set them ablaze—and not merely metaphorically. In the USSR and throughout the communist world, churches were ignited, dynamited, obliterated. As communists in the West assured Christians that they wanted to shake hands with them, communists in the East and elsewhere handcuffed them and blew up their churches.

To say that communists wanted to obliterate religion was no mere matter of expression. In places like Bolshevik Russia, it was a literal process.

The desire to smash religion was shared by communists in America, even if it did not descend to the level of Marxist kingpins ordering in the wrecking balls to the nation's cathedrals. Mercifully, Marxists never seized the reins of power in the United States. We were spared their wrecking balls, at least physical ones.

But while America's communists could not get their arms around church edifices, they did their best to take a metaphorical ax to religious belief where and when they could. They knew which religion was their most vexing foe. That knowledge was displayed in one particularly striking line from the November 1946 testimony of erstwhile American communist leader Louis Budenz, who said of the Catholic Church in particular but also of religion generally, "The Communists everywhere plan to wage war on the Catholic Church as the base for obliterating all religion."

What Budenz said was backed more strongly and widely—regarding Christendom more broadly—by the likes of other former leading American communists—in particular, Ben Gitlow. Gitlow spoke to American Christianity generally, particularly the mainline Protestant denominations.

What Budenz and Gitlow warned about is distressing to this day.

"War Upon the Catholic Church"

Louis Budenz was a top American communist in the 1930s. He would also become a leading ex-communist, and an ex-atheist.

Recall that it was Budenz who, in the *Daily Worker*, had openly challenged Fulton Sheen to prove that communists were against religion. Sheen took up that challenge with typical panache. Budenz was so won over by Sheen's arguments that he ultimately became one of the era's most well-known converts of Sheen. Yes, Fulton Sheen brought Louis Budenz into the Catholic Church, back to the faith of his youth. Quite remarkably, almost hilariously, the priest managed to bring Budenz back into the fold while the *Daily Worker* editor's name was still on the newspaper's masthead. If the comrades around the office had known that, well, you could have probably heard them howl from the other side of the Brooklyn Bridge. Sheen brought Budenz into the Church along with his wife and three daughters.[422]

By the mid-1940s, Budenz was ready to offer some serious public penance for his past sins with communism. This included his important testimony before Congress on November 22, 1946.

By this point, the former managing editor of the *Daily Worker*, the official newspaper of Communist Party USA, had left the party and become an assistant professor of economics at Fordham University and at the University of Notre Dame. He had been a party member for ten years, six of which he served prominently as a member of the national committee.[423]

Budenz recounted those details in his testimony. He also spoke to (among other things) what he called "the present tactics of the Communists in regard to the Catholics." He had come to Washington that day in part to call attention to those tactics.[424] Budenz stated:

> I mentioned also the question of the Catholic Church, and I raise that because today it is a question that is of concern to every American, and it's part of the tactics of Communists as I learned them. I was one of those who were fooled into believing that in America there could be cooperation between the Communists and the Catholics.
>
> I found that was considered undesirable from the Communist viewpoint, but beyond that I learned toward my latter days in the Communist Party from material I read in the *New Times*, which is now the name of the Communist International magazine, that the Communists everywhere plan to wage war on the Catholic Church as the base for obliterating all religion.

Budenz also noted that certain Protestants (including communists posing as Protestants) were exploited in this strategy. He said that this policy had been outlined in an article by a left-wing Protestant publication, titled simply *Protestant* magazine. "This policy was developed in an article to which I shall call your attention setting forth the ideas that I learned," said Budenz, "namely, of the program to arouse the Protestants against the Catholics in this country as a means of causing confusion in the United States."

Budenz generously said that he had "enough confidence in the American Protestants to know that that is not going to succeed, but I have to point to this because it is in black and white in an official article." The article actually had been "worked up" by one of Budenz's comrades from CPUSA's political committee, clearly showing that there were intimate connections between the party and this Protestant publication. Budenz stated:

I knew about this before I left, and pointed to it very temperately in my statement as I left. This matter was presented to me in a conference by the comrade who worked up the material for this article for the political committee. He advised me the aim was to extend the work of the *Protestant* magazine. That is a magazine whose name is "Protestant," but which is engaged largely in being anti-Catholic and the responsible Jewish organizations have recently condemned it, as you may know. That view of the extension of the *Protestant* work against Catholics was confirmed by this article of V. J. Jerome in *Political Affairs* in April 1946, in which he links up the Catholic Church with American imperialism, and in which he shows what he calls the great wealth of the Catholic Church and says there has been no sufficient Protestant reaction. That immediately tells the comrades to go out and pose as Protestants and arouse that reaction, for when a Communist reads an article he puts it into action. In this article the recent attack on Cardinal Spellman by the Communist councilmen in New York City was endorsed as being proper Communist tactics when it was feasible to do so. In other words, here is outlined a program which is directly opposed to the alleged outstretched-hand idea which the Communists formerly said they stood for when they needed to rally everybody, including the Catholics, to the defense of the Soviet Union against the efficient German war machine. This renewed program of war upon the Catholic Church is contained in the April 1946 issue of *Political Affairs* as part of their tactics within the United States today.

From there, Budenz's comments went to the matter of religion generally, prompted by the chairman of the committee, Congressman Rankin, who asked, "Mr. Budenz, is it not a fact that communism is opposed to all kinds of religion?" Budenz answered, "That is correct. A totalitarian regime, especially one built on the materialistic interpretation of history, cannot permit any organization of religion except as a servile tool of the all-powerful state." Rankin asked Budenz if Karl Marx's infamous assessment, "Religion is the opium of the people," was "Communist doctrine . . . before you went into the party, and all the time you were in the party." Budenz replied:

> That was the principle, although, you see at that time they had the policy of the outstretched hand, which was the result of the People's Front Policy and they contended that they wanted cooperation between all religions and the Communists, or specifically the Catholics and the Communists.
>
> However, I would like to say this to sort of bring this to a point: The fact of the matter is, those who sought collaboration, like myself as an individual, as one member of the party, did so on the basis that this outstretched-hand policy would lead to better relationship between the two groups, and that was roughly in line with the policy of the Communists at that time.
>
> Now, it was written by Elizabeth Flynn in the *Daily Worker* at the time I left the party that you could have any religion you chose and remain in the Communist Party. That is not true. You cannot have any religion, except where you are in a particular religion and it serves the purpose of the party to keep you there. Even there, as Lenin pointed out, the party must fight religious ideology. The leaders of the party are not permitted to hold any religious belief.

As further proof of this, Budenz invoked the statement of Gilbert Green at the 1935 convention of the Communist International—the Comintern's so-called People's Front convention. In that statement, said Budenz, which represented the policy of America's Young Communist League, headed by Green, Green pointed out that when his fellow communist youth came into association with religious youth, they did allow these youth to continue to go to church, but in such a way as not to interfere with "our atheistic principles." As Budenz put it, "He [Green] was there explaining to the Communists that atheism was their standard, but sometimes in working with youth they had to be more lenient, and, of course, that meant that they would try to wean those youth away from religion entirely. That was Lenin's instructions years ago."

Here again, as the likes of Earl Browder and William Z. Foster would have averred, these religiously inclined communists (non-party leaders, importantly) could, temporarily, keep their juvenile religious superstitions, so long as they were in the process of ultimately liquidating those beliefs. Their church attendance would be tolerated for the time being, but not permanently.

They would be ultimately tolerated by atheistic communists about as much as atheistic communism tolerated all religion. As Lenin said, they must fight religious ideology.

Ben Gitlow's Testimony

Even more instructive than Louis Budenz's testimony was that of Ben Gitlow. Budenz had offered a mere morsel compared to the buffet of material Gitlow served up.

Gitlow, too, was a major Communist Party USA figure. In fact, he had risen higher than almost anyone next to Earl Browder and William Z. Foster. He twice ran as the party's candidate for vice president of the United States (1924 and 1928) and served on the Executive Committee of the Soviet Comintern. Budenz had never traveled to the Soviet Motherland, but Gitlow had done so on several occasions.

After a long silence upon leaving the party in 1929, Gitlow emerged to testify before Congress (first in 1939) and to write two major books, *I Confess* (1940) and *The Whole of Their Lives* (1948),[425] where he laid out a litany of disturbing facts about CPUSA's relationship with Moscow, such as its members' "fanatical zeal" for the Motherland and "its ultimate victory over the capitalist world,"[426] and revealing details of espionage and Soviet funding of the American Communist Party. As to the latter, Gitlow's figures itemized the Comintern's sending CPUSA $100,000–150,000 annually (1922–29), its infusing $35,000 to launch the *Daily Worker* (1924), and its providing tens of thousands of dollars to American union bosses, funding which continued still. For blowing the whistle, Gitlow earned the enmity of the Comintern and its American hacks. In an October 1939 memo to the Executive Committee of the Comintern, Pat Toohey, CPUSA's representative in Moscow, wrote a summary of Gitlow's Congressional testimony and denounced him to Soviet bosses as a "stool-pigeon and provocateur."[427]

Our interest here is Ben Gitlow's testimony before the House Committee on Un-American Activities on July 7, 1953, seven years after Louis Budenz's testimony. Among the most shocking material was his information on how the American Communist Party and the Comintern penetrated the mainline denominations, particularly the Episcopal Church and the United Methodist Church. Gitlow made clear that the best agent for the party (or worst depending upon your point of view) and the Comintern was the Rev. Harry Ward, especially via his commandeering the enormously damaging front-group the Methodist Federation for Social Action. The material from Gitlow on Ward and his organization is plainly stunning. He made clear that the Rev. Ward might have been one of the most duplicitous clergymen of the twentieth century. Reading this material will prompt readers to shake their heads at what scoundrels and inveterate deceivers men like Ward were. One wonders how the American mainline churches survived the treachery of men like this. In significant ways, they never fully did. Such church leaders wreaked havoc in the mainline denominations and generally throughout many Christian churches in America and the West, helping lunge them to the left, and prompting many Protestants to flee into more conservative denominations and into countless independent, non-denominational churches. The residual effects are still felt today, and the residual forces are still at work continuing the job.

Unlike Budenz, who spoke powerfully but briefly and mentioned the Catholic Church as being in communist crosshairs, Gitlow spoke powerfully but at much greater length and without a single mention of the Catholic Church. He was asked about "all" of the Christian faith, but his comments were mostly directed at Protestant churches generally, and the Methodist Church specifically. This was instructive—an accurate indicator of the reality. One will see throughout these excerpts from the official transcript of Gitlow's testimony, published by the US Government Printing Office, that Gitlow's use of the word "church" was properly printed with a lowercase *c*. That was because he was indeed speaking of the Christian/Protestant "church" generally (the exception came when he spoke of specific denominations, such as "the Methodist Church").

Gitlow's testimony in July 1953 took up almost seventy pages in the official on-the-record transcript, almost a third of which dealt with Ward and the Methodist Federation for Social Action. Every page of it deserves to be read. Here I will at best summarize some of the highlights, taken from about five thousand words of material transcribed for this book. The below quoted material is taken verbatim from the GPO published testimony.[428]

Exploiting and Destroying the Church

Gitlow began his testimony by sharing his communist-socialist bona fides, starting with his joining the Socialist Party in 1907 before helping to launch the Communist Party in America in 1919, for which he became one of the very top leaders throughout the next decade. He ran on the Communist Party ticket for everything from mayor of New York City to governor of New York, as well as (as noted) vice president of the United States. He had been so central to directing the party that by 1929 he had risen to the pinnacle as general secretary of the Communist Party of the United States—until his disagreements with Joseph Stalin got him expelled that same year. It would be difficult to find a more committed comrade. Gitlow was one of countless examples of comrades who got the ax for not offering 100 percent fealty to the Kremlin at every waking moment.

Gitlow was asked to testify specifically that day to "the matter of Communist infiltration of religious institutions." He did not disappoint.

The questioning of Gitlow was begun by the House Committee's chief counsel, Robert Kunzig. Here are excerpts from the official transcript:

> *Mr. Kunzig.* Now, Mr. Gitlow, the main purpose for which you have been invited to testify before this committee at this time is to give from your extensive background your experiences in connection with the relationship of the Communist Party to religion.
>
> Would you in brief, please, trace the position of the Communist Party on the question of religion and its policies, if any, in the matter of Communist infiltration of religious institutions? . . .
>
> *Mr. Gitlow.* I believe that the basic atheistic position of world communism to religion has not changed from the inception of the Communist movement to date. The questions of the strategy and tactics which the Communists use for the purpose of exploiting the church, clergy, and the followers of the church for its own purposes are not in contradiction with the basic atheistic position and final goal of the destruction of the church as a superstitious institution in the service of capitalism and imperialism.
>
> *Mr. Kunzig.* Will you please elaborate on that, Mr. Gitlow?
>
> *Mr. Gitlow.* I think a number of references should prove beyond a shadow of a doubt that the Communist movement is an atheistic movement.[429]

At this point in his testimony, Gitlow cited a pamphlet edited by the executive committee of the Komsomol, the youth organization of the Communist Party of the Soviet Union, which laid out what communists themselves called "The 10 Commandments of Communism." Published in the Moscow newspaper *Bolshevist*, they were printed in the excellent 1950 book *The Vatican and the Kremlin*, by Camille Cianfarra, the Vatican correspondent for the *New York Times*, who reported extensively on relations between the Vatican and the Kremlin.[430] Here were the ten commandments, as printed verbatim in the congressional record:

1. Never forget that the clergy is the most powerful enemy of the Communist state.
2. Try to win your friends over to communism and remember that Stalin, who has given a new constitution to the Russian people, is the leader of the anti-God army, not only in the U.S.S.R. but throughout the world.
3. Convince your friends not to have any contact with priests.
4. Watch out for spies and report saboteurs to the police.
5. Make sure that atheist publications are distributed among the largest possible number of people.
6. A good young Communist must also be a militant atheist. He must know how to use his weapons and be experienced in the art of war.
7. Wherever you can you must fight religious elements and prevent whatever influence they might have on your comrades.
8. A true "godless" must also be a good police agent. It is the duty of all atheists to guard the security of the state.
9. Support the godless movement with your money, which is especially necessary for our propaganda abroad where funds, under present circumstances, can only be spent secretly.
10. If you are not a convinced atheist you cannot be a good

Communist or a real Soviet citizen. Atheism is indissolubly bound to communism. These two ideals are the pillars of Soviet power.

Gitlow quoted these from Cianfarra, who quoted from a pamphlet published by the Komsomol. Kunzig, in turn, asked Gitlow if this remained the position of the Communist Party in the United States, from its founding in 1919 to that day. "It was identical," said Gitlow, who then quoted further material, this time from a pamphlet titled "The Communist Program," which was an analysis of the principles of the Russian Communist Party by none other than Nikolai Bukharin, one of the chief leaders of the Bolshevik Revolution, behind only Lenin and Trotsky. The Bukharin pamphlet was published in the United States in 1920 by the Contemporary Publishing Association, one of the early underground publishing organizations of the Communist Party. It stated:

All these considerations explain the program of the Communists with regard to their attitude to religion and to the church. Religion must be fought, if not by violence, at all events, by argument. The church must be separated from the state. . . .

There is a poison called opium. When it is smoked sweet visions appear. You feel as if you were in paradise, but its action tells on the health of the smoker. His health is gradually ruined, and little by little he becomes a meek idiot. The same applies to religion. There are people who wish to smoke opium, but it would be absurd if the state maintained at its expense—that is to say, at the expense of the people—opium dens and special men to serve them. For this reason the church must be—and already is—treated in the same way. Priests, bishops, archbishops, patriarchs, abbots and the rest of the lot must be refused state maintenance. Let the believers, if they wish it, feed the holy fathers at their own expense on the fat of the land, a thing which they, the priests, greatly appreciate.

To say this was a hard, distasteful, cynical view of religion would be an obvious understatement. Nonetheless, it was fully consistent with the long-accepted communist view of religion: Religion was a seductive drug, a poison, an opiate that when smoked produces sweet visions, hallucinations, turning the junkie into a "meek idiot." The priests were like the dealers; they peddle the junk to hook the addicts who sit stupidly in the pews.

What was the Soviet Comintern's position on religion? It was the same. Kunzig asked Gitlow that very question. In reply, Gitlow quoted from official Comintern literature: "One of the most important tasks of the cultural revolution affecting the wide masses is the task of systematically and unswervingly combating religion—the opium of the people."

"The Infiltration of Religious Organizations"

Robert Kunzig then asked Ben Gitlow about the Communist Party in the United States having "adopted a policy for the infiltration of religious organizations." Had that taken place? Gitlow's answer was quite illuminating. The exchange should be absorbed in full for its richness of disturbing detail, right down to individuals named:

> *Mr. Gitlow.* The policy in those days was framed in such a way that the members of the Communist Party could infiltrate church organizations for the purpose of conducting their propaganda among them, for enlisting their support for Soviet Russia and for the various campaigns in which the Communists were interested.
>
> *Mr. Kunzig.* Mr. Gitlow, the House Committee on Un-American Activities is interested, of course, in the valuable background of material which you are giving, but they are also interested in specific examples. Can you cite any specific examples of these tactics to which you are referring?

Mr. Gitlow. Certainly. The Russian Communists were the first to exploit ministers of the United States and through them, the church organizations, for the purpose of spreading propaganda in favor of Communist Russia and for the building up of a pro-Soviet sentiment among church people in America and among Americans generally.

I will, if I may, make mention of a few of the prominent American religious leaders who were used for that purpose in the early 1920's: Dr. Kirby Page, Dr. Sherwood Eddy, Jerome Davis, Dr. Harry F. Ward, the Rev. Albert Rhys Williams, and others. In reference to Albert Rhys Williams, it is interesting to note his biography. Albert Rhys Williams was a graduate of the Hartford Theological Seminary. He was a minister and director of the Maverick Church and Forum of Boston, Mass. When he went to Russia he became a Communist and got a job as assistant in the Commissariat of Foreign Affairs in the Soviet Government. He became a secret member of the Communist Party of the United States. He worked for the Communists in preparing propaganda to foment a Communist Revolution in Germanry [sic]. He organized the International Legion in the Red Army.

In 1943 and 1944 Albert Rhys Williams, a paid agent of the Soviet Government, a secret member of the Communist Party, nevertheless, had such prominence in the United States that he became a lecturer at Cornell University for the years 1934 to 1944. He was also a contributing editor to the Survey Graphic, the leading magazine in the field of philanthropy and social service in the United States. . . .

Mr. Kunzig. Did the Communist Party of the United States in the early 1920's enlist the support of church people for its campaigns and in support of the Communist Party, its activities in Soviet Russia?

Mr. Gitlow. It certainly did, for the number of ministers that actively supported the Communist Party in those days, though not as large as it is today, was, nevertheless, impressive. The outstanding clergymen among them were Dr. Harry F. Ward, Bishop William Montgomery Brown, Jerome Davis, William B. Spofford, and Albert Rhys Williams. The one that I know was a Communist Party member was Bishop William Montgomery Brown. The others cooperated closely with the Communist Party, and in the political committee of the Communist Party their activities on behalf of the Communist Party were continuously discussed.

We see here an unequivocal affirmation from Gitlow that members of the Communist Party had a policy to infiltrate church organizations in order to carry out propaganda among them "for enlisting their support for Soviet Russia and for the various campaigns in which the Communists were interested." And this was done not merely by American members of the Communist Party but by "Russian Communists," who, said Gitlow, "were the first to exploit ministers of the United States and through them, the church organizations, for the purpose of spreading propaganda in favor of Communist Russia and for the building up of a pro-Soviet sentiment among church people in America and among Americans generally." That is a remarkable statement.

Gitlow then named names of those exploited, underscoring, however, that not all were exploited. For example, Episcopal Church Bishop William Montgomery Brown was a Communist Party member. This is no surprise. Bishop Brown, known as "the bad bishop," was so heterodox in his Christianity (and blatantly pro-Marxist) that he was eventually tried for heresy and deposed for his teachings. He was expelled from the Episcopal Church. Still, he had attempted to foster his heresy and pro-communism from within.

Gitlow also knew Albert Rhys Williams to have been a "paid agent of the Soviet Government," as well as a secret member of the

Communist Party. Williams had become a prominent lecturer in the Ivy League, at Cornell University. A Congregationalist who had attended Hartford Theological Seminary, Williams was gushingly pro-Bolshevik, to the point that every person in that congressional hearing would have nodded in assent when Gitlow named him among the Soviet sympathizers.

Truth be told, not a person named by Gitlow would have made anyone in that room flinch: neither pro-Soviet lieutenants such as Episcopal Church Bishop William B. Spofford and Jerome Davis nor others like Dr. Sherwood Eddy, a New England blueblood who was a product of Phillips Andover Academy, Yale, and Princeton Theological Seminary.

Kunzig's questions along these lines for Gitlow continued. He next asked him how the communist penetration came about. This led to a key explication by Gitlow of the communist tactic of the "united front."

> *Mr. Kunzig.* Can you tell us how the Communists infiltrated the religious field?
>
> *Mr. Gitlow.* Before I answer that question I believe it will help the committee to get a better understanding of the Communist technique if I deal briefly with the tactic of the united front adopted by the Communists in 1922 after they realized that their militant policy for instigating a revolution in Germany and then throughout Europe and the world had failed. The united-front policy by Lenin and approved by the Comintern became the official policy of the Communist Party of all countries, including the Communist Party of the United States. Its implementation in the United States resulted in the formation by the Communist Party of many united-front organizations and the initiation of a number of united-front actions.
>
> The united-front tactic enabled the Communists to greatly increase the effectiveness of their infiltration activities. The

united-front tactic was first directed toward the development of pro-Soviet sentiment and support of the Soviets; second, to build up support for the Communists in the trade unions and to create the organizations and conditions for their capture by the Communists; and third, to spread Communist propaganda, incite discontent among the people, undermine the loyalty of the American people and to divide them on religion, national, racial, and economic lines.

Kunzig immediately zeroed in on the religious element. He asked Gitlow explicitly what the policy of the united front had to do with the infiltration of religion. That conversation piqued the interest of everyone, including the longtime chairman of the committee, Pennsylvania Democrat Francis E. Walter, who jumped in:

> *Mr. Gitlow.* The united-front policy enabled the Communists to widely expand their infiltration activities on the religious field because instead of using the Communist Party directly in enlisting the support of the clergymen and laymen who were pro-Soviet and supported the Communist Party and its activities, the Communist Party could enlist them through the front organizations, and on the specific issues of the united front. It was, for the Communists, for men and women operating in a field hostile to communism, to operate in the name of a front organization instead of in the name of the Communist Party. The front organization served as a shield to protect those individuals who were Communists or who explicitly carried out the Communist Party instructions from the charge that they were Communist agents. Besides, on specific issues the Communist Party, through the front organizations, was able to enlist a large number of individuals to follow its line, who under other circumstances would not do so. . . .

Mr. [Congressman Francis E.] Walter. And by "united-front organizations" technically is meant organizations which are part and parcel of the Communist movement?

Mr. Gitlow. No. United-front organizations are organizations which are organized by the Communist Party through which they can enlist on specific issues the support of other organizations which are not Communist organizations and in which they can enlist the support of individuals who will go along with the Communist Party on a specific issue, but will not join the Communist Party on the issue of communism.[431]

Here Gitlow offered important eyewitness affirmation of what we have seen in this book: the united-front tactic was pursued by communists in Moscow and in the United States, begun by the Comintern and initiated as official policy by the Communist Party of every country. The tactic enabled these members of the Communist Party to "greatly increase the effectiveness of their infiltration activities," particularly in the churches. Those who were targeted and tapped in this strategy were not communists but liberal dupes exploited by communists.

Kunzig asked Gitlow about his specific role and what he witnessed among leaders of the Comintern in Moscow. What Gitlow described, particularly about the role of the Rev. Harry Ward in fostering communism in pre-Mao China, is very disturbing.

Mr. Kunzig. You were a member of various important committees of the Comintern and the Profintern.[432] Did you, when you were in Moscow, ever discuss the question of Communist infiltration of religion with the leaders of the Comintern?

Mr. Gitlow. The matter came up in Moscow, not only in reference to the infiltration of religion in the United States, but also in the Far and Near East.

Mr. Kunzig. Will you give us some specific instances?

Mr. Gitlow. My first visit to Moscow was in 1927 when I attended as a delegate of the American Communist Party the enlarged sessions of the executive committee of the Comintern. During my stay in Moscow, I also attended the sessions of the Anglo-American Secretariat, the organization committee of the Comintern, headed by Piatnitsky, had private sessions with the man in charge of archives of the Comintern who also headed the Comintern's agitprop department,[433] sessions of which I also attended, and in addition had a long conference with Stalin. At the meetings of the Anglo-American Secretariat, also at meetings of the executive committee of the Communist International and of its organization department, the question of the American Communist Party's activities on the religious field was discussed. At these meetings the Communist Party was directed to intensify its efforts to draw the religious elements into the party's united-front activities. . . .

At the sessions of the organization department, the importance of establishing good contacts with the religious organizations so that the Communists could infiltrate the missions in China and use them for Communist purposes, was given serious consideration and special attention was drawn to the effective work which Dr. Harry F. Ward did for communism in China.

This raised the antennae of the House committee members and its counsel. Robert Kunzig paused to ask Gitlow if he was claiming that Dr. Ward had engaged in direct communist propaganda when he was in China in 1925. Gitlow responded emphatically in the affirmative: "Certainly. . . . All the lectures delivered in China by Dr. Ward had for its main purpose bolstering up the position of the Communist movement in China and winning support of the Chinese intellectuals and Christians in China for the Chinese Communist movement and for Soviet Russia." Gitlow said that Ward's lectures in China in

1925 were highly appreciated and "discussed at length in Moscow at the Comintern." He said that Comintern officials judged that "clergymen with Dr. Ward's point of view, using the cloak of religion, could render service of inestimable value to the Communist cause in China and to Soviet interests."

Beyond lectures, Gitlow flagged the Rev. Ward's work for the group the Society for Technical Aid to Russia, which had been organized upon instructions of the Soviet government. It was used to facilitate travel into the Soviet Union by issuing visas and passports on behalf of the Bolshevik government. That organization, said Gitlow, "greatly aided the movement of Soviet spies into and out of the United States. It served as an important industrial espionage agency for the Soviet government in both the United States and in Canada."

In short, summed up Gitlow, Ward's Methodist Federation for Social Action was directly "tied into the China conspiracy."

That treasonous connection was not merely underhanded but nefarious and tragic. At that point in time, communism had a snowball's chance in Hades of gaining momentum in China. The likes of Rev. Harry Ward, however, did their damnedest. They would do whatever they could to bring Mao Zedong to power. By 1949, they got their wish, and China soon became the single greatest killing field in the history of humanity, entirely at the hands of Mao's Marxists. No other despot in the long, sordid history of communism racked up a death total like Mao's.

And particularly infuriating for the world's Methodists is that among the first groups booted from Mao's China were the Methodist missionaries. No other group of Western missionaries had made greater inroads, but Mao and his Marxists—the buddies of Rev. Ward and his radical Methodist Federation for Social Action—sent them packing. They showed them the road out of China. To this day, of course, China remains communist and suffers under religious repression.

Communist Infiltration of Religion as "Major Policy" of CPUSA and Moscow

Ben Gitlow would give more testimony regarding Ward's doings in China, but our focus in this chapter is communist infiltration among American Christians. Kunzig questioned Gitlow on that topic directly.

> *Mr. Kunzig.* When did the Communist infiltration of religion become a major policy of the Communist Party of the United States?
>
> *Mr. Gitlow.* It certainly did. On August 20, 1935, with a full delegation of the Communist Party of the United States present, a resolution was adopted unanimously dealing with the preparation of the imperialists for a new world war.

Here was remarkable specificity, with Gitlow tagging a year, month, and date to an actual resolution—as well as a place: Moscow. What did it say? He quoted from the resolution, which included the "religious" among the groups targeted in the united front. According to Gitlow, this resolution declared, "The establishment of a united front with social-democratic and reformist organizations (party, trade unions, cooperative, sport, and cultural and educational organizations), and with the bulk of their members, as well as with mass national liberation, religious, democratic, and pacifist organizations and their adherents, is decisive in the struggle against war and its Fascist instigators in all countries."

Gitlow explained that this resolution was "very specific for it states that a united front on the part of the Communists and the organizations they control, with religious organizations and their adherents, is decisive in the struggle against war and fascism." He said that the resolution was passed by the Seventh World Congress of the Communist International and "proves that Communist infiltration of the religious field was decided upon in Moscow as a major policy. Those who declare that such infiltration of religion, especially the Christian churches, is a figment of the imagination, either do so to hide the astounding facts about such infiltration or because they are too stupid to see or realize what is going on."

Kunzig then asked Gitlow if communists in America had played a part in formulating the policy of the Comintern for the "infiltration of the religious field." "The American Communists played quite an important part," answered Gitlow, who had come to this hearing very well prepared for precisely such questions. He brandished a report made directly to Comintern officials in Moscow by Gil Green, head of the Young Communist League of the United States, which stated:

> We are influencing larger masses of youth and are accepted by large numbers of them as a constructive force. In these organizations we found innumerable functionaries and cadres to fight with us against reaction. In the course of less than a year our Young Communist League built 175 units within these mass organizations and through these began to anchor the united front from below.
>
> At the second American Youth Congress, the Young Communist League delegation was faced with many complicated questions, any one of which if handled in a broad way could have resulted in a break in the united front. For example, the question of religion. Many of the religious groups were skeptical about uniting with Communists, although they were against fascism, because they feared that was a trap to force our atheistic views upon them. This problem was solved by simply agreeing to permit all religious youth in the Congress to hold church services Sunday morning. This did not compromise the Communist youth and yet showed to the masses of religious youth that this was not a united front against religion but against political reaction.

It is instructive that communists were willing to momentarily set aside their contempt for religion to make this concession in the overall service of forging a united front. It was worth the price, for now.

Kunzig then asked Gitlow, "Did the Communist infiltration of religion, on an intensified scale, begin in the United States before the decisions of the Seventh World Congress of the Comintern in 1935?" That was a keen question by Kunzig, no doubt cognizant of prior activities, having done his preliminary research. Gitlow answered, "It actually was in full swing in the United States in 1934. The Seventh World Conference of the Comintern only reiterated and greatly stressed, as I have already indicated, what had always been the policy of the world Communist movement."

Kunzig proceeded to ask Gitlow about the primary organizations involved in carrying out a literal "Communist conspiracy" regarding religion. Here again, Gitlow named names, starting with the elephant in the Marxist living room: the Rev. Harry Ward's unique gang of radical Methodists.

> *Mr. Kunzig:* What were the main organizations through which the Communist conspiracy in religion was carried out?
>
> *Mr. Gitlow.* The Methodist Federation for Social Action and organizations patterned after it in the other religious denominations and the united-front organizations set up by the Communist Party. The united-front organizations which recruited thousands of ministers, through which the Communist infiltration of religion was carried on on a grand scale and was highly successful, were the American League Against War and Fascism, later changed to the American League for Peace and Democracy, and the American Youth Congress.

Quite significantly, Gitlow here affirmed what many had suspected regarding just how far left and pro-Moscow were Ward's Methodist Federation for Social Action and the united-front organizations "set up by the Communist Party." These organizations recruited *thousands of ministers*, most of them presumably dupes, through which American Marxists in the Communist Party carried out their infiltration of religion "on a grand scale."

Kunzig then asked Gitlow about what kind of an organization was the Methodist Federation for Social Action. Gitlow's answer was chilling, and to this day should make faithful Methodists concerned about far-left radicals seeking to sabotage their church from within shudder. Gitlow stated, "The Methodist Federation for Social Action, originally called the Methodist Federation for Social Service, was first organized by a group of Socialist, Marxist clergymen of the Methodist Church, headed by Dr. Harry F. Ward. Dr. Ward was the organizer, for almost a lifetime its secretary and actual leader. He at all times set its ideological and political pattern. Its objective was to transform the Methodist Church and Christianity into an instrument for the achievement of socialism."

Gitlow's words jarred every member of Congress in that hearing room. He confirmed the worst fears and suspicions: the Rev. Harry Ward and his cell of Marxist-socialist clergymen had sought nothing less than to convert the Methodist Church and Christianity as a whole into an instrument for socialist victory.

Gitlow further explained that the group had been established in 1907, twelve years before the organization of the Communist Party of the United States in Chicago in 1919. "The outbreak of the Bolshevik Revolution in Russia in November 1917," Gitlow explained, "had a tremendous effect upon the Socialist ministers of this organization and especially upon Dr. Ward. When the Communist Party was organized in 1919, Dr. Ward was already a convinced Communist with a few insignificant minor reservations. By 1920 he was already, though not yet a member of the Communist Party, cooperating and collaborating with the Communist Party." Note the words "not yet." And this collaboration of Dr. Ward with the Communist Party, Gitlow emphasized, was fully reflected in the "expressions and activities" of the Methodist Federation for Social Action.

Gitlow detailed that Harry Ward, naturally, did not act alone. Among the "inner hard core" of the Methodist Federation was Jack R. McMichael, who Gitlow testified was a member and leader of the Young Communist League. McMichael was elected the organization's executive secretary after Ward relinquished his leadership post, no doubt because the reverend's plate was full. The churchman's ideological cup had runneth over. So many front groups, so little time.

Regardless, Ward had been the brain and face and hand behind the Methodist Federation for Social Action, and still remained in the group and highly active. This was Harry Ward's baby. This organization was, in essence, "a Communist cell headed by Ward, which functioned under the direction of the Communist Party. . . . The Methodist Federation for Social Action was always in the grip of this Communist Party cell and was therefore an instrument through which the Communist Party operated on the religious field."

Ben Gitlow wanted every member of that congressional committee to grasp just how unusual was the Methodist Federation for Social Action. He implored Congress to understand that the organization was comprised of communist Methodists—that is, of Methodists who were communists. Said Gitlow, "The Methodist Federation for Social Action is a membership organization made up entirely of Methodists. It does not affiliate other organizations with it. The Communist Party is not included as an affiliate. The organization is a Communist Party instrument controlled by the Communist Party through the Communist cell secretly operating as a Communist Party disciplined unit in the federation."

This was staggering testimony. Ward's Methodist Federation for Social Action was not a typical left-wing organization of "social justice" clergy lamentably albeit innocently hoodwinked by conniving communists. To the contrary, testified Gitlow under oath, the Methodist Federation for Social Action was, flat out, by creation, a communist organization itself. The goal of the Methodist Federation for Social Action was to dupe others, to mislead others, to hood-wink others. It was not made up of suckers but of communist and pro-communist ministers looking to reel in suckers—that is, dupers, as opposed to dupes. It was a direct instrument of the Communist Party, controlled and directed by the Communist Party. And as for the Rev. Ward—who, it bears repeating here, was co-leader and one of the founders of the American Civil Liberties Union—he was a "convinced Communist" "cooperating and collaborating with the Communist Party."

Hundreds of Pages of Stooges

How far did these tentacles reach into the wider United Methodist Church flock? Kunzig asked just that, and Gitlow's answer was again shocking:

> *Mr. Kunzig.* Did the Communists infiltrate the Methodist Church?
>
> *Mr. Gitlow.* In the infiltration of the Methodist Church, the Communists were highly successful. To detail the extent of the Communist infiltration of the Methodist Church, the people who served the Communists in the Church consciously and those who were its stooges, would take several hundred pages of testimony.

Kunzig asked Gitlow if he could name the principal individuals involved in the infiltration of the Methodist Church. Gitlow replied very specifically: "The principle individuals involved in the Communist conspiracy to subvert the Methodist Church for Communist purposes are: Dr. Harry F. Ward, Rev. Jack R. McMichael, Rev. Charles C. Webber, Rev. Alson J. Smith, Dr. Willard Uphaus, Margaret Forsyth, Rev. Lee H. Ball, and Prof. Walter Rautenstrauch." Each of these names could receive detailed examination here, but such would go beyond the scope of what is necessary in this book.

All had the typical credentials. For instance, Rev. Charles C. Webber, the first manipulator named after Ward and McMichael, was likewise a joint product of Union Theological Seminary (where he was on the faculty) and of Columbia University (where he received a master's degree).

Equally alarming, however, was the extent of their influence among the wider Methodist flock. Moreover, their organization operated without official sanction from the United Methodist Church, no doubt infuriating the UMC leadership, or at least those among the leadership who were not left-wingers. Gitlow explained:

> The Methodist Federation for Social Action operated, though it was an unofficial organization, as if it had the official sanction of the Methodist Church. Its limited, small membership, fluctuating between 2,000 and 10,000, is dominated by a handful of Communists who never officially avowed their Communist affiliations. The Communists in the organization maintained an alliance with militant, revolutionary Socialists, who were not under Communist discipline, but who nevertheless went along with the Communists. The Communists operated within the Methodist Federation for Social Action on the premise that it was important to keep within the Methodist Federation for Social Action all the Socialist, leftist, pacifist, and the so-called liberal and progressive elements just so long as they went together with the Communists on specific issues.

It seems odd that Gitlow would describe this as a "limited, small membership," given that a membership of several thousand, or two thousand to ten thousand, is quite substantial. Then again, Gitlow was surely familiar with even larger webs spun by Communist Party USA and the Comintern.

Kunzig asked Gitlow to spell out the connections between the Methodist Federation for Social Action and the leading communist-front organizations that he had mentioned with important roles in the Communist Party infiltration of religion. Gitlow thus responded with still more upsetting details, again revealing his intimate knowledge of the players involved, noting that the Methodist Federation for Social Action was affiliated with and "collaborated most closely with" the American League Against War and Fascism, the American League for Peace and Democracy, and the American Youth Congress. He duly added that it had been "no accident" that Dr. Ward, chairman of the Methodist Federation, became chairman of both the American League Against War and Fascism and the American League for Peace and Democracy, and served in that capacity for many years. Likewise no accident, the Rev. Jack R. McMichael became chairman for many years of the American Youth Congress.

When asked pointedly by counselor Kunzig if Dr. Ward used his position as chairman of the American League Against War and Fascism "to aid the Communist conspiracy for the infiltration of the churches," Gitlow responded without hesitation, "He did." Gitlow then quoted from an article Dr. Ward wrote in the August 1934 issue of *Fight*, which was the official publication of the American League Against War and Fascism. Titled "Churches and Fascism," Ward wrote:

> They live narrow starved lives with no knowledge of economics or politics, no interest in science, no contacts with literature or art. Their religion supplies them with an opiate that takes them into the dream world. They are the natural followers of a powerful demagogue who can deceive them with vague promises and revolutionary phrases. When their economic security is gone or threatened, their undisciplined emotions can quickly be turned into hate of the Jew, the Communist, the Negro. The only preventative serum that will make them immune from these poisonous germs is propaganda in emotional terms that enables them to locate the real enemy. The people who come to know that the capitalist system is the source of their economic

troubles are not easily led to chase and beat scapegoats. *To work at that task the American League Against War and Fascism needs to get members in all religious organizations. [emphasis original]*

That is an astonishing statement from a minister. In fact, given such sentiments, including describing religion as an opiate that floats the folks in the pews into a dream world, one is tempted to wonder if the Rev. Harry Ward was really even a *Christian* minister. Was he an atheist-communist plant—a wolf in sheep's clothing? Writings like this beg the question.

The committee's inquiry went on, with Kunzig asking about other officials in the Methodist Federation of Social Action who were perhaps also officials of the American League Against War and Fascism. Again, the encyclopedic Gitlow named still more names, all of which are probably beyond the scope of this book, with the overall point of the Marxist infiltration having been made clear.

But alas, one final exchange between Kunzig and Gitlow is worth accentuating, for reasons which will be apparent:

> *Mr. Kunzig.* You stated that the Communist infiltration of religion was decided upon at the World Congress of the Comintern on August 20, 1935, as a major Communist united-front tactic. Did Moscow follow up this resolution with an appeal to the clergymen of the world?
>
> *Mr. Gitlow.* It did.
>
> *Mr. Kunzig.* In what form was the Soviet appeal to the clergymen of the world made?
>
> *Mr. Gitlow.* The drive, on a world scale for the Communist infiltration of religion, was started by Romain Rolland's famous letter to the clergymen of the world, first issued in September 1935, printed in the Communist and pro-Soviet press of the world. It first appeared in the United States in the November 1935 issue of *Soviet Russia Today.*

Romain Rolland was a strange French writer who won the Nobel Prize in literature. He was part spiritualist, part Freudian, part mystic, part socialist. Gitlow quoted a significant passage from that November 1935 issue of *Soviet Russia Today*, which was a key pro-Soviet, communist-front publication: "The results are gigantic. You and your friends can go and see for yourselves. For the U.S.S.R. today is accessible to all and its doors are wide open. You will see a social faith which is equal to, and in my mind, surpasses all the religious faiths, for it is at the service of the entire human future."

This appeal from Rolland to the clergy of the world, of all religious denominations, which, said Gitlow, the Frenchman was forced to write at the behest of the Communist International and the Soviet Government, "contains unvarnished the statement that communism as practiced in the Soviet Union surpasses all religious faiths, therefore, leaving the conclusion that it should become the accepted religion of mankind." Again, one is reminded of Ronald Reagan's description of Marxism-Leninism: "that religion of theirs."

Counselor Kunzig asked Gitlow the million-dollar question: "Why are the Communists so interested in enlisting the support of clergy and in infiltrating religious organizations of all kinds?" Gitlow answered that "religion through the clergy and its various institutions interlocks with and influences practically every field of human endeavor." He rattled off "important contact points," such as military chaplains (and thus the armed services), education, children, church missions, social agencies, foundations, philanthropy, publishing ("the religious organizations maintain large and extensive publishing houses and publish numerous magazines, pamphlets, and leaflets dealing with almost every subject interesting mankind"), and more. In all, religion was "an integral part of the cultural life of the country," from education to business to politics. Gitlow summed up, "The Communists would consider themselves fools and idiots to neglect such an important field as the religious field, for religion exerts its direct influence on life, it can truthfully be said, from the cradle to the grave."

They would indeed. And they sadly found many fools and idiots to enlist in their grandiose cause of infiltrating churches—for the purpose not of promoting the Christian religious faith but, rather, of obliterating it.

CHAPTER 10

"THE DEVIL DOTH QUOTE THE SCRIPTURE"

MANNING JOHNSON ON THE INFILTRATION OF THE CHURCH

Shortly after Ben Gitlow testified before Congress came Manning Johnson, who, like Gitlow and Louis Budenz, was a prominent ex-communist. He was particularly well-known as a leading African-American communist. Johnson, too, witnessed "Uncle Joe" Stalin (as FDR affectionately called Stalin) and his USSR ordering around Communist Party USA. He left the party in disgust.

Johnson had served on the National Negro Commission, an important subcommittee of the National Committee of the Communist Party. It was important because of the vigorous push by CPUSA and the Comintern to attempt to organize black Americans into a segregated "Negro Republic" in the South.[434] That National Negro Commission, said Johnson, was created "on direct orders from Moscow to facilitate the subversion of the Negroes." He soon realized the full extent to which "the Negro is used as a political dupe by the Kremlin hierarchy."[435]

Several top white communists, such as James S. Allen (an alias used by Sol Auerbach), Robert Minor, and Elizabeth Lawson were placed on the commission and ran the show. These white communists, said Johnson, "wielded more power than the nominal Negro heads of the Commission. In a word, they are like white overseers."

Moreover, "Every Negro member was aware of the fact that these white overseers constituted the eyes, the ears and the voice of the Kremlin."

The black man was expected to follow the dictates of Sol and the white masters. Good Negro communists were to be unquestioning Negro communists, who sat quietly and did as they were told. A good black communist listened to the white communist—his comradely master. For all their bluster about elevating blacks, this was how communists treated their African-American brothers.

Particularly egregious, Johnson alleged that white women were exploited by Communist Party leaders as sexual objects to be employed against black men in the party. "I observed how white women communists are used as political prostitutes," wrote Johnson, "cohabiting with high-level Negro communists in order to spy on them." He asserted, "This information is invaluable to the red hierarchy in their relations with their Negro lickspittles. In top red circles, this is known as 'bedroom politics.'" The information procured by the white female communists was then transmitted to the white male communists as handy blackmail material against the black male communists, in case they got out of line—maybe did some back-talking, got a little "uppity" with the white folks. The black reds were basically being used as Uncle Joe's Uncle Toms.

According to Johnson, the conveyor belt of information then went from these "Negro lickspittles" to various "progressive groups," which were, in fact, a wider coalition of communists, fellow travelers, sympathizers, and liberals that "constitute the vehicle on which the reds pin their present hope of victory."

What Johnson concluded of communists' usage of blacks also applied to their exploitation of women, whether in America or the Soviet Union or elsewhere: "when communists unite with and support them [women] today," he warned, it must be kept in mind that "it may be necessary to denounce them tomorrow and the day after tomorrow hang them."

Thus, in the end, blacks and women were indeed treated like everyone else under communism: everyone could be abused and sometimes even executed.

Much more could be said about that, but our focus here is how communists exploited and infiltrated religion. Manning Johnson had some particular valuable insights into how communists viewed not just blacks and women but religious people. Congress was particularly interested. The nation was interested. The churches were interested.

Destruction Through Infiltration

Manning Johnson's testimony before Congress was given on July 8, 1953. His primary questioners were the committee's lead counsel, Robert Kunzig, and Congressmen Kit Clardy of Michigan and Gordon Scherer of Ohio. What he had to say is extraordinary. This chapter draws from a transcribed excerpt of roughly seven thousand words.[436]

Johnson spoke to the Christian faith in America generally: "The Communists discovered that the destruction of religion could proceed much faster through infiltration of the church by Communists operating within the church itself." Here, Johnson, like Gitlow, meant the Christian church or Christianity generally. In his uses of "the church," Johnson never once specified the Catholic Church. He spoke broadly of Christian churches, almost exclusively Protestant churches, even as some Catholic authors have tried to suggest otherwise.[437] He did once mention in his testimony "the superstition of Rome," which was a reference to the Roman Catholic Church. By and large, however, Johnson spoke of Christianity as a whole. Most significant was his statement that communists determined and "discovered" that the destruction of religion could proceed much more rapidly by infiltrating the church and operating from within.

Manning Johnson began by stating that communists believed that every communist had a "duty" to extricate himself from the "supernatural bondage" of religion and to liberate the masses from that bondage:

> *Mr. Johnson*: When I first joined the Communist Party, the district organizer, Peter Chaunt, C-h-a-u-n-t, and a member of the district bureau and the district committee of the Communist Party by the name of Otto Hall, talked at great length to me on the subject of communism and religion. The essence of what they said was that man made God, not God made man, and that the duty of every Communist is to rid himself of the supernatural bondage of religion; that religion is used by the powers that be in order to keep the masses of the people in docile submission to exploitation. Therefore, the liberation of the masses of humanity is dependent upon their emancipation from religious ideology.

Johnson himself experienced that. During the time he was an active member of the Communist Party, he was not atheist. He explained to the congressional committee, "I hid my religion. I committed the grievous sin of hiding it. I outwardly accepted the atheistic anti-religious program of the Communists, but secretly in my heart I retained my religious convictions. Of course, that was an awful struggle, an internal struggle, a struggle between two different and opposing philosophies, the philosophy of charity and the philosophy of hate. Sometimes I wonder how I did that tightrope walking." In fact, added Johnson, now that he had left the party, he had joined a Baptist Church in New Jersey and attended church services in New York regularly.

Johnson explained how the Communist Party indoctrinated its members via "so-called lessons of indoctrination, they gave me Lenin's writings on religion." Counsel Kunzig asked when and where this happened, and about the materials Johnson received:

Mr. Kunzig: When and where was this given to you, Mr. Johnson?

Mr. Johnson: This was in Buffalo, N. Y., when I first joined the party, in 1930.

Mr. Kunzig: Do you have any samples of any printed instruction which was given to you?

Mr. Johnson: Yes, I do have. I was given the pamphlets and booklets that were written by Bishop William Montgomery Brown. He was a prominent Episcopalian bishop who was expelled from the church because of heresy. He devoted the balance of his life to a war on religion. He published such books as the *Bankruptcy of Christian Supernaturalism, Heresy*,[438] and others. The Communist Party received a large supply of these antireligious pamphlets, and they circulated them very extensively. They either gave them away or sold them.

Mr. Kunzig: Throughout the United States of America?

Mr. Johnson: Yes, throughout the United States.

Mr. Scherer: Let me just ask one question. You have here with you this morning some of the books and pamphlets of Bishop Brown to which you have referred; have you not?

Mr. Johnson: Yes, I have.

Mr. Scherer: Would you just for the record say which ones are in your possession at this time?

What Manning Johnson then proceeded to furnish was of compelling interest, and very enlightening as to the thinking of these leftist ministers—specifically, Bishop William Montgomery Brown, the Episcopal bishop (mentioned earlier in the Gitlow testimony) who was ultimately expelled from his denomination for heresy. He was the so-called "bad bishop." Johnson had brought a copy of Bishop Brown's multivolume *Bankruptcy of Christian Super-naturalism*, volumes 1, 2, and 3. He also toted along a copy of Brown's *Communism and Christianity*, where he quoted from page 210: "Christianism is nothing to either the owners or workers in the sky, for its God and heaven, devil and hell are lies, and neither religious Christianism or political republicanism or democratism, not to speak of the other evils of religion and politics, offers the workers aught on earth. Capitalism is the god of this world, of no part of it no more than of these United States, and capitalism is to the laborer a wrong, lying, murderous devil, not a good divinity."

That is a shocking set of beliefs from an ordained minister. But Bishop Brown was a shocking man. By this point, Brown was deceased, and Johnson informed the committee that the late Episcopal bishop had willed his entire estate to the Communist Party. Not to his church but to the party.

Manning Johnson here added the one reference he made in his testimony to the Roman Catholic Church, which had been in Bishop Brown's crosshairs, as it was for his fellow communists: "I may also state that the main theme of Bishop Brown was to banish gods from the heavens and capitalists from the earth for the science of Moscow against the superstition of Rome [i.e., the Roman Catholic Church]."

Johnson noted that Bishop Brown not only wrote such books for adults but he also wrote books for children in order to indoctrinate them in atheism. Said Johnson, "He also issued antireligious material for children. . . . When I was a member of the Communist Party, the Communist Party paid special attention to the indoctrination of the youth. They in fact issued special bulletins instructing leaders and teachers with regard to the type of training for the youth."

Johnson affirmed that during the period of his membership in the Communist Party there was never any deviation from the basic antireligious line. There was, however, a change in what he called "the tactical application of the Communist Party's antireligious policy." This tactical change was made in 1932 at a meeting he attended of the national committee of the Communist Party in New York, "at which time Earl Browder made a speech to the committee in which he said that our aim should be to draw the religious element into the movement before we convinced them to become atheists. In other words, to reverse the old policy of convincing the worker and farmer to become an atheist before he became active in the Communist Party movement. As Browder put it, that old policy was like putting the cart before the horse."

Counsel Kunzig was on to this: "In other words, if you cannot completely destroy religion, would you say that the correct phraseology would be that it is best to attempt to infiltrate it first and then later destroy it?" Johnson answered, "I would say that the policy then was to first get the worker and the farmer involved in Communist activities, and in the course of his involvement in these activities you steadily indoctrinate him in the antireligious philosophy of the Communist Party."

Johnson noted that this stood contrary to previous procedure whereby the communist first approached the average worker and farmer with an antireligious program and policy. The result of this was that the Christian worker was antagonized, and a wall of resistance was built up "between the party and the religious element in America." The new policy aimed to break down this wall of resistance by "getting the Christian element in, thereby getting the Communist Party out of the rut of sectarianism in which it had fallen."

But at the same time, said Johnson, the Communist Party pursued both tracks. It continued its antireligious propaganda while simultaneously revising its tactical approach toward the Christian element in order to draw in sympathetic Christians: "Once they got them in, they continued to indoctrinate them in their antireligious program."

Counsel Kunzig thus pivoted to the matter of the united front. He asked Johnson to describe that front. Johnson explained:

> The united front was a development of a new tactical line by the Communist International in 1935. This new tactical line was developed at the seventh world congress of the Communist International in Moscow in 1935. Georgi Dimitrov, general

secretary of the Communist International, presented this new tactical line to the seventh world congress. Now, the essence of it was to infiltrate churches, trade unions and all other organizations through the process of involving them into a so-called united front on the basis of a program presented to them by the Communist Party.

Now, the united front was a coalition or an alliance of the church, trade unions, farm and youth and women's organizations of the Communist Party, under Communist Party leadership and for the promulgation of the Communist Party program. It was a step in the formation of a people's front government, which of course is a form of transition to proletarian revolution and the seizure of power in a given country. As Dimitrov said, the united front is useful, but the final salvation is in a socialist revolution. The united front is used for revolutionary training of the masses.

Notably, Johnson thereby had backed Ben Gitlow's testimony regarding where and when this new tactical line had started: in Moscow in 1935. And the ultimate goal was not Christian salvation, of course, but the "final salvation" of a socialist revolution.

Dagger to the Heart of the Church

Robert Kunzig pushed on to the crucial related question of Earl Browder's "outstretched hand." Johnson's description is striking. He explained that the outstretched hand was the "new united-front policy of the Communist International applied all over the world." Again, using lowercase *c* to refer to the wider Christian church all over the world, he said that this was "the extension of the hand of friendship and cooperation to the church, while in the other hand holding a dagger to drive through the heart of the church." In other words, it was a ruse whereby communists could get the churches involved in united-front activities so communists could bring to the "religious element in America" their antireligious program. The goal was to educate the masses in the revolutionary program and policy of the Communist Party, "to prepare them ideologically and organizationally for the overthrow of the Government of the United States."

The outstretched hand concealed a knife.

As evidence to back his provocative assertions, Johnson entered into his testimony some documents for the record. First among them was the *Communist*, the theoretical organ of Communist Party USA, specifically an article titled "The United Front: The Key to Our New Tactical Orientation," written by Earl Browder. Johnson referenced pages 1076–77. He characterized Browder's argument as communists conceding that their old tactical orientation was wrong and thus had to be changed because new conditions had arisen. Nothing had changed from the obeisance to the teachings of Marx, Engels, Lenin, and Stalin, but tactics had to be adjusted in order to achieve practical success—at least for now. Johnson noted that Dimitrov himself had pointed out that the united-front tactic, which (in Johnson's characterization of Dimitrov) "is aimed at getting control of the churches, is not a digression from the basic position of the Communist Party; that is, the struggle for revolution, the conquest of power, but merely a reconstruction of tactics in accordance with changing situation. It is the tactic to draw wide masses into revolutionary class struggle where the working people, both Christians and Jews, will be welded into a millionfold strong revolutionary army, led by the Communist International under the leadership of Stalin at that time."

These tactics, said Johnson, were brought out by Dimitrov, who invoked Greek history, the Battle of Troy, the Trojan horse, as the best model for what they were trying to do. He quoted Dimitrov: "Comrades, you remember the ancient tale of the capture of Troy. Troy was inaccessible to the armies attacking her, thanks to her impregnable walls, and the attacking army, after suffering great losses, was still unable to achieve victory until, with the aid of the Trojan horse, it managed to penetrate to the very heart of the enemy's camp." In other words, said Johnson, what Dimitrov was saying "is that if you cannot take over the churches by frontal attack, take them over by the use of deception and guile and trickery, and that is exactly what the Communists practice in order to infiltrate and subvert the church and prepare them for the day when they would come under the hierarchical and authoritarian control of Moscow."

Communists were employing Trojan horse tactics.

Manning Johnson then gave some specifics to explain how this played out. He noted that the leaders of the Communist Party "had an eye toward the millions of people in the churches, and this policy was designed specifically to reach the millions in the churches." Party officials had done their homework. Johnson said that as early as 1931 the Communist Party actually did a survey of churches in the United States "which was published by certain international pamphlets." In the pamphlet titled "The Church and the Workers," by Bennett Stevens, could be found a survey of the Christian churches, their membership, and holdings. Johnson read what Stevens said about the wider Christian church. He said that the survey "was not prepared without instructions from the Communist Party, because when pamphlets of this kind, according to my knowledge and experience, are written and published, they are published under instructions of the top leadership of the Communist Party, both in America and abroad, because such pamphlets are sent to the Soviet Union where they are evaluated, and on the strength of them the policy for the Communist Party of America is formulated, and not only for America, but throughout the world." He said that the survey showed how many people in America were connected with Christianity, a key reality "not lost to the men who sit in the Kremlin and are formulating policy for the American party." Johnson quoted:

> The churches are effective propaganda agencies, for they reached a membership of 50 million persons in 1930. That capitalists

are conscious of this fact is shown by the liberality of their donation to the churches. As one of his many contributions to the Episcopal Church, J. P. Morgan paid the expenses involved in publishing the revised Book of Common Prayer. John D. Rockefeller, Jr., in addition to building a $7-million church in New York, gives millions to Baptist colleges and other religious enterprises. In 1929 gifts to Protestant churches of the United States amounted to $520 million. The churches are not spiritual institutions, but are in themselves powerful, wealthy, capitalist corporations, and as such have special church-property investments, and churches spent $817 million in immediate expenses in 1926. Only a very slight portion of this went to benevolencies. The following table indicates the value of church property and expenses in some of the larger sects of the United States.

Again, CPUSA officials had done their research.

As Johnson described it, they then went on to give an estimate of the value of church property in the United States—something of keen interest to materialistic, anti-spiritual communists already inclined to see the churches and their capitalist supporters as bloodsuckers. Johnson explained that the author of this article, Bennett Stevens, went on to say that "religion cannot be reformed, whatever its doctrine and ritual, that it remains an agency by which the capitalist class enforces its control. The program of those who want to reform existing religion must therefore be rejected."

That was the longtime teaching, of course, of Karl Marx.

The significance of this, said Johnson, is that the Communist Party had already, in 1931, "seen the need of getting into the churches where 50 million Americans are, and this survey and surveys made after this one was made, constituted a very important factor in determining the Communist policy in infiltrating the churches and religious organizations."

The policy and the conclusion were one of infiltration.

Congressman Scherer then asked the impressively prepared Manning Johnson for further documentary evidence. To that end, Johnson offered a statement by William Z. Foster in the *Communist* (August 1939 edition, pages 702, 703), quoting from Foster's article, "Secondary Aspects of Mass Organization." Said Foster, "Religion is another extremely important secondary aspect of American mass organization. Inevitably a social current so well organized and so deeply ingrained in the mind of the masses as religion has exerted a far-reaching effect upon the people's mass organization of all types throughout their entire history." Comrade Foster conceded "a very serious mistake of the American left wing during many years," which had been "its attempt arbitrarily to wave aside religious sentiments among the masses." This had backfired. Foster acknowledged the intention of the outstretched hand to reverse that error: "In recent years, however, the Communist Party, with its policy of 'the outstretched hand,' has done much to overcome the harmful left-wing narrowness of former years and to develop a more healthy cooperation with the religious masses of the people in building the democratic front."[439]

Precisely that course was being pursued by America's Marxist-Leninists.

The United Front: "School for Communism"

Manning Johnson's testimony at this point further rang alarm bells. He heralded the fact that the success of the united-front policy had enabled the Communist Party to "come in contact with thousands of ministers and millions of people who make up their congregations all over the country." He said that "the fact that they were successful in the so-called outstretched-hand policy" was clearly stated by Earl Browder in his book *What Is Communism?* Johnson quoted from page 147 of the book: "It is significant that the Communist Party, more than any other labor group, has been able to achieve successful united fronts with church groups on the most important issues of the day. This is not due to any compromise with religion as such on our part. In fact by going among the religious masses we are, for the first time, able to bring our antireligious ideas to them."

Note: no compromise with the religious. The idea was not for communists to warm to religion but to bring atheistic communism to the religious.

This prompted Robert Kunzig to zero in: "In other words, you would say, would you not, Mr. Johnson, that on the basis of your personal experience and knowledge the united front is the medium through which people were educated to communism?" Johnson answered, "That is correct." In a really jarring statement, Johnson added, "The united front is a school for communism. It is the instrument to bring the Communist Party program and policy to millions of people throughout the length and breadth of the country."

Kunzig asked Johnson if it would it be correct to say that there was actually party recruiting occurring through the united front. "Yes, there was," affirmed Johnson. "The whole purpose of the united front was to bring the Communist Party into contact with millions of people from whom they had before been isolated in order to indoctrinate them, to educate them and train them in Communist policy and orient them along the path of revolutionary struggle."

At this juncture in his questioning, Johnson introduced into the congressional record an excerpt from the report to the Tenth National Convention of CPUSA, done on behalf of the central committee by General Secretary Browder. The date was May 1938. In reference to the matter of communists training those involved in united-front activities, Browder had stated, "We propose to make the education of our leading people, the Marxist-Leninist training, the central task of the whole party. It shall not be confined to the members of the central committee and State leaders, but extended to a broad new circle of leaders for the States and sections and for party leaders in the mass organizations, trade unions, youth, Negro, farm, cultural, women's, religious, national groups, and other organizations."

Johnson here interjected that "the main purpose of this educational process of religious leaders is for the overthrow of the Government of the United States. The party, according to my knowledge and experience, realized that without subverting the millions of persons in the church, revolution in the United States is unthinkable; it is impossible. For that reason, a corps of trained persons was necessary who would be in a position to work successfully toward this end among the churchgoers."

As further evidence, Johnson cited *Fight* magazine, which was the official organ of the odious front-group, the American League Against War and Fascism. In the April 1934 issue (page 34), *Fight* had declared:

> This means that those who would use what resources are available in the churches to fight the development of fascism must be prepared to show the people in the churches that there is no way out under the profit system and that the only way they can get the better life that is within their reach is to take ownership and control out of the hands of the few, put it into the hands of the many, and develop a planned economy for the purpose of realizing the classless society. Then the emotions and ideals that will otherwise be misled by the Fascists will be directed to the defeat of the real enemy of the people—the capitalist system— and will be given a constructive outlet in the building of a new order. To work at this task the American League Against War and Fascism needs to get members in all religious organizations.

Note carefully what this set forth: the imperative to get members inserted and implanted in all religious organizations. Yes, *all* religious organizations. They would be marshalled together as part of a committed fighting force to defeat the "real enemy" of the people: the American capitalist system.

Kunzig here paused to ask Johnson which individual was the

chairman of the American League Against War and Fascism, knowing the answer Johnson would provide: the Reverend Harry F. Ward. The counselor was ready to focus the spotlight in that direction. The specter of the Rev. Ward was haunting the hearing room yet again.

> Mr. Kunzig: When you were a member of the Communist Party did you know him as a member of the Communist Party?
>
> Mr. Johnson: Yes; he was a member of the Communist Party while I was a member.
>
> Mr. Kunzig: Did you meet with him as such?
>
> Mr. Johnson: Yes, I did.
>
> Mr. Kunzig: Would you characterize him as a prominent member of the Communist Party?
>
> Mr. Johnson: I would say that he is the Red dean of the Communist Party in the religious field.

Here the discussion shifted just a bit, or at least away from Ward for the moment.

They discussed the matter of training leaders for work in the united front. "The training of leaders for work in the united front is of major importance to the success of the Communist Party's program," said Johnson. "For that reason we had considerable discussions in the central committee and in the sections and districts and State committees of the Communist Party on methods of work among religious elements." Johnson personally participated in these discussions on both national and lower levels in the Communist Party. He presented to the committee the substance of some of those discussions that were aimed at educating party members on "how to work among the religious element." He quoted William Z. Foster directly: "Communists must ever be keen to cultivate the democratic spirit of mutual tolerance among the religious sects in the people's mass organizations. A still greater lesson for us to learn, however, is how to work freely with religious strata for the accomplishment of democratic mass objectives, while at the same time carrying on our basic Marxist-Leninist educational work."

Continuing along that line, said Johnson, communist leaders instructed him and his fellow comrades "in the use of deceit in dealing with religious elements." That colorful exchange between Johnson and Kunzig is worth quoting verbatim.

> Mr. Kunzig: Was deceit a major policy of Communist propaganda and activity?
>
> Mr. Johnson: Yes, it was. They made fine gestures and honeyed words to the church people which could be well likened unto the song of the fabled sea nymphs luring millions to moral decay, spiritual death, and spiritual slavery. An illustration of this treachery, I might point out, is smiling, sneaky Earl Browder, for example, who was vice chairman of the American League Against War and Fascism, greeting and praising ministers and other church workers participating with him in the united front, antiwar activities, while secretly harboring in his heart only contempt for them and for the religion that they represented.

As evidence of how the likes of Browder trained others in the use of such deceit, Johnson again quoted from Browder's 1936 book *What Is Communism?* "It is true that we have learned to be much more careful about the quality of our mass work in this field. We take pains not to offend any religious belief. We don't want to close the minds of religious people to what we have to tell them about capitalism, because of some remark or action offensive to their religion. We can well say that the cessation of ineffective, rude, and vulgar attacks upon religion is a positive improvement in our work."

This returned the attention of everyone in that hearing room to what Manning Johnson called the "major organizational form of the united front in which the churches were involved"—the American

League Against War and Fascism. According to Johnson, this was "the key Communist Party front. There was no other Communist Party front in all of the solar system of organizations of the Communist Party that involved so many ministers, churches, and religious organizations." In fact, warned Johnson, this organization was "the key to the infiltration of the church, and as a result of the successful infiltration and penetration they were able to involve these ministers in every other Communist front through the years, even down to the present time."

Through the vehicle of the American League Against War and Fascism, the Communist Party was able to involve ministers in every communist front up through that present day.

Maybe looking to extend a little Christian charity to some of those ministers regrettably taken in, Kunzig said to Johnson, "Undoubtedly the great, great number of ministers who were involved one way or another in this or other Communist-front groups were loyal citizens and fine, good, religious men who were completely duped; is that not true, Mr. Johnson?" Johnson made a critical distinction between the ringleaders and those they misled. Many of the latter were in fact dupes.

> Mr. Johnson: There were quite a few of them who were duped, but the Communist clergymen and fellow travelers and those under Communist Party discipline were not duped. They were fully conscious and fully aware of what they were doing. They were the small minority that utilized their position to infiltrate and seek to subvert the majority of the clergy in the interests of the aims and objectives of the Communist Party of the United States.
>
> Mr. Kunzig: It was an example of a small minority attempting to influence, control, and use the majority of good, decent clergymen?
>
> Mr. Johnson: Yes; that is true, because I know from my own

experience in working in labor organizations, for example, that we had an organization with 10,000 members, and there were only about 60 or 70 Communists, and we controlled the organization. So with small minority of ministers who work in an organized manner, they can always win over and subvert and dupe the majority who are disorganized and are individualistic.

With merely a small group of, say, sixty to seventy, communists could redirect an organization of ten thousand. Impressive but sad. All that was needed was a small albeit dedicated cell of organized ministers. The ringleaders spearheading the front-group that was the American League Against War and Fascism knew how to manipulate. That brought the conversation right back to Rev. Harry Ward and friends.

Kunzig wanted to direct Johnson's and the committee's attention to this "very vital and important organization so that the true picture of the true work of this organization may become clear on this record." He asked Johnson to explain to the committee how this group was organized, who headed it, and in general its purposes and functions. Johnson was a rare eyewitness. He related to Kunzig and the committee that he had actually sat in on the very meetings of the national committee of the Communist Party in New York City for the formation of the American League Against War and Fascism. The league had been a literal communist plot from the outset, with Communist Party USA, at that meeting, taking its orders from and working with the Soviet Comintern. "The substance of these discussions was that the Communist International had formed an organization known as the World Congress Against War," explained Johnson, who added that the head of that organization was Henri Barbusse, a leader of the Communist Party of France and a confidante of Joseph Stalin. "The American party was instructed by the Communist International to form the American League Against War and Fascism." That organization, said Johnson, was officially set up at what communists had organized as their first "United States Congress Against War," held in

New York City in 1933, an event attended by Barbusse, who also was instrumental in its organization and direction.

According to Johnson, the purpose was crystal clear: "The policy of this particular front—that is, the American League Against War and Fascism—was to involve the religious organizations into Communist Party activities generally to exploit the tremendous antiwar and anti-Fascist sentiment that exists among the religious masses." And that was why, said Johnson, the Rev. Harry F. Ward was selected to head the American League Against War and Fascism: "The party conclusion was that because he was a minister, he would be able to draw in churches, and secondly, that he would be able to draw in labor because of his imposing record as a clergyman of some standing and note. In other words, they considered him the ideal head for the organization."

This, said Johnson, was proven to be a good decision because the American League Against War and Fascism was able, "through exploiting the antiwar and anti-Fascist sentiments among the clergymen and among church people generally, to involve millions of people in supporting" its program.

He noted that because the majority of the American people are peace-loving and democratic and opposed to war and fascism, such a campaign had tremendous appeal. Nonetheless, added Johnson at length:

> When such a campaign like the one against war and fascism is used as a cover to attack our government, our social system, our leaders, when it is used as a cover to attack our law-enforcement agencies and to build up mass hate against them, when it is used as a cover for the transmission of intelligence information to Soviet Russia, when it is used as a cover for Soviet espionage, when it is used as a cover for infiltration and subversion of our churches, seminaries, youth organizations, when it is used as a cover to undermine national security, when it is used as a cover

to sabotage industry and transportation, when it is used to prepare and to influence and win over millions in support of the
foreign policy of an alien government, namely, Soviet Russia,
against our own country, when it is used as a cover to defend
Communists, the sworn enemies of our great heritage, when
it is used as a cover for preparing millions of people ideologically and organizationally for the overthrow of the United States
Government, then that is a different matter altogether.

That was quite a mouthful from Johnson—in one sentence. And
note, for our interests in this book, the particularly poignant line
within that long sentence—namely, that this particular campaign
and organization was used as a cover for infiltration and subversion
of American churches and seminaries. "That is the program as it was
worked out in the central committee," said Johnson, "and that was
the program that was advocated by the American League Against
War and Fascism when I was not only a member of it, but a member
of the national committee."

Infiltration of Protestant Denominations and Seminaries

To re-emphasize, this infiltration and subversion of American
churches and seminaries was, by Johnson's testimony, a Protestant
effort among fellow Protestants. At least he made no mention of
Catholic churches and seminaries. Johnson spoke of "the program
of the Communist Party for the infiltration of the various Protestant
denominations on the basis of conditioning them mentally, organizationally for the overthrow of the Government of the United States."

Johnson identified the radical-left publication the *Protestant* as
the print flagship for this effort. "The Protestant Digest [*The Protestant*] was first published in 1938 while I was a member of the party,"
said Johnson, "and in the party circles it was discussed as one of the
Communist-front publications that had as its aim and purpose using
first the infiltration of the Protestant denominations; secondly, to

carry the materialist, antireligious policy of the Communist Party into the religious denominations under the guise of religion." He said that the *Protestant* even went so far as to provide ministers with pro-communist material for sermons to deliver to congregations at regular Sunday services.

In sum, such was the breadth and depth of Manning Johnson's remarkable testimony in July 1953. Robert Kunzig asked him to conclude with a summary of the overall manner in which communists had attempted to "infiltrate and poison the religious organizations of America wherever possible." Johnson's reply was chilling, and it shines the light on the dark designs of what the likes of Earl Browder and Communist Party USA had really been up to amidst their sweet words about extending an "outstretched hand" and working with Christian believers for peace and harmony:

> Once the tactic of infiltrating religious organizations was set by the Kremlin, the actual mechanics of implementing the "new line" was a question of following the general experiences of the living church movement in Russia where the Communists discovered that the destruction of religion could proceed much faster through infiltration of the church by Communist agents operating within the church itself.
>
> The Communist leadership in the United States realized that the infiltration tactic in this country would have to adapt itself to American conditions and the religious makeup peculiar to this country. In the earliest stages it was determined that with only small forces available it would be necessary to concentrate Communist agents in the seminaries and divinity schools. The practical conclusion, drawn by the Red leaders, was that these institutions would make it possible for a small Communist minority to influence the ideology of future clergymen in the paths most conducive to Communist purposes.

We see once again the power, understood by communists so terribly well (and by the radical left in America to this day), of a tightknit group of committed organizers and what they could accomplish by igniting a ripple effect. A small minority of agents planted in the seminaries and divinity schools could influence the ideology of future clergymen in a way most conducive to Marxist purposes.

Johnson paused to add a critical point on how these radical leftists sought to politicize and ideologize the pulpit, tugging these churches away from their spiritual mission to a material one: "In general, the idea was to divert the emphasis of clerical thinking from the spiritual to the material and political." This meant a formation based on communist doctrine and the communist program "to weaken our present society and prepare it for final conquest by Communist forces." They would divert clerical thinking from "matters of the soul" to political-ideological matters.

And surfacing again in his testimony was the red dean, the Rev. Ward, captain of the Marxist-Leninist ship trolling the water for suckers. Seminaries were aggressively targeted:

> The Communists had some small forces in the seminaries and under the leadership of Harry F. Ward. These were quickly augmented by additional recruits and siphoned into the divinity institutions by manipulations of Communist cells in the seminaries. This infiltration into seminaries was expedited by the use of considerable forces the Communists had in educational institutions which were eligible for hire by divinity organizations. The plan was to make the seminaries the neck of a funnel through which thousands of potential clergymen would issue forth, carrying with them, in varying degrees, an ideology and slant which would aid in neutralizing the anti-Communist character of the church and also to use the clergy to spearhead important Communist projects.

Communists thus created cells and "small forces" in seminaries.

These in turn were quickly augmented by new recruits promoted up and "siphoned into the divinity institutions" and "educational institutions." This was an actual "plan" to reorient the seminaries as "the neck of a funnel" to generate potentially "thousands" of clergymen who would uphold, in varying degrees, "an ideology and slant" that at the least would neutralize anti-communist elements in the wider Christian church and, at best, would exploit the clergy to "spearhead" important efforts of value to the communist cause.

How successful was this effort?

"This policy was successful beyond even Communist expectations," asserted Johnson. "The combination of Communist clergymen, clergymen with a pro-Communist ideology, plus thousands of clergymen who were sold the principle of considering Communist causes as progressive, within 20 years, furnished the Soviet apparatus with a machine which was used as a religious cover for the overall Communist operation ranging from immediate demands to actually furnishing aid in espionage and outright treason."

Yes, outright espionage and treason. Now that's a serious matter.

Moreover, the cohesiveness of these particular communists— directed in the service of a carefully preconceived plan of operation— was always among their greatest assets. "The Communists have an advantage in religious organizations due to the fact that their forces within religious groups are well organized as a totalitarian group which, operating as a highly mobile force, works unceasingly toward a premeditated program," said Johnson. "This gives this destructive element a great tactical advantage over all others in the religious organizations who deal with religion as individuals, operating ethics on the basis of an individual conscience before God."

And what kind of numbers were we talking about? By Manning Johnson's estimate, the number of trained forces by American communists reached into the thousands:

In the early 1930s the Communists instructed thousands of their members to rejoin their ancestral religious groups and to operate in cells designed to take control of churches for Communist purposes. This method was not only propounded, but was executed with great success among large elements of American church life. Communists operating a double-pronged infiltration, both through elements of Communist-controlled clergy, and Communist-controlled laymen, managed to pervert and weaken entire stratas of religious life in the United States.

Communists in churches and other religious organizations were instructed to utilize the age-old tradition of the sanctity of the church as a cover for their own dastardly deeds. Through Reds in religion, we have a true living example of the old saying: "The Devil doth quote the Scripture."

The devil does quote the Scripture. He had the audacity to quote it directly to Jesus Christ, but in his own deceptive way—twisting and manipulating it. When he tried to tempt Christ with the material of the world, the Son of God corrected Satan, noting that man does not live on bread alone. Man is also a spiritual being. You cannot solve the problem of man by bread alone. Communists promised their flock the deception that man's plight could be resolved by bread, by the strictly material and not the spiritual. "From each according to his abilities, to each according to his needs," said Marx, misquoting the Scripture just slyly enough, with yet another deception.

But twentieth-century communists were especially slick. They would enlist clergymen (some duped, others doing the duping) to quote the Scripture to the flock. "The Communists learned that the clergyman under their control served as a useful 'respectable face' for most of their front activities," averred Manning Johnson. "In this way the name of religion was used to spearhead the odious plots hatched by the agents of antireligious Soviet communism."

And yet, even with such large numbers, extending into the

thousands, communists knew that the *quality* of the manipulators was always more important than the quantity. "Communist strategists counted the effectiveness of their forces not so much on numbers alone, but on the importance of individuals loyal to communism in key spots where a small group can influence large numbers and create havoc by controlling a sensitive spot," said Johnson. "Thus one professor of divinity, lecturing to future clergymen, who in turn will preach to thousands of churchgoers, is, in the long run, more dangerous than 20 Red preachers singing the praises of communism from the pulpit."

The best multiplier effect was generated by having the best initial sources to start the multiplication process. One really skilled pro-Marxist professor of divinity, smart and cautious with the language he used, could be far more influential than a couple dozen big-mouthed preachers less polished in their leftist proselytization efforts.

The same was true, said Johnson, for a communist agent holding an important position in a church publication that reaches large multitudes of the churchgoing public. "One practical effect of Red influence in church publications is to tip off scores of pro-Soviet clergymen, who are only too glad to receive sermon material through the medium of a church publication," said Johnson. "The large backlog which the Communists have in the writing and journalistic field make it easy for them to infiltrate religious publications and organize new publications representing the Communist slant in church circles."

Johnson concluded with another scary demonstration of how shrewdly communists could operate with a small band of true believers worming their way through an institution from the inside. Behold his jarring numbers: "It is an axiom in Communist organization strategy that if an infiltrated body has 1 percent Communist Party members and 9 percent Communist Party sympathizers, with well-rehearsed plans of action, they can effectively control the remaining 90 percent. . . . In the large sections of the religious field, due to the ideological poison which has been filtered in by Communists and pro-Communists through seminaries, the backlog of sympathizers and mental prisoners of socialistic ideology is greater than the 10 percent necessary for effective control."

In other words, a trusting flock could, in the deceitful hands of a few bad shepherds, be led to spiritual slaughter. Or, in the case of the communist world as it existed in the USSR and behind the Iron Curtain, and in places like China, and, later in the killing fields of Cambodia and in Korea and Vietnam, *physical* slaughter as well as spiritual. All in the name of the sweet promises of communism and its preachers.

The devil doth quote Scripture indeed.

CHAPTER 11

"OVER A THOUSAND COMMUNIST MEN"

INFILTRATION OF CATHOLIC SEMINARIES?
BELLA DODD'S CLAIMS

Manning Johnson was back before the House Committee five days later, on July 13, 1953.

Attorney Robert Kunzig asked Johnson for further detailed testimony about the Methodist Federation for Social Action. Johnson reiterated that Rev. Harry Ward's group had been "invaluable to the Communist Party" in its united-front organizations and campaigns. The group had been invaluable "because through it the party was able to get contact with thousands of ministers all over the country."

Yes, *thousands*. By this, Johnson meant thousands of "affiliated" ministers who were broadly sympathetic to the aims of the communist front-group and the social-justice buttons it was shrewdly pushing—albeit pushing subtly and carefully so as to try to avoid appearing too blatantly pro-Soviet. Effective manipulation required fastidious skill and cunning.

This prompted Michigan Congressman Kit Clardy to ask Johnson, "You mean they could contact ministers who had not the slightest idea about the sinister purposes and background of what they were trying to do?" Johnson answered, "That is correct. They had the contact, a wealth of contact, established and built up over the years with ministers in every section of the country who were easily and quickly involved in various united-front activities, consequently giving these Communist-front movements an aura of respectability the like of which they could not get except for the tremendous amount of faith people have in religion and the church."

This exchange prompted the committee's counsel to bring into the conversation a name that had not been raised to Johnson in his previous testimony the week before: a lady named Bella Dodd.

Dodd had testified before the committee a few weeks prior. Kunzig related to Johnson that Dodd had spoken of her personal knowledge and involvement with the Communist Party in New York in creating what Kunzig referred to as "sucker lists." These were "sucker lists of distinguished citizens, scientists, and professional people throughout the country whom they used whenever they needed distinguished fronts to cover up their purposes. These people did not know what their names were being used for." Kunzig applied these to the preachers that Johnson had spoken of at great length, asking Johnson, "Is the testimony that you are giving with regard to these ministers an identically similar situation?"[440]

Johnson answered, "Yes, only with this exception, that there were a number of ministers who actually knew what they were doing." Some were suckers, but others were not. Not all were naïve and innocent. Some of the ministers baited the hooks to catch the suckers. They were fishers of men—communists casting out for men to reel in for the cause.

Congressman Clardy clarified that Bella Dodd had indicated that "the vast majority" were suckers—dupes. There were a few who knew they "were lending themselves to Communist purposes, but most of them did not."

But alas, what of those who knew? Who were they? How many of them? In this chapter, which is focused on Bella Dodd's handiwork, we will explore how many of these clergymen were Roman Catholic. Manning Johnson and Ben Gitlow had flagged Protestant clergy, but what about Catholic priests? Had communists placed a bull's-eye on Catholic seminaries?

The Tantalizing Case of Bella Dodd

That controversial and fascinating question is one which has reemerged with renewed rigor in recent years as the Roman Catholic Church deals with the awful scandals that are the byproduct of unholy, unfaithful men in the priesthood. In her accounts, Bella Dodd said, "Yes," the communists had, in fact, orchestrated a major infiltration of American Catholic seminaries in the 1930s and 1940s.

I have been asked increasingly in recent years about this claim of a major infiltration, to the point where I had no choice but to investigate it myself. The source cited is always Bella Dodd, whose claims from over a half century ago remain raw. Who was she? Could she have been involved in something like this? And could something like this have been pulled off?

We should understand first and foremost that Bella Dodd, who was a dedicated communist activist tasked with organizing educators via teachers' unions, would have been undoubtedly aware of how such things worked. Few professions were sized up by communists quite like the teachers' unions. Dodd desired and flatly pursued the infiltration of the teaching profession with thousands of communists. That being the case, and with such tactics being her expertise, it would not be a surprise if her comrades sought her assistance to try to infiltrate the priesthood as well.

Dodd (1904–69) was born and raised a nice little Catholic girl in New York by her Italian-immigrant parents. Baptized with the beautiful name Maria Assunta Isabella, the innocent child would one day morph into a rabid Marxist. That fundamental transformation took shape in college. Bella initially attended Hunter College. All was fine until the day that Bella and her friend Ruth Goldstein enrolled for courses at Columbia University. This "work at Columbia" would ruin her, at least for a time, as it would so many innocents, such as Thomas Merton and Whittaker Chambers, both of whom became communists there.

There, said Bella in her eye-opening memoir *School of Darkness*, she "discovered the John Dewey Society and the Progressive Education Association" and, of course, the Columbia Teachers College. That college was home to legendary education "progressive" John Dewey, founding father of American public education. Professor Dewey, who was pro-communist, is honorary president for life of the National Education Association. Bella soon realized "what a powerful effect Teachers College would have on American education." She was especially influenced by Dr. George Counts, who, like his pal Dr. Dewey, had made pilgrimage to Moscow to pay homage to the Motherland.[441]

She also thereby discovered what a powerful effect the Communist Party could have, as Bella moved into the education front and joined the party (a natural next step after Columbia). She earned her law degree from NYU (rather than finishing her doctorate at Columbia, where she earned a master's) and became a self-described and highly engaged "card-carrying Communist." In March 1943, she consented to become "an open Party leader" in order to more fully untether and unleash her ideological activities. In no time, those activities inevitably became a major hindrance to her marriage and family life, which was verboten according to her comrades who insisted that she could not be a good communist and have children. "The bourgeois family as a social unit was to be made obsolete," she was instructed. She obeyed. The party pushed her into "industry."

Bella also turned her back on her faith, becoming "anti-clerical."[442] Religion likewise, of course, was absolutely verboten.

After many years of incessant activism, Dodd eventually became very disillusioned. She could only take so much: the lies, the conniving, the evildoing, the harassment and intimidation by party enforcers. In fact, before she could leave the party, her comrades expelled her. She later shared a harrowing moment when one of the leading party honchos, the austere Alexander Trachtenberg, confronted her: "We want to ask you a few questions," said an accusatory Trachtenberg in his thick German accent. "We hear you attacked the Cominform." (The Cominform was the rebranded name for the Comintern after World War II.) It was the usual treatment of Communist Party members held in suspicion. "I've been ill, Comrade Trachtenberg," Bella said in her defense. "I guess I'm all right now."[443]

That was the only reasonable explanation. Only a *sick* person, after all, would doubt the Cominform.

Trachtenberg, for the record, was identified by Whittaker Chambers as the "head of GPU" in the United States—that is, the notorious Soviet military police, a successor to the Cheka.[444] He was a charter member of the American Communist Party and its cultural commissar. He was also the head of International Publishers, which had a monopoly on the publication and distribution of communist and Soviet books and pamphlets. "Trachtenberg once said to me," recalled Dodd in her memoir, "that when communism came to America it would come under the label of 'progressive democracy.' 'It will come,' he added, 'in labels acceptable to the American people.'"[445] These were benign labels like progressive, liberal, and democracy. She repeated this in slightly more detail in a major speech at Fordham University in 1950, where she said that Trachtenberg had told her in New York in 1944: "When we get ready to take the United States, we will not take it under the label of communism; we will not take it under the label of socialism. These labels are unpleasant to the American people, and have been speared too much. We will take the United States under labels we have made very lovable; we will take it under liberalism, under progressivism, under democracy. But take it we will."[446]

Bella was a dutiful comrade on the education front. That was where she thrived in her party work. She became a union leader and organizer. The teachers, said Dodd, "were used on many different fronts" by the Communist Party. This was fundamental, she said, "to establish a Soviet America," the designation used by CPUSA leaders to describe their new Comintern-directed country upon their "victory in America." (Again, William Z. Foster's book was titled *Toward Soviet America*.)[447]

Bella would later greatly regret what she did. As a teacher who was a leader in the union, she was especially concerned about how communists manipulated children through the educational system. "There is no doubt in my mind that the Communists will use the schools and every other educational medium," she told the US Senate. "They will use every educational medium . . . from the nursery school to the universities."

Like Lenin before them, and the cultural Marxists that followed, they saw education as indispensable to inculcating their far-left agenda. "Give me four years to teach the children," asserted Lenin, "and the seed I have sown shall never be uprooted."[448]

Generally, Bella was a hardcore party hack and agitator, overt and covert. More overtly, she was (impressively) an actual editor at *New Masses*, where she served under Whittaker Chambers while he was secretly spying for the Soviet GRU.[449] Covertly, she was involved in so many deceitful and nefarious front operations that it is hard to find sympathy for her even after she repudiated them and repented. She was, for instance, an organizer for the insidious American Peace Mobilization, arguably the most duplicitous front-group ever to exist in America. Bella was an organizer in that scam. She was so visible that she was photoed and featured in the left-wing magazine *PM* on August 1, 1940 in an article titled "These Women Don't Want Their Menfolk Conscripted." There, Bella was featured among one hundred other delegates of the Trade Union Women's Committee for Peace. The caption of the photo says, "Dr. Bella V. Dodd, center, holds batch of petitions asking President Roosevelt to keep America out of war." Posing as an apostle of peace, Bella was following orders from the Kremlin. Such is just one photographic proof, in real-time, of her vigorously assisting a front-group effort that enlisted a substantial number of Protestant ministers and their congregants. In the photo, she feigns a look of sweet innocence, even as she was fronting and lying for Stalin and Molotov.

Bella was a ringleader in that effort. On September 3, 1940, in Chicago, one of the crucial initial meetings in the founding of the American Peace Mobilization, Bella (listed officially in the program guide as representing the American Federation of Teachers) was elected a "permanent officer" of the mobilization. She would remain one of its principle organizers and stalwarts. She also, in keeping with the same brazen about-face of other party stooges to Stalin, instantly flipped and became pro-war the minute that Hitler betrayed Stalin. When the American Peace Mobilization was ordered by the Kremlin and CPUSA to become the American *People's* Mobilization, Bella saluted the red flag of her masters. On a dime, Bella Dodd was ready to grab her gun and urge American women everywhere to conscript their menfolk.[450]

This was just one of innumerable communist schemes that Bella was part of. She was so active that her name appears forty-one times in the index of the important "Appendix IX" report compiled by Congress in 1944. The woman seemed to be involved in every lousy communist front-group or operation under the sun. She was without shame. No wonder she was ultimately so wounded that she fell to her knees one day and came to Fulton Sheen and the Roman Catholic Church for healing.

The Hand of Fulton Sheen

Bella Dodd would not crawl out of the pit of her communist atheism for years. Helping her climb out was Fulton Sheen, who brought her back into full communion with the faith of her youth.[451]

Sheen had not initiated the contact. Bella wrote about the process openly in 1954 in *School of Darkness*. She recalled that it was the fall of 1950 and she had been in Washington testifying. A friend, Congressman Christopher McGrath, who represented her old East Bronx neighborhood, discerned her unease and anxiety and asked if she would like to visit a priest. "You look harassed and disturbed, Bella. Isn't there something I can do for you?" He sensed she was in danger and might need protection. When she refused security, he suggested prayer and a priest: "Bella, would you like to see a priest?"[452]

The years of communist atheism had hardened Bella to that very prospect, but now she felt it was something she could no longer resist. "Yes, I would," she said with an intensity that surprised herself. He responded, "Perhaps we can reach Monsignor Sheen at Catholic University." Working with his secretary, Rose, McGrath arranged for Bella to meet Sheen at the priest's home later that evening.

On her way there, Bella felt the "tiny flame of longing for faith within me." Even then, she felt like looking for an "easy exit" as Sheen walked into the room, "his silver cross gleaming, a warm smile in his eyes." Her reservations vanished. He held out his hand: "Doctor, I'm glad you've come." He observed, "Dr. Dodd, you look unhappy." She said, "Why do you say that?" Sheen replied, "Oh, I suppose, in some way, we priests are like doctors who can diagnose a patient by looking at him."[453]

She began to cry as he put his hand on her shoulder. When the conversation seemed to reach a dead end, Sheen led her gently into a small chapel, where both bowed before a statue of Our Lady, the Ave Maria. Like a little girl again, Maria Assunta Isabella felt a peace, stillness, calm.

When they left the chapel, Sheen gave Dodd a rosary. "I will be going to New York next winter," he told her. "Come to me and I'll give you instructions in the Faith." On her way to the airport, she said she thought about "how much he understood." With an unexpected sense of serenity, she held that rosary tightly all the way to New York.[454]

Christmas approached that 1950, and Bella's longing continued. On Christmas Eve, she found herself alone, wondering, riding a bus, searching, until she came upon a Midnight Mass at St. Francis of Assisi Church on New York's West Side. It was packed. She wedged her way in. She prayed over and over, "God help me. God help me." When Midnight Mass ended, she walked the streets alone for hours, but she felt different; she felt a "warm glow of hope." "I knew I was traveling closer and closer to home," she wrote later, "guided by the Star."[455]

She was on a different walk now. Bella began praying every day and attending daily Mass at Our Lady of Guadalupe on West Seventeenth Street. She met the group of religious men, the Christophers, whose motto is, "It's better to light one candle than to curse the darkness," a school of darkness that Bella was trying to escape by rekindling the light of her Catholic faith. She began reading, including Augustine's *City of God*, and also Aquinas. It was Easter season, 1951, and she got back in touch with Fulton Sheen, visiting him at his offices at the Society for the Propagation of the Faith on East Thirty-Eighth Street. She thus began to receive weekly instruction in the faith from Sheen, taken by his keen logic and reasoning and patient telling of the love of God for man, of man's longing for God, of the words of Christ, and of the founding of Christ's Church. She read long into each night.

By Easter of 1952, with a year of intense instruction, Sheen felt that Bella Dodd was ready. Reasonably certain that she had been baptized as an infant in her little native town in Italy, she received a conditional baptism. On April 7, 1952, the anniversary of her mother's birthday, she was baptized by Sheen in the baptismal font of St. Patrick's Cathedral. Afterward, Sheen heard her first confession and gave her absolution. At Mass the next morning, he gave her Holy Communion.

"It was as if I had been ill for a long time," she would later recount, "and had awakened refreshed after the fever had gone. . . . I seemed to have acquired a new heart and a new conscience. . . . An order and peace of mind returned to my life."[456]

Infiltration of Catholic Seminaries

Amid all of her subsequent reports of what communists had done inside America, the most sensational bombshell that Bella dropped was her reported claim that communists had infiltrated and flooded churches and seminaries, and that she personally helped recruit over 1,000 "communist men" (by some accounts, 1,100, and by others, 1,200) into Catholic seminaries. The provenance of that claim is itself controversial and demands care and nuance.[457]

In her public testimonies, Bella Dodd spoke primarily to the matter of communist infiltration of the teachers' unions and teaching profession. That was her main area of responsibility for the Communist Party. Those details were pervasive throughout her memoir, her testimony before the US Senate, her speeches around the country, and in contemporaneous articles about her and in obituaries at the time of her death.[458] Unfortunately, one cannot find in these same sources companion statements about her work in helping to place communists in seminaries. Nonetheless, she did seem to make such statements, albeit much less frequently—as I will note below. Looking back at the record, I suspect a possible reticence by Bella to speak to this highly sensitive matter, maybe because she was not as directly involved as she was as an education expert for the party working to infiltrate education. I also think she might have been not only embarrassed by the religious infiltration but humiliated and sorrowful in a way that she did not feel concerning the other fields she had worked to penetrate.

An entrance to the official *Congressional Record* at the time of her death by Congressman John Rarick might have alluded to this: "Bella Dodd spent the rest of her life combatting the evil forces working for the destruction of the United States," stated Rep. Rarick. "She testified before Senate and House committees and gave information to the F.B.I. Much of her testimony was given in executive hearings and has never been made public. Some of this testimony was so damning to important figures that even the stenographic notes have disappeared. In open hearings she was warned again and again not to mention names, so careful were the legislators to protect the 'innocent.'"[459]

One wonders to what extent Bella's information on the infiltration of Catholic seminaries might have appeared in those statements. Quite amazingly, Bella Dodd's FBI file has never been released, even as thousands of other provocative and highly sensitive FBI files on major Cold War figures from the Rosenbergs to Whittaker Chambers have been released for many years. For this book, I filed a Freedom of Information Act request for Bella Dodd's FBI file.[460] That FOIA remains submitted without release almost a year after it was submitted. Dodd's file is still classified, over a half century after her death.[461]

That being the case, what are the (public) sources that document Bella Dodd's alleged claims of infiltration of Catholic seminaries?

Many voices in the Catholic world have written of Bella's supposed claim. Unfortunately, their documentation (or lack thereof) is almost always unreliable. It is typically asserted that Bella addressed this issue in her famous Fordham speech and in her riveting (public) congressional testimony. That is inaccurate. So, where and when did she say it?

One of the leading authorities on the subject is Dr. Mary A. Nicholas, a retired MD and expert on Dodd who, among other sources she has probed, has interviewed the legendary Dr. Alice von Hildebrand on this precise question. Widow of the renowned German theologian Dietrich von Hildebrand, Alice, who, as of this writing is ninety-seven years old, knew Dodd personally, going back to their time together at Hunter and Fordham. Dodd herself directly told Alice about these precise efforts. Alice says that Dodd told her that the number of men she recruited was "approximately 1,200."[462] I have exchanged many emails on this subject with Dr. Nicholas over the years, and she has copied me on several emails with Alice von Hildebrand.

No one has dug into Bella's life like Mary Nicholas. She has produced an unpublished biography of Bella, an impressive work of meticulous research that deserves to be published. Mary confirmed to me that she likewise has been unable to find a specific speech transcript in which Bella directly addressed the issue of an infiltration of seminaries or divulged hard data.[463] In her unpublished manuscript, Dr. Nicholas marshals five forms of attestation for Bella's words, which she summed up for me in our email correspondence: 1) Bella's words as recalled and quoted by Alice von Hildebrand; 2) a sworn affidavit from Johnine Leininger, a close friend of Bella who heard her speak of the infiltration; 3) Fulton Sheen's comments about an infiltration (Sheen does not openly name Dodd as his source, though Dodd likely was); 4) testimony from Albert Vassart of France regarding the 1936 order from Joseph Stalin that Sheen would publicly speak of (Dodd did not give a date); and 5) testimony from Manning Johnson.[464]

Among these, as laid out in the previous chapter, Manning Johnson spoke more of infiltration generally among Protestant churches. I dealt with him at length. The other sources, however, have credence regarding the Roman Catholic Church, particularly Vassart, Leininger, and Sheen.

Albert Vassart

As noted earlier, Albert Vassart was a leader in the French Communist Party and its official representative to the Soviet Comintern. He had been summoned to Moscow in April 1934, where he received orders to create a French popular front—*Le Populaire*—between the French Communist Party, the French Socialist Party, and a wider united coalition. His experience is significant, albeit perhaps related mainly to France.

According to the US Senate, Vassart later (after he broke from the French Communist Party) admitted to and spoke of an infiltration of seminaries. This was reported in a major 1960 study on Soviet propaganda done by the Senate Judiciary Committee. "Contrary to what might be expected," the report stated, "churches are also highly infiltrated." Here, the report noted the case of France, citing Albert Vassart specifically, and pointed to seminaries and even to religious orders, naming a specific Moscow edict: "In 1955, a former member of the French Communist Party, Albert Vassart, revealed that in 1936 Moscow had sent out an order to have sure and carefully selected members of the Communist Youth enter seminaries and become priests. Others infiltrated the religious communities, particularly the Dominicans."[465] The report gave no further details, including whether or to what degree this applied to seminaries, priests, and Dominicans in the United States. Of course, the Dominicans are an international group.

Unfortunately, the report gave no further details on where Vassart said this. It did not clarify if this was restricted mainly to France or not. Still, the committee, composed of very serious men, veteran senators such as the likes of Democrats (far and away the majority) Thomas Dodd and James Eastland and Republicans like Everett Dirksen, needs to be taken seriously. And yet, the lack of details is frustrating.

The report added that the infiltration went beyond the Christian religion. It had been especially active, the report claimed, among Buddhists in Asia—Cambodia, Thailand, Burma.[466] It summed up, "Infiltration of all churches is one of the major tasks of the Soviet propaganda apparatus."[467]

The Leininger Affidavit

Much more helpful in affirming Bella Dodd's alleged claims is a crucial affidavit from Johnine Leininger.

The Leininger affidavit was certified by a notary public in Lavaca County, Texas on November 30, 2004 and signed by both Johnine and her husband, Paul. Mary Nicholas owns a copy and shared it with me. I have a PDF. The photocopy is not particularly good (hardly unusual for historical documents), but it is readable.

The affidavit attested that "at a large public meeting in Orange County, California in the 1960's, I was present in an auditorium filled to capacity with 600 to 800 people who had come to hear a former Communist Party official give an expose of the infiltration of the Communist Party into every facet of American life." That official was Dr. Bella Dodd. Leininger gave examples of the penetration that Dodd detailed in various elements of labor, including teachers' unions. Leininger also attested to what Dodd had said about an infiltration of seminaries: "In the late 1920's and 1930's, directives were sent from Moscow to all Communist Party organizations. In order to destroy the Catholic Church from within, party members were to be planted in seminaries and within diocesan organizations. Dr. Dodd said, 'I, MYSELF, PUT SOME 1,200 MEN IN CATHOLIC SEMINARIES.'" Leininger added, "Dr. Dodd also detailed the influence being implemented in the Vatican itself by Cardinals who were members of the Communist Party. She said she knew the truth of her statement because 'I KNOW WHO MY CONTACTS WERE!'"

Leininger said that Dodd shared this information because she had returned to her Catholic faith and was "truly repentant of the damage she had caused," including to "her Church and the American way of life."

Leininger added that both she and her husband often quoted and passed along Dodd's testimony:

> Especially when public scandal and dissent by high Church officials caused irreparable harm to the Body of Christ. This dissent was more open and obvious beginning in the 1960's. Massive infiltration within seminaries and teaching and formation programs appear to be the only explanation. . . . It became

obvious that the Roman Catholic Church had been the victim of a massive Communist/Masonic infiltration. . . . Today we are witnessing the results of a well organized, diabolical plan whose blue print was laid over 70 years ago and patiently implemented. The Communist goal of destroying the American way of life could only be accomplished if her most formidable opposition—the Roman Catholic Church—was infiltrated, compromised and ultimately destroyed.

This November 2004 Leininger affidavit is one of the best eyewitness forms of evidence to what Bella is said to have stated.

Alice von Hildebrand's Witness

Likewise crucial, and to be taken eminently seriously, is the witness of Alice von Hildebrand, who has been vocal about this matter for a very long time, affirming it many times in the many decades since she long ago first met Bella Dodd.

Alice was born in 1923 and has gone on to live a long life. She came to the United States from Belgium in 1940, early in World War II, as the Nazi war machine was gobbling up the continent and her homeland. It was in America that she met Dietrich von Hildebrand, the renowned Catholic scholar and theologian and escapee from Hitler, who was among the first and most prominent theologians to speak out against the Nazi madman. Dietrich was thirty-four years her senior. She met him at Fordham University, where she was a student and he was a professor. They would marry in 1959, after the death of Dietrich's first wife. Dietrich died in 1977. Alice picked up his torch and his legacy, becoming a widely respected Catholic scholar in her own right, frequently appearing in Catholic media, particularly on EWTN television, where she hosted several series and participated in various documentaries.

As of this writing, in 2020, it has been seven decades since Alice was first told by Dodd in the early 1950s about the infiltration of the seminaries. Alice knew Dodd from their time together at Hunter College in New York City, where Alice began teaching after World War II.

As noted, I myself have been privy to emails from Alice (via third party, specifically Mary Nicholas) affirming Bella's statement on the seminaries. Better, Alice has gone on the record on camera in videotaped interviews widely available on the internet. One such statement, procured by Michael Voris in an interview with Alice, was posted by Voris on YouTube on January 29, 2016.[468] There, Alice stated, "The Church has been infiltrated. I repeat these words: *the Church has been infiltrated.*" She said of Bella Dodd, "Bella Dodd gave a talk in Orange, California, in which she declared publicly—I repeat, *publicly*—that in the course of the 20 years of activities for the communists she recruited some 1,100 young men, with neither faith nor morals, that entered seminaries. And they were so superbly trained that it was not that easy to detect them, because in many ways they seemed to be orthodox."

Alice said they spread their "poison." They "spread it out and it worked fantastically."

Alice has repeated this many times, again well into the current century. In a 2001 print interview, she stated, "It is a matter of public record, for instance, that Bella Dodd, the ex-Communist who reconverted to the Church, openly spoke of the Communist Party's deliberate infiltration of agents into the seminaries. She told my husband and me that when she was an active party member, she had dealt with no fewer than four cardinals within the Vatican 'who were working for us.'"[469]

That, too, is obviously alarming. Alice's assessment rises above and beyond American seminaries to the highest echelons of the Church in Rome.

Breaking Down Bella's Numbers

Before considering other assessments, including what Fulton Sheen had to say, we should pause and try to assess whether the planting of 1,100 or 1,200 men in US seminaries by the likes of Bella Dodd seems even feasible.

Could Bella and fellow communists have done this? Actually, such a number was hardly out of bounds given what she was accustomed to as a communist organizer for teachers' unions in New York State from 1936 to 1938. She wrote of their organizing success, "At its peak the Union boasted ten thousand members, and in it the Communist Party had a fraction of close to a thousand. Among them were Moscow-trained teachers and men and women who had attended the sixth World Congress of the Comintern."[470]

Think about these numbers, particularly in light of the possibilities for penetrating the priesthood: If Bella and the reds could manage to help place a thousand communists in the teachers' union in one state, tantamount to 10 percent of all union members, then placing a thousand communists in seminaries nationwide might not seem an overwhelming task. Notably, though the teachers' unions would come under significant attack because of their obvious radicalism, Bella said that by 1941 the communist element remained virtually unshaken, with about one thousand of the four thousand union members still being communists—a striking one-quarter of all union members.[471]

And not surprisingly, these communists, working in cahoots and concealing their ideological sympathies, actually had control of the union. By 1936, said Bella, "the Communists had control."[472]

For the record, a thousand communist teachers was easily doable in New York, which had the largest number of communists of any state—by far. New York was home to the vast majority of American Marxists. It was the headquarters of Communist Party USA and publications such as the *Daily Worker*, the *New Masses*, and others, and it was the home of commie hot-spots such as Columbia University. This was no secret to anyone, least of all to the FBI. As presented in a declassified March 2, 1948 document, directed to D. M. Ladd, assistant director of the FBI, and titled "Redirection of Communist Investigations," there were "approximately 30,000" Communist Party members in the New York City area alone. Remarkably, the document reported that "almost 50% of the Communist Party members in the United States are located in the New York area."[473]

The document further noted that the New York Office of the FBI had accumulated 1,168 Security Index cards on these CPUSA members in New York. That, too, is striking. Americans placed on the federal government's Security Index were deemed (as this FBI document itself stated) "dangerous" or "potentially dangerous"—meaning they were considered as potential collaborators with a foreign power against the United States; in this case, with Stalin's Soviet Union. If a war broke out between the United States and USSR, these people could have been placed under immediate arrest because of their loyalty oath to Stalin's Soviet Union, which they swore upon becoming official Communist Party members.

Another document from this period, a February 21, 1948 FBI letter from J. Edgar Hoover to D. M. Ladd, reported that these thirty thousand New York communists were organized and "controlled" through "1,016 clubs." They were spread out among the four boroughs of New York City.

So, if Bella and comrades wanted to round up a thousand communists to try to infiltrate American seminaries, they need not look far. There were walking all over the pavement in New York City.

How many priests existed nationwide in the late 1930s? In 1936, there were 30,250 Catholic priests in the United States, consisting of 20,836 diocesan clergy and 9,414 priests in religious orders. Importantly, this was the start of an upswing that would eventually reach a peak number of 59,892 priests by 1967.[474]

As for seminarians, in 1936 there were 23,579 students in Catholic seminaries, which likewise would more than double by 1965 (before plunging after Vatican II). According to the *Official Catholic Directory*, in 1965 there were 48,992 seminarians; by 1970, the total plummeted to 28,819.

As noted by Dr. Paul Sullins, a priest and sociologist at the Catholic University of America, "Given an eight-year formation track, then, about 3,000 men would enter seminary each year; about 2/3 would drop out before ordination." Sullins notes that Dodd's claim "is thus plausible by the numbers, especially if she meant 'by 1936' or 'since 1936' or 'around 1936,' not that all 1100 entered seminary in 1936." Sullins also notes that 1936 was an unusually high year for number of seminarians, higher than any year until 1948.[475]

This very large number of seminarians and priests from the 1930s underscores an obvious point for this discussion: As daunting as Bella's 1,100–1,200 figure might initially appear, upon closer inspection it may not seem so impossible, especially for someone who had placed a thousand communist teachers in a teachers' union of only four to eight thousand members. Placing roughly a thousand priests among a mass of over one hundred thousand priests and seminarians surely looked not only doable to Bella but probably a cinch.

That said, whether Bella and her comrades achieved just that is something I cannot confirm with available hard evidence today, so many years down the road. And yet, here is a crucial reality: As we can see in these pages, especially in the material on Browder, Budenz, Gitlow, Johnson, the outstretched hand, the Comintern, CPUSA, and the vigorous activities in 1937 and 1938, the year 1936 indisputably fits the timeline. For the seminaries to have been a focal point of the communist effort to influence Catholics makes perfect sense. And targeting seminaries meant, of course, targeting future priests, the leaders of the flock.

Fulton Sheen on the Infiltration of Seminaries

Someone else who spoke to this effort was a man of highest renown in the American Catholic Church in the twentieth century: Fulton Sheen.

Before sharing Sheen's statement on suspected infiltration, it might be worth emphasizing his reliability. Sheen lived not only a prolific life with his writing and his speaking, particularly on all matters of the Church and studying and dealing with communism, but a holy life as well. His life was so noted for its holiness that the Vatican in 2012 declared him "venerable," meaning that he demonstrated remarkable and unusual holiness and virtue. The cause for the canonization of Fulton Sheen has been in process for years. In 2014, the Vatican's Congregation for the Causes of Saints unanimously approved a miracle attributed to Sheen's intercession.

Thus, we should commend Sheen not only for his media stature but for his honesty, integrity, and reliability.

Fulton Sheen always made headlines. He was a headline. He was the headliner every time he spoke and at every event he attended. But on April 28, 1952, he made headlines for a statement he made not in the United States but in Rome, and specifically on the subject of communist infiltration of the Church.

"Sheen in Rome Says Red Agents Tried to Infiltrate the Priesthood," reported the front page of the *New York Times* that April 28, running a piece reported by the Associated Press. The article was not long, but it certainly grabbed readers' attention:

> Rome, April 27—American Communists were under secret orders in 1936 to infiltrate the Roman Catholic priesthood, Bishop Fulton J. Sheen said today.
>
> The 57-year-old Auxiliary Bishop of New York, speaking before an overflowing congregation in the American Catholic Church of Santa Susanna, said:

"In 1936 the [Communist] wolves went into the forces which control public opinion. There was hardly a prominent newspaper commentator who did not have a Communist secretary, although he or she did not necessarily know it.

"This was the beginning of the planting of forces of evil communism within the religious communities to destroy them from within. A call for volunteers to enter religious orders and make the great sacrifices of the life of a seminarian was made at a secret Red meeting in a large [American] city."

The year that Sheen gave accords perfectly with the year that Albert Vassart had given.

How to interpret this? Where was Sheen getting his information?

As an obvious starting point, one is apt to think he heard it from Bella Dodd. The dates of the Sheen-Dodd timeline are conspicuously congruent with Sheen's statement. Sheen made this statement in Rome on April 27, 1952. He had just received Bella Dodd into the Church three weeks earlier. He heard her first confession on April 7, 1952, after a year of giving her instruction in the faith.

It would seem certain that Sheen must have heard this from Bella Dodd during that time. Maybe he heard it from her in the confessional, or privately from her outside the confessional. Moreover, note the date and place that Sheen gives: "secret orders in 1936" and a "large [American] city." That was precisely when Bella was organizing and inserting a thousand communist teachers into teachers' unions in New York City. In fact, Bella was tasked with organizing the teachers' contingent that marched in New York's huge May Day parade that year, where she commandeered a mass of five hundred marching teachers who were secretly communists.[476]

The year 1936 was a busy one for Bella, as she was also ordered by the party to organize committees of striking seamen against ship owners. Thus, she was organizing not only teachers and seamen, but also doing trade union work for the old A.F. of L. She had her hand in more than merely the teachers' front.[477] Bella also pointed to a "prodigious effort" made by Moscow in 1936 to marshal communists worldwide to Spain to fight for the communists in the Spanish Civil War.[478]

If Bella was not Fulton Sheen's source, maybe the Vatican was. Note the place: Rome. Perhaps Sheen learned of such orders given from Moscow while he was in Rome in late April 1952. He regularly met with the pope himself while in Rome, as he had been doing since the 1930s. He could have easily learned something from Pius XII or Vatican staff in 1952, or perhaps even earlier from Pius XI in the 1930s. Both popes had always encouraged Sheen in his research and exposés of communism. "Pius XI had told him to study Karl Marx and communism," wrote Sheen biographer Thomas Reeves, "and never to speak in public during his pontificate without exposing their fallacies. Fulton took the charge to heart and began an intensive study of Marxist literature."[479] Pius XI was pope from 1922–1939, and his close aide, Cardinal Eugenio Pacelli, the Vatican secretary of state, became Pius XII in 1939, holding the chair of St. Peter until 1958.

Unfortunately, the *New York Times* article offers no further details, and neither do key Sheen books and pamphlets on communism, such as his *Communism and the Conscience of the West*, *The Tactics of Communism*, *Communism and Religion*, and *The Church, Communism and Democracy*. Sheen's 1937 book, *Communism Answers Questions of a Communist*, which had responded to Louis Budenz and the outstretched hand offer, gave no indication of Sheen contemporaneously knowing about a 1936 edict by the Kremlin to penetrate American seminaries. One can fairly assume that Sheen most likely heard of that charge from Bella Dodd; the timeline fits.

The only other possible insight into the infiltration issue provided in the article is the next-to-last paragraph, which stated, "Although he did not mention him by name, Bishop Sheen strongly indicated in his sermon that the case of Alighiero Tondi, 44, Italian Jesuit priest who has just 'embraced the Communist idea,' parallels American Communist infiltration. Communist propagandists have been stressing the defection of Tondi strongly."[480]

Alighiero Tondi, a Jesuit who became a communist and left the order after sixteen years, was a case well-known in Italy, but not in the United States, and which history (at least in the English world) has forgotten about. He seems to have been a mole for the Kremlin inside the Vatican, though whether he began that way as an atheistic, pro-communist plant and infiltrator is something I do not know. He turned on the Vatican, yes, and sided with and supplied Moscow.

So, could Sheen have learned from the Vatican in late April 1952 about a secret order from Moscow issued in 1936? Sure. But it also seems likely (if not more likely) that he learned about it from Bella Dodd in early April 1952. It also could be that he learned about it first from Bella earlier that month and then followed up and learned still more from the Vatican later in the month.

In my estimate, the totality of what exists on and off the record suggests this was information that Sheen might well have learned privately from Bella, and not for public attribution. That would also explain why the priest never publicly divulged his source for the information.

Solanus Casey on the Threat to Seminaries

Finally, one truly venerable American Catholic who offered a partial testimony to at least knowing of some such activity was Blessed Solanus Casey, another popular and holy twentieth-century priest.

Casey, 1870–1957, was the first man born in the United States to be declared "venerable" by the Roman Catholic Church. He was a gentle soul widely hailed for kindness, holiness, and virtue. Many gifts and even reported cases of miraculous healings were credited to his intercession and literal touch. The Capuchin-Franciscan friar was born to Irish-Catholic parents who raised him in Minnesota.

He would spend long stints in novitiates, churches, and monasteries in Wisconsin, Michigan (Detroit), New York (Yonkers, Manhattan, Brooklyn), and Indiana (Huntington). He died on July 31, 1957. On July 11, 1995, Pope John Paul II declared him venerable, noting the "proven evidence" of the theological and cardinal virtues "exercised to a heroic degree by the Servant of God, Francis Solanus Casey, a professed priest of the Order of Friars Minor Capuchin."[481]

The biographer of Casey is Michael H. Crosby, OFM Cap., who was appointed by the Vatican as the official "External Collaborator to the Relator" for his cause for canonization. In his biography of Casey, Crosby, no big fan of vocal American anti-communists, shares a 1955 letter from Casey on the subject of communist infiltration into the Church. Crosby prefaced the letter by seeming to equate the anti-communism of the 1950s with hysterical anti-communism, or at least with discredited "McCarthyism." "Solanus's support of the anticommunism of [Father] Charles Coughlin in the thirties shifted easily to McCarthy," wrote Crosby. "McCarthy found communists in movie studios, the halls of Congress, and all sorts of places in between."[482]

Of course, there actually were communists in the movie studios— every single member of the Hollywood Ten was a formal member of Communist Party USA, which they joined in the Stalin area[483]—and in the halls of Congress, the White House, the State Department, the Labor Department, the Commerce Department, the Department of Agriculture, and all sorts of places in between. Crosby, however, dismisses these established facts as "paranoia." "Given such para-noia around the omnipresence of communists," he writes, "Solanus's natural naivete and gullibility could be exploited with stories about communists penetrating the ranks of the church as well."

Quite the contrary, Crosby is naïve as to the very real threat posed by communism and the extent of its successful infiltration in numer-ous areas of American life. I mention this not to be hard on Crosby, for whom the subject of domestic communism is not his field or area of expertise, but rather because his skepticism lends credence to him being willing to present a letter from Solanus Casey—whom he rightly admired in this hagiographical work—on the threat of communism in that period. He clearly does not share Casey's concerns, yet is honest enough to present the letter as written.

As for the letter itself, it was written on January 15, 1955, to a Dominican sister in Grand Rapids, Michigan, listed as "Sister M. Bernice." Solanus Casey wrote clearly and unequivocally:

> There is such a thing as "red communism" stealing into convents and monasteries. Very clever young men have been known to offer themselves as candidates for the Order who have turned out after months, sometimes after years, to have been nothing more than secret promoters of unrest and red communism. Such candidates, I have heard of and in one case at least have known to show themselves very clever and experienced and naturally older than real promising candidates. They are in their late 20's or even middle 30's and, of course, are not fervent at all, even though they keep the rule fairly to the letter.
>
> Of course, to suspect anyone deliberately without a conscience [sic] observance and prayer, is a rather dangerous course. Nevertheless, self-preservation and "charity begins at home" where right order and charity always must begin. Superiors especially are expected to be on the alert concerning any subject who persists in refusing to speak to, or associate with any other member of the religious family.[484]

This is a compelling testimony by a holy man of God. A cynic might want to shrug off Casey's suspicions of communists "stealing into convents and monasteries" as having perhaps been gleaned from Fulton Sheen's published claims, or those of Bella Dodd, or even (as Crosby suggests) from a naïve gullibility influenced by the likes of Coughlin and McCarthy. Such an interpretation, however, would be a failure to read Casey's words carefully. Note that Casey, while not expressing knowledge of a vast infiltration by hundreds or thousands throughout Catholic seminaries, personally had knowledge of "such a thing" as "very clever young men" who had offered themselves as candidates within his particular Capuchin Order. He had "heard of" "such candidates" (plural) and "in one case" knew of such a candidate. He even described what they were like: very clever, experienced, older (late twenties or middle thirties), and "not fervent at all, even though they keep the rule fairly to the letter." He shared specific detail of what he had heard or seen.

Obviously, Casey's testimony to Church infiltration is limited to what he saw and personally witnessed within his own community. That is true for any direct witness of anything. Nonetheless, it is the testimony of a highly honorable and demonstrably holy man of integrity. One can only wonder how many forgotten biographies, memoirs, diaries, and letters mentioning communist infiltration exist from that era.

Of course, our fears of what might have happened to American seminaries are nothing compared to what actually happened to seminaries behind the Iron Curtain.

CHAPTER 12

"THEY KEPT A TAB"

SEMINARIES, CHURCHES, AND CLERGY
BEHIND THE IRON CURTAIN

Roman Catholic Church aside, there is no question that communists sought to penetrate various Protestant denominations and inter-church organizations, especially groups like the National Council of Churches and the World Council of Churches. As noted earlier, J. B. Matthews in April 1962 produced his report "A Compilation of Public Records of 658 Clergymen and Laymen connected with the National Council of Churches." A powerful leftist-activist group of "social justice" Protestant ministers in America, the NCC was notorious for echoing the Moscow-CPUSA line.[485]

Bella Dodd was asked pointedly about the NCC and kindred spirits in one of her many public speeches. During the Q&A session after an hour-and-a-half long talk, an audience member inquired, "Are there communists in the clergy in the National Council of Churches?" Dodd replied generally, "As a member of the Communist Party I did know of the fact that the Party subsidized hundreds of young men to go into ministry. They went into the more liberal churches."[486]

Here Bella meant particularly the mainline Protestant churches, and she was speaking to the United States. And yet, the United States was a mere microcosm of an aggressive global effort by Marxists.

Well beyond attempts to penetrate seminaries, churches, and

influence clergy in the United States, it is crucial to understand that communists did that and much more behind the Iron Curtain—in countries throughout Eastern Europe and certainly within the USSR. An extensive analysis of those efforts would require a separate book. In fact, others have written such books.

Here, I will make brief note of just some of that information, in part to further underscore the point that what Marxists had achieved in the Communist Bloc emboldened them to try the same in the United States. To be sure, they would never match in America that same level of insidious success. Nevertheless, they were inspired by their victories inside the Soviet empire. And what they did is yet another example of how the ideology of Karl Marx went beyond merely hating religion; it inspired its adherents to slither into the very houses of worship where the religious sought safety, security, comfort. Communists' sheer contempt for religion came to mean that they could not keep their covetous hands off it. They wanted to not only denounce it in their writings but to eliminate it from the face of the earth.

Spying Against God

To fully survey the array of communist activities inside churches on the other side of the Berlin Wall is unnecessary. I will call attention to a few recent works by other writers and some examples of my own.

As this book neared completion, Elisabeth Braw published *God's Spies: The Stasi's Cold War Espionage Operation Inside the Church*.[487] She concentrated on the former East Germany, stronghold of the infamous secret police, the Stasi (the Ministry for State Security). Braw shows the disturbing lengths taken to control churches in East Germany, the area that had been home to Martin Luther. The Lutheran Church was far and away the dominant church across East German territory. The Stasi made its inroads there.[488]

Braw's book highlights four specific "pastor agents" and the recruiting work of a Stasi official named Joachim Wiegand (still living and interviewed by Braw), who headed up the Stasi's so-called "Church Department," formally known as Department XX/4. These pastor agents, states Braw, were "very active," engaging in regular clandestine meetings with Stasi contacts and "extensive cooperation over many years," agreeing to "spy on their fellow human beings," including their own congregants. They had varying motivations. Some did it for the money—a "depressingly" small sum, notes Braw. Others cooperated because they felt they were helping causes like "peace" by curtailing "anti-militarism" in post-war Germany. Regardless, notes Braw, these pastors "betrayed and sold out their friends and acquaintances."[489]

How many pastors were in the pocket of the Stasi? Exact numbers are hard to pin down, given that the scrupulous East German secret police meticulously shredded stacks of incriminating records the moment the Berlin Wall fell. Braw estimates that of roughly 180,000 everyday East Germans who served the Stasi as collaborators or agents of some sort, "it's safe to say that there were several hundred over the years" who were pastors. This also meant, she adds, that the Stasi "really kept a close eye" on seminaries, from which it "very cunningly" recruited students and professors.[490]

Another historian who has given special attention to the Stasi and declassified material from East Germany is John Koehler, the former AP reporter who wrote *Spies in the Vatican: The Soviet Union's Cold War Against the Catholic Church.*[491] Koehler, who looked more closely into the Catholic Church than did Braw, examined how priests and possibly even bishops and cardinals were coopted. Koehler includes chapters with names like "Spies Penetrate the Papal Sanctum" and "A Potpourri of Spies."

Koehler's best material likewise dug into Stasi Department XX/4, which was also tasked with surveillance of the Catholic Church in East Germany, and the role of the infamous Markus Wolf and his HVA (*Hauptverwaltung Aufklaerung*), which was second only to the

KGB as the Communist Bloc's most formidable espionage service. Wolf was one of the leading spymasters of the Cold War.[492] Koehler offers groundbreaking research on cases such as the controversial German Monsignor Paul Dissemond, long justifiably suspected as having been an unofficial collaborator and Stasi informer, though he would always plead innocence.[493]

Outside of East Germany, Koehler flagged the sinister role of the Soviet KGB under the odious Yuri Andropov, who would one day give the green light to the Kremlin's single most audacious act: its attempt to assassinate Pope John Paul II smack in the middle of St. Peter's Square on May 13, 1981, the Feast Day of Our Lady of Fatima, tapping the Bulgarians and Turk Mehmet Ali Agca as co-conspirators and hitmen.[494] Well before that notorious act, Andropov was maneuvering against churches. Though he headed the KGB at the time of the crime against the pope, the assassination attempt was merely his prized crowning touch to a longer campaign attempting to assassinate Christianity entirely. He ran the KGB from 1967 to 1982, its longest-serving head, even surpassing its founder Felix Dzershinsky and the henchman Lavrenti Beria. Back further still, Andropov played a suitably dastardly role in the deaths of thousands of Hungarians in the Red Army invasion of October–November 1956—adequate training to assume the helm at Lubyanka.

When Andropov took the reins at KGB headquarters, he ordered a systematic reorganization of its directorates and duties. This included an upswing in surveillance activities and control of religious groups. That responsibility became the duty of a newly created Fifth Directorate. Among the religious entities of utmost special interest to Andropov was the Vatican. In 1969, he ordered an intensification of espionage operations against the Holy See. Such was John Koehler's central focus in *Spies in the Vatican*. "Besides the prime target, the pope, he [Andropov] was particularly interested in the activities of Archbishop Agostino Casaroli," wrote Koehler of Cardinal Casaroli, who become the Vatican's principal Kremlin accommodationist, managing the Holy See's policy of *Ostpolitik*, which warmly embraced Eastern Europe's communist despots. He was the face and heart of Pope Paul VI's strategy to get along with communists in the hope they would like the Vatican and lessen their persecution of the faithful.[495]

How comprehensive was Andropov's order to expand espionage operations against the Holy See? Koehler stated, "Eventually, every department of the Church had been infiltrated."[496]

That success by Andropov and the KGB came at the expense of Pope Paul VI and Cardinal Casaroli, whose olive branch to Moscow was chewed up and spit back in the Vatican's face.

Targeting John Paul II

There were countless incidents like this orchestrated by the Kremlin in Eastern Europe during the Cold War, profoundly troubling efforts to sully some of the most redeeming and triumphant moments of the Church in its battle against Soviet communism. Consider, for instance, John Paul II's glorious return to his Polish homeland from June 2 through June 11, 1979, which has rightly been called "nine days that changed the world."

The world watched every step of that visit as the pope told his countrymen to "Be not afraid." He began with an opening homily in Warsaw's Victory Square on June 2, where he boldly declared, "There can be no just Europe without the independence of Poland marked on its map." The Kremlin was apoplectic, and Poles were ecstatic, chanting, "We want God! We want God!"

This was a game-changer in the Cold War confrontation, inspiring the likes of Ronald Reagan, watching news coverage of the epic papal visit on his television in his home in California, to assert, "That's it, that's it, that's it! The pope is the key, the pope is the key, the pope is the key!" He turned to his top aide Richard V. Allen and said, "Dick, we need to find a way to get elected and reach out to this Polish pope and the Vatican and make them an ally."[497] Reagan, not yet elected president, knew that this new pope one day could help him take down Soviet communism. The Soviets knew, too, just what a mortal threat this Polish pope was to their empire. Only a few months later, on November 13, 1979, the Soviet Central Committee met in Moscow and issued a chilling edict to do whatever was within the realm of their panoply of deadly possibilities to stop this menace sitting in the Chair of St. Peter.

It was there, at that moment, on that dreary day in Moscow, that John Koehler and others believe that Moscow had laid out "an order for assassination," formally determining to "get physically close" to the pope (and not to kiss his ring). SISDE (the *Servicio per le Informazioni a la Sicurezza Democratica*), the security service for the Italian government, concluded that the nine members of the Soviet Central Committee that day had thereby resolved a plan for the "physical elimination" of John Paul II.[498]

Some will debate those specifics.[499] But what is not debatable is that that edict was indisputable affirmation that the pope's dramatic return to Poland had so alarmed the Soviets that they felt John Paul II had to be stopped by whatever means possible, beyond (the edict concluded) typical Kremlin means of "disinformation and discreditation." Communist officials were already tracking his every move. They watched his pilgrimage to Poland every step of the way. They launched a massive damage-control operation code-named LATA '79 (meaning SUMMER '79). This included 480 Polish SB agents (the SB was the Polish secret police) who monitored Karol Wojtyla's moves and tried to generate whatever problems they could. The devious operation included seven moles that infiltrated the pontiff's orbit, one of them a clergyman acting in the spirit not of Jesus but of Judas. Yet more clergy from outside Poland, such as the German Benedictine Eugen Brammertz, were reportedly part of the effort. The accused Benedictine betrayer allegedly worked with the Stasi, which established a special working group to foul up the papal pilgrimage.[500]

For communists, this was standard operating procedure. While tens of millions of Poles readied to be inspired, thousands of communist operatives readied themselves for their usual deviltry.

The Soviets worked arduously with their stooges in the Polish communist regime to line up Polish clergy willing to betray their native son and shepherd. Father Konrad Hejmo was one of those alleged to have been an informer. He would remain so close to the papal entourage that he was placed in charge of Polish pilgrims visiting Rome. Hejmo has denied this charge, but no less than Cardinal Glemp, who was hardly a reckless anti-communist, firmly said of Hejmo: "Certainly he was a spy. The documents and papers that were made public last year prove it." Glemp was referring to documents released in 2005 by the Polish National Remembrance Institute.[501]

There remains endless suspicion to this day regarding certain clergy that might have spied on or betrayed St. John Paul II throughout his historic papacy and even back home in his beloved homeland. Authors such as myself in my book *A Pope and a President* and George Weigel, biographer of John Paul II, have written about these suspicions. It is a sad saga of treachery.

A Hundred Communist Students?

There are still more shocking accounts of backstabbing and infiltration and deception that could be cited from other books, albeit with varying levels of reliability. Two particularly controversial books made remarkable claims, though of dubious authenticity. I will mention them only briefly. To neglect them would make them conspicuous by their absence.

Many readers of this chapter will expect a reference to the 1972 book *AA-1025: The Memoirs of an Anti-Apostle* by a French Catholic nurse named Marie Carré, who claimed to have come upon a mysterious diary (thus the word "memoirs") found in the possession of a priest brought to the hospital after a fatal car crash in the 1960s.

The priest was alive when he arrived but died a few hours later. He was, purportedly, a communist who had secretly entered the Catholic priesthood to help destroy the Church from within, as his cryptic diary is said to say. First published in French, it was soon translated into English in 1973 and has been reprinted several times.[502] I have attempted to read the book but find it confusing and frustrating and cannot confirm its legitimacy. Still, the book is known within certain circles, and what it postulates certainly seems feasible and could have happened. But again, I cannot affirm its assertions.

Similarly, a likewise enigmatic book read by many and dismissed by many (and seems less apocryphal than *AA-1025*) is the sensational Italian bestseller *Via col vento in Vaticano*, published in English as *Shroud of Secrecy: The Story of Corruption Within the Vatican*.

Published in Italy in 1999, *Shroud of Secrecy* was composed by a small group of anonymous Vatican prelates who called themselves "the Millenari." The authors are listed on the cover as just that, "the Millenari." The book was an alarming exposé of corruption, fraud, abuse, immorality, graft, and still more scandals in the Vatican. It flagged sabotage from within by conspirators ranging from freemasons to communists. It became a runaway bestseller, and the Vatican hierarchy moved swiftly to cease its publication and distribution and to identify its authors. This merely accelerated the demand for copies, which soon exceeded over one hundred thousand in sales.[503]

The one author who bravely came forward and acknowledged his role was Monsignor Luigi Marinelli, who, in turn, was ordered to appear before the court of the Holy See, the Sacra Romana Rota. He refused, daring the Vatican to instead pursue him in secular courts. He would eventually leave Rome altogether, escaping the pressures there.

Chapter 17 of *Shroud of Secrecy* is titled "Communism in the Vatican." Befitting the book's style and penchant for anonymity, it is vague, sparse, not footnoted, and does not sufficiently provide enough names or extended details. It does, however, quote an intriguing incident related by Don Pasquale Uva, founder of the House of Divine Providence in Bisceglie, Italy (located in southern Italy on the Adriatic Sea). Father Uva in 1956 had invited into his fraternity a new aspiring priest from the Basilicata, a young man named "Sanomonte" (no other name provided in the book). Sanomonte was an infiltrator for the Communist Party, pilfering documents for the local Communist Party offices, until he made a mistake by unintentionally handing material to a local Christian Democrat who he confused for a comrade. Sanomonte was sent home, the police were informed, and Fr. Uva, the rector of the house, reported the incident to the appropriate ministry in Rome, which reprimanded Uva for not acting more quickly.[504]

The case of Sanomonte is offered by the Millenari as an almost casual example of the stark claim they provide at the beginning of the chapter: "In 1935, the [Italian] secret service indicated that, during those years [or year], approximately 100 Communist students had infiltrated the seminaries and novitiates of Western Europe where, feigning a true religious vocation, they prepared to become priests. Once ordained, the party intended to place them in the most important and sensitive positions in their respective national churches."[505]

That assertion by the Millenari fits the timeline of this book and the information provided to the US Congress and other investigative authorities and sources. It is surely accurate at least in terms of broad intention, perhaps off only when it comes to the exact number of communist students estimated.

According to the Millenari, this would have a multiplier effect in the seminaries: "During the sixties and seventies [1960s and 1970s], the phenomenon became so serious that there were conflicts and protests over the many Communist priests in the seminaries and novitiates." The Millenari gave the quiet example of Fr. Uva and Sanomonte as well as higher-profile examples like Cardinal Mindszenty's mistreatment by the *Ostpolitikers* Cardinal Casaroli and Pope Paul VI. The Millenari rightly referred to Mindszenty as one of "many martyrs of this policy" of *Ostpolitik*.[506]

The Millenari concluded that the likes of Lenin, Stalin, and others of their ilk came to realize that the key to doing the most damage to the Church was to corrupt it from within.[507]

Russian Orthodox Seminaries

Above all, the communists wreaked their worst havoc inside the predominant church in their own backyard. That brings us to the elephant in the Bolshevik living room: the Russian Orthodox Church.

The Russian Orthodox Church was penetrated, manipulated, and in many aspects controlled by the Soviet government. Readers familiar with that history will immediately nod in agreement.

Within the initial years and decades of the Bolshevik takeover, the Russian Orthodox Church was brutalized by the Marxist thugs unleashed by Lenin and Trotsky and Stalin. The stories are too many and too sad. The persecution by these devils became so overwhelming that the Russian Orthodox Church succumbed to a lamentably high degree of control by the communist regime as a tragic calculated tactic for survival. That submission merely enabled the manipulation to run still deeper.

"The alternative to collaboration could very well have meant complete liquidation of the [Russian Orthodox] Church's hierarchy and organization," wrote the *New York Times*' Vatican correspondent, Camille Cianfarra. "There were other grave reasons, in addition to the necessity of avoiding extinction, which counselled a policy of collaboration with the Government." Most remarkable among these, and totally forgotten in the West today, is that the Russian Orthodox Church surrendered to become a tool of the Soviet government (to quote Cianfarra) "in order to unite all Christians and make Moscow the Rome of the Twentieth Century."[508]

Both the Bolshevik leadership and Russian Orthodox Church leadership alike wanted to contest Rome's leadership as the primary head of the world's Christians. Cianfarra put it this way:

> Tactically, the Soviet Union embarked on two simultaneous drives. It favored every initiative of the Russian Orthodox Church to establish its authority and influence over all the other national Eastern Churches, and carried out religious persecutions designed to break the hierarchical organizations of the Catholic Church. Both offensives had as their immediate aim to detach the Catholic episcopate and clergy from Rome and establish "national" Catholic Churches which would no longer recognize the Pope as their supreme religious authority. The overall goal was that of placing the Catholic Church under State control, as the Kremlin had so successfully done with the Russian Orthodox Church, the penultimate step towards fully accomplishing Lenin's ultimate objective of utterly destroying all religions and securing the triumph of atheistic materialism.
>
> This strategy had the advantage of furthering the advent of communism in countries outside the Soviet Union and of aiding Soviet plans for political hegemony in Europe. The Orthodox Church was to be used as a magnet to unite all Christians in Russia and within the Russian sphere of influence and thus build a strong Moscow-dominated Orthodox front to oppose the Catholic Church under the authority of Rome.[509]

Of course, Pope Pius XII fought this tooth and nail, which is why Stalin and the Kremlin would smear him as "Hitler's Pope."[510] And as for the Russian Orthodox Church, it capitulated, albeit never easily or comfortably, but enough. The Kremlin would allow the Russian Orthodox Church to continue to exist so long as it could be wielded as a cudgel against the Roman Catholic Church.

The Bolshevik leadership went so far as to provide air transport and subsidize trips by Patriarch Alexej when he was willing to be employed as a mouthpiece for Stalin at various ecumenical councils outside the USSR. When Alexej visited Palestine, Syria, and Egypt in May 1945, he made the following statement at a reception given in his honor by the Metropolitan of Beirut: "May God make ever stronger the ties which bind our peoples. I am moved by your esteem for our Red Army and our beloved leader, Joseph Stalin, who succors all those in need."[511]

The patriarch was succoring Stalin, the bad boy who buttered his bread, and he was bowing to the communist-atheist Red Army, so long as it did not drop the guillotine on his Church.

This was what the "Bolshevization" of the Russian Orthodox Church looked like, even as the flock and so many ministers toiled to not genuflect to the unholy church of Marxism-Leninism. It was a tough line to toe and a tricky course to navigate for these churches throughout the Soviet Bloc. In countries like Romania and Bulgaria, beholden to regimes placed under the jackboot of Moscow, the episcopate of the respective national Orthodox Churches likewise was forced to follow the shameful example of many of their Russian brothers.[512]

As for Rome, it did not bend one bit. When in Romania the liberal priest Andrea Agotha convened a "Congress" of some forty Catholic clergy in the town of Targu Mures on April 27, 1950 to discuss creating a "democratic" (pro-Communist Party) Church, Pope Pius XII immediately excommunicated them once he received the news in Rome.[513]

Here were yet more reasons for the Kremlin to scream, "Hitler's Pope!"

So be it, the Roman Catholic Church would fight infiltration. Pius XII was in Rome, not in Moscow. Of course, not that Rome was a picnic in those days of Benito Mussolini. During the dark days of World War II, including when Mussolini was finished but the Nazis were still encamped, the pontiff had already been the effective ruler of Rome. He would not leave, even if the enemies were inside the gates.

"This is where Christ told Peter the Church should be built," Pius XII affirmed. "And here is where the Pope will remain."[514]

The KGB "Kept a Tab on Every Student in the Seminary"

The reality of Bolshevik control of the Russian Orthodox Church is unsurprising. This was the Soviet Union, after all—an unrestrained totalitarian dictatorship and police state where religion was brutally repressed. What wasn't banned was controlled. What was permitted was exploited. This was true of Russian Orthodox Church seminaries. One such eyewitness testimony, heretofore unpublished, is the account of Vladimir Rusak.[515]

Rusak was born in 1949 in Baranovichi, Belorussia. He entered seminary—namely, Zagorsk Theological Academy—as a young man in his early twenties, in 1972.

Vladimir had already been accustomed to a life of religious harassment by the government. When he was in high school and middle school, he and other religious kids ventured to go to church if there was a religious holiday during the week. He remembers the school principal standing at the church entrance warning and trying to bar them from attending the religious service. "He would try to stop us from getting through with his own body and his hands spread open so we wouldn't be able to go to church," says Vladimir. "So that was absolutely clear: you're not allowed to worship God." He recalled that religious items and articles, such as wearing a crucifix to school, were strictly forbidden. They "got their crosses ripped off, which was a normal action of things if you wore a cross to school. You were not allowed to wear it."

Thus, Vladimir knew that taking the especially audacious step of attending seminary would make him an even greater affront to communist principals in the USSR. He learned that right away.

Asked about the degree to which seminaries in the Soviet Union were controlled by the government, Vladimir answered, "Of course, the KGB was trying to control all the students, they kept a tab on every student in the seminary. And sometimes they would be interrogated on a face-to-face basis." The KGB inquisition usually began by asking students, "Well, you are a patriot of your country, why are you here?" The implication was that these men either served the Soviet state or they served God; they could not do both. He said, "They wanted to hear that the country, the Motherland, came first and God second."

Starting from that basis, the KGB controllers then went to a higher level of personal intrusion into the space of the seminarian and his brothers: "And then they start chipping away on a more serious basis. 'What if you hear something or see something that's not really *Soviet*? Will you tell us about it?' Many students would say, 'Absolutely not, I'm not going to rat anyone out, because that means somebody else's life would be in danger.' . . . And then the next stage of that conversation, they'd slowly try to involve the students into working with the KGB as an agent, an undercover agent."

Vladimir did not know which fellow seminarians he could trust. He was unaware which were directly working for the KGB, "but they had enough informants to really keep them supplying [the KGB] with all kinds of information." He knew of two occasions where fellow students were actually "dismissed and discharged" from the seminary for "uncorrect political views."

The penetration was thorough. Asked if he and other seminarians feared the presence of electronic listening devices, Vladimir responded briefly and assuredly, "Sure." No doubt this also included monitoring phone conversations and intercepting and reading mail. Hence, he was always "very careful" what he did.

Naturally, the KGB learned through this process which seminarians might then be counted upon as future informers and servants to the Soviet government as they rose through the ranks. Conversely, they also learned which seminarians were "obstinate" and would need ongoing surveillance throughout their careers. They would continue to be watched ever more carefully once they moved into positions of influence among the flock in their churches or elsewhere. That included Vladimir, who had been pegged as among the devout and stubborn.

Vladimir graduated from the Zagorsk Theological Academy in 1977. He was then employed in the publishing department of the Moscow Patriarchate. There, he dangerously gathered a unique collection of documents on church-state relations in Russia after 1917—not a rosy portrait. He attempted to write a history of the Russian Orthodox Church under Soviet rule—again, not a pretty picture. The regime was not happy with his manuscripts. Part of his work was smuggled out and published in the West. The other part was confiscated by the KGB. To this day, he does not know where it is.

Vladimir was arrested in April 1986, despite the introduction of Mikhail Gorbachev's widely touted *glasnost*, promising religious freedom. He was sentenced to seven years in Soviet prison camps (i.e., the Gulag). He was released early, in 1988, as a sign indeed of better times as *glasnost* did begin bearing fruit. After the Berlin Wall fell and the USSR ultimately collapsed, Vladimir came to the United States.

The case of Vladimir Rusak is one of thousands that could be told. The persecution he faced was standard operating procedure for religious persons in the USSR. To attend seminary in the Soviet Union, within the Russian Orthodox Church, was to live under the continuous gaze of KGB surveillance.

Infiltration and "Hatred of the Faith" in Romania

As a final example from the communist world, a coda to bring this up to date, Pope Francis on June 2, 2019 traveled to Blaj, Romania, to beatify seven communist-era bishops of the Eastern Rite Catholic Church who perished from harsh treatment, including in confinement in prison, which, as the Rev. Richard Wurmbrand always emphasized—and which the horrific Pitesti Prison grimly showcased—in Romania, meant torture.

These new blesseds—Valeriu Traian Frentiu, Vasile Aftenie, Ioan Suciu, Tito Livio Chinezu, Ioan Balan, Alexandru Rusu, and Iuliu Hossu—were, as Francis put it, killed "in hatred of the faith" between 1950 and 1970. The Catholic community in Romania during this period had been "put to a harsh test by a dictatorial and atheistic regime. . . . All the Bishops and faithful of the Greek-Catholic Church and those of the Latin rite Catholic Church were persecuted and imprisoned."[516]

The Romanian communist government, brutal from the late 1940s until the communist collapse there on Christmas Day 1989, when dictator Nicolai Ceausescu was executed, tried to force members of the Eastern Rite Catholic Church into the Orthodox Church, because the Communist Party (there as in Moscow) had the Orthodox Church influenced if not subdued. *Reuters* reported on the Francis visit, "After World War Two, Romania's Communist authorities confiscated properties of the Eastern Rite Catholic Church and ordered its members to join the majority Orthodox Church, which was easier for the party to control."[517]

This is yet another example, of so many that could be cited, of how communists captured and often outright controlled certain churches—in this case, again, the Orthodox Church.

"The Smoke of Satan"

The devil seemed to have a field day strutting through numerous pews and seminaries and clouding the minds of many ministers in the twentieth century, with ripple effects still reverberating through their churches to this day.

"The smoke of Satan has entered the Church," said Pope Paul VI in June 1972, forebodingly, in a reference to the devil's influence at myriad levels. He was referring not necessarily to the infiltration of spies at the Vatican, though his words in retrospect seem apt, particularly regarding any smoke emanating from fires ignited by the Kremlin.[518]

In truth, the smoke of Satan had entered many seminaries and many churches, Protestant and Catholic alike. It is hard to adequately measure the damage done. But we all know what has happened: the number of seminarians, church attendance, and the percentage of Americans and Europeans who believe in God have all plunged. By the end of the 1970s, Churchmen such as Fulton Sheen were rightly pronouncing that the culture of Christendom in the West was dead; Christianity was hanging on, but Christendom was no more. As we enter the third decade of the twenty-first century, that sad fact is abundantly clear.

Of course, to lay all the reasons for this disaster at the feet of Marxism-Leninism would be a vast oversimplification—truly not giving the devil his due. The grand deceiver operates on so many levels and with such diabolical cleverness. Still, though far from the only factor, communists could take credit for a not insignificant amount of the harm done, if for nothing else for the confusion they have sown.

One can point to the confusion created by heretical concepts, such as those found in so-called Liberation Theology, promoted chiefly by the Jesuits, which became very popular and influential in Latin America.[519]

We know, of course, that Liberation Theology was pervaded with Marxist sentiment. Some ultimate insiders, such as Lt. Gen. Ion Mihai Pacepa, the leading Romanian spy chief who defected to the West in the late 1970s, have gone so far as to claim that Liberation Theology was created by the KGB. "The movement was born in the KGB," states Pacepa unequivocally, "and it had a KGB-invented name: Liberation Theology." Pacepa, a very high-level Communist Bloc intelligence official, gave specific details: "The birth of Liberation Theology was the intent of a 1960 super-secret "'Party-State Dezinformatsiya [Disinformation] Program' approved by Aleksandr Shelepin, the chairman of the KGB, and by Politburo member

Aleksey Kirichenko, who coordinated the Communist Party's international policies. This program demanded that the KGB take secret control of the World Council of Churches (WCC), based in Geneva, Switzerland, and use it as cover for converting Liberation Theology into a South American revolutionary tool."[520]

That is a very provocative testimony that many will want to dispute, especially left-leaning Catholics. Fair enough, though it is rather difficult to trump Pacepa's firsthand experience. He was personally involved in these schemes at the highest level.

What is beyond dispute is that the smoke of Satan in the form of communism had crept under many a seminary and church door and infected many clergy and, worse, laity. The resultant smog oozed into the pews, and still clouds Christendom to this day.

PART 5

THEY ARE LEGION

CHAPTER 13

"THE WORLD'S WICKEDEST"

MINIONS, PAGANS, WEIRDOS, RADICALS

We arrive now at the final part of this book, where the length could double, even triple, as we glance at a motley crew of creatures generated when Marxism went cultural and sexual in the twentieth century. Karl Marx desired to ruthlessly criticize all that exists, to blow up traditional absolutes, and to invent an entirely new order. This cast of disciples would seek to do just that, no doubt going places that even Marx and Engels could have scarcely imagined. Writing this section of the book was painful enough, but the years of torturous reading that have gone into it is downright dreadful. It is not for the faint of heart.

Exploring the thoughts (too generous of a word, really) of these ideological madmen (and madwomen) is a somber sojourn into a world of stupidity, an exercise in self-immolation. It is a waste—fruitless, useless, depressing, damaging. The amount of time and energy needed to adequately understand and then explain and convey these idiotic ideas is plainly not worth the human investment and spiritual grief. The practitioners of the ideas in this chapter and the one that follows—especially the perverse men of the Frankfurt School—were intellectually and spiritually vapid. Their notions were inane, yes, but they were also dark. Indeed, it would not be so bad if their ideas were just dumb. Their ideological nostrums were toxic, sometimes literally deadly, and poisonous to the soul.

At one point near the end of my off and on compilation of this section of the book—off and on because one must take long breaks in order to preserve one's peace of soul amid wading through this execrable twaddle—I simply walked away from a six-inch stack of highlighted material and notes and decided that enough was enough. As one can see in the endnotes, I have suggested further reading for anyone who ventures to shove through this mental sewage.

Throughout this book, we have encountered some sordid individuals whose crude ruminations produced great evil—Marx, Engels, Lenin, Trotsky—and lesser-knowns who did not slaughter the masses but, nonetheless, in the name of communism, operated by deceit, disinformation, manipulation, misinformation, infiltration—the likes of Bakunin, Foster, Browder, Ward, Bella Dodd in her bad days. Here in this chapter, we will meet still more toilers in this dubious vineyard. Here, too, are some freaks who did harm in their own way. They have names not like Mao and Che and Fidel and the other usual suspects who the world already knows too well, but names like Crowley, Duranty, Hay, Reich, Benjamin, Alinsky, Millett, the Frankfurt School—more elusive targets off the radar, and who the world should know more about, at the least because they serve as subtle (or not so subtle) markers and cautionary tales of the consequences of these ideas.

There are so damned many. And damned they were by what they inflicted on themselves, on the young they miseducated, and on the world they infected. They are legion. And communism was a giant collective petri dish for cultivating them and their virulent concoctions.

Some of these individuals delved into the occult, particularly those in the intellectual cesspool that was Germany, but also in the United Kingdom and the United States. They began their vulturous descent in the late nineteenth century, following the *Communist Manifesto*, in some cases as an alternative to the failure or abandonment of the revolutionary dreams of Marx and Engels. "Things changed in the second half of the 19th century, after the disappointment of 1848," writes Stephen Schwartz. "Radicalism in politics and occultism intersected in the UK and US for some time, exemplified by Annie Besant, who began as a fighter for the rights of working women and ended up in Theosophy."[521] (Theosophy—another absurd idea.)

Few living today have the personal experiences with the communist movement that Stephen Schwartz had. He was born in 1948 to a father who was Jewish and a mother who was the daughter of a Protestant minister, though both were non-practicing and, in fact, anti-religious. As an infant, Stephen was baptized in a Presbyterian church and began a lifelong quest for spiritual and political meaning. At first, he became a communist, an extremely well-informed one, to this day retaining a library of knowledge in his mind. He ultimately rejected that god that failed. Today he is a Sufi Muslim.[522] His intimate knowledge of American communism is hard to surpass—including its sillier and darker elements—from the nineteenth to the twentieth centuries and still today.

"The CPUSA was a hotbed of sickos," Schwartz wrote to me. He quickly flags Herbert Aptheker as a dubious example. Aptheker, hailed as the "theoretician" of Communist Party USA, is infamous even among the left not only for defending the Soviet invasion of Hungary in 1956 but for molesting his daughter, Bettina. Bettina Aptheker, a well-known, open member of CPUSA, today is chair of Women's Studies at the University of California at Santa Cruz.[523] Divorced and now married to a woman, she applies her Marxism culturally and fights for lesbian, bisexual, homosexual, "queer," and transgender rights. Like so many classical Marxists, her radicalism became cultural and sexual.

"The infamous Stalinist Herbert Aptheker systematically raped his own daughter," states Schwartz, "as did others I knew. They thought they answered to a higher morality."[524] Rattling off other examples, some of which will be noted in this chapter, Schwartz went on, "NAMBLA [North American Man-Boy Love Association] was founded by a Trotskyist who considered pedophilia a form of antibourgeois rebellion. And then there were the lovely Weather-men."[525] He goes on and on, listing groups like the "Spartacist" International Communist League, before sighing in disgust, "So much garbage, so little time."[526]

Indeed, so much garbage, so little time, so little space, and only so much that one can take as a researcher compiling it and as a reader digesting it.

So, where to begin? The better question: where to stop? Stop one must, for one's own self-preservation. Let's start in chronological order with maybe the wickedest of them all: Aleister Crowley.

The Great Beast: The Magick Cult of Aleister Crowley

Aleister Crowley (1875–1947) was known as "The Great Beast" and dubbed "The Wickedest Man in the World," titles he happily assumed.[527] He was an occultist and was widely accused by contemporaries of being a Satanist, though certain other weirdos and admirers and devotees claim he was not. But what even his defenders acknowledge is that he and his cogitations and practices fully inspired a long line of Satanists who credit him as their inspiration. His influence on modern Satanism, and the features of his "esotericism" that were adopted into contemporary Satanism, are undeniable.[528]

Crowley performed all sorts of strange magic, or "magick," if not black magic, and crowned that with macabre other-worldly sexual perversity, especially shocking for his time at the turn of the nineteenth to the twentieth century. At the age of twenty-one, he conveniently came into an inheritance, ensuring that he would never need to get a real job. Like Marx and Engels, Crowley used his old man's hard-earned money to play around with his goofy ideas. Also at age twenty-one, he fell in love with a man called "Herbert" who (says Crowley biographer and admirer Tobias Churton) was known for performing a cross-dressing act "inspired by a famous Parisian lesbian." Such acts became part of the Crowley legend, symptomatic of the bizarre sexual-spiritual-occultist performances for which he was infamous.[529]

The pagan cult of Crowley employed ritualistic sex as part of its "Gnostic Mass" that inverted and mocked not only the Roman Catholic Mass but, no doubt, Christianity *en masse.* Crowley based his philosophy on his bizarre Law of Thelema, a religious principle expressed in the creed, "Do what thou wilt shall be the whole of the Law." It was a precursor to the sixties credo, "If it feels good do it," albeit more sinister.

A Wikipedia entry retrieved at the time of this writing, which stood virtually unchanged a year later, and which is the first item that pops up in a search of Crowley, stated this (warning: prepare to be very confused):

> The Baphomet of Lévi was to become an important figure within the cosmology of Thelema, the mystical system established by Aleister Crowley in the early twentieth century. Baphomet features in the Creed of the Gnostic Catholic Church recited by the congregation in *The Gnostic Mass*, in the sentence: "And I believe in the Serpent and the Lion, Mystery of Mysteries, in His name BAPHOMET."
>
> In *Magick (Book 4)*, Crowley asserted that Baphomet was a divine androgyne and "the hieroglyph of arcane perfection:" Seen as that which reflects. "What occurs above so reflects below, or As above so below."

Is that weird enough? The explanation prattles on, plowing ahead with still more incomprehensible lunacy:

> The Devil does not exist. . . . 'The Devil' is, historically, the God of any people that one personally dislikes. . . . This serpent, SATAN, is not the enemy of Man, but He who made Gods of our race, knowing Good and Evil; He bade 'Know Thyself!' and taught Initiation. He is 'The Devil' of The Book of Thoth,

and His emblem is BAPHOMET, the Androgyne who is the hieroglyph of arcane perfection. . . . He is therefore Life, and Love. But moreover his letter is *ayin*, the Eye, so that he is Light; and his Zodiacal image is Capricornus, that leaping goat whose attribute is Liberty.

For Crowley, Baphomet is further a representative of the spiritual nature of the spermatozoa while also being symbolic of the "magical child" produced as a result of sex magic. As such, Baphomet represents the Union of Opposites, especially as mystically personified in Chaos and Babalon combined and biologically manifested with the sperm and egg united in the zygote.

This is what people find when they search online for "Aleister Crowley" and his ridiculous creed of "Baphomet," and it does generally accord with what more respectable biographers of Crowley have reported as they endeavored to ascertain whatever in hell the man had summoned up. I share this mumbo-jumbo here to illustrate to readers what they might not believe if I tried to describe it myself.

Trying to pin down Crowley's politics is largely a futile exercise unworthy of the hazards. He was consumed with spiritual matters more than political-ideological ones, though the circles that he ran in were considerably left of center, hanging with communists, socialists, and various "free love" progressives. He was certainly not anti-communist, and he particularly approved of Marxism's anti-Christian element. As one biographer writes, "What Crowley liked about Nazism and communism, or at least what made him curious about them, was the anti-Christian position and the revolutionary and socially subversive implications of these two movements. In their subversive powers, he saw the possibility of an annihilation of old religious traditions, and the creation of a void that Thelema, subsequently, would be able to fill."[530] As with Marx, here was a tool to take down the Judeo-Christian order.

Still, to my knowledge, he was not an open communist or activist.

Crowley, did, however, have some odd political bedfellows from within the communist movement, including one Walter Duranty.

The Demented Case of Walter Duranty

One of many sleazy individuals who had a relationship (that includes the physical) with Aleister Crowley was Walter Duranty, long known to scholars and contemporaries and colleagues as the *New York Times'* notorious "Man in Moscow," the mendacious reporter who filed terribly misleading reports on Stalin's forced famine against the Ukraine in the 1930s, where five to ten million men, women, and children starved to death.

Amazingly, Duranty would be awarded the Pulitzer Prize, despite his woefully misleading and scurrilous journalism. Duranty would report, including in articles with titles like "Russians Hungry, but Not Starving" (March 31, 1933, *New York Times*): "Here are the facts. . . . There is no actual starvation or deaths from starvation, but there is widespread mortality from diseases due to malnutrition. . . . These conditions are bad, but there is no famine."[531] This was not simply erroneous reporting. Duranty knew otherwise. He told William Strang at the British embassy on September 26, 1933 that as many as ten million people had already died. He also personally told Eugene Lyons (UPI's Moscow correspondent) that he estimated the total number of famine victims around seven million. Malcolm Muggeridge would call Duranty "the greatest liar of any journalist I have met in fifty years of journalism." Even the esteemed man of the left, Joseph Alsop, would denounce Duranty as a "fashionable prostitute" in service of communists.[532]

The Kremlin wined and dined Duranty, who licked it all up. The Soviets lavished him with food and booze (while Ukrainians tried to eat grass), a chauffeured car, assistants, and a handy cook-secretary-turned-mistress named Katya, who (Lenchen-like to Karl Marx) put her full self at the disposal of the *Times'* feted "Man in Moscow."

She bore Duranty a son in the process. Eugene Lyons suspected that Duranty was flatly on the Kremlin's payroll; at the least, he was a recipient of the Bolsheviks' generous subsidies.[533]

But Katya and the Bolsheviks were not Duranty's only romance. There was also his intimacy with the Great Beast himself. Even many of those familiar with Duranty's perverse reporting were unaware of his perverse relationship with Aleister Crowley.

According to Duranty's biographer, S. J. Taylor, a respected scholar whose definitive work on her subject was published by the top academic press—Oxford University Press—Duranty and Aleister Crowley had sex together. While the precise lurid details are not completely clear, it looks like they had threesomes with a woman they shared, though they might have engaged in direct homosexual conduct together. They did "exchange their semen," according to the account. That exchange was part of the cult ritual.[534]

Taylor introduces Crowley to readers as the man who "commonly referred to himself as 'Beast 666,' the great Anti-Christ predicted in the Book of Revelation," who in his late thirties, when hooking up with Duranty, was already referring to himself as "the Great Magister" and "the Wickedest Man in the World." When he encountered Walter Duranty, Aleister Crowley was going through "something of a crisis." He had just crossed the channel from London to Paris, "there to practice the black arts and magico-sexual rituals to which he had dedicated the preceding dozen or so years of his life." He was now sensing a certain "inhibition," as he put it, a fear that his chosen path might be closing up. "Fortunately," writes Taylor, "he was saved when he made the acquaintance of a man some eight years his junior, but wise already in the ways of the world. That man was Walter Duranty."[535]

Apparently, Crowley's conscience had been bothering him. He was for the first time in his life having second thoughts about the "great quest" he had set before himself, even falling into depression. "It was Duranty," records Taylor, "who helped him [Crowley], as he put it, 'win out.'"

Taylor says that the relationship between the two men "was cemented by the pair's common interest in smoking opium and in a woman." This woman, the epitome of the "Scarlet Woman," as Taylor describes her, was named Jane Cheron. Crowley described the French seductress as "a strange and venomous flower" and a fellow "devotee of that great and terrible god, Opium."

Karl Marx and Friedrich Engels spoke of the opium of the masses. Here was the opium of Walter Duranty, Aleister Crowley, and Jane Cheron.

Crowley was turned on by the "inexpressible evil" he discerned in the she-devil, Cheron, a perfect partner—as Taylor put it—for the world's wickedest man. Taylor writes of how Duranty, too, dug into the evil woman along with Crowley. The two men "routinely shared the favors of" Jane Cheron, "just as they shared an interest in dope. It was an affable *ménage à trois*: sex with the one partner, drugs with the other, a little magic on the side."

The Christmas season of 1913 was a curious one for Duranty and Crowley. It was another chance to engage in their dark world of sexual-spiritual sacrifice and mis-pleasure. On December 1, 1913, Duranty went to work for the *New York Times*. S. J. Taylor describes the twisted tryst between the *Times'* Man in Moscow and Crowley and friends on December 31, every word of which should be read and soaked in so as to grasp the full dimensions of Duranty's and Crowley's perversity:

> On December 31st, "the last day of the vulgar year 1913," Aleister Crowley began the first of twenty-three ritualistic happenings called "the Paris workings." They were aimed at evoking the gods Jupiter and Mercury. The first ceremony toward achieving this end was to receive the sacrament "from a certain priest, A.B." which Crowley proceeded to do at 5:35 p.m., as recorded in his diary, a precise account of his varied and excessive life.

Priest A.B. was Walter Duranty, and what receiving the sacrament meant, in effect, was "that Crowley received his semen." Precisely how this was accomplished was never fully disclosed; nevertheless, it was recorded that participants in "the Paris workings" were given over to painting "prime pantacles" in various preordained places, jumping from one spot to another vigorously, and chanting "*Sanguis et Semen! Sanguis et Semen!*" (Blood and Semen! Blood and Semen!) along with more lengthy Latin recitations. Duranty translated most of the verse concocted by the pair, "he being the better Latinist."

Jesus Christ offered his body and blood. Roman Catholic priests, *in persona Christi*, have long consecrated bread and wine. Walter Duranty and Aleister Crowley befouled semen and blood for their ritualistic-pagan "sacrament."

S. J. Taylor further described the spectacle that was the "Paris workings" in all their glorious detail:

> The sixteenth "working" was perhaps the most impressive of the twenty-three. Crowley "became inspired and entered a trance," in which he was given instructions to place a wax phallus, carved earlier, into "a besica" (a shallow dish in the shape of "the yoni" or female pudendum) and that a sparrow or pigeon should be slain before the Accendat, the sacrifice taking place while chanting these words, *Nunc flavi Jovi spumantem sanguine saevo Passerum* (Now I have blown to Jupiter a sparrow foaming with fierce blood) or "other such words as may be suggested by the Art-Bachelor W.D."
>
> Then, during the ceremony, Crowley cut the figure four on the breast of another partner named Victor Neuburg, encircled his head with a chain, and flogged him on the buttocks. The pair recited another of Duranty's verses in Latin before attempting to commit sodomy. Since neither man was in actual fact homosexual,[536] the attempt was a failure—as were presumably

the "Paris workings" themselves in their goal of raising the specters of Jupiter and Mercury in Crowley's apartment.[537]

This was sick stuff. Certainly demented. The ritualistic element smacks of not only blasphemy but certainly a form of pagan activity (perhaps even bordering on the demonic). Imagine this behavior from the *New York Times'* feted Pulitzer winner. One of the top reporters in the world, soiled by the Great Beast, his strange political bedfellow. Perhaps it was fitting private behavior for a man who would lie to the world about the deliberate starvation of millions of people by a murderous communist tyrant in the Kremlin.

Harry Hay: Gay Communist Pioneer

A related example is the case of Harry Hay. If ever atheistic communism bestowed a secular saint of "gay communism," it was Harry. He was a pioneer.

Harry Hay (1912–2002) was a radical political activist, dubbed by his biographer, Stuart Timmons, as the "founder of the modern gay movement,"[538] and by Hay expert Will Roscoe as the "founder of gay liberation."[539] Roscoe underscored Hay's unique role in fashioning a strange trinity of "Marxism, Native American revivalism, and New Age spirituality," all of which shaped his work to advance the gay and transgender movements.

Perhaps Hay's most spectacular achievement was his shrewd tactical move to portray homosexuals as a "minority" class, a crucial step in getting the wider liberal left to protect, accept, and ultimately advance them. Liberals are suckers for a minority movement that they are sympathetic to, and thus this worked masterfully, particularly as the left went secular, sexual, and cultural. "Without the idea of Gays as a cultural minority," writes Roscoe, "there would be no Gay identity and no Lesbian/Gay movement today." This "cultural minority thesis," says Roscoe, has been Hay's "most profound and lasting contribution."[540] Roscoe and many others would rightly call this a "profound contribution" by Harry Hay.[541]

It was a Marxist operating on the cultural and sexual front that made this happen. Harry Hay's triumph is one of a cultural-sexual Marxist. As we will see, the work of these cultural-sexual Marxists would constitute a revolution within the communist movement, one that pervades it to this day.

I caution researchers about citing Wikipedia as a source, but I do so here because it surprisingly and consistently describes Harry Hay exactly right, warts and all. That is surprising because Wikipedia entries often go very soft on leftists and hardcore communists.[542] For Harry Hay, however, the Wikipedia entry at least six years running (I began checking it in 2014) has been spot-on accurate not only in characterizing his shocking communist work but his still more shocking sexual radicalism. States Wikipedia, "Hay was a prominent American gay rights activist, communist, pro-pedophilia activist (NAMBLA), and . . . founder of the Mattachine Society, the first sustained gay rights group in the United States, as well as the Radical Faeries, a loosely-affiliated gay spiritual movement."[543]

Among these, NAMBLA is the infamous North American Man-Boy Love Association, which advocates for pedophilia and pederasty and seeks to abolish age-of-consent laws to allow adult men to have sex with boys.[544] The organization gives pause even to the most sexually accepting "progressives." It encourages adult men to find and "make love" to young boys. It encourages grown adult men to become wondrous "boy lovers." Its founder was a committed communist: David Thorstad, a prominent gay rights activist, a former president of New York's Gay Activists Alliance, a member of the Trotskyist Socialist Workers Party, and a staff writer for the Trotskyists' brutal newspaper, the *Militant*.[545] Thorstad had begun "enjoying" homosexual experiences at age nine.[546]

Harry's biographers state that he himself was never a member of NAMBLA, but they do not hesitate to note that he was a vigorous defender, as he made clear in written and spoken word. That is a controversial position (mercifully) even among leftists. In fact, Harry's position was a natural extension of the fact that he himself had been initially a man-boy lover. His first homosexual experience came when he, as a young teen, was taken by an older man. Harry had been (by his own description) "jail-bait" to his man-lover.[547]

Harry hence spit with rage at Senator Jesse Helms (R-NC) and other conservatives, not to mention anti-NAMBLA Democrats and liberals and homosexuals, for "selling NAMBLA down the river." It pained an almost hysterical Hay to see his fellow gay brothers and sisters denounce their NAMBLA brethren as "child molesters."[548] Harry did not see it that way. As even his Wikipedia entry acknowledges, he spoke up at several NAMBLA meetings and spoke out in support of relationships between adult men and boys as young as thirteen.[549]

Also noted in the Wikipedia description of Hay is the organization the "Radical Faeries," a left-wing cultural-spiritual-ecological and (self-admitted) pagan group. "Our shared values include feminism, respect for the Earth, and individual responsibility rather than hierarchy," says the organization's website. "Many of us are Pagan (nature-based religion)." The website has a page dedicated strictly to Harry, who it calls the "Father of the Radical Faeries."[550]

The Radical Faeries should not be laughed off by the politically incorrect among us. It should be of interest if not concern at least because of the ability of such "shared values" to maneuver into the arms of the ever-evolving, constantly *progressing* wider left—ideas now gaining popularity and firmly making their way into the mainstream. This includes the realm of the radical redefinition of gender. The Radical Faeries' positions include supporting a form of transgenderism called "two-spirit," which was explicitly championed by Harry Hay. This is noted clearly in communist literature, including this piece from *Workers World*, which details Harry Hay's work in "two-spiritism:" "Two-Spirit is the language that many Native [American] people have chosen instead to describe those with diverse gender expression, sexualities and sexes."[551]

Again, this should not be shrugged off as silliness by readers. In 2016, "two-spirit" became one of the thirty-one official gender identity options approved by the New York City council for public employees.[552] Of course, a "choice" among an array of thirty-one gender options is hardly unconventional nowadays. As an indicator of the warp-speed of today's LGBTQ movement and progressives generally, Facebook by 2017 was listing seventy-one gender options, and in 2019, the BBC came under fire for an instructional video teaching kids that there are "100, if not more" gender options.[553]

Here, too, Harry Hay was ahead of his time, a trend-setter.

"Harry Hay's broad study of same-sex love throughout the changing history of the organization of human society and the method of his approach are achievements in themselves," records *Workers World*. "He also made some important contributions of thought." Among these was fathering a "two-spirit" option for today's transgender warriors.

Harry began vigorously pushing these ideas in the 1970s, when the Radical Faeries took off. They even established several "collectives" in rural areas in the mid-1970s and started their own publication, titled *RFD: A Magazine for Country Faggots*. They also started a group called "the faery circle" out of the Haight Street apartment in San Francisco of writer Arthur Evans. Evans wrote about this pagan circle in his 1978 book *Witchcraft and the Gay Counterculture* and in articles for the homosexual publications *Out* and *Fag Rag*.[554]

The faery men were assigned various neo-pagan names connected to Mother Earth, named for various animals, trees, Native Americans, and stars and constellations. These were names like Crazy Owl, Morning Star, Neon Snowflake, Rosy-Fingered Don, Flower, and Marvelous Persimmon. Some took names from popular culture, such as "Judy Jetson," from the TV cartoon *The Jetsons*. Some were named for snakes, and these Radical Faeries literally hissed at one another. The names were captured in a circulated Faerie Directory, which evolved into a more sacred named Holy Faerie Database.[555]

It is crucial to pause here to understand the obvious environmental thread in this. The Radical Faeries preached a Mother Earth stewardism/paganism. This was but one of numerous Marxist-environmentalist fusions. That is a key point. Many modern communists have taken refuge in the environmental movement.[556]

Again, Harry was a pioneer in all of this, a veritable spiritual leader and inspiration. He personally shared what he called his "Fairy Vision," urging his fellow radical faeries to spread their wings: "Fairies everywhere must begin to stand tall and beautiful in the sun," Harry exhorted in July 1980. "Fairies must begin to throw off the filthy green frog-skin of Hetero-imitation and discover the lovely Gay-Conscious not-MAN shining underneath." To achieve such a fundamental transformation in human nature, Hay urged "re-working all previously developed systems of Hetero thought." That included reappraising previous information concerning key New Age and Pagan philosophies, or, as Hay put it, "all the data we previously have gathered concerning Shamanism and Magick."[557]

Yes, "Magick." Remember Aleister Crowley?

Harry and the Temple of the Great Beast

Speaking of whom, Harry Hay had been involved in some seriously shady stuff throughout his life, but one incident merits particular mention. Almost casually mentioned in the definitive biography of Hay (and not on his Wikipedia page) was the time that he served as organist (in the year 1935) for the Los Angeles lodge of the Order of the Temple Orientis, or OTO, the notorious anti-Christian spiritual-sex-occultist movement of Aleister Crowley.[558]

For the record, I have no knowledge that Hay ever met Crowley, but Harry did connect with some of Crowley's disciples. Harry actually played the organ at these services in the Los Angeles chapter of OTO. He was hired by his lesbian friend and fellow actor Regina

Kahl, a large woman who was a high priestess in the OTO, as were two other friends, a pair of lesbian sisters known simply as "the Wolfe sisters." According to Harry's reminiscences to his biographer, the temple was run by a "frail" man named Wilfred Smith, who lasciviously performed "exorcisms" on attractive young men.[559]

"A gong sounded and we'd get to the chapel by ladder," Harry remembered of the start of the "Mass." "The congregation sat in pews facing a sarcophagus behind a gauze curtain. Regina, in a flowing robe, slit the veil with a sword and out came Wilfred wearing a snake diadem and a red velvet cape made from a theater curtain." Wilfred would ritualistically announce, "I am a man among men," before taking Regina, a much larger person than Wilfred, to whom he would say, "Come thou virgin, pure and without spot."[560]

As this spectacle proceeded, Harry would bang upon the keys of the organ into a slow dirge. The ceremony in the temple thus commenced.

This must have even had a chill upon the otherwise intrepid future founder of the pagan Radical Faeries. Hay's biographer notes that Harry would "frequently" drop into his childhood Catholic parish the same day to try to "balance his sacrilege" at the OTO lodge.[561] There must have been a lingering sense that something wasn't quite right. That is a notable point by biographer Stuart Timmons, who elsewhere said that Harry had previously rejected his Catholic upbringing and essentially had never turned back.

Harry had been raised Roman Catholic, attending St. Gregory Catholic Church on Ninth and Norton Streets in Los Angeles. His decisive split had come Easter Sunday 1927, when Harry attended required confession with other parishioners. The priest apparently knew from another boy in the church, whom Harry had been kissing, that the two had been doing something not permitted. Harry finished his confession with no mention of this transgression. The priest pressed Harry to continue confessing. He asked Harry, "Have you finished?" When Harry assured Father Follen that he had finished, the priest snapped at him, "You have not!"[562]

The priest demanded that Harry admit his guilt and repent. Harry refused. "I wasn't sorry, and there was nothing for me to confess," he explained later. The priest reached around the confessional, grabbed Harry by the collar and the belt, marched him to the front of the cathedral, and then pushed him out of the church, kicking open the door. "Don't you come back until you are ready to say you're sorry," he allegedly barked.

Harry never did. At age fifteen, he left that church for good.

From Gay to Red

Another flirtation that Harry's Church (the Roman Catholic one, not the Crowley one) would not have approved of was his growing romance with the ideology of Bolshevism, far deadlier than paganism.

For this budding communist homosexual, the homosexuality had come first. And it came with great profusion, as Harry was a sexual juggernaut, vigorous in the homosexual lifestyle from an early age. His biographer writes of Hay's "sexual flurry" in his early twenties, just as he began eyeing up Marx and Engels. Harry told his biographer that he engaged in "two or three affairs a day between 1932 and 1936." That would equate to over a thousand instances of homosexual intercourse with other men per year, and at a time when gays were in the closet. The closet could not contain Harry's hyperactive libido. Hay's biographer points to these "affairs" as a sign of Harry's "restless" nature.[563]

Harry would have insisted that he was a born a homosexual. But he was not born a communist. For that, Harry needed a special mentor. He needed "Grandpa Walton."

Harry Hay's politics through the 1930s grew increasingly radical, but his leap into the lap of the communist movement was chaperoned by one of his dearest lovers, actor Will Geer, who many readers will know as "Grandpa Walton" from the hit 1970s TV show *The Waltons*.

"I was madly in love with Bill," said Hay of Geer.[564]

Harry met Geer in February 1934, as a fellow actor performing at a local theatre. Many sexual encounters followed, as did their bond over radical politics. In July 1934, he joined Geer in some agitation and propaganda on behalf of union strikers in San Francisco. The next year, he and Geer worked together organizing migratory workers in the San Joaquin Valley. That year he and Geer also formed a group called the Hollywood Theatre Guild, and he became active in the "progressive" Hollywood Film and Photo League, with all sorts of added communist front-groups to follow, such as the American League Against War and Fascism.[565]

Harry had snuggled into the ideological arms of Geer. Really, it was Will Geer who mentored Harry into the Communist Party. Harry was already steadily drifting left, but it was Geer who plunged him into a "total immersion" of hardcore political activism.[566] He escorted Harry from the homosexual orbit into the communist orbit. Geer was multi-talented, playing music with a communist folk-group called the Almanacs, which alternately included Woody Guthrie, Pete Seeger, and Burl Ives ("Have a Holly, Jolly Christmas"), and which strummed pro-Stalinist propaganda. Harry likewise performed with both Guthrie and Seeger.[567]

To Harry, Grandpa Walton wasn't the red under the bed; he was the red in the bed. And Harry would never really let go, even after Geer married a woman and had children. When Geer died in 1978, a jealous Harry, in the mode of bitchy spurned lover, crudely boasted to Geer's widow at his funeral, "I had him first."[568]

For a perfectly telling statement of what a passionate communist Harry's paramour was, Will Geer once said that his greatest fear was "people who believe you can't change human nature."[569] Such is totalitarian communism in a nutshell. Lenin and Marx and Trotsky and every cultural Marxist would wholeheartedly agree with that sentiment.

The Geer relationship brought Harry to the bosom of Communist

Party USA, which he joined in 1934, merely a few months after taking Geer's hand. Whittaker Chambers's biographer described Chambers joining the party as Chambers having at long last "found his church."[570] Harry Hay's biographer said the same. "To come into the CPUSA," wrote Stuart Timmons, "involved almost religious feelings" for Harry. No question. Harry affirmed, "Joining the Party actually was like joining the Holy Orders in earlier centuries. Party ways and outlooks dominated your everyday consciousness from then on. Except that instead of manifesting the City of God on earth, you were creating the International Soviet, that shall be the Human Race, as one sang in the final line of the [Communist] 'Internationale.'"[571]

Harry Hay became a devout commie. He went to communist central, New York City,[572] where between 1939 and 1942 he began haunting the party's library and drinking deep from its literature. He read Marx and Engels studiously. He even took advanced courses in Marxist theory with the intent of becoming a teacher for the party. In fact, he would hit the classroom not only in New York but when he returned to Los Angeles, where he taught alongside other comrades, such as future Hollywood Ten leader John Howard Lawson.[573]

Harry was a very active comrade in New York throughout the 1940s. He was also married at that time. He and his wife, Anita, had wed in September 1938 in a backyard garden of a home in downtown Los Angeles. Typical of many communists, they were married by a Unitarian minister (whereas Harry was an ex-Catholic, Anita was Jewish). The Rev. Steve Fritchman happily accommodated their wish to omit any "God stuff" from the ceremony.[574] The couple soon moved to New York, returning to Anita's family's roots, where they immediately signed up with the Communist Party's huge district office, the largest in the nation.

Sexually, Harry was in agony during this time, trying to remain faithful to his wife despite his overwhelming urges to have very frequent sex with men. They couldn't hold it together and divorced after thirteen years of marriage.

The Communist Party and Homosexuals

Today, the Communist Party in America has rolled out the red carpet for all manners of sexual libertinism, as it happily and ruthlessly criticizes every traditional norm. CPUSA and publications like *People's World* are robust advocates for the entirety of the left-wing LGBTQ agenda. But it was not always that way.

In Harry Hay's day, Communist Party USA was not a totally hospitable place for homosexuals for a number of reasons, primarily because of their susceptibility to blackmail. The lifestyle made them "automatic security risks," as acknowledged by Harry's lawyer, Frank Pestana. Harry himself said that "homosexuals were forbidden membership in the Party, according to its own constitution."[575]

Hay biographer Stuart Timmons notes, "The Party strictly prohibited homosexuals from joining and did not acknowledge homosexuality as anything more than the degenerate phase of a decadent system." But Timmons's own sources later in his book suggest the larger reality was more complicated. He quotes several sources, from Harry himself to Dorothy Healey, the infamous "Red Queen" of Southern California, insisting that the party was not "homophobic." Those perceptions vary, but there was no question the party realized (correctly) that homosexuals were a security risk because of their blackmail potential. In fact, a humorous assessment comes from Nicholas von Hoffman, biographer of Joe McCarthy aide Roy Cohn, who observed, "The only thing the State Department and the Communist Party agreed on was that homosexuals were security risks." Party officials were even known to hurl accusations of homosexuality against non-homosexuals who had been booted from the party for political reasons.[576] Such dirty smears were classic Leninist "morality," with the ends justifying the means.

But though officially opposed, Timmons notes that an "unofficial subpolicy" existed below the surface; that is, exceptions were made for effective comrades who were doing excellent work and were avoiding situations that could subject them to blackmail. Timmons said that Harry was one such comrade; for him, an exception was made.[577]

That was indeed the case, until Harry felt that his cover was being blown, or in jeopardy of being compromised. With that, he decided—on his own—to leave the party for the best of the party. Thus, contrary to what has been interpreted, Harry was not expelled from CPUSA; he left on his volition.

One more consideration should be added. This one comes from the Soviet side, which would have been particularly concerned about blackmail because CPUSA answered to the Kremlin.

Respected Cold War researcher John Barron, in his classic book *KGB: The Secret Work of Soviet Secret Agents*, maintained that the Kremlin distrusted homosexuals less because of blackmail risk than because it judged homosexual men "at war with themselves." The KGB deemed them emotionally if not mentally unstable. They were rejected as potential spies or agents of influence because they were viewed as unreliable and a risk of treason.

"Contrary to popular supposition, the KGB is not primarily interested in homosexuals because of their presumed susceptibility to blackmail," wrote Barron. "In its judgment, homosexuality often is accompanied by personality disorders that make the victim potentially unstable and vulnerable to adroit manipulation. It hunts the particular homosexual who, while more or less a functioning member of his society, is nevertheless subconsciously at war with it and himself." Barron continued, "Compulsively driven into tortured relations that never gratify, he cannot escape awareness that he is different. Being different, he easily rationalizes that he is not morally bound by the mores, values, and allegiances that unite others in community or society. Moreover, he nurtures a dormant impulse to strike back at the society which he feels has conspired to make him a secret leper. To such a man, treason offers the weapon of retaliation."[578]

Such a psychological assessment is not surprising from the Soviets. For the KGB, then, an American communist who was a homosexual might have been devoted to the cause but could not be relied upon to serve the Soviet Union, certainly not as a spy, because of the inherent risk of betrayal. The homosexual was not emotionally stable. That was the Kremlin's perspective.

One could examine all of these varying views at length, but the point here is that, as Hay's biographer Stuart Timmons put it, Harry concluded that "even under the best of circumstances" he would be a "liability" to the party, and "so he recommended his own expulsion as a security risk because of his homosexuality."

Thus, Harry left CPUSA in 1951 after roughly seventeen years as a member. That same year he joined a group of homosexual communists from the Los Angeles area in forming the so-called Mattachine Society, the pioneering organization of gay communists.[579]

Notably, these homosexual communists in the Mattachine Society described themselves as "progressives."[580] Here, too, Hay gave his total religious-like devotion, just as he had to the Communist Party. Stuart Timmons said that Harry cast himself into the cause of the Mattachine Society with "evangelical fervor." The group, like CPUSA, assumed a "missionary nature."[581]

The guys in the Mattachine Society would spread the gospel of Marx and Lenin, albeit from a "gay" perspective.

Alas, there is much more to the multifaceted life of Harry Hay. As to our interests here, the "progressive" Harry remained an aggressive advocate for homosexual rights and never relinquished his support of Stalinism.[582]

To the likes of gay communists like Harry Hay, homosexuals were to be sympathetically presented to the public as a new victim class. In a creative appropriation and extension of Marxist theory, they could be constituted as a new bourgeoisie to refashion the revolution and reject the old order. Here was an ideal group to undermine traditional norms. Here was a handy tool—eventually an entire "civil rights" movement—to fundamentally transform society's understanding of human nature. Ultimately, their cause could be employed to redefine everything from marriage to the understanding of the nature of human sexuality itself.

Harry Hay and others like him were true trailblazers, for such was the next iteration of the evolving specter of communism, as certain twentieth- and twenty-first-century heirs to Marx picked up the ideology and added the colors of the rainbow to the traditional red. Marxism embarked on a brave new course, a new road both sexual and cultural. This, as we shall see, was the revolutionary road less traveled by (among others) the Frankfurt School and the sixties radicals. Unfortunately, they were incredibly successful, and it is now a most busy highway in the twenty-first century.

CHAPTER 14

"THE SPECTER OF THE FRANKFURT SCHOOL"

MORE MINIONS, PAGANS, WEIRDOS, RADICALS

"A specter is haunting the sociological enterprise," writes Zoltan Tarr, "the specter of the Frankfurt School."[583]

The Frankfurt School haunted much more than sociology. Its ghosts are still present. And that brings us to another perverse assortment of Marxist minions, pagans, weirdos, and radicals.

It also brings us to yet another crucial word of caution: Trying to discern the inane and impenetrable ideas of the men of the Frankfurt School is a soul-crushing exercise in futility. One must spend years scouring pages and footnotes of thick volumes (mostly in untranslated German) trying to arrive at a vague flickering of understanding at what in the devil's name these madmen were thinking about. It would be bad enough if this venture was simply a waste of one's time—especially given the sacrifice of more edifying reading—but what is worse is the strain and toxicity to the intellect and the soul. One is struck again and again at how some Godless intellectuals (especially German ones) can descend into such rank intellectual vacuity, ambiguity, and downright stupidity. For the researcher, this is particularly exhausting and frustrating, as what should be a straightforward project to dig out certain concepts for incorporation into a book becomes a massive maze of the mind—a vexing effort to figure out what these sordid men were devoting their despairing lives to. Theirs was the work of lunatics. The Frankfurt School was a veritable devil's den of derangement.

Early in the twentieth century, from the smoldering embers of Marxist-Leninist theory, arose a fiery field of fanatics who came to be known collectively as the Frankfurt School. These Marxists were all about culture and sex. The Frankfurt School protégés were neo-Marxists, a new kind of twentieth-century communist less interested in the economic/class ideas of Marx than a remaking of society through the eradication of traditional norms and institutions. They brought to Marxist theory not a passion for, say, more equitable tax policy or reallocation of private property but rather tenets of psychology, sociology, and Freudian teaching on sexuality.

These men developed a kind of Freudian-Marxism, or "Freudo-Marxism," integrating the extraordinarily bad but influential twentieth-century ideas of Sigmund Freud with the extraordinarily bad but influential nineteenth-century teachings of Karl Marx. This was no match made in heaven. The noxious Marx had conjured up the most toxic ideas of the nineteenth century, whereas the neurotic Freud had cooked up the most infantile ideas of the twentieth century. Swirling the insipid ideas of those two ideological-psychological basket cases into a single malevolent witch's brew was bound to uncork a barrel of mischief. The Frankfurt School was the laboratory and the distillery for their concoction, and the children of the 1960s would be their twitching guinea pigs and guzzling alcoholics. The flower-children, the hippies, the Yippies, the Woodstock generation, the Haight-Asbury LSD dancers, the sex-lib kids would all drink deep from the magic chalice, intoxicated by lofty dreams (more like hallucinations and bad acid-trips) of fundamental transformation of the culture, country, and world. And a generation or two still later, they would become the nutty professors who mixed the Kool-Aid for the millennials who would merrily redefine everything from marriage to sexuality to gender, wittingly or not serving the Frankenstein monster of cultural Marxism by doing so.

To be sure, the Frankfurt School of the 1930s was certainly not issuing joint statements calling for, say, same-sex marriage—such would have been considered pure madness in any day before our own. Nonetheless, this cabal's comprehensive push for untethered, unhinged sexual openness with no cultural boundaries or religious restrictions cracked the door for almost anything down the road. When God and tradition and ancient norms are said to no longer exist, anything and everything is permissible.

For these neo-Marxists, orthodox Marxism was too old and too limiting; it was too narrow, too restrictive, too reactionary even, too controlled by the Comintern and its ironclad party discipline that strong-armed national communist parties from upon high in Moscow. That rigidity prevented these more freewheeling neo-Marxists from initiating the rampant cultural transformation they craved, which included revolutionary changes in marriage, sexuality, gender, and family. Above all, these Frankfurt leaders were left-wing/atheistic academics and intellectuals who looked to the universities as the home-base to instill their ideas—and who, most of all, spurned the churches. Marx and Freud were the gods who, they were sure, would not fail them.

Rather than organize the workers and the factories, the peasants and the fields and the farms, they would organize the intellectuals and the academy, the artists and the media and the film industry. These would be the conveyor belts to deliver the fundamental transformation.

There were many key figures from the Frankfurt School: Georg Lukacs, Herbert Marcuse, Max Horkheimer, Theodor Adorno, Erich Fromm, Franz Neumann, the Soviet spy Richard Sorge, Wilhelm Reich, Walter Benjamin, and others. The school began in 1923 as the Institute for Social Research at the University of Frankfurt in Germany. It is also sometimes called Goethe University, fittingly and frighteningly enough. Karl Marx would have been proud. The

Frankfurt School in the 1930s would pick up and relocate to the United States, as its members (most if not all of them Jews) fled Hitler's atrocious Final Solution.[584]

Fully revisiting all of that history with each of those figures would be too much for present purposes. Here I will highlight only two of them: Wilhelm Reich and Walter Benjamin. Two is more than enough.

Wilhelm Reich's Revolution

Born in March 1897 in Austria-Hungary, Wilhelm Reich was the perturbed son of secular Jewish parents who did not raise him in the faith, or any faith. His father, Leon, was an angry man, who abused his children and his wife. Wilhelm said he lived in "great fear of his beatings." He could not recall his "austere father" of "ferocious temper" ever "having cuddled or treated me tenderly at that time—nor can I recollect feeling any attachment to him."[585]

Sex would become little Wilhelm's obsession throughout his life, as is evident in his autobiography, appropriately titled *Passion of Youth*, which is sex-saturated from the opening pages. By paragraph five, where he tells us of his first memories, he is already writing about sex—as a four-year-old. He shares his "erotic sensations of enormous intensity" as a mere child of four and a half. He enthusiastically conveyed his experience from one afternoon at that very young and innocent age when he jumped into bed with the family nursemaid, climbed on top of her, lifted her dress, "reached feverishly for her genitals," and for about ten minutes had his way with her (which she strangely allowed to continue), stopping only out of fear of his father discovering them.[586]

Wilhelm constantly fantasized about having sex with everyone from the babysitter to his mom. "Since I always bathed with Mother," wrote Reich, "sexual feelings regularly stirred within me and I often attempted to undress Mother with my eyes." He also enjoyed and relished his many days imbibing in chronic masturbation—that is, his self-admitted "intense pleasure in masturbating."[587]

By the time he was just eleven years old, the seemingly pre-pubescent Reich was already having daily intercourse with another of the family servants, a cook. "She was the first to teach me the thrusting motion necessary for ejaculation," Reich anxiously informs us. "From then on, I had intercourse almost every day for years—it was always in the afternoon, when my parents were napping."[588]

It didn't stop there. When a woman around the house was not available to lust or thrust over, little Wilhelm turned to the farm animals, watching them mate, gazing at their genitals, and sexually stimulating them himself. "One of my favorite activities was to go into the stall at noon," he recalls for his readers, taking them on a tour of the strange Reich barn and stable, "while all the farmhands were eating or sleeping. I wantonly enjoyed observing the genitals of both male and female animals. While doing this, I always had an erection." Eventually, the excitement overtook young Wilhelm, who could not resist: "One day I grew so excited looking at the animals that I took a whip with a smooth grip, turned it around, and thrust the handle into the vagina of a mare. The animal was surprised at first but then seemed to enjoy it. She spread her legs wide and began to urinate while I had an orgasm (without ejaculation). From then on, I did this every day and extended my activities to other mares as well." This went on for about two months until Reich (mercifully) felt a sense of disgust and decided to stop.[589]

If Reich were around today, his progressive pals might have him arrested for molesting animals—though surely not for his rampant sexual desires toward and activities with humans, for which Reich would become a leading light to the New Left (more on that in a moment).

Such is chapter one of Reich's autobiography: a vivid picture of a boy dropping his trousers impulsively to engage in excessive mastur-bation and penetration and borderline sadomasochism and bestiality.

In all, it is a perfect image and metaphor for the no-boundaries sexuality of cultural Marxism.

Given such extreme predilections from the time of toddlerhood, it was an inevitable, perfect match when Reich found his true love in the teachings of Sigmund Freud, another sexual screwball and moral weirdo.

Reich first met Freud in 1919 and asked him for a tutorial and list of writings on sexology. Freud obliged. By 1922, Reich was working as a "physician" for Freud's psychoanalytic clinic.

It was the 1920s in elite Europe, which meant that the Soviet Comintern was in full bloom and that intellectuals in the academy and elsewhere were filling their pipes with smoky dreams of a Marxist utopia. To that end, Wilhelm Reich would encounter his second god when he dug into the writings of Marx. He joined the Communist Party in Austria in 1928 and visited the USSR the next year, where he lectured and was received openly—even as the Bolsheviks would eventually blanch at Reich's soon-to-come wacky screeds on sexuality. Wilhelm was a little too wild for the Soviets.

Reich by then was well on his way in search of a grand unifying theory of Freudianism and Marxism. He ultimately did so in his revolutionary sexual manifesto, *The Sexual Revolution*. The book made him famous. Wilhelm Reich was the man who thereby coined the term "The Sexual Revolution."[590] Today, the likes of *The New Yorker* hail him as the "Father of the Sexual Revolution."[591] He was widely read by the 1960s New Left—the children of the sexual revolution.

Reich's book is a sick piece of work. It was first published in German in 1930 and in English in 1945.[592] It was banned from circulation in the United States by a US court order in 1954 and by the FDA in 1956, as much on mental, psychological, and physical health grounds as moral ones.[593]

In his preface to the fourth edition (published in 1949),[594] Reich immediately started into a vigorous defense of "the genital rights of children adolescents," which, he noted, he began pioneering from a

Marxist-socialist perspective in 1928 when he founded his Socialist Society for Sexual Consultation and Sexual Research in Vienna. He lamented how it was deemed "unthinkable for parents to tolerate sexual play, let alone to regard such manifestations as part of a natural, healthy development. The mere thought that adolescents would satisfy their need for love in the natural embrace was horrifying. Anyone who even mentioned these rights was slandered." Reich regretted that even fellow socialists and communists, not to mention members of all religious denominations, had resisted these "attempts to guarantee the love life of children and adolescents." Thus, he and his group "fought for the rights of children and adolescents to have a natural love life." This would be his "great revolution." He would battle for "the naturalness of genital self-gratification for the child."[595]

In the preface to the third edition (published in 1945), Reich likewise championed "the love life" and "free life expressions of newborn infants, of small children, adolescents, and adult men and women." Yes, *newborn infants*. He insisted not only that "sexual intercourse during puberty is a natural and self-evident need" but that "the sexual needs of infants and adolescents are completely natural and justified."[596]

For Reich, as he explained carefully in this book, this was endemic to the "Freudo-Marxism" from which he was operating. He laid out this "new revolutionary ideology" and "ideological endorsement of sexual gratification" at length. He also identified the Church as one of his primary opponents—namely, "the Church as a sex-political organization of patriarchy."[597]

With great foresight into the chaos to come decades later in America, particularly during the sixties when sexual revolutionaries like Kate Millett would use language exactly like this, Reich understood even back then that his ideas would be better received in the United States than in Russia. He saw the USSR as "reactionary in terms of sex politics, while the United States . . . must be described as at least progressive in its sexual politics." America would be a riper target.[598]

It would indeed.

Reich's atheistic views—which were atheistic-*Marxist* views—cannot be separated from this crowning work of his. To be sure, his faith sojourn would become a complicated one. By the end of his life, his hostility toward religion and the religious seemed to mellow. He cooled somewhat in his outright contempt for religious belief, or at least of spirituality, becoming increasingly sympathetic toward spiritual concerns.[599] By 1951, he surprisingly wrote an interesting and complicated book titled *The Murder of Christ: The Emotional Plague of Mankind.* While that book is sympathetic to Jesus Christ, it rejects Christ's Messianic divinity and the teachings of the apostles and Christianity.[600] He believed that Christ mistakenly believed he was the Messiah. Reich felt that the simple teachings of Jesus, which he appreciated and liked, had become hopelessly distorted and erroneously mystified through centuries of Church rule. He also rejected Jewish teachings, including those that Christ invoked in his Messianic mission.[601]

Reich would, to his credit, according to two of his biographers, turn fully against the occult and so-called "psychic phenomena."[602]

At the time of the writing of his *The Sexual Revolution*, however, Wilhelm Reich was ensconced in the pit of his atheist-Marxist-Freudian worldview. Two scholars of Reich, W. Edward Mann and Edward Hoffman, note that the earliest statements from Reich on religion came during the late 1920s, when he was closely involved with first the socialist and then the communist movements. They observe, "He adopted the conventional Marxist attitude toward religion: one of general contempt. He believed that religious feeling was indeed the opiate of the masses and one of the chief means by which the ruling class maintained its hold." In particular, "Reich regarded orthodox religion as simply a major social institution by which political revolution was repressed." He also shared the view of Freud (who called himself a "godless Jew") that all religion was based on illusion—at best a kind of psychological crutch (Marx's view as well).[603] Reich asked, "How can seemingly intelligent and rational people believe the most illogical and preposterous things in the name of religion?"[604]

Reich particularly disliked the religious "taboos" against sexual "expression" that he believed the churches had irrationally established. This he called a "compulsory suppression of sexuality," which included "the struggle to resist the temptation to masturbate," a desire "experienced by every adolescent and every child" (particularly the young Reich).[605]

In all, what we have here in Wilhelm Reich, *pater familias* of the Sexual Revolution, was a bizarre and amoral (and obviously immoral) form of sexuality, fully at odds with the Church. This was a direct product of his Freudianism and his atheistic Marxism. Here was a man fully separated from a religious tradition, whether Jewish or Christian, and who thus proceeded to invent his own sexuality and morality—his own rules and his own truths. Even that might not be so bad if his ideas were confined merely to himself and his farm animals. But unfortunately, the children of the sixties were eagerly awaiting his ideas and embraced his calls for unrestrained sexual expression.

Wilhelm Reich, Freudian-Marxist, had launched a sexual revolution.

Satan and Walter Benjamin

Another purveyor of despair from the Frankfurt School worthy of mention is Walter Benjamin.

Benjamin was born in July 1892 in Berlin and raised in that same European Babylon as Wilhelm Reich.[606] For his mis-education, he haunted some of the same universities that corrupted the minds of Karl Marx and other would-be transformers of human nature—namely, the University of Berlin and the University of Freiburg. His closest colleagues in the Marxist world were Bertolt Brecht, the playwright dubbed "Minstrel of the Soviet GPU" (a pal of America's Hollywood reds), and Theodor Adorno, a veritable virtuoso of destructiveness. Via Adorno and Max Horkheimer, the mastermind behind the financing and operating and relocating of the Frankfurt School to the United States,[607] Benjamin was able to secure Frankfurt School money for his projects. His most famous work was his last, *On the Concept of History* (1940).[608]

Like other members of the Frankfurt School, Walter Benjamin was Jewish, and thus likewise (fortunately) escaped the Nazis in the 1930s but (unfortunately) took his chaos elsewhere. He fled to Paris, where for the first of several times he considered killing himself. He met a tragic end when, in September 1940, he committed suicide in Catalonia, Spain. His nostrums for the West at large were likewise suicidal, as he joined his Frankfurt School comrades in seeking death for the best traditions and timeless truths the West had to offer. Benjamin stands out with Reich as among the weirdest of the cultural Marxists (no small feat, as the likes of Georg Lukacs offered stiff competition). And like Reich, he was a man who seemed to have tapped into some dark forces.

Benjamin's early post-modern worldview was heavily impacted by what he perceived as the failures of the "old way" of doing things. World War I had demonstrated in Benjamin's mind that the traditional, capitalist economic-political order was doomed. The carnage of the war and Nietzsche's death of God moved him into an aesthetic existentialism that left him hungering for a "great transformation."[609] But that wasn't all.

Walter Benjamin had a fascination with the satanic and the "daemonic," the latter in particular playing a role in his conception of "critical practice."[610] Writers on Benjamin contend that he preferred the term "daemonic" for its political significance. Among them, Donna Roberts and Daniel Garza Usabiaga offer a succinct exposition of the role of the satanic in Benjamin's writing in their work *The Use Value of Lucifer: A Comparative Analysis of the Figures of Lucifer and Satan in the Writings of Roger Caillois and Walter Benjamin in the 1930s.*[611]

While in his Parisian exile following the Nazi takeover, Benjamin became acquainted with surrealist thought.[612] Surrealism had a long tradition of dabbling in the satanic. That tradition had origins in the Dadaist movement, an artistic movement which critiqued "bourgeois culture." Dada harbored a disdain for established authority, especially the established religious order. (Dada, or Dadaism, was an early twentieth-century avant-garde art movement popular in certain European circles.) Hugo Ball, the leader of Dada art, viewed himself as a heretic, and did a yeoman's job showing it. On one occasion, Ball gave a performance which he described as a "synthesis of the romantic, dandyish, and demonic theories of the nineteenth-century."[613] Ball fancied dressing as a "magical bishop" while performing ceremonies which mocked traditional Christianity.[614]

The surrealists launched a variety of attacks against Christianity via both visual and written works of sacrilege during the 1920s and 1930s.[615] For example, Man Ray's *Monument a D.A.F. de Sade* (1933) featured an inverted cross which framed a female buttock.[616] Similarly, the surrealist Lewis Kachur's work *The Blessed Virgin Chastises the Infant Jesus Before Three Witnesses* depicted the Virgin Mary (complete with halo) holding down the infant Jesus while spanking his bare bottom.[617] (If these guys were around today, they would be prime candidates for a grant from the National Endowment for the Arts.)

Drawing from this Romantic/Surrealist pit, Walter Benjamin integrated his interpretation of the daemonic. To be sure, while Benjamin supposedly never fully systematized his notions of the satanic/daemonic, he did reference or tap into these concepts in several of his works.[618] Sometimes in quite disturbing ways.

For instance, Paul Klee's famous monoprint *Angelus Novus*, or New Angel, is central to Benjamin's integration of the philosophy of history (for which Benjamin is best known).[619] Benjamin went so far as to not only interpret the image but purchase the actual print in 1921. The painting is often referred to as Benjamin's "angel of history."

Benjamin's understanding of *Angelus Novus* evolved over time, but by 1933, he was ascribing satanic qualities to the monoprint. He discerned in the Angel "satanic features—with a half suppressed smile" and clawed feet that "preferred to free men by taking them."[620] His long-time friend Gershom Scholem candidly observed in his essay "Walter Benjamin and his Angel" that Benjamin understood *Angelus Novus* to have "satanic attributes."[621] Scholem noted that Benjamin's observations came during a "satanic phase," during which Benjamin smoked hashish as a means of "profane illumination."[622]

Yet again, here was another Marxist smoking opium and having hallucinations if not supernatural visions. When Marxists made fun of "the masses" and their religious opium, maybe they should have looked in the mirror.

Benjamin seemed to especially like *Angelus Novus* as a symbol of rebellion against the *repressive* status quo, particularly the Western culture of "commodity."[623] One scholar of Benjamin writes that his interpretation of the New Angel was lapped up by other leftists, who came to relish Benjamin's rendering, thus elevating the *Angelus Novus* to the level of "icon of the left."[624]

Walter Benjamin's interest in Satanism is as complex as it is unsettling. At its core, however, he seemed to view Satan as a triumphant symbol of rebellion (recall that Michael Bakunin acknowledged Satan for similar reasons, and we will see that Saul Alinsky did as well). Note, then, the similarity between Benjamin's understanding and that of Surrealist/Romantic Satanism: both viewed the moral status quo of Western civilization as repressive, and Satan as liberatingly triumphant against "moral authoritarianism."

For the record, the modern Church of Satan claims atheism. The Church of Satan's official website states, "We do not believe in God, we are atheists."[625] (This is eerily verbatim to Vladimir Lenin's October 1920 statement on behalf of Soviet communists: "We do not believe in God."[626]) In fact, the website asserts, "we do not believe in Satan as a being or person."[627]

This begs the question: if the Church of Satan does not actually believe that Satan exists, then why does it invoke him as its namesake? Its answer: "Satan . . . is a symbol of pride, liberty, and individualism."

Again, that is the spirit of Bakunin and other Marxists and socialists we have seen in this book.

What is particularly clear is that these Satanists seek to remove God from the center of the universe and replace God with man—akin to communists' goals. To repeat, as Whittaker Chambers said of communists' first and most fundamental ambition: *Ye shall be as gods.*

To the Church of Satan—echoing yet again Karl Marx's buddy Michael Bakunin—Satan represents rebellion against the *artificial constraints* placed upon man by religion, specifically Christianity. *The Satanic Bible* preaches the complete rejection of any creed that invokes the "authority of a 'divine' nature." There is also a rejection, then, not just of the Creator, but of any notion of the existence of a natural law let alone a biblical law—of a set system of moral codes and absolutes. Thus, Satanism offers its adherents a system of their own to rebel against these "constructs."

That brings us back to Walter Benjamin. Both Benjamin and the Church of Satan draw from Satan as a preferred symbol of rebellion. The Western/Christian tradition is not merely spurned but despised.

One could take this connection further and draw a parallel between Satanism and the so-called "critical theory" pioneered by the Frankfurt School. The Frankfurt School sought to dispel a traditional/Christian understanding of society and instead desired to set society free from the constraints of historical Western culture. As Max Horkheimer noted, the goal of critical theory is "to liberate human beings from the circumstances that enslave them."[628] These "circumstances" are the traditional Western institutions and moral norms that have held together the Judeo-Christian world for millennia.

For culture-focused Marxists, these institutions had to be dismantled. Literally speaking, to hell with them.

Critical Theory's Insidious Roots

Alas, this brings us to a closer understanding of critical theory. What is often termed (for better or worse) "cultural Marxism," or Marxism operating on the cultural front, is more often or formally referred to in the academy as "critical theory."[629]

Today, in the twenty-first century, much of the more culturally inclined Marxism flies under that banner. There are entire academic departments at universities dedicated to critical theory. Tellingly, most of these academic proponents of Marxism are not economics or political science professors, or historians, most of whom know better, but faculty from English departments. Only in our intellectually bankrupt universities could these vapid viewpoints get a following let alone a hearing.

There seems to be an ever-widening panoply of these Marxists. The numbers evolve as the Marxism itself evolves. Today, there are even *gender* Marxists in the academy. There are, for instance, self-described "queer theorists" and academicians engaged in "intersectionality" who are Marxists focused on cultural work.

Above all, these Marxists are about culture. Culture, culture, culture.

If one Googles "critical theory," the first thing that pops up is a boxed definition that states: "**crit·i·cal the·o·ry**, *noun*, a philosophical approach to culture, and especially to literature, that seeks to confront the social, historical, and ideological forces and structures that produce and constrain it. The term is applied particularly to the work of the Frankfurt School."[630]

That is precisely correct. Note the words "culture" and "Frankfurt School." Modern critical theory has grown out of that early Freudian-Marxism of the Frankfurt School.

Jason A. Josephson-Storm, a scholar who published a book on the subject with the University of Chicago Press in 2017, states in his systematic examination, "I locate the origins of much of critical theory in the occult milieu of fin-de-siecle France and Germany, where an alternative to modernity arose that presented itself first and foremost in reference to spiritualism, paganism, Hermeticism, mysticism, and magic." He focuses specifically on the controversial German poet and neo-pagan mystic Ludwig Klages—namely, Klages's influence on a number of key critical theorists, particularly Walter Benjamin.[631]

For the record, Josephson-Storm is hardly alone among scholars in making this connection. In their 1992 journal article "Ludwig Klages (1872-1956) and the Origins of Critical Theory," Georg Stauth and Bryan S. Turner likewise "challenge the traditional view that the Frankfurt School and critical theory were primarily (even exclusively) influenced by the legacy of classical Marxism." They, too, point to Klages (among other sources) and highlight the thought of Walter Benjamin.[632] They and still other scholars, such as Nitzan Lebovic of UCLA, have underscored (likewise in refereed journal articles) Benjamin's fascination with the *Lebensphilosophie* thinking of Klages.[633] Further back, friends and contemporaries wrote of how Benjamin went to Munich to seek out Klages, whose writings "attracted him greatly."[634]

This is not an exhaustive presentation of the literature (academic or popular) on this subject. More articles could be cited. The point is that what I am laying out here was not my invention nor my exaggeration. Critical theory has many dubious tentacles that reach well beyond Marxism into other forms of paganism, esotericism, Magick, if not occultism.[635]

Importantly, Josephson-Storm does not endeavor to condemn or even criticize critical theory. Not at all. His tone appears sympathetic. Nonetheless, his research takes him to those conclusions, most notably in his chapter "Dialectic of Darkness: The Magical Foundations of Critical Theory." That chapter, and the entire book, is extremely illuminating. To cite just one of numerous disturbing examples, he discusses the influence of Klages and his Cosmic Circle (and its occult philosophy) not only on Benjamin but on leading Frankfurt

School members and even founders, such as Max Horkheimer, Theodor Adorno, Georg Lukacs, and Jurgen Habermas—all of whom, Josephson-Storm notes, had read and cited Klages's work.[636] (Habermas took his PhD at the University of Bonn, the haunt of Marx and Bruno Bauer.) He sees in all of it an "uncanny resemblance" between critical theory and "the heart of magical philosophy."[637]

"All told," sums up Josephson-Storm, "it would appear that critical theory's proximate other was the occult."[638]

This was a Marxist philosophical system that was not merely anti-Christian but indisputably pagan, if not demonic. Here was another disturbing confluence of the devil and Karl Marx.

Lucifer and Saul Alinsky

Speaking of disturbing confluences, the inspirations behind famed radical Saul Alinsky are likewise troubling and hard to pin down. Not hard to find, however, is his acknowledgment to Lucifer, which comes at the start of his most famous work, *Rules for Radicals*. Kicking off his opus to radicalism and community organizing, Alinsky offered this curious opening acknowledgment: "Lest we forget at least an over-the-shoulder acknowledgment to the very first radical: from all our legends, mythology, and history . . . the first radical known to man who rebelled against the establishment and did it so effectively that he at least won his own kingdom—Lucifer."

Yes, Saul Alinsky, icon of the political left, whose admirers include Hillary Clinton and Barack Obama, commenced his magnum opus—the one for which he is hailed by progressives, a book not only read by Clinton but used as a text by Obama in Chicago as a teacher of community organizing—with an acknowledgement of the devil.[639] He directed his readers' gaze to Satan as a glorious "rebel." His evocation is very similar to Bakunin's in his 1871 magnum opus *God and the State*, which lauded Lucifer as "the eternal rebel, the first freethinker and the emancipator of worlds."

To avoid overstatement and hyperbole, we should clarify that it would not be quite accurate to say that *Rules for Radicals* is "dedicated" to Lucifer, as is often claimed by Alinsky's detractors. (It is also hard to criticize them for making that assumption.) Looking at the book carefully, it appears to be dedicated to one person: there is a page at the start of the book that says simply, "To Irene." On the page prior to the Irene dedication is a list of "Personal Acknowledgements," where Alinsky lists four friends: Jason Epstein, Cicely Nichols, Susan Rabiner, and Georgia Harper. Following the Irene page is another page, the controversial one, in which Alinsky offers three quotes, the first from a Rabbi Hillel, the second from Thomas Paine, and the third from Alinsky himself, giving his nod to Lucifer. One well-known fact-checking source on the web, Snopes.com, describes this as "three epigraphs on an introductory page."[640] That is a fair and acceptable way to characterize it. And the third of the three is an "epigraph" (if you will) to Satan.

But we should not let Alinsky off the Luciferian hook.

Alinsky elsewhere had more favorable things to say about that first rebel and radical, and particularly Satan's dominion in the netherworld. He was asked about the acknowledgment in his March 1972 interview with *Playboy* magazine near the end of his life, a swan song that every Alinsky aficionado knows about. The exchange came at the very end of the interview, with *Playboy* apparently judging it a fittingly provocative close to the extremely lengthy discussion:

> PLAYBOY: Having accepted your own mortality, do you believe in any kind of afterlife?
>
> ALINSKY: Sometimes it seems to me that the question people should ask is not "Is there life after death?" but "Is there life after birth?" I don't know whether there's anything after this or not. I haven't seen the evidence one way or the other and I don't think anybody else has either. But I do know that man's obsession with the question comes out of his stubborn refusal to

face up to his own mortality. Let's say that if there is an afterlife, and I have anything to say about it, I will unreservedly choose to go to hell.

PLAYBOY: Why?

ALINSKY: Hell would be heaven for me. All my life I've been with the have-nots. Over here, if you're a have-not, you're short of dough. If you're a have-not in hell, you're short of virtue. Once I get into hell, I'll start organizing the have-nots over there.

PLAYBOY: Why them?

ALINSKY: They're my kind of people.

"They're my kind of people," said Alinsky. "Hell would be heaven for me." Alinsky averred that he would "unreservedly choose to go to hell." That is frightening. Theologians often comfort repentant sinners fearing the flames of hell by assuring them that one must deliberately choose hell to end up there. Well, Saul Alinsky determined that such was his choice, unreservedly so.

Like Karl Marx's character in "The Pale Maiden," Alinsky was willing to forfeit heaven by choosing hell.

When I first Googled the Alinsky-*Playboy* interview several years ago, I found the aforementioned excerpt posted at (among other places) a Satanist website. There, the author, in an article titled "Saul D. Alinsky: A role model for left-wing Satanists," writes of the exchange, "I'm not sure whether Alinsky really was a Satanist/Luciferian of some sort or whether he was just joking. He may well have been just joking."[641]

An Alinsky supporter, a liberal friend of mine, shrugged this off as a joke, as Alinsky allegedly being facetious. I asked my friend how she knew that. She admitted that she did not, not for certain. And if those statements and nods to Lucifer and hell were something of a joke, they are not very funny.

Another online fact-checking source, *PolitiFact*, adds this caveat:

"The rest of the book [*Rules for Radicals*] includes no real discussion of Lucifer or Satan, though it does talk about the way people demonize political opponents so that others see their opponents as 'devils.'"[642]

Indeed it does. And that is not particularly amusing either. One of Alinsky's most infamous rules is to isolate the target and vilify it. This was the thrust of Alinsky's final and most egregious rule for radicals (no. 13): *"Pick the target, freeze it, personalize it, and polarize it."* He advised cutting off the support network of the person and isolating the person from sympathy. He cruelly urged going after people rather than institutions because people hurt faster than institutions. That is most assuredly not what Jesus would do.

As for Alinsky's politics, they are not easy to discern. Many conservatives reflexively tag Alinsky a communist, but that is not nuanced enough. The man was maddening, as were his politics. He was pro-communist, and unquestioningly the quintessential radical, but he was certainly no textbook Marxist-Leninist, nor a member of the Communist Party.

One writer, *National Review*'s Stanley Kurtz, has studied Alinsky and pegs him well, calling him a "democratic socialist" who "worked closely for years with Chicago's Communist Party and did everything in his power to advance its program. Most of his innovations were patterned on Communist Party organizing tactics." Kurtz adds that Alinsky "was smart enough never to join the party. . . . From the start, he understood the dangers of ideological openness. He was a pragmatist, but a pragmatist of the far left." Kurtz adds, "So Alinsky supported the central Marxist tenet of public ownership of the means of production. Unlike the New Left, however, Alinsky had no expectation of reaching that end through swift or violent revolution. He meant to approach the ultimate goal slowly, piecemeal, perhaps over generations, through patient organizing efforts at the local level."[643]

This was much more akin to the Fabian-socialist model adhered to by many American progressives and "democratic socialists." It was the call of evolution rather than revolution. It was the Marxist-communist-socialist call of public ownership of the means of production, but without Lenin's love of violence.

Kurtz puts it well. I would add the crucial caveat that though Alinsky was not a doctrinaire communist in ideology, he was very favorable to communism. Alinsky himself said he was never a Communist Party member but did not shy from working with party members. "I knew plenty of Communists in those days, and I worked with them on a number of projects," said Alinsky in his *Playboy* interview. "Back in the Thirties, the Communists did a hell of a lot of good work." He added emphatically, "Anybody who tells you he was active in progressive causes in those days and never worked with the Reds is a goddamn liar. Their platform stood for all the right things." He contended that "the party in those days was on the right side and did considerable good."[644]

That is quite a testimony for a purported non-communist: note that Alinsky contended that the Communist Party "stood for all the right things," that it "was on the right side," and that it "did considerable good." He was referring to the Communist Party of the 1930s; the height of the Stalin era. This was precisely the period that American Communist Party members pledged a loyalty oath to Stalin's USSR and toward the goal of a Moscow-directed "Soviet America." Those were Alinsky's pals that he worked with, who did a *hell of a lot of good work*.

And so, Saul Alinsky was not a communist? Technically, formally, no—even as, ideologically, and physically, he was not far removed from the party.

In his 1972 interview with *Playboy*, nearing the end of his life, Alinsky stated, "I've never joined any organization—not even the ones I've organized myself. I prize my own independence too much. And philosophically, I could never accept any rigid dogma or ideology, whether it's Christianity or Marxism."

That was certainly true of Christianity. There were no

acknowledgments to Christ at the start of *Rules for Radicals*. No, only to Lucifer.

Kate Millett: Mao of Women's Lib, High Priestess of Feminism

Likewise nothing to laugh at were the antics of Kate Millett, one of the early faces of the National Organization for Women (NOW), and one of the leading feminists of the 1960s and 1970s. Kate was not only a feminist but a Marxist.

Millett was the author of *Sexual Politics*, her dissertation at the communist hotbed Columbia University. It became a cultural juggernaut when published in 1970. There, she decried the "patriarchy" of the monogamous nuclear family. The book landed Kate on the cover of *Time* magazine on August 31, 1970, which dubbed her the "high priestess" and "Mao Tse-tung of the Women's Movement." Her angry book served as the bible, the feminist-Marxist manifesto, of women's lib.[645] *The New York Times* referred to *Sexual Politics* as "the Bible of Women's Liberation."[646]

The best witness to Millett's long life, mindset, destruction, and demons is her sister, Mallory. Mallory had suffered her own inner turmoil at the hands of the university system before rediscovering her faith and eventually pulling herself out of the clutches of the cultural-Marxist beast. Amid the sixties revolution, Kate implored Mallory to "come to New York," where she and her female comrades were "making revolution!"[647]

Mallory went to Kate's gathering in New York, thus becoming an eyewitness not only to how unhinged the left had become but to what was festering within the culture rotted by the maggot of Marxist ideology. Mallory remembers:

> I stayed with Kate . . . in a dilapidated loft on The Bowery as she finished her first book, a PhD thesis for Columbia University, "Sexual Politics."

It was 1969. Kate invited me to join her for a gathering at the home of her friend, Lila Karp. They called the assemblage a "consciousness-raising-group," a typical communist exercise, something practiced in Maoist China. We gathered at a large table as the chairperson opened the meeting with a back-and-forth recitation, like a Litany, a type of prayer done in the Catholic Church. But now it was Marxism, the Church of the Left, mimicking religious practice:

"Why are we here today?" she asked.

"To make revolution," they answered.

"What kind of revolution?" she replied.

"The Cultural Revolution," they chanted.

"And how do we make Cultural Revolution?" she demanded.

"By destroying the American family!" they answered.

"How do we destroy the family?" she came back.

"By destroying the American Patriarch," they cried exuberantly.

"And how do we destroy the American Patriarch?" she replied.

"By taking away his power!"

"How do we do that?"

"By destroying monogamy!" they shouted.

"How can we destroy monogamy?"…

"By promoting promiscuity, eroticism, prostitution and homosexuality!" they resounded.[648]

Mallory says that the comradely sisters then proceeded with a sustained discussion on how to advance these goals. "It was clear they desired nothing less than the utter deconstruction of Western society," she said. How would they do this? They would do so via the method laid out by the cultural Marxists, by the Frankfurt School, by the spirit of Antonio Gramsci and the "long march through the institutions" of the culture, from media to education. They would "invade every American institution. Every one must be permeated with 'The Revolution.'"

Mallory watched it unfold and unravel. She also witnessed the cultural wreckage. Today she speaks tragically of encountering women in their fifties and sixties who fell for this "creed" in their youth and now cry themselves to sleep many countless nights grieving for the children that they will never have and that they "coldly murdered because they were protecting the empty loveless futures they now live with no way of going back." "Where are my children?" they cry to Mallory. "Where are my grandchildren?"

Those children were sacrificed at the feminist altar of abortion.

"Your sister's books destroyed my sister's life!" Mallory has heard numerous times. "She was happily married with four kids and after she read those books, walked out on a bewildered man and didn't look back." The man fell into despair and ruin. The children were stunted and deeply harmed. The family was profoundly dislocated and there was "no putting Humpty-Dumpty together again."

Kate Millett: Marxist, feminist, advocate for gay rights, for new sexuality, for new spousal relationships, and on and on. She channeled her revolutionary energies into a campaign to take down marriage and family, the backbone of American society. And she practiced what she preached. Though she was married, she practiced lesbianism, becoming bisexual. She had started that lifestyle at Columbia while writing *Sexual Politics*. This would, predictably, end her marriage to her husband, who found the trashing of these norms unnatural and detrimental to the health of their marriage. Of course, to many in our brave new world, this makes Kate a heroine. Today, the bio for Kate Millett at the "GLBTQ" website hails her as a "groundbreaking" "bisexual feminist literary and social critic."[649]

Kate Millett's Demons

Most disturbing about Kate is just how far she descended into a darker world. Her sister, Mallory, believes Kate was demonically possessed. Obviously, that is a major charge, one not levied lightly, but Mallory, today a devout Catholic, and who not only studied Kate intimately—they shared a bedroom (bunk beds) when they were growing up—has done her share of theological exploration. She has expressed that observation to me many times in emails and phone calls, and has openly shared it with others in interviews and on websites. She has not been reticent about it.

"I've always thought and said that Kate was a definite case of possession," Mallory wrote to me in one email. "Our elder sister Sally tells me that Kate was nuts when she was four and that when I was born in her sixth year she was poised over my bassinet plotting my murder and not in the normal way of a child whose babyhood has been usurped. Sally said that she was a real menace from the beginning. I don't think she was ever in the faith."[650]

The reference to the faith refers to the family's Roman Catholic roots. Kate went to St. Mark's grade school in St. Paul, Minnesota, from kindergarten through eighth grade—with nuns as teachers all the way. She also attended the elite girls' Convent School in St. Paul, Derham Hall. She was expelled multiple times. "I have no idea when she left the Church," Mallory writes, "as she was irreverent her whole life."[651]

As to this vexing matter of Kate's diabolical side, Mallory wrote to me on another occasion, "She was definitely possessed, Paul. There's no question." She recalls how Kate could fly off the hinges and in an instant become an "outrageous lunatic." She recalled family reunions at Kate's home in New England, which would start on a Thursday with the feminist Kate surprisingly turning into a delightful homemaker and laying out a "wonderful spread" in classic New England home fashion. These would start on a Thursday, with the whole family there and Kate "just delightful." By Saturday and then Sunday morning, however, one could feel (literally) a stark change in Kate's behavior and the overall ambience. "By Sunday morning, she was brooding," said Mallory, "and you were just waiting for her to pop." According to Mallory, "By Sunday afternoon, she would be literally on her back kicking her legs in the air screaming. It was just awful. My poor mother. She was just so distraught by this every time."[652]

My first conversation with Mallory was a long, chilling one early in the afternoon of Friday, April 7, 2017, while I was driving on the Pennsylvania Turnpike en route to Reston, Virginia. We talked for close to two hours. We could have kept going. She was a fan of my previous writings, especially my 2015 book *Takedown*, and was pleased that for that book I had used her September 2014 *FrontPage Magazine* article on Kate.[653] She wanted to open up to me about her famous feminist sister.

Mallory herself had been an actress and was close to some well-known Hollywood figures. She had been through a lot in her life, but was now a very devout Catholic in faithful standing with the Church. One can sense a penitential feel from Mallory, seeking to find reparation and healing.

Mallory proceeded to say to me that Kate was "crazy and insane— sadistic, evil, and dangerous." She shared with me for the first time her older sister's account that from the moment that Mallory was in the bassinet, Kate gave her an ominous look as if she wanted to reach out and strangle her. "From the day I was in the bassinet, she wanted to kill me."

Here she also offered what she believed was a spiritual explanation for this behavior: she said she believed that her Marxist sister was demonically possessed. Mallory conceded that some people think she is crazy when she says that. She even proffered that diagnosis to two priests who gave her funny looks. Nonetheless, she told the priests, "Listen to me. I understand this stuff. I have a sister—a very famous sister—who is possessed. I know what I'm talking about." She said there is no other explanation for Kate's lifelong pattern of outrageous and ruinous and vicious behavior that could not be fixed or corrected. She is convinced of it.

Mallory had not spoken to Kate since 1993, at their mother's funeral. Her mother always looked at Kate with sympathy in a way that a mother would look painfully at her most messed-up child. Her dying mom asked Mallory to take "good care" of Kate once she was gone. Mallory rebuffed her mother, "I'm sorry, Mom, but there's no way." She said she had to break from Kate because Kate would destroy her.

Mallory spoke from experience. Of all the Millett kids, Mallory was the one who always got stuck in the room with Kate because Mallory was, by nature, "the helper." But unfortunately, this was dangerous. Mallory lived in New York and had a psychiatrist advise her that when she got in these situations where she was stuck with Kate, she should simply leave: "Walk away. Simply get up and walk away." Mallory replied, "But how do I do that?" The psychiatrist told Mallory to simply say to Kate, "I need to go to the bathroom," and then leave and don't come back. Mallory said this was so simple as to be laughable, but it worked. Otherwise, until that point, she had not been able to break free from Kate's grip. She said, "Kate would effectively hold you hostage in the same room with her, beating you down, tormenting you, threatening you, brooding over you." She said she seriously thought that one of those days Kate would try to kill her. She truly did believe that.

Mallory said that Kate lived in darkness for decades following the death of their mother, with her feminist "minions" surrounding her. Mallory said these "minions" were all women—acolytes, disciples, all of whom practically worshipped Kate. She was like their guru. Mallory said that these were "old aging lesbian feminists" who "all sleep with each other, and all worship Kate." Kate was like their cult leader.

Mallory told me pointedly that one could see by looking into Kate's eyes and face that she was highly abnormal. Mallory returned to the "demonic" point: she said that when she would talk to Kate, Kate's face would take on "forms." This made Mallory think that Kate had "something inside of her."

A pained Mallory says the one thing that has most baffled and saddened her about life generally has been to observe how her "crazy" sister's "lunatic" ideas managed to rapidly sweep through the culture and country. She remains "blown away" at how within "a couple of years" it seemed like "every university" in America had her sister's warped book (*Sexual Politics*) on syllabi as required reading. "It just doesn't make sense, Paul," she told me. "How did something like that happen?"

It is a great question, Mallory—a vexing one, a sad testimony to the flawed human condition. It is also a timeless, agonizing question: what explains the inexplicable attraction of the idiotic ideas of the likes of Marx and Engels, Marcuse and Reich, Harry Hay and Walter Benjamin, or those of the Frankfurt madmen and Kate Millett? How do human beings fall prey to such awful notions?

"Evil Itself"

Beyond my own discussions with her, Mallory Millett would go on to relate these sentiments to others, including in a notable February 2018 interview with *FrontPage Magazine*.[654] Those remembrances are worth quoting not only as further affirmation of what Mallory told me privately but as further (public) extension of what Mallory witnessed. Note her descriptions of Kate's "evil," her "darkness," her raging, ranting, "eyes rolling in her head" and "frothing of the mouth:"

> She was the most disturbed, megalomaniacal, evil and dishonest person I have ever known. She tried to kill me so many times that it's now an enormous blur of traumatizing horrors. She was a sadist, a torturer, a deeply-engrained bully who took immense pleasure in hurting others. Incorrigible and ruthless, she was expelled multiple times from every school she attended. I spent

my childhood with heart hammering as I tiptoed through the house so as not to be noticed by the dreadful Kate. Our mother was helpless, paralyzed with terror in the face of Kate.

It's a grinding hardship to bring oneself to write such harsh things about one's own blood. It took some bucking up for me to start telling the truth. . . . I spent decades laboring to reason her into the light. . . .

This was especially true after an incident when I was trapped alone with Kate in an apartment in Sacramento for a week and she did not allow me to sleep for five days as she raged and ranted, eyes rolling in her head, frothing at the mouth and holding chats with "little green men." Not knowing a single person in Sacramento, I had nowhere to turn. Too terrified to go to sleep, I wasn't sure she even knew who I was but I could imagine a butcher knife thrust into my back as I slept. Big sister Sally came from Nebraska to rescue me.

After that there was an enormous effort by the family wherein we all took Kate to court for legal commitment in Minnesota. She hired a male feminist hotshot New York lawyer and managed to swim back out into the world to hurt, menace, and harm ever more people.

Kate had many handmaidens. Mallory notes that her radical sister had "enablers everywhere" on all seven continents—more groupies, acolytes, minions, who "worshipped" her.

Mallory also recalled in this 2018 interview with *FrontPage Magazine* the "consciousness-raising sessions" in New York City. She underscored that these girls wanted to normalize a host of evils and taboos that even included Satanism and witchcraft:

In 1969 I attended consciousness-raising sessions in New York City with my sister, Kate, where a group of 10-15 women sat around a long oval table and plotted the New Feminist

Movement and the founding of NOW. Their template was Mao's China and the group confessionals conducted in each village in order to "cleanse the people's thinking." The burning objective of Kate's "consciousness-raising" was "the destruction of the American family," as she deemed it "a patriarchal institution devoted to the oppression and enslavement of women and children."

They went on to form NOW and, with that organization, achieve their stated goal of taking down the Patriarchy through a massive coordinated promotion of promiscuity, eroticism, prostitution, abortion and homosexuality. Their proposed method was to infiltrate every institution in the nation: the universities, the media, primary and secondary schools, PTAs, Teachers Unions, city and state governments, the library system, the executive branches of government as well as the judiciaries and legislatures.

One of their most desired results was the smashing of every taboo in Western culture. Imagine that! Think of that alone! The normalizing of every taboo: polygamy, bestiality, Satanism, pornography, promiscuity, witchcraft, pedophilia—all activities which rot the human soul and city.

The reaction to this interview posted at the website of *FrontPage Magazine* was quite expressive, with readers not shying from menacing language. When one reader wrote that Kate was not crazy but evil, Mallory herself jumped into the discussion in the readers' comments section and stated emphatically, "I entirely agree with you." Further down in the discussion, Mallory iterated unequivocally that she believes that Kate was demonically possessed: "I have come to understand that Kate was, indeed, possessed and from what I can discern it was probably an early event, most likely before I was born. There was an energy from her that was inexplicable, illogical, demonic and, to any reasonable person, terrifying. She could tear through a room of people like a storm of flying razor blades. A friend who didn't know her once told me she was seated next to Kate (in the 1980's) at a charity dinner and was struck by her demeanor: 'the darkest person I've ever met.......as if she had a black aura.'"

Even if this behavior "was clinically diagnosed as insanity," said Mallory, "for me it was always evil itself."

In sum, Mallory has been on the record for a long time saying these things about Kate. To quote just one more example, back in a June 2014 piece, referring to her larger family, she said that Kate "demonized us."[655]

Practicing the Sexual Politics She Preached

Aside from the dark roots of whatever might have possessed Kate Millett, the fruits of her Marxist ideology were palpably toxic, not just upon the public but her own life.

Kate practiced the sexual politics she preached. She had long ago abandoned her long-suffering, faithful husband not for men but for numerous other women she hopped in bed with. This included lesbian orgies that slithered into the realm of the pagan. Mallory described to author Carrie Gress a harrowing episode one Halloween evening at Kate's loft apartment. Gress recorded:

> Upon entering [Kate's apartment], there was a long, low table with twelve placements topped by a plate, a bowl of water, and sharp knife resting on it. In front of each place setting were twelve completely naked women, sitting cross legged on cushions. The naked woman at the head of the table was wrapped by a ten-foot boa constrictor. Dumbstruck and appalled, Mallory and her friend watched in horror. They were invited to join in the ritual, but they told Kate that they were just there to observe, which seemed to suit Kate since they were only willing to take off their shoes. "As they took their eyes off us to resume their ritual," Mallory explains, "we tiptoed to our shoes and crept out

running down those flights like bats out of hell. My feet barely touched the steps until we burst out onto the Bowery, shaking and huffing in shock and terror."[656]

Kate Millett, feminist founder, even tried to aggressively get her own sister, Mallory, in bed with her. What Mallory witnessed among Kate and her cohort was a mix of Marxism, atheism, paganism, witchcraft, the occult, and a flat-out psychotic if not demonic element as well.[657]

Ultimately, Kate's dance with the dark side ended one morning in Paris, September 6, 2017, a week shy of her eighty-third birthday. She collapsed from a massive heart attack.[658] At her side was her "wife," Sophie Keir.

Mallory got the news from her sister Sally. "I was flooded with such indescribable relief that she could no longer spread her filth, lies and misery, nor could she go on threatening the lives and safety of others," said Mallory. She immediately recalled one such occasion from Kate: "Once, she wrote an entire book describing her deep passion for her lover, Sita. Sita's response was to kill herself. My biggest anxiety about Kate has always been that one day she would take out a family of five on the Saw Mill River Parkway as—laced with liquor, wine, lithium, marijuana, and God knows what else—she hurtled, ranting and raging, up that difficult road. For many years I have braced for that call in the night."

Mallory was relieved. Kate's doting fans, however, mourned; they grieved the passing of their Marxist-feminist heroine.

Kate's funeral was held at a church whose members neither openly embrace Jesus Christ nor the Father—namely, the Fourth Universalist Society, a Unitarian church on Central Park West in New York City. In its glowing obituary, the *New York Times* celebrated not only the late high priestess of women's lib but the "foot soldiers and commanders" of feminism in attendance at Kate's death service: Gloria Steinem, Phyllis Chesler, the actress Kathleen Turner—who was there as "a stand-in for both Hillary Clinton and Robin Morgan"—and even the bizarre Yoko Ono, a buddy of Kate for over fifty years. The congregants at the "church" were led by folk singer and activist Holly Near in bellowing a piece titled "Singing for Our Lives," which Near wrote after gay pioneer Harvey Milk was murdered. "Everyone seemed to know the words," wrote the *Times* reporter. "Ms. Ono joined hands with Ms. Keir and Ms. Chesler."[659]

What a hollow way to go. But it was a fitting dirge to the life of Kate Millett.

The funeral spectacle would have been bad enough if it had reflected merely Kate's perversities. But perhaps saddest of all, Kate's radical sexual politics have become her country's and culture's sexual politics as well, to the point that this author of *Sexual Politics*—this woman—was legally able to marry another woman in the new America, with few batting an eyelash. She pivoted from classical Marxism to cultural Marxism, from economics to sex, from redistributing wealth to stumping for same-sex marriage and "LGBTQ rights." It took America a few decades, but all the hard work by secular progressives in the schools and the universities eventually brought the masses in line with the very ideas of Kate Millett that Americans once considered insane and evil.

Marx's minions may not have secured an economic revolution, but they have triumphed in their cultural revolution.

PART 6

CONCLUSION

CHAPTER 15

"FUNDAMENTAL TRANSFORMATION"

MARX'S ENDURING SPECTER

"We are five days away from fundamentally transforming the United States of America." So declared Barack Obama in Columbia, Missouri on October 30, 2008, on the cusp of his historic presidential election. He predicted a "defining moment in history" to "give this country the change we need."[660]

It was a striking statement, boldly revolutionary, perhaps surpassed only by the response of those in attendance, who, rather than pausing to reflect upon such an audacious assertion, wildly applauded. To be sure, Obama enthusiasts would have ecstatically cheered anything he said at that moment. He could have promised everyone a magical unicorn. Obama himself admitted to serving as a kind of "blank screen" upon which Americans desiring some warm and fuzzy "hope and change" could project whatever they wanted.

But even then, the words "fundamentally transform" should have set off alarm bells. Americans generally don't do fundamental transformation. They make changes, yes, small and large, but the remarkable system conceived by the American founders—especially remarkable for its stability—was not devised for a single man to enter the White House and initiate a fundamental transformation. Who among us—other than the most radical revolutionaries—actually

379

want to *fundamentally transform* the nation of Washington and Jefferson and Adams and Madison and Lincoln and the Roosevelts and Kennedy and Reagan? Many people think America has many problems, but those can be addressed without a *fundamental transformation*. Ask professors who teach history or political ideologies and they will tell you that totalitarian communism, Marxism-Leninism, is the ideology that seeks fundamental transformation.

Recall that in *The German Ideology* (among others), Marx and Engels said that in order to achieve "communist consciousness, and for the success of the cause, it is necessary that man himself should suffer a massive change." This change must come through "a revolution," a process of "overthrowing" the old "filthy yoke and . . . founding a new society only in a revolution." Marx repeatedly urged nothing less than the creation of a "new world." His "generation," he insisted, like the Jews that Moses led out of the wilderness, must "conquer a new world" and "must also perish in order to make room for the people who are fit for a new world."[661] Communists would play the role of sacrificial savior to deliver a new secular covenant for the new world.

Such is the totalitarian task of communism. Indeed, the textbook definition of totalitarianism, which I have scribbled on the chalkboard every fall semester at Grove City College since 1997, is to fundamentally transform—specifically, to seek to fundamentally transform human nature via some form of political-ideological-cultural upheaval.

So, that being the case, I winced when Barack Obama said that, and then felt sick to the stomach when I watched people blissfully and blindly applaud. Such blithe *unthought* is disturbing to see from inhabitants of a nation founded upon the extraordinarily thoughtful and stable principles of 1776.

And yet, Obama's two-term presidency no doubt marked a turning point. The country did seem to begin a fundamental transformation in that period and through the 2010s.[662]

That fundamental transformation, however, did not happen in areas hoped for (or feared) in 2008, or that Obama perhaps even had in mind let alone dared to mention in Columbia, Missouri. It has not been a fundamental shift in attitudes regarding the role of government, taxation, regulations, economics, class, or even healthcare, where Obama had his signature legislative achievement. It did not happen in foreign policy.

The reality is that the true fundamental transformation in America (and the West generally) has come in the realm of culture, notably in matters of sexual orientation, gender, marriage, and family. The shift there has been unprecedented and far beyond anyone's imagination in 2008. It was signaled most conspicuously in June 2015 when the Obama White House—the nation's first house—was illuminated in the colors of the "LGBTQ" rainbow on the day of the *Obergefell* decision, when the Supreme Court, by a one-vote margin, rendered unto itself the ability to redefine marriage (theretofore the province of biblical and natural law) and imposed this new "Constitutional right" on all fifty states. If ever there was a picture of a fundamental transformation, that was it. And that was just one of countless "accomplishments" heralded and boasted of by the Obama administration. In June 2016, to celebrate the one-year anniversary of *Obergefell,* the White House press office released two extraordinary fact sheets detailing President Obama's vast efforts to promote "LGBT" rights at home and abroad.[663] Not only was it telling that the White House would assemble such a list, and tout it, but the sheer length of the list was stunning to behold. There was no similar list of such dramatic changes by the Obama White House in any other policy area. Such achievements included the infamous Obama bathroom fiat, through which, according to Barack Obama's executive word, all public schools were ordered to revolutionize their restrooms and locker rooms to make them available to teenage boys who want to be called girls.

Looking back, it is in the understanding of human sexuality, its subversion really, that Barack Obama left his stamp upon the United States. One can hope the stamp is not indelible.

From there, the culture's fundamental transformation has hit warp speed, with the number of optional "gender identities," for instance, expanding exponentially. Changes there, more than anywhere, seem irreversible by anything other than the miraculous, by anything short of a religious revival or unforeseeable dramatic shift in spiritual-moral thinking.

As noted, the New York City council offers public employees the option of choosing from thirty-one different "gender identities," including pioneering gay communist Harry Hay's "two-spirit" option. Of course, that is nothing compared to Facebook, which at various times since 2014 has listed fifty-one gender options, fifty-three, fifty-six, fifty-eight, and seventy-one, or to the BBC, which (as of 2019) teaches children that there are more than one hundred and counting.[664]

Where does it end? Truly no one knows.

The political left's cultural revolution on the sexual-gender-family front is ubiquitous, as is its intolerance of any dissenters. We see it in the culture of fear and intimidation by the self-prided forces of "diversity" and "tolerance" who viciously seek to denounce, dehumanize, demonize, and destroy anyone who disagrees with their brazen newfound conceptions of marriage and family, even as their inventions are at odds with the prevailing position of 99.99 percent-plus of human beings who have bestrode the earth since the dawn of humanity. Instead, traditional Christians are the ones portrayed as the outliers, as abnormal, as extremists, as bigots, as "haters."

That is a fundamental transformation of a culture and a nation. That is evidence of a true revolution by the heirs of Marx and other radicals.

"The Most Radical Rupture in Traditional Relations"

To "fundamentally transform." Here was, in essence, an inherently Marxist goal declared to a sea of oblivious Americans, whether Barack Obama explicitly or fully understood or meant it himself. It is highly doubtful that Obama had Marx (or a Marcuse or Millett or Reich) on the mind at that moment.[665] Obama was merely riding a wave that began as a ripple over a century or so ago. And typically, most of those surfing or floating along have little notion who or what helped give the initial push.

Nonetheless, the goal of Karl Marx and the Marxist project from the outset was one of fundamental transformation, permanent revolution, and unrestrained criticism of everything—nothing less than "the ruthless criticism of all that exists."[666] Marx's ideas were so radical, and so (as Marx openly conceded) "contrary to the nature of things," that they inevitably lead to totalitarianism; that is because they *are* totalitarian in the strictest sense, as they seek to transform human nature and the foundational order. We have seen passages from Marx to that effect throughout this book. Here is a short summary:

- Marx in the *Manifesto* said that communism represents "the most radical rupture in traditional relations."
- Marx in the *Manifesto* acknowledged that communism seeks to "abolish the present state of things."
- Marx in the *Manifesto* stated that "they [the Communists] openly declare that their ends can be attained only by the forcible overthrow of all existing social conditions."
- Marx in the close of the *Manifesto*: "Communists everywhere support every revolutionary movement against the existing social and political order of things."
- Marx in a letter to Arnold Ruge called for the "ruthless criticism of all that exists."
- Marx had a favorite quote from Goethe's *Faust*, "Everything that exists deserves to perish."

- Marx in his essay declaring religion "the opium of the people" said that "the criticism of religion is the beginning of all criticism." (Recall that in that essay he used the word "criticism" twenty-nine times.)

Beyond ruthless criticism, there was ruthless abolition. The word "abolition" is omnipresent throughout Marx's writings. As Robert Payne noted, the word almost seems to jump off every page of the *Manifesto*.[667] "And after he has 'abolished' property, family, and nations, and all existing societies, Marx shows little interest in creating a new society on the ruins of the old," observed Payne. "He had written in a poem to Jenny that he would throw a gauntlet at the world, and watch it crumble. Comforted by her love, he would wander through the kingdom of ruins, his words glowing with action, his heart like the heart of God. The *Communist Manifesto* was the gauntlet he threw at the world."[668]

It was indeed. Marx's more benign modern defenders want to characterize Lenin and Stalin and other tyrants as aberrations of Marxism, as the nasty totalitarians seeking to annihilate the old order. In fact, they were merely following Marx, the ultimate revolutionary and rebel. Karl Marx wanted to burn down the house long before Lenin and Stalin were even born.

Lenin himself would profess the same, as is likewise clear throughout his statements. As merely one case in point, consider again his seminal 1920 speech to the Third All-Russia Congress of the Russian Young Communist League, published in *Pravda* in October 1920. That speech was quoted in this book at length for its many striking statements against religion. Equally significant, however, was Lenin's expressed task to immediately set about abolishing and fundamentally transforming the old order. "Comrades, today I would like to talk on the fundamental tasks of the Young Communist League," Lenin began to the six hundred delegates at the October 1920 Congress. "It is the youth that will be faced with the actual task of creating a communist society. For it is clear that the generation of working people brought up in capitalist society can, at best, accomplish the task of destroying the foundations of the old."[669]

Vladimir Lenin—communist, Bolshevik, self-anointed keeper of the Marxist flame, half namesake of Marxism-Leninism—could not have been clearer: the "task" was to destroy the foundations of the old.

The "whole point here," said Lenin, was "the transformation of the old, capitalist society; the upbringing, training and education of the new generations that will create the communist society cannot be conducted on the old lines." The teaching, training, and education of youth "must" be directed to that goal: "Only by radically remolding the teaching, organization and training of the youth shall we be able to ensure that the efforts of the younger generation will result in the creation of a society that will be unlike the old society, i.e., in the creation of a communist society."

Note the unmistakable language from Lenin: "destroying the foundations of the old," "the transformation of the old," "radically remolding."

Here, Lenin pointed back to Marx, as he always did, as the "genius" inspiration. "He was a genius," Lenin told his beaming young comrades, particularly because of Marx's goal of radically and critically reshaping everything. "He [Marx] critically reshaped everything that had been created by human society, without ignoring a single detail," said Lenin, speaking of Marx here in almost omnipotent terms. "He reconsidered, subjected to criticism, and verified on the working-class movement everything that human thinking had created."

No doubt that was true of the man who called for the ruthless criticism of everything that exists. He and Lenin were of the same mind.

The old schools were so loathsome, averred Lenin: "The old schools produced servants needed by the capitalists. We must therefore abolish them." The new "aim," said Lenin, was simple: "learn communism." He told the youth: "You have to build up a communist society. . . . You must be foremost among the millions of builders of a communist society in whose ranks every young man and woman should be." Every young man and woman should proceed in that total task at hand. No exceptions. "You must train yourselves to be communists," demanded Lenin. "To be a communist means that you must organize and unite the entire young generation." As for "the old society," said Lenin, "We had to destroy all that, and overthrow them." This meant "overthrowing the tsar, overthrowing the capitalists, and abolishing the capitalist class."

Thus, communism would become the central guiding principle and force in the lives of youth. "This generation should know that the entire purpose of their lives is to build a communist society," insisted Lenin. "The members of the [Young Communist] League should use every spare hour to improve the vegetable gardens, or to organize the education of young people at some factory, and so on."

Such was the mission field, a literal field, or a factory floor. That was mission territory for the disciples to sow the harvest. Communism was the alpha and the omega. It was truly like a religious calling, a new order.

It was to be a fundamental transformation.

The March Through the Institutions

This call to total transformation resonates today among cultural and sexual Marxists. While very different from classical Marxists in their cultural-sexual as opposed to economic thinking, they bear a crucial commonality with their forebears in this ongoing objective of fundamental transformation via criticizing all that exists, especially traditional Judeo-Christian values and institutions. The original ambition of an economic/class-based revolution has failed. And so, instead, today's Marxists—including throughout Communist Party USA, once the home of classical Marxism—have gone cultural and sexual.

This newly evolved form of Marxism is so radical in its redefinition of human nature that Karl Marx himself would blush and find it bewildering. When I first drafted this chapter, the lead article at CPUSA's website was titled "The Capitalist Culture of Male Supremacy and Misogyny"—a piece breathtaking in its cultural radicalism.[670] It personifies the communist movement's thrust today. Truly, at any given day, an article like that can be found at the CPUSA website or at its flagship publication, *People's World*. That is where modern Marxists in America now stand.

As noted, this cultural Marxism began to emerge not on May 5, 1818, with Marx's birth, but over a hundred years later with the birth of what came to be known as the Frankfurt School.

As shown, these 1920s and 1930s German Marxists were Freudian-Marxists for whom orthodox/classical Marxism was too limited. They and their disciples, especially in America and the wider West in the 1960s, lusted for revolutionary changes in sexuality and in culture. The universities would be their factory floor. They would rally students, the academy, the arts, the media, film—the forces of cultural change.

Even then, one can look at the Frankfurt School's cultural Marxism not as a replacement for classical Marxism but as the accelerator pedal for a wheezing, stalling vehicle. The cultural Marxist fully agrees with the classical Marxist that history passes through a series of stages on the way to the final Marxist utopia, through feudalism and capitalism and socialism and ultimately to the classless society. But the cultural Marxist recognizes that communists will not get there by economics alone. In essence, cultural Marxists shrewdly realized that the classical Marxists would utterly fail to take down the West with an economic revolution; capitalism would always blow away communism; the masses would choose free markets. Cultural Marxists understand that the revolution requires a cultural war over an economic war. Whereas the West—certainly America—is not vulnerable to a revolt of the downtrodden trade-union masses, it is eminently vulnerable when it comes to, say, sex or porn. Whereas a revolution for wealth redistribution has been unappealing to most citizens of the

West, a sexual revolution would be irresistible. Put the bourgeoisie in front of a hypnotic or seductive screen, and it would be putty in your hands.

In this book, we have looked at key figures of the Frankfurt School, including Georg Lukacs, Walter Benjamin, *The Sexual Revolution*'s Wilhelm Reich, and (among others) Herbert Marcuse, whose bizarre meanderings swept up the sixties New Left, making Marcuse an ideological guru to the radicals who today are tenured at our universities.

Not to be forgotten on the cultural front, however, is a critical figure, a non-German. At the age of thirty-five, in 1926, Antonio Gramsci was arrested in his native Italy by Mussolini and spent the last eleven years of his life in prison, where he would write, write, and write—compiling a master volume of thirty-three *Prison Notebooks*.[671] Samuel Gregg calls Gramsci perhaps "the most dangerous socialist in history."[672]

Gramsci, too, looked to culture. If the fundamental transformers of the radical left truly wanted to win, then they needed to first seize the so-called "cultural means of production;" that is, culture-forming institutions such as the media and universities and even churches. Gramsci himself foresaw societal transformation coming about by what others have characterized as a Gramscian "long march through the institutions."[673] That is, the institutions of the culture.[674]

Not until leftists came to dominate these institutions would they be able to convince enough people to support their Marxist revolution. "This part of his thesis was like manna from heaven for many left-wing Western intellectuals," writes Gregg of Gramsci. "Instead of joining a factory collective or making bombs in basements, a leftist professor could help free society from capitalist exploitation by penning essays in his office or teaching students."

The heirs of Gramsci, like the ideological progeny of Marx and Lenin and the Frankfurt School, insisted on the need to question everything, including moral absolutes and the Judeo-Christian basis of Western civilization. They needed to frame seemingly benign conventions as systematic injustices that must be exposed. This is where we got professors fulminating against everything from "the patriarchy" to "white imperialism" to "transphobia." By the twenty-first century, even biological sex was no longer considered a settled issue.

There was no traditional institution off limits to the cultural left.

In fact, so "critical" was the cultural-Marxist Left of everything, it would brand itself as "critical theory." Today, there are entire academic departments and programs dedicated to "critical theory" and offshoots such as "queer theory" and "gender ideology." Barack Obama's alma mater, Occidental College, is hardly an anomaly in boasting a Department of Critical Theory and Social Justice, which at its website promises to instruct wide-eyed students in the principles of "Marxism, psychoanalysis, the Frankfurt School, deconstruction, critical race studies, queer theory, feminist theory, postcolonial theory."

For the cultural-Marxist left, "critical theory" is the *zeitgeist*, the prevailing spirit of the age. Michael Walsh dubs it "the cult of critical theory," the playground of "The Devil's Pleasure Palace," the instrument for what he rightly calls "the subversion of the West." To quote the sixties radicals, *hey, hey, ho, ho, Western civ has got to go*.[675]

Perhaps most frustrating to those standing aghast at this destruction is that the typical Starbucks-sipper redefining marriage and gender has no clue that she may be complicit in a vast cultural Marxist revolution.

Sam Gregg puts it well: "The worst part of Gramsci's legacy is that it has effectively transcended its Marxist origins. His outlook is now blankly taken for granted by millions of teachers, writers, even churchmen, who have no idea that they are committed to cultural Marxism."

That is so agonizingly true. And so, adds Gregg, "the vast structures of cynicism which Gramsci's ideas have built, which honeycomb Western society today, will prove much tougher to dismantle than the crude cement blocks of the old Berlin Wall."

They will indeed. The people of Berlin had no problem recognizing the concrete wrongness of the wall that corralled them. But try telling same-sex marriage supporters that what they support is concretely wrong, or that it somehow might have evolved from certain Marxist origins. They will either give you a blank stare or laugh in your face.

The Never-Ending Search for the Newest Victim Class

In a crucial respect, classical Marxism and cultural Marxism will always bear an essential, enduring commonality—one that explains a lot about today's modern left.

Both classical Marxists and cultural Marxists see history as a series of struggles that divide the world into hostile/antagonistic groups of oppressors and the oppressed. Both seek out victim groups as the anointed group that will also serve as society's redeemer group.[676] The victim group becomes the agent for emancipation in ushering in the new and better world. The Marxist must always, then, be on the search for the newest victim class which, in turn, must always be made aware of its victimization. Its "consciousness" must be raised.

In classical Marxism, this was simple: the victim group was identified by class/economics. It was the proletariat. It was the factory worker.

In cultural Marxism, this has not been so simple, because the culture is always changing: the victim group is constantly being searched for anew by the cultural Marxist. The group one year might be women, the next year African Americans, the next year another group. Today, there's a hard push by cultural Marxists to tap the "LGBTQIA-plus" (*People's World* frequently uses that expansive label) movement as the championed victim group: lesbians, gays, bisexuals, transgenders, "queer" persons, "intersexuals," "asexuals," and on and on.

Thus, a leading cultural Marxist like Angela Davis (mentored by

Herbert Marcuse) could stand at the January 2017 Women's March in Washington, DC before a sea of oblivious girls wearing pink hats modeled after their genitalia and recite a litany of politically correct grievances. In her casting about for victim groups, the former Communist Bloc cheerleader hailed the transgendered Chelsea Manning, "trans women of color," "our flora and fauna," and "intersectional feminism," and denounced "white male hetero-patriarchy," misogyny, Islamophobia, and capitalist exploitation.[677]

Victims, victims, victims.

Davis, who twice ran on Communist Party USA's presidential ticket, and in 1979 was awarded the Lenin Peace Prize by the Kremlin in Moscow, did not mention CPUSA but LGBTQ, not Marx but Manning, not Bolshevism but transgenderism. She spoke not about class but culture. She knew she would find allies not in railing against property rights but in ranting for "marriage rights."

That is the tack throughout the modern communist movement.

It is very revealing that the "About" section of the website of *People's World*, successor to the Soviet-funded *Daily Worker* and the leading mouthpiece of American communism, singles out a label that would have had Marx and Engels scratching their heads: "cultural workers." It states, "Today, *People's World* offers a daily news platform for the broad labor-led people's movement—a voice for workers, the unemployed, people of color, immigrants, women, youth, seniors, LGBTQ people, cultural workers, students and people with disabilities."[678]

They are looking less for *factory workers* than *cultural workers*. Forget the factory floor—that project failed long ago. Communists tried to organize the steelworkers, the autoworkers, the teamsters, the coal miners. It didn't work. (West Virginia coalminers in 2016 voted for Donald Trump.) The new recruiting ground is the classroom floor, the campus, the university, the schools. That is where the cultural workers who can usher in the fundamental transformation are being sought and being found. These modern cultural revolutionaries are succeeding magnificently in redefining everything from marriage and family to sexuality and gender.

This is where today's Marxists in America and the West are toiling hard. They are working diligently on the cultural front. That is where they are confident that they can finally take down the West and its Judeo-Christian bedrock that Marx and a long line of disciples looked to smash.

Critical Theory and Critical Marx—or the Devil Is in the Details

Clearly then, perhaps the most important link between cultural Marxism and the classical Marxism of Marx, of Lenin, and of Marx's immediate implementors and longtime admirers is found in the very name that cultural Marxism has assumed in the academy. In a way, it is maddeningly frustrating—seemingly almost willfully deceptive, one suspects—that the academy has chosen or clung to the term "critical theory" to covertly fly the banner of cultural Marxism; such is a more palatable label to shop its wares, to market its ideological snake-oil. Knowing they would get flagged openly advertising an academic program titled Cultural Marxism, no doubt alarming college alumni and trustees alike, shrewd academic leftists instead went with the more innocuous and ambiguous Critical Theory. And yet, that said, "*critical* theory" perfectly describes what cultural Marxists do best: they criticize.

By seeking to tear down the old, especially the traditions they detest, they are acting in the mold and spirit of Karl Marx, and of Lenin. They may not be able to tell you a century or mere decade henceforth what will be erected in its place, but they do agree on the need to bulldoze the house. Give them not a screwdriver but a sledgehammer.

And yet, like neo-Marxist pioneer Herbert Marcuse with his notion of "repressive tolerance" (he urged "intolerance against movements from the Right, and toleration of movements from the Left"), they only blast to smithereens the things they don't like. They are willing to tolerate all sorts of novel inventions, from new forms of "marriage" and sexuality to endless gender options. They actually *don't* criticize quite everything, but instead only the things they don't like. Like liberals and progressives who beam about "diversity" and "tolerance," critical theorists and cultural Marxists vilify only those who depart from their newfangled vision for the world and humanity. If you agree with their fundamental transformation, then you are good and accepted. If you disagree, then prepare to be boycotted, turned into a pariah on social media, lynched by Twitter mobs, pursued by lawyers and dragged into court. *You* are not to be included under the rainbow umbrella of "diversity," which, it turns out, is not as multi-colored as they had led the world to believe. This is their great tolerance-diversity fraud. Sadly, 90 percent of them in their *zeitgeist* (maybe *vortex* would be a better word) often do not even realize the phoniness. Such has been their university brainwashing that they do not seem to have the mental wherewithal to discern these contradictions. One is tempted to call it a hoax, but that would suggest they are aware of it.

Welcome to the maddening tyranny of moral relativism that is the common feeding trough of the left en masse, whether a progressive, a "liberal," a critical theorist, a cultural Marxist. And alas, that is the toxic cup from which they imbibe, the chalice that unites them in their fundamental transformation of the Judeo-Christian West.

The Modernist Heresy

This fundamental transformation is a byproduct of the new modern spirit. The forces of modernism have sought nothing less.

"Modernism aims at that radical transformation of human thought in relation to God, man, the world, and life, here and hereafter," states the *Catholic Encyclopedia*.[679] It is a threat that the Church did not notice just today. To the contrary, these modernist forces caught the Church's attention early in the previous century, as Marxism was taking flight and in some countries taking hold.

One man who saw it coming, or something like it, was Pope Pius X, whose encyclical on the Modernists, formally known as *Pascendi Dominici Gregis*, was published in 1907. It called modernism the "synthesis of all heresies." Modernism had to be condemned in order to protect the faith, including from enemies not only outside but inside the gates. These modernists were not merely Marxists or communists or socialists but a wider panoply of leftists, pagans, progressives, moral relativists, cultural relativists, human-nature redefiners, fundamental transformers. Their enemies were absolutes, religion, tradition. They believe in change, reform, evolution, progression—that is, "progress." They favored then and favor still not an *enduring moral order* (Russell Kirk's description of conservatism) but an *ever-evolving order*. They reject the very notion of an unchanging moral order based on biblical and natural law. They believe that truths and values can and do evolve, change, *progress* along with or relative to society, culture, norms, history. They reject that there is such a thing as "abiding truths," a "storehouse of wisdom" to preserve and conserve, or what G. K. Chesterton called a "democracy of the dead" always worth considering and consulting.[680]

Pius X warned of the "many roads" of Modernism that lead "to atheism and to the annihilation of all religion." We face a terrific danger as each and every person renders unto itself his or her own individual interpretation of truth and reality. Eventually, each person becomes his or her own god. Soon enough, it ends in Karl Marx's ultimate goal: the undermining if not annihilation of religion.

The Anonymous Power

Such being the case, then who or what is today's Western world ultimately following? Who or what is whispering in our ears? Who or what is silently prodding the culture? Is it the same murky force to which Karl Marx penned his sordid prose?

Perhaps a trenchant insight into all of this is a phrase coined by Joseph Ratzinger, who would become Pope Benedict XVI: "the anonymous power." It seems a poignant portent of where we are culturally, socially, ideologically, theologically, at this troubling juncture in history.

Today, as in every era, though at a pace unseen before, we see and suffer through many dangerous fads and fashions, especially since the nineteenth century. Whether we are dealing with silly, destructive, *old* ideas like Marxism, Freudianism, or even the ugly Freudian-Marxism of the Frankfurt School, or dealing with silly, destructive, *new* ideas like transgenderism, gender ideology, the ever-expanding "LGBTQ" movement (again, already morphing into what many label "LGBTQIA+), "intersectionality," critical theory, queer theory, or whatever the latest trend, these often-toxic ideas—old or new—share a few notable commonalities:

First, there is the sheer sophistry of these *concepts* (in as much as they deserve to be called "concepts") and their inherent violation of common sense. Worse, the sophistry is so self-evident, particularly to anyone schooled in a Christian/Catholic worldview with a well-formed conscience, moral compass, and intellectual tradition. Second, there is the matter of the sheer harmfulness of these ideas in and beyond their time; the cultural carnage, the human wreckage, the soul damage. Third, there is their fleeting quality, their ephemeral nature, which is never clear to enough people, as so many get sucked into the vortex. Amid the prevalence and dominance of these pernicious doctrines, countless human beings get swept up. Fourth, and maybe most frustrating, is the reality that many of these concepts have a strange tendency to simply slither into the night and vanish. But even as they might seem to mercifully disappear into the dustbin of history, they often have a tendency to hang on, linger, reemerge in a slightly altered form, and to continue to corrode. For instance, we thought that the very recent victory of the West in the

Cold War had killed communism. Quite the contrary, the ideology has bounced back with a shocking appeal among a very high number of Millennials.[681]

From whom or what do these concepts draw their power?

Joseph Ratzinger spoke of what he called the "anonymous power" that dictates prevailing fads and fashions. He related the phrase to a much earlier but defining time in history, a decidedly theological and Christological moment: Judas's betrayal of Jesus. "Judas is neither a master of evil nor the figure of a demoniacal power of darkness but rather a sycophant who bows down before the anonymous power of changing moods and current fashion," Benedict stated. "But it is precisely this anonymous power that crucified Jesus, for it was anonymous voices that cried, 'Away with him! Crucify him!'"

By this rendering, Judas was a mere sycophant to what Benedict dubbed "the anonymous power" of "changing moods and current fashion." This highly influential power lives on in modern times, of course. It never seems to go away. It is a power that one cannot always get a handle on, or visibly discern, but it is there, with its terrible effects, looming large and holding tremendous sway over the crowd.

It was indeed that same anonymous power, manifest in the form of anonymous voices, which yelled at Jesus, "Away with him! Crucify him." We know not their faces. But we know they handed Christ over.

Mere days earlier, the same people had been hailing Christ with hosannas, begging him to heal them, watching his miracles in awe, welcoming him into their homes and towns. And just like that, they turned on him.

There have been so many ideas and ideologies in which we have discerned such anonymous power at work: Marxism, Freudianism, Freudian-Marxism, the twisted notions of a Wilhelm Reich, a Walter Benjamin, a Herbert Marcuse, a Mikhail Bakunin, a Bruno Bauer, an Aleister Crowley, a Harry Hay, a Kate Millett, those which inspired the diabolical brutality in places like Pitesti prison in Romania or

60 Andrassy Street in Hungary. Consider the martyrs and suffering witnesses such as the Rev. Richard Wurmbrand or Cardinal Joseph Mindszenty, tortured in the name of a vapid ideology of class warfare. Then consider the militant push by secular progressives throughout the West to redefine God's plan for marriage and family and gender. The same spirit is there, almost in the ether, the air we breathe. It is a spirit which has the force of a veritable cultural tsunami. On TV and Twitter and Facebook and the web, it is overwhelming.

Our Western world is comprised of legions of sycophants to the anonymous power of changing moods and current fashion. Whatever the latest fads, no matter how contrary to the moral law and natural law, from redefining marriage to even redefining one's God-given and nature-given gender, modernist democratic majorities step forth to ride the wave and board the latest bandwagon.

It is what some call the *zeitgeist* (a German term, fittingly), the prevailing spirit—a phrase that Ratzinger, as a German, would know. R. Emmett Tyrrell Jr., founding editor of *The American Spectator*, refers to this as the *Kultursmog* ("culture smog," another German term, fittingly). Benedict attributed slightly more contour to this spirit or smog, calling it an "anonymous power" that seems to almost have form and presence, and is perhaps inspired by a darker force altogether. And it indeed is felt everywhere in every age, albeit cleverly assuming an always-altering manifestation.

Who or what is driving it? Well, no one can really say, or see. Who is the leader, the face? Nobody. If there is any driving "philosophy" that rules the modern world, it is the dictatorship of relativism, in which everyone is his or her own guiding power. Such is another apt phrase of Benedict that goes hand in hand here.

In his final homily after the death of John Paul II, given just before the College of Cardinals convened to choose him as the next pope, Cardinal Ratzinger called out a "dictatorship of relativism."[682] What prompted his words were the readings that day, April 18, 2005. He was quoting Ephesians 4:14, where St. Paul warned of people being "tossed here and there, carried about by every wind of doctrine" (Eph 4:14).

As Ratzinger noted with exclamation, "This description is very timely!" He explained:

> How many winds of doctrine have we known in recent decades, how many ideological currents, how many ways of thinking. The small boat of the thought of many Christians has often been tossed about by these waves—flung from one extreme to another: from Marxism to liberalism, even to libertinism; from collectivism to radical individualism; from atheism to a vague religious mysticism; from agnosticism to syncretism and so forth. Every day new sects spring up, and what St. Paul says about human deception and the trickery that strives to entice people into error (cf. Ephesians 4:14) comes true.
>
> Today, having a clear faith based on the Creed of the Church is often labeled as fundamentalism. Whereas relativism, that is, letting oneself be "tossed here and there, carried about by every wind of doctrine," seems the only attitude that can cope with modern times. We are building a dictatorship of relativism that does not recognize anything as definitive and whose ultimate goal consists solely of one's own ego and desires.

This captures powerfully the phenomenon to which I have struggled to affix a label. In fingering the various extremes, Ratzinger fittingly named Marxism first, with a litany of other variants of Modernism following. Yes, every day it seems a new sect pops up, with people so easily deceived, tricked, enticed. Whoever is behind the dramatic success of that moral relativism which lies at the root of Modernism (and Marxism) is who or what has succeeded in nearly destroying western civilization. No doubt, the devil to whom, as we have seen, Karl Marx gave such chilling attention has had a hand in it all.

Communism became an ideology of deception and of infiltration, manipulation, exploitation—trickery, dupery. Just ask the likes of Ben Gitlow, Louis Budenz, Manning Johnson, Bella Dodd. Maybe even ask William Z. Foster, Earl Browder, Harry Ward—assuming they would ever admit to enticing people into error. Or ask those who foresaw it and warned of it: Popes Pius IX, Leo XIII, Pius X, Pius XI, Pius XII, John Paul II.

So many victims would succumb, tossed here and there, carried about by every wind of doctrine.

On the positive side, Ratzinger recommended how to avoid this pitfall, and the answer is one that has remained true for two thousand years:

> We, however, have a different goal: the Son of God, the true man. He is the measure of true humanism. An "adult" faith is not a faith that follows the trends of fashion and the latest novelty; a mature adult faith is deeply rooted in friendship with Christ. It is this friendship that opens us up to all that is good and gives us a criterion by which to distinguish the true from the false, and deceit from truth. . . .
>
> The other element of the Gospel to which I wanted to refer is Jesus' teaching on bearing fruit: "It was I who chose you to go forth and bear fruit. Your fruit must endure" (John 15: 16).

Ratzinger repeated that exhortation, especially for his fellow priests: "We have received the faith to give it to others—we are priests in order to serve others. And we must bear fruit that will endure."

It is Christ's faith that endures. It is Christ's Church that endures. Ratzinger would have agreed with G. K. Chesterton, who said, "The Catholic Church is the one thing that saves a man from the degrading slavery of being a child of his age."

A child of his age, captive to the currents of the dictatorship of relativism and the dictates of the anonymous power. That describes the West today. Amid the winds of all these foolish philosophies that have come and gone, and are still coming and going, even if we do not realize it, the Church truly is the one thing that saves a man from the degrading slavery of the futile doctrines that toss him about like an infant.

"All people desire to leave a lasting mark," stated Ratzinger in that April 2005 homily. "But what endures? Money does not. Even buildings do not, nor books. After a certain time, longer or shorter, all these things disappear. The only thing that lasts forever is the human soul, the human person created by God for eternity."

Spirit of Truth vs. Spirit of the Age and Marx

"If you marry the mood or the spirit of the age," warned Fulton Sheen, "then you will be a widow in the next one. These fashions simply do not last."[683]

Sheen affirmed that "we've got to have some principles that do not change to live by." In order "to think well, one has to have principles that are independent of space and time. By which one can live. We know that these principles exist, and we know there's such a thing as truth simply because there's a *logos*, there's an intelligence behind the universe."

Those are the abiding truths, the first things, the permanent things, the enduring moral order. Individuals do not invent these anew. They are there. And it is the sacred duty of the Church, with its deposit of the true faith, to protect and cultivate, to maintain and proclaim them.

It is the Church, Sheen ardently argued, that keeps a man and a woman on the straight and right path: "Why is a romance very much, like Chesterton says, like driving a chariot, six wild horses, driving them down a mountain lane, road? And on either side of this mountain road, there's a ravine here, precipice here, chasm here and a pit here. And the thrill of following truth is to drive those horses straight down that line." Sheen set that image and model against the ideologies and isms of his day:

> Oh, it's the easiest thing in all the world to be a rightest, for example, in politics. All you gotta do is tumble over. The easiest thing in the world to be a leftist. Just fall over. Let go. It's the easiest thing in the world to be an Arian in the fourth, fifth century. Easiest thing in the world to tumble into some mood today. Very easy to be a communist. Just as simple as falling off a log. Very easy to be a Nazi, all you gotta do is fall into the other side. So, the great romance of truth therefore consists in going to this straight line, knowing the pitfalls, driving the horses of truth directly, and seeing all of these errors and moods, prostrate and fallen and forgotten. But driving ahead, reeling but erect, that's the romance of thinking, that's the joy of truth.

The truth was to be found in Truth itself, in Himself. And Sheen was certain most of all that Truth existed in the Church that He, Jesus Christ, founded upon Peter, the rock upon which He built His Church. That Church would provide the foundation for surviving age after age and all the corrosive ideologies and isms and spirits that pervade it. The Church offers a constant reminder to people of the principles that do not change and which thus are those to live by, and those which will protect us from being children of our age.[684]

No wonder Karl Marx and his minions hated religion. It halts their essential project to fundamentally transform.

Sheen said that the Church is a rock, stable and sure: "The ideas of the Church are like her vestments; always well-dressed but never the slave of passing fashion." He said, "The Church knows after 1900 years' experience that any institution which suits the spirit of the age will be a widow in the next one."[685] Sheen averred that the main problem with modern systems is that they are steered by the spirit of the age and the evolution of the world.[686] They fill the air with noxious ideas toxic to the soul. They infuse the atmosphere with particulates of whatever anonymous power will choke the lungs and cloud the mind.

In the case of atheistic communism, those have been no ordinary pollutants. A legacy of over one hundred million dead, not to mention the robbing of so many basic liberties and the incalculable harm to so many souls has been nothing short of diabolical—truly a satanic scourge, a killing machine. The effects of that dance of death have been pernicious. Its specter endures. It is one of the worst modernist heresies and fruitless works of darkness. It plagues us to this day.

To borrow from Marx, hellish vapors still rise up around us. To what extent do those vapors emanate from the Prince of Darkness who sold that blood-dark sword about which Marx, as a young man, waxed poetic? The one that unerringly stabbed within the soul that went mad until the heart was utterly changed and the soul forfeited heaven by choosing hell.

Hellish vapors indeed. Marx saw something there.

If Karl Marx might have erred his way into one insight of value for understanding this damnable mess, maybe that was it. Our duty must be to struggle against those hellish vapors, to not breathe them in. We must battle against and expose the powers of darkness that continue to pervade this modern world.

ACKNOWLEDGMENTS

This book is a product of many years of sordid knowledge that I have unfortunately accumulated through the lamentable occupational hazard of studying, writing about, and teaching Marxism and the history of communism. I would much rather write about something happier like, oh, baseball. But alas, this is my lot in life. And I am grateful to several student assistants who suffered with me through the (unenviable) unique research for this particular book and its particularly awful subject matter.

Among my Grove City College students, I want to pay special thanks to Hannah Lutz, Ian Worrell, Erin McLaughlin, and Zach and Jennifer (whose last names I've left out because they have sensitive positions). Among these students, many had to wade through the same ideological-mental manure that I did. Ian dealt with Aleister Crowley and Walter Benjamin and their impenetrably stupid and outright wicked concepts. My deepest apologies to Hannah and Jennifer, who stumbled into the sick, gross material on Crowley and Walter Duranty. My apologies, too, to their parents. Such are the unexpected pitfalls of researching these perverse people. One can scarcely imagine the levels of depravity one might encounter. Leave it to Marxists to break the mold every time. It is never pretty. Also, Jennifer and Hannah highlighted and read more biographies of Karl Marx and his family than any well-adjusted human being should ever have to endure in a lifetime.

I would like to thank Doug Grane for his timely advice that I not ignore Pope Pius X's warnings of the "Modernist heresy" in his brilliant *Pascendi Dominici Gregis*. I saw Doug at a talk that I was giving at the Union League Club in Chicago in March 2019. He's an old grad-school classmate of mine from the School of International Service at The American University in Washington, DC. I hadn't seen him in over twenty-five years. Doug suggested a full book on the Modernist heresy, which indeed someone ought to pursue at this time of full-blown Modernist heresy in the West. Few warnings have proved as prophetic as that of Pius X over a century ago. I wanted to ensure that *Pascendi Dominici Gregis* at least got its due in this book. At that same talk in Chicago, another old friend, Jameson Campaigne, suggested that I do a full edited volume on the Church's encyclicals on communism and socialism. That, too, was beyond the scope of my plans, but it was a good reminder that I not neglect at least a cursory summary of some of those encyclicals in this book.

Special gratitude, of course, goes to the good folks at TAN Books and Saint Benedict Press: John Moorehouse made this book happen, pursuing me to pick up the project after I had shelved it for quite a while because of its unpleasant nature. Nonetheless, John, like me, knew the book had to be done. I likewise thank Kevin Gallagher and so many others on the editing and production side who toil behind the scenes. Among them, Nick Vari did an excellent job copy editing. Between John and Nick, this was one of the smoothest editing processes I've ever experienced over a life of writing probably close to twenty books.

Finally, perhaps an odd and unexpected acknowledgment: I thank the saints. That is, favorite saints and religious writers of mine such as St. Catherine of Siena, St. Faustina, Pope St. John Paul II, Francis of Assisi, Padre Pio, Fulton Sheen, and Dante, among others. After painful days of reading these awful Marxists and wanting to flush away their mental-ideological sewage polluting my mind, I took refuge each evening in the edifying thoughts of the saints. Their direct connection to the divine, to Truth itself, allowed me to purge the toxic nonsense I had to read each day from the miserable purveyors of Marxist bilge that was a regrettable part of my day job. It is often said that one should not go to bed at night bitter or angry, whether with a spouse or whatever. I would add that one should not go to bed at night with bitter Marxist filth on the mind.

I thank the saints for a heavenly place to turn each night for peace of soul. And to them and the entire cloud of witnesses in the Church, I ask for intercession and prayer for me, for my family, and for the souls of every person mentioned in this book. And yes, that certainly includes Karl Marx as well.

ENDNOTES

1. Stephane Courtois et al, *The Black Book of Communism* (Harvard University Press, 1999), pp. 3-4.

2. Malia in Courtois, *Black Book*, pp. xvii-xviii.

3. Courtois, *Black Book*, p. 4. Some contributors to the book, namely, Nicolas Werth and Jean-Louis Margolin, disassociated themselves with the number 100 million, claiming that it was approximated and not completely accurate. See Ron Radosh, "The Black Book of Communism: Crimes, Terror, and Repression," *First Things*, February 2000. Also see: Robert Stacy McCain, "Communism's Atrocities Detailed in 'Black Book,'" *Washington Times*, September 21, 2000.

4. See website of the Victims of Communism Memorial Foundation: https://www.victimsofcommunism.org/memorial.

5. Malia in Courtois, *Black Book*, p. x.

6. Courtois, *Black Book*, p. 4.

7. See Alexander Yakovlev, *A Century of Violence in Soviet Russia* (New Haven, Conn.: Yale University Press, 2002), p. 32; Alexander Solzhenitsyn, *Alexander Solzhenitsyn Speaks to the West* (London: The Bodley Head, 1978), p. 17; and Lee Edwards, editor, *The Collapse of Communism* (Stanford, CA: Hoover Institution Press, 1999), p. xiii. Edwards cites figures by political scientist R. J. Rummel, who draws on the research of Solzhenitsyn, Robert Conquest, and others, thereby estimating that the USSR was responsible for the death of 61.9 million from 1917-87.

8. See Rummel's classic book, *Death by Government* (New Brunswick, NJ: Transaction Publishers, 1994), which is posted online at https://www.hawaii.edu/powerkills/NOTE1.HTM.

9. Edwards, *The Collapse of Communism*, p. xiii.

10. The latest figures of 70-million plus by Mao are recorded in the seminal work, by Jung Chang and Jon Halliday, *Mao: The Unknown Story* (New York: Knopf, 2005). On Mao, the *Black Book* records 65 million dead (page 4).

11. See my discussion in the North Korea section of Paul Kengor, *The Politically Incorrect Guide to Communism* (Washington, DC: Regnery, 2017).

12. During the sixty-four-year Spanish Inquisition period (1481–1545), the highest earliest estimates, which, according to the latest scholarship, were far too high, were that some 31,912 were killed. See the early authoritative work on the subject: J. A. Llorente, *A Critical History of the Inquisition of Spain* (1823), pp. 575–83.

13 Located in "Ronald Reagan: Pre-Presidential Papers: Selected Radio Broadcasts, 1975-1979," January 1975 to March 1977, Box 1, RRL. For a full transcript, see: Kiron Skinner, Annelise Anderson, and Martin Anderson, editors, *Reagan: A Life in Letters* (NY: Free Press, 2003), pp. 10-12.

14 I say this as the author of full spiritual biographies of books with titles such as *God and Ronald Reagan: A Spiritual Life*, *God and George W. Bush: A Spiritual Life*, and *God and Hillary Clinton: A Spiritual Life*. Those books covered each of their subjects biographically from first to last page.

15 I will discuss this later with the case of the late Rev. Richard Wurmbrand specifically.

16 Marx's only son, young Edgar, wrote a letter to his father in March 1854 addressing him as "My Dear Devil." Richard Wurmbrand makes a big deal of this letter in his book *Marx & Satan*, aptly wondering what son would address his father this way. (Wurmbrand, *Marx & Satan*, p. 46.) Sympathetic biographers of Marx, if they mention the letter at all, say nothing about such a strange choice of greeting one's father. (See, for instance: Gabriel, *Love and Capital*, p. 240.) Personally, I am not sure what to make of this one. I do not want to overstate its significance, especially if the salutation was done playfully, as one imagines and hopes it oddly was, but I also do not want to ignore it. Marx actually adored Edgar, and was heartbroken when Edgar died. Readers can make of the salutation what they will. In the larger scheme of Marx, however, it at least warrants suspicion. Full citations: Richard Wurmbrand, *Marx & Satan* (Wheaton, IL: Crossway Books, 1986); and Mary Gabriel, *Love and Capital: Karl and Jenny Marx and the Birth of a Revolution* (New York: Little, Brown, 2011).

17 These, too, I will deal with. It is not always entirely clear when these are used playfully or figuratively. Marx's detractors opt for the latter, whereas his hagiographers either opt for the former or say nothing at all.

18 That most assuredly applies to my spiritual biographies of Ronald Reagan, George W. Bush, and Hillary Clinton.

19 Robert Payne, *Marx: A Biography* (NY: Simon & Schuster, 1968), pp. 315, 317. Tellingly, Francis Wheen does not make fun of Robert Payne for this statement or Payne's wider treatment of Marx's "demons," unlike Wheen's treatment of Richard Wurmbrand's statements on Marx and the devil. Wheen takes Payne more seriously, probably because Payne is an academic and not a pastor or a seeming right-wing anti-communist. See Payne quoted in Francis Wheen, *Karl Marx: A Life* (New York: Norton, 1999),, p. 3.

20 Earl Browder, *Communism in the United States* (New York: International Publishers, 1935), p. 335.

21 Browder, *Communism in the United States*, p. 55.

22 Engels letter to Marx dated November 23-24, 1847, posted at: https://www.marxists.org/archive/marx/works/1847/11/prin-com.htm.

23 https://www.marxists.org/archive/marx/works/1844/manuscripts/comm.htm#44CC4.

24 https://www.marxists.org/archive/marx/works/1845/german -ideology/ch01a.htm#a4.

25 Among other sources, the authoritative www.marxists.org historical archive states that on August 28, 1844 "Marx and Engels meet in Paris; this is the beginning of a lifelong friendship and joint work." https://www.marxists. org/archive/marx/bio/marx/lifeandwork.htm.

26 See my treatment of this subject at length in Paul Kengor, *Takedown: From Communists to Progressives, How the Left Has Sabotaged Family and Marriage* (Washington, D.C.: WND Books, 2015). In that book, I deal at length with the question of to what extent Marx and Engels literally desired the "abolition" of the family. Since the publication of that book in 2015, I have noticed this line from Robert Payne's 1968 biography of Marx: "He is perfectly serious when he demands the abolition of the family." See Payne, *Marx: A Biography*, p. 173.

27 Karl Marx, "Suppression of the *Neue Rheinische Zietung*," *Neue Rheinische Zietung* (final issue), no. 301, May 18, 1849, posted at https://www.marxists.org/archive/marx/works/download/Marx_Articles_from_the_NRZ.pdf. Note: Marx was editor-in-chief of *Neue Rheinische Zietung*.

28 Payne, *Marx: A Biography*, p. 113.

29 Payne, *Marx: A Biography*, pp. 144-46.

30 See Grigori Zinoviev, "Lenin: Speech to the Petrograd Soviet Celebrating Lenin's Recovery from Wounds Made in the Attempt on His Life," August 30, 1918, posted at https://www.marxists.org/archive/zinoviev/works/1918/lenin/ch18.htm.

31 Quoted in V. I. Lenin, "Can 'Jacobinism' Frighten the Working Class?" first published in *Pravda* No. 90, July 7 (June 24), 1917, and later published in *Lenin Collected Works*, Vol. 25 (Moscow: Progress Publishers, 1977), pp. 121-22. Posted online at https://www.marxists.org/archive/lenin/works/1917/jul/07a.htm.

32 Quoted by Trotsky, *The History of the Russian Revolution*, p. 395. See 1932 edition translated by Max Eastman and posted online at https://www.marxists.org/archive/trotsky/1930/hrr/index.htm.

33 These Lenin letters are quoted in Alexander Solzhenitsyn, *Alexander Solzhenitsyn Speaks to the West* (London: The Bodley Head, 1978), pp. 48, 54.

34 One Hegel scholar wrote, "Hegel is a Christian, but not an orthodox one by the Nicene Creed. He denies the precedence of the Father, from whom the Son and the Spirit proceed. He denies that lordship is the meaning of divinity, so that Christ manifests divinity only as the risen Lord. The true definition of divinity is Spirit. But Hegel is not an ancient Gnostic like Marcion or Valentinus. He does not denigrate the body as the kingdom of the devil. He affirms the incarnation and construes natures as the logos made flesh, as spirit, i.e., the infinite Christ. He is a modern, Joachimite Gnostic: world history is the story of the logos making itself flesh in the rational state and human rights. . . . [Hegelian philosophy] is still Christian even if not

orthodox. To be a heretic one must after all first be a Christian." See Clark Butler, *New Perspectives on Hegel's Philosophy of Religion* (Albany, NY: SUNY Press, 1992), pp. 139, 141.

35 Kenneth Alan, *Explorations in Classical Sociological Theory* (Thousand Oaks: Pine Forge Press, 2005), p. 72.

36 See Raines, *Marx on Religion*, p. vii.

37 What communists and socialists (including Marx and Engels and Lenin and even Mao, among others) mean by "democracy" is very different from what modern Americans mean by it.

38 Grant Havers, "A Christian Hegel in Canada," *Modern Age*, Winter 2019, p. 51.

39 See McLellan, *Karl Marx: A Biography*, p. 25.

40 Grant Havers, "A Christian Hegel in Canada," *Modern Age*, Winter 2019, p. 54.

41 See Sperber, p. 63.

42 Sperber, *Karl Marx: A 19th Century Life*, pp. 65-66.

43 Sperber, *Karl Marx: A 19th Century Life*, pp. 65-66, 69.

44 Fulton J. Sheen, *The Church, Communism, and Democracy* (New York: Dell Publishing), p. 138.

45 McLellan, *Karl Marx: A Biography*, p. 34.

46 See, among others, McLellan, *Karl Marx: A Biography*, p. 26; Gabriel, *Love and Capital*, p. 29; and Sperber, *Karl Marx: A 19th Century Life*, p. 73.

47 Sperber, *Karl Marx: A 19th Century Life*, p. 66.

48 See Friedrich Engels, *Ludwig Feuerbach and the End of Classical German Philosophy*, first published in 1886, translated and published in 1946 by Progress Publishers, posted at https://www.marxists.org/archive/marx/works/1886/ludwig-feuerbach/ch01.htm#013.

49 Quoted in McLellan, *Karl Marx: A Biography*, p. 34; and Wheen, *Karl Marx*, pp. 31-32.

50 Sperber, *Karl Marx: A 19th Century Life*, p. 73.

51 Sperber, *Karl Marx: A 19th Century Life*, pp. 74-75.

52 Wheen, *Karl Marx*, p. 34.

53 Wheen, *Karl Marx*, pp. 40-42.

54 "Loutish philistine" is Wheen's description; "untrustworthy egoist" is Marx's. Wheen, *Karl Marx*, pp. 41-42.

55 Wheen, *Karl Marx*, pp. 41-42.

56 **See** Payne, *Marx: A Biography*, pp. 104, 439-40.

57 Payne, *Marx: A Biography*, pp. 439-40.

58 See version posted online at Marxists.org: https://www.marxists.org/reference/archive/bakunin/works/godstate/index.htm. All of the quotations herein are pulled from that online version.

59 This is stated by Alinsky in the opening page of his magnum opus *Rules for Radicals*.

60 Karl Marx, introduction to "A Contribution to the Critique of Hegel's Phi-

losophy of Right," published in *Deutsch-Französische Jahrbücher*, February 7 and 10, 1844 (in Paris), posted at https://www.marxists.org/archive/marx/works/1843/critique-hpr/intro.htm.

61   See, for instance, Acts 4 and Matthew 25. Scholars debate this.

62   Marx, introduction to "A Contribution to the Critique of Hegel's Philosophy of Right."

63   For one analysis and case in point, see Peter Thompson, "Karl Marx, part 1: Religion, the wrong answer to the right question," *The Guardian*, April 4, 2011, posted at https://www.theguardian.com/commentisfree/belief/2011/apr/04/karl-marx-religion.

64   There are two common translation of this Sept. 1843 letter to Arnold Ruge. One states that Marx calls for: "the *ruthless criticism of the existing order*." (Italics are Marx's.) In another translation, Marx states, "I am referring to *ruthless criticism* of all that exists." (Italics are Marx's.) See https://www.marxists.org/archive/marx/works/1843/letters/43_09-alt.htm and https://www.marxists.org/archive/marx/works/1843/letters/43_09.htm.

65   On this, see Payne, *Marx: A Biography*, pp. 127-30.

66   Quoted by Thomas M. Magstadt and Peter M. Schotten, *Understanding Politics: Ideas, Institutions, and Issues* (NY: St. Martin's Press, 1993), p. 39.

67   Karl Marx, *The Class Struggles in France* (New York: HOUSE, 1964), p. 114.

68   Karl Marx, "The Communism of the *Rheinischer Beobachter*," *Deutsche-Brusseler-Zeitung*, September 12, 1847, published as Marx, "The Social Principles of Christianity," in Saul K. Padover, ed., *On Religion: Karl Marx*, The Karl Marx Library, Volume V (New York: McGraw-Hill Book Company, 1974), pp. 93-94.

69   Marx wrote this in his 1844, *Estranged Labor*. See John Raines, ed., *Marx on Religion* (Philadelphia: Temple University Press, 2002), p. 11; and version posted online at https://www.marxists.org/archive/marx/works/1844/manuscripts/labour.html/.

70   Payne, *Marx: A Biography*, p. 82.

71   This is one version of several similar such translations adapted from Aristotle's classic *Politics*. My colleague Robert R. Reilly uses this particular rendition. Another translation, taken from the late Benjamin Jowett's seminal translation, speaks of how "innovations" (also translated as "revolutions" or "revolutionary changes") can "creep in through the private life of individuals." A more recent translation by contemporary Aristotle scholars Irwin and Fine states, "And since people's private ways of life also lead them to revolution . . ." Two of my philosophy colleagues at Grove City College convey a strict Greek translation that reads "on account of private lives."

72   Modern biographer Francis Wheen, a leftist who is highly sympathetic to Marx and goes through great lengths to defend him and to dismiss almost anything obviously negative about the man, rips Richard Wurmbrand in the introduction to his biography. He laughs at this "bizarre book published in 1976 by a famous American hot-gospeller, the Reverend Richard Wurm-

brand, author of such imperishable masterpieces as *Tortured for Christ* ('over two million copies sold')." This is very uncharitable by Wheen. Wurmbrand was, in fact, tortured for Christ, and that chilling book explains why and how, which is why one can still find it on the shelves of probably over a million Christian households to this day. Why Wheen would deride him as an "American hot-gospeller" is hard to imagine (other than Wheen simply not liking the man); Wurmbrand was a Romanian who escaped to America after escaping the communist prisons in Romania in which he was brutalized for his faith. He actually never fit the mold of what one might envision as a "hot-gospeller."

My one defense of Wheen's attack on Wurmbrand is that I agree with Wheen that Wurmbrand does not offer hard proof for some of his more extreme charges against Marx, such as Marx's possible participation in things that "reminds us of the inversions of the Satanic black mass" or perhaps involvement in a "highly secret Satanist church." Many of these very-heated charges by Wurmbrand likewise frustrated me because of the lack of proof provided. Nonetheless, I grant far more authority to Richard Wurmbrand on the subject of communist torture and even Satanic influences and practices than I do Francis Wheen. Wurmbrand experienced those things. In fact, black Masses and worse took place in the prison of Pitesti in Romania, which Wurmbrand wrote about in *Tortured for Christ*. I will note that in the pages ahead.

Wheen argues against holding Marx and Marxism even partly responsible for the ideology that killed so many. I am convinced after reading Wheen that even if he personally found evidence of Marx engaging in outright Satanism, he would come up with a way to shrug it off. See Francis Wheen, *Karl Marx: A Life* (NY: W. W. Norton, 2001), pp. 2-4.

[73] See Paul Johnson, *Intellectuals* (New York: Harper & Row, 1988); Gary North, "The Marx Nobody Knows," in Yuri Maltsev, ed., *Requiem for Karl Marx* (Auburn, Alabama: Praxeology Press, Auburn University, 1993); Mark Skousen, *The Big Three in Economics: Adam Smith, Karl Marx, and John Maynard Keynes* (New York: M. E. Sharpe, 2007); and Murray Rothbard, *An Austrian Perspective on the History of Economic Thought* (Auburn, Alabama: Edward Elgar Publishing, 2006).

[74] See Bruce Mazlish, *The Meaning of Karl Marx* (New York: Oxford University Press, 1984).

[75] Robert Payne, *The Unknown Karl Marx* (New York: New York University Press, 1971).

[76] Even then, Payne was not the first to notice the strange religious side of Marx. Among others, see North, "The Marx Nobody Knows," pp. 75-77.

[77] Payne, *The Unknown Karl Marx*, p. 57.

[78] Payne, *Marx: A Biography*, pp. 59, 67.

[79] See Payne, *Marx: A Biography*, p. 73; and Johnson, *Intellectuals*, p. 55.

[80] Again, see https://www.marxists.org/archive/marx/works/1843/letters/43_

09-alt.htm and https://www.marxists.org/archive/marx/works/1843/letters/43_09.htm.

81   Payne, *The Unknown Karl Marx*, p. 57. On Lewis and Dante, see Marsha Daigle-Williamson, *Reflecting the Eternal: Dante's Divine Comedy in the Novels of C. S. Lewis* (Peabody, Mass.: Hendrickson Publishers, 2015).

82   Johnson, *Intellectuals*, p. 54.

83   Payne, *Marx: A Biography*, p. 59.

84   Payne, *Marx: A Biography*, p. 62.

85   Payne, *The Unknown Karl Marx*, p. 57.

86   Payne, *The Unknown Karl Marx*, pp. 59-60.

87   Payne, *The Unknown Karl Marx*, p. 60.

88   Wurmbrand, *Marx & Satan*, p. 15.

89   Payne, *The Unknown Karl Marx*, pp. 62-63.

90   Payne, *The Unknown Karl Marx*, p. 63.

91   Payne, *Marx: A Biography*, p. 63.

92   Payne, *Marx: A Biography*, p. 64.

93   Payne, *Marx: A Biography*, p. 64.

94   For further details, see the excellent sleuthing of Payne in Payne, *Marx: A Biography*, pp. 64-65.

95   Payne, *The Unknown Karl Marx*, p. 63; and Payne, *Marx: A Biography*, p. 59.

96   See the Old and New Testaments, Isaiah 7:10-14 and Luke 1:18-24, respectively.

97   Retrieved from Wikipedia, May 17, 2016.

98   See https://www.marxists.org/archive/marx/works/1837-pre/verse/verse21.htm.

99   See the Chilean black-metal band that calls itself "Ilkim Oulanem."

100   Payne, *The Unknown Karl Marx*, p. 60.

101   That is certainly an assertion that I cannot attest. See: Payne, *Marx: A Biography*, pp. 68-69, 72.

102   Johnson, *Intellectuals*, pp. 54-55.

103   Payne, *The Unknown Karl Marx*, pp. 60-61.

104   Ibid, p. 62.

105   Ibid, p. 63.

106   Payne, *Marx: A Biography*, pp. 67, 73.

107   Payne, *Marx: A Biography*, pp. 68, 73.

108   Wurmbrand, *Marx & Satan*, p. 19.

109   Payne, *The Unknown Karl Marx*, pp. 63-64.

110   See https://www.marxists.org/archive/marx/works/1837-pre/verse/verse24.htm.

111   Wurmbrand, *Marx & Satan*, pp. viii, 25.

112   Ibid, p. 25.

113   https://www.marxists.org/archive/marx/works/1843/critique-hpr/intro.htm.

114   "Letter from Heinrich Marx to son Karl," Trier, March 2, 1837, published in

Marx-Engels Collected Works, Vol. 1, pp. 670-73, posted at www.marxists.org. Also see post at http://www.historyisaweapon.com/defcon6/letters/papa/ 1837-fl2.html. David McLellan uses a translation that reads this way: "I feel myself suddenly invaded by doubt and ask myself if your heart is equal to your intelligence and spiritual qualities, if it is open to the tender feelings which here on earth are so great a source of consolation for a sensitive soul; I wonder whether the peculiar demon, to which your heart is manifestly a prey, is the Spirit of God or that of Faust. I ask myself—and this is not the least of the doubts that assail my heart—if you will ever know a simple happiness and family joys, and render happy those around you." David McLellan, *Karl Marx: A Biography* (London: Papermac, an imprint of Macmillan, 1995) p. 1. Mary Gabriel, another top and highly sympathetic biographer of Marx, uses the same translation of the letter posted at www.marxists.org. Gabriel finds the letter "poignant." See Gabriel, *Love and Capital,* p. 28.

115 See Raines, *Marx on Religion,* p. 15.

116 Payne, *Marx: A Biography,* pp. 17-18.

117 See Jonathan Sperber, *Karl Marx: A 19th Century Life* (New York: W.W. Norton/Liveright, 2014), pp. 6-7, 11; and Mary Gabriel, *Love and Capital,* p. 16.

118 McLellan, *Karl Marx: A Biography,* p. 2.

119 Sperber, *Karl Marx: A 19th Century Life,* p. 17. Mary Gabriel pegs the year of Heinrich's conversion as 1817. Mary Gabriel, *Love and Capital,* p. 16.

120 Sperber, *Karl Marx: A 19th Century Life,* pp. 18-20.

121 Gabriel, *Love and Capital,* p. 16.

122 Sperber, *Karl Marx: A 19th Century Life,* pp. 18-20.

123 McLellan, *Karl Marx: A Biography,* p. 6.

124 Sperber, *Karl Marx: A 19th Century Life,* p. 23; and Gabriel, *Love and Capital,* p. 17.

125 There are signs of this even in his August 1835 essay, "The Union of the Faithful with Christ," which he wrote as a seventeen-year-old student fulfilling his religious requirement for graduation from high school. At first glance, this seemingly nice reflection on the fifteenth chapter of John's Gospel is absent of some of the crucial fundamentals of the Christian faith and life.

126 See Padover, *On Religion: Karl Marx,* pp. xiv-xv.

127 Marx, "A Contribution to the Critique of Hegel's Philosophy of Right," posted at https://www.marxists.org/archive/marx/works/1843/critique-hpr/ intro.htm.

128 Karl Marx, "The Decay of Religious Authority," *New York Tribune,* 1854, printed in Raines, *Marx on Religion,* pp. 188-89.

129 For some modern scholarly, respected books (readable, not lengthy) on the Crusades, a subject that Christians ought to understand much better, especially since the Crusades are used as a club to beat Christianity, I recommend the works of Professor Jonathan Riley-Smith (Cambridge University), *The*

Crusades: A History, and *What Were the Crusades?*, and Professor Thomas Madden (Saint Louis University), *The New Concise History of the Crusades*. Madden has also produced an edited volume, *Crusades: The Illustrated History* (University of Michigan Press, 2004). Also released more recently (2009) is Rodney Stark's *God's Battalions: The Case for the Crusades*.

130 Marx, "The Decay of Religious Authority."

131 Saul Padover, ed., *The Letters of Karl Marx* (Englewood Cliffs, New Jersey: Prentice-Hall, Inc., 1979), p. 239; and Sperber, *Karl Marx: A 19ᵗʰ Century Life*, p. 544.

132 Sperber, *Karl Marx: A 19ᵗʰ Century Life*, p. 544.

133 Marx, "Excerpts from *Das Capital*," published in Raines, *Marx on Religion*, p. 202.

134 Sperber, *Karl Marx: A 19ᵗʰ Century Life*, p. 27.

135 See Payne, *Marx: A Biography*, pp. 50-51. My translation comes from Payne. Also see version, "Letter from Marx to His Father," November 10, 1837, posted at https://www.marxists.org/archive/marx/works/1837-pre/letters/37_11_10.htm.

136 Payne, *Marx: A Biography*, p. 52.

137 Payne dates the letter as December 10, 1837. Other sources date it as December 9, 1837. Here I have used the source posted at www.marxists.org, which is a fuller and complete version. It is taken from *Marx-Engels Collected Works* Vol. 1 (NY: International Publishers, 1975), pp. 685-91: http://www.historyisaweapon.com/defcon6/letters/papa/1837-fl7.html.

138 Payne, *Marx: A Biography*, pp. 54-55.

139 Payne, *Marx: A Biography*, p. 77.

140 One of the most influential early accounts of Marx's family life was Otto Ruhle, *Karl Marx: His Life and Works* (NY: Viking Press, 1929). Also considered landmarks were the collections done by German socialist Franz Mehring. Among more recent works, I will draw particularly from four sympathetic accounts by Marx biographers Francis Wheen, Mary Gabriel, Jonathan Sperber, and David McLellan. By frequently citing Wheen and Gabriel, who often engaged in extremes to defend the worst of Marx (especially Wheen), I am hoping to avoid charges of an excessively one-sided bias. Moreover, as a Christian scholar, I do a feel moral responsibility to do my best to try to be fair to every subject, even a man who unleashed such a deadly ideology. Finally, I will add here that I believe the most original and elegantly written biographical work on Marx remains the fascinating research of Robert Payne, particularly his groundbreaking 1968 book. I have also drawn from older, negative biographical examinations of Marx by strident anti-Marxists, notably Paul Johnson and Fulton Sheen.

141 Quoted in Johnson, *Intellectuals*, p. 74.

142 Quoted in Fulton J. Sheen, *The Church, Communism, and Democracy* (New York: Dell Publishing), p. 140.

143   Mary Gabriel, whose perspective on all such negative Marx things is the complete opposite, always applying the utmost positive interpretation toward Marx, writes, "Some biographers have accused Marx of inexcusable callousness toward his father, claiming that he did not attend his funeral because he had better things to do. That is a misrepresentation of events. Having just left Trier, Karl did not return for the funeral because it would have been impossible to make it there on time, and in any case, he had said his goodbyes." Gabriel, *Love and Capital*, p. 31.

144   Sheen, *The Church, Communism, and Democracy*, p. 140.

145   Payne, *Marx: A Biography*, p. 316.

146   Sheen, *The Church, Communism, and Democracy*, p. 140.

147   Sheen, *The Church, Communism, and Democracy*, p. 140.

148   Sheen, *The Church, Communism, and Democracy* (, p. 140.

149   Payne, *Marx: A Biography*, p. 339.

150   Sheen, *The Church, Communism, and Democracy*, p. 141.

151   Gabriel, *Love and Capital*, p. 303.

152   See, among others, Gabriel, *Love and Capital*, p. 304; and Wheen, *Karl Marx*, pp. 262-63.

153   Payne, *Marx: A Biography*, p. 339.

154   This Prussian police report is infamous and often quoted. See, among others, Johnson, *Intellectuals*, p. 73; Gabriel, *Love and Capital*, pp. 234-35; and Wheen, *Karl Marx*, p. 170.

155   Johnson, *Intellectuals*, p. 73. See also McLellan, *Karl Marx: A Biography*, p. 256; and Payne, *Marx: A Biography*, pp. 347-48.

156   Payne, *Marx: A Biography*, p. 343.

157   Payne, *Marx: A Biography*, pp. 346, 349; and "Letter from Karl Marx to Friedrich Engels," January 20, 1864, printed in Raines, *Marx on Religion*, p. 238.

158   McLellan, *Karl Marx: A Biography*, p. 311; and Sperber, *Karl Marx: A 19ᵗʰ Century Life*, pp. 350-51.

159   Johnson, *Intellectuals*, p. 73; and Payne, *Marx: A Biography*, p. 350.

160   Troy Jollimore, "The private life of Karl Marx," *Salon*, September 18, 2011.

161   Karl Marx and Friedrich Engels, *Reminiscences of Marx and Engels* (Moscow: Foreign Language Press, 1959), p. 281.

162   Payne, *Marx: A Biography*, p. 108.

163   For more, see Payne, *Marx: A Biography*, p. 63.

164   Gabriel, *Love and Capital*, pp. 46, 237.

165   Eleanor married and took the name Eleanor Aveling. See Karl Marx and Friedrich Engels, *Reminiscences of Marx and Engels* (Moscow: Foreign Language Press, 1959), pp. 252-53. Also see Wheen, *Karl Marx*, p. 215.

166   Gabriel, *Love and Capital*, pp. 286, 364.

167   Payne, *Marx: A Biography*, p. 317.

168   Payne, *Marx: A Biography*, p. 317.

169   Payne, *Marx: A Biography*, pp. 316-18.

170 Payne, *Marx: A Biography*, pp. 132-38.

171 Payne, *Marx: A Biography*, p. 315.

172 Gabriel, *Love and Capital*, p. 79.

173 Sperber, *Karl Marx: A 19th Century Life*, p. 259.

174 Troy Jollimore, "The private life of Karl Marx," *Salon*, September 18, 2011.

175 Sheen, *The Church, Communism, and Democracy*, p. 140.

176 Johnson, *Intellectuals*, p. 77. See letters in McLellan, *Karl Marx: A Biography*, pp. 212-13, 241-47.

177 Sperber, *Karl Marx: A 19th Century Life*, p. 256.

178 Sperber, *Karl Marx: A 19th Century Life*, p. 257.

179 Sperber, *Karl Marx: A 19th Century Life*, pp. 293-94.

180 Gabriel, *Love and Capital*, pp. 5-7, 244-45.

181 See Wheen, *Karl Marx: A Life*, p. 249; Gabriel, *Love and Capital*, pp. 5-7; Sperber, *Karl Marx: A 19th Century Life*, pp. 347-48; and McLellan, *Karl Marx: A Biography*, p. 306.

182 McLellan, *Karl Marx: A Biography*, pp. 248, 252.

183 The best presentation of this episode was done by Jonathan Sperber. See Sperber, *Karl Marx: A 19th Century Life*, pp. 262-63.

184 Gabriel, *Love and Capital*, p. 81.

185 Johnson, *Intellectuals*, pp. 79-80; and Payne, *Marx: A Biography*, pp 255-59. Payne does note that Lenchen was tough and took no guff from Karl. She could give it right back to him. Still, he nonetheless paid her squat and exploited her shamelessly.

186 Payne, *Marx: A Biography*, p. 260.

187 McLellan, *Karl Marx: A Biography*, p. 249.

188 Gabriel, *Love and Capital*, pp. 212-14.

189 Sperber, *Karl Marx: A 19th Century Life*, pp. 262-63.

190 Wheen, *Karl Marx*, p. 49.

191 Johnson, *Intellectuals*, pp. 78-80.

192 Sperber, *Karl Marx: A 19th Century Life*, pp. 469-70.

193 Wheen, *Karl Marx*, p. 350.

194 Sperber, *Karl Marx: A 19th Century Life*, pp. 469-70.

195 Quoted in Padover, *The Letters of Karl Marx*, p. 338.

196 Mary Gabriel, "Marx's Not-So-Marxist Marriage," *The Daily Beast*, September 21, 2011.

197 Some sources claim three daughters committed suicide; some claim only one. No doubt at least two of them did. The sources on this vary terribly.

198 Payne, *Marx: A Biography*, p. 453.

199 Johnson, *Intellectuals*, pp. 78-80.

200 Johnson, *Intellectuals*, pp. 62, 78-79.

201 Marx wrote this in November 1882, still fourteen years after Lafargue and Laura married. See Wheen, *Karl Marx*, p. 291.

202 Email correspondence with Stephen Schwartz, June 14, 2018.

203 Sperber, *Karl Marx: A 19th Century Life*, p. 496.

204 Though Wheen does quote those insults, he remarkably writes of Marx's offensive, horrid tract on "the Jewish Question:" "Some passages from 'On the Jewish Question' have an equally rancid flavor if taken out of context—which they usually are." Wheen adds, "In spite of the clumsy phraseology and crude stereotyping, the essay was actually written as a defence of the Jews." To the contrary, Marx's essay is pure anti-Semitic tripe and should not be defended. If the likes of Wheen found an essay like this in the past of a conservative it would be hoisted on a petard to forever label the writer a vile anti-Semite. Wheen, *Karl Marx*, pp. 55-56.

205 Quoted in Padover, *The Letters of Karl Marx*, p. 338.

206 See Dmitri N. Shalin, *Pragmatism & Democracy* (New Brunswick, NJ: Transaction Publishers, 2011), p. 197; Wheen, *Karl Marx*, p. 55; and Johnson, *Intellectuals*, p. 62.

207 Walter Williams, "Marx's racism," nationally syndicated column, June 21, 2006.

208 Padover, *On Religion: Karl Marx*, pp. 169-92. The following excerpts and quotations from "On the Jewish Question" are taken from Padover's edition.

209 Padover, *On Religion: Karl Marx*, p. xiii.

210 Sperber, *Karl Marx: A 19th Century Life*, pp. 128-29.

211 Sperber, *Karl Marx: A 19th Century Life*, pp. 65, 129.

212 Payne, *Marx: A Biography*, pp. 130-31.

213 Sperber, *Karl Marx: A 19th Century Life*, p. 133.

214 Sperber, *Karl Marx: A 19th Century Life*, p. 91.

215 Payne, *Marx: A Biography*, p. 82.

216 See Johnson, *Intellectuals*, p. 56.

217 Sperber, *Karl Marx: A 19th Century Life*, p. 133.

218 Shalin, *Pragmatism & Democracy*, p. 197; and Williams, "Marx's racism."

219 Weikart, who quotes this letter, argues that despite Marx "probably father[ing] an illegitimate child," he was nonetheless "apparently a model husband and remained faithful to his wife." Weikart wrote this in 1994, perhaps prior to his knowledge of more recent research on Marx's woefully poor conduct as a husband. Of course, a husband who fathers an illegitimate child to the family's young nanny is not a model or faithful husband.

220 Quoted by Richard Weikart, "Marx, Engels, and the Abolition of the Family," *History of European Ideas*, vol. 18, no. 5, 1994, p. 668. Marx's defenders will probably want to argue that he was speaking tongue-in-cheek, given the high cost of a man (especially a man like Marx) financially supporting a large family (as opposed to a single man with no such obligation). Personally, I'm inclined to a less charitable interpretation, given the realities of Marx's life and attitudes. Notably, Mary Gabriel does not defend it. Gabriel, *Love and Capital*, p. 239.

221 McLellan, *Karl Marx: A Biography*, pp. 305 and 311; and Sperber, *Karl Marx: A 19th Century Life*, p. 466. Also see translation by Mary Gabriel, who quotes the statement from Marx as: "What could be more asinine for people

of wide aspirations than to get married at all." Gabriel, *Love and Capital*, pp. 265 and 338. On Jenny's miseries, also see Gabriel, pp. 77, 244-45, 264-65, 287-90, 299.

[222] Wheen, *Karl Marx*, p. 291.

[223] Most online and other biographical accounts list Jenny's death as December 2, whereas some older accounts list December 5.

[224] See Gabriel, *Love and Capital*, p. 490; Wheen, *Karl Marx*, p. 376; and Payne, *Marx: A Biography*, p. 486.

[225] Sperber, *Karl Marx: A 19th Century Life*, p. 541.

[226] Gabriel, *Love and Capital*, pp. 504-5; and Sperber, *Karl Marx: A 19th Century Life*, pp. 396, 546-47.

[227] See Johnson, *Intellectuals*, pp. 78-80; and Payne, *Marx: A Biography*, pp. 513-14.

[228] On Shaw as a dupe, see Paul Kengor, *Dupes: How America's Adversaries Have Manipulated Progressives for a Century* (Wilmington, Delaware: ISI Books, 2010), pp. 10, 54-55.

[229] Payne, *Marx: A Biography*, pp. 513-14.

[230] Payne, *Marx: A Biography*, pp. 515, 525-30; and Wheen, *Karl Marx*, pp. 385-86.

[231] Gabriel, *Love and Capital*, pp. 591-94.

[232] Payne, *Marx: A Biography*, p. 532.

[233] Gabriel, *Love and Capital*, pp. 591-94.

[234] Franz Mehring, *Karl Marx: The Story of His Life* (Ann Arbor, Michigan: The University of Michigan Press, 1962), p. 88.

[235] Ibid.

[236] Ibid, p. 89.

[237] Sperber, *Karl Marx: A 19th Century Life*, p. 139.

[238] Sperber, *Karl Marx: A 19th Century Life*, pp. 138-41.

[239] David McLellan refers to it as a "satirical poem" written by Edgar Bauer, the brother of Bruno. He refers to it as such, with Edgar Bauer as the author, in the text of his biography of Marx on page 27. In the accompanying footnote, however (footnote 103, carried on page 55), he lists the poem's *co-authors* as Bauer and Engels. See McLellan, *Karl Marx: A Biography*, pp. 27, 55. To the contrary, Franz Mehring records the author of this poem is Friedrich Engels, which was published as *A Christian Epic*, written in four cantos. See Mehring, *Karl Marx: The Story of His Life*, p. 92. The authoritative website, www.marxists.org, which is the most up-to-date of all these sources, posts all four cantos with Engels as the sole author—at least at the time of this writing. Still another excellent source, albeit publishing his biography way back in 1968, when the provenance of the poem might have been in question, is Robert Payne, and Payne lists the author as Edgar Bauer. Payne, notably, makes no intimation that the poem was anything but serious. He also says that the poem was written about the various members of the Doctors' Club, with each of the leading members described at some length, including the

stanza on Marx. See Payne, *Marx*, p. 81.

How to reconcile these differing opinions among serious, good biographers? I believe this might be the answer: Edgar Bauer and Friedrich Engels were both part of the Doctor's Club. Edgar Bauer already knew Marx very well, whereas Engels was about to meet him, and obviously come to know him very well. Perhaps Edgar Bauer had drafted a portion of this longer "poem" on Marx (and many various other assorted, rambling things) and then Engels joined in and expanded upon it, with both thus sharing in some degree of authorship. The precise lines which each man wrote is not totally clear among biographers.

240   Mehring, *Karl Marx: The Story of His Life*, p. 92.

241   Quoted in Mehring, *Karl Marx: The Story of His Life*, pp. 92-93.

242   Again, Payne credits the authorship of the poem to Edgar Bauer, which is perhaps even more significant because, as Payne notes, at the time of the writing of this poem Edgar knew Marx well, and Engels did not. What is much more important to Payne, and really to all of us, is not what this passage might say about the author but the subject—that is, about Marx. Payne, *Marx*, pp. 81-82.

243   For consistency, I will stick with my first translation.

244   Ibid.

245   This is the recollection of Edward Aveling, the husband of Marx's daughter Eleanor. Quoted in Karl Marx and Friedrich Engels, *Reminiscences of Marx and Engels* (Moscow: Foreign Language Press, 1959), p. 316.

246   Weikart, "Marx, Engels, and the Abolition of the Family," pp. 665-67.

247   See, among others, H. Kent Geiger, *The Family in Soviet Russia* (Cambridge, Mass.: Harvard University Press, 1968), p. 11; and Weikart, "Marx, Engels, and the Abolition of the Family," p. 657.

248   Weikart, "Marx, Engels, and the Abolition of the Family," pp. 665-66.

249   Frederick Engels, *The Origin of the Family, Private Property and the State* (New York, NY: International Publishers, 1942), p. 67.

250   Engels, *The Origin of the Family, Private Property and the State*, p. 67.

251   Engels, *The Origin of the Family, Private Property and the State*, p. 67.

252   Geiger, *The Family in Soviet Russia*, pp. 20-21, 33.

253   The "opiate of the masses" remark is well-known. The source for the quote, "communism begins where atheism begins," is Fulton J. Sheen, *Communism and the Conscience of the West* (Indianapolis and NY: Bobbs-Merrill, 1948). Sheen, who spoke and read several languages, translated the quote into English from an un-translated Marx work. See also. Sheen, *The Church, Communism, and Democracy*, pp. 138-39.

254   Marx and Engels, *The Communist Manifesto*, p. 74.

255   Quoted in John Koehler, *Spies in the Vatican* (NY: Pegasus Books, 2009), p. 1.

256   See chapter 11, "Communism and Religion," in Bukharin's *The ABC of Communism*, written in 1920, first published in English in 1922, published

by Penguin Books in 1969, and posted online at https://www.marxists.org/archive/bukharin/works/1920/abc/11.htm.

[257] Quoted in Archie Brown, *The Gorbachev Factor* (NY: Oxford University Press, 1996), pp. 291-92.

[258] As cited by Richard Pipes, *Communism: A History* (NY: The Modern Library, 2001), p. 98.

[259] Leon Trotsky, "Speech to the Thirteenth Party Congress," May 26, 1924. In *The Challenge of the Left Opposition: 1923-1925*, Naomi Allen ed. (New York: Pathfinder Press, 1975), p. 161.

[260] Kennan's seminal work was his "Sources of Soviet Conduct," published in the elite journal *Foreign Affairs* in July 1947. The article publicly presented his secret/historic "Long Telegram" sent from Moscow in February 1946.

[261] Reagan, "The President's News Conference," January 21, 1982.

[262] A handwritten draft of the text is on file at the Reagan Library. Located in "Ronald Reagan: Pre-Presidential Papers: Selected Radio Broadcasts, 1975-1979," April 1977 to September 1977, Box 2, RRL. Reagan, "Religious Freedom," radio broadcast, July 31, 1978.

[263] The opening line in the introduction to a volume of collected works of Vladimir Lenin on religion begins, "Atheism is a natural and inseparable part of Marxism, of the theory and practice of scientific socialism." See V. I. Lenin, *Religion* (London: CPGB-ML, 2012), p. 5, posted at http://ciml.250x.com/archive/lenin/english/lenin_religion.pdf. The original edition of this volume was first published by International Publishers, specifically, the Little Lenin Library, in New York in 1933.

[264] Lenin, "Socialism and Religion," first published in *Novaya Zhizn*, December 3, 1905. Translation taken from V. I. Lenin, *Collected Works*, Vol. 10 (Moscow: Progress Publishers, 1965), pp. 83-87. www.marxists.org/archive/lenin/works/1905/dec/03.htm.

[265] Edward Aveling quoted in Karl Marx and Friedrich Engels, *Reminiscences of Marx and Engels* (Moscow: Foreign Language Press, 1959), p. 316.

[266] Lenin, "Socialism and Religion," first published in *Novaya Zhizn*, December 3, 1905. Translation taken from V. I. Lenin, *Collected Works*, Vol. 10 (Moscow: Progress Publishers, 1965), pp. 83-87. www.marxists.org/archive/lenin/works/1905/dec/03.htm.

[267] Bukharin, "Communism and Religion."

[268] Lenin, "Socialism and Religion," *Novaya Zhizn*, December 3, 1905.

[269] Lenin, "Socialism and Religion," *Novaya Zhizn*, December 3, 1905.

[270] Lenin, "The Attitude of the Workers' Party to Religion," first published in *Proletary*, No. 45, May 26, 1909. Translation taken from V. I. Lenin, *Collected Works*, Vol. 15 (Moscow: Progress Publishers, 1973), pp. 402-13. See www.marxists.org/archive/lenin/works/1909/may/13.htm.

[271] Dean Dettloff, "The Catholic Case for Communism," *America Magazine*, July 23, 2019. https://www.americamagazine.org/faith/2019/07/23/catholic-case-communism. Also see the defense of the article by *America Mag-*

azine's editor-in-chief, Matt Malone, S.J., "Why we published an essay sympathetic to communism:" https://www.americamagazine.org/politics -society/2019/07/23/why-we-published-essay-sympathetic-communism.

272   Lenin, "The Attitude of the Workers' Party to Religion," first published in *Proletary*, No. 45, May 26, 1909. Translation taken from V. I. Lenin, *Collected Works*, Vol. 15 (Moscow: Progress Publishers, 1973), pp. 402-13. See www.marxists.org/archive/lenin/works/1909/may/13.htm.

273   On Lenin's use of the term "useful idiots," see my discussion in Kengor, *Dupes*, pp. 2-3.

274   See Lenin, *Religion*, pp. 18, 26, 41.

275   Lenin, *Religion*, p. 9.

276   Another translation of the word is "necrophily." Lenin, Letter to Maxim Gorky, written November 13 or 14, 1913. First published in *Pravda*, No. 51, March 2, 1924. Translation taken from V. I. Lenin, *Collected Works*, Vol. 35, (Moscow: Progress Publishers, 1976), pp. 121-124. See www.marxists.org/ archive/lenin/works/1913/nov/00mg.htm.

277   See James Thrower, *God's Commissar: Marxism-Leninism as the Civil Religion of Soviet Society* (Lewiston, NY: Edwin Mellen Press, 1992), p. 39.

278   See J. M. Bochenski, "Marxism-Leninism and Religion," in B. R. Bociurkiw et al, eds., *Religion and Atheism in the USSR and Eastern Europe* (London: MacMillan, 1975), p. 11.

279   Quoted in Dmitri Volkogonov, *Lenin: A New Biography* (NY: The Free Press, 1994), p. 373.

280   This item is published in Yakovlev, *A Century of Violence in Soviet Russia*, p. 157.

281   The Third All-Russia Congress of the Russian Young Communist League took place in Moscow from October 2-10, 1920 and was attended by an estimated six hundred delegates. Lenin addressed the first session the evening of October 2. The transcript was published in *Pravda* on October 5, 6, and 7, 1920. It also appears in Lenin's *Collected Works*, volume 31. See posting at: https://www.marxists.org/archive/lenin/works/1920/oct/02.htm.

282   Lenin, Letter to Maxim Gorky, written November 13 or 14, 1913.

283   See Daniel Peris, *Storming the Heavens: The Soviet League of the Militant Godless* (Ithaca, NY: Cornell University Press, 1998).

284   Quoted in Pipes, *Communism: A History*, pp. 68-69.

285   Quoted in Barry Lee Woolley, *Adherents of Permanent Revolution: A History of the Fourth (Trotskyist) International* (Lanham, MD: University Press of America, 1999), pp. 4-5.

286   Among others, see Woolley, p. 5.

287   Alexander Solzhenitsyn, "Men Have Forgotten God," Templeton Prize Award speech, May 10, 1983.

288   This is not to say that the Russian leaders before the Bolsheviks were model "Christians," or that they were all Christians. The point, however, is that, generally, their *attitude* toward Christianity was far less hostile than that of

the Bolsheviks.

[289] Yakovlev, *A Century of Violence in Soviet Russia*, pp. 155, 163.

[290] See Thrower, *God's Commissar*, p. 64; Jennifer McDowell, "Soviet Civil Ceremonies," *Journal for the Scientific Study of Religion*, Vol. 13, No. 3, 1974, pp. 265-79; and Powell, "Rearing the New Soviet Man," in Bociurkiw and Strong, *Religion and Atheism in the USSR and Eastern Europe*, pp. 160-65.

[291] W. Bruce Lincoln, *Red Victory: A History of the Russian Civil War* (NY: Simon and Schuster, 1989), pp. 476-77.

[292] Hedrick Smith, *The Russians* (London: Sphere Books, 1976), p. 396.

[293] See, among others, Yakovlev, *A Century of Violence in Soviet Russia*, pp. 162-67; Smith, *The Russians*, p. 396; Lincoln, *Red Victory*, pp. 476-77; and "A Restored Look for the Long-Ignored Churches of Russia," Associated Press, July 23, 1976, p. B3.

[294] Lincoln, *Red Victory*, p. 474.

[295] On this, see Alexander Solzhenitsyn, *The Gulag Archipelago, 1918-1956* (NY: Harper and Row, 1974), pp. 37-38.

[296] Volkogonov, *Lenin*, pp. 374, 380.

[297] See Kengor, *A Pope and a President: John Paul II, Ronald Reagan, and the Extraordinary Untold Story of the 20th Century* (Wilmington, Delaware: ISI Books, 2017), pp. 28-31; Volkogonov, *Lenin*, pp. 29, 325-27, 345-51; and Yakovlev, *A Century of Violence in Soviet Russia*, pp. 155-61.

[298] Volkogonov, *Lenin*, pp. 376-78.

[299] Yakovlev, *A Century of Violence in Soviet Russia*, p. 168.

[300] James Billington, "Christianity and History," 125th anniversary lecture series, Grove City College, Grove City, Pennsylvania, September 27, 2001.

[301] Radzinsky speaking in interview for A&E Biography of Joseph Stalin, "The Red Terror."

[302] Mikhail Gorbachev, *Memoirs* (NY: Doubleday, 1996), p. 328.

[303] Mikhail Gorbachev, *On My Country and the World*, (NY: Columbia University Press, 2000), pp. 20-21.

[304] See Paul Dixon, "Religion in the Soviet Union," Marxist.com, April 17, 2006, first published in *Workers' International News* in October 1945, posted at http://www.marxist.com/religion-soviet-union170406.htm. See also Yakovlev, *A Century of Violence in Soviet Russia*, p. 164.

[305] This passage is taken from an article, "A Life of Lasting Thankfulness," by Reverend Yuri Sipko, member of the Russian Union of Christian Baptists. Article excerpt is included in transcript of interview with Sipko. Correspondence received by author June 21, 1998.

[306] Richard Wurmbrand, *Tortured for Christ* (Bartlesville, OK: Living Sacrifice Book Company, 1998), p. 65.

[307] H. W. Crocker III, *Triumph: The Power and Glory of the Catholic Church* (NY: Three Rivers Press, 2001), pp. 407-8.

[308] "Dry," said Sheen, because he primarily suffered mental torture rather than being physically annihilated like martyrs of old.

309 Jozsef Cardinal Mindszenty, *Memoirs* (NY: Macmillan Publishing, 1974).

310 Again, see "The Communist War on Religion," posted at www.globalmuse-umoncommunism.org.

311 See Bertram D. Wolfe, *A Life in Two Centuries* (Stein and Day, 1981), pp. 403-4.

312 Wurmbrand, *Tortured for Christ*, pp. 33-38.

313 See https://www.thegenocideofthesouls.org/public/english/video-historians/, retrieved July 30, 2019.

314 The citations are reprinted below as they appear at the website.

315 Virgil Ierunca, *The Pitesti Phenomenon*, Paris, 1981, p. 37.

316 Eugen Magirescu, *The Devil's Mill: Memories of Pitesti Prison*, Editura Fronde, Alba-Iulia, Paris, 1994, p. 6.

317 Eugen Magirescu, *The Devil's Mill*, in Memoria no. 13, p. 38.

318 Ion Balan, *The Prison Camp Regime in Romania, 1945-1964*, Fundatia Academia Civica, 2000, p. 225.

319 Alin Muresan, *Pitesti: The Chronicle of an Assisted Suicide*, Polirom, Bucharest, 2008.

320 Alin Muresan, *Pitesti: The Chronicle of an Assisted Suicide*, Polirom, Bucharest, 2008.

321 Costin Merisca, *The Pitesti Tragedy*, Jassy, 1997, p. 70-71.

322 Justin Stefan Paven, *The Hell of Pitesti*, in Memoria, no. 22, p. 66.

323 Yakovlev, *A Century of Violence in Soviet Russia*, pp. 7-8, 158.

324 Yakovlev, *A Century of Violence in Soviet Russia*, pp. 8, 26-27, 87, 155-68.

325 Pope Pius IX, *Qui Pluribus (On Faith and Religion)*, November 9, 1946, posted at https://www.papalencyclicals.net/Pius09/p9quiplu.htm.

326 In their critical 2013 book *Disinformation*, Ion Mihai Pacepa and Ron Rychlak chronicled the crass art of Kremlin deception, an effort with no moral scruples, and one particularly aimed at defaming, maligning, and slandering religious individuals. Pacepa, a former Romanian general, was the highest-ranking intelligence official to defect the Soviet bloc, and a witness to many of the events the book describes. Pacepa and Rychlak gave special attention to the scandalously successful case against the vehemently anti-communist Pope Pius XII, who was public enemy no. 1 to Stalin at the start of the Cold War. They show that the attack against Pius was launched with a 1945 Radio Moscow broadcast that first echoed the bald-faced lie of a smear, "Hitler's Pope." The Soviets understood that Pius XII was a mortal threat to their ideology and thus manufactured their big lie that Pius had been pro-Hitler. They embarked on an unholy crusade to destroy the pope, his reputation, scandalize his flock, and foment division among faiths. For the Soviets, this became a standard tactic. They would sling the pro-Nazi charge at numerous Church figures like Cardinals Mindszenty and Stepinac (Yugoslavia) and Wyszynski (Poland).

327 Here's a full post: http://geocities.ws/caleb1x/documents/communism. html. And here's a post from a Catholic website based in Brazil (in the orig-

inal Latin): http://www.montfort.org.br/eng/documentos/decretos/antico-munismo/. A very important question is raised in the comments section of this latter website: "This decree from Pius XII's Holy Office, confirmed by John XXIII in 1959 is still valid. . . . The penalty for those who disobey the prohibition of aiding communism (or its variants) under any aspect (including voting for filo-communist parties) is automatic excommunication." This is a crucial question with undeniable modern relevance, especially given that the leading Jesuit publication, *America*, 70 years later, in July 2019, scandalously published an outrageous piece titled "The Catholic Case for Communism," written by *America*'s Canadian correspondent who (Rod Dreher reports) is a member of the Canadian Communist Party.

328   See my article: Paul Kengor, "Vatican II's Unpublished Condemnations of Communism," *Crisis Magazine*, November 30, 2017. This section is adapted from that article.

329   The source is Matthew Cullinan Hoffman, who I interviewed for the November 2017 article for *Crisis*.

330   Thomas C. Reeves, *America's Bishop: The Life and Times of Fulton J. Sheen* (Encounter Books, 2001), pp. 87-88.

331   Reeves, *America's Bishop*, p. 88.

332   Sheen, *The Church, Communism and Democracy*, pp. 61, 122, 138.

333   Kathleen L. Riley, *Fulton J. Sheen: An American Catholic Response to the Twentieth Century* (Staten Island, NY: Alba House, 2004), p. 149.

334   The full quote from Pope Francis is: "The Marxist ideology is wrong. But I have met many Marxists in my life who are good people." Francis said this in December 2013 to the Italian newspaper *La Stampa*. The issue of Francis and communism is complicated. Francis, admittedly, doesn't have much of a track record of papal statements or actions against communism. Two instances stand out: For one, Pope Francis in Rome in April 2017 lamented "the many Christians killed by the demented ideologies of the last century." It is assumed that this was a reference to communism, which it surely was, even as communism or Marxism was not singled out by name even once by Francis. The same was true for a slightly clearer occasion in June 2019 in Romania, where Francis beatified seven communist-era bishops. On this occasion, Francis said that the martyred bishops had "endured suffering and gave their lives to oppose an illiberal ideological system that oppressed the fundamental rights of the human person." Once again, Francis did not once mention communism or Marxism. The accusations that Pope Francis is soft on communism are justified. It might be more accurate to say that he is simply silent on communism. For a highly critical assessment of Francis on communism, coming from a colleague and very negative source who nonetheless has done his homework on Francis, including visiting and digging deep into his Argentinian roots, see George Neumayr, "Where Bergoglio Buried His Communist Mentor," *The American Spectator*, August 28, 2019. Neumayr provides a decidedly different treatment from the likes of Francis

biographer Austen Ivereigh. Still, it is hard to dispute Neumayr's alarming facts on Francis, particularly Francis's early roots with Latin American communist Esther Ballestrino de Careaga.

335   In 2015, the word "socialism" was the most looked-up word at Merriam-Webster.com. That reflects the growing interest, but it also reflects the enduring confusion over what the word means. That confusion has always been aided by those wielding the term. Ask ten socialists to define socialism and you'll get ten different answers. See Alex Adrianson, "Socialism Can Never Work," *The Insider* (Heritage Foundation), Spring 2016, p. 2.

336   The name change came in 1903 when these Russian socialists split into two factions, the Bolsheviks and the Menshaviks. See, among others, Pipes, *Communism: A History*, pp. ix-x.

337   See Bertram D. Wolfe, "A Party of a New Type," in Milorad M. Drachkovitch and Branko Lazitch, eds., The Comintern: Historical Highlights—Essays, Recollections, Documents (New York: Praeger), pp. xi, 20.

338   The full title is *The State and Revolution: The Marxist Theory of the State & the Tasks of the Proletariat in the Revolution*, written in August-September 1917 as Lenin was in hiding from the Provisional Government and mere weeks before he spearheaded the October Revolution. For a year at least, Lenin had argued the need for such a theoretical work applied to practical realities, and this was his major stab at providing one. See (among others) the introductory notes provided to *The State and Revolution* at www.marxists.org.

339   He stated this in his *Mater et Magistra, Encyclical on Christianity and Social Progress*, May 15, 1961.

340   Pope John Paul II, *Centesimus Annus*, May 1, 1991, posted at: https://w2.vatican.va/content/john-paul-ii/en/encyclicals/documents/hf_jp-ii_enc_01051991_centesimus-annus.html.

341   See *Catechism of the Catholic Church*, nos. 1883-94; and David A. Bosnich, "The Principle of Subsidiarity," *Religion & Liberty* (published by the Acton Institute), Vol. 6, No. 4, July 20, 2010.

342   See, for example, various congressmen using this in reference to Bella Dodd's testimony during their exchange with Manning Johnson: Hearing Before the Committee on Un-American Activities, U.S. House of Representatives, 83rd Congress, First Session, "Investigation of Communist Activities in the New York City Area—Part 7 (Based on the Testimony of Manning Johnson)," July 13, 1953 (Washington, D.C.: U.S. Government Printing Office, 1953), pp. 2202, 2216, 2217. See link posted at: https://archive.org/details/investigationofcnyc0708unit/page/2202.

343   Both were published by Circuit Riders, Inc., located in Cincinnati, Ohio.

344   Melish took up two pages, whereas his son, William Howard Melish (more on him in a moment), took up nine pages. Together, they filled pages 102-12 of the "20.5%/Episcopal" compilation.

345   In the 1920s, Roger Baldwin was very pro-Soviet, pro-communist, and worked closely with the Communist Party and its members, but didn't join

the party. The Hitler-Stalin Pact in 1939 was his wake-up call, as it was for many liberals. He began purging communists from the ACLU national board. After World War II, Baldwin became very anti-communist and even shared information with the FBI. He, too, is a remarkable story of political redemption when it came to communism.

346 See Kengor, *Dupes*, pp. 62-64, 188.

347 See Kengor, *Dupes*, pp. 62-64, 306-8.

348 In HUAC's July 1953 report on communist activities in the New York City area, there are more references to Harry Ward than any other figure—twice as many as the next most-cited figure: Earl Browder. "Investigation of Communist Activities in the New York City Area—Part 5," Committee on Un-American Activities, U.S. House of Representatives, 83rd Congress, 1st Session, July 6, 1953 (Washington, DC: GPO, 1953), pp. 2284, 2291.

349 Alas, while Ward remained a dupe, there was a measure of redemption for Roger Baldwin. Baldwin eventually, after the Red Terror, after the Great Purge, after the Ukrainian famine, after the Hitler-Stalin Pact, after millions of rotting corpses, after the gulag, after the communists had violated every imaginable civil liberty, awakened to the stench of the Soviet system. He finally saw communism, and communists, as a genuine concern. By the early 1950s, Baldwin began insisting that ACLU officers take a non-communist oath. Call Baldwin crazy, but he figured that any ACLU member who held allegiance to "totalitarian dictatorship" was not truly serious about civil liberties. Perhaps they were publicly exploiting American civil liberties to privately support a nation (the USSR) that had no civil liberties? Yes, they were.

350 "Investigation of Un-American Propaganda Activities in the United States," Special Committee on Un-American Activities, House of Representatives, 78th Congress, Second Session, on H. Res. 282, App. Part IX, Vol. 1 (Washington, DC: GPO, 1944), p. 431.

351 William Z. Foster, *Toward Soviet America* (NY: International Publishers, 1932), pp. 272-73.

352 Among others, see the discussion in Paul Hollander, *Political Pilgrims* (NY: Harper & Row, 1983), p. 64.

353 See Jean Wagner, *Black poets of the United Sates: From Paul Laurence Dunbar to Langston Hughes* (Chicago and Urbana: University of Illinois Press, 1973), p. 435; and Faith Berry, *Langston Hughes: Before and Beyond Harlem* (NY: Citadel Press, 1992), pp. 296-97.

354 Email correspondence with Herb Romerstein, April 16, 2007 and June 23, 2007.

355 This exchange appears in "Investigation of Un-American Activities and Propaganda," Special Committee on Un-American Activities, 75th Congress, House of Representatives, January 3, 1939, pp. 18-21. See posting at https://archive.org/details/investigationofu1939unit/page/18.

356 Martin (M.Y.) Latsis, the ferocious Latvian. In *The Red Terror in Russia*, published in Berlin in 1924, the Russian historian and socialist Sergei Mel-

gunov cited Latsis, one of the first leaders of the Cheka, as giving this order to his thugs on November 1, 1918. This quote has been cited by a number of sources. Most recently, see Courtois, *Black Book*, p. 8. Among other sources that cite this quote, see Brown, *Doomsday 1917*, p. 173; and Leggett, *The Cheka*, pp. 463-68.

357   Earl Browder, *Report to the 8ᵗʰ Convention, Communist Party* (NY: Workers Library Publishers, 1934), p. 104.

358   "Conditions of Admission to the Communist International," *Party Organizer*, February 1931, p. 31.

359   Quoted in "Structure and Function of Party Units," *Party Organizer*, February 1931, p. 2. As further evidence of such thinking, M. J. Olgin, communist and Browder colleague, said during FDR's first year in power, "The Communist Party of the U.S.A. is thus part of a worldwide organization which gives it guidance and enhances its fighting power. Under the leadership of the Communist Party the workers of the U.S.A. will proceed from struggle to struggle, from victory to victory, until, rising in a revolution, they will crush the capitalist State, establish a Soviet State, abolish the cruel and bloody system of capitalism and proceed to the upbuilding of Socialism." M. J. Olgin, *Why Communism?* (NY: Workers Library Publishers, 1933), p. 95.

360   Browder, *Communism in the United States*, p. 334.

361   Browder, *Communism in the United States*, p. 337.

362   Browder, *Communism in the United States*, p. 338.

363   I write about this at length throughout my book on Frank Marshall Davis. See Paul Kengor, *The Communist: Frank Marshall Davis, the Untold Story of Barack Obama's Mentor* (New York: Mercury Ink, Simon & Schuster, 2012), pp. 34-44.

364   Browder, *Communism in the United States*, pp. 294, 349.

365   Browder, *Communism in the United States*, p. 336.

366   Browder, *Communism in the United States*, p. 337.

367   Herb Romerstein and Eric Breindel, *The Venona Secrets* (Washington, D.C.: Regnery, 2000), pp. 412-13.

368   Romerstein and Breindel, *The Venona Secrets*, p. 413.

369   See" "Pacelli Lunches With Roosevelt," *New York Times*, November 6, 1936; and Kengor, *A Pope and President*, pp. 54-56.

370   See Charles R. Gallagher, *Vatican Secret Diplomacy: Joseph P. Hurley and Pope Pius XII* (New Haven: Yale University Press, 2008), pp. 87-88.

371   See the foreword to the 2018 paperback edition of my book, *Dupes*, as well as other chapters in the book on FDR.

372   For the record, *Divini Redemptoris* was released in March 1937, though it was merely the latest in a long line of anti-communist statements from the Vatican dating back to at least 1846.

373   Romerstein and Breindel, *The Venona Secrets*, pp. 412-13.

374   "Browder Offers Aid to Catholics," *The New York Times*, May 29, 1938.

375   Earl Browder, *A Message to Catholics* (New York: Workers Library Publishers,

1938). Document is available online at: https://www.marxists.org/archive/browder/message-catholics.pdf.

[376] This is widely understood by anyone who belonged in or has studied the Comintern and international communist movement. For a quick summary, see Kengor, *Dupes*, pp. 20-33.

[377] Robert Service, *The End of the Cold War: 1985-1991* (NY: Public Affairs, 2015), pp. 95-98.

[378] Browder, *A Message to Catholics*, p. 3.

[379] See Celie and Albert Vassart, "The Moscow Origin of the French 'Popular Front,'" in Milorad M. Drachkovitch and Branko Lazitch, eds., The Comintern: Historical Highlights—Essays, Recollections, Documents (New York: Praeger), pp. 112 and 234-52.

[380] Celie and Albert Vassart, "The Moscow Origin of the French 'Popular Front,'" pp. 246-47, 257, 311.

[381] Celie and Albert Vassart, "The Moscow Origin of the French 'Popular Front,'" pp. 251-52.

[382] Celie and Albert Vassart, "The Moscow Origin of the French 'Popular Front,'" pp. 235-36.

[383] See Kengor, *Dupes*, pp. 160-81.

[384] Browder, *A Message to Catholics*, p. 3.

[385] Browder, *A Message to Catholics*, p. 7.

[386] See Shawn Ritenour, *Foundations of Economics: A Christian View* (Eugene, Oregon: Wipf & Stock, 2015).

[387] Browder, *A Message to Catholics*, p. 7.

[388] Browder, *A Message to Catholics*, p. 8.

[389] Browder, *A Message to Catholics*, p. 8.

[390] For an in-depth examination, see Paul Kengor, *Takedown: From Communists to Progressives, How the Left Has Sabotaged Family and Marriage* (Washington, DC: WND Books, 2015).

[391] Browder, *A Message to Catholics*, p. 15.

[392] "Catholics Reject Communist Plea," *The New York Times*, July 31, 1938.

[393] Fulton J. Sheen, *Communism Answers Questions of a Communist* (New York: The Paulist Press, 1937).

[394] Sheen's most powerful exposition on the communist war on the family appears in chapter seven of his 1948 work, *Communism and the Conscience of the West*.

[395] Sheen, *Communism Answers Questions of a Communist*, p. 33.

[396] See discussion in Kengor, *A Pope and a President*, pp. 72-73, 82-83.

[397] Sheen, *Communism Answers Questions of a Communist*, pp. 34-35.

[398] Sheen, *Communism Answers Questions of a Communist*, pp. 38-39.

[399] "Open Letter to Browder By Editors," *The Catholic Worker*, Vol. VI, No. 4, September 1938, pp. 1-2.

[400] See discussion in Paul Kengor and Robert Orlando, *The Divine Plan: Ronald Reagan, John Paul II, and the Dramatic End of the Cold War* (Wilmington,

DE: ISI Books, 2019), pp. 40-47.

401　See J. B. Matthews, *Odyssey of a Fellow Traveler* (New York: Mount Vernon Publishers, 1938).

402　Matthews, *Odyssey of a Fellow Traveler*, pp. 59-64.

403　John R. Erickson, "A disappointed man," *WORLD Magazine*, November 7, 2015.

404　We see here with the likes of Thomas a crucial difference between socialists of old and those of today: the ones of old were oftentimes religious, whereas those of today are often secular and anti-religious. One continuing thread, however, is the Religious Left: there have long been religious leftists in American history. They have long carried the banner of "social justice," arguing in particular for heavy levels of wealth redistribution.

405　Matthews, *Odyssey of a Fellow Traveler*, p. 96.

406　Matthews, *Odyssey of a Fellow Traveler*, p. 115.

407　See the numerous examples throughout Matthews, *Odyssey of a Fellow Traveler*.

408　Matthews, *Odyssey of a Fellow Traveler*, pp. 9-10. Matthews here cites Earl Browder, *Communism in the United States* (New York: International Publishers, September 1935), p. 335.

409　Matthews, *Odyssey of a Fellow Traveler*, p. 9. Matthews cites Browder, *Communism in the United States*, p. 55.

410　Matthews, *Odyssey of a Fellow Traveler*, p. 9. Matthews quotes from D. Z. Manuilsky, *The Work of the Seventh Congress*.

411　Matthews, *Odyssey of a Fellow Traveler*, p. 208.

412　Matthews, *Odyssey of a Fellow Traveler*, pp. 208-9. Here Matthews cited the *Daily Worker*, February 9, 1938.

413　Matthews, *Odyssey of a Fellow Traveler*, p. 209. Here Matthews cited Bennett Stevens, *The Church and the Workers*, p. 31.

414　Once again: Matthews, *Odyssey of a Fellow Traveler*, p. 209—citing Bennett Stevens, *The Church and the Workers*, p. 31.

415　Matthews, *Odyssey of a Fellow Traveler*, p. 209. Here Matthews cited Corliss Lamont, *Soviet Russia and Religion*, p. 21f.

416　Matthews, *Odyssey of a Fellow Traveler*, p. 209. Here Matthews cited Corliss Lamont, *Soviet Russia and Religion*, p. 19.

417　See Kengor, *Dupes*, pp. 68-79.

418　Matthews here was quoting from general (unnamed) communist literature. Matthews, *Odyssey of a Fellow Traveler*, p. 210.

419　Matthews, *Odyssey of a Fellow Traveler*, p. 211. Here Matthews cited the *Daily Worker*, January 14, 1938, p. 6.

420　Matthews, *Odyssey of a Fellow Traveler*, p. 211. Here Matthews cited editions of the *Daily Worker* from January 21, 1938, January 24, 1938, and February 16, 1938.

421　Matthews, *Odyssey of a Fellow Traveler*, p. 212.

422　See Reeves, *America's Bishop: The Life and Times of Fulton J. Sheen*, pp. 170-

73.

[423] Testimony of Louis Francis Budenz, Hearing Before the Committee on Un-American Activities, U.S. House of Representatives, 79th Congress, Second Session, "Investigation of Un-American Propaganda Activities," November 22, 1946 (Washington, D.C.: U.S. Government Printing Office, 1946), pp. 1-2, 31-33. See link posted at https://archive.org/details/investigationofu1946unit/page/n5.

[424] Budenz's testimony before the House Committee on Un-American Activities came on November 22, 1946. The key part of his testimony excerpted here from the official transcript runs from the bottom of page 31 to the middle of page 33.

[425] Benjamin Gitlow, *I Confess: The Truth About American Communism* (New York: E.P. Dutton, 1940); and Benjamin Gitlow, *The Whole of Their Lives* (New York: Scribner's, 1948).

[426] Gitlow wrote, "Not only does the Communist Party member give every moment of his time to the cause but every dollar he can spare as well, often giving much more than he can afford." Gitlow, *I Confess*, 289.

[427] This document is in the Comintern Archives on CPUSA, Fond 515, Opis 1, Delo 4084. See also Romerstein and Breindel, *The Venona Secrets*, 20-21.

[428] "Testimony of Benjamin Gitlow," Hearing Before the Committee on Un-American Activities, U.S. House of Representatives, 83rd Congress, First Session, "Investigation of Communist Activities in the New York City Area—Part 6," July 7, 1953 (Washington, D.C.: U.S. Government Printing Office, 1953), pp. 2145-79. Gitlow's testimony runs from pages 2069-2136. The key material on Ward and his Methodist Federation for Social Action is on pages 2074-95. What follows is excerpted from those pages. See link posted at: https://archive.org/details/investigationofc0506unit/page/2032.

[429] "Testimony of Benjamin Gitlow," Hearing Before the Committee on Un-American Activities, U.S. House of Representatives, July 7, 1953, pp. 2072-73.

[430] See Camille M. Cianfarra, *The Vatican and the Kremlin* (New York: E. P. Dutton & Co., 1950), pp. 62-63. Cianfarra also wrote the 1944 book *The Vatican and the War*. He died tragically on July 25, 1956 during a collision of two large passenger ships off the coast of Nantucket (en route from Spain). The tragedy killed two of his children as well.

[431] "Testimony of Benjamin Gitlow," Hearing Before the Committee on Un-American Activities, U.S. House of Representatives, July 7, 1953, pp. 2077-78.

[432] The Profintern, which existed from 1921 to 1937, was formally known as the Red International of Labor Unions. The name was a contraction derived from the Russian "Professionalye Soyuz Internationalnye." See https://www.marxists.org/history/international/profintern/index.htm.

[433] The term "agitprop" is a contraction that refers to agitation and propaganda. The Soviets ran an actual Department of Agitprop.

434   See Paul Kengor, *The Politically Incorrect Guide to Communism* (Washington, DC: Regnery, 2017), pp. 287-97; and Kengor, *The Communist*, pp. 37-41.

435   The information in this section comes from chapter one of Manning Johnson's *Color, Communism and Common Sense*.

436   Hearing Before the Committee on Un-American Activities, U.S. House of Representatives, 83rd Congress, First Session, "Investigation of Communist Activities in the New York City Area—Part 7 (Based on the Testimony of Manning Johnson)," July 8, 1953 (Washington, D.C.: U.S. Government Printing Office, 1953), pp. 2145-79. See link posted at https://archive.org/details/investigationofcnyc0708unit/page/n3.

437   I have encountered several Catholic authors who took the liberty of inserting the word "Catholic" and inaccurately creating an uppercase *C* for "Church" in Manning Johnson's testimony. These authors quote the testimony this way: "the Communists discovered that the destruction of religion could proceed much faster through infiltration of the [Catholic] Church by Communists operating within the Church itself." (See, for example, Taylor Marshall in his 2019 book with Sophia Institute Press, *Infiltration: The Plot to Destroy the Church from Within*, p. 86.) That is an inaccurate rendering. It is not how the original testimony of Manning Johnson reads, was printed, or was intended. In the official transcript printed by Congress's Government Printing Office, it reads this way: "the Communists discovered that the destruction of religion could proceed much faster through infiltration of the church by Communists operating within the church itself." The mistake is probably an honest one by Catholics who assume that "church" means "Catholic Church," or who simply have cited the mis-rendering by others.

438   Note: Manning Johnson is probably here referring to William Montgomery Brown's book, *My Heresy: The Autobiography of an Idea*. Johnson can be forgiven for referring to it strictly as *Heresy*.

439   See article posted at https://www.marxists.org/history/usa/pubs/communist/v18n08-aug-1939-The-Communist-OCR.pdf. The Communist would change its name to *Political Affairs*, the longtime title of what was known as "the theoretical journal" of Communist Party USA. https://www.marxists.org/history/usa/pubs/communist/index.htm.

440   Hearing Before the Committee on Un-American Activities, U.S. House of Representatives, 83rd Congress, First Session, "Investigation of Communist Activities in the New York City Area—Part 7 (Based on the Testimony of Manning Johnson)," July 13, 1953 (Washington, D.C.: U.S. Government Printing Office, 1953), pp. 2202-3. See link posted at https://archive.org/details/investigationofcnyc0708unit/page/2202.

441   Bella V. Dodd, *School of Darkness* (NY: Devin-Adair, 1954), pp. 3, 33-35, 39-41, 42-43. On George Counts' Moscow pilgrimage with John Dewey, see Kengor, *Dupes*, pp. 66, 102.

442   Dodd, *School of Darkness*, pp. 47, 60, 159.

443   Bella Dodd, *School of Darkness*, p. 214.

444 Whittaker Chambers, *Witness* (New York: Random House, 1952), pp. 242, 264.

445 Bella Dodd, *School of Darkness*, p. 150.

446 This speech by Bella Dodd can be listened to online. Click the following link and go to the 1:09:35 marker for this particular passage: https://www.youtube.com/watch?v=37HgRWTsGs0.

447 Again, see the very revealing book by CPUSA head William Z. Foster, *Toward Soviet America*.

448 This quote is well-established. For a current source who documents it nicely, see Barry Popkin, who, among other bona fides, is a contributor to the *Oxford English Dictionary*. Popkin at his website lists at least a half-dozen contemporaneous books (all by reputable, leading publishers of their day, such as MacMillan and Viking) with very similar variations of the quote, including Harry Greenwall's *Mirrors of Moscow* (1929), Bruce Hopper's *What Russia Intends* (1931), Margaret (Reibold) Craig-McKerrow's *The Iron Road to Samarcand* (1932), Thomas Woody's *New Minds: New Men?* (1932), and Walter Duranty's *Duranty Reports Russia* (1934). Duranty, of course, was the Pulitzer Prize-winning (and infamous) *New York Times* correspondent on Moscow. Duranty reported the Lenin quotation this way: "Give me four years to teach the children, and the seed I shall have sown will never be uprooted" (page 175 of his book). http://www.barrypopik.com/index.php/new_york_city/entry/give_me_four_years_to_teach_the_children. In addition to Popkin, also see S. Doniger, "Soviet Education and Children's Literature," *The Journal of Educational Sociology*, vol. 8, no. 3, 1934, pp. 162-67.

449 On Dodd at *New Masses*, see "Investigation of Un-American Propaganda Activities in the United States," Special Committee on Un-American Activities, House of Representatives, 78th Congress, Second Session, on H. Res. 282, App. Part IX, Vol. 3 (Washington, DC: GPO, 1944), also known simply as "Appendix IX," pp. 1350-52 and 1453.

450 See "Investigation of Un-American Propaganda Activities in the United States," Special Committee on Un-American Activities, House of Representatives, 78th Congress, Second Session, on H. Res. 282, App. Part IX, Vols. 1, 2, and 3 (Washington, DC: GPO, 1944), also known simply as "Appendix IX," pp. 433, 443, 446, 449, 1366, 1632, 1672, 1771, 1778.

451 Sheen also brought back to the faith Louis Budenz, bringing the *Daily Worker* editor—whose name at the time of his reversion was still on the masthead—into the Church along with his wife and three daughters. Thomas C. Reeves, *America's Bishop: The Life and Times of Fulton J. Sheen* (Encounter Books, 2001), pp. 170-73.

452 Bella Dodd, *School of Darkness* (New York: 1954), pp. 230-31.

453 Dodd, *School of Darkness*, pp. 231-37; and Fulton J. Sheen, *Treasure in Clay* (New York: Doubleday, 1980), p. 263.

454 Bella Dodd, *School of Darkness* (New York: 1954), pp. 231-33.

455 Dodd, *School of Darkness*, p. 237.

456   Dodd, *School of Darkness*, pp. 240-45.

457   Merely Googling or checking YouTube for the source of Bella's assertion is fruitless. Posted audio claiming that she spoke of 1,000 or 1,100 or 1,200 men in seminaries in her memoir, before Congress, in a speech at Fordham, in a speech at Utica, fails every time to produce the exact line from the memoir, from her congressional testimony, from her speeches at Fordham or in Utica. Documentaries quoting her giving the number do not actually produce the precise where and when. Online sources will run audio of a Bella Dodd speech and then stop it and over-lay the alleged quote about seminaries, without citing its provenance. It is a frustrating endeavor. Nonetheless, it appears that she did say it, albeit not in any of those venues.

458   See "Bella Dodd, Former Red, Dies," *Washington Post*, May 1, 1969; and "Dr. Bella V. Dodd Dies at 64," *The New York Times*, April 30, 1969.

459   The Honorable John R. Rarick, *The Congressional Record—Extensions of Remarks*, May 15, 1969, p. E4036.

460   I filed the FOIA via an attorney friend and colleague who deals with FOIAs on a day-to-day basis. He likewise has been surprised at the lack of progress on this particular request.

461   The lack of response could well be the usual inefficiency of the federal bureaucracy. I do not know how many others have filed FOIAs for Bella Dodd's file. It would, however, be a big surprise if I were the first and only to submit a FOIA request for her FBI file. The federal government has acknowledged the request, but the file still has not been released.

462   Hildebrand seems to have used phrases like "approximately 1,200" and "some 1,100."

463   As recently as a May 7, 2019 email exchange, Mary Nicholas told me again: "In terms of something Bella said in writings, the answer remains no."

464   Email correspondence with Mary Nicholas, September 7, 2018. Though I have read Mary's manuscript, I attempted first to write this chapter without her notes (about six months had passed since I had last looked at the notes), constructing my own narrative first, and only then going back to her account for what I might have missed. I did this so as not to duplicate her work and to see if I could come to similar conclusions prior to revisiting her case. I do disagree with her citing of Manning Johnson. Overall, however, I do not dispute her conclusions.

465   "The Technique of Soviet Propaganda," A Study Presented by the Subcommittee to Investigate the Administration of the Internal Security Act and Other Internal Security Laws, Committee on the Judiciary, U.S. Senate, 86th Congress, Second Session (Washington, D.C.: U.S. Government Printing Office, 1960), p. 7. See link posted at https://babel.hathitrust.org/cgi/pt?id=uiug.30112039644817;view=1up;seq=3.

466   I noted earlier how Pol Pot and his Khmer Rouge were a product of European universities, specifically in France. This particular report, issued in 1960, a decade and a half before Pot and his genocidal thugs took power

in Cambodia (in 1975), prophetically stated, "European universities are so contaminated [by Marxist propaganda] that the Communist and para-Communist movements of Asia and Africa can be said to have been nurtured in them." "The Technique of Soviet Propaganda," Committee on the Judiciary, U.S. Senate, p. 7.

467 "The Technique of Soviet Propaganda," Committee on the Judiciary, U.S. Senate, p. 8.

468 "Exclusive Interview with Alice von Hildebrand," Michael Voris, Church-Militant.com, January 28, 2016, posted on YouTube at https://www.youtube.com/watch?v=CKLBvvlabgw.

469 "Present at the Demolition," an interview with Dr. Alice von Hildebrand, *The Latin Mass Magazine*, summer 2001, posted at http://www.latinmass-magazine.com/articles/articles_2001_su_hildebran.html.

470 Dodd, *School of Darkness*, pp. 83, 93-94.

471 Dodd, *School of Darkness*, p. 130.

472 Dodd, *School of Darkness*, p. 94.

473 This document was an inter-office "Office Memorandum: United States Government," basically an official internal FBI document, written by J. P. Coyne to "Mr. Ladd," who was D. M. Ladd. Both were high-level government officials. Ladd was the FBI's assistant director.

474 This data comes from the Official Catholic Directory and was provided by the Rev. Donald Paul Sullins, M.Div., Ph.D., Research Associate Professor of Sociology at the Catholic University of America in emails April 14-15, 2019. I am very grateful to Dr. Sullins for his assistance.

Still today, after decades of steady, precipitous decline, there are some 37,000 priests in the United States (and about 5,000 current seminarians), down from roughly 60,000 in 1970. According to the US Conference of Catholic Bishops, in 2018 there were 37,302 priests and 4,856 seminarians. See http://www.usccb.org/about/public-affairs/backgrounders/clergy-religious.cfm. On statistics, since 1970, when there were 59,192 total priests, see the data maintained by Georgetown's Center for Applied Research in the Apostolate: http://cara.georgetown.edu/frequently-requested-church-statistics/.

475 Email from Dr. Paul Sullins, April 15, 2019.

476 Dodd, *School of Darkness*, p. 85.

477 Dodd, *School of Darkness*, pp. 78-83.

478 Dodd, *School of Darkness*, pp. 86-90.

479 Reeves, *America's Bishop*, pp. 86-87.

480 Also in the *New York Times* of April 28, 1952 was a shorter accompanying article, titled "Sheen Leaves for Paris: Sheen Says Reds Had Church Spies," reported by United Press, also on page 1 of the newspaper. It noted that Father Alighiero Tondi "had left the [Jesuit] order and has become a Communist. Such actions involve automatic excommunication." The piece noted that Tondi "had been a Jesuit for sixteen years" prior to "his conversion to communism," which he outlined in a lengthy article in the pro-communist

Italian newspaper *Il Paese*.

481 Michael H. Crosby, *Thank God Ahead of Time: The Life and Spirituality of Solanus Casey* (Cincinnati, OH: Franciscan Media, 2009), p. 1.

482 Crosby, *Thank God Ahead of Time: The Life and Spirituality of Solanus Casey*, p. 192.

483 See Kengor, Dupes, pp. 226-27. That book includes each five-digit Communist Party USA membership number of each of the Hollywood Ten, as do other books, such as Allan Ryskind's excellent 2015 work, *Hollywood Traitors: Blacklisted Screenwriters—Agents of Stalin, Allies of Hitler* (Washington, D.C.: Regnery). For a quick reference, see my April 2015 review of Ryskind's book posted online at the website of the Institute for Faith & Freedom, https://www.faithandfreedom.com/hollywoods-blacklist-and-agents-of-stalin-and-hitler/.

484 Letter published in Crosby, *Thank God Ahead of Time: The Life and Spirituality of Solanus Casey*, p. 193.

485 The introduction to the "658/NCC" compilation report (written by M. G. Lowman) was careful to caution: "The reader of these records of leftist affiliations should guard with the utmost care against the assumption that these men and women of the National Council of Churches are Communists, Communist sympathizers, or Communist Party members. Any such assumption should be avoided with respect to the group of 658 as a whole and with respect to any individual member of the group." That is a fair warning. Even then, there is no question that some if not many of the 658 were communists.

486 The audio of this speech is posted online, albeit not reliably sourced. It is, however, indisputably Dodd. As the details of the speech reveal, it was given in New York State, and after her baptism under Sheen and after her 1953 Senate testimony. References are also made to McCarthy, who is spoken of in present tense. (He died in 1957.) The speech would thus have taken place sometime between 1953 and 1957. See https://www.youtube.com/watch?v=37HgRWTsGs0.

487 Elisabeth Braw, *God's Spies: The Stasi's Cold War Espionage Operation Inside the Church* (Grand Rapids, Michigan: Eerdmans, 2019).

488 Elisabeth Braw interviewed on "Kresta in the Afternoon," Ave Maria Radio Network, September 16, 2019.

489 Braw on "Kresta in the Afternoon."

490 Braw on "Kresta in the Afternoon."

491 John Koehler, *Spies in the Vatican: The Soviet Union's Cold War Against the Catholic Church* (New York: Pegasus Books, 2009).

492 Koehler, *Spies in the Vatican*, pp. 153-54.

493 Koehler, *Spies in the Vatican*, pp. 136-51.

494 See my extended analysis throughout Kengor, *A Pope and a President*.

495 See Kengor, *A Pope and a President*, pp. 151-55.

496 Koehler, *Spies in the Vatican*, pp. 9, 15, 169.

497 See our interview with Allen in Paul Kengor and Robert Orlando, *The Divine Plan: John Paul II, Ronald Reagan, and the Dramatic End of the Cold War* (Wilmington, Delaware: ISI Books, 2019), pp. 104-5.

498 Koehler, *Spies in the Vatican*, pp. 87-88. Also see *A Pope and a President*, which deals with the November 13, 1979 meeting and the implications more than any other recent book.

499 George Weigel, for instance, questions whether the edict was an on-the-record order for assassination. Robert Orlando and I discuss this, including the pros and cons, at length in our book *The Divine Plan*.

500 I cannot affirm the accuracy of these reports. Thus, I note that the priest has been accused and alleged and reported to have engaged in such things. See George Weigel, *The End and the Beginning* (New York: Image, 2011), pp. 110-11.

501 See "Vatican Informers Spied on Pope John Paul II," *National Catholic Register*, September 17-23, 2006.

502 My edition is the 1991 edition published by TAN Books.

503 My edition is the version translated from Italian by Ian Martin and published by Key Porter Books in Toronto in the year 2000. The original 1999 was published in Italy by Kaos Editions (*Kaos Edizioni*, located in Milan) in February 1999.

504 The Millenari, *Shroud of Secrecy*, pp. 168-70.

505 The Millenari, *Shroud of Secrecy*, p. 167.

506 The Millenari, *Shroud of Secrecy*, pp. 167-71.

507 The Millenari, *Shroud of Secrecy*, p. 171.

508 Camille M. Cianfarra, *The Vatican and the Kremlin* (New York: E. P. Dutton & Co., 1950), pp. 66-67. See Cianfarra's examples of persecution on pages 49-56, among others.

509 Cianfarra, *The Vatican and the Kremlin*, pp. 68-69.

510 For a summary of the origins of the communists' reprehensible smear "Hitler's Pope," see chapter 7 of my *A Pope and a President*, which, among others, cites the important work of scholar Ron Rychlak as well as the other recent literature on the subject.

511 Cianfarra, *The Vatican and the Kremlin*, pp. 72-73.

512 Cianfarra, *The Vatican and the Kremlin*, pp. 74-80.

513 Cianfarra, *The Vatican and the Kremlin*, pp. 115-16.

514 Cianfarra, *The Vatican and the Kremlin*, p. 28.

515 I interviewed Rusak on April 21, 2017 at Grove City College in Grove City, Pennsylvania.

516 Hannah Brockhaus, "Pope in Romania: Martyred bishops gave their lives for fidelity to the Church," *Catholic News Agency*, June 2, 2019.

517 "Pope warns of divisive ideologies in homage to communist-era martyrs," Reuters, June 2, 2019.

518 Pope Paul VI said this in a June 29, 1972 homily. Also see Paul VI's 1972 encyclical, "Confronting the Devil's Power," posted at https://www.papalencyclicals.net/paul06/p6devil.htm.

519   Dean Dettloff, "The Catholic Case for Communism," *America Magazine*, July 23, 2019. Also on the Jesuits, see Malachi Martin, *The Jesuits: The Society of Jesus and the Betrayal of the Roman Catholic Church* (New York: Simon and Schuster, 1987).

520   "Former Soviet spy: We created Liberation Theology," *Catholic News Agency*, May 1, 2015, posted at https://www.catholicnewsagency.com/news/former-soviet-spy-we-created-liberation-theology-83634.

521   Email correspondence with Stephen Schwartz, June 11, 2018.

522   See Stephen's description, "Why I Chose Islam Instead of Judaism," Jewcy.com, February 19, 2007, posted at http://jewcy.com/post/why_i_chose_islam_instead_judaism.

523   On Herb and Bettina Aptheker, see my discussion in *Dupes*, pp. 306-11.

524   Bettina Aptheker has written openly about her father sexually abusing her. See Bettina Aptheker, "'Did I ever hurt you when you were a child?'" *Los Angeles Times*, October 15, 2006.

525   I have written about the members of the Weathermen and Weather Underground (particularly Mark Rudd, Bill Ayers, and Bernardine Dohrn, among others) at great length in my books *Dupes* and *Takedown*, with the latter focused on the sexual-moral views and practices of this sordid gang of Marxist-progressive revolutionaries. I recommend those treatments for readers not faint of heart.

526   Email correspondence with Stephen Schwartz, June 11, 2018.

527   John Symonds, The Great Beast: *The life and magick of Aleister Crowley* (London: Macdonald and Co., 1971).

528   See the definitive work Asbjorn Dyrendal, "Satan and the Beast: The Influence of Aleister Crowley on Modern Satanism," in Henrik Bogdan and Martin P. Starr, eds., *Aleister Crowley and Western Esotericism* (NY: Oxford University Press, 2012).

529   John Preston, "Aleister Crowley: The Biography by Tobias Churton: review," *The Telegraph*, September 7, 2011.

530   See Marco Pasi, *Aleister Crowley and the Temptation of Politics* (London and New York: Routledge, 2014), pp. 52-53, 73-77.

531   Walter Duranty, "Russians Hungry, but Not Starving," *New York Times*, March 31, 1933, p. 13.

532   See Douglas McCollam, "Should This Pulitzer Be Pulled?" *Columbia Journalism Review*, November/December 2003; Robert Conquest, *The Harvest of Sorrow* (New York: Oxford University Press, 1986), pp. 308-9; S. J. Taylor, *Stalin's Apologist* (New York: Oxford University Press, 1990), p. 205; and Mark Levin, *Unfreedom of the Press* (New York: Threshold Editions, Simon & Schuster), pp. 166-70.

533   Douglas McCollam, "Should This Pulitzer be Pulled?" *Columbia Journalism Review*, November/December 2003.

534   S. J. Taylor, *Stalin's Apologist: Walter Duranty: The* New York Times*'s Man in Moscow* (New York: Oxford University Press, 1990), pp. 35-37.

535   The following account comes from S. J. Taylor, *Stalin's Apologist*, pp. 29-37.

536   Presumably Taylor meant to imply that both men were bisexual. They both had sexual relations with women and, it certainly seems, engaged in some sort of physical if not sexual relations with men and with each other.

537   Taylor, *Stalin's Apologist*, pp. 36-37.

538   Stuart Timmons, *The Trouble with Harry Hay: Founder of the Modern Gay Movement* (White Crane Books, 2012).

539   Will Roscoe, ed., *Radically Gay: Gay Liberation in the Words of Its Founder* (Boston: Beacon Press, 1996).

540   Roscoe, *Radically Gay*, p. 5.

541   Timmons, *The Trouble with Harry Hay*, p. 169.

542   For instance, the Wikipedia entry on Obama's mentor, Frank Marshall Davis, is sugarcoated beyond any semblance of accuracy when it comes to Davis's communist activism. It is plainly outrageous and mendacious in its whitewashing of his CPUSA membership and overall intense communist commitment, neither of which typically are even mentioned there.

543   Wikipedia entry retrieved July 1, 2016.

544   This is widely known. The Wikipedia entry for NAMBLA accurately describes the group as "a pedophilia and pederasty advocacy organization in the United States" that "works to abolish age-of-consent laws criminalizing adult sexual involvement with minors." See https://en.wikipedia.org/wiki/North_American_Man/Boy_Love_Association, retrieved July 20, 2019.

545   Even Wikipedia, which often censors this kind of material regarding leftists it likes, includes all of these facts on Thorstad. They are included in Wikipedia entry for David Thorstad and they are also included in the Wikipedia entry for NAMBLA, which lists Thorstad as the group's founder. Wikipedia entry retrieved (again) on May 8, 2020, https://en.wikipedia.org/wiki/North_American_Man/Boy_Love_Association.

546   See David Thorstad, "Why I'm Skipping Stonewall 50," *CounterPunch*, June 21, 2019, posted at https://www.counterpunch.org/2019/06/21/why-im-skipping-stonewall-50/; and Matt C. Abbott, "Admitted pederast accuses me of spreading a lie," Renew America, August 12, 2010, posted at http://www.renewamerica.com/columns/abbott/100812.

547   See Roscoe, *Radically Gay*, pp. 302-10.

548   Roscoe, *Radically Gay*, pp. 302-10 and 363.

549   Wikipedia entry retrieved May 8, 2020, https://en.wikipedia.org/wiki/Harry_Hay.

550   Website of the Radical Faeries, retrieved June 29, 2016. http://www.radfae.org/.

551   Leslie Feinberg, "Hay studies ancient history, finds pride," *Workers World*, July 14, 2005. http://www.workers.org/2005/us/lavender-red-42/.

552   See Peter Hasson, "New York City Lets You Choose From 31 Different Gender Identities," *The Daily Caller*, May 24, 2016. The list of gender options is posted online by the New York City Commission on Human Rights:

http://www.nyc.gov/html/cchr/downloads/pdf/publications/GenderID_Card2015.pdf.

553 This was widely reported. See, among others, "BBC films teaches children of '100 genders, or more,'" *The London Times*, September 8, 2019, posted at https://www.thetimes.co.uk/article/bbc-films-teach-children-of-100-genders-or-more-7xfhbg97p.

554 Timmons, *The Trouble with Harry Hay*, pp. 282-83.

555 Timmons, *The Trouble with Harry Hay*, p. 304.

556 See my section, "Watermelons and climate communists," in Kengor, *The Politically Incorrect Guide to Communism*, pp. 262-63.

557 Hay wrote this on July 5, 1980. See Roscoe, *Radically Gay*, pp. 254-64.

558 I do not know how long Harry did this, but he did so at least in the year 1935, perhaps give or take a few years before or after. See Timmons, *The Trouble with Harry Hay*, pp. 83-84; and Will Roscoe, *Radically Gay*, p. 356.

559 Timmons, *The Trouble with Harry Hay*, pp. 83-84.

560 Timmons, *The Trouble with Harry Hay*, p. 84.

561 Timmons, *The Trouble with Harry Hay*, p. 84.

562 Stuart Timmons does not give the first name of Father Follen, and I was unable to definitively identify it.

563 Timmons, *The Trouble with Harry Hay*, p. 70.

564 Timmons, *The Trouble with Harry Hay*, p. 75.

565 Roscoe, *Radically Gay*, p. 356; and Timmons, *The Trouble with Harry Hay*, p. 72.

566 Timmons, *The Trouble with Harry Hay*, p. 72-76.

567 Roscoe, *Radically Gay*, p. 357; and Timmons, *The Trouble with Harry Hay*, p. 141.

568 Timmons, *The Trouble with Harry Hay*, p. 323.

569 Timmons, *The Trouble with Harry Hay*, p. 76.

570 See Sam Tanenhaus, *Whittaker Chambers: A Biography* (NY: Random House, 1997), pp. 56-67.

571 Timmons, *The Trouble with Harry Hay*, p. 108.

572 Recall the earlier citation of the March 2, 1948 FBI document reporting that "almost 50% of the Communist Party members in the United States are located in the New York area."

573 Roscoe, *Radically Gay*, p. 39; and Timmons, *The Trouble with Harry Hay*, pp. 134-35.

574 Timmons, *The Trouble with Harry Hay*, pp. 115-16.

575 Timmons, *The Trouble with Harry Hay*, pp. 178, 206.

576 Timmons, *The Trouble with Harry Hay*, pp. 205-7.

577 Timmons, *The Trouble with Harry Hay*, pp. 121 and 178.

578 John Barron, *KGB: The Secret Work of Soviet Secret Agents* (NY: E. P. Dutton & Co., 1974), pp. 206-7.

579 Different sources and scholars place different dates on this, some saying 1950, and others saying 1951. Roscoe says that Hay resigned from CPUSA

in 1951 after having joined the Party in 1934, and that Mattachine was officially formed in 1951. Timmons, to the contrary, says that Mattachine was founded in 1950. See Roscoe, *Radically Gay*, pp. 37-8, 358-59; and Timmons, *The Trouble with Harry Hay*, p. xx.

580 Harry and gang referred to themselves as "us progressives." These men initially came together through the Progressive Party presidential bid of Henry Wallace in 1948, which was a rallying point for American communists. Timmons, *The Trouble with Harry Hay*, pp. 150-53.

581 Timmons, *The Trouble with Harry Hay*, p. 108.

582 Stephen Schwartz told me, "Harry Hay was a Stalinist to the end. I know this from an unimpeachable source." Email from Schwartz, June 14, 2018.

583 Zoltan Tarr, *The Frankfurt School: The Critical Theories of Max Horkheimer and Theodor W. Adorno* (New Brunswick, NJ: Transaction Publishers, 2011), p. 2.

584 The two best scholarly books on the Frankfurt School and its history are Rolf Wiggershaus's *The Frankfurt School*, published in 1994 by MIT Press (nearly 800 pages in length, with translations of German writings that no other scholar in English has published), and Martin Jay's *The Dialectical Imagination*, published in 1996 by the University of California Press.

585 Wilhelm Reich, *The Passion of Youth: An Autobiography, 1897-1922* (New York: Farrar, Straus, and Giroux, 1988), pp. 4-5, 9. The book was published posthumously and was edited by Mary Boyd Higgins and Chester M. Raphael.

586 Reich, *The Passion of Youth: An Autobiography, 1897-1922*, p. 6.

587 Reich, *The Passion of Youth: An Autobiography, 1897-1922*, p. 13.

588 Reich, *The Passion of Youth: An Autobiography, 1897-1922*, p. 25.

589 Reich, *The Passion of Youth: An Autobiography, 1897-1922*, pp. 21-22.

590 See entry at http://www.marxists.org/glossary/people/r/e.htm#reich-wilhelm.

591 Ariel Levy, "Novelty Acts," *The New Yorker*, September 19, 2011. Another source who merits this title is arguably Alfred Kinsey, whose sexual anarchism was possibly to the left of even Reich.

592 I will here quote from the 1974 edition, translated by Therese Pol and published by Farrar, Straus, and Giroux. Full citation: Wilhelm Reich, *The Sexual Revolution: Toward a Self-Regulating Character Structure* (New York: Farrar, Straus, and Giroux, 1974). This book starts with prefaces from the second edition (1936), third edition (1945), and fourth edition (1949).

593 See informational post at the Wilhelm Reich Trust website, http://www.wilhelmreichtrust.org/sexual_revolution.html, retrieved July 19, 2019.

594 Reich noted in the fourth edition that the book was "virtually unchanged" from the first edition.

595 Reich, *The Sexual Revolution*, pp. xi-xiv.

596 Reich, *The Sexual Revolution*, pp. xvi-xvii.

597 These statements come from the preface to the 1936 edition of the book in

German, written by Reich in November 1935. See Reich, *The Sexual Revolution*, pp. xxvi-xxviii and xxx.

598   He wrote this in the preface to the third edition, in 1945: Reich, *The Sexual Revolution*, pp. xv-xvi.

599   The best and most extended analysis of this is: W. Edward Mann and Edward Hoffman, *The Man Who Dreamed of Tomorrow: A Conceptual Biography of Wilhelm Reich* (Los Angeles: J. P. Tarcher, 1980), which includes a foreword by Reich's daughter, Eva Reich. See especially pages 182-97.

600   See the discussion by Myron Sharaf, *Fury on Earth: A Biography of Wilhelm Reich* (New York: St. Martin's Press, 1983), pp. 396-97.

601   Mann and Hoffman, *The Man Who Dreamed of Tomorrow: A Conceptual Biography of Wilhelm Reich*, pp. 191-92, 194.

602   See Mann and Hoffman, *The Man Who Dreamed of Tomorrow: A Conceptual Biography of Wilhelm Reich*, pp. 188.

603   See chapter 12, "*The Future of an Illusion*," in Ben Wiker, *10 Books That Screwed Up the World* (Washington, D.C.: Regnery, 2008), pp. 165-76.

604   Mann and Hoffman, *The Man Who Dreamed of Tomorrow: A Conceptual Biography of Wilhelm Reich*, pp. 182-85.

605   Mann and Hoffman, *The Man Who Dreamed of Tomorrow: A Conceptual Biography of Wilhelm Reich*, pp. 186-87.

606   Berlin in this period was a haunt of every sort of demon. The licentiousness, the immorality, the culture was wicked. It is no surprise the creatures that emerged from this milieu in the first of half of the twentieth century. Ralph de Toledano would describe it as a kind of "European Babylon."

607   On the financing of the Frankfurt School move, see Toledano, *Cry Havoc!*, pp. 78-83.

608   See posting at: https://www.marxists.org/reference/archive/benjamin/1940/history.htm.

609   Kam Shapiro, "Walter Benjamin, the Kabbalah, and Secularism," *AJS Perspectives: The Magazine for the Association for Jewish Studies*, Spring 2011.

610   Eric Jacobson, "Metaphysics of the Profane: The Political Theology of Walter Benjamin and Gershom Scholem" (New York: Columbia University Press, 2003), p. 245, n67.

611   Donna Roberts and Daniel Garza Usabiaga, *The Use of Lucifer: A Comparative Analysis of the Figures of Lucifer and Satan in the Writings of Roger Caillois and Walter Benjamin*. http://www.academia.edu/6014358/The_Use_Value_of_Lucifer_A_Comparative_Analysis_of_the_Figures_of_Lucifer_and_Satan_in_the_Writings_of_Roger_Caillois_and_Walter_Benjamin_in_the_1930s Accessed: 11/14/2016.

612   Roberts and Usabiaga, *The Use of Lucifer*.

613   Roberts and Usabiaga, *The Use of Lucifer*, p. 1.

614   Roberts and Usabiaga, *The Use of Lucifer*, p. 1.

615   Roberts and Usabiaga, *The Use of Lucifer*, p. 2.

616   Ray Man, "Monument a D.A.F. de Sade (1933)," Art Stack: The World's

favorite art. https://theartstack.com/artist/man-ray/monument-a-d-f-de-sa accessed: 11/12/2016

617 Ernst, Max, "The Blessed Virgin Chastises the Infant Jesus Before Three Witnesses (1926)" artnet http://www.artnet.com/magazineus/features/kachur/kachur7-21-05_detail.asp?picnum=2 accessed: 11/12/2016

618 Roberts and Usabiaga, *The Use of Lucifer*, p. 5.

619 Benjamin's interest in aesthetics and art criticism permeated throughout his works. This more esoteric, non-analytical approach to philosophy is characteristic of Benjamin's work.

620 See, among others, David Biale, *Gershom Scholem: Kabbalah and Counter-History* (Cambridge: Harvard University Press, 1982), pp. 136-38 and n94; and Roberts and Usabiaga, *The Use of Lucifer*, p. 6.

621 Roberts and Usabiaga, *The Use of Lucifer*, pp. 5-7.

622 Roberts and Usabiaga, *The Use of Lucifer*, pp. 10-11.

623 Roberts and Usabiaga, *The Use of Lucifer*, pp. 6-7.

624 See Otto Karl Werckmeister, *Icons of the Left: Benjamin and Einstein, Picasso and Kafka After the Fall* (Chicago: University of Chicago Press, 1997), p. 9.

625 Church of Satan's official website, F.A.Q. Fundamental Beliefs, http://www.churchofsatan.com/faq-fundamental-beliefs.php, accessed: 11/12/2016

626 As cited earlier, see posting at: https://www.marxists.org/archive/lenin/works/1920/oct/02.htm.

627 Ibid.

628 Max Horkheimer, *Critical Theory* (New York: Seabury Press, 1982), p. 244.

629 For an extended discussion of the term "cultural Marxism" and how the very term itself is misunderstood today, see my piece: Paul Kengor, "Cultural Marxism and Its Conspirators," *The American Spectator*, April 3, 2019, posted at https://spectator.org/cultural-marxism-and-its-conspirators/.

630 This definition appeared throughout 2019 as I checked several times during the writing of this book.

631 Jason A. Josephson-Storm, *The Myth of Disenchantment: Magic, Modernity, and the Birth of Human Sciences* (Chicago: University of Chicago Press, 2017), pp. 209-39.

632 Georg Stauth and Bryan S. Turner, "Ludwig Klages (1872-1956) and the Origins of Critical Theory," *Theory, Culture & Society*, Vol. 9, 1992, pp. 45-63.

633 Nitzan Lebovic, "The Beauty and Terror of *Lebensphilosophie*: Ludwig Klages, Walter Benjamin, and Alfred Baeumler," *South Central Review*, Vol. 23, No. 1, Spring 2006, pp. 23-39.

634 See *Gershom Scholem, Walter Benjamin: The Story of a Friendship* (Philadelphia: The Jewish Publication Society of America, 1981), pp. 19-20.

635 And yet, as an indicator of the messiness of these ideas, debates, and the difficulty of drawing conclusions, making observations, and avoiding sweeping and unfair generalizations, see, for instance, Theodor Adorno's critique of occultism as "the metaphysic of the dopes," cited in this larger discussion of

Adorno: Cary J. Nederman and James Wray Goulding, "Popular Occultism and Critical Theory: Exploring Some Themes in Adorno's Critique of Astrology and the Occult," *Sociological Analysis*, Vol. 42, No. 4, Winter 1981, pp. 325-32. Moreover, entire books with titles like *Freud, Jung, and Occultism* have been done (by author Nandor Fodor, published in 1971). These subjects are a black hole that can suck the researcher into a vortex with no end in sight, and into an intellectual tailspin not worthy of any individual's time and energies. It is intellectual trash—dead ideas that not surprisingly long ago earned their death.

636   On Benjamin specifically, see Josephson-Storm, *The Myth of Disenchantment*, pp. 226-36.

637   Josephson-Storm, *The Myth of Disenchantment*, p. 215.

638   Josephson-Storm, *The Myth of Disenchantment*, p. 239.

639   See Paul Kengor, "The Hillary-Alinsky-Lucifer Connection," *The American Spectator*, July 26, 2016.

640   David Emery, "Did Saul Alinsky Dedicate 'Rules for Radicals' to Lucifer?" *Snopes.com*, July 20, 2016, posted at https://www.snopes.com/fact-check/saul-alinsky-dedicated-rules-for-radicals-to-lucifer/.

641   Diane Vera, "Saul D. Alinsky: A role model for left-wing Satanists," *Theistic Satanism*, 2005, posted at http://www.theisticsatanism.com/politics/Alinsky.html.

642   Angie Drobnic Holan, "What Ben Carson said about Hillary Clinton, Saul Alinsky and Lucifer," *PolitiFact*, July 20, 2016, posted at https://www.politifact.com/truth-o-meter/article/2016/jul/20/what-ben-carson-said-about-hillary-clinton-saul-al/.

643   Stanley Kurtz, "Why Hillary's Alinsky Letters Matter," *National Review Online*, September 22, 2014.

644   Alinsky said this in his 1972 interview with *Playboy* magazine. It is known as "The Interview with Saul Alinsky, Part Ten," and available on many admiring progressive websites.

645   See "The Liberation of Kate Millett," *Time* magazine, August 31, 1970; and Lily Rothman, "Obituary: Kate Millett," *Time* magazine, September 14, 2017.

646   Barbara Hardy, "De Beauvoir, Lessing—Now Kate Millett," *The New York Times*, September 6, 1970.

647   Mallory Millett, "Marxist Feminism's Ruined Lives," FrontPageMagazine.com, September 1, 2014. https://www.frontpagemag.com/fpm/240037/marxist-feminisms-ruined-lives-mallory-millett.

648   Mallory Millett, "Marxist Feminism's Ruined Lives."

649   See http://www.glbtq.com/literature/millett_k.html, retrieved December 12, 2014.

650   Email correspondence with Mallory Millett, November 27, 2017.

651   Email correspondence with Mallory Millett, November 27, 2017.

652   Phone conversation with Mallory Millett, February 2, 2019.

653 Mallory Millett, "Marxist Feminism's Ruined Lives," FrontPageMagazine. com, September 1, 2014. https://www.frontpagemag.com/fpm/240037/ marxist-feminisms-ruined-lives-mallory-millett

654 Mark Tapson, "My Sister Kate: The Destructive Feminist Legacy of Kate Millett," FrontPageMagazine.com, February 7, 2018. https://www.front-pagemag.com/fpm/269251/my-sister-kate-destructive-feminist-legacy -kate-mark-tapson

655 "Millett: No Gun Ever Killed Anyone," TruthRevolt.org, June 2, 2014, posted at https://www.truthrevolt.org/commentary/millett-no-gun-ever-killed-anyone.

656 Carrie Gress, *The Anti-Mary Exposed: Rescuing the Culture from Toxic Femininity* (Charlotte, NC: TAN Books, 2019), p. 75.

657 Gress, *The Anti-Mary Exposed*, pp. 73-74, 76.

658 Email correspondence with Mallory Millett, November 22, 2017.

659 Penelope Green, "Feminism's A-List Attends Kate Millett's Memorial in New York," *The New York Times*, November 10, 2017.

660 "Obama Rallies Columbia, Missouri," *RealClearPolitics*, October 30, 2008, posted at https://www.realclearpolitics.com/articles/2008/10/obama_ral lies_columbia_missour.html.

661 See earlier citation.

662 See Paul Kengor, "Fundamental Transformation: The 2010s, the LGBTQ Decade," *National Catholic Register*, January 2020.

663 "FACT SHEET: Obama Administration's Record and the LGBT Community," White House Press Office, June 9, 2016, posted at https://obamawhite house.archives.gov/the-press-office/2016/06/09/fact-sheet-obama-adminis trations-record-and-lgbt-community; and "FACT SHEET: Promoting and Protecting the Human Rights of LGBT Persons," White House Press Office, June 29, 2016, posted at https://obamawhitehouse.archives.gov/the-press-office/2016/06/29/fact-sheet-promoting-and-protecting-human-rights-lgbt-persons.

664 See earlier citations regarding the New York City Council and the BBC. For Facebook and the 51, 53, 56, 58, 71 "gender options," see pieces at the *Daily Beast*, *Huffington Post*, *Slate*, ABC News, and the *London Telegraph*, posted at https://www.thedailybeast.com/what-each-of-facebooks-51-new-gender-options-means; https://www.huffpost.com/entry/facebooks-gender -identities_b_4811147; https://slate.com/technology/2014/02/facebook-custom-gender-options-here-are-all-56-custom-options.html; https://abc news.go.com/blogs/headlines/2014/02/heres-a-list-of-58-gender-options -for-facebook-users/; and https://www.telegraph.co.uk/technology/face book/10930654/Facebooks-71-gender-options-come-to-UK-users.html.

665 I have addressed many times in books and articles and commentaries the question and degree of Barack Obama's sympathy for socialism, communism, Marxism. I deal with it at length in my book on Obama's mentor, *The Communist: The Untold Story of Frank Marshall Davis, Barack Obama's Mentor*

(NY: Mercury Ink / Simon & Schuster, 2012), where I quote at length communists who knew Obama in college, including the president of Occidental College's Marxist organization at the time. I believe there is no question that Obama was a communist in college; in fact, prior to arriving at college. By the time of his presidency, I believe he was more of a general leftist, albeit a radical leftist in certain respects, particularly on cultural issues. He is symptomatic of where many Marxists have drifted, namely, to culture. The source I interviewed for *The Communist*, Dr. John Drew, still discerned in President Obama much of the "Marxist mental architecture" and mindset he had seen from Obama in college, including on some class and economic issues. Drew, for the record, was a cultural Marxist, a big fan of Herbert Marcuse and other Frankfurt School writers. See Kengor, *The Communist*, pp. 249-62.

666   As cited earlier, see Marx's September 1843 letter to Arnold Ruge, posted at https://www.marxists.org/archive/marx/works/1843/letters/43_09-alt.htm and https://www.marxists.org/archive/marx/works/1843/letters/43_09. htm.

667   "Seems" is the operative word. The word "abolition" or "abolish" does not appear on every page, but at times it certainly seems so, given how frequent and striking is such language from Marx.

668   Payne, *Marx: A Biography*, p. 173.

669   The Third All-Russia Congress of the Russian Young Communist League took place in Moscow from October 2-10, 1920 and was attended by an estimated six hundred delegates. Lenin addressed the first session the evening of October 2. The transcript was published in *Pravda* on October 5, 6, and 7, 1920. It also appears in Lenin's *Collected Works*, volume 31. See posting at https://www.marxists.org/archive/lenin/works/1920/oct/02.htm.

670   Michelle Kern, "The capitalist culture of male supremacy and misogyny," *People's World*, March 25, 2018, posted at http://www.cpusa.org/article/ the-capitalist-culture-of-male-supremacy-and-misogyny/.

671   The definitive English translation of Gramsci's work is Joseph Buttigieg's (father of Pete Buttigieg) translation of Gramsci's vast volume, *Prison Notebooks* (*Quaderni del carcere*), published by Columbia University Press in 1992.

672   Samuel Gregg, "The Most Dangerous Socialist in History," *The Stream*, July 25, 2016.

673   There is debate over who first used the phrase "long march through the institutions" to describe Gramsci's goal and strategy. Most current online sources credit a West German (naturally) Marxist writer and student activist of the 1960s named Rudi Dutschke.

674   Of Gramsci's thirty-three notebooks, Notebooks sixteen and twenty-six deal with "Cultural Topics" I and II, respectively. Even then, cultural is a consistent theme throughout the *Prison Notebooks*.

675   Michael Walsh, *The Devil's Pleasure Palace: The Cult of Critical Theory and the Subversion of the West* (NY: Encounter Books, 2017).

676   On the Proletariat as the victim and redeemer group in Marxist theory, see

Professor Martin Malia's introduction to the Penguin-Signet Classics edition (1998 and 2011 editions) of the *Communist Manifesto*, pp. 14-15.

677   See Paul Kengor, "Women's Marchers, Unite!" *The American Spectator*, January 24, 2017.

678   See "About People's World," posted at https://www.peoplesworld.org/about-the-peoples-world/.

679   See discussion by Joseph Pearce, "How the Modernists Made 'Ecumenical' a Dirty Word," *Crisis Magazine*, November 26, 2019.

680   See Wilfred McClay, ed., *Russell Kirk's Concise Guide to Conservatism* (Washington, D.C.: Regnery, 2019), pp. 2-6.

681   We have all seen the numerous polls of Millennials saying positive things about communism and even saying that they prefer communism and socialism over capitalism. In retrospect, a turning point came in 2011, when a major study by Pew Research Center found that 49 percent of Americans aged eighteen to twenty-nine have a positive view of socialism, exceeding the 43 percent with a positive view of capitalism. Three years later, in 2014, a survey by *Reason Magazine* and the Rupe Foundation did a deeper dive. It found that 53 percent of those aged eighteen to twenty-nine view socialism favorably. Not long after that survey, Gallup turned up a gem, learning that 69 percent of Millennials said they would be willing to vote for a socialist as president of the United States of America—a country founded on the antithesis of socialist principles. They did just that in 2016, contributing mightily to Bernie Sanders's twelve million votes in the Democratic Primary. That is the data in the country that won the Cold War and defeated communism. As I write, the latest survey by Victims of Communism Memorial Foundation (conducted by YouGov), released in November 2019, shows that 36% of Millennials say they approve of communism, and 22% believe "society would be better if all private property was abolished."

682   "Homily of his Eminence Cardinal Joseph Ratzinger, Dean of the College of Cardinal," Vatican Basilica, April 18, 2005, posted at http://www.vatican.va/gpII/documents/homily-pro-eligendo-pontifice_20050418_en.html.

683   Fulton Sheen, "How To Think," Life Is Worth Living, originally broadcast in 1955, https://www.youtube.com/watch?v=FmMBLTz6Pp8.

684   Fulton Sheen, "How To Think," Life Is Worth Living, originally broadcast in 1955, https://www.youtube.com/watch?v=FmMBLTz6Pp8. See minute markers 19:29-23:12.

685   Fulton J. Sheen, *War and Guilt* (Huntington, Indiana: Our Sunday Visitor, 1941), pp. 138-39.

686   Reeves, *America's Bishop*, p. 54.

INDEX

JAMES MEANS

and the

PROBLEM OF MANFLIGHT

During the Period
1882-1920

by his son
JAMES HOWARD MEANS, M.D

SMITHSONIAN INSTITUTION
WASHINGTON, D. C.
1964

Smithsonian Publication 4526

CONTENTS

INTRODUCTION

UNDER the date of May 30, 1899, there was received in the office of the Secretary of the Smithsonian Institution, my distinguished predecessor Dr. Samuel Pierpont Langley, a letter from a 32-year-old aeronautical enthusiast, which read:

The Smithsonian Institution

I have been interested in the problem of mechanical and human flight ever since as a boy I constructed a number of bats of various sizes after the style of Cayley's and Pénaud's machines. My observations since have only convinced me more firmly that human flight is possible and practicable. It is only a question of knowledge and skill just as in all acrobatic feats. Birds are the most perfectly trained gymnasts in the world and are specially well fitted for their work, and it may be that man will never equal them, but no one who has watched a bird chasing an insect or another bird can doubt that feats are performed which require three or four times the effort required in ordinary flight. I believe that simple flight at least is possible to man and that the experiments and investigations of a large number of independent workers will result in the accumulation of information and knowledge and skill which will finally lead to accomplished flight.

The works on the subject to which I have had access are Marey's and Jamieson's books published by Appleton's and various magazine and cyclopaedic articles. I am about to begin a systematic study of the subject in preparation for practical work to which I expect to devote what time I can spare from my regular business. I wish to obtain such papers as the Smithsonian Institution has published on this subject, and if possible a list of other works in print in the English language. I am an enthusiast, but not a crank in the sense that I have some pet theories as to the proper construction of a flying machine. I wish to avail myself of all that is already known and then if possible add my mite to help on the future worker who will attain final success. I do not know the terms on which you send out your publications but if you will inform me of the cost I will remit the price.

Yours truly, WILBUR WRIGHT

The Smithsonian Institution, then as now and for all the past 117 years, has devoted its facilities to "the increase and diffusion of knowledge among men" in accordance with the terms of the

v

bequest of its founder, James Smithson of England. Long before this now-famous letter from Wilbur Wright came to the Smithsonian, the Institution had included aeronautics among its many fields of study and publication and had reprinted articles by a number of the pioneers of flight.

With the reply to Mr. Wright's letter, a selection of these articles was sent gratis to him. They were: "Empire of the Air," by Louis-Pierre Mouillard of France; "The Problem of Flying" and "Practical Experiments in Soaring," by Otto Lilienthal of Germany; "Story of Experiments in Mechanical Flight," by Samuel P. Langley; and "On Soaring Flight," by E. C. Huffaker of Mississippi. The list of books for recommended study include "Progress in Flying Machines," by Octave Chanute (New York, 1894); "Experiments in Aerodynamics," by Samuel P. Langley (Washington, 1891); and "The Aeronautical Annual" for 1895, 1896, and 1897, edited by James Means of Boston.

These "Means Annuals," as they were called, contained writings of outstanding authorities who were interested in the study of the problems of human flight. James Means, the editor of "The Aeronautical Annual," was himself a serious experimenter with aeronautical models, kites, gliders, and various apparatus for studying the mysteries of the air. He had learned much from reading of the efforts by others, and so he wished to advance the art and science of aeronautics by making readily available to other students and experimenters the epitome of what had gone before. These "Annuals" provided a valuable service at a critical time toward the close of the 19th century which had witnessed thousands of efforts to solve these problems. Experimenters, then and now, often learn as much from previous failures as from successes. Thus, the "Annuals" were especially useful in showing many examples of aeronautical efforts.

On June 14, 1899, Wilbur Wright sent a letter of appreciation for this informational service to the Secretary of the Smithsonian Institution, and in later years his brother Orville recalled their studies of the history of human flight with the statement:

> On reading the different works on the subject we were much impressed with the great number of people who had given thought to it, among these some of the greatest minds the world has produced. But we found that the experiments of one after another had failed. Among these who had worked on the problem I may mention Leonardo da Vinci, one of the greatest artists and engineers of all time; Sir George Cayley, who was among the first of the inventors of the internal combustion engine; Sir Hiram Maxim, inventor of

the Maxim rapid fire gun; Parsons, the inventor of the turbine steam engine; Alexander Graham Bell, inventor of the telephone; Horatio Phillips, a well-known English engineer; Otto Lilienthal, the inventor of instruments used in navigation and a well-known engineer; Thomas A. Edison; and Dr. S. P. Langley, Secretary and head of the Smithsonian Institution. Besides these there were a great number of other men of ability who had worked on the problem.

Certainly the great Wright brothers learned much from these efforts of their predecessors by reading "The Aeronautical Annuals." Similarly, hundreds of other pioneers in aviation have benefited through the foresight and discernment of James Means. Today, copies of the "Annuals" are among the great classics of aeronautical literature. They are, of course, long out of print and are treasured by the fortunate few who own them.

Every close reader of these "Annuals" wonders why they were not continued through 1898, 1899, and into the next century, which on December 17, 1903, through the success of Wilbur and Orville Wright, brought to magnificent realization the first flight by man in a heavier-than-air craft under power and control. Students and historians and engineers, after reaching the last page of the 1897 Annual, must begin a search in many scattered publications to find a continuation of the record of research in aeronautics.

The public has known little of the story of James Means who provided this service. Why did he come to gather together these wonderful "Annuals"? Did he produce other publications? What were his own contributions to aeronautics? Now, thanks to the work of his distinguished son, Dr. James H. Means, we have this long-needed biography. The author was a student at both the Massachusetts Institute of Technology and Harvard University. He received both his bachelor and doctor of medicine degrees from Harvard. He has had a distinguished career as an investigator. From 1924 to 1951 he was Jackson Professor of Clinical Medicine at the Harvard Medical School and Chief of the Medical Services of the Massachusetts General Hospital. He is internationally known for his research on the physiology and pathology of the thyroid gland.

In the present book, therefore, the distinguished son of a distinguished father has performed a great service for aviation. Throughout the world scientists and engineers and lay students of aviation and its history will find interest and inspiration in its pages. They will form a distinct addition to the record of a man whose work at the turn of the century did much to advance aviation and to whom all who are interested in the history of flight will be forever indebted. All who enjoy the benefit of reading this book will, I am sure, join with me in thanking Dr. James Howard Means, the son of James Means, for giving us this delightful and significant publication.

LEONARD CARMICHAEL
Secretary of the Smithsonian Institution
January 1963

FOREWORD

WHEN James Means discontinued publishing his Aeronautical Annual in 1897, the conquest of the air was already in sight. Mouillard (1881) in France and Lilienthal (1886) in Germany had demonstrated the feasibility of gliding or soaring flight, and Langley in this country had shown by flights of self-propelled models that an inherently stable airplane was possible.

However, two advances in the art were necessary but both came quickly; first, the light gasoline engine that evolved from early automobile experiments and, second, lateral control by warping the wings that appeared on the Wright brothers' glider of 1900. In 1903 the Wrights made the first powered, sustained, and controlled airplane flight in history.

Means, through his friend Octave Chanute, followed these developments with interest and attended the Wrights' 1908 demonstration for the War Department at Fort Myer, Va. He also attended the first international flying meet in France in 1909, where the stars of the new generation of flyers performed: Bleriot, Farman, Breguet, Curtiss, and others. Not without interest to the gentlemen of Means's circle was the 1910 Harvard flying meeting at Squantum Meadows, where Claude Grahame-White of England, in a French Bleriot monoplane, won $10,000 by flying out to Boston Light and back.

Aviation in the years before the first World War showed enormous vitality, and Means was naturally anxious to follow developments. He wished to participate somehow and undertook to invent a visual scheme for signaling, a catapult for getting airplanes off the ground quickly, a device for converting an airplane into a parachute when in trouble, an inclinometer to show the aviator his angle of pitch, and a simplified control system using a single lever to control pitch, yaw, and roll. In this latter invention, which was many years ahead of its need, Means thought of the instinctive control of a bicycle and proposed to standardize airplane controls.

One can conclude that Means's real contribution to the art of aviation came from his publication of the Aeronautical Annual during the years when experimenters with kites, gliders, and models were active. It is to be regretted that he did not continue this publication, because there was a real need to diffuse the knowledge acquired by the early flyers. His thinking of what might be helpful led to several inventions that were not really practical for the then state of the art.

I came to M. I. T. in 1909 as a graduate student in naval architecture with an interest in the possibilities of aeronautics for the Navy. My professor, Dr. E. B. Wilson, took me to supper at Mr. Means's house in Boston to hear the talk about what the flyers were doing here and abroad. It was a fascinating evening, and I was much impressed by the wide interest and helpful attitude of a cultivated Boston gentleman. It was clear that James Means had no intention of engaging in the highly competitive airplane business, but it was equally clear that he was fascinated by what was going on and anxious to know about advances in the art, and that he wished to be helpful. He had had a hand in spreading knowledge of the new art of flying and probably felt somewhat left behind by its rapid development under international competition, presumably in anticipation of the war to break out in Europe in 1914.

JEROME C. HUNSAKER

Cambridge, Massachusetts
February 12, 1962

PREFACE

FOR MANY years I have wanted to write this memoir of my father. Several abortive starts have been made, the first shortly after his death in 1920, but owing to the demands of my own professional activities they all miscarried. At last, however, in my retirement I have happily been able to accomplish this purpose. It will be understood that my competence lies not in aeronautics—I am a physician —but there is no one left now who remembers my father's life in as much detail or intimacy as I do; that is why I have undertaken to write this story.

Many persons have taken an interest in this project and have given me both encouragement and editorial help. I am particularly indebted to Professors Jerome C. Hunsaker and Ross A. McFarland, who, by their sustained interest, really got me to the point of writing. And I have to thank Hunsaker also for his fine Foreword. Professor Neal B. DeNood, who for years has taken an interest in my writings, also has given me cheer in the present undertaking. My thanks are due to him. I wish to thank also Mrs. Elizabeth Kelleher for skillfully translating my rather illegible chirography into good typescript.

I am very grateful to Mr. Charles H. Gibbs-Smith of England. Through reading his excellent book *The Aeroplane, an Historical Survey* I have broadened my understanding and appreciation of man's accomplishments in flight. Mr. Gibbs-Smith has kindly given me permission to quote some passages from his book where they are pertinent to my father's writings.

I wish especially to express my deep gratitude to Mr. Paul E. Garber, Head Curator and Historian of the National Air Museum, Smithsonian Institution, who has with great devotion and meticulous care done an expert editorial job on the manuscript which I could hardly have obtained anywhere else, and has skilfully assembled the illustrations and prepared the index. He has also helped me in innumerable other ways. Mr. Crocker Wight, former Navy transport pilot, also has read the manuscript carefully and in an editorial spirit. I am grateful to him, too. Thanks are due to Mr. David C. Crockett for his special assistance. Generous help toward the expense of publication has been received from Messrs. L. W. Cabot, Ward M. Canaday, Edward Mallinckrodt, Jr., and from my cousin Mrs. Ellen F. Loomis.

J. H. M., 1963

Chapter I

THE MAN

IN THE YEAR 1879 a young man sat on the stern of an ancient steamship and watched the flight of gulls. He was a business-man, on a business trip, but the slow progress of his vessel over summer seas, from Panama to San Francisco, caused delightful relaxation and left him content to devote each day to the quiet contemplation of nature. Especially the gulls, which followed the ship endlessly, fired his imagination. Of them he wrote, "As I watched these birds day after day, I became fascinated with the grace and beauty of the creatures themselves, and with their mar-vellous evolutions. Our ship, with her ponderous engines, seemed to tremble with the toil of her own progress, while those creatures of the air, suspended upon their gracefully curved wings, kept pace with her, seemingly without effort." (*Manflight,* 1894, p. 4.)

To trace the train of thought lighted in my father's brilliant mind by this experience is the task I have set myself, but first I must tell something of the man himself and of his intellectual versatility. To be sure, he was a businessman by vocation, but it will presently appear that he also had the mind of a scientist and philosopher and the soul of a poet. It was these traits which deter-mined the course of his life.

James Means was born (1853) and brought up in the Congrega-tional parsonage of the then rural district of Dorchester, Massa-chusetts. As a boy he was not allowed to do upon the Sabbath any of the things that are likely to give pleasure to the normal civilized human being of today. I mention this because it has some bearing on his attitude toward life. In fact, it made an agnostic of him intellectually, though emotionally he was so deeply religious that later he wrote an essay which sought to prove, in pure logical style, the existence of God. Apparently this was purely for the good of his own soul, for the manuscript never saw the light of day until I found it among his papers after his death.

Of what my father told me of his early life I have some vivid memories. With the house in which he lived I was thoroughly

1

familiar. It was a fine early Victorian affair with lawn, trees, and gardens all about it and situated in the midst of a pleasant countryside. Through the years the growing city has engulfed all these, but the white Meeting House of which my grandfather was pastor still stands proud as ever. In spite of its strict religious atmosphere my father's boyhood as he used to tell me of it seemed for the most part normal enough. Various tales he took pleasure in recounting. One was that of my grandfather's Irish gardener of whom my father was very fond. On being asked why he did not volunteer to go to the Civil War he made the sage reply, "Maisther Jaimie, life is a swate swate thing." This same Hibernian also suffered for a time because his scalp seemed to him to be too tight for his head. However, after placing a ladder in the elm tree and sawing off a limb betwixt the ladder and the trunk, he sustained a trauma which had the remarkable effect of completely curing the affliction.

My grandfather's predecessor in the Second Congregational Pulpit was the Reverend John Codman. He had a seafaring son, Captain John. One story of Captain John, which my father loved, concerned an episode in which the captain overheard some parishioners knocking the parental sermon as they emerged from meeting. Captain John promptly felled the chief offender with a sock on the jaw. The Reverend Codman censured his son saying, "John, John, you never should have done it on the Sabbath."

The first evidence that I have found of my father's scientific bent is his graduation essay at the Dorchester High School. This effort, written in the year 1869, when he was sixteen years old, and in a fine Macaulayan style, concerns the blessings conferred upon mankind by more than a century of steam. My father's personality was very well integrated, and this appears even in this early writing. The poetry in him thrilled to the romance of scientific discovery, and his intellect became active in the contemplation of scientific achievement. His sentiments and reason were in harmony. He was during his whole life the applied, rather than the pure, scientist. His point of view was fundamentally humanitarian. The use of scientific discovery for the benefit of man was his ideal; indeed, I might say his religion. Although the quest for truth for its own sake may have been his credo, the use of truth for the good of man was his main objective. All this emerges even in the schoolboy essay. For example, in summary he says, "Thus we see that the different countries of the earth are brought near to each other by this mighty agent, and the manufactures which steam enables them to produce are interchanged between them, and if as time rolls on the different nations of the earth shall become united as one, and shall carry on as one family the great enterprizes of civilization, we may truly boast that steam has *helped* to bring about this glorious result." That this proximity and easy intercourse might one day loose the powers of destruction was to him then, and indeed pretty much throughout his life, unthinkable. In the good genius of man, in the possibility of what nowadays is called "the good life," he thoroughly believed. Idealistic in theory, and in practice, he was close to Utopian in his philosophy of living; in business, in politics, and in science, this idealism constantly appears.

If the reader at this point pictures to himself an anemic young prig, I will tell him at once that he is wrong. The youthful James was a red-blooded, passionate, and handsome young blade. This is easily proved by the fact that at twenty-two we find him in the crow's-nest of an ancient bark, bound for Fayal, reading Byron. The voyage was undertaken to assuage a broken heart. Apparently it did that, and more. It saw, for example, the beginning of a habit which persisted into middle life, that of writing letters to the *Boston Transcript*. So abundant are such letters in the scrapbooks [1] he has left that one is tempted to credit him largely with the long survival of that journal. One of his admirers told me years afterward that he cut out all these newspaper articles of my father's and kept them pasted end to end in a roll in his pocket! He did not say whether he rolled them on a corncob. In the letters from the Azores the Byronic influence strongly conditions his perception of the beauties of the islands. His descriptive technique, however, is more in the style of the "Swiss Family Robinson." Let me give a sample.

One of the most remarkable craters in the whole Atlantic is the Caldeira of Fayal. It is in the centre of the island, about 4,000 feet above the sea. A small party of adventurers started off one day to ascend the mountain and explore the crater. Having packed our dinner baskets, and hired the services of a muleteer with donkeys, we mounted our fiery steeds and began our journey. Like all of the mountain pathways, the one over which we rode was full of beauty; after an ascent of nine miles we found ourselves at the edge of the crater; we had heard much about this famous Caldeira, but now we found all our expectations realized. If the reader will imagine to himself a gigantic basin in the form of an inverted truncated cone, with a circumference of five miles at the top, a depth of 1,700 feet,

---

[1] These scrapbooks are now in the possession of the National Air Museum.

and a level bottom two miles and a half in circumference, then he will have some idea of what we saw before us as we stood on the edge and looked down into the crater. It is not known how long this volcano has been extinct; there are other craters in the island which are known to have been active a century ago, but this one has probably been at rest much longer. The sides of the basin are overgrown with shrubbery, the bottom is carpeted with soft turf, and in the centre is a large pond in whose mirrorlike depths the green sides of the crater are reflected.

After we had satisfied ourselves with the view from the top, we began the descent into the crater. The sides were very steep and the path was quite slippery, but we had tramped so much during our wanderings that we were in good training, and did not find the paths difficult. When we reached the bottom of the basin we found the scene still more strange and impressive. A circle of blue sky over our heads, and all around us the high walls of brilliant green, with here and there a silver cascade trickling over the rocks.

We admired the wild beauty of the place until a feeling within us told us that it was time to eat dinner, and forgetting our aesthetic enjoyment, we gave way to the stronger impulses of our nature. We climbed to the top of the crater and opened our baskets.

Whatever philosophers may say concerning the nobleness of the mind of man, they must still confess that there remains in him yet a good deal of the animal. What should we have cared for the beautiful scenery while we felt within us the pain of hunger.

As has been said, we opened our baskets; the rapidity with which the viands disappeared proved the keenness of our appetites. When we had finished our repast and supplied the wants of the inner man, we were again fitted to enjoy the charming scenery which we found before us in descending to the sea. When we had been traveling upward our backs were turned on the view below, but now as we turned our faces homeward we had spread before us a broad prospect that was glorious beyond description.

For the first two miles we had a view of the whole eastern part of the island; the city of Horta seemed insignificant, and our barque riding at anchor in the bay looked like a child's toy vessel. Across the water the peak of Pico showed his summit above the clouds.

After riding about three miles we turned off into a narrow bridle path that led down to Flamingo Village; the path was narrow, steep, and winding; it was bordered on both sides with tangled thickets of wild-rose bushes which formed a continuous archway over our heads; the glimpses of the white houses of the village which dotted the valley below us were very pleasing as seen through the openings along the path.

We reached our hotel after our twenty-mile jaunt without feelings of weariness and passed a pleasant evening on our veranda, enjoying the sound of the dashing surf and the sight of the mountain clothed in his sombre robes of darkness.

So powerfully, in fact, did the beauty of the islands work upon the but recently love-wounded soul of this sentimental, practical, and probably bumptious young man that we next find him plunging headlong into higher art criticism. Evidently he had no inhibitions at this stage and possessed considerable, rather naive, conceit. In a letter, this time to the *Boston Journal,* he undertakes to put Ruskin in his place for having the effrontery to praise Turner.

When the author [Ruskin] shows us the importance of truth in art we assent to his statements, but when he gives boundless praise to a painting in which truth is ignored, we marvel at his inconsistency.

Now if we look at this picture of the 'Slave Ship' we shall see these faults so plainly that we cannot admire the work, but can only wonder at the ignorance of the artist. First, let us observe the forms of the waves. There is no motion suggested; they are as blocky as if carved in wood; no wind that ever ruffled the sea could make waves in this form; no conflict of wind and tides could compel the waters to assume such shapes; and yet Ruskin says that this is the 'noblest sea ever painted by man!'

No artist should dare to attempt to paint the sea unless he has lived on it and acquainted himself with all its moods. Turner was a landsman;[2] he knew nothing of the mystery of the great deep; he made the grossest errors in painting his ships. In one of his paintings may be seen a sail held aloft by nothing but the stiffness of its canvas, for the spar that held it is gone.

We have not the space here to describe all the absurdities of this painting. Many a time have we seen the glorious sunsets of the mid-Atlantic and wished that some artist might have the genius which should enable him to transfer to his canvas the gorgeous combinations of color, but the daubs and splashes of Ruskin's ideal painter do not suggest to us anything but mere paint and canvas.

Alas poor Turner! Clearly the parent could not be reached through paint and canvas. Poetry was a form of expression he understood better.

Following his graduation from high school, young James spent one year at Phillips Academy at Andover and following that a year

---

[2] And yet Thomas Craven (1931) in "Men of Art" assures us that Turner from childhood "rode down to the sea in ships, got the hang of them, mastered them, every rope and spar, made himself a sailor."

at the Massachusetts Institute of Technology. He left the Institute to go into business. What influences, if any, either Andover or Tech had upon his intellectual or emotional life I have not been able to discover. I do know that he thought the "theologs" on the top of Andover Hill were a priceless bunch of hypocrites.

On leaving Tech he went to Brookfield, Massachusetts, to learn shoe manufacturing in a factory belonging to an uncle. After a year or two of apprenticeship, so to speak, with what seems now to me amazing enterprise and audacity, he borrowed $5,000 from his grandmother, hired a small factory in Brockton, Massachusetts, and became a shoe manufacturer, and capitalist, overnight. This was in 1878 when he was twenty-five years old.

His business career, which lasted but fifteen years, is worth some scrutiny, for it strongly reflects his character. In modern parlance he was a good salesman. He also was fundamentally inventive. He had a new idea about the shoe business, and he sold it to the public. This was that the retail price of a trademark shoe should be determined by the manufacturer, for the protection alike of retailer and purchaser. He at once took out his trademark, "James Means Shoe," advertised very heavily, and quickly built up a lucrative business. He really had the vision of mass production and believed in the wide sale of standard articles at low prices. The James Means Shoe retailed as low as $2.50 and $3.00 a pair and was of excellent quality. He adhered to the principle that moderate profits and large volume of business are better for all concerned than large profits on a small volume of business.

In 1883 with a younger brother he formed a partnership known as James Means & Co. with offices at 41 Lincoln Street, Boston. I can recall being taken there as a very small boy and playing with certain blocks, which I now believe to have been the zinc plates for shoe advertisements. A larger factory was built in Montello, Massachusetts, and although of wood it is still functioning, now as a manufactory of leather bags and other leathergoods.

By 1893 my father had amassed a sufficient amount of capital from this business to yield him an income which he considered adequate to support his family in the way he wished. He therefore retired in order that he might have leisure to indulge in intellectual pursuits more to his liking than mere moneymaking. The piling up of money for its own sake was distasteful to him. As we shall see, he had other things he preferred to do. Ownership in the precious trademark, however, he retained, and for years afterward he leased it out to other manufacturers, always making the terms such that his ideals of business were satisfied.

All during his brief but successful business career my father's aggressive honesty and idealism were manifest by his attempts to better the conditions of the working man and by certain political activities. Indeed, at this period, he took a lively interest in politics and economics and had a strong sense of social responsibility. A scrapbook full of letters he sent to newspapers has preserved for us his social and political philosophy. He invariably expressed his ideas with simplicity, force, and utter candor. I never knew him to dissemble on anything, and he was no respecter of persons.

In 1884, having been a Republican, he refused to support James G. Blaine, the then Republican candidate for President. Becoming an ardent Mugwump, he was one of a "Committee of One Hundred" which went to New York in that year to pledge its support to Grover Cleveland, the Democratic candidate. In 1888 he served as a member of the Common Council of the City of Boston. In that same year and later he carried on active propaganda in favor of tariff reform and free trade. In addition to many newspaper articles he attacked the protectionists in a pamphlet entitled "Oppressive Tariff Taxation," which was published by the Massachusetts Tariff Reform League (1888) and dedicated "To my employees."

On the cover of this appeared a cartoon which aroused considerable interest at the time. It depicted the working man painfully struggling uphill and bearing on his back not only the "protected" manufacturer but also a great burden like that of Christian in *Pilgrim's Progress,* labeled "Tariff Taxes" and "Protection for the Poor Working Man." The working man remarks, "Protection may be a good thing for me, but I cannot quite see how." In a diagram also there are shown fourteen unprotected Peters taxed to pay protected Paul, who in turn is "poorly paid, notwithstanding the fact that the Peters are taxed to protect him. Who has got the money? The kind-hearted 'protectionists', the 'friends of the poor working man', have it in their pockets. There are fourteen Peters to one Paul in this country, but the protectionists do not say much about Peter; they are always talking about Paul. When you ask them how they can consider it right and just to tax Peter to pay Paul, they answer, 'Oh Peter has his loss made up to him by the general prosperity of the country.' Then they turn their backs and walk off, jingling in their pockets the money they have taxed out of Peter. Isn't that an easy way out of it?" That hard times are not due to overproduction was another of his firm convictions.

In 1891 my father felt very strongly that neither of the two great national parties fully supported the policies needed to promote social justice. In company with a few other men of like opinions, he sent out circulars calling for the formation of a new party and asking for the signatures of those in favor of its platform. Most of those to whom the circular was sent were Mugwumps, or men of independence who clung loosely to parties, but followed instead their consciences and their intellects.

The new party held as its chief tenets the belief in "honest money," a gold standard, and a tariff for revenue only. This circular met with a favorable response from many men, and signatures were forwarded in such numbers as to be almost overwhelming. Other circulars and many newspaper articles and pamphlets followed; the ideas of the new party, later to be called the "Columbian Party," were set forth in many places. Newspapers in widely separated parts of the country took up the matter and commented upon it, some with favor, many with disapproval and even ridicule. The number of men who gave their names in approval continued to increase, and the work of bringing to the public the importance of its two tenets of honest money and a tariff for revenue only went steadily on for more than a year, in spite of all discouragements.

The idealism which was so essential a part of my father's character made him willing to devote his time, his thought, and his money, selflessly, furthering what he felt to be in the best interest of his country. Moreover, although the Columbian Party did not become a formal organization as he hoped it might, he did not desist from his efforts until he felt that its declarations, forcefully made in many places, had to an appreciable extent influenced public opinion in favor of its policies.

Chapter II

THE PROBLEM

Let us now rejoin my father on the stern of the S.S. *Constitution*.[1] Having observed in what an effortless manner the gulls kept up with the ship in calm weather, he thought, nonetheless, that come a strong head wind they would then have to do some work with their wings to maintain such a station.

At last such conditions were encountered off Point Concepcion, California, "with a fierce wind blowing directly in our teeth, and above us and all around the gulls filled the air." Again their flight seemed effortless, "on pinions which were apparently quite motionless, they rose and dipped, thus conquering the gale."

I can readily believe that my father was right about the wind because, sixty or so years later, I too voyaged from Panama to San Francisco, and just such a gale as he describes was blowing at Point Concepcion, and there were still plenty of gulls.

My father thus formed his first aeronautical concept as a result of his voyage on the Pacific, and he first published an account of this experience in 1884 in an article entitled "Manflight" in the *Boston Transcript,* from which I will quote.

> Notwithstanding the long leisure for observation and study, I could not at that time solve the problem of flight; but those attempts were not quite without result; since then I reached one con-

---

[1] My friend the historian Mr. Robert E. Peabody has kindly prepared the following memorandum on this vessel:

"The *Constitution,* on which your father went to California, was a wooden ocean-going side-wheel steamship of 3,575 tons built in New York in 1861 for the Pacific Mail Steamship Co. From 1862 to 1879 she ran in the Pacific Mail Line between Panama and San Francisco, and if your father went on her in 1879 it must have been about her last voyage, as the records indicate she was broken up in San Francisco in that year. You will find a fine description of the *Constitution* in Kathryn Hulme's delightful life of her grandfather, Captain John Cavarly, 'Annie's Captain' (Little Brown, 1961). Captain Cavarly commanded the *Constitution* in 1864 when she was considered the last word in modern ships. There is a good picture of the *Constitution* in the Mariners' Museum, Warwick, Va., which is reproduced in 'The Panama Route' by John H. Kemble (University of California Press, 1943). This book also gives a good description of travel to California via Panama in the days before the transcontinental railways were built."

9

clusion which I still hold firmly, namely, that the capability of a bird —or a mechanical contrivance—of sustaining itself in the air depends not so much upon the exercise of a vast amount of power, or comparative lightness of the body sustained, as upon a *correct application of that power.*

It is interesting to insert here a similar statement in a letter written from Dayton, Ohio, March 2, 1906, by Wilbur Wright to Augustus Post, who was then Secretary of the Aero Club of America. It was a detailed report of the Wright brothers' progress from 1900 to date, and it listed their best flights of 1905 culminating in that of October 5—24⅕ miles in 38 minutes and 3 seconds. Quoting from the closing paragraph:

From the beginning the prime object was to devise a machine of practical utility rather than a useless and extravagant toy. For this reason extreme lightness of contruction has always been resolutely rejected. On the other hand every effort has been made to increase the scientific efficiency of the wings and screws in order that even heavily-built machines may be carried with a moderate expenditure of power. The favorable results which have been obtained have been due to improvements in flying qualities resulting from more scientific design and to improved methods of balancing and steering. The motor and machinery possess no extraordinary qualities. The best dividends on the labor invested have invariably come from seeking more knowledge rather than more power.

I cannot but wonder whether the germ of that significant statement might have been my father's text written 22 years before and which may well have been read by Wilbur Wright as he continued with his program—as described in his wonderful letter of 1899 to the Smithsonian—"to avail myself of all that is already known. . . ."

My father concludes: "I advanced no further than this; accompanying the idea, however, came the conviction that, if this view were correct, the time was not far distant when the brain of man, which had solved so many problems, would reach the solution of this one also."

His voyage over, business affairs claimed my father's attention to such an extent that apparently for several years he gave no further thought to aeronautics. Then one day he happened on "a publication of some English aeronautical society," in which his attention was attracted by the description of a machine for navigating the air. He took a dim view of the unnamed author's proposal, but the encounter brought back the recollection of the

Pacific gulls, and his interest in aerial navigation was reawakened. This time it remained awake for the rest of his life. He realized that to pursue such an interest he must read the literature, and so he seized with avidity everything he could lay hands upon which had a bearing on the subject and obtained information covering the period from the Montgolfier brothers "to the present date." Just when this date was I have no record, but it could not have been later than 1884. As a matter of fact, in a short autobiographical sketch which my father wrote in 1913, only seven years before his death, he said that he "first became interested in aviation in 1882 by reading Dr. J. Bell Pettigrew's article in the 9th edition (1879) of The Encyclopaedia Britannica, an article entitled 'Flight'." He also quoted from Pettigrew as follows: "The balloon is in no sense a flying machine. . . . The balloon is passive; the flying creature is active. . . . The balloon is controlled by the wind, the flying creature controls the wind: . . . Weight, however paradoxical it may appear, is necessary to flight. Everything which flies is vastly heavier than the air."

Reading Pettigrew clearly was not the beginning of my father's interest in aviation because it postdates the gull episode; however, Pettigrew made a great impression on him. The *heavier-than-air* idea would not leave his mind. Indeed, it never did. Of balloons, even powered ones, he always remained skeptical.

After he had done considerable reading, my father proceeded to write a critical review which is marked by candor and perspicacity. This appears in the 1884 paper "Manflight," already mentioned.

First he gives a classification of "air vessels" which, if we added jets and rockets, would serve very well today. Five classes he recognized:

I. *"Buoyant vessels,"* that is, any kind of lighter-than-air varieties.

II. *"Winged machines,"* by which he meant a birdlike affair equipped with wings and motive power to flap them; "ornithopters" we call them today.

III. *"Screw machines"* and it is evident that what he had in mind for this class is what we now call helicopters.

IV. *"Aero-plane machines, using the aeroplane in combination with one or more elements from the preceding classes."* He used "aeroplane" not as we do, rather improperly, to denote an entire craft, but in the sense of Pettigrew to mean "a thin, light, expanded structure intended to float or rest upon the air, and calculated to afford a certain amount of support to any body attached to it."

Thus what we call wings, tails, flaps, and ailerons would all be aeroplanes in the Pettigrew sense. Airfoil is perhaps the best modern equivalent.

V. *"Combination machines, including those which combine two or more elements of the foregoing classes."* To understand why practical air navigation had not yet been accomplished (1884) he searched for the faults of machines already designed. "A little study," he said, "shows us that buoyant vessels are entirely without value, and that the abandonment of them has been a step in advance." The whole development of rigid and nonrigid dirigibles was to continue long after his statement. Nevertheless, it seems to me now (1964) that in the very long view my father was correct. Of machines with flapping wings he was utterly scornful.

> Some English scientists have gone into the most tedious and useless analyses of bird flight with a view to its mechanical reproduction. It will not be difficult to show why these endeavors are useless. Nature is a good teacher, and the models which she furnishes have helped many an inventor to accomplish his task. But too close an imitation of Nature is in many cases more of a hindrance than an aid. To illustrate this point, and to show the folly of attempting to construct winged machines, let us suppose the world to have wanted a locomotive. If the inventor had looked to Nature for his model, he would probably have chosen, as being the most powerful, the elephant. Then, if he followed the method of those who are trying to solve our difficulty by a study of wing movements, he would have constructed a vast machine with legs and levers! . . .
>
> It is quite right for us to study Nature that we may learn principles; but, if we attempt to make the same application of power, we do not progress.
>
> In mechanics we find that the form of power which can be most readily utilized is rotary; so we may say that in mechanics the foundation of motion is revolution. But in the animal world revolution is unknown; all propelling power, whether of beast, bird, or fish, is applied by oscillatory movement. The reason for this is not far to seek. Living creatures are dependent upon the circulation of the blood. Revolution necessitates the existence of an independent revolving body.

In brief, then, the application of power to a body to propel it must be oscillatory if that body be a living one; it must be rotary if the body be mechanical. Of course, neither my father nor hardly anyone else at that time thought of propelling aircraft by the jet or rocket principle, yet rockets had been discharged into the sky for entertainment since the days of ancient China, and their historic use in warfare is recalled in "The Star Spangled Banner."

When father got to his class IV, he was very wrong. In the case of "aero-planed machines" he claimed that there was "another false principle."

> Those who advocate the use of the aero-plane claim that, as we find these passive surfaces assist the flight of the bird, therefore they should enter into the construction of the machine for mechanical flight. If our future air-ship were to be made with oscillating wings, the claims might not be unreasonable. The aero-plane lends aid to the flight of the bird because the action of the bird's wings is intermittent; the passive surfaces act while the active surfaces are idle; but it has been shown that the action of the future air-ship must be continuous, because no machine could be constructed of sufficient strength to withstand the strain of intermittent action; therefore, the introduction of a passive surface into a machine whose action is continuous would be useless, because it could only derive power by detracting from that of the continuously acting surface at the expense of the latter.

The idea that a "passive surface," if of a right shape, could impart lift if propelled through the air by a continuously acting force, e.g., such as that delivered by "aerial screws," had not as yet occurred to him, although it had to others, e.g., Henson, 1842 (see Chapter IV). Some years later he did some experimenting with kites. He would not have made this mistake if he had already had this experience.

In his 1884 paper he finally approached the question "What must the future air-ship be?" And the answer he came up with was the helicopter! He designed one in his imagination and took us for an imaginary (and prophetic) flight in it! A large screw on a vertical shaft, from which hung a car, and a small screw on a horizontal shaft—the former for lift, the latter for propulsion—were the direct elements involved. To prevent rotation of the car he recommended two screws for lift, revolving in opposite directions. At one end of the car was the tractor screw, at the other a horizontally acting rudder ("aero-plane"). Of course, he could not build his ship because there was then no sufficiently light and powerful motor.

Octave Chanute, in his important history of aviation, *Progress in Flying Machines* (1894), makes the following comment on my father's dream-aircraft of those days:

> A somewhat similar proposal is made in a pamphlet published in 1891 [reprint of 1884] by Mr. James Means of Boston, but he gives

only a scanty glimpse of the arrangement by which he thinks the problem could be solved. He proposes one screw on a vertical shaft, sustaining a car, with a pair of widely extended vertical planes, to prevent rotation of the apparatus, and concludes by saying: "If you want to bore through the air, the best way is to set up your borer and bore."

Our knowledge of the action of aerial screws is almost wholly experimental; and it would seem, in the present chaotic state of theory as applied to the screw, as if this remark of Mr. Means was almost as comprehensive and reliable as anything on the subject of aerial screws which has been published up to the present time. The writer feels quite certain that it contains in a condensed form as much reliable detailed solid information as several mathematical articles of considerable complexity which he has consulted, and it will be seen, by closely analyzing Mr. Means' suggestion, that after its entire adoption in the spirit in which it is made, there would be little left to be desired in the development of aerial screws.

In 1891 my father reprinted (privately) the 1884 paper on "Manflight" together with an addendum containing a plan for an improved helicopter type of aircraft. In this he dispensed with the smaller tractor screw and in its place substituted rudders which would have the action of the elevator of a modern aircraft, by means of which the vertical propeller shaft could be inclined at will and thus used to direct the machine in a horizontal course.

In the preamble to this addendum he recognizes that the great problem of manflight naturally falls into three divisions: (1) that of overcoming gravity, (2) that of steering the machine, and (3) that of alighting. This last was the one Darius Green did not thoroughly understand, but my father did! At the conclusion of

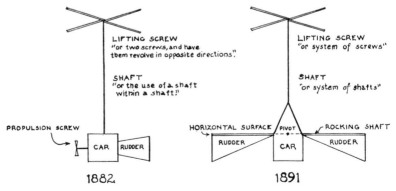

FIG. 1.—Schematic conceptions of helicopters. Copied from *Manflight*, 1891.

this addendum he mentions recent articles by Maxim and by Langley in which "much attention seems to be given to aero-planes." He goes on, however, rather tenaciously to restate his 1884 position that aeroplanes are useless! "Is it not evident that at the moment of starting or stopping, the aero-plane, being a passive surface, is nothing but a dead weight? Where is its efficacy? It is entirely from active surfaces that we must derive our support. These," e.g., a screw, "may be active while the car is at rest. Passive surfaces never. To have lifting power, the aero-plane must have an enormously rapid motion through the air; this at times it cannot have, so let us throw it away and substitute the screw." He had not then grasped the idea that one can have both, an aeroplane giving lift by being moved through the air by a propeller. He had, however, correctly grasped the principle which he learned from the "Pacific gull in a gale of wind" that any flying creature, or contrivance, must have weight combined with power properly applied, and not mere lightness. "When we have learned this much," said he, "we have nothing more to learn from nature."

In January 1893, after more cogitation on matters aeronautical, he ventured into print again with two articles, one in the form of a letter to the *Boston Transcript*, the other to Frank Leslie's weekly. For some reason, quite unknown to me, he elected to sign both of these contributions with the pseudonym John Meade.

The one in the magazine, entitled "The Scientific Value of Flying Models," begins with a fervent appreciation of Langley. By his paper "Experiments in Aerodynamics," Langley, so my father thought, had "probably marked the dawn of a new era in the history of the human race." The problem of aerial navigation, he continued, may be divided as follows:

1. To show that the attraction of gravitation can be overcome by mechanical means.
2. To adapt the motors we already have to the needs of mechanical flight.
3. To direct and control the movements of an aerial machine.

Langley, he submitted, had already solved the first of these problems; that of motors, he believed, was rapidly advancing. He recalled his first paper, "Manflight," of nine years before and said that great progress in the lightening of motors had been made since that date.

The third problem, control, he believed was uppermost at the time of writing.

Supposing [said he] that the air when violently attacked is for our practical purposes a solid; supposing also that we have a sufficiently light motor, we still know very little about starting, steering, balancing, and alighting. Concerning these matters we must learn by experiment. It is quite evident that to experiment at first with apparatus of full size will be sheer extravagance; we must therefore consider *what is the scientific value of flying models?*

Hundreds of successful flying models have been constructed, but in past years they have been looked upon as toys, and they have not been regarded with respect for the simple reason that Professor Langley's great demonstration was yet to come. Now these models are no longer toys; they are dignified objects of science.

And then followed a sentence indicating clearly my father's basic philosophy concerning aeronautical research. "While it is true that the success of a model will not prove that its larger type will succeed, it is also true that the failure of a model *will* prove the failure of its larger type, and it therefore seems highly probable that *any measure of success with full-sized apparatus must be preceded by complete success with flying models."*

He believed that the successful machine of the future would contain three primary elements: a screw or screws, a plane surface or surfaces, and a motor. How to dispose of these elements as to proportion, shape, and arrangement was the practical problem.

Some examples of past accomplishment in this direction are next cited, Cayley, Henson, Penaud, etc. He reverts also to his own suggestion of a helicopter type of machine in his 1884 paper. But he emphasizes that anyone wishing to design a flying model should above all things study Langley.

The real objective of his papers, so he stated, was to awaken interest in flying models among "ingenious mechanics, and if, after having secured their patents, designers should wish to take part in competitive trials of their models, it would be well to establish certain standards of dimension for models." A "regatta" for flying models was what he had in mind. Two points in these remarks are very revealing of his orientation: the mention of patents and of regattas. Although he regarded aeronautics as a science, practical advancement in it must be by trial and error, invention and competition. Furthermore, the inventor, who must derive his support from his inventions, must patent them, else they might be stolen from him. It should be recalled that my father's instincts had been those of business before they became modified by those of science.

Toward the end of this paper my father made some remarks

which amazed, indeed, in view of his usual pacifistic attitude, almost shocked me. "It seems reasonable," he said, "to suppose that the flying model will be developed into the aerial torpedo, and that, in its turn, into the practical flying-machine." This sounds like a premonition of the buzz bomb of World War II! "These machines," he went on, "would perhaps meet half-way between the contending forces and attempt to destroy each other, and the nation which can bear the heaviest taxation to swell its torpedo fund will probably be the winner." Some prevision—what?

The January 21, 1893, *Boston Transcript* article, the complete title of which is "Manflight—the Last Mechanical Problem of the Century," has the same theme, promotion of interest in manflight, but different variations. Again Langley comes in for praise, and a number of other contributors are cited. It is interesting that several of these published their ideas in popular monthly magazines, as had Langley and Means, possibly because it was thought that the subject should be of wide popular interest, or because special media for aeronautics had hardly appeared at that time. The possibility that man could sustain himself in the air by his own muscular effort, not by flapping wings, but by turning a screw, is aired in this paper, not with enthusiasm, but apparently for completeness. The idea seems to be that for steady flight, after momentum has been gained, relatively little energy is required. It is suggested that it might be comparable to that exerted by a racing bicyclist. I am sure my father did not think this would apply in the case of his helicopter. "In terrestrial locomotion," he opined, "men used their legs before they used steam boilers, and it is reasonable to suppose that they may well begin with their legs in aerial locomotion."

"Man remains earthbound in spite of the fact that for thousands of years the birds have been telling him that he might fly." This has been due to man's "gigantic misconception as to the true nature of air"; he has "regarded air as having about the same sustaining power as a vacuum." A charming little notion of the evolution of a flying machine from a thistledown is interesting in this connection (see fig. 2).

A thistle-down (A) is said to float in the air. It does not actually float, it sinks very gradually. It does not quite hold its own altitude. Man, in order to fly, *does not need to hold up his own weight;* the air will do most of that—he has simply to condition himself like the inert thistle-down, and then provide himself with mechanical ap-

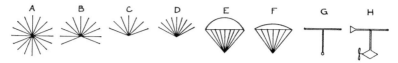

FIG. 2.—Evolution from thistledown to parachute to airplane.

pliances whereby his muscular power may enable him to a *little more than hold his own altitude.* That is, he must make himself just a little superior to the thistle-down.

The thistle-down as shown at A is a parachute in embryo. The succession of figures shows the process of evolution. The parachute is an aero-plane in embryo; the former cannot be driven through the air, flatten it out and give it sharp edges and you have the latter as shown at G. Here you find an improved thistle-down, that is one that offers the extreme of resistance vertically and the extreme of non-resistance horizontally. Add the motor and the screw and the vertical rudder as shown at H, and you have an improved form of the machine which is said to have been proposed by Sir George Cayley in 1810.

It seems that he even looked upon himself as a dreamer and/or a prophet, for he included this poetical sentiment from Tennyson's "Locksley Hall" in his 1884 paper:

For I dipt into the future, far as human eye could see,
Saw the Vision of the world, and all the wonder that would be;

Saw the heavens fill with commerce, argosies of magic sails,
Pilots of the purple twilight, dropping down with costly bales;

Heard the heavens fill with shouting, and there rain'd a ghastly dew
From the nations' airy navies grappling in the central blue.[2]

With release from the cares of business, he lost no time in becoming the active experimenter. Somewhere between 1891 and 1894, probably because of the reading he had done, he lost interest in helicopters and embraced instead support of a heavier-than-air apparatus, with airfoils possessing velocity, as the principle by

---

[2] I believe my father was one of the first to bring this remarkably prophetic verse to the attention of aeronautical enthusiasts. It has often been quoted since, notably by the President of the United States in 1928 at the International Civil Aeronautics Conference. Perhaps if my father had lived to see our current efforts in the United Nations to develop more amicability among nations he might have added the next four lines to this quotation:

Far along the world-wide whisper of the south-wind rushing warm,
With the standards of the peoples plunging thro' the thunder-storm;
Til the war-drum throbb'd no longer and the battle-flags were furl'd
In the Parliament of man, the Federation of the World.

which man would achieve flight. The fact that, given velocity, an aeroplane can sustain weight quickly taught him that there is no necessity to depend exclusively on the vertical thrust or pull of a power-driven screw to lift a flying machine into the air. All that is needed, when it is equipped with wings, is power to keep it in horizontal flight.

In 1894 he published a second pamphlet, entitled "The Problem of Manflight," which gives evidence of a more extensive study of the literature than did the first one. On its cover was a drawing showing Otto Lilienthal making a flight in his birdlike motorless glider. This article starts off with the statement that "as the century draws to its close the interest in the subject of aeronautics steadily increases. There already exists a keen curiosity to know what the aerial machine of the future is likely to resemble," and farther on, "the investigators of this subject are now divided into two camps: on the one side there are men who, like Mr. Maxim, are endeavoring to construct machines which will carry motors and therefore be self-propelling; on the other side there are men like Mr. A. M. Wellington, who maintains that a motor is unnecessary and that wind power is sufficient."

Of course now we know that both were right. At any rate, by this period of his life my father had become convinced that any flying machine, with or without motors, needed wings, and for himself he began making experiments with unpowered gliding models—"soaring machines" he then called them—soaring being to glide in the air with passive airfoils unaided by flapping. Actually he was returning to his first aeronautical love, the gull, and he never again left it, or at least its derivatives. The watchword became wings, whether on a bird (I don't recall his ever mentioning insects or bats, but they fly, too) or on a flying machine.

About this time he developed the idea that flight might become useful to man even in the absence of a motor through the use of gliders making descents at very gentle declinations and so covering a considerable distance. The captive balloon, he felt, would be useful in giving gliders their initial elevation. This does not seem to be one of the brightest of his ideas, although J. J. Montgomery used free-ascending hot-air balloons for launching gliders in 1905. Very wisely my father emphasized repeatedly that the first point to be mastered was the perfection of the control of the glider, and, although he believed that motor flight eventually would come, he put that as a thing to be attacked after mastery of the first, thus foreseeing the procedure followed by the Wright brothers. He always maintained that a great deal could be learned from gliding models regarding the proper design of sustaining surfaces, the center of gravity, and other aerodynamic features and ventured to say that it was far wiser to develop a successful small unmanned model than risk the lives of men in poorly designed powered apparatus. The great Samuel Pierpont Langley was similarly minded. Lilienthal, who was not, made 1,000 or so successful flights before he lost his life in gliding.

The lesson learned from the gull and other soaring birds was that they can remain aloft indefinitely without any flapping of wings and even gain altitude so long as they take advantage offered by the movement of the air. The gull had taught that what is needed is velocity, which can be gained by gliding downward. With velocity so acquired, momentum is gathered by which horizontal, or even ascending flight, can be obtained until momentum is lost. "Altitude sacrificed," said my father, "becomes velocity or momentum, and momentum sacrificed becomes altitude." A take-off for either bird or machine is something else again. Either it must be by means of a swoop from a place of high altitude, e.g., the top of a cliff, or a rising current of air, or by the active flapping of wings, or the whirling of a propeller. But my father at this point was only incidentally interested in take-offs. What he wanted to study experimentally was how the angle of descent of a motorless glider can be brought to a minimum. "What speed," he asked, "may we expect of an improved soaring machine, and upon how gentle a decline can we hope to see it maintain its initial velocity?"

As was characteristic of him, he made use of an analogy:

> When a railway car is at rest upon a smooth steel track having a down grade of one and twenty-three one-hundredths feet in every one hundred feet, it will remain at rest if undisturbed; but let it be once started downward by ever so slight an impulse and it will run down the track, gaining velocity to the end of the grade. It encounters the head resistance of the air, and the friction of the track, but an aerial machine would encounter only air resistance; is it not, therefore, reasonable to suppose that a dirigible aeroplane would in a calm, maintain its initial velocity while running upon a down grade of air of one foot in every one hundred feet? If so, an altitude of ten or twelve hundred feet would send a soaring machine eighteen or twenty miles, and greater altitudes would give longer flights, if, as may be supposed, the rarefaction of the air can be offset by an increase in velocity. These are surmises, but the way to learn is to experiment with soaring machines.

PLATE 1.—James Means, 1853-1920. Drawing by Pietro Pezzati.

PLATE 2.—Wright brothers' glider of 1902 being tested as a kite.

No. 1.

ONE DOLLAR.

The
Aeronautical
Annual.

1895.

Edited by JAMES MEANS.

BOSTON, MASS.:

W. B. CLARKE & CO.,

340 WASHINGTON STREET.

PLATE 3.—The cover—similar for all three issues.

PLATE 4.—Sir George Cayley, 1773-1857.

PLATE 5.—William Samuel Henson, 1805–1888, and his proposed airliner, 1842.

PLATE 6.—Otto Lilienthal, 1848–1896, and his glider of 1894

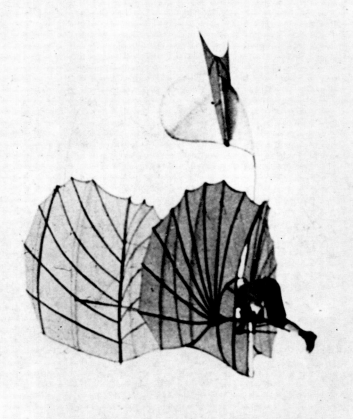

PLATE 7.—Lilienthal's biplane glider, 1896.

PLATE 8.—Sir Hiram Maxim, 1840-1916, and his steam-powered aircraft, 1894.

PLATE 9.—Scale models of Chanute gliders, one-fourth size, in the National Air Museum, gift of Octave Chanute.

PLATE 10.—Octave Chanute, 1832-1910.

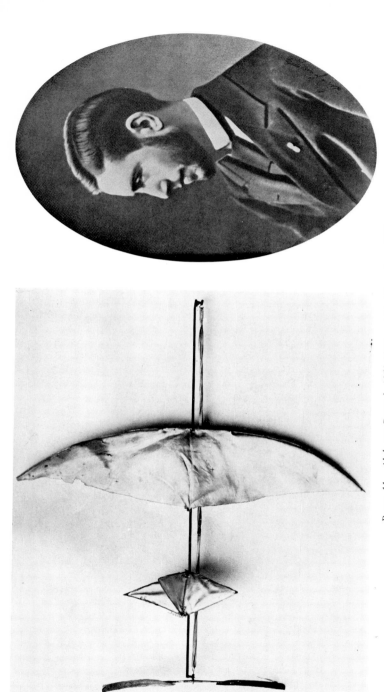

Plate 11.—Alphonse Penaud, 1850-1880, and his *Planaphore*, 1871.

PLATE 12.—A. Lawrence Rotch, 1861-1912.
(Photo courtesy of U. S. Department of Agriculture.)

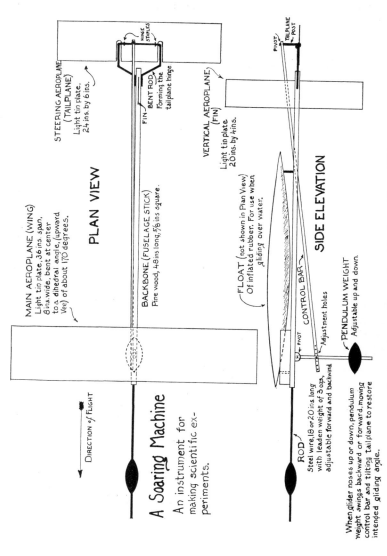

FIG. 3.—A soaring machine designed by James Means, 1893.

And this is what he began doing immediately after retiring from business in 1893, if not a bit earlier. He designed and built his own gliding models, "soaring machines," in a small workshop in his private house, 196 Beacon Street, Boston. In the Charles River Basin outside his window he had plenty of gulls and coot and ducks as well, to look at.

A blueprint and description of his first soaring machine were published in the pamphlet of 1894. He labeled it "an instrument for making scientific experiments." Although I was only eight years old at the time, I can remember this apparatus very clearly. It was made of light tin plate and pine wood. Its planes were all just that—flat surfaces. A horizontal plane served as elevator, and a fixed vertical one as a sort of forerunner of the fin. It was supposed to function, as do the feathers on an arrow, to maintain, as far as possible, a straight line in a plane perpendicular to the earth's surface. These two devices were carried at the rear end of the soaring machine as are an elevator and fin in the tail assembly of the modern aircraft. Stability, both vertical and horizontal, as well as dirigibility, was clearly in my father's thinking from the beginning of his experimenting. In this first model, however, he aimed only at controlling the inclination of glide, and this he attempted to do by connecting the elevator with a free-swinging pendulum. The pendulum to operate an automatic elevator had been patented as early as 1888 by Beeson.

"In November, 1893," he wrote, "I launched several of these machines from the balcony of the tower of Boston Light, and more recently I have experimented from the top of the cliffs at Manomet, Mass. The former place is an ideal one for the purpose of experiment, being as it is, one hundred and eleven feet above the sea with a straight drop of seventy or eighty feet. Unfortunately, a gale of wind was blowing when I visited the light, and two out of the three machines were total failures, being badly bent by the wind before they were launched. The third machine righted itself before reaching the ground, but the pendulum . . . was too light to do efficient work." None of these mishaps daunted him in the slightest. On the contrary, it was through them that the hobby was launched, that was to give him enjoyment and intellectual satisfaction for many years.

Chapter III

EXPERIMENTING
AND PROMOTING

IN THE spring of 1894, having since the previous autumn designed and built a much improved model, my father again went to the sand cliffs at Manomet, Massachusetts, this time equipped with six "machines" of the new type. The design of these showed a distinct advance over that of the year before, described in the preceding chapter. The dimensions and configuration resembled much more closely those of a modern aircraft. The ratio of wing spread to over-all length became greater. The wings themselves became curved airfoils, instead of flat planes, as in the first attempt. Also he discovered lighter and more flexible building materials. He still retained the pendulum to operate his elevator automatically and had some trouble with oscillation, but one machine made a horizontal flight "of about two hundred feet, before alighting." This evidently was very gratifying to him.

Directly after this, having liberated himself from what he regarded as the shackles of business, he established the family for the summer in a cottage in York Harbor, Maine, and set to work in earnest. "I spent," said he, "the greater part of my time in working at the bench and in the field." I well remember the attic workshop he fixed up, in which he built his models and from the window of which he sometimes launched them. The neighbors, I am sure, considered him eccentric, if not even a little balmy, but this did not disturb him in the least.

His better building materials showed his practical ingenuity. The "backbone" of his structure was of light wood (pine, I think), and its wings of about three feet span were fashioned from a pair of umbrella ribs, bent to whatever degree he wished and covered with tightly stretched and varnished silk. For his tail assemblies he found Japanese fans made of bamboo and paper to be very satisfactory. He soon abandoned his attempts at automatic stabilization

23

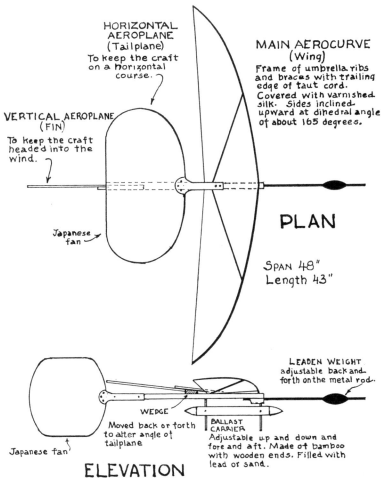

FIG. 4.—A soaring machine designed by James Means, 1894.

by means of pendulums and narrowed his study to that of shape and size of airfoils and center of gravity. After noting the glide of a model, he would alter some one factor slightly and try again. In this way of trial and error he improved the performance of his gliding model considerably. Indeed, of his final model of the summer of 1894 he had this to say: "Having altered my design after every trial, I can now offer to experimenters the drawing of an instrument which will, I think, be useful to them in beginning a series of investigations. It involves no new principle, but as the result of experiment it is proportioned in such a way that it will soar instructively. Whatever the merits or the faults of the design may be, its dimensions are given, and anyone may test it."

This was indeed a modest statement. In retrospect I have little doubt that if his model were blown up to mansize, and equipped with proper controls, a modern glider pilot would be able to fly it. Possibly it was of better design than that of the contemporary apparatus in which Otto Lilienthal lost his life.

During the summer of 1894 he began using kites to get his soaring machines aloft, and a byproduct of this was that he later developed an interest in the kite itself as an instrument worthy of study in relation to manflight. The soaring machines were sent up dangling from the kite string 100 to 150 feet below the kite. A gadget with a slow match burned through the string holding the model and, in due course, freed it to soar. His progress, however, was slow during that summer because calms and light winds were so prevalent that often there were no more than three or four days a month when the wind was sufficient for kite flying and glider launching. Therefore to get to a greater height than his kites could give him he went in September to Mount Willard in the White Mountains, New Hampshire. There is a precipitous descent there of 800 to 900 feet where he hoped to get good results. He went provided with twenty gliders all ready to put together. After trials of seven or eight he found that most of them were caught in eddies of wind which turned them inward and wrecked them against the face of the cliff. His gliders and hopes were indeed dashed, but not his spirits. "The remaining instruments," he said, "I still hold, hoping at some future time to launch them from a captive balloon." I cannot discover, however, that he ever carried out this plan. Instead, he went in for bigger and better kites.

During the next three summers, 1895 through 1897, he expanded his operation. He hired an unused old shop about a mile up the York River and engaged an M.I.T. student, Charles W. Bowles '94, as assistant. Various types of kites, some very large, were built and flown. Often, with other boys, I would bicycle, or row, upriver to watch the kites and the soaring machines that occasionally were turned loose from them.

I think the kite became an object of interest to my father in its own right, because he recognized that after all it was no less a species of flying machine than his gliding models. Actually the analogy is closer to the power-driven aircraft than to the glider. A

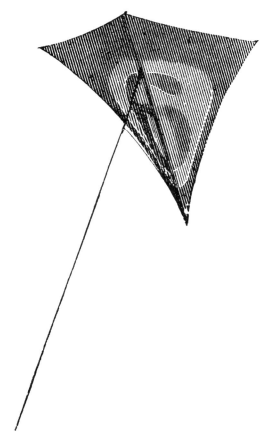

Fig. 5.—A Malay Kite, as modified by William A. Eddy.

power-driven aircraft remains aloft because its airfoils are forced through the air by a propeller. Should its engine fail, it would at once have to go into a downward glide, or crash. A kite's airfoils are not propelled through the air by a power plant but are held against the wind by a string. Should the wind cease or the string break, the kite, too, would come down, unless by a shift forward of its center of gravity it, also, could be put into a downward glide.

My father's direct objective in his studies of kites was to determine what forms of kite fly with the greatest steadiness and efficiency and what is the best way to make a kite a weight carrier. His approach to these questions was experimental—to try out the various types and compare their performance one with another. Only tailless kites were given any consideration. Although a tail may impart stability to a kite in flight, it was regarded as so obviously inefficient a device as not to be worth spending time on.

Although a number of types of tailless kites were studied, in the beginning two soon emerged as the most promising. These were the Malay, which is a diamond-shaped kite, and the Hargrave, or Australian box kite. Many variants of these were made, flown, and studied in the summers of 1894 through 1896. Some of them were very large and required large reels to control the strings. The chief observations made were on the angle in the vertical plane at which the kite would fly and on the pull upon the string measured in pounds. By means of an extra line to a flying kite running through

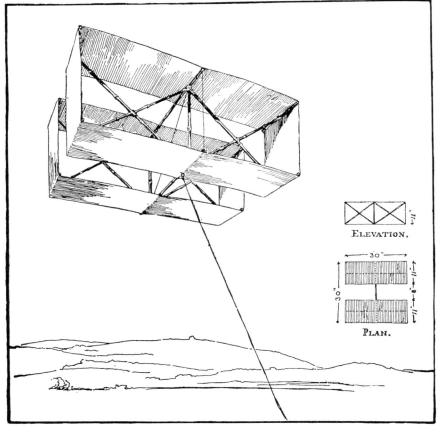

Fig. 6.—Hargrave Kite, 1893.

a pulley, weights were raised to the kite itself and note taken of its effect on the kite's behavior. As to practical uses of kites it had even been suggested, so my father said, "by some experimenters in aeronautics that the successful aerial machine of the future will be so designed that it may be raised in the air as a kite and while remaining anchored will act as one." To this proposal he wisely replied that it seemed to him "that the development of the kite must progress further before the correctness of this view can be determined, for we do not yet know the possibilities of the kite." And continuing, he opined as follows: "It is presumable that the flying machines of the future will be of various types and various speeds. When we consider the low average velocity of the wind, we are led to think that only low-speed machines will act as kites in ordinary winds. Even if this be so, the practices of kite-designing and kite flying seem likely to give us useful knowledge."

So interested in fact did my father become, for a time, in kites, that he wrote, "During the season of 1895 so much time was given to kites that I have not been able to carry my soaring-machine experiments as far as I had hoped to do." Thus he had added kite-flight to bird-flight in his approach to manflight.

One amusing episode of the kite experiments occurred when, in flying a large triple Malay kite, after 3,166 feet of string were out, the line parted. "What became of the kite," said my father, "I have not learned. Boone Island is six miles from shore and ten miles from where the kite left the ground; fishermen near this island last saw the kite and reported it as very high in the air and rapidly

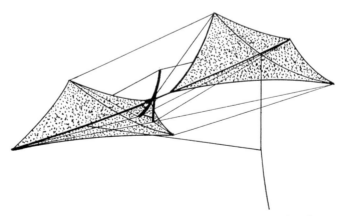

FIG. 7.—Double Malay Kite, 1896. Designed by C. H. Lamson of Maine. One of the many types built and flown by James Means.

travelling seaward. Measurement upon the reel showed that the kite had carried away about 1,400 feet of string, and, as a well-balanced kite with a drag-line of just the right length—as this seemed to be—is self-regulating, I think the kite must have travelled until it came to a calm spot."

On April 20, 1895, my father issued "A Memorandum" entitled "The Development of the Kite." I still have the manuscript in my possession. It reads as follows:

The practical flying machine of the future must be so well-designed and well-proportioned in all its parts that, in a fresh breeze, it may be anchored to the ground by a long line, and, acting as a kite, ride as steadily to its anchor as a ship rides when anchored.[1]

There are many reasons for thinking that any aerial machine which will not do this will be too unstable to make a successful free flight.

If this be so, then every improvement which is made in the kite will help the solution of the main problem of aerial navigation. By a process of evolution the kite may be developed into a practical soaring machine lacking only the motor for screw-propulsion, which will, when added, make it a practical flying-machine. The ideal kite—of any size—will fly infinitely near the zenith and will be controlled by an infinitely small line.

Any kite when steadily flying is in equilibrium. Three forces act on any flying kite, (1) the wind, (2) gravity, and (3) the cohesion of the string.

The pull upon any kite string is a resultant of two components, (1) lift, (2) drift [drag].

The meaning of the former word is self-evident. *Drift* is the pressure of the wind which tends to carry the kite directly to leeward. The meaning of the word *drift* may be made clearer by stating that in a flying-machine moving horizontally in free flight the resistance to its onward movement would be called *drift*. To the casual reader the word *drift* is a misleading one.

It is evident that when a kite is properly designed the string may be relieved of a part of the pull which is caused by component number one. This may be done by making the kite a weight carrier. It being desirable in the extreme to increase the efficiency of the kite as a weight carrier our greatest efforts in designing should be to obtain the maximum of lift with the minimum of drift. When these

---

[1] As though in confirmation of this statement, the Wright brothers made preliminary tethered tests of their gliders of 1900, 1901, and 1902 which directly preceded their powered flyer of 1903. All their gliders flew successfully as kites, and thereby the brothers learned much about their lift, stability, and balance.

are reached, the kite soars with its weight infinitely near the zenith controlled by an infinitely small string.

I have found by experiment that when large kites are made according to proportions found good in small prototypes that the large ones are much steadier than the small ones. The difference in their conduct reminds one of the difference between a small boat which bobs about and a large yacht which moves majestically.

I am therefore led to infer that if a kite having six or eight feet for its greatest dimension is designed and proportioned and weighted so that its conduct is satisfactory, its reproduction on a Lilienthal scale will give a kite which will carry up a man's weight and be controlled by a very small line.

A kite so made would naturally have such fine balance of parts that it would be in itself, when cut loose, an improved soaring-machine, to which a motor could be added when, after practice, the art of steering it had been fully learned.

During the winters of those years in which my father spent his summers testing soaring machines and kites, he was busy in his library at 196 Beacon Street, Boston, studying, writing, and making contacts with the leading men of the day in experimental aeronautics. Outstanding among these were Langley and Chanute. Both of these men were his friends from the early nineties until the time of their deaths. They often came to our house when visiting Boston. I can remember them both rather clearly, at least how they looked, not what they said. To a small boy the bearded Langley had an almost Jovian aura about him, whereas the French-born Chanute with his mustache and imperial was more fascinating than awe-inspiring. I am sure that my father was corresponding with other leaders in the field at this time, such as Sir Hiram Maxim and Otto Lilienthal, but I have no recollection of their being present at our house.

It was during these years, too, that my father's penchant for promoting scientific inquiry came clearly to the fore. He wanted to draw as many people as possible into the experimental study of aeronautics and to give them both help and encouragement. He thoroughly believed that competition could be productive of progress and that offering prizes could stimulate competition.

First he tried to involve the Federal Government. "It is needless," he said, "to advert to the fact that a universal highway would be a boon to humanity, for that is generally recognized. There are many reasons for thinking that the problem of aerial navigation can be solved before the close of the present century, if the United

States government encourages investigation and experiment. When we consider the great progress which, during the present century, has been made in other sciences and useful arts, we see plainly how the science and the useful art of aerial navigation have, until recently, been languishing since the days of Cayley, who experimented and wrote well in the early part of the century (1800-1809). The science of aerial navigation may properly be called the neglected science."

Consequent to propaganda of this type, a bill "to secure Aerial Navigation" was introduced in December 1893 in the United States Senate. It died in committee (Interstate Commerce), but two years later, December 1895, a second bill with broader provisions was drafted by my father and introduced to the Senate by Senator Henry Cabot Lodge. This bill, S-302, 54th Congress, offered a prize of $100,000 to anyone who could construct an apparatus which would, to the satisfaction of a committe of three appointed by the Secretary of War, navigate the air at a speed of not less than thirty miles an hour and be capable of carrying passengers and freight weighing a total of at least 400 pounds. Furthermore, a time limit was set to January 1, 1901. The implication was that this flight would be motor driven. The bill, however, offered a second prize, this one of $25,000, to encourage the development of gliding flight. To win this, the practicability of safely navigating the air in free flight for a distance of one mile in a descending line with loss of not more than sixty-six feet of altitude must be demonstrated. My father was chiefly interested in the second prize, because, as he said, for years he had been trying to convince people of the extreme importance of the development of the motorless soaring-machine (in modern parlance, glider).

The founding and fostering of societies which would stimulate interest in "the neglected science" constituted another of my father's pet interests. Such societies had been founded abroad before his day. The first was the Société Aerostatique et Meteorologique de France, founded in 1852, and next the Aeronautical Society of Great Britain, founded in 1866. In America, Chanute attempted to start an American Aeronautical Society in 1890, but the time was not ripe and the plan was not fulfilled. Thus it remained for a growing coterie of local enthusiasts in Boston, of which my father was a leading spirit, to be the pioneers in such an undertaking. They formed themselves into the Boston Aeronautical Society on May 2, 1895. Professor William H. Pickering of the Harvard Astronomical Observatory was chosen president. Was this a premonition of astronautics? Albert A. Merrill became secretary. The membership was limited to twenty, and the activities included fortnightly meetings at which papers on aeronautical subjects were read and discussed. Nearly all the members were active experimenters, and they felt that their society had a useful work before it and that their field would be an ever-widening one. It certainly has been.

My father's profound belief in the advantage of free exchange of ideas and collaboration is well exemplified by the following passage:

> Maxim speaks of Lilienthal as a parachutist, and likens him to a flying-squirrel. He also says that his (Lilienthal's) experiments do not assist us at all in performing actual dynamical flight.
>
> Lilienthal, after alluding to the unwieldiness of Maxim's machine, says, "After all, the result of his labors has only been to show us how not to do it."
>
> If any two men should be friends rather than foes, these are the two. Each has certain ideas and qualifications which the other lacks, and it is the greatest of pities that they cannot clasp hands over the watery channel. [Annual, 1895, p. 169.]

How true these remarks have proved is shown by the fact that after all the great achievement of the Wright brothers consisted essentially in the attachment of a motor to a successful glider, the child as it were of the Lilienthal machine.

What my father urged was cooperation rather than selfish rivalry in furthering the best interests of what he called "the neglected science," but he also believed in friendly competition, as shown by his interest in prizes.

Chapter IV

THE AERONAUTICAL
ANNUAL

In 1913 my father wrote a short autobiographical note in which he says, speaking of himself in the third person:

At the end of 1894 having produced the usual amount of wreckage, he had a fair gliding model and the question arose, what next?

One day it occurred to him that, scattered over the world there were several others who were experimenting, as he was, in ignorance of what others were doing and probably duplicating each other's failures. He thought that if he could gather the best of the world's literature on the subject and publish it, it might bring experimenters together thus preventing waste of effort.

This led him to the publication of the Aeronautical Annual.

Having no contributors he found it necessary to make the first volume largely historical. The 1895 number (the first) contains the wheat from many bushels of chaff. It was sent to every experimenter in the world whose name and address Mr. Means could find and to the public libraries of the United States in all cities having populations of 100,000 or more.

This brought him into correspondence with the scattered experimenters and brought him contributors, so that when the second number was published (1896), it contained the best that the world had to offer at that time. The third number, 1897, kept up the standard established in No. 2.

When the time came to prepare a fourth number it was found that material was lacking and as the circulation had been almost entirely gratuitous, it hardly seemed worth while to issue a padded number, so only three were issued.

When one looks at the proliferating, padded advertisement-supported journals of today (1960's) this decision of my father's seems extraordinarily enlightened.

From the vantage point of more than sixty years later it seems likely that the Aeronautical Annual was my father's most important contribution in the field of aeronautics. It made him known the world over among its devotees. There was but little if any basic science related to flying at that time. I cannot find the word research in any of my father's writings. Rather it was the day of the inventor and practical experimenter, and he evidently realized this when at the conclusion of his experiments with gliding models he asked, "What next?" He could not go further with the experimental approach, since he lacked the necessary technological training. The switch to the literary approach was natural. For a modern (1960) and unbiased appraisal of the Annual we may take this from C. H. Gibbs-Smith's *The Aeroplane:*

> Of less stature than Chanute, but of considerable importance during this period, was another American, James Means. Like Chanute, he was determined to disseminate as much information about flying as possible, being convinced that mechanical flight would one day be achieved; so in the three illustrated volumes of *The Aeronautical Annual* (1895-97) he collected, edited, and issued the most significant papers he could find on current developments, including the work of Lilienthal, Chanute, Langley, Hargrave, and others, and also performed a valuable service by reprinting some of the classic papers by Cayley and Wenham, besides giving bibliographies and other useful material. These admirable volumes, which were also issued in London, were read and studied by everyone seriously interested in heavier-than-air flight, and provided them with valuable data and encouragement. The dedication by Means in the last volume (1897), six years before the Wrights flew, reads: "To the memory of those who, intelligently believing in the possibility of mechanical flight, have lived derided, and died in sorrow and obscurity." Happily, he lived to see the aeroplane become a practical vehicle.

The Annual, even its appearance, was unique and distinguished. An octavo paperback in light blue, its front cover in dark blue print bore a reproduction of an old engraving portraying Bellerophon, on Pegasus, slaying the Chimera, a mythical example of attack from the air, perhaps more appropriate than the editor could have imagined. The spine bore, in bold vertical type, the words "The Aeronautical Annual," followed by the year. This ensemble gave the Annual a high visibility even in the company of many other books. The title page described the Annual as being "devoted to the encouragement of experiment with aerial machines, and to the advancement of the science of aerodynamics."

A certain degree of whimsicality on my father's part also pervades the first volume. Old cuts of fabulous flying creatures, the roc giving air transport to three elephants, a witch flying through the air on the devil, and other oddities, including caricatures of one sort or another took his fancy. His love of poetry also appears in quotations from Burns and Homer.

This first volume takes off with Leonardo da Vinci, whom the editor introduces with this bit:

> The story which tells of the sad fate of Icarus [again the classic touch] is but one of many which may be found in the pages of antiquity showing that from time immemorial man has longed to fly. Yet, these tales are but traditions, and, search as we may, no written records of the study of the great problem of flight are to be found until we come to the manuscripts of Leonardo da Vinci, who died three hundred and seventy-five years ago.

The frontispiece, also, is Leonardo—a fine reproduction in color of his famous self portrait in red chalk, the original of which was then in the Royal Library, Turin. Da Vinci, whose genius was universal, busied himself, of course, with the problem of mechanical flight, along with all of his other interests. His desire seems to have been to construct mechanical wings, an ornithopter in other words, and to this end he studied the anatomy of the wings of birds, especially the arrangement of their bones and feathers, and produced drawings to show how they might be imitated.

He also made observations of birds in flight and wrote a treatise on the subject from which several quotations are made in the Annual, as for example this (p. 13):

> The kite and other birds which beat their wings little, go seeking the course of the wind, and when the wind prevails on high then they will be seen at a great height, and if it prevails low they will hold themselves low.

> When the wind does not prevail in the air, then the kite beats its wings several times in its flight in such a way that it raises itself high and acquires a start, with which start, descending afterwards a little, it goes a long way without beating its wings, and when it is descended it does the same thing over again, and so it does successively, and this descent without flapping the wings serves it as a means of resting itself in the air after the aforesaid beating of the wings.

But Leonardo was not completely satisfied with the ornithopter idea. He also designed a helicopter and a parachute. According to Gibbs-Smith (1960), however, both of these "were casually 'thrown off' in little more than marginal sketches and not returned to." They were, nonetheless, as subsequent history has proved, original inventions of paramount importance.

After Leonardo, nothing of real significance happened in the progress of manflight until three centuries later when a solitary scholar, Sir George Cayley, Bart., of Yorkshire, appeared upon the scene. Cayley has been judged by present-day authorities as the "true inventor of the aeroplane" and a great genius in the history of aviation, as well as in other fields. Almost a second Leonardo he seems to have been.

It was fitting, therefore, that the editor of the Annual should have placed, next after Leonardo, a work of Cayley's on "Aerial Navigation," originally published in three parts in Nicholson's Journal for November 1809 and the February and March issues of 1810.

I can find no mention of Cayley in my father's writings prior to the first Annual. I presume it was during his search of the literature in preparation for this volume that he came upon Cayley. I do know that he had started his library of works on aeronautics some years before that and that he procured various important items in the book shops of London and on the continent. Among these were complete sets of Nicholson's Journal, a scientific monthly of some distinction, and of the "Reports of the Aeronautical Society of Great Britain" (1866-1893). Both of these he prized highly, and it was very likely in the former that he discovered Cayley.

The particular contributions of Cayley, selected for the Annual, portray vividly the great breadth of this man's interest in aeronautics. They start off with an exposition of how futile it is for man to expect to fly by artificial wings attached to his arms à la Daedalus. Cayley thought it unlikely that man could do much with the power of his own musculature even if in an apparatus that made it possible to apply this power with the greatest possible effectiveness. Extra power would be necessary for sustained flight, but it need not be great, after good velocity has been attained. To gain velocity, he realized, would take the major portion of the power. The steam engine had been invented by Watt forty years before the time of Cayley's observations, but Stephenson's locomotive was still two decades in the future. Cayley, however, entertained the idea of using steam to propel a flying machine, and he understood very well that it must be light, strong, well stabilized, and dirigible. To attain maximum lightness of his engine he proposed a water-tube boiler and estimated that an engine with fuel and water for an hour's flight need not exceed 163 pounds. He got the idea from the French that gunpowder could be burned as a light fuel. Apparently he intended to apply his power to beating wings on the ornithopter principle.

He also mentions making gliding models of various sizes, the largest of which he called his "noble white bird." According to Gibbs-Smith (1960), toward the latter part of his life Cayley built a glider which sustained a man for a short flight, his own coachman, in fact! Cayley appears also to have been the first to use the whirling arm to test airfoils, which he did in relation to his gliding models. I was rather astonished to find that the editorial comment on Cayley in the Annual (1895, p. 161) was limited to the following:

> Sir George Cayley made what he called his "noble white bird," but unfortunately, so far as known, he left no mechanical drawing with dimensions and weights. Had he included such a drawing in his published articles, it would have been a help to later investigators. Since Sir George's day there have been many accounts published of the performances of soaring devices, but most of these fail to give the detailed drawings with weights and dimensions which are needed to give to such accounts their highest value to workers.

The third article, Thomas Walker's "Treatise on the Art of Flying by Mechanical Means" (p. 49), was a truly fantastic piece of writing. This man was clearly no charlatan, of which there were many in the aeronautics of those days. His words have the ring of sincerity. But the flight which he achieved was merely that of his own fancy. He presented a most handsome example of the error of overconcluding from one's data.

He had been engaged in his studies concurrently with Cayley, for he says (pp. 52, 53) in the preface of his treatise:

> When my work was just ready for the press (it was published in 1810) I was much surprised at the account a friend gave me of what he had seen that day upon flying, in a monthly journal. I immediately procured a sight of it, and found it to be an ingenious paper written by Sir George Cayley, and I own I was astonished at the perusal. I conceived it to be very extraordinary that two persons, not having the least knowledge of each other, should be publishing their thoughts at the same time upon such a subject; nor was I less surprised to find the subject treated of there in a manner so rational and far superior to anything I have ever seen before.

This certainly was said in good sporting spirit. It is worth recording that both of these would-be aeronauts came from Yorkshire, Hull in the case of Walker.

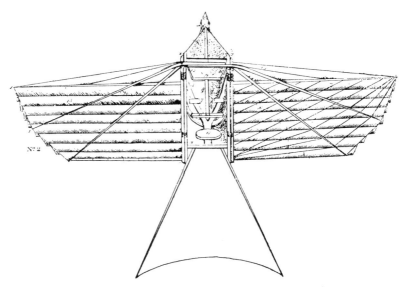

FIG. 8.—Proposed aircraft of Thomas Walker, 1810.

On his title page Walker is described as a portrait painter. Perhaps he was, but there is nothing further said in the treatise about that. What he does appear to have been was a competent ornithologist, and his approach to manflight was clearly via birdflight. He evidently had had considerable experience in studying the anatomy of the wings of birds and observing their flight, all the way from the hummingbird to the condor. Of the latter he gives a most interesting account. Condors may weigh up to 50 or 60 pounds and can carry more than their own weight of prey. This puts them weightwise almost in a class with man, and since their wingspread is as much as thirteen feet or more, he concluded that a wingspread of sixteen feet or so should sustain a man.

Cayley and Walker were both attacking the problem of manflight, and both believed that its solution would lie in a flying machine of the ornithopter type (i.e., with flapping wings). But there all similarity between them ceases. Cayley was a true experimenter, while Walker was largely an armchair philosopher. In intellectual stature Cayley was by far the greater of the two. Walker's naive confidence in his own untested theories is incredible. It is well exemplified by the following statements (Annual, 1895, p. 54):

The natural history of birds has particularly occupied my attention, and that enviable faculty which they possess of flying, has greatly excited my curiosity, and led me to that study by which I have obtained a *true knowledge* of the mechanical principles by which they fly, a knowledge which I do not hesitate to declare has hitherto remained undiscovered, although it has been the object of the study and contemplation of many of the most eminent philosophers of past ages.

[And a bit farther on] My invention for attaining the art is founded *entirely upon the principles of nature;* and although these principles are as old as the creation, they have never, until now, been properly attended to.

He would give directions he said (p. 56) "for making a machine wherein a man may sit, and, by working a pair of wings with a lever, be able to ascend into the air, and fly with as much safety and ease as a bird."

Then comes the alibi: "Although I have, for many years, been extremely anxious to bring the machine into effect, and am very sanguine in my expectations of success (for I positively assert that flying cannot be accomplished on any other plan than the one I propose), I, unfortunately, have ever found myself unable, from my professional avocations and other circumstances, to put it in practice, or I should long since have made the experiment." However, he decided to publish it anyway in "the hope that the lovers of the arts and sciences, when I have laid before them a scheme so practicable, will readily be induced, for the honour of science and our country, to contribute to the means of bringing it into practice, and demonstrate to their fellow mortals how they may gain a perfect dominion over another element." Apparently he got no takers!

Walker's concept of the mechanics of birdflight is encompassed in the following paragraph (pp. 62, 63):

When a bird, by the power of its pectoral and deltoid muscles, puts its wings into action and strikes them downwards in a perfectly vertical direction upon the air below, that air being compressed by the stroke of the wings makes a resistance, by its elastic power, against the underside of the wings, in proportion to the rapidity of the stroke and the dimensions of the wings, and forces the bird upwards; at the same time the back edges of the wing being more weak or elastic than the fore-edges, they give way to the resisting power of the compressed air, which rushes upwards *past the same back edges,* acting against them with its elastic power, and thereby *causes a projectile force,* which impels the bird forwards; thus we see that by one act of the wings the bird produces both *buoyancy* and *progression.* When the tail is forced upwards, and the wings are in action, the birds ascends and forced downwards it consequently descends; but the most *important use of the tail is to support the posterior weight of the bird,* and to prevent the vacillation of the whole.

And so, on this interpretation of the correctness of which he had no doubt whatever, he proceeded to describe how he would build his flying machine, of the success of which he was entirely sanguine. In fact, said he, "having discovered and explained . . . the natural mechanical means by which birds accomplish flying," and having built his machine in accordance therewith, there could not "remain *a doubt of success."*

Briefly, what he described was a birdlike apparatus flapping its wings in the manner described and steering with its tail. The man, pilot we may perhaps call him, or pilot and human motor in one, was to be encased in a birdlike fuselage to which were attached the wings and tail. So far as I can discover it was never built, much less flown.

There is no editorial comment on Walker in the Annual. Why the paper was included is anybody's guess! Perhaps merely because it is entertaining reading and to discourage future ornithopterists.

We now leap ahead a half century to June 27, 1866, when the first meeting of the Aeronautical Society of Great Britain was held. This was a very important date in the history of aeronautics and marked a transition from what had been largely empiric work by amateurs to more basic approaches by scientifically trained men. The editor of the Annual (p. 136) had this to say of the British Aeronautical Society's reports:

> The best of the world's knowledge of aeronautics is to be found in the two thousand pages of these reports. The organization has never been a large one, and probably years will pass by before the importance of its twenty-nine years of work will be fully understood and appreciated. Even as the missal painters kept art alive during the Dark Ages, so has this band of men kept aeronautics alive during the years in which their branch of science has been by the many regarded almost as a pseudo-science. The editor wishes to make the fullest acknowledgment of the debt he owes to this society.

At this first meeting of the Aeronautical Society of Great Britain a paper was presented by F. H. Wenham entitled "On Aerial Locomotion and the Laws by which Heavy Bodies Impelled through Air are Sustained." A learned paper exceeding in scientific merit anything which had gone before, it very appropriately was reprinted

FRANCIS
WENHAM

Fig. 9.—Francis Wenham, 1824–1908. (Courtesy *N.Y. Times.*)

in full in the Annual. I have a reprint of this bearing Wenham's autograph, which he presented to the Boston Aeronautical Society.

Wenham starts off with the statement that the resistance of a surface of defined area, passing rapidly through yielding media (such as air), may be divided into two opposing forces, one arising from the cohesion of the separated particles and the other from their inertia "which according to well-known laws, will require a constant power to set them in motion . . . therefore a weight, suspended from a plane surface, descending perpendicularly in air, is limited in its rate of fall by the weight of air that can be set in motion in a given time."

"If," he continues, "a weight of 150 lbs. is suspended from a surface of the same number of square feet, the uniform descent will be 1,300 feet per minute, and the force given out and expended on the air, at this rate of fall, will be nearly six horse-power; and, conversely, this same speed and power must be communicated to the surface to keep the weight sustained at a fixed altitude." This would be the case of a parachute descending vertically, or of any other heavier-than-air body moving through the atmosphere.

When the "heavy body" is a bird, or a man-made glider in flight, driven by some propelling force, it is sustained by the impingement of air (or wind of flight) upon the inclined surfaces of its wings. Like Cayley and Walker before him, Wenham sought explanations by studying the flight of birds and the aerodynamic properties of their wings. He found that the shape and dimensions of wings are closely related to the kind of flight engaged in by the several species studied.

As did my father but fifteen years or so earlier, Wenham observed the flight of gulls from the stern of a steamship. He did not mention the gulls' use of upward currents, as my father did, but was interested rather in the angle of the wings in straight head-on flight. Said Wenham:

> He [the gull] has just dropped astern, and now comes on again. With the axis of his body exactly at the level of the eyesight, his every movement can be distinctly marked. He approaches to within ten yards, and utters his wild plaintive note, as he turns his head from side to side, and regards us with his jet black eye. But where is the angle or upward rise of his wings, that should compensate for his descending tendency, in a yielding medium like air? The incline cannot be detected, for, to all appearance, his wings are edgewise, or parallel to his line of motion, and he appears to skim along a *solid* support. No smooth-edged rails, or steel-tired wheels, with polished axles revolving in well oiled brasses, are needed here for the purpose of diminishing friction, for Nature's machinery has surpassed them all. The retarding effects of gravity in the creature under notice, are almost annulled, for he is gliding forward upon a *frictionless* plane. There are various reasons for concluding that the direct flight of many birds is maintained with a much less expenditure of power, for a high speed, than by any mode of progression. [Annual, 1895, pp. 86-87.)

Wenham studied the wings and flight of many birds, and this led him to some basic aerodynamical knowledge. The wandering albatross (see Jameson in bibliography) particularly attracted his attention as a species for man to emulate in designing his flying machines. "A bird for endurance of flight probably unrivalled." It can glide hour after hour on practically motionless wings. The important point about the albatross is that whereas it has a wing-spread of some fifteen feet the width of the wing at its greatest point is only eight or nine inches. The wing of a bird or other flying creature is both a sustaining and propelling organ. At high speed it has been found that "the whole sustaining power approaches toward the front edge." Wing surface alone does not suffice; length is the important factor. "The wings of all flying creatures," said Wenham further, "whether of birds, bats, butterflies, or other insects, have this one peculiarity of structure in common. The front, or leading edge, is rendered rigid by bone, cartilage, or a thickening of the membrane; and in most birds of perfect flight, even the individual feathers are formed upon the same condition" (p. 102).

In designing airfoils Wenham kept these facts in mind and for practical testing he invented and used the wind tunnel. Instead of moving the airfoil through the air, he moved the air past the airfoil.

Wenham also made extensive studies of airscrews. The emergence of the airscrew was gradual. Its ancestor undoubtedly was the windmill. In the case of the latter, the wind turns the blades. The screw propeller is merely the opposite. Driven by an extraneous

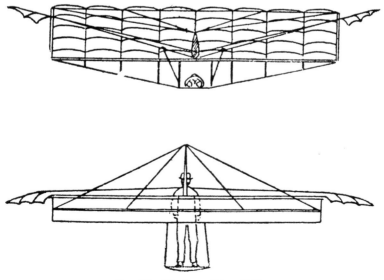

Fig. 10.—Wenham glider, 1866.

force it creates a wind. The blades of an airscrew are airfoils, no less than are wings, and the same aerodynamical laws apply to them.

Wenham designed and built a man-sized glider, but I can find no record that he got off the ground in it. According to his calculations, the wingspread required for such a device would have to be sixty feet. This being, as he thought, structurally impractical, he resorted to the superposed plane principle introduced by Cayley. With five such planes, one above the other, the total functional lifting edge of the airfoils could amount to sixty feet, although the actual width of the aircraft would be but twelve. These multi-plane gliders gave rise subsequently to the familiar modern type of biplane whether glider or powered.

When Wenham had concluded, the president of the Society, the Duke of Argyll, made some comments from the Chair. One of these, at least, was extraordinarily penetrating and farseeing. "I think it is quite certain," said His Grace, "that if the air is ever to be navigated, it will not be by individual men flying by means of machinery; but that it is quite possible vessels may be invented, which will carry a number of men, and the motive force of which will not be muscular action" (p. 110).

The remaining third of Annual No. 1 is made up of short pieces of most miscellaneous nature.

A selection of letters between Benjamin Franklin and some of his scientific friends, on the subject of ballooning is followed by "a few words" by the editor "about a great hope." The great hope, of course, was that it would turn out that the invention of the balloon heralded the conquest by man of the circumambient atmosphere of his planet. It has actually by no means met such promise. Franklin is reported to have replied to the question What good is a balloon? with the further question What good is a baby? To the former question, we can now answer, "not much." I suppose it was to make clear this point that my father included these balloon items in the Annual. From the beginning of his interest in aeronautics he had always held to the belief that the usefulness of the balloon would be very limited. The career even of the rigid dirigible he predicted would be transient. Many of the great Zeppelin-type airships came to tragic endings. When the U.S. Navy's *Akron* was lost on April 5, 1933, I wrote to the *Boston Transcript* reminding them of the remark of my father's which they had published almost half a century before, namely, that "buoyant vessels are entirely without value." The sister ship of the *Akron*, the *Macon*, succumbed two years later, and the tragic loss of the *Hindenburg* in 1937 was the end of the great lighter-than-air airships. The Navy continued with its smaller blimps for another quarter century, but finally in July 1961, I read that the last remaining ones were about to be liquidated.

Next we come to the statement of a principle derived by Langley from some of his experiments (1891). "If," said he, "in aerial motion, there be given a plane of fixed size and weight, inclined at such an angle, and moved forward at such a speed that it shall be sustained in horizontal flight, then the more rapid the motion is, the *less* will be the power required to support and advance it." Langley submits that, paradoxical as this seems, it is nevertheless true.

The editor's comment is this: "Since Samuel Pierpont Langley has, beyond any question, been the first to discover, to state, and to prove this great law of the economy of high speeds, the editor feels justified in naming it *Langley's Law.*" It has obvious bearing on the work of Cayley, Wenham, and others.

In 1910 Wilbur Wright, in a letter to Dr. Charles D. Walcott, Langley's successor as head of the Smithsonian, wrote: "The law itself contains some elements of truth, but it also contains elements of error, and the form of statement is such that its general effect has been to mislead readers and give them false ideas."

To me it would seem that Langley, at that early stage of his studies (1891), had not properly conveyed his understanding of the relation between supporting power and propelling power, that is: surface vs. thrust. He had undoubtedly observed that the faster a wing surface is moved, the more weight can be supported by it, and, conversely, the faster an aerodynamic object is moved, the less wing surface is needed to support it. If Langley had substituted the word "surface" for "power" he would have been more correct. In other words, the increase in power needed to attain greater speed is somewhat offset by the decrease in surface required to support the object as speed increases (the thin ice phenomenon).

From Langley the Annual (p. 129) jumps back to Charles Darwin, who in 1834, while on the voyage of the *Beagle,* made notes, as had Walker before him, on the flight of the condor. These interested my father. Except when these birds were rising from the ground, Darwin could "not recollect ever of having seen one of these birds flap its wings." And about this mode of flight, Darwin made this penetrating comment: "In the case of any bird soaring, its motion must be sufficiently rapid, so that the action of the inclined surface of its body on the atmosphere may counterbalance its gravity. The force to keep up the momentum of a body moving in a horizontal plane in the air (in which there is so little friction) cannot be great, and this force is all that is wanted." So Darwin contributed to aerodyamics as well as to evolutionary biology.

"Wise upon Henson" is the title of the next item. John Wise, an American balloonist, had authored "A System of Aeronautics" in 1850. In this he gave a description of a flying machine designed and patented by an Englishman, W. S. Henson, in 1842. Henson's "Aerial Steam Carriage," as he called it, apparently never got beyond the drafting board and a powered model which failed to fly, but in pictorial form it achieved considerable publicity in the *Illustrated London News* and elsewhere. An imaginative picture of it, showing some remote resemblance to a modern aeroplane flying over the city of London is very familiar. Henson had designed a light steam engine which was to operate a pair of pusher-type propellers. The affair was designed to be launched from an inclined plane which would give enough speed for the take-off, after which the propellers would only "be called upon to repair the loss of velocity due to air resistance." Altogether, though never built, this machine indicated a rather accurate power of prophecy on the part of the inventor.

After the Henson piece, a table of wind velocities for the year 1892 was thrown in for good measure, and following that a bibliography of aeronautics.

My father's article entitled "The Problem of Manflight," which was published in pamphlet form in 1894, was also reprinted in the 1895 issue of the Annual. And the closing piece is entitled "Editorial." This sets forth so clearly my father's philosophy regarding manflight up to that time that I shall quote it (p. 160);

> Since the foregoing pamphlet was published, about a year ago, I have become more than ever firmly convinced that the soaring-machine is, of all others, the instrument by which we must, for the present, acquire knowledge.
>
> With all due respect to those who are constructing machines to start along the ground with motors, I still express the opinion that such machines are less instructive than are soaring machines launched from considerable heights. The reason is this. The art of steering machines of the former kind has only been partially acquired, consequently long flights of such do not occur, and their conduct can be studied for a very brief time only. But the soaring-

machine, with the potential energy of lead for its motor, when launched from a captive balloon at a considerable height, must, of necessity, declare itself for a considerable length of time and teach the observer new things with every new flight. Every movement is instructive to the designer, and no hasty wreck can occur to deprive him of the opportunity for study. When a soaring machine which will carry four or five hundred pounds of lead or sand-bags has been satisfactorily designed, then will it be time to consider motors. To trust valuable motors to machines before we have successfully carried sand-bags uses up appropriations faster than is necessary.

After the soaring machine is sufficiently improved, the adding of a motor—if such be found necessary—will be the adding of a new force which will tend to throw the machine out of equilibrium; yet the power can be applied very gradually so that we may learn to counteract the disturbance of the equilibrium which it causes.

How astonished my father would have been if, at that point, he could have seen his great-grandsons putting little toy model aeroplanes into splendid flights, powered by tiny gasoline motors; or, contrariwise, grown men taking off from some high mountain in graceful motorless gliders and soaring among the high peaks as easily as a condor!

His prognostications on the aeroplane include this interesting statement: "Writers frequently express the opinion that aerial machines, when they come into use, will first be applied to the purposes of warfare. I venture to predict otherwise. It seems likely that the earliest use of aerial machines will be for purposes of sport, and most interesting sport it will be." The subsequent history of the motorless glider vindicates a fraction of his prophecy, but, unhappily, how wrong he was on war.

Everything moved more slowly in the nineties than now. There was much less hurry and tension. There was no need for tranquilizers. Therefore, this prediction need not surprise us: "The present revival of interest in the subject of aeronautics leads many writers confidently to predict a solution of the great problem at an early date; yet I venture to say that the more one studies the subject the more plainly he sees the enormous difficulties which are still unconquered, and the more inclined he is to think that many years will elapse before any travelling in the air becomes an important feature in the daily life of the human race. Yet these very difficulties are what give the subject its extreme fascination" (p. 169). The development, however, was faster than he could have dreamed.

Also within the pages of this editorial is a description of my father's improved soaring machine, already mentioned in Chapter III.

The objective of bringing together the world's best literature on aeronautics, for inspirational purposes, seems to have been well met in Aeronautical Annual No. 1. The aim was not to write a comprehensive history of aeronautics, but rather to make some of the giants readily available. The selection of Leonardo, Cayley, and Wenham as the top flight was very sound. The period from Leonardo to the middle 1890s, taking off from birdflight and ringing the changes on it in ways occasionally profound, but usually crude and unenlightened, finally saw the last ornithopter duly buried. No manned ornithopter ever actually got off the ground in sustained flight. The interest in birdflight, however, survives even today, but it is the soaring flight of birds, not the flapping, that has proved helpful to man in his conquest of the air. My father clearly sensed all this from the start. After a brief attention to helicopters, his interest lay chiefly in the development of aircraft having fixed birdlike wings. He did not foresee, or live to see, that the helicopter was also destined to play a significant role in manflight.

His hope for the first Annual my father expressed as follows: "If this compilation should happily bring any new workers into the field of aeronautical experiment, the hopes of the editor will be amply fulfilled."

I have in my possession a letter from the Wright brothers dated January 5, 1908, and signed by Orville. It contains the following sentence: "The old Annuals were largely responsible for the active interest which led us to begin experiments in aeronautics."

Another letter from Orville Wright to my brother, Philip A. Means, dated November 12, 1921, contained the following passage:

> The Aeronautical Annuals of 1895-96-97 contained the best collection of reprints from that work of the earlier experimenters in aviation that had appeared up to this time, and I do not know of a better collection today. Your father showed rare good judgment in his selections, separating most of the good work from the mass of worthless matter which had been published.
>
> Your father's work was of great benefit to us, and I think of my personal acquaintance with him with affection.

Thus indeed were my father's hopes fulfilled beyond all possible expectations.

Chapter V

THE SECOND ISSUE, 1896

UNLIKE the first, the second Annual was concerned with contemporaneous work. The title page bears the words "Devoted to the Advancement of the Neglected Science." It starts off with an original article (specially requested by the editor) by Otto Lilienthal on "Practical Experiments for the Development of Human Flight." This title exactly described the field in which Lilienthal became one of the stars of first magnitude.

Born in 1848 in the German province of Pomerania, he had been interested in manflight from early youth. With a younger brother he had experimented with flapping wing devices of one sort or another. But he was no mere ardent amateur in experimental aeronautics. He graduated in engineering in Berlin just before the Franco-Prussian war. After serving through that war in a Guards regiment, he opened a manufactory of machinery in which he developed and brought to production many of his own inventions. All during this time he continued to study problems of manflight, but now he could bring to bear on them his professional knowledge of engineering. The study of birdflight was always his take-off point. He believed that by scientific investigation of the manner in which birds stay aloft and propel themselves through the air, man could learn to do something of this sort also. He made precise observations of birds in flight, and investigated such matters as the shape of airfoils, wind resistances and the like.

In 1889 he published a famous paper, "Der Vogelflug als Grundlage der Fliegekunst." Shortly after this, he decided that one could not conquer the air from the drafting room, but must actually get out with one's apparatus in the wind and try to fly it. He wrote (Annual, 1896, p. 9):

> One can get a proper insight into the practice of flying only by actual flying experiments. The journey in the air without the use of the balloon is absolutely necessary in order to gain a judgment as to

the actual requirements for an independent flight. It is in the air itself that we have to develop our knowledge of the stability of flight
so that a safe and sure passage through the air may be obtained, and
that one can finally land without destroying the apparatus. One must
gain the knowledge and the capacity needed for these things before
he can occupy himself successfully with practical flying experiments.

Lilienthal was convinced that human flight could not be brought
about by any single invention but would have to be achieved by
gradual development.

In free flight through the air [he continued] a great many peculiar
phenomena take place which the constructor never meets with elsewhere; in particular, those of the wind must be taken into consideration in the construction and in the employment of flying apparatus.
The manner in which we have to meet the irregularities of the wind
when soaring in the air can only be learned by being in the air itself.

[And again] The only way which leads us to a quick development
in human flight is a systematic and energetic practice in actual flying
experiments. These experiments and exercises in flying must not only
be carried out by scientists, but should also be practised by those wishing for an exciting amusement in the open air, so that the apparatus
and the way of using it may by means of common use be quickly
brought to the highest possible degree of perfection.

The question is therefore to find a method by which experiments
in flying may be made without danger, and may at the same time be
indulged in as an interesting amusement by sport-loving men . . .
These conditions are easily fulfilled. One can fly long distances with
quite simple apparatus without taxing one's strength at all, and this
kind of free and safe motion through the air affords greater pleasure
than any other kind of sport.

Lilienthal next describes his apparatus and procedures. The
former was equipped with airfoils "very like the outspread pinions
of a soaring bird." A light wooden framework covered with cotton
twill was all that he used. "Sailing apparatus" he called it, and the
method of use was "to hold the frame with the hands, the arms
resting between cushions, thus supporting the body." The legs
were left free for running or jumping. A tail assembly with vertical and horizontal planes was used, but only for stability. They
were immobile. His procedure was to start running with the
apparatus from the top of a small hill, into the wind, until lifted
off into a glide. All steering was done by movements of the body,
especially his legs, thus changing the center of gravity in the desired
direction.

He gives simple directions for all maneuvers, taking-off, landing, dealing with shifting air currents, etc. He almost sounds like a mother bird teaching her young to fly.

In five years Lilienthal made over a thousand glides and introduced many improvements in his apparatus. One of his advanced types is shown in Plate 7. In this one he had come to the biplane which he found had several advantages, including greater lift and better stability. He had a conical hill built, 30 meters in height, from which he could take off into the wind whatever its direction, just like a wise old gull. As he gained experience he became bolder and made many experiments in the wind. He became quite familiar with upward currents and often was carried by them to higher elevations than his take-off point. On one occasion he was lifted vertically from the top of the hill by a gust of wind.

There can be no doubt that Lilienthal became a very expert glider pilot, one of the first the world had known. He accomplished flights of several hundred yards often with numerous ups and downs in them. Although throughout his career he had certain hankerings for wing-flapping, and even believed that motor flight would be achieved by the ornithopter principle, it was nevertheless his mastery of gliding flight which put him in the category of the human albatross or condor, and not at all in that of the pigeon.

His chief delight was battling turbulent winds, and he claimed that when one worked up to this slowly, and had acquired sufficient skill, this sort of thing could be done without danger. But alas, this belief finally cost him his life. His fatal crash was on August 9, 1896, in a monoplane glider. The frontispiece of Annual No. 2 showed his biplane glider.

My father, I know, had a great admiration for Lilienthal and was saddened by his death, which he looked upon as needless. The two were agreed that everything possible should be learned from birdflight and that gliding flight should be perfected before motor-driven flight was attempted. My father felt that everything possible should be learned from models before human life was risked. Lilienthal entrusted himself to the air from the beginning and paid the price at the early age of 48.

Following Lilienthal's paper the Editor has a three-page whimsical little divertissement on "Wheeling and Flying." "The slow development of the flying machine in its early stages," said he, "finds its analogue in that of the bicycle. The admirable wheel (that is what they called the bicycle in the gay nineties) of today is the product of more than eighty years of careful thought and experiment." The choice of this analogy was not as farfetched as it might seem today. In the mid-1890s nearly all able-bodied persons were riding bicycles, not merely to get about, but because it was the rage. The automobile in those days was in its infancy, seen on American streets only rarely, and the horse was a more expensive form of transportation than the bicycle. The bicycle held the stage, at least for a brief interval. To quote the Annual again (p. 24):

> It is not uncommon for the cyclist, in the first flush of enthusiasm which quickly follows the unpleasantness of taming the steel steed, to remark, "Wheeling is just like flying." This is true in more ways than one. Let us note the points of resemblance. Both modes of travel are riding upon the air, though in one case a small quantity of air is carried in a bag and in the other the air is unbagged. There are many who believe that in order to travel upon air it is not necessary to put the air in a bag; they not only believe this but they know it has been done. Lilienthal has done it many times, and the Lilienthal machine is to flying what the wheel of 1816 was to pneumatic wheeling. The Lilienthal machine seems likely to lead to important things, yet there are men who say of the inventor: "He cannot fly up, he can only fly down, he is a parachutist, a flying squirrel, he has not solved the great problem." True he has not solved it, but he has given a partial solution which will place his name on the role of the immortals.

And now from gliding flight we jump to power-driven flight, or at least an approach to it. Hiram S. Maxim is the figure that addresses us. He was a down-East Yankee, at least he was born in 1860 in Sangerville, Maine, and apparently he was a congenital inventor. Early in his career he transplanted himself to England where he founded an arms company. Later this was consolidated with the Vickers firm and finally Vickers and Armstrong, which produced some of the famous fighting planes of World War I. In 1884 Maxim invented the Maxim machine gun, and numerous other inventions in the munitions line stood to his credit. Presumably as a reward for all this, in 1901, he was knighted.

Maxim, according to his article in the Annual, had been interested both in natural and artificial flight for many years. He had made extensive observations on the flight of birds, always from the aerodynamical point of view. He made calculations of the amount of energy used by them in flying and the amount of work performed. He had studied the flight of gulls from the sterns of steamers, as had my father. He compared the flappers, e.g., ducks, with the soarers, e.g., the albatross. The latter practically live in the air with relatively little expenditure of energy circling constantly to take advantage of air currents. The former, expending much more energy, fly in straight lines to reach some point with greatest possible speed.

Maxim also studied wind currents as betrayed by the surface of the waters. The size and direction of waves and the alternation of rough and smooth areas gave him the notion that the atmosphere is in constant motion with rising and descending currents, as well as horizontal winds—the very stuff for gliding flight.

Always the experimentalist, he made extensive studies of the aerodynamical properties of airfoils, both of propellers and wings, by means of a whirling arm, and also of a primitive wind tunnel.

Despite his evident interest in soaring flight, when it came to his own major contribution to practical aeronautics he leaped at once to power. His objective, as he stated it, was "to make a large machine heavier than air that would lift itself from the earth by dynamic energy generated by the machine itself." Evidently he believed that this should be achieved before free flight was attempted. His "first idea," he said, "was to construct a machine with two large screws on vertical shafts." In other words, a helicopter, but it appears he soon abandoned this for screws on horizontal shafts. Actually he caused to be constructed, at great expense, a rather horrendous gadget with six or so airfoils and two large propellers, operated by a specially designed light steam engine. The whole was mounted on a platform with flanged wheels which ran on a track. He seems to have given very much more attention to the designing of the motor and propellers, for which he had his engineering competence, than to the actual flying elements of his airship.

Maxim's objective was to discover whether such an apparatus could maintain itself aloft under its own power. The track had over-and-under rails on each side, the lower rails being for the wheeled gear to roll on, and the upper rails for the wheels to rise against and roll along underneath if and when the aircraft lifted. He could not allow it to go into free flight because it was completely nondirigible. On one of the test runs, the upward pull against the inverted rail was so great that an axle of the apparatus was bent and the machine damaged. Maxim seemed to think that this was a great achievement and that he had proved that "a flying machine is now possible without the aid of a balloon in any form." Satisfied with this and because of the great expense, he discontinued his experiments. He felt sure that future experimentors would take on where he left off and with the advantages of the knowledge already gained would be able to construct a practical flying machine which would be a great advantage to mankind. He was very sanguine indeed!

My father, I know, regarded Maxim's work as important, but now, as we look at it after sixty-five years, it seems unimpressive. Gibbs-Smith sizes it up in this way:

> A study of the machine, and his own description of it, reveals that he had a sound but limited knowledge of wings, despite his elaborate tests; had made considerably advanced experiments in propeller design; and, with his excellent steam engine, had produced enough lift to raise the machine at the expense of nearly everything else that is necessary for a practical aeroplane. He had made no proper provision for, nor study of, stability and control in the air; and when all is considered, from the standpoint of practical aviation, it was time, money and effort wasted, as this otherwise eminent man contributed nothing to the progress of flying."

Could two approaches to the same ultimate objective, namely manflight, be so far apart as Lilienthal's and Maxim's?

Of my father's several pioneer aeronautical contemporaries, he was probably most closely in touch with Chanute. He had read some of Chanute's writings by 1894, or perhaps earlier, that is to say, prior to the publication of Chanute's famous work "Progress in Flying Machines."

In Annual No. 2 (p. 60) my father included a short biographical sketch of Chanute, reprinted from Engineering News, 1891, and also an article by Chanute, entitled "Sailing Flight." This continued in Annual No. 3 (1897, p. 98). Also in No. 3 Chanute describes his own experiments with gliders.

Octave Chanute was born in Paris in 1832 but came to the United States when six years old and spent the rest of his life there. He was educated chiefly in New York as a civil engineer and entered upon the practice of his profession in 1849. His work had to do with the construction of railroads and their appurtenances. From 1853 on he was based in Chicago. Not a word is said in the piece in the *Engineering News* of 1891 about his interest in aeronautics, but Gibbs-Smith (1960, pp. 18, 32) tells us that Chanute went abroad in 1875 and met Wenham, and that ever after he read whatever aeronautical literature he could find. In the early nineties Chanute came also upon Lilienthal and was evidently deeply impressed.

He supported Lilienthal's philosophy that it was necessary for experimentors to make full-sized gliders and get into the air themselves in order to have direct flying experience.

In 1896 Chanute did just that. He set up a camp—Camp Chanute —among the sand dunes at the southern end of Lake Michigan, where with a team of coworkers he made an extensive series of experiments in gliding flight. It was essentially an extension of the trail blazed first by Lilienthal, with further development of the motorless glider. We shall return to it a little later.

Chanute's article on "Sailing Flight" in Annual No. 2, with continuation in No. 3, we can consider together. It starts off with these interesting remarks:

> The soaring, or as the French term it more properly, the sailing flight (vol-a-voile) of certain species of birds, that is to say their power of progressing through the air and of translating themselves at will without any flapping action whatever, has always seemed such a mechanical paradox that its very existence has been questioned by those who have not carefully observed the performance of birds.
>
> That a bird should float on outstretched wings high in air for hours, with no muscular exertion whatever save the passive one of keeping his wings rigidly extended, seems so preposterous, so much against all our mechanical instincts and experience of the law that expenditure of energy is necessary to produce locomotion, that even when the feat of soaring is first witnessed, the mind doubts the evidence of the eyes and seeks for some undetected movement to account for the forward advance."
>
> Yet there is nothing more certain than that the soaring birds are supported and propelled without flap of wing. It is generally conceded by observers that they extract from the wind the energy necessary to the performance, but the exact way in which this is done is not at all agreed upon. [Annual, 1896, p. 60.]

Chanute cites considerable literature on birdflight, much of it by French observers, but does not find in any of it the precise measurements that would be necessary to test the authors' theories "by numerical examples and computations." Therefore he determined to gather such data for himself. He gave consideration to several species of soaring birds and found that the greatest of them were inaccessible to close or convenient observation so, like several of his contemporaries in the field, he became a gull-watcher.

His account of his observations on these obliging creatures is vivid and fascinating, and he gives us a classification of the several types of birdflight which is useful for analytical purposes. It is as follows (p. 62):

Rowing Flight	Ordinary progression by flapping	e.g., Ducks, Geese, etc.
Hovering Flight	Remaining over one fixed point	Hummingbirds
Gliding Flight	Sliding over the air on fixed wings	Pigeons, Swallows
Soaring Flight	Sailing with occasional flaps	Hawks, Eagles, etc.
Sailing Flight	Utilizing the wind alone	Excelled in by Vultures, Albatross, etc.

Of this it can be said that the term "rowing flight" has not survived, though one can concede that it is more truly descriptive than flapping. Restricting "gliding flight" to a brief slide through the air, like a boy sliding on ice after a run, is not consistent with modern usage, nor does the distinction between "sailing" and "soaring" seem to contribute very much of importance. Nowadays all airplanes have fixed wings—none can flap—and the only aircraft that can hover is the helicopter. It is interesting that in Chanute's list of examples he did not mention the gull. But it is evident that the gull, although probably a soaring bird by preference; may employ steady flapping flight when it has to go somewhere either in a calm or against the wind.

The gulls, said Chanute, "are absolutely fearless of man." (We'll say they are, and that was before their population explosion, too.) They "will float or fly within 15 to 30 feet of him while performing their evolutions, so that more may be learned of the minute acts of soaring from them in an hour than from months of observations of other birds which soar comparatively high in the air." Chanute, as did Maxim and my father, liked especially to view gulls from the sterns of steamships. The several elements of their flying, which he observed in this manner were, "1st, Starting or getting underway. 2nd, Sailing, or soaring on the wind. 3rd, Balancing or maintaining equilibrium. 4th, Alighting, including stopping the motion."

The take-off from the surface of water, always into the wind, when there is any, Chanute recognized as of necessity a power affair, that is to say, assisted by much flapping. When starting from a high perch, whence a downward glide could be gone into directly, gulls exercise a minimum of flapping, perhaps none, before gaining enough momentum to sustain soaring flight, or, as we would say today, to become airborne. A gull can leave a high perch, he observed, execute a variety of maneuvers, and return to the perch "without furnishing a single stroke of the wing."

Of the act of balancing, he has this to say (pp. 72, 74):

> As the wind varies in intensity, or as the birds wish to rise or to fall, they are constantly changing their angle of incidence and their poise. This is done by advancing or moving to the rear the tips of wings, which are stretched out in a soaring attitude. The movement is slight, and, as the writer suspects, is also automatic. It alters the poise at once fore and aft, and the bird either rises or falls, or he restores the adjustment between his own speed and that of the wind.
>
> If he wants to wheel to one side, a manoeuvre which is done very gracefully, he apparently increases the flexion of the wing on the side to which he wants to turn, the body tilts to that side in consequence of its disturbed balance, and the bird wheels to that side. The same result is also thought to follow the advancing of one wing more than the other, but the writer does not feel that his observations are quite conclusive on that point.
>
> But most of the continual balancing is effected with the head and feet, which, when the wind is at all gusty, are almost constantly in action. The fore and aft balancing is sometimes effected with the head alone, the neck being stretched out or drawn in, or it may be swung from side to side to preserve the transverse equilibrium. Often, however, the legs also come into action. When in full sailing activity in a steady breeze, they are rigidly extended out back under the tail, but when a gust of wind compromises the balance, the legs drop downward, making an angle at the knee, and the feet are adjusted as required to preserve the fore and aft balance, by altering the leverage due to their weight, making thus an adjustable pendule of great efficiency.

How like all this sounds to Lilienthal's description of how he used his own body to stabilize and steer his motorless glider! The several alighting maneuvers of the gull are also described vividly. None of these could be executed by any man-made aircraft.

The continuation of Chanute's article on "Sailing Flight," which appeared in Annual No. 3 (p. 98), is a masterly critique of all the many theories which had been advanced to account for the paradox of the sailing flight of birds, in order to solve the mystery of how the birds "extract energy from the wind." Most of the previous theories were incomplete or fragmentary and without quantitative considerations, and none, so far as Chanute knew, had "published full mathematical computations showing just how the sailing bird is supported and propelled, at the speeds of wind and bird, and at the angles of incidence observed. This last is what he set himself to do, but first he grouped the previous theories and discussed the pros and cons of each. He recognized eight groups as follows:

(1) Assimilates sailing flight to kite action.
(2) Assumes rising trends in the winds.
(3) Supposes different coefficents on front and rear of birds.
(4) Surmises propulsion to be obtained by tacking and circling.
(5) Believes energy to be derived from combination of gravity and wind.
(6) Believes energy to be drawn from the different speeds of wind strata.
(7) Believes energy to be drawn from intermittency of wind force.
(8) Believes energy to be drawn from variations in wind direction.

The kite action theory Chanute attributes to Count d'Esterno, who, in 1864, likened the sailing bird to a kite, in which the weight replaced the action of the string. This is all right as far as it goes, but it fails to show how forward propulsion can be obtained except on the inference that altitude and speed can be interchanged without loss, but that would involve perpetual motion!

Of the important role of ascending currents of air in sailing flight, Chanute seems well convinced, but not quite that it is the whole story. Pénaud[1] as early as 1875 held such a view, and Maxim (1896) was completely convinced of it. There are, Maxim believed, ascending and descending columns of air, generally separated from each other by distances varying from 500 feet to 20 miles, which soaring birds seek out and utilize. This theory compares the soaring bird to a ship sailing close-hauled upon the wind, the force of gravity replacing the effect of the keel.

Chanute seems willing to accept all this, but he is troubled by certain observations seemingly incompatible with it. "Its defect," said he, "is that it is not complete, for careful observation shows that while local ascending trends of wind are not uncommon, they are indeed very frequent, yet sailing birds are sometimes seen to perform their feats perfectly when every test shows the mean wind to be horizontal. I saw for instance, at Tampa, Florida, in February, 1893, three buzzards advance half a mile dead against the wind,

---

[1] Alphonse Pénaud (1850-1880) of France was first to use twisted rubber bands to rotate the propellers of experimental model aircraft. He devised successful small forms of an airplane, ornithopter, and helicopter, and, in 1876 with Paul Gauchot designed a very advanced airplane having a tapered wing, twin propellers, retractable landing gear, and other features later proven practical. His untimely death deprived the science and art of flight the probable further accomplishments of a great genius.

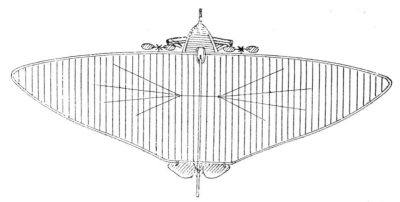

Fig. 11.—Proposed aircraft, designed by Pénaud and Gauchot, 1876.

on a level course, without one single flap, while the smoke from the tall chimney of the adjoining hotel laundry, the top of which was about at the same level as the birds, indicated that the wind was quite horizontal." But we may retort that the buzzards were, presumably, not flying exactly where the smoke was!

We may skip theories under groups 3 and 4 and come to 5, "Combination of Gravity and Wind." The theories advanced under this title, says Chanute, "are based upon the assumption that what we call the 'wind' blows as a practically uniform current of air, regular both in velocity and direction. Many eminent scientists hold, however, that for the sailing bird a uniform current is equivalent to a calm, and they brush aside all the above theories except Pénaud's, upon the ground that it is not physically possible for sailing flight to occur in a uniform current."

A very pertinent letter of Lord Rayleigh, published in *Nature,* April 5, 1883, is quoted as follows (p. 109):

I premise that if we know anything about mechanics, it is certain that a bird, without working his wings, cannot, either in still air or in a uniform horizontal wind, maintain his level indefinitely. For a short time such maintenance is possible at the expense of an initial relative velocity, but this must soon be exhausted." This is gliding flight in the Chanute sense. "Whenever, therefore, a bird pursues his course for some time without working his wings, we must conclude either (1) that the course is not horizontal, (2) that the wind is not horizontal, or (3) that the wind is not uniform. It is probable that the truth is usually represented by (1) or (2); but the question I wish to raise is whether the cause suggested by (3) may not sometimes come into operation.

"This brings us," said Chanute, "to the three groups of theories which suppose energy to be derived by the bird from irregularities in the wind." It seems that there is abundant evidence that the air is never still. There are detectable changes in its velocity and direction of movement. Direction may change in either horizontal planes or vertical, or of course both. The concept is brought out of constant turbulence or unrest, even when seemingly there is a perfect calm. The observation of the behavior of smoke indicates such a condition. Invariably it indicates some degree of billowiness. It is on the presumption of such a state that Langley rested his theory of the "internal work of the wind." Langley had recorded fluctuations in wind velocity, and A. F. Zahm [2] had tabulated changes in wind direction, and these facts, together with experiments of his own in gliding manflight, led Chanute to the concept that the movement of the air is essentially rolling in character. He believed that as it has no inertia "smoke immediately partakes in a large measure the motion of the air, and that its curlings represent the conditions which must be met in free flight."

Having thus reviewed all the theories of sailing flight, of which he had knowledge, Chanute points out that none of them take account of the shape of the birds themselves and that no mention seems to have been made of the cross sections of the wings of sailing or other birds. He had, however, investigated this himself and found a striking difference between soaring and nonsoaring birds. The former, he found, have a downward-projecting lobe at the front, and the radius of curvature at about one-quarter of the distance back of the front edge is sharper on the under side than on the upper side of the wing. Not only do the nonsoarers have thinner wings, but also the curvature is nearly the same on the upper and lower surfaces. These divergences led him to the inference that difference in shape of wings alone may account for the fact that one class of birds can extract energy from the wind which other classes cannot. He made many computations bearing on these matters and finally (p. 127) sums up in these words,

Upon the whole, sailing flight cannot yet be said to be accounted for in all its phases. Its full explanation requires that it shall be shown

---

[2] Albert Francis Zahm (1862-1954), aerodynamicist and author, who developed the first wind tunnel in America, conducted numerous tests of airfoils and fusiforms, headed the Smithsonian's Langley Memorial Laboratory in 1913, was research engineer with the Curtiss Aeroplane Co., 1915-1916; and director of the U.S. Navy Aerodynamic Laboratory from 1916 until he filled the Guggenheim Chair of the Aeronautics Division of the Library of Congress in 1929, retiring in 1945.

how the bird extracts energy from the wind, that the conditions assumed actually exist at the time of the particular evolution considered, and that the manoeuvres of the bird will produce the observed result. This must be supported by quantitative calculations based upon actual observations of the speeds of the wind and of the bird, the angles of incidence with their coefficients, and the distances traversed horizontally and vertically, so that a good deal more is required than has yet been presented in order to carry conviction.

It may be added that the simplest and most satisfactory explanation thus far is that which assumes ascending columns or trends of wind to exist at opportune times and places, but that it does not account for cases in which all observers are agreed that the wind is horizontal.

The contributions of Lilienthal, Maxim, and Chanute are the best meat of Annual No. 2. The volume, however, contains a number of shorter pieces of variable importance.

W. H. Pickering, for example, has a brief note entitled "How a Bird Soars." Pickering was an astronomer, and so his normal field of enquiry was in space, not air. Certainly he has not given any comprehensive answer to the question raised by his title. He does, however, make an interesting point about gusts and claims priority for it (1889). If in the course of circling soaring flight a bird "happens to be travelling at right angles to the wind, when the gust strikes him he will surely be turned round, almost in spite of himself, so as to face the gust. If the bird does face the gust, it will certainly raise him to a higher level" (p. 78).

My father's great interest in kites, in their relation to aeronautics, has been stressed in Chapter III. In view of this, it is not surprising, therefore, to find in Annual No. 2 a block of six papers all related to this subject. The first of these, "The Relation of the Wind to Aeronautics," is by A. Lawrence Rotch, director of Harvard's Blue Hill Meteorological Observatory. It is interesting that Pickering, the astronomer, and Rotch, the meteorologist, were both members of the Boston Aeronautical Society. Rotch had made considerable use of kites, at Blue Hill, primarily for meteorological purposes, not aeronautical. Nevertheless he submits that what the meteorologist can contribute to our knowledge of wind currents is bound to have significance for the aeronaut. The gist of what he has to say is that the atmospheric air is in constant motion, up or down, around the compass, and ever changing in velocity. S. P. Fergusson, also of the Blue Hill Observatory, adds a note on how to construct kites to make them durable and of what materials. The Editor gives consideration to the kite "as an instrument of value." His remarks at this point are essentially those already reported in Chapter III.

J. B. Millet, another member of the Boston Aeronautical Society, has a short paper on the Malay kite, another on the Hargrave. As noted earlier, the former is an irregular diamond-shaped kite, the latter a box kite. Millet found the Malay best in light winds, the Hargrave in strong winds. Sometimes he flew one of each, in tandem, on the same string. More of the same was presented by I. H. Lamson.

The greatest (and last) splash in the field of kites in relation to manflight, known to my father, was made by no less a man than Alexander Graham Bell. From about 1895 on Bell spent much time experimenting with kites at his place at Baddeck on the Bras d'Or lake, Cape Breton, Nova Scotia. He invented the tetrahedral cellular kite, which lent itself to endless development through proliferations of tetrahedra, giving the suggestion of a vast honeycomb. In 1907 he produced a mancarrying kite which on December 6 of that year was towed off the lake carrying Lt. T. E. Selfridge, U. S. Army, aloft for a brief time. The kite was damaged after alighting, but Selfridge escaped, only to suffer a fatal concussion in 1908 in a crash landing after flying as a passenger with Orville Wright. His was the first tragic sacrifice to the development of the powered airplane. In 1909 Bell built still another huge tetrahedral kite, equipped with propeller and engine, which he tried to fly as an aircraft off the frozen lake. It demonstrated some lift but had excessive drag and did not fly. After one more attempt with another tetrahedral aircraft, also unsuccessful, Bell did not pursue the matter further. I can find nothing about Bell's kite research in the Aeronautical Annuals, but I do know that one summer my father went to Baddeck to visit him and observe the tetrahedral kites in action. I cannot remember the year, but it must have been in the late nineties. I can recall, very vividly, hearing my father describe the experience.

Consideration of a valuable paper by A. M. Herring on "Dynamic Flight" will be postponed to Chapter VI because Herring has a second paper in Annual No. 3, and the two can best be discussed together.

The so-called editorial of this second issue of the Annual, which is actually a potpourri of very miscellaneous short bits, opens with an invitation to "Experimenters in All Parts of the World" to send in for publication accounts of their experiments.

The Editor states that he is frequently asked "What about Dr. Langley's recent experiments?" and says that in reply "The only answer now to be made is that Dr. Langley is not yet ready to give the public the results of his recent researches. . . . The reports of his work which have appeared in the public prints during the past year or two have been unauthorized and misleading." Sic.

Next comes an invitation to the "master of some sailing-ship" to bring back "the skins of one or two very large albatrosses." I do not think this ever got any takers. Would the master of a sailing-ship shoot an albatross? Would he have been a reader of the Aeronautical Annual?

A passage on "Motors" comes next. Reference is made to a statement of Maxim's that his experience indicates that "the flight of man is possible, even with a steam engine and boiler." He advises young engineers interested in aviation to explore thoroughly the possibilities of petroleum motors. The Editor says he has been looking into these himself and believes that the current interest in automobiles will accelerate the development of such fuels.

Flapping wings vs. screw propellers also claimed the editorial attention. He repeated the view he had expressed before that whereas rotating parts cannot be part of living organisms, flapping wings are ill suited to mechanical flight.

Next follow some further items on kites, and finally the Editor, in his jocular vein, for a sign-off reverts to the Lilienthal-Maxim line with this:

If Lilienthal and Maxim, each of whom possesses qualifications which the other lacks, were together exiled to a lonely island in the South Seas, with ample commissariat, and plenty of material, machines, tools, and fuel, and then if their ships were burned and they were told to fly home—but I pause,—the Annual isn't a novel: it is a very serious publication, and prithee remember that it *is* an Annual, and that another number will be asking your kind attention about twelve months hence. Till then, adieu.

Chapter VI

THE THIRD ISSUE, 1897

A PROGRESS note by the Editor, for the year 1896, follows the title page of Annual No. 3. "The advance toward the full solution of the problem of manflight," said he, "which was made in the year 1896 was greater than that of any previous year. Saving the sad death of Lilienthal, the chronicler's pen has only good news to tell."

In times past the extreme difficulty of determining what were the best methods of work was the deterrent which kept investigators from entering the field of aeronautics, and consequently the world's workers were comparatively small in number.

Now, this condition of affairs no longer pertains, for the demonstrations of 1896 were such that the best lines for investigators to follow are very clearly marked out. These lines, three in number, distinct, yet convergent, are as follows:

(1) The development of the self-propelled aerodrome.
(2) The development of the motor-less air-sailer.
(3) The development of the motor.

In each of these departments of work there is now a well-defined point of vantage which is accessible to every intelligent experimenter who is inclined to carefully study the ground already traversed, and so to fully understand the results already reached.

The frontispiece of the third Annual was a portrait of a distinguished-looking bearded gentleman, in full academic costume, Samuel Pierpont Langley, Ph.D., LL.D., D.C.L., Secretary of the Smithsonian Institution. The volume opens with a memoir of him by Commander Francis M. Green, U.S.N., Ret., which discloses that Langley was born in 1834 in Roxbury, Massachusetts, and that he graduated from the English High School in Boston in 1851. "As his inclinations tended strongly to mathematical and mechanical pursuits he was not sent to college, and at that time none of the opportunities for higher scientific education now existing at the Massachusetts Institute of Technology and other similar institutions of learning were available for young students." Young Langley, under these circumstances, could find nothing more appropriate to his interests than to enter an architect's office. He actually practiced architecture for some years, but it wasn't really what he wanted. Finally in 1865 he succeeded in getting into astronomy, a subject which had interested him from youth. A succession of academic jobs with advancement then ensued, during which time he made important contributions in the field of solar physics. In 1887 he became Secretary of the Smithsonian Institution, and it was there that he had the opportunity to continue the pursuit of another boyhood interest, flight.

In 1891 and 1893 the Institution published papers by Langley that were to become famous, the first entitled "Experiments in Aero-dynamics" and the second "The Internal Work of the Wind." In 1896 he made successful flights with unmanned powered model "aerodromes" driven by propellers and minute steam engines.

At this point (pp. 8-10) a long quotation from Chanute on Langley is inserted. It is so enlightening on both men that I will requote it in its entirety.

In my judgment the principal contributions thus far made by Doctor Langley to the science of aerodynamics consist in his having given to physicists and searchers firm ground to stand upon concerning the fundamental and much-disputed question of air resistances and reaction.

When I was in Europe, in 1889, I inquired into the state of knowledge on this important question, and found utter disagreement and confusion. There were numerous formulae, promoted by various physicists, but these gave such discordant results that arrangements were being proposed in France to try an entire set of new experiments, with air currents to be procured by an enormous fan-blower. A fair idea of the state of knowledge can be had from Professor Marey's careful work on "Le vol des oiseaux," published in 1890. Oblique pressures were then still generally held to vary according to the Newtonian law, or as the square of the sine of incidence, although this gives but five to ten per cent of the true reactions at acute angles of incidence.

Doctor Langley has shown us, by experiment, the general accuracy of which cannot be questioned, that the empirical (based on experiments) formula of Duchemin is sufficiently correct to calculate the radiations upon planes; so that the French, who had ignored this formula since 1836, now claim its inception and accept it (as they do some wines) *retour d'Amérique*. Doctor Langley has also shown us that the variation of the center of pressure on an inclined plane, observed by Sir George Cayley and by Avanzani as well as by Kummer, follows approximately the law formulated by Jossel, so that now, for the first time, searchers are enabled to calculate the sustaining power, the resistance, and the center of pressure of a plane, with confidence that they are not far wrong; and this, together with the further law, formulated first by Doctor Langley, that within certain limits "the higher speeds are more economical of power than the lower ones," has made it possible to assert that the problem of artificial flight is not insoluble as theretofore affirmed by many of the most eminent scientific men.

Whether Doctor Langley's scientific labors in this department of physics will soon result, like those of the preceding secretaries, in the practical application of his discoveries to the use of mankind, it is perhaps too early to assert positively. I think, myself, that they will so result before many years, but there are so many intricate questions to be solved before commercial success can be achieved that another generation may pass before the problem of flight is fully solved.

Moreover, Doctor Langley's labors and discoveries are by no means over. He has thus far published only the result of his investigations on planes, while saying in the penultimate paragraph of his summary that it is not asserted that planes are the best forms to use. Lilienthal and Phillips have since shown that concave-convex surfaces are more efficient forms, and it is very much to be desired that Doctor Langley shall next publish some data concerning such forms.

The practical development of a scientific truth is somewhat like the growth from a new seed. We recognize the existence of the plant, we ascertain some of its virtues, but we cannot tell its full uses, how soon it will mature, nor how large the tree will be.

It is significant, however, that, prior to the publication of Doctor Langley's work, it was the rare exception to find engineers and scientists of recognized ability who would fully admit *the possibility* of man being able to solve the twenty-century-old problem of aviation. Professor Joseph LeConte, in the *Popular Science Monthly,* of November, 1888, has very recently taken the ground, flatly, "that a pure flying-machine is impossible." This was probably based on the fact that the then-accepted formula of Newton, and the calculation of Napier and other scientists, if correct, rendered the solution practically impossible. Since the publication of "Experiments in Aerodynamics," however, it is the exception to find an intelligent engineer who disputes the *probability* of the eventual solution of the problem of man-flight. Such has been the change in five years. Incredulity has given way, interest has been aroused in the scientific question, a sound basis has been furnished for experiment, and practical results are being evolved by many workers. Much remains to be discovered concerning curved surfaces, with which alone practical flight is likely to be achieved, but when this is accomplished it is probable, in my judgment, that the beginning of the solution will be acknowledged to date back to the publication of Doctor Langley's book, and that he will be distinguished as Secretary Henry is now with regard to the development of electrical appliances.

Langley's article in Annual No. 3 is entitled "Story of Experiments in Mechanical Flight." He starts off by saying: "The subject of flight interested me as long ago as I can remember anything, but it was a communication from Mr. Lancaster, read at the Buffalo meeting of the American Association for the Advancement of Science, in 1886 which aroused my then dormant attention to the subject."

His approach to the problem of manflight was, like Maxim's, from the beginning, through the development of motor-driven aircraft. Having found the literature, from his point of view, rather barren, he set about to find out for himself and in his own way "what amount of mechanical power was requisite to sustain a given weight in the air, and make it advance at a given speed." This seemed to him to be "an inquiry which must necessarily precede any attempt at mechanical flight."

His aeronautical experiments began in 1887 at the Allegheny Observatory near Pittsburgh with the construction of a whirling arm, 60 feet in diameter, driven by a steam engine. To the outer end of this arm planes of different shapes were mounted so that their angles of incidence could be changed and their air pressures and other reactions measured at various speeds. The results of his studies with this equipment were published by the Smithsonian Institution in 1891, under the title "Experiments in Aerodynamics." The whirling arm had been used by various investigators before Langley, and the wind tunnel, a much better instrument for aerodynamical testing, had been introduced as early as 1871 by Wenham and Browning. From the results of his experiments Langley concluded that one horsepower rightly applied could sustain over 200 pounds in the air at a horizontal velocity of somewhat over 60 feet per second. This being true, he concluded further that mechanical flight was, therefore, possible with engines they were able to make at that time, that is to say, if the art of properly applying the power produced, could be achieved.

In 1889 Langley continued his efforts to acquire the art of flight, by the ingenious method of testing stuffed birds upon his "whirling arm." A frigatebird, a condor, and an albatross were so tested. The results were disappointing and led to the conclusion that a stuffed bird could not be made to soar except at speeds much greater than what serves to sustain a living one. And subsequently experiments with actual flying models showed that for a given sustaining surface much greater power must be exerted to carry a given weight than nature finds it necessary to employ.

From 1891 to 1896 Langley made an extensive series of experiments with flying models. He made the extraordinary etymological error of calling all these "aerodromes." The Greek word δρομος can mean a race course. It can properly be applied to an airport, and has been, but not to an aircraft. However, while discussing Langley we may use it in the sense he intended. He began experimenting with rubber-driven models of the Pénaud type but soon decided that the length of flight possible with them was so short as to be unsatisfactory for research, and so he presently switched to steam. The construction of a steam-driven aerodrome he recognized as a formidable task, but after investigating the capacities of condensed air, carbonic acid gas, electricity, hot-water engines, inertia motors, and gas engines, he decided to proceed with the construction of a suitable steam engine. It is interesting to us today that he made no mention at that time of gasoline! In 1901, however, he came to it, but of that more later.

Langley's series of experiments with his *aerodromes* was an Odyssey of frustration after frustration with final (at least partial) success. Toward the close of 1893 a model from which the *bugs* of previous ones were believed to have been removed was ready for actual trial in the air. But now there arose a new problem, not faced before, namely that of launching, and thereby ensued another "long story of delay and disappointment" over how to obtain a successful launch.

For his launching device, Langley unhappily chose the catapult principle which involved shooting the aerodrome off a houseboat moored in the Potomac. It was not until after a series of disasters had occurred that the *bugs* were got out of the launching device also. Late in 1895 "success finally came."

Langley's article leaves us with that admission, but it is followed immediately by an eyewitness account of the flights of the successful *aerodromes* by no less a one than Alexander Graham Bell. For over a year Bell had observed flights of Langley's aerodromes, but

it was one by "Aerodrome No. 5" on May 6, 1896, that he describes
in detail. The central body, or fuselage of this aircraft was built
entirely of metal; the wings and tail were wooden frames covered
with cloth.

Bell's description of the flight of May 6, 1896, is as follows:

Through the courtesy of Dr. S. P. Langley, Secretary of the
Smithsonian Institution, I have had, on various occasions, the
privilege of witnessing his experiments with aerodromes, and
especially the remarkable success attained by him in experiments
made upon the Potomac river on Wednesday, May 6, 1896, which
led me to urge him to make public some of these results.

I had the pleasure of witnessing the successful flight of some of
these aerodromes more than a year ago, but Dr. Langley's reluctance
to make the results public at that time prevented me from asking
him, as I have done since, to let me give an account of what I saw.

On the date named two ascensions were made by the aerodrome,
or so-called "flying-machine," which I will not describe here further
than to say that it appeared to me to be built almost entirely of
metal, and driven by a steam engine which I have understood was
carrying fuel and a water supply for a very brief period, and which
was of extraordinary lightness.

The absolute weight of the aerodrome, including that of the
engine and all appurtenances, was, as I was told, about 25 pounds,
and the distance from tip to tip of the supporting surfaces was, as I
observed, about 12 or 14 feet. The method of propulsion was by
aerial screw-propellers, and there was no gas or other aid for lifting
it in the air except its own internal energy.

On the occasion referred to, the aerodrome, at a given signal,
started from a platform about 20 feet above the water, and rose at
first directly in the face of the wind, moving at all times with
remarkable steadiness, and subsequently swinging around in large
curves of, perhaps, a hundred yards in diameter, and continually
ascending until its steam was exhausted, when, at a lapse of about
a minute and a half, and at a height which I judged to be between
80 and 100 feet in the air, the wheels ceased turning, and the
machine, deprived of the aid of its propellers, to my surprise did
not fall, but settled down so softly and gently that it touched the
water without the least shock, and was in fact immediately ready
for another trial.

In the second trial, which followed directly, it repeated in nearly
every respect the actions of the first, except that the direction of its
course was different. It ascended again in the face of the wind,
afterwards moving steadily and continually in large curves accompanied with a rising motion and a lateral advance. Its motion was,
in fact, so steady, that I think a glass of water on its surface would

have remained unspilled. When the steam gave out again, it repeated for a second time the experience of the first trial when the steam had ceased, and settled gently and easily down. What height it reached at this trial I cannot say, as I was not so favorably placed as in the first; but I had occasion to notice that this time its course took it over a wooded promontory, and I was relieved of some apprehension in seeing that it was already so high as to pass the tree-tops by 20 or 30 feet. It reached the water 1 minute and 31 seconds from the time it started, at a measured distance of over 900 feet from the point at which it rose.

This, however, was by no means the length of its flight. I estimated from the diameter of the curve described, from the number of turns of the propellers as given by the automatic counter, after due allowance for slip, and from other measures, that the actual length of flight on each occasion was slightly over 3,000 feet. It is at least safe to say that each exceeded half an English mile.

From the time and distance it will be noticed that the velocity was between 20 and 25 miles an hour, in a course which was taking it constantly "up hill." I may add that on a previous occasion I have seen a far higher velocity attained by the same aerodrome when its course was horizontal.

I have no desire to enter into detail further than I have done, but I cannot but add that it seems to me that no one who was present on this interesting occasion could have failed to recognize that the practicability of mechanical flight had been demonstrated. [Annual, 1897, pp. 26-27.]

Following Bell there is a page by the Editor giving more detailed specifications of Aerodrome No. 5, together with scale drawings of the same. Undoubtedly these were obtained directly from Langley. "In action," the Editor says, "the boiler evaporates about one pound of water per minute. Flights could be greatly lengthened by adding a condenser and using the water over and over again, but as Dr. Langley says, the time for that will come later."

It is believed that Langley had decided to give up his experiments after the successful flights of 1896, but in 1898 he was asked by the President of the United States to construct a full-sized, man-carrying aerodrome, for it was thought that it might have military usefulness. Langley consented to do this, but first he built a quarter-sized model powered with a gasoline engine. This had the distinction of being, in 1901, the first gasoline-powered airplane ever to fly. The full-sized edition was ready for trial in 1903. Two attempts were made over the Potomac (October 7 and December 8, 1903), with a human pilot aboard. In both cases the launching apparatus failed to release the aerodrome as intended and the craft went into the river. The pilot, Charles M. Manly, was not injured. After these misfortunes the Government lost interest and withdrew its support, and that was the end of Langley's attempts to achieve mechanical flight. The use of catapult launching was a factor in his undoing. If, as Gibbs-Smith suggests, he had used a wheeled undercarriage and a flat field he could safely have made as many tests and adjustments as he pleased. But this is much easier to see now than in Langley's day.

For a present-day estimate of Langley, I have been fortunate enough to receive the following in a personal letter from Professor Hunsaker.

Langley's powered models flew over the Potomac with "inherent stability," for long flights. This may be the "break through" that Lanchester and Pénaud foretold with flying toys. Also, Langley had the most advanced light power plant designed and built for him by his young engineer, Charles Manly. Manly's engine could have made Langley's machine fly, if successfully launched.

Langley was no engineer and was off base in expecting an inherently stable airplane to be steered like a boat. The Wrights invented control about three axes. Planes have been flown with horizontal and vertical rudders only, but are no good in rough air, or for landing on a windy day.

We now return to Chanute and learn of his own experiences during experiments in the field. Under the title "Recent Experiments in Gliding Flights," he tells (p. 30) of the work done at Camp Chanute among the "desert sand hills" at the southern end of Lake Michigan, thirty miles from Chicago, in the summers of 1896 and 1897. It is a very vivid and personal account in which we see man's advance toward flying in the making.

After having, for a number of years, studied the physical principles underlying flight, and having extensively reviewed the experiments of others, Chanute decided that the actual achievement of artificial flight by man involved the study of at least ten separate problems which he listed as follows:

(1) The resistance and supporting power of air.
(2) The motor, its character and energy.
(3) The instrument for obtaining propulsion.
(4) The form and kind of apparatus.
(5) The extent of sustaining surfaces.
(6) The material and texture of the apparatus.

(7) The maintenance of the equilibrium.

(8) The guidance in any desired direction.

(9) The starting up under all conditions (in modern parlance, take-off).

(10) The alighting safely anywhere.

Man must devise means, he said, for observing and mastering all these conditions. Today (1963) it may be said that all have been accomplished except Nos. 9 and 10. The "all" of No. 9 and the "anywhere" of No. 10 are still not within the picture for an airplane, although helicopters, VTOL (vertical take-off and landing), and convertiplanes have greatly extended the flexibility of aircraft.

The terrain selected for the field experiments seems to have been ideal. The sandhills had been piled up by the wind blowing sand from the beach. At the point chosen they rose to about 70 feet above the lake and slanted in every direction of the compass so that it was always possible to take off into the wind. The site also had the advantage of extreme remoteness which afforded the necessary privacy. Chanute had no desire to be invaded by the press or curiosity seekers.

Chanute's party included, besides himself, A. M. Herring and W. P. Butusov, both of whom had had previous experience with gliders, and A. M. Avery, electrician and carpenter. They went into camp, for the first time, on June 22, 1896, and during their stay in the sandhill region made many successful glides with several types of gliders. This was true experimental research, for they observed each flight with scientific precision, to discover errors in both construction and operation of each model, and at once took steps to correct them.

Herring had previously built himself a Lilienthal apparatus and made gliding flights with it (see pl. 6). This he rebuilt for Chanute and also constructed a new one after Chanute's own design. About 100 glides were made with the former, but evidently considerable discontent with it developed, and finally on June 29, it was decided to discard it, and it was accordingly broken up.

"This decision," said Chanute (p. 35), "was most unfortunately justified on the 10th of the succeeding August, when Herr Lilienthal met his death while experimenting with a machine based on the same principle, but with two superposed sets of wings.[1] This deplorable accident removed the man who has hitherto done most

---

[1] Chanute was wrong. It was a monoplane glider.

to show that human flight is probably possible, who was the first in modern times to endeavor to imitate the soaring birds with full-sized apparatus, and who was so well equipped in every way that he probably would have accomplished final success if he had lived." [2]

Having abandoned the Lilienthal design, the group proceeded forthwith to test Chanute's. This differed from the former in that the effort to achieve stability and direction was undertaken by movements of the wing rather than by shifting the position of the body of the aviator. The design was indeed something new and different, providing as it did for 12 wing panels (each 6 feet long and 3 wide) arranged in pairs both sides of center and above one another. Each was pivoted at its root to a central frame, so that it could move fore and aft, this action being restrained by springs. After making a few glides with this arrangement "a series of changes was tried to ascertain what was the best grouping and the best distance between the wings in order to obtain the maximum lift and the greatest steadiness. The paths of the wind currents in each arrangement of the wings were indicated by liberating bits of down in front of the machine, and, under their guidance, six permutations were made, each of which was found to produce an improvement in actual gliding flight over its predecessors."

In the final arrangement to which these experiments led, five pairs of wings had "gradually accumulated at the front, and the operator was directly under them, while the sixth pair of wings formed a tail at the rear; and being mounted so as to flex upward behind in flight, preserved the fore and aft balance." This form of the apparatus was found to be steady, safe, and manageable in winds up to 20 miles per hour. About 100 glides were made with it, after which Chanute and his associates packed up and returned to Chicago for shop work. It was Chanute's feeling that during the two weeks' experience he had learned more about the practical requirements of flight than in all the years of the study of the principles involved, and of experiments. "The latter," he said (p. 37), "are instructive . . . but they do not reveal all the causes for the vicissitudes which occur in the wind. They do not explain why models seldom pursue exactly the same course, why they swerve to right or left, why they oscillate, or why they upset. When a man is riding on a machine, however, and his safety depends upon the observance of all the conditions, he keenly heeds what is happening

[2] There are two articles by Lilienthal in Annual No. 3 and a memorial. See pages 75, 84, and 92 of that issue. Also, Chanute should have identified Lilienthal as "one of the first." Lilienthal had several predecessors in gliding flight.

to him, and gets entirely new and more accurate conceptions of the character of the element which he is seeking to master."

One of the chief things learned was the inconstancy of the wind. As shown by Zahm, Rotch, and others, it is continually varying both in direction and velocity. *The wind gusts also,* so it seemed to Chanute, *seem to come in as rolling waves*—that is to say, rotating at higher speed than the general forward movement.

In Chicago they reconstructed the first glider of Chanute and built another on a different principle. This latter started off as what we would call a triplane but, after trial the lowest plane was removed so that it became a biplane. "Aerocurve," Chanute called this glider because its wings were not flat but slightly curved—concavity down, of course. This was to become Chanute's final and best glider. One may call it *the* Chanute glider.

A third apparatus was built after a plan of Butusov's. It closely resembled one experimented with by Le Bris between 1855 and 1868. Le Bris had been a sea captain, and during his voyages he observed the flight of the albatross. He patterned his aircraft after that bird. Gibbs-Smith (1960) regards him as one of the earliest pioneers in practical flying. Certainly he was ahead of his time in the matter of launching. He had his machine placed in a cart and driven along a road, taking off in this way. Apparently he did get airborne in at least one short glide. It is very interesting that Butusov, like Le Bris, had been a sailor, and done some albatross watching himself. Moreover, Du Temple, who in the 1850's succeeded in constructing a model aeroplane powered first by clockwork and later by steam, which took off under its own power, sustained itself, and landed safely, was also a sea-faring man—a French naval officer. According to Gibbs-Smith, Du Temple's apparatus was the first powered aeroplane to sustain itself in the air.

The three machines being ready, one reconstructed, two newly built, the Chanute party repaired again to the sandhills on August 20, 1896. This time they went five miles farther east where the hills were higher and the seclusion greater. The company was the same with the addition of a young surgeon, Dr. Ricketts, who found nothing professional to do but got a good experience as cook!

The first trial was with the so-called aerocurve. A few glides were made with it in its triplane form. Then it was reduced to a biplane which became its permanent form. In two weeks' time, "scores and scores of glides were made with this machine." "It was found steady, easy to handle before starting, and under good control when under way—a motion of the operator's body of not over two inches proving as effective as a motion of 5 or more inches in the Lilienthal machine." Sometimes a point was reached during a glide higher than the take-off. "The machine made steady flights and easy landings, and was not once broken in action." It was considered safer and more manageable than the Lilienthal machine, which they had tested.

Chanute's remarks about the limitation of their flying are of interest:

> We performed nothing like continuous soaring with any of the machines. The fluctuations of the wind were entirely too irregular to be availed of; for a wind gust, which tossed a machine up, was almost immediately succeeded by a lull which let it down again. If we had had a long, straight ridge, bare of trees at its summit, and a suitable wind blowing at right angles thereto, we would have attempted to have sailed horizontally along the top of the ridge, transversely to the ascending current. This maneuvre is frequently and easily performed by the soaring birds over the edge of a belt of trees. They ride across the face of the ascending aerial billow, decomposing its upward trend into propulsion as well as support. The feat should be performable by man, and should, in my judgment, be attempted before circling flight is tried. It requires, of course, that the equilibrium shall be first mastered, and also that the angle of flight shall be flatter than with our machines. [Annual, 1897, pp. 46-47.]

Finally the Butusov apparatus was given a trial. The Chanute-designed craft, like the Lilienthal before them, were all light enough to enable the operator, for his take-off, to run with them until air-borne. The Butusov, however, was too heavy for that. It became necessary, therefore, to build an inclined trestle for its launching. The fixed position of the trestle slowed up the experimenting because it involved waiting for a favorable wind. A few launchings were accomplished, and the machine became airborne for brief moments. It appeared to be "moderately stable," but it glided at too steep an angle to be useful without alteration. The season then being too far advanced [September 27, 1896], it was decided to return to the city.

"Such," said Chanute, "were the experiments. They occupied an aggregate of seven or eight weeks in the field, they were carried on without the slightest accident to the operators, and they made manifest several important conclusions."

These were: (1) It is reasonably safe to experiment with full-sized machines, if the writings of Lilienthal be previously studied.

(2) Experiments with full-sized machines, carrying a man, are likely to be more instructive than experiments with models. (3) It is probably possible to evolve an apparatus with automatic stability in the wind, but that in order to do so there must be some moving parts, apart from the man, in order to restore the balance as often as it is compromised. (4) The problem of automatic stability will be most easily worked out with a light apparatus, so light as to enable the operator to carry it with ease, and so arranged as to enable him to use his legs in landing. (5) It will require a good deal of experimenting to adjust the working parts, before it will be safe to try to perform soaring feats in the wind. (6) The incessant fluctuations of the wind, which so greatly complicate the problem of maintaining automatic stability, probably result from the rotary action of its billows. (Annual, 1897, p. 52.)

In his final paragraph, Chanute says that he does not know how much further he will carry these experiments. They were all made wholly at his own expense in the hope of gaining scientific knowledge and without expectations of pecuniary profit. Commercial flying, he thought, was a long way off. It would have to be achieved by a process of evolution.

Chanute, however, went again to the sandhills for field work in 1897. My father went to Camp Chanute that summer and observed the gliding. I vividly recall his enthusiastic accounts of it upon his return. I have in my possession a letter of his dated September 15, 1897, in which he says, "I am on my way to visit Mr. Chanute in Chicago and to see his experiments with gliding machines." Between 1897 and the time of his death in 1910, Chanute played the role of elder statesman in aeronautics, giving much moral support and counsel to the Wright brothers. His last contribution, "Recent Progress in Aviation," was published the year of his death in the Annual Report of the Smithsonian Institution.

Octave Chanute, in his important history of aviation, *Progress in Flying Machines,* 1894, makes the following comment on my father's dream aircraft of those days.

A somewhat similar proposal is made in a pamphlet published in 1891 by Mr. James Means of Boston, but he gives only a scanty glimpse of the arrangement by which he thinks the problem could be solved. He proposes one screw on a vertical shaft, sustaining a car, with a pair of widely-extended vertical planes, to prevent rotation of the apparatus, and concludes by saying: "If you want to bore through air, the best way is to set up your borer and bore."

Our knowledge of the action of aerial screws is almost wholly experimental; and it would seem, in the present chaotic state of theory as applied to the screw, as if this remark of Mr. Means was almost as comprehensive and reliable as anything on this subject of aerial screws which has been published up to the present time. The writer feels quite certain that it contains in a condensed form as much reliable detailed solid information as several mathematical articles of considerable complexity which he has consulted, and it will be seen, by closely analyzing Mr. Means' suggestion, that after its entire adoption in the spirit in which it is made, there would be little left to be desired in the development of aerial screws.

Two papers by Chanute's collaborator, A. M. Herring, an engineer, appear in the Annuals. In No. 2 there is "Dynamic Flight" and in No. 3 "Recent Advances toward a Solution of the Problem of the Century," i.e., manflight.

In the first of these the author stresses the vital need, in the advancement of a new science, for systematic series of experiments made by thoroughly competent investigators. "In aeronautics until very recently, these have been conspicuous by their scarcity. There is, however, enough knowledge of the action of air on planes to make it easy in a theoretical consideration "to prove that dynamic flight is not only possible with light and powerful machinery, but that the power required at high speed is so small as nearly to bring flight within the limit of man's unaided strength. But," he added very wisely, "theoretical considerations omit many of the conditions which have to be met in practice. In the actual machine the conditions which arise cause a necessary waste of power many times greater than that originally allowed in even very liberal estimates."

Herring started off with models in order by experiment to find and eliminate faults in their design. He was early interested in stability and for a while tried pendulums, as did my father, but soon abandoned them. The best solution of the stability problem he said, "is to be found in such surfaces, and their arrangement relative to each other, as will remain undisturbed by the changes in the wind. This, which has been the object of very much of my experimental work, for a long time seemed almost a hopeless task, but I believe it has at last been attained—not perfectly, but nearly so."

From very early in his work Herring was interested in power. Power-driven aircraft were undoubtedly his final objectives. In 1890 he built a model, powered by a twisted rubber band, which gave a very creditable performance. We might describe it as a monoplane type of aircraft, about 4 feet from wing tip to wing tip, with a horizontal and vertical tail assembly, and two propellers,

16 inches in diameter, one pusher, one tractor, arranged in tandem. It was very light, and could make flights up to 135 feet in length at a speed of 12 to 16 feet per second. It was a very impressive device, at least as judged by its creator's account of it in the Annual. In 1891, Herring made a similar machine, this one powered by a tiny steam engine. This also gave excellent results. With it he made studies of its mechanical efficiency, lifting power in relation to area of supporting surfaces, expenditure of energy, etc.

In 1894 he constructed three full-sized gliders in order to learn airmanship, and also to determine the amount of power required to maintain a man and machine in flight.

Herring ended this first paper (p. 101) with a prophesy which I find admirable: "Many of the foremost workers on the flying-machine problem are firm believers in the possibility of man learning to soar by utilizing the forces of the wind, as the birds do, but for my own part, if this be ever accomplished, I believe it will be long after the air has been navigated by steam. This, in spite of the difficulties which a few years ago seemed unsurmountable, is not only a probability but is apparently a certainty of the near future." This prophesy, if we substitute "power" for "steam," has just about been fulfilled.

In his second article Herring stresses the importance of solving the problem of manflight. Briefly he lists the highspots of what had been done to the time of his writing. Like my father he took a

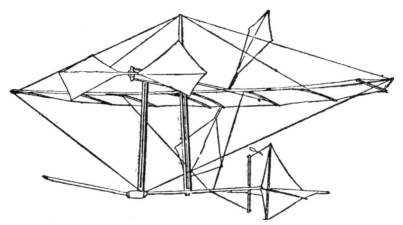

Fig. 12.—Model airplane, made and flown by Augustus Herring with push-pull propellers, powered by twisted rubber bands. Dr. A. F. Zahm described the distance flown by one of these models as "all the way across the street."

dim view of balloons, and although he could see theoretical value in helicopters he doubted whether they could be given enough power to be useful. The ornithopter principle he thought offered nothing practical.

He was deeply interested in the problem of stability and bent his efforts to develop devices which would preserve the equilibrium of an aircraft automatically. He did considerable work in the Lilienthal type machines which he built himself and in which he made several improvements, among others in the manner in which the weight of the operator was carried. Lilienthal rested on his elbows, Herring on bars under his armpits. The center of gravity was thus lowered, and the operator had more freedom of motion. He emphasizes the gain which Lilienthal made by switching to "double deckers." In other words, he moved to the biplane.

Herring also made extensive studies with the Chanute glider and added stabilizing devices to it. He also began making glides with extra weight aboard with a view to discovering whether the time had come to add an engine. He even built a light gasoline engine, which showed clearly where he was aiming, but I cannot find evidence of its having functioned aloft in an aeroplane.

Herring paid hearty tribute to Chanute to whom he was doubtless very useful.

Annual No. 3 contains a memorial to Lilienthal, translated from the German of Karl Müllenhoff. It was from this that I drew the biographical data presented on pages 49-51. There are also three other brief items of Lilienthal's in Annual No. 3, also translated from the German originals.

The first of these, "Our Teachers in Sailing Flight" (p. 85) is a choice bit of aerodynamical ornithology. Our teachers are, of course, the birds, and they have taught us very much, but Lilienthal's statement that "all perplexities concerning light motors, and specu-lations on the amount of power required for flying, are relegated to the background by the fact that the power of the wind alone is sufficient to effect any kind of independent flight" is somewhat too broad. If he had omitted the words "any kind" it would be accepta-ble. It is the soaring birds, of course, with which he is concerned. He concedes that the turkey buzzard and the gull are good instruc-tors but gives the palm to the stork, which lives so intimately with man in the lowlands of northern Germany. "Being convinced," said Lilienthal, "that Father Longlegs is just made for our instructor in flying, I kept a great many young storks, some years ago, whose attempts at flying have given me many explanations in flying technics. As soon, however, as their proficiency extended to soaring, when rising above the tree-tops, they felt the magnificent bearing-effect of the wind, and ventured into higher regions, they joined other wild storks, and so ended all further observation."

In one small village, however, where there were storks' nests on most of the roofs he made many observations. When the wind in the lower strata had "a velocity of six to eight meters" (sic) the storks did not move their wings at all. They soared close above the house tops or high in the sky, in any direction they pleased, with the wind, against the wind, or sideways. They circled to ascend to higher air strata. They only flapped when moving between houses or trees, that is, in places protected from the wind.

The second piece, which is an extract from a longer article, is entitled "At Rhinow." In this Lilienthal describes (pp. 92-93) a crash from which he learned the necessity of extreme care in making changes in air-sailing machines. He wrote:

> In my experiments made before Easter from the still higher mountains near Rhinow, I perceived that I had to bear with the upper part of my body a good deal towards the back to prevent my shooting forward in the air with the apparatus. During a gliding flight taken from a great height this was the cause of my coming into a position with my arms outstretched, in which the centre of gravity lay too much to the back; at the same time I was unable—owing to fatigue—to draw the upper part of my body again towards the front. As I was sailing at the height of about 65 feet with a velocity of about 35 miles per hour, the apparatus, overloaded in the rear, rose more and more, and finally shot, by means of its *vis viva,* vertically upwards. I gripped tight hold, seeing nothing but the blue sky and little white clouds above me, and so awaited the moment when the apparatus would capsize backwards, possibly ending my sailing attempts forever. Suddenly, however, the apparatus stopped in its ascent, and, going backward again in a downward direction, described a short circle and steered with the rear part again upwards, owing to the horizontal tail which had an upward slant; then the machine turned bottom upwards and rushed with me vertically towards the earth from a height of about 65 feet. With my senses quite clear, my arms and my head forward, still holding the apparatus firmly with my hands, I fell towards a greensward; a shock, a crash, and I lay with the apparatus on the ground.

Can this be beaten for intrepidity? Lilienthal escaped with minor injuries, and the machine was not damaged at all. All during the moments he was facing death he was making scientific observations of great importance. He attributed his escape to an elastic recoil-bar which he had attached for the first time before that very flight!

The third Lilienthal item is on "The Best Shapes for Wings." "The primitive idea," he said, "that the desired effects could be produced by means of flat wings has now been abandoned, for we know that the curvature of birds' wings gives extraordinary advantages in flying. . . . The most important point as regards this form of the wing will always be the curvature of its profile." In birds, owing to the position of the bones of the wing, the front edge of the wing is thickened, but it can be shown that this thickening produces a favorable effect in sailing flight.

A paper by E. C. Huffaker on "The Way of an Eagle in the Air," I find especially intriguing. Actually the word eagle, having been used in the title, appears nowhere in the text—hawks and vultures, yes—but no eagles. The eagle is used, no doubt, symbolically, as the king of the great soaring birds.

Huffaker appears to have been a well-versed aerodynamical ornithologist and also an experimentalist. He has given us a clear account of a very extensive series of studies with model gliders, aimed at throwing light on how these birds accomplish their mastery of the air. He goes along in general with the theory that the soarers gain altitude by taking advantage of rising air currents. If I understand him right, he suggests that in vigorous flapping these birds may at times create down drafts which on striking the earth may give rise to up-currents which the bird may then use in his take-off. It sounds to me a bit like a boot-strap operation, and yet he may have envisioned what a modern helicopter pilot calls "ground effect," which is an increase in lift due to bounce-back reaction from the ground at low altitudes.

For his experimental work Huffaker constructed model gliders which he called "artificial birds" and gives working drawings and descriptions of them. With them, he says, he made thousands of experiments. Observation of flights and readjustment of surfaces, as indicated by performance, constituted his method of procedure. He claimed to have obtained glides as long as 1800 feet with a fall not exceeding one in ten when no wind was blowing. The model had a wingspread of 40 inches and area of two square feet. It carried 11 ounces of lead in the form of plates nailed to the body. His chief problem turned out to be lateral stability. "A model properly balanced," he said, "should maintain at all times a position approximately horizontal, under varying wind velocities." He succeeded in this respect to such a degree that, as he described the glides, models could be carried to a great height by strong winds upon a hillside, and rise and fall without careening or plunging. "I do not doubt," he said, "that it is possible to construct a model which would remain in the air an indefinitely long time." It would seem to me that Huffaker approached more closely, with his models, the performance of the soaring birds themselves than anyone else up to his time of writing. He foresaw, indeed, the man-carrying motor-less glider of today!

A short article by Hiram Maxim on "Screw-propellers Working in Air" follows next. In this study he determined the thrust and slip of air-screws under various conditions—very important basic knowledge, but rather technical for the general reader. More for the light it throws on Maxim than on air-screws, I will quote his final paragraph:

> In regard to future experiments, I would say that the gun business has been very lively during the last year,[3] that I have had much new experimental work to do, and that I have had very little time to devote to flying machines. I, however, have obtained very large premises with plenty of room, where I hope to resume experimental work as soon as I have time.

And finally we find a very important contribution by Percy S. Pilcher on "Gliding Experiments." Pilcher was an English engineer inspired to experiment with full-sized gliders by Lilienthal. Like Lilienthal he gave his life (1899) in the crash of one of his own gliders. Gibbs-Smith (1960) speaks of him as "the pioneer who might well have made a practical powered aeroplane before the Wright brothers." He had aimed in that direction for a couple of years or so before his death, and had actually built a motor, but had not completed the aircraft in which it was to be installed. He mentions this in the article in Annual No. 3. Very sportingly he tells that he had seen photographs of Lilienthal's apparatus by 1895, the year in which he constructed his first machine, but that he purposely did not go to see Lilienthal until he had made his own, so that he would not copy his details. Up to the time of his writing he had made three machines, and a fourth, which was to be powered, was being built. Like Huffaker, with his models, he found that one could dispense with a vertical rudder, but that a horizontal one is indispensable. He learned the dangers of the dihedral angle

---

[3] Maxim had invented a machinegun and was at that time receiving orders for them from many nations.

in aeroplane wings, and following Cayley he employed the wheeled undercarriage and made some take-offs by being towed into a light breeze on it. There can be no doubt that Pilcher played an important role in the progress of manflight.

A "Miscellany" of sorts is appended to Annual No. 3. Some of the highspots in it are: Compressed CO_2 with which to power model aircraft—a ballistic study of various objects shot through the air—description of a keeled kite—a measurement of the speed of flying ducks (about 50 miles an hour).

A short dissertation on the albatross from Alfred Newton's *Dictionary of Birds* compared the wing design of that bird with other soarers and cited Professor Hutton as disagreeing with the Duke of Argyll and Dr. Pettigrew that the extremely long and narrow wings of the albatross are the best for soaring flight. The vulture and the condor, with much broader wings, soar extremely well, also.

There is also a most interesting quote from Lilienthal, dated April 17, 1896, less than four months before his death:

> I am now engaged in constructing an apparatus in which the position of the wings can be changed during flight in such a way that the balancing is not effected by changing the position of the centre of gravity of the body. In my opinion this means considerable progress, as it will increase the safety. This will probably cause me to give up again the double sailing surfaces as it will do away with the necessity which led me to adopt them.

The most important item in the Miscellany in my view is a statement of Albert Ross (not albatross, although the latter might have made the statement too if he could talk!), as follows: "If a bird can soar (i.e., gain altitude without expending energy from within) in a moving horizontal wind, then he can also soar in a calm, for when he is in flight in the wind referred to, he is in a relative calm as soon as the resistance of the wind has overcome his inertia. There must be air *resistance* against his wings if he is to derive energy from the air, and when his inertia has been overcome (if we understand the properties of the air) there can be no resistance against his wings, excepting that which is caused by the gravity of the bird, and gravity has never been found to give back to a body any more energy than that of which it deprives it." I almost cheered when I came upon this statement, the truth of which seems obvious. I had been searching for such a statement throughout my reading of the Annuals, but this was the first time I found it! A corollary to it had been expressed by my father, in his "Problem of Manflight" pamphlet of 1894, thus—"There is no calm for the aeroplane. Give it altitude and it can gain velocity, and velocity gives the wind of flight."

Annual No. 3, like the previous two, closes with an Editorial. In this the Editor starts off with one of his pet subjects, the importance of studying flying models. His major reason for favoring these is humanitarianism. "We have now reached," said he, "the stage of experiment where it is necessary to use all possible persuasion to keep reasonably near *terra firma* those persons who have nothing but the courage of ignorance to equip them for ventures in the air."

He lists subjects which can suitably be studied by means of model aircraft, e.g., automatic devices for preserving equilibrium, disposition of surfaces, placing of screws, curves of surfaces, relation of weight to area, relation of power to weight, effects of elasticity in sustaining surfaces.

In view of the world situation today, the following words of the Editor cannot but promote nostalgia:

> I have tried to make a strong plea in behalf of the flying model. It seems to me that, whatever its limitations may be, it can lessen the risks to life and limb. We are fortunate that we live in a time of peace, when such things are the first to be thought of. If we were at war, it would be necessary to call for recruits who would risk their lives in making glides from captive balloons, for if we did not do that some other nation would, and when bags of explosives are dropped into the smoke-stacks of multi-million dollar battleships, it will cause a revision of opinions concerning the balance of power of the world.

Next follows a passage on motive power for flying models, followed by an encomium on certain meteorological research being done at the Blue Hill Meteorological Observatory.

Then there is a note on a man-carrying glider designed by Gustav Koch in Germany. An important feature was that his design provided a horizontal position for his pilot, a position proposed earlier by Wenham, and later used by the Wright brothers.

It was toward the close of this Editorial that I found, for the first time, any mention by the Editor of the financial support of research. There were no grants in aid, from either government or foundations. Langley had had a grant from the U. S. Government, but this was exceptional, and it will be recalled that it was not renewed when the Government lost faith in him. Chanute has told us that he

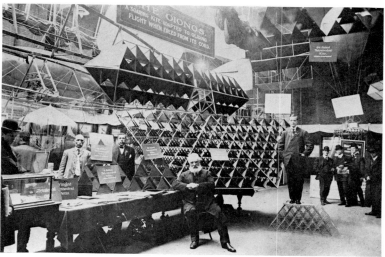

PLATE 13.—Alexander Graham Bell, 1847-1922, exhibiting his tetrahedral kites at an aeronautical show in New York City, 1906. (Photo from William J. Hammer collection.) Upper: Bell's Cygnet II, powered kite, 1909. (Photo Bell collection.)

PLATE 14.—Samuel Pierpont Langley, 1834-1906, wearing the academic robe of doctor of civil law of Oxford University, 1894.

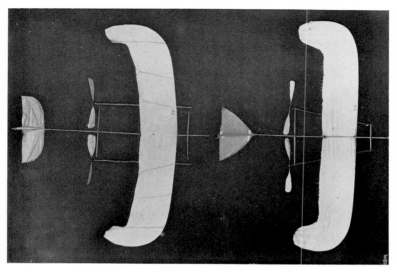

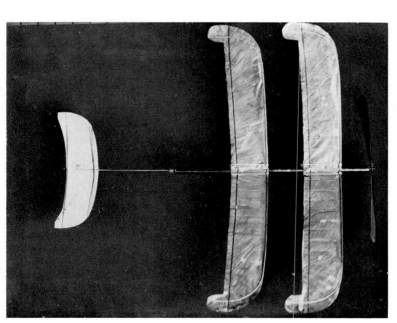

Plate 15.—Experimental model airplanes designed and tested by S. P. Langley. The model at the left shows an early form with tandem wings. These models were powered by rubber bands in torsion.

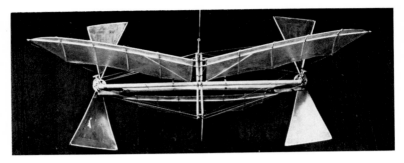

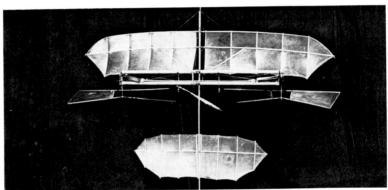

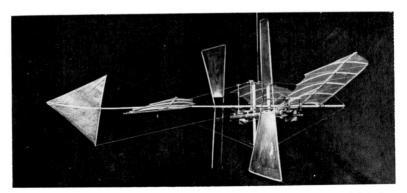

PLATE 16.—Langley developed more than thirty types of these small models before "graduating" to the larger steam-powered aerodromes. These illustrations are three views of the same model. It was powered by rubber bands stretched in tension.

PLATE 17.—Catapult launching of Langley's steam-engined Aerodrome No. 5, on May 6, 1896, over the Potomac River near Quantico, Va. At left, model in flight. (Photo by A. G. Bell.)

PLATE 18.—Flight of Langley's one-quarter-sized unmanned aerodrome, June 18, 1901. The first gasoline-engined, heavier-than-air craft in the world to fly.

PLATE 19.—Tests of Chanute gliders. The pilot of the biplane glider was Augustus Herring, an assistant to Chanute and Langley, who contributed two articles to the Annual.

PLATE 20.—Percy Pilcher, 1866-1899, and *The Hawk*, 1896.

From a drawing from life
done at Le Mans by the
Artist — 1908

Leo Mielziner
1924

PLATE 21.—Wilbur Wright, 1867-1912. Drawn from life by Leo Mielziner.

PLATE 22.—Orville Wright, 1871-1948, pilot of the first powered and controlled flight by man in a heavier-than-air craft, near Kitty Hawk, N. C., December 17, 1903.

PLATE 23.—Wright brothers' airplane at Fort Myer, Va., September 12, 1908; world record flight with passenger, 9 minutes 6⅓ seconds, Orville Wright, pilot, with Maj. George O. Squier.

PLATE 24.—Glenn Curtiss, 1878-1930, winning the speed event, at a speed of 47 miles an hour in the First International Air Meet, Rheims, France, August 29, 1909.

was obliged to finance all his own experiments. What the Editor said on the subject was this:

The length of time which it will take to reach a complete solution of the problem of mechanical flight will depend largely upon the amount of money contributed to pay the expenses of experimenters.

Money so contributed may easily be wasted, and there are never wanting men who eagerly affirm that a certain amount of money placed in their hands will surely bring the solution of the problem.

Then after a few aeronautical town topics the volume comes to an end.

Chapter VII

THE ANNUALS
IN PERSPECTIVE

U P TO the time when Annual No. 3 left the press it is quite clear that my father had every intention of continuing publication of the periodical. For example, the issue of 1897 closes with the following passage:

> The date of issue of this, the third number of the Annual, is May 25, 1897. It was necessary this year to postpone publication in order to give the leading contributors ample time to complete their articles. Last year the Annual was published in February, and it is hoped that future numbers may appear in that month, so that experimenters may have more time to study the previous season's work before arranging their summer plans. Contributors will please send in their articles for No. 4 some time during November, 1897.

Some of the contributors to No. 3, also, indicated their expectation to make further contributions. For example, Pilcher said, "I hope with the new machine with the engine that I shall be able to obtain results worth reporting in your next Annual, but 'we shall see what we shall see'." But alas both Pilcher and the Annual were soon to die.

To clinch the matter further I will quote the following notice which appeared at the end of Annual No. 3.

> Experimenters in all parts of the world are invited to send, for publication in *the next number of the Annual* [italics added], concise accounts of their experiments. Contributors will kindly note the following: (1) The Editor is not to be held responsible for rejected manuscripts, drawings, or photographs. (2) In describing experiments, contributors are requested to send photographs, and also working-drawings of those pieces of apparatus which they consider their best. (3) Well-illustrated descriptions of experiments with the following kinds of apparatus are especially desired: Gliding machines; Self-propelled models; Motors; Screw propellers. (4) All photographs should be distinct, or they cannot be satisfactorily re-

produced. All drawings should be in very black ink on white paper or tracing cloth, and they should be sufficiently well executed to be photo-engraved without re-drawing. (5) Accuracy, explicitness, and conciseness of statement are desirable in the extreme. (6) Please state if any of the text or illustrations have been in print before, and, if so, where. Please give dates of all experiments. [Annual, 1897, p. 176.]

The reasons which induced my father, between May 1897 and February 1898, to let the Annual die, he gave in his Autobiographical Note of 1913 (see page 33): too little good material and too great cost to himself—he was publishing almost gratis. As in the case of many fine works, the acclaim is good, but the sales are poor! In retrospect, I find it a sad thing that he felt obliged to do this. Had he waited a few years there would have been an abundance of material, and had he obtained the services of an enterprising publisher it might well have been made a growing concern. It might be going even yet!

Shortly after my father's death, in 1920, I gave these my own thoughts on the subject: "The publication of the Annual was discontinued after the 3rd volume because Mr. Means felt it had served its purpose. By that time the science had begun to progress. One cannot but be impressed throughout Mr. Means' writings, by the generous spirit with which they were contributed. His aim always was to promote interest in what he believed to be a neglected science, and in a problem which he always felt would ultimately be solved to the great benefit of mankind."

Looking back at all this from 1963, I remember a number of things clearly. Vivid recollections linger of my father busying himself with his aeronautical papers, etc., in the library at 196 Beacon Street. It was a large pleasant room overlooking the Charles River Basin, then tidal. No dam had yet been built, nor were there any buildings of M.I.T. on the farther shore. Tech was still on Boylston Street in those days, and the area it now occupies was largely one of mud flats at low tide, with some coal pockets and other wharves in the background.

The room was booklined and contained a huge writing table, at which my father did the major portion of his literary and editorial work. All his aeronautical books and papers were there, and particularly a series of huge scrapbooks with cuttings on manflight and related matters, from every conceivable source. These are now in the Smithsonian Institution, Washington. When he needed a respite he would go to the large central plate-glass window and do a little aerodynamical birdwatching. Here he could always refresh his mental picture of the soaring flight of the gulls and compare it with the flappings of coots and other wildfowl.

An ornate-paneled wooden mantlepiece bore this friendly message, carved in the wood:

Lass uns gemütlich beim
Feuer sitzen

On the hearth beneath there often was, in winter, a fire of cannel coal burning. Beside it, I can see in my mind my father chatting with a distinguished friend, or writing vigorously at the big table. He was very apt to tell me what he was up to, and he even gave me little jobs, such as making a line drawing for him from time to time. I was greatly interested in his work and was excited by what he was doing.

Although the Annual died, a phoenix, of sorts, did, however, arise from the ashes. "Epitome," my father called it, "Epitome of the Aeronautical Annual." Indistinguishable in size and format from the original annuals, it appeared upon the scene in 1910. It was dedicated "To the Students of Aviation," and on the flyleaf was printed:

The three numbers of the Aeronautical Annual mentioned on the title-page being now out of print, the Editor has selected several of the most important articles and reprinted them here.

This compilation has for its primary object the encouragement of those who are just beginning the study of aviation.

In the effort to reach a good understanding of the achievements of today the student may do well to learn of the work of the path-finders.

Although the Editor has added very little criticism of his own of the material selected for reprinting in 1910 from the three Annuals, even so we may read his mind a bit or explore his likings, by noting what he chose and what he discarded—what he considered as of the most significance or importance. For a starter he omitted Leonardo. Leonardo was one of the first to devise an air screw and therefore was among the giants in aeronautics, but he had it revolve in a horizontal plane, as a helicopter, not in a vertical plane, for propulsion. By 1910 my father had lost interest in helicopters, as he had earlier with ornithopters and balloons, and had become convinced that the promising lines of development would be in motorless gliders on the one hand and power-driven aeroplanes on the other. The great accomplishments of Cayley and Wenham he certainly appreciated, and he thought that Henson had at least a promising concept of a flying machine. Walker was dropped, and I would think properly so.

Everything of Lilienthal's that appeared in the Annuals is repeated in the Epitome, and one of two contributions by Maxim. Single papers by Pilcher, Langley, Bell, Pickering, and the Editor were also reprinted. Maxim's paper acquired a poetical motto, from Erasmus Darwin, in the Epitome:

> Soon shall thy arm, unconquered steam, afar
> Drag the slow barge, or drive the rapid car;
> Or on wide waving wings expanded bear
> The flying chariot through the field of air.

Of Cayley's paper the Editor remarked in 1910 that it was "especially interesting as showing that even at that time (1809-1810), there was at least one man who was intelligently experimenting and giving careful thought and study to the subject of aviation." And on Lilienthal we find this:

> The epoch-making work of Otto Lilienthal gave ocular demonstrations of two facts which before his time had been generally disbelieved.
>
> First: That it is possible for a man, in free flight, using extended surfaces of moderate dimensions, to derive support from the impact of the air upon those surfaces without the aid of the buoyant power of a gas lighter than air.
>
> Second: That it is possible for a man, in free flight, to acquire a fair degree of control of an aeroplane apparatus.

A little new material did find its way into the Epitome. For the two articles of Chanute's in Annuals Nos. 2 and 3 on "Sailing Flight" there is substituted a newer article entitled "Soaring Flight," which appeared first in *American Aeronautics,* April 1909. In this paper Chanute returned, after twelve years, to the fundamental problem of avian soaring flight. His earlier computations were all right as far as they went, so he believed, but they had not totally clarified the mystery. "It was stated," said Chanute (that is, in the 1896-97 articles), "that a gull in its observed maneuvers, rising up from a pile head on unflapping wings, then plunging forward against the wind and subsequently rising higher than his starting point, must either time his ascents and descents exactly with the variations in wind velocities, or must meet a wind billow rotating on a horizontal axis and come to a poise on its crest, thus availing of an ascending trend."

But it was not demonstrated that variations of wind gusts and movements of birds were always synchronous. The observed spiral soaring in light winds, apparently horizontal, or even in calms, was not accounted for. Chanute joined forces with Langley's one-time assistant, Huffaker, and studied buzzards in eastern Tennessee to get more data. Speeds of buzzards in the air were determined by timing the rate of movement of their shadows on the ground. The inclination of their flights above or below the horizon was estimated by observing how the light of a low sun struck them. If it hit their backs they were descending. Air resistances were determined for a stuffed buzzard in a wind tunnel.

> This particular buzzard weighed in life 4.25 pounds, the area of his wings and body was 4.57 square feet, the maximum cross-section of his body was 0.110 square feet, and that of his wing edges when fully extended was 0.244 square feet.
>
> With these data, it became surprisingly easy to compute the performance with the coefficients of Lilienthal for various angles of incidence and to demonstrate how this buzzard could soar horizontally in a dead horizontal calm, provided that it was not a vertical calm and that the air was rising at the rate of 4 or 6 miles per hour, the lowest observed, and quite inappreciable without actual measuring. [Such light upward airs they ascertained by watching thistledown.]

At the end of this paper, which is an extremely important one, Chanute gives a list of what would be the "requisites and maneuvers to master the secrets of soaring flight." That is to say, by man. We need not repeat all these directions, but here are a few samples:

> Obtain an initial velocity at least 25 feet per second before attempting to soar.
>
> Circle like the bird. Simultaneously with the steering, incline the apparatus to the side toward which it is desired to turn, so that the centrifugal force shall be balanced by the centripetal force. The amount of the required inclination depends upon the speed and the radius of the circle swept over.
>
> Rise spirally like the bird. Steer with the horizontal rudder, so as to descend slightly when going with the wind and to ascend when going against the wind. The bird circles over one spot because the rising trends of wind are generally confined to small areas or local chimneys, as pointed out by Sir H. Maxim and others.
>
> Once altitude is gained, progress may be made in any direction by gliding downward by gravity.

And finally this prophesy: "The bird's flying apparatus and skill are as yet infinitely superior to those of man, but there are indications that within a few years the latter may evolve more accurately proportioned apparatus and obtain absolute control over it." [Epitome, 1910, p. 82.]

How right he was! A decade later the Germans were further fulfilling Chanute's prediction. They were driven into that channel by the restrictions placed on them in military flying, by their conquerors.

Another new item in the Epitome was by Professor A. Lawrence Rotch on "The Relation of the Wind to Aerial Navigation." He had had, it will be recalled, a paper in Annual No. 2, which in effect was on what meteorology had to offer to aeronautics. The new one, written for the Epitome in 1910, outlined the progress in this field since the earlier paper was published.

The Editor, as was his wont, preceded Rotch's paper with a little biographical sketch of Rotch himself, a close personal friend, and followed it with an account from the April 1910 *Technology Review,* of the Blue Hill Observatory, which Rotch created. The former piece included a portrait of Rotch, the latter a view of the Observatory.

In his paper Rotch indicated what progress had been made in the study of upper air currents by means of sounding balloons. He hinted that the smart airplane pilot would search for a favorable air current—premonition of the jet stream perhaps.

In the windup of the Epitome we find first a Miscellany, as in Annual No. 3, then an Editorial, as in all the Annuals. The first begins with some reprints from the Miscellany of No. 3. Then follow some new and more recent bits. An especially choice one is the following:

In September, 1901, Mr. Wilbur Wright in addressing the Western Society of Engineers said: 'If I take this piece of paper, and after placing it parallel with the ground, quickly let it fall, it will not settle steadily down as a staid, sensible piece of paper ought to do, but it insists upon contravening every recognized rule of decorum, turning over and darting hither and thither in the most erratic manner, much after the style of an untrained horse. Yet this is the style of steed that men must learn to manage before flying can become an every day sport. The bird has learned this art of equilibrium, and learned it so thoroughly that its skill is not apparent to our sight. We only learn to appreciate it when we try to imitate it. Now, there are two ways of learning how to ride a fractious horse; one is to get on him and learn by actual practice how each motion and trick may best be met; the other is to sit on a fence and watch the beast a while, and then retire to the house and at leisure figure out the best way of overcoming his jumps and kicks. The latter system is the safest, but the former, on the whole, turns out the larger proportion of good riders. It is much the same in learning to ride a flying-machine; if you are looking for perfect safety, you will do well to sit on a fence and watch the birds, but if you really wish to learn, you must mount a machine and become acquainted with its tricks by actual trial.' [Epitome, 1910, p. 213.]

Next we find some references on motorless flight and a page of recommended reading, listing articles on aeronautics published in the Annual Reports of the Smithsonian Institution, dated from 1892 to 1908, all valuable to students of aviation.

There is a short passage in which the Editor tells prospective readers where they can find the now out-of-print Annuals.

A chronology of "Memorable Events—Flights with Motor Aeroplanes," from Kitty Hawk to 1910, concludes the Miscellany.

The Editorial in the Epitome I find disappointing, not so much for what it says as for what it omits. Here would have been the place to give a critical review of pre-Wright progress in manflight and to relate it to what had happened since. Instead, the Editor in his imaginative way, using his favorite analogy, the railway, contents himself with looking briefly into the future, from, be it remembered, the year 1910.

Naturally enough the Epitome drew some fan mail. I will insert here just two of these letters, which are of a sort, considering their sources, to give much satisfaction.

A. F. Zahm, Cosmos Club, Washington, D. C., June 7, 1910, to James Means:

> I wish to thank you very heartily for the two copies of reprinted articles of the famous Aeronautical Annual.[1] I have placed one of the copies in the library of this Club and kept the other for my own library, as you wished.
>
> The Annual was so valuable in its day that I have often wished it could have continued yearly up to the present time, giving the substance of the most important papers that appear each year in the aeronautical journals.
>
> What would you think of a contest flight from Boston to Washington? I had thought of proposing such an event but Mr. Curtiss anticipated me by proposing a flight from New York to Washington, and since then we have been at work on that proposition. It will,

---

[1] That is to say, the Epitome.

however, cost us between $40 and $50 per mile to secure a flight. Rather a fancy price. Don't you think so?

General James Allen, Chief Signal Officer, U. S. Army, Washington, on June 1, 1910, to James Means, Boston:

I appreciate very much your thoughtfulness in sending me your Annual [2] for 1910, and find it most interesting. I am sure you are as pleased as we all are with the success of Mr. Curtiss in flying from Albany to New York City. It is hard to say whether such features impress our Government with the necessity of doing something or whether they simply take it as a matter of course, but I feel that next year Congress will take up the matter seriously.

Lieutenant Foulois with the Wright machine has been at San Antonio, Texas, all winter and is flying from time to time. I noticed in the paper yesterday that he had been up the day before for something over an hour. We cannot do very much with only one aeroplane and one officer. In the near future I hope to see a fleet of aeroplanes.

As I attempt, mentally, to digest the three issues of the Aeronautical Annual as a whole, the chief thing that emerges is the very clear derivation of manflight from birdflight. The early devotees were, we might say, aerodynamical bird watchers or disciples of ornithologic aeronautics. Although many other types of animals—bats, reptiles, insects—have learned to fly, their impact on manflight has been negligible. It is from the birds that man has learned, and we owe them a great debt of gratitude. It is perhaps retributive that, having profited so much from them, without ever having thanked them, we should now find ourselves being sabotaged by them occasionally, when they imperil our aeroplanes by plugging the engines' air-intakes, or interfere with the runways which we make of their breeding grounds.

As we have seen throughout the writings in the Annuals, there are two main types of avian flight, flapping and soaring. Some species of birds, gulls, for example, use both (not simultaneously) seemingly with equal facility. Others such as pigeons, use chiefly flapping. Hummingbirds use only flapping, and that at an incredibly fast rate. As is true of all species, and of all functions, the design of the bird has been evolved to serve most efficiently, the function which the struggle for existence has forced upon it. Of course, the two have evolved together. But we should note that all species,

---

[2] This letter marks the time when the U.S. Air Force consisted of *one aeroplane and one pilot!*

except man, have had to adapt to new environments by evolving the machinery of adaptation as integral parts of their own bodies. Only man can build himself a mechanical flying machine. The bird, bat, reptile, or insect, which has a need to fly, has to become the flying machine itself. Man flies by means of mechanisms; other creatures by their own organs.

Naturalists distinguish between divergent and convergent evolution. If the path of evolutionary progress divides, and by one branch a foreleg is converted into a wing, while by another it remains a foreleg, that is *divergent* evolution; and if by a third branch the foreleg becomes a finlike organ, that is still more divergent evolution. The opposite situation is that in which organs of very different structure and function, in phyla far removed from one another in the evolutionary tree, are modified to serve a similar function, in order to invade a (to them) new and promising environment, the air for example, in which case it is necessary for them to develop wings. The wings of birds, mammals, reptiles, and insects have many features in common, regardless of their origin, because these are the requisites of the medium. If the organism cannot meet them, it cannot fly. This is *convergent* evolution.

When we jump to man, who builds his wings, instead of growing them on his body, we find he too has to meet these requirements. Is it any wonder then that the pioneers in aeronautics were very much preoccupied with the flight of birds? Of course not, but why were they not interested also in the flight of other flying creatures? I think the answer is that of all flying creatures, at least those that are with us today, only the birds can soar, and not all of them, at that. The soaring birds are in a small minority compared with the flappers, and the thousands of species of flying insects all are flappers.

Man cannot fly by flapping, at least after many trials over centuries, he has never succeeded in doing so. As long as he remains motorless, man can keep company with the soaring birds. Indeed the modern motorless glider is a very fair imitation, so far as form goes, of an albatross. But, when man resorts to power, he must in applying it, make use of principles totally different from those used by the lower creatures. If man cannot fly by flapping wings, no more can any subhuman creature apply power to flight, as my father pointed out in his 1884 paper (see page 12), by means of anything involving rotating parts. Man has left the birds, so far as powered flying goes, although he may yet learn other things from them, and he can still become enraptured by the beauty of their movements in the air.

We must in passing take cognizance of the type of flight exemplified among birds, not only by the hummingbirds, but among insects by innumerable species: the type of flight characterized by very rapid flapping, and the ability to hold to a point in the air, or change direction of flight almost instantly. The hummingbird moth, an insect, gives a magnificent imitation of the bird in the general manner of its flight. Here is convergent evolution of a high order.

The dragonflies are especially noteworthy in this connection. In a text on insects [3] I found it stated that they are among the strongest and most graceful of all insects. "Their flight is so perfect that it has been seriously suggested that flying machines should be modeled after the flight mechanisms of these insects." As a matter of fact, the Brazilian aviator Alberto Santos-Dumont named one of his aircraft the "Demoiselle," but in this case the demoiselle was a dragonfly!

The variety of birds studied by the pioneers is impressive. Leonardo in his treatise on the flight of birds was concerned chiefly with the kite (bird) and other great soarers. Cayley, contemplating the bird (species not specified) said, "There is no proof that, weight for weight, a man is comparatively weaker than a bird; it is therefore probable, if he can be made to exert his whole strength advantageously upon a light surface similarly proportioned to his weight as that of the wing to the bird, that he would fly like the bird." The difficulty lies in the word *advantageously*. It is difficult, yet recently shown to be possible, for a man to apply his own muscle power advantageously to propel an aircraft for a short distance. But he does not have to if soaring conditions are present. After he is airborne, he needs no power except to operate his controls. It is on the take-off only that power is indispensable, and if there is any extrinsic power available from wind or position (e.g., from a high perch) no intrinsic power is needed for take-offs. The key to flying is to gain velocity. "Many birds," said Cayley, "and particularly waterfowl, run and flap their wings for several yards before they can gain support from the air. The swift is not able to elevate itself from level ground. The inconvenience under consideration arises from very different causes in these two instances. The supporting surface of most swimming birds does not exceed the ratio of $\frac{4}{10}$ths of a square foot to every pound of their weight: The swift, though it scarcely weighs an ounce, measures eighteen inches in extent of wing. The want of

---

[3] *The Insect Book,* by L. O. Howard. Doubleday, New York, 1905.

surface in the one case and the inconvenient length of wing in the other, oblige these birds to aid the *commencement* of their flight by other expedients; yet they can both fly with great power, when they have acquired their full velocity."

Cayley went to the birds not only to gain understanding of flight itself, but for hints on structure of wings, also. Being engaged in designing a mechanical wing, he notes:

> The hollow form of the quill in birds is a very admirable structure for lightness combined with strength where external bracings cannot be had; a tube being the best application of matter to resist as a lever; but the principle of bracing is so effectual, that, if properly applied, it will abundantly make up for the clumsiness of human invention in other respects; and should we combine both these principles, and give diagonal bracing to the tubular bamboo cane, surfaces might be constructed with a greater degree of strength and lightness, than any made use of in the wings of birds.
>
> The surface of a heron's wing is in the ratio of 7 square feet to a pound. Hence, according to this proportion, a wing of 54 square feet would weigh about 7¾ pounds; on the contrary the wings of water-fowl are so much heavier, that a surface of 54 square feet, according to their structure, will weigh 18½ lb. I have in these instances quoted nearly the extreme cases among British birds; the wing I have described may therefore be considered as nearly of the same weight in proportion to its bulk as that of most birds. [Annual, 1895, pp. 44-45.]

Walker, we have already noted, was very much of an ornithologist, but not much of an engineer. He appears to have known more about condors than any of his competitors. He was very fond of bird watching and hostile to hunters!

Of all birds, however, gulls have been the object of more aerodynamical bird watching than any others. Wenham, Chanute, Means, Maxim, and others were all gull-watchers, and it would seem that this species (the herring gull) is the best all-around avian flight instructor for man. He is vastly more accessible than any of the other good soarers, easier to watch, and capable of more types of flight than more specialized species. The gull indeed has been creating several different types of scientific interest lately. To the ecologists and conservationists he presents pressing problems because he is having, like us, a population explosion. And then his family and social life are very alluring to such investigators as Tinbergen.

Lilienthal found the stork equally convenient for study, and as good a subject as the gull, but the stork would not do for us, as it is unknown in North America. The albatross is very important but remote to reach, and Wenham, at least, found the pelican very interesting.

The mass of information in the Annuals, as well as showing the derivations of manflight from birdflight, gives clear indication of the direction of progress in aviation achieved by the experimental method.

Experimenters (this is the term my father often used for them) fell into several categories and pursued their goals by different routes. There were those who believed that gliding flight should be mastered before attempting motorized flight and there were some, including the Editor of the Annual, who believed that a great deal of work should be done with models before human life was risked in questionably designed machines. There is no point now in trying to figure out which of these approaches was the best. All of them were used, and all probably contributed to the total progress that was made.

What finally happened, of course, was that the Wrights installed a light motor and propellers in their fifth aircraft, derived from their third glider. Their first glider, made in 1900, was somewhat similar to Chanute's earlier one. By means of this combination, on December 17, 1903, at Kitty Hawk, North Carolina, the Wrights made their power-propelled-and-controlled flight which gave practical aviation to the world. From the point of view of the nature and development of aircraft, it is extremely interesting that the Wrights had tested their general form of apparatus before it was motorized, both as a glider and as a kite.

There is an essential unity of all winged aircraft. To stay aloft all they need is an adequate and proper impingement of air upon their airfoils. Whether this is secured by the force of gravity, by holding them against a wind, or by propelling them through the air by power-driven screw propellers, makes no qualitative difference in final result. The aircraft has relative air speed in any of the three cases. The kite does not have ground speed, but it stays aloft just the same, because it has relative air speed.

In any field of thought and exploration, progress is made by fits and starts, and innumerable persons contribute to it, some in big ways, some in very tiny ones. But rarely can any single person be given exclusive credit for a major advance or change in direction. The way is prepared for him by the prior contributions of many others. Putting several pieces together to make a new and original whole is the mark of genius, but even this cannot be achieved unless others have first provided the pieces. There is also often a bit of luck as to who first reaches a goal. Lilienthal or Pilcher, for example, had they not been killed, might have antedated the Wrights in giving practical powered flight to man. So too, conceivably, might Langley, had he not been rather insistent in using a catapult for launching his large "aerodrome."

The Annuals portray all these strivings of the pre-Wright era, and leave us in 1897 with human gliding flight a *fait accompli*, and practical powered flight fully ready to be born.

The following letter is a very happy epilogue to the Annuals.

May 26, 1897

My dear Mr. Means:

I have your postal card of 24 and as I fear that the Annual will not reach me in time for me to tell you what I think of it before your departure, I write to bid you "bon voyage" and to tell you what I think of you.

I congratulate myself every day upon having formed your personal acquaintance, I am deeply sensible of my good fortune in having apparently won your friendship and I thank you heartily for the many kindnesses I have received at your hands.

I think you are doing a great work for the inchoate art of Aviation by the publication of your Annual, and that should success be achieved as soon as you indicated a few days ago, your name will remain permanently connected with it.

Wishing you a prosperous journey and all sorts of happiness, I beg you to present my best regards to Mrs. Means.

Yours very truly,
O. CHANUTE

Chapter VIII

INVENTING

IN 1897, when the Annual was discontinued, my father was forty-four years old, and he had come again, I suspect, as he had in 1894, to the point of asking himself, What next? Actually from 1897 to 1899 there was a brief period of doldrums in the progress of aeronautics in general, and this, I dare say, affected my father as it seems to have many others. He was a gentleman of leisure, but he had a mind which could tolerate no intellectual idleness. From his conversation, bits of which I can recall—I was in prep school and living at home at the time—it was quite evident that he was as passionately interested in the problem of manflight as ever he had been. He kept in touch with what was going on in the field and corresponded with a number of key people.

For example, early in 1897 we find such entries as these in his diary:

Jan. 6th '97	Arrived Chicago, 7 P.M.
" 7th	At about 10 A.M. called on Mr. Chanute, 413 East Huron St. First time I had met him after long correspondence. Lunched with him and talked till 3 P.M. Evening A. M. Herring called on me.
Jan. 8th	With Mr. Chanute in the A.M. I lunched with Herring and dined with Mr. Chanute and spent the evening.
Jan. 9th	Mr. Chanute lunched with me. Left at 5:30 P.M. on Penna Limited.
" 10th	Arrived 6 P.M. at Washington Shoreham Hotel.
" 11th	Called on H. C. Lodge (Senator) about Senate Bill 302. Called on Prof. Langley who showed me his latest aerodromes and put me in the hands of J. E. Watkins, Coast Survey, Pat. Office. Again to Smithsonian and with Mr. Watkins in the Museum. Left at 3:15 P.M. by Federal Express.
" 12th	At 8:30 A.M. arrived 196 Beacon St., Boston.

99

Then after a trip to Europe with my mother and brother we have these diary entries:

Sept. 15, '97   Arrived Chicago. Mr. Chanute met me at station.
"   16th   At Camp Chanute.
"   17th   At Camp Chanute.

It was thus that his epistolary acquaintance with Chanute of many years' standing ripened into warm personal friendship. There is not much further to be got from the diary. It never consisted of more than scattered and brief recordings of facts, nothing of ideas, opinions, or emotions. After 1897 there are no entries on aviation, merely itineraries of numerous travels.

A voracious reader, he had an omnivorous appetite for things scientific and dipped into the literature in many directions. He made friends with a number of the faculty of M.I.T., from whom he gained a variety of new insights, some of which he passed on to me before I had encountered them at all in my own formal education.

It was in 1899 that the great crescendo in the progress of aviation began. This was the year the Wright brothers started active experimentation with a large kite, flown with four lines so that its panels could be twisted to test the effect on lateral control. In 1900 they built a biplane glider and tested it at Kill Devil Hills, near Kitty Hawk, North Carolina, where they had terrain much like that which Chanute had at the southern end of Lake Michigan. Indeed, it was he who suggested this locale to them. They flew their glider as a kite and improved their famous wing-warping method of providing lateral stability. By 1903, having done a great deal of gliding with several aircraft, the Wrights were ready to install an engine to drive two pusher propellers in a machine specially built for the purpose, "The Power Flyer." In this on December 17, 1903, they made what has been styled "The First Powered, Sustained, and Controlled Aeroplane Flights in History," shaking the world thereby.[1] They took off from level ground; in other words, it was a completely motorized take-off. No gravity or catapult was used at all. Practical motorized flight developed fast in the early years of the Twentieth Century. Chanute had visited France in 1903 and undoubtedly gave great impetus to flying on the continent of Europe through his descriptions of the Wrights' successes. It was also in 1903 that Langley made attempts (unsuccessful) to launch his

_____
[1] This airplane now hangs in the Smithsonian Institution, National Air Museum.

full-scale "aerodrome." The French took to flying like ducks, not to water but air. They tried various types of airplanes, monoplanes (Bleriot, 1907; Lavavasseur's "Antoinette," Santos-Dumont's "Demoiselle," 1909), and box-kite types such as Santos-Dumont's, Voisin's, and Farman's. In 1904 Esnault-Pelterie used the trailing-edge aileron which soon displaced wing-warping for lateral stability.

Glenn Curtiss, after the Wrights, was the next highly successful American. In 1909 Bleriot flew the English Channel in a small, light monoplane, thus giving the British a major subject for thought in the field of defense of their island. From Kitty Hawk to Lindbergh's trans-Atlantic flight was 24 years, and from that to a man in orbit around the earth in space was but 34 years more! Commercial flying developed fast after Lindbergh's feat inspired public confidence in aviation. The air-transport activities of the armed forces during World War II gave further impetus to such acceptance. In the United States there was a great proliferation of airlines—perhaps too much. The growth of the manufacture of aircraft into an important industry was great at this time. Manflight became part of the culture, both military and civilian, but not to any great extent as a sport (except with gliders), as my father had expected.

Needless to say, until his death in 1920 he followed all aeronautical developments closely and was eager to see the flying with his own eyes. His opportunity to do this came in 1908. The War Department had advertised for bids for the construction of aeroplanes for the Army, and the Wrights' bid had been accepted. The contract called for certain test flights, and it was some of these that my father witnessed at Fort Myer, Virginia.[2]

Two communications from him on the subject are extant. He was staying as a guest at the Cosmos Club in Washington when he wrote. The first of these, a postcard to my mother, dated September 9, 1908, read:

> The 9th of Sept. will be a memorable day in American history. As you have seen by the papers Mr. Wright (Orville), this evening broke his own record of the morning, then took on a passenger and made a flight of seven minutes.

> He is now quietly sitting down just as though this day were like any other day!

---

[2] The flights at Fort Myer, Virginia, in September 1908 were all made by Orville Wright. Wilbur was in Europe at the time making flights and arrangements to sign contracts with foreign manufacturers to make the Wright aeroplane, under the brothers' foreign patents.

My father wrote to me from Washington on September 11, 1908, as follows:

> I suppose the best way to get a letter from you is to give you one to answer.
>
> When I got as far as that it was time to start for Fort Myer. I am in one of the officers' tents and one of them is now saying over the telephone, "Mr. Wright will fly about five." In the postal I sent your mother last evening, I did not fully explain why the flight yesterday, though short, was remarkable. As Mr. Wright put it to me, the conditions were like this. If you were to take your bicycle and substitute for the turning bar a lever working fore and aft and then get on and try it for the first time, it would not be exactly easy to steer gracefully. Your job would be on terra firma, that is practically what Mr. Wright had to do in the air yesterday. The perfect balance of the new machine as shown yesterday is very encouraging to Mr. Wright. . . . It is perfectly delightful here in Washington. The members of the Cosmos are almost all men of science, and I am learning lots of new things every day. Two days ago Dr. Zahm (Prof. of Physics in the Catholic University of America) with whom I had quite a correspondence ten or twelve years ago, took me out to his laboratory where he has been for years carrying out a series of experiments on air resistances, and he showed me his most interesting apparatus. Lieut. Selfridge is here in the tent. He is one of Dr. Bell's "June Bug" operators.[3] Yesterday I went up the Washington Monument with Dr. Zahm. I will add a P.S. later about the flight. . . .
>
> 7:15. Superb flight. Five and one half times around the Parade Ground, alighting like a feather.

But tragedy was to follow quickly. Only a week later Orville Wright took Selfridge up as a passenger and crashed from a height of 75 feet. Selfridge died in about two hours as a result of his injuries, and Wright was injured. The crash was determined to

---

[3] Lieutenant Selfridge's association with Dr. Alexander Graham Bell's kite experiments has been mentioned on page 62. Others in the group with Dr. Bell were J. A. D. McCurdy and F. W. Baldwin, young graduate engineers, and Glenn H. Curtiss, who had developed reliable engines for his motorcycles and for airships. This group formed the Aerial Experiment Association whose object was "to get into the air." Branching away from tetrahedral cells, they first made a biplane glider in which they learned to coast on the air. Then followed four powered airplanes. Their first, the "Red Wing," made a flight of 319 feet on March 12, 1908. In the second, the "White Wing," Selfridge learned to fly, thus becoming the first military officer in the world to pilot an airplane. The third airplane, named "June Bug," had flown over one kilometer July 4, 1908, winning the Scientific American Trophy, and was thus fresh in my father's mind when he was writing to me in the above letter. The Association's fourth airplane, "Silver Dart," was completed after Selfridge's death and became the first airplane to fly in Canada, February 23, 1909.

have been due to a crack in a propeller blade causing an imbalance which violently shook the aeroplane, breaking a wire and pulling the rudder out of proper alignment. As my father was deeply interested in furthering the attainment of safety in flight, this episode was very shocking to him.

The year 1909 was characterized, as Zahm (1911) put it in his book *Aerial Navigation,* by "strenuous competitive flying." Handsome prizes were offered by various newspapers and societies. A new type of flying man was emerging to compete for these—the aviator or pilot in the modern sense, the successor to the gliding men of the preceding generation—Lilienthal, Chanute, Pilcher, etc. The new men were full of zeal and possessed by a competitive spirit. They made, and broke, records not only for distance but also for speed and altitude, thus vindicating my father's early belief in the efficacy of prizes in stimulating progress in manflight.

The first international aviation meeting was held at Rheims, France, in August 1909. Its official name was "Grande Semaine d'Aviation de la Champagne." Coming six years after Kitty Hawk, it can be said to have been the blossoming of the seed planted in 1903, the coming of age party, so to speak, of practical motorized aviation.

The various aviation stars, the men of the new generation of flyers, were there—Bleriot, Farman, Breguet, Latham, Paulhan, Curtiss, Santos-Dumont, and others. The Wright brothers did not attend. Wilbur had given many exhibition flights in France the summer before (1908). Two Wright aeroplanes were flown at Rheims piloted by others. Glenn Curtiss was the only United States pilot who participated. In addition to contests for distance, height, and speed, there seems to have been a certain indulgence in aerobatics at this meet, undoubtedly amazing and perhaps terrifying to the spectators in the grandstand.

My father went to France and attended this meeting. He met and talked with many of the young airmen and came home full of enthusiasm which I recollect vividly. He made another scrapbook from the postcards and programs he had collected at this event.[4]

The Rheims meeting was a truly historic occasion, for it established manflight as a practical achievement. Aviation became a *fait accompli* and set the pace and pattern for further contests. Progress was made with extraordinary rapidity in the years thereafter. The Second International meeting took place at Belmont Park, Long

[4] Now in the National Air Museum.

Island, New York, in October 1910, under the auspices of the Aero Club of America.

There was also a meeting of some note in Boston (the Harvard-Boston) in the summer of 1910. I attended this meeting with my father and have a vivid memory of it. As we arrived at the field a Wright aeroplane flew directly over us and went into a steep bank and a tight turn. It was the first time I had ever seen an airplane in flight, and it made a deep impression on me. Various stunts were pulled off; one, really rather childish, consisted of dropping a baseball from a plane to be successfully fielded by a professional baseball player, stationed at a selected spot to receive it. I recall the performances of two English flyers at this meet.

Claude Graham-White, who had made a reputation in the London-Manchester race, came to Boston equipped with a sleek monoplane. It was really a beautiful aircraft. We were watching Graham-White as he circled around the field, when suddenly he shot off tangentially and headed for the open sea. He passed out of sight, but in 30 minutes or so he returned and made a successful landing. He had flown around Boston lighthouse, a total distance of 33 miles, and had won a prize of $10,000 offered by the *Boston Globe*.

Another Englishman, A. V. Roe, arrived with a triplane. We saw him make a good take-off in this contraption. It was well powered, for it made a steep ascent after take-off. Then the pilot swerved sharply to the left and went into a steep bank but seemed unable to steer out of it. The aircraft came to an attitude in the air in which the long axis of its wings was nearly vertical. In this position it rapidly sank to the ground hitting first on its left wing tips, which seemed to crumple under the weight of it, as well they might. We saw an ambulance hasten to the wreck and extract the pilot, who was rushed to the first-aid station nearby. Fortunately, Roe was not badly hurt. He appeared soon after at a dinner, and in later years he became the founder of the Avro aircraft manufacturing concern. Finally he was knighted.

Great distance flights in 1910 were made in ever-increasing numbers—London to Manchester, transalpine, Albany to New York, New York to Philadelphia and return, etc., etc. Early airmail flights began in various places in 1911 and transport of passengers in multiplace airplanes. Progress was also being made in design and construction of airplanes. Experiments were tried with new types. The profession of the airplane pilot was growing rapidly. The airplane industry was getting under way also; and all this, just prior to World War I, meant that aviation would play a great role in that war—which it did, and thereby gave a great impetus to progress in civilian aviation.

My father, no doubt, had a great yearning to take an active part of some sort in the march of events in aviation. He could not be content merely with the role of fan or kibitzer. He wanted to be a genuine contributor to the design and development of aircraft or their accessories. He presumed that he possessed enough knowledge of the principles involved and enough ingenuity to do this successfully. And who can say that he did not have these? He came to think that the way for him to proceed lay in the realm of invention. He firmly believed in competition in the practical development of ideas and in survival of the fittest for industry. He also was convinced that inventors or innovators who came up with something new and promising should lose no time in applying for patents on it. A precedent had been set for this, in aviation, by Chanute, who had repeatedly urged the Wrights to secure their basic patents as soon as possible. Most of their competitors did the same, so that there ensued an amazing lot of litigation over patent infringements in the making of airplanes.

I do not think there was any great commercial motivation behind my father's procuring of patents. He did not have any intention of going into the business of manufacturing any of his aeronautical inventions, as he had shoes in his earlier days. He rather hoped to find other manufacturers who would undertake to produce his inventions under license and pay him royalties.

His first patent (U.S. 922709) was granted on May 25, 1909, for a signaling device for airplanes. He had become conscious that when flight came into common use it would be necessary for airplanes to be able to communicate with the ground and vice versa, and between one another. He set to thinking about that problem, and what came to his mind was in the category of sky-writing, although that did not materialize in the usual sense of the word until 1922. What my father proposed to do was to write on the sky, by means of puffs of smoke, messages in the dots and dashes of the Morse code. This was before radio telegraphy had become available for such a purpose, but not long before. In fact, within the year McCurdy both sent and received messages by wireless from an airplane in flight.

Fɪɢ. 13.—The Means Signaling device sending Morse Code, spotting artillery fire.

My father named his invention THE JAMES MEANS AERIAL SIGNAL and described it as follows:

The object of this apparatus is to provide a system whereby visible or audible signals may be transmitted automatically or otherwise from a motor-propelled or other aerial machine.

It consists in part (a) of an automatic transmitter actuated by clock-work or otherwise; (b) of a receptacle containing material[5] which may be used intermittently injected into the exhaust pipe of the engine, and which when so injected causes well defined puffs of black smoke to appear in the wake of the aerial machine.

These puffs of smoke may be long and short corresponding to the dots and dashes of the Morse code, or they may be numerical signals showing as one, two, or more dots suitably spaced according to the code used.

When the aerial machine carries an extra man the signals may be controlled by him, in which case the automatic transmitter would not be used. [From brochure, 1909, advertising the patent.]

The volume, duration, and spacing of the smoke puffs may be regulated by a perforated ribbon or by a notched disk forming a part of the mechanism of the automatic transmitter.

Then very practically he adds: "The open end of the exhaust pipe is placed where the smoke puffs are undisturbed by the rush

[5] As, for example, carbon black.

of air from the propellers" (or in modern parlance, "prop-wash").

He had a notion that his aerial signal might have important military uses:

> Secrecy being 'the soul of strategy' it seems probable that the art of war is about to undergo important modifications.
>
> However valuable wireless telegraphy may be for some purposes, it is inadequate in the matter of bringing information from within the enemy's lines. That service can only be rendered by rapid flying machines.
>
> Many aviators are on the alert to win distinction at the beginning of this era of practical flying. Some try for duration of flight, some for velocity, some for records in travel over difficult country. All of these efforts will aid in the development of the military flying-machine, and it is certain that high honors will be deserved and will be received by successful aviators.
>
> Yet after all, the question which military authorities of all nations are asking is this: "What practical and useful military service can the flying-machine render in the immediate future?"
>
> In answer to this, words and prospectuses are useless; an ocular demonstration is necessary to convince. The designer and the operator of the first flying-machine which proves to be completely adaptable to the needs of military scouting will win great distinction.

And then the old business instinct comes to the surface in these words:

> I call the attention of the designers, constructors, and operators of successful flying-machines to my Signalling Apparatus.
>
> My invention is patented in the U.S. and Canada and patents are pending in European countries.
>
> Under certain conditions which will fully protect me in all of my patent rights, I will make arrangements with the builders of flying-machines in regard to the use of my signalling apparatus. I therefore invite correspondence, etc., etc.

Despite his characteristic peaceful inclinations, my father bent every effort to capture the interest of the military in his aerial signal. He communicated with General James Allen, Chief Signal Officer of the Army, who arranged for a field trial of the James Means Signal under Army auspices, on October 13, 1911. My father had a young assistant, Ripley Bowman. At College Park, Maryland, a site near Washington which had been leased by the Army for aviation purposes, Bowman, with the apparatus, was taken aloft in a Wright airplane. Purely for demonstration purposes a tank of compressed carbon dioxide was used to provide the blast of air to discharge the puff of lamp black. It was not desired to run the risk of promoting engine trouble by hooking directly into the exhaust pipe during these experiments. On October 13 Bowman wrote from Washington to my father, who was unable to be present at the trials: "Just back from a most successful afternoon at College Park. I had the apparatus up for twenty minutes in Lt. Kirtland's Wright, and the officers stationed on the ground had absolutely no difficulty in reading everything I sent to them. They were all very much pleased with the way it has worked out—but not half as tickled as I." More tests were made the following day. The official report of the participating officers, however, included the following passage: "Because of the short time of visibility of the puffs, and because of the impossibility of distinguishing same at a distance greater than four or five miles, it is thought that the device is not practicable for general military use."

In reply to a *post hoc* query of my father's, General Allen explained that "the idea intended to be conveyed was that from our experience with wireless telegraph it is believed that it is superior to any visual system now known." This seems to have been the coup de grace, so far as the U.S. Military were concerned.

Also, there is evidence that the U.S. Government had little interest in military aviation at that point. The Army as early as November 1909, then possessing an air force of one Wright aeroplane, was pressing for an appropriation to buy more planes and the wherewithal to train some officers to operate them. By January 1911, things had begun to move a little. To help them along, my father sent to each of his Senators, Henry Cabot Lodge and W. Murray Crane, a letter which, because it reflects so clearly his thinking of that time, I will quote in toto.

Boston, January 12, 1911.

Dear sir:

May I ask if you will kindly consider a few arguments which I herein present favoring an Army appropriation for aeronautical purposes?

As you may wonder why a civilian should address a senator upon a military subject, let me say that for thirty years I have been deeply interested in this subject and I have at all times done what I could to advance the science of aviation.

I spent several days in Washington last month and I am fairly familiar with the present status of aeronautics in the minds of legislators.

I am aware that public opinion is, in a vague way, strongly in favor of almost any kind of retrenchment. It is, I believe, this state of public opinion which prevents the subject of military aeronautics from receiving in Congress the careful investigation which it deserves.

The cost of supplying the Army with the twenty aeroplanes which it wants would be comparatively small. In reply to this a legislator might say, "What of that? There are hundreds of other small items which are just as worthy of consideration; if we make appropriations for one we might as well make them for all."

The vital question just now is, would the latter point be well taken?

Believing firmly, as I do, that our legislators are making a great mistake I would give my reasons for that belief:

1. Legislators, very properly, take business views of these questions. Undoubtedly many of them are saying, "The Europeans are developing the military aeroplane at their own expense, all we have to do is to let them perfect it and when they have done so we can copy their best designs." The answer to this is that the development of the scouting machine is only a part of the military problem, the other part is the training of *men.* The aviators who are now being trained for exhibition purposes are without the guidance of military experts and consequently are learning little or nothing of the art of making useful observations and communications.

2. It is a mistake for a government to remain in blindness concerning a great military invention. In the case of Ericsson the efforts of a few civilians brought before the Government the revolving turret which the inventor had for years been vainly trying to introduce. The proposition which he made was very simple; he said, "When you want to point a gun, it isn't necessary to turn the whole ship around; put the gun in a turret and turn the turret." Nobody in authority in Europe or America could grasp that idea.

3. Here is a proposition almost as simple as the foregoing. From the earliest times the cavalry has been 'the eye of the army.' From this time on armies will be provided with a far more efficient organ of vision, the aeroplane. Is it too early for the Government to begin to train, *under its own military experts,* a score of men who will be able to discern *and understand* whatever may be visible upon a field of manoeuvres? Is it not a mistake to delay in this matter?

4. Whatever may be the state of public opinion concerning retrenchment, the amount of money here concerned is insignificant. A sum less than the cost of *one submarine* would put military aviation upon a new basis here in America.

5. If two men, Langley and Chanute (in addition to all the rest that they did), could promote the science of aviation by giving to it

dignity, it would seem that the United States Government has power to exert great influence by ceasing to ignore the science which so many men are now striving to advance. Further, if the Government very promptly leads off with a score of machines and observers, the hundreds of civilians who are working at private expense will profit by the example of the men who may be intelligently working under the supervision of military experts.

6. Foreign nations have a larger number of workers in aviation than we have. We should think now of 1911, not of 1912; progress this year in America will depend to no small extent upon the willingness of Congress to provide a moderate fund.

7. Is it not quite possible that the object mentioned may be worthy in the sense that Ericsson's invention was worthy? If so, will not legislators make a mistake if they fail to give the matter prompt and careful consideration?

Very respectfully,

(Signed) JAMES MEANS

A week later General Allen was able to write my father as follows.

Washington, January 20, 1911.

I have your letter of January 12th, and in reply I am very glad to say to you that an appropriation of $125,000 for the purchase of aeroplanes has passed the House of Representatives. The bill will go to the Senate next week, where we have assurances it will be passed; so your letters to Mr. Crane and Mr. Lodge were very timely, as Mr. Lodge is on the Military Committee, and he will no doubt do all he can to send it through the Senate. I know that you will be glad to know that at last we are going to make a start, and I hope even with the small amount we have to do some serious work. The money will not be available until the 1st of July, but in the meantime arrangements can be made for the purchase of machines; so I hope by the early autumn to have a number of officers in the air."

(Signed)   J. ALLEN
Brigadier General,
Chief Signal Officer of the Army

As World War I was threatening in Europe, at the time this correspondence was taking place, it can easily be understood that the United States was in no sense forehanded in its preparations for defense or offense in the air.

My father decided to look abroad. He had printed and distributed in suitable places certain circulars about his signal. One of these displayed a blindfolded young soldier labeled "ARTILLERIST

German, French, British, Russian, or Italian." Thus included were future combatants of both sides. The artillerist was described as a "master of gunpowder. . . . Unblind him by using the JAMES MEANS AERIAL SIGNAL."

He also launched an advertising campaign in foreign military journals and in 1912 had ads in the *Deutsches Offizierblatt,* and *Kriegstechnische Zeitschrift,* Berlin; *l'Aerophile,* Paris; and the *Broad Arrow,* the *Army and Navy Gazette,* and *Flight,* London. All these carried a full description of the apparatus. "It is the only reliable aerial signal ever invented," so this inventor proclaimed.

He described the signal's use thus: "The aeroplane flies in circles above the target [a pot shot it would seem for antiaircraft artillery], and, the instant a shot strikes, the aerial observer signals where it strikes as follows: T for target, O for over, L for left, R for right, S for short."

In another small broadside entitled "Military Scouting from Aeroplanes," the following statements, among others, are made: "Axiom —Air Scouts are useless unless they are able to report what they see." "Apart from wireless telegraphy only two methods of reporting have been fully described in military journals. One method is for the observer to write a message, place it in a tin box and drop it. Such a message may easily be lost." "The other method is by using the James Means Aerial Signal. It is today the only reliable apparatus in the world for this purpose."

His awareness of his chief competitor, radio, and his understanding of the jamming of radio transmission are set forth in the following passage:

I believe that I am rendering a service in the development of the flying-machine in asking now if it is not possible that the military authorities of the world are making a great mistake in assuming that 'wireless' aerial signaling will be dependable in time of war?

If the Governments find it necessary to make laws to protect themselves from the amateurs in time of peace, what will happen in the event of war, when powerful disturbers, producing all wave lengths, are certain to be quickly constructed and brought into action?

The selective method has met with some success but its dependability in the presence of all-wave-length disturbers remains undemonstrated.

The experiments and investigations concerning wireless telegraphy from aeroplanes are sure to go on; the defects are plainly visible; they may possibly be overcome. Is it safe for the military authorities to take as a working hypothesis that they will be overcome?

SHOULD VISUAL AERIAL SIGNALING BE IGNORED?

All this publicity resulted in only one take, namely with the Louis Breguet Company of Paris. This concern entered into a contract with my father to manufacture the Aerial Signal under license. A Paris despatch published in the *Boston Transcript* under date of February 2, 1914, stated that the apparatus "is being tried aboard French army aeroplanes and dirigibles, as a result of the difficulties encountered in the use of wireless." Also, "The Means system, which, it is expected, will be generally adopted especially in artillery units or for an air fleet consists of etc., etc." Further comments on the Aerosignal will be made in the next chapter.

In the meantime let us consider my father's next patented idea, which is quite contemporaneous with the signal. His experience had taught him that as the speed of airplanes increased the problem of getting them airborne would become increasingly difficult. He gave thought, therefore, to problems of launching. Whether the unsuccessful outcome of Langley's attempts to launch his motor-driven manned aeroplane had anything to do with the interest cannot be determined accurately, but at least it well might have done so. Langley's very elaborate launching mechanism, when put to the test, let him down. The Wrights used a catapult and rail for launching and skids for landing from 1904 until July 21, 1910, when it is recorded that they began making experiments with wheels. By that time most other "flyers" were using wheeled undercarriages and were making take-offs by rolling on wheels over smooth flat surfaces until enough speed was attained to lift the aircraft from the ground. Why the Wrights were so slow in adopting what would seem to be the simplest method for launching is difficult for me to understand. Prior to this and after September 1904 their catapult launching device involved the use of a truck running on a track which was laid down facing the wind—Langley's method on the ground, so to speak. My father undoubtedly pondered on these things and came up with some ideas of his own which led to a flock of four patents, granted on May 25, 1909, the same day as that for the signal. They were for four different types of launcher.

The basic problem was how to give an adequate speed to become airborne in a relatively short distance at the time, 1909. There were, of course, no airfields (or aerodromes) with proper runways in the modern sense, yet it was obvious that if the airplane was to realize its potentialities for practical flight (especially in military usage) it must have a wide range of ability in taking off and alighting.

In promotion of his launching devices, my father had this to say:

The supporting power of an aeroplane increases approximately as the square of the velocity. If a machine be designed for a speed of sixty miles per hour, its sustaining surfaces need be less than half of the area required in a machine designed to travel at 40 miles per hour. The ideal structure to meet the conditions of varying speeds is found in the wing of the bird. When gliding at low speeds the maximum of surface encounters the air; when gliding at high speeds the minimum of surface encounters the air; when gliding at high speeds the wings are "reefed," exquisitely reefed, in that the shafts of the feathers trailing aft are so placed as to cause the minimum resistance to the onward motion of the bird.

At the present it seems that the motor-aeroplane, if it is to have in the future high efficiency at both high and low speeds, must include some device, not necessarily similar, yet analogous in function to the bird's reefing apparatus. It is not possible to set limits to the ingenuity of man, yet if with the strength of materials which he can command he is ever able in a motor-aeroplane to quickly reef his sustaining surfaces and at the same time sufficiently reduce head resistance caused by the framework which must support his reefing device, it will be a triumph of the inventive faculties.

I interrupt here to point out that my father's foresight of more than a half-century ago is being realized in today's developments. The use of wing flaps is one example. They are becoming a familiar sight to passengers on airliners, who have observed that, as the airplane is poised at the end of the runway, a broad wide surface starts emerging from the trailing edge of the wing. The pilot is adding more area to increase the lift for take-off. When the airplane has gained altitude and leveled off, these flaps are drawn back into the wing, restoring the wing to its original area. But when he is approaching his airport of destination, the pilot again extends the flaps, usually about the same time that he lowers the wheels. The bird is spreading out its wings and feet for the landing. The passenger feels a distinct slowing down and the pilot gets a better grip on the air. Before long the airplane is back on the ground.

The Navy pilot, faced with the problem of getting his thousand-plus-knots fighter down from the substratosphere and onto the deck of his carrier, which looks like a little sliver on the ocean far below, is grateful for the buttons he can push and wheels he can turn to make slots and slats and spoilers and flaps ruffle out the feathers in his wings so that before long he will be in the approach pattern and soon after will walk into the ward room aboard ship.

I notice from the illustrations of the proposed all-purpose fighter, the TFX, that consideration is being given to varying the angles at which the wing extends from the body, so that the best selection of wing attitude can be made in accordance with varying flight conditions. Other examples could be given of adjustable-wing airplanes including the Bell X-5 and the Grumman F10F, and foreign types as well, all strengthening the projection of my father's belief that a wing should be made adaptable to varying flight requirements.

Now, let us continue the quotation:

> Lacking the device just indicated, it seems that in the near future in designing airplane machines we must content ourselves with high efficiency at the desired speed only.
>
> Suppose we desire a speed of sixty miles per hour. The surface which is most efficient at that speed has so little lifting power at low speeds that it seems desirable to have launchers which can give to the machine an initial velocity equal or nearly equal to the desired maximum speed.
>
> It is difficult to see how an efficient aeroplane designed for a sixty-mile speed could get into the air in any desired direction without a powerful launcher, unless we suppose it to carry a motor having reserve power and to start from even ground of ample area. The lack of the latter has been a great hindrance to progress in aviation.

The modern airport and the catapult launchers aboard naval carriers would seem to have overcome these difficulties.

The James Means launchers constitute four variations of a single basic plan which the inventor describes thus:

> My invention relates to apparatus for launching flying machines. In a flying machine of the aeroplane type a certain high initial velocity in the direction opposite to that of the wind is desirable for soaring, and this velocity which varies according to conditions is best imparted to the machine by means extraneous thereto so that the weight of the machine may be a minimum.
>
> The object of my invention is to provide a simpler and efficient apparatus for launching flying machines whereby any desired initial velocity may be imparted to the machine in a direction toward any point of the compass.

It was proposed to meet these indications by means of a rotatable table, traversed in one of its diameters by a track, either of rails or grooves, along which an aircraft could be quickly whisked into a speed sufficient to permit it to become airborne, when it reached the end of the track—in other words, to shoot it off the end of the track into free flight and continue in the same by means of its own power plant, and propeller(s).

In two of the four types, acceleration was to be provided by clutching an endless cable as is done in customary cable cars. The pilot could operate the clutching and releasing mechanism, as does the operator of a cable car. Any convenient extrinsic prime mover could be used to drive the endless cable. In the other two types the accelerating impulse was to be provided by means of a large cylinder and piston, operated by compressed air.

For military purposes the inventor believed that "it will be necessary to have portable launchers which can be quickly taken apart, carried to the chosen place" by whatever transport might be available, "and quickly reassembled."

All these James Means launchers are, of course, of the nature of catapults. To my knowledge there followed no general development or use of catapults with landplanes until recently, when I learned that the U.S. Marine Corps is testing such a device for expediting the take-off of heavy aircraft from small fields. But in my father's time as soon as it was found that with a wheeled undercarriage an aircraft could take off from the ground, or on pontoons or with a hull from the water, solely with its own power, interest in devices to do for it what it could do for itself, quickly subsided.

On board warships, however, the catapult has come into its own. The flattop or carrier has vindicated my father's foresight.

My father's aeronautical cogitations continued unabated after he had delivered himself of the launchers. On October 5, 1909, he took out a patent on a safety device by which in case of emergency the pilot could, by throwing one lever, convert the aircraft itself into a sort of parachute and simultaneously cut the motors. The idea was that the aircraft would thereupon sink slowly and safely to the ground. It was not, I should think, one of his brightest ideas. To my inexpert mind the proposal sounds utterly impractical, nor can I find any evidence that it was ever tested.

On June 27, 1911, our inventor patented yet another device, namely, an "aeronautical clinometer." An instrument, this was to inform a pilot of how much, if any, inclination from the horizontal his aircraft might have assumed. It was described as "having in combination two separated spherical glass plates, a globule of mercury enclosed between the same, and means for varying the separation of said plates, whereby said globule may be tightly compressed and its movement restrained." The lower plate was to be blackened, and the upper etched in concentric circles and radii. The instrument worked on the principle of a carpenter's level but was modified into a circular bowl-like form with the mercury globule at bottom-center. With this instrument mounted in an airplane with the rim of the bowl horizontal to the line of thrust and the wing tips, the globule would move in whichever direction the airplane was tilted. So simple and ancient was it in principle that it is almost incredible that it was found patentable. But it was. Recently a pilot friend of mine expressed admiration for this invention, his only criticism being that it would require the pilot to look directly down into it—an awkward position when flying. Clinometers have, however, been developed by later inventors into frontal-viewing instruments which have glass tubes containing liquids, a vertical tube showing inclinations of climb and descent, and a horizontal or slightly-curved tube indicating lateral balance. An example, the Rieker type, can be seen in the National Air Museum on the instrument panel of Lindbergh's *Spirit of St. Louis.*

It is interesting to me that, while flying was still in its low-altitude infancy, my father foresaw the need for such an instrument to aid the aviator when "flying blind."

My father's next invention, which was to be his last and in my opinion his best, consisted in a unified control system for operating aeroplanes. Patents on it were granted in 1909 and 1911. In all his inventions there was his double purpose or hope of increasing either safety or efficiency of operation. He called this device:

THE JAMES MEANS CONTROL
For
Flying Machines
(Based upon the principles of
Mental Automatism.)

I think he may have contributed to both safety and efficiency with this.

All his inventions resulted from considerable study. He sought for the important practical problems and tried to solve them. He came to the conclusion that if aeroplanes were to become widely used it would be extremely important from the safety point of view to have their controls standardized. He got good support for this opinion in the following passage from the *Army and Navy Gazette* (London), January 4, 1913:

The time is rapidly coming, and the quicker the better, when controls will have to be standardized. The point is one of particular importance to the military pilot, who may be called upon to navigate machines of different types. If the necessity of standard-

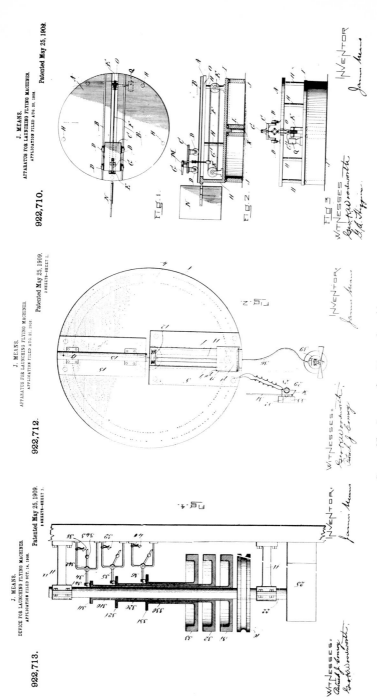

PLATE 25.—Patents for Means launching apparatuses.

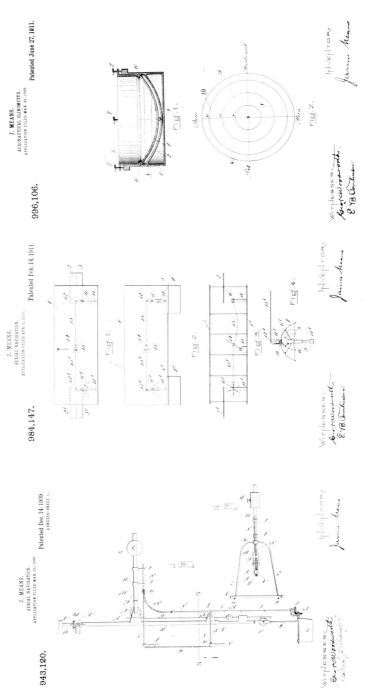

PLATE 26.—Patents for the Means control, the yaw-steering device, and the clinometer.

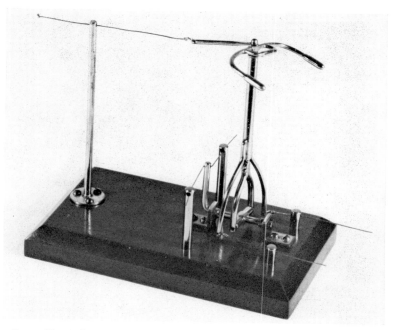

Plate 27.—Scale models of Means Control and of the Heinrich Monoplane of 1909. This airplane used the James Means control. Both models are in the National Air Museum.

PLATE 28.—The James Means Memorial prize medal established in 1926 at the Massachusetts Institute of Technology by Dr. James H. Means in memory of his father. It was originally awarded to an undergraduate of the Institute for an essay on an aeronautical subject, but since 1950 it has been awarded to the graduating senior who, in the opinion of the heads of the Department of Aeronautics and Astronautics, shows the greatest professional promise in these sciences, considering all factors of character, scholarship, and knowledge as evidenced in a written thesis. A cash award is included.

PLATE 29.—Engineers' Club Dinner honoring Orville Wright at the Massachusetts Institute of Technology, June 12, 1916. James Means is standing, second from the right; Alexander Klemin, then instructor at M.I.T. is at his left, and Dr. Jerome Hunsaker is at Means's right. In front, seated, is Dr. Alexander Graham Bell, and Orville Wright is seated second to his right. The photograph shows only a portion of those present, who included Glenn Martin, Lester Gardner, Roy Knabenshue, Godfrey Cabot, Paul Litchfield, Alan Hawley, Oscar Brindley, and other leaders in engineering, education, and aeronautics.

ization is clear, the particular standard to be adopted opens a wide field for discussion, which may be profitably dealt with upon another occasion.

On this he commented:

I fully agree with this in the main, although I should have liked to see the words *without undue haste* inserted after "the quicker the better." This may seem like emphasizing a trivial thing, but it is really far from doing that. The author speaks of one control, having natural movements, which has been used for many years and with which most remarkable things have been done, as having for its obvious disadvantage "its radical departure from accepted standards."

It seems to me it is too early in the development of the flying machine to pay much attention to "accepted standards" in matters of standardization. Many of these accepted standards are positively bad. We must always remember that a man likes a thing which he has mastered and the more difficult for him it was to learn to use it, having once mastered it, the harder it is for him to see merit in a simpler thing which is much easier to learn. I think that all those who follow the developments in aviation and who have never learned to fly with a bad control will agree with me that all controls which use levers moving fore and aft to correct lateral balance are bad.

There is only one way to fix upon a standard control and that is by making records of success *or failure* in teaching pupils.

If a man undertakes to invent a new control, he must ask himself just what it is that he has to do. Certainly it is this, to provide the shortest cut between the brain and the machine. He will then decide whether the flyer shall use hands, feet or both; and whether or not he shall use the shoulders.

I have consulted brain specialists in this matter of connecting the brain with the machine, and regret that I cannot quote their exact language, but the impression left on my mind is this, that one must not divide the current, that if the hands can do it all, it should so be done. This brings us to a single lever control actuating three elements, i.e., for longitudinal, lateral and directional control. Of course, the fingers may be used to actuate electrical connections.

My father was much imbued with the automaticity of bicycle riding and wanted to make it as easy and natural to drive an aeroplane as to ride a bike. In the further development of this idea he had this to say:

Mental automatism in balancing may be illustrated by the experience of the novice learning to ride the bicycle. If he is able to keep from falling he does so by extremely rapid thinking which is represented by wabbling. When after some practice, the learner ceases to wabble, he has ceased to think; his motion is even and graceful.

The mental automatism which he has then acquired is as complete as that which enables him to balance without thought in walking.

The novice in flying makes his initial flight under the most favorable conditions when he is able to make use of previously acquired mental automatism. In the matter of balancing, the less he has to unlearn the shorter will be the process of learning. Bicycle handle-bars, unlike steering-wheels, are, in his case, already mentally associated with the act of balancing.

In bicycle riding the swaying of the body is in harmony with the swaying of the machine. The shortest way to proficiency in flying is found in bringing about harmony in the movements of the man and those of the flying machine.

This form of the JAMES MEANS CONTROL is designed first and above all to enable the aviator to take the fullest possible advantage of the mental automatism which he has previously acquired in balancing the bicycle.

As the flying machine is now being developed everything points toward a standardization of control.

That very desirable end will be reached by the survival of the fittest control. The fittest, whichever it may prove to be in the future, will be the one with which, other things being equal, the art of flying is seen to be most easily learned and continuously practised with the fewest accidents.

The modern airplane has a certain number of airfoils which are movable, and the position of which is under the control of the pilot, and a certain number which are fixed or immobile. In the first category are the rudder, ailerons, elevator, and the wing flaps; in the second, the wings, the horizontal stabilizer, and the vertical tail fin. By means of the control column, "stick" or "joystick," the pilot can move the elevator and ailerons. By means of his feet he operates the rudder.

My father planned to exercise all controls through the stick. He mounted a bicyclelike handlebar on its top (see diagram, fig. 14), and had this to say about its operation:

It will be seen in the diagram that the balancing motions of the aviator are natural, that is to say, in actuating the lateral and longitudinal rudders the movement of the handle-bars is in the direction which the swaying of the aviator's body would take if he sought to correct by his weight the rolling or pitching.

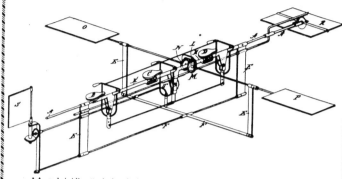
Fig. 14.—Advertisement for Means Control.

In examining the drawing, it will be seen that there are three kinds of movement of the handle-bar:

(1) both hands forward or aft. (2) Both hands right or left, and also, (3) the ordinary bicycle steer which moves the vertical rudder.

These movements may be made either independently or simultaneously. To illustrate the former:

Both hands aft elevates the bow.
"   "   forward depresses the bow.
"   "   to the right elevates port side.
"   "   "   " left   "   starboard.

Another advantage of the James Means Control was that it lent itself well to training purposes. Sticks and pilots' seats could be set up in tandem for as many as desired.

In designing a machine for a plurality of flyers the tandem arrangement is the only one which economizes power in locating the seats.

When we consider the strenuous endeavors which are being made to reduce the head resistance it seems remarkable that some designers still place their men side by side, thus wasting power.

There will be those who will say that my father was but a dreamer, and this may well be true. However, he was a dreamer who dreamed realistically and who exerted himself adventurously to make his dreams come true. He patented the signal, the launchers, and the control in Canada, Great Britain, France, and Germany, as well as in the United States, and his patent lawyers did their utmost to find foreign manufacturers who would exploit the patents under license. I am sure that he sank a lot of money in these promotional activities and that he got little if any return on any of it. Only the French showed any active interest. The firm of Louis Breguet at Douai, France, made a few signals and investigated the control a bit. There is a large file of letters from firms which had been solicited. For the most part they expressed polite interest and regrets that they could not make use of the patents. The Avro Company in Manchester, England, wrote with extreme candor regarding the control to my father's lawyers as follows:

We saw particulars of this in an advertisement in the American Press some time ago, and we rather think it has been offered before. It is therefore evident your client is spending a lot of money in his endeavours to get his idea placed.

Of course, it is hardly in your province, but you would certainly be doing him a great kindness if you let him know candidly that he will never place it.

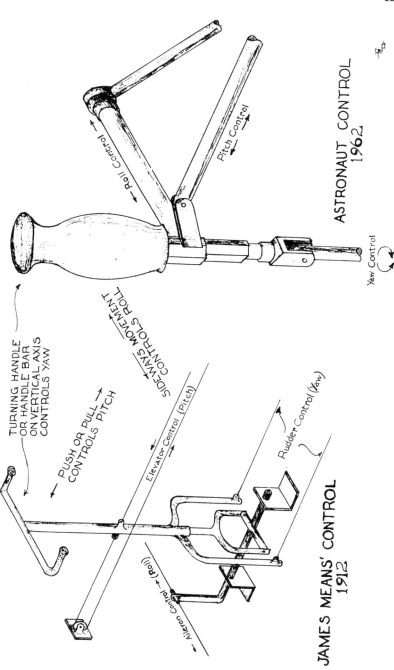

ASTRONAUT CONTROL
1962

Roll Control

Pitch Control

Yaw Control

TURNING HANDLE
OR HANDLE BAR
ON VERTICAL AXIS
CONTROLS YAW

PUSH OR PULL
CONTROLS PITCH

SIDEWAY'S MOVEMENT
CONTROLS ROLL

Elevator Control (Pitch)

Rudder Control (Yaw)

Aileron control (Roll)

JAMES MEANS' CONTROL
1912

Fig. 15.—Comparison of Mercury Astronaut's left-hand control with Means Control—a half century between.

If Mr. Means would just take a few lessons in flying he would then cease hoping, for he would then see and understand why his invention is really useless.

This letter was signed by A. V. Roe, the man my father and I had seen crash his triplane the year before at Boston. On this somewhat somber note, I will rest my own account of my father's brief period as an inventor in the field of aeronautics. It puts me in mind of his dedication to the first issue of the Aeronautical Annual (see pages 46-47). The culmination of it all follows in the next chapter, in which my father and my brother, who traveled together in Europe in the summer of 1912, speak for themselves.

But before we come to that I must tell about a more recent and very pertinent little episode. It was in the Smithsonian's National Air Museum. The head curator and historian, Paul E. Garber, was showing me about. Presently he led me up to a Mercury capsule, the one that had actually taken astronaut Alan Shepard into space. There was a large opening through which we could look into it. A mannequin of the astronaut was in place. "Do you see where his right hand is?" said Garber. The mannequin's hand was grasping a knob surmounting a control column. "The manipulation is the same as in your father's control," Garber added. "This one works on the same principle. It can be moved fore and aft, sideways, or twisted, just as in the James Means Control, thus controlling the position of the capsule in three-dimensional space, only this astronaut's control exerts its function by activating directional jets, instead of airfoils, as in the case of the airplane control."

Later on Mr. Garber called the attention of astronauts Shepard and Glenn to this resemblance, and he told me they agreed that there is a similarity.

In the same building, on a wall panel illustrating outstanding persons associated with aeronautics during the pioneer period, a photograph of my father is included. Nearby is a small scale model illustrating the elements of the James Means Control, and in a display case with other scale models of airplanes of the Early Bird era there is one of the Heinrich monoplane, which was designed, built, and flown on Long Island by Arthur and Albert Heinrich. The original airplane used my father's control, and the scale model has a miniature of it in the cockpit.

It is gratifying to know that in the national aeronautical and astronautical collections, my father has his place.

Chapter IX

FAREWELL JOURNEY

IT IS fitting, I think, to close this memoir with a rather firsthand account of my father's final efforts to promote his ideas in the field of practical flying. Fortunately, I have two letters which tell the story and give a vivid impression of my father and an understanding of his motivation and orientation to his prime interest. I shall quote from them quite extensively.

In the summer of 1912 my father and my brother, the late Philip Ainsworth Means, made a tour of Europe together, which is the subject of this chapter. My father was fifty-nine years old at the time, and my brother was twenty. The latter had just completed his sophomore year in Harvard College. Later he became a noted archeologist, especially in the region of the Andes and other parts of Spanish America.

The first letter in question is from my father to my mother.

London, August 23, 1912

Here we are back in London again.

We left Paris on Tuesday and went to Amiens, went to Douai on Wednesday, had the latter part of the day in Amiens, and came here yesterday via Boulogne-Folkestone.

Last Monday P. went to Chartres, and I took an interpreter and an auto, and made the rounds of the Aeroplane Factories just outside of Paris, at Neuilly, Lavellois, Billancourt, etc. I visited the establishments of Farman, Nieuport, Bleriot, Esnault-Pelterie, Morane and others. They were very agreeable, and glad to show me whatever I wanted to see. It was some satisfaction to me to find that my name was not unfamiliar to them. I made no business propositions to any of them, for reasons which I will mention presently. I talked Signal and found them interested. In most cases I talked with principals; had pleasant chats with Bleriot and the younger Farman.

Philip had a fine day at Chartres, and says that the Cathedral is wonderful.

123

I am, as you know, more interested concerning the Breguet concern than any other, and I have felt that if I could get to their headquarters and make friends with Louis Breguet, it would be the best thing that could happen. That is why I thought it best not to talk business in Paris.

Wednesday morning, as I have written, P. and I went to Douai.

Louis Breguet had his outer office posted with signs about short visits, and the value of time, etc., and we found him busy indeed and a little bit indifferent at first, as though he wanted to get back to the things he had in hand, but, as I talked Signal to him (through Philip and B's private secretary as interpreters), he seemed to forget his other things, and at last I was pleased to hear him say to his secretary—'Tell Mr. Means that I am very much interested in this.' To make a long story short, he has requested me to send him all the details about Mr. Clarke's work, so that he might test the apparatus on one of his machines.

I may here interpolate that all of the army men and aeroplane designers to whom I have put the question agree that at present my Signal is the only practical one so far proposed. I believe I have written this before.

Then we turned to the question of Control and Patents.

I asked him whether I should deal with the British Breguet Company or with the French, and he said "deal with us."

I told him that my policy in Patents is to pursue a course exactly opposite to that which has been followed by the Wright Companies; that I believe those who have Patents which may resemble each other should work for harmony.

He asked me for the date of my application for my earliest Control Patent. I showed him my broad claims and the date, March 2nd., 1908. I asked him for the same data in regard to his. He brought it out. It is a narrow Patent, and the application was not filed until 1909.

Breguet frankly admitted that my Patent must take precedence of his.

After we had finished our business talk, he said he wanted to take me out to his Aerodrome, some kilometers out; we all got into his auto, and he drove us out, at a wicked rate of speed. It is a fine flying field—and what a fine lot of Breguet machines he showed us! He had me climb into the machines, and went into all sorts of details whenever I asked him a question.

Then we drove back, and B. said it was his busy day and he must be excused. He deputed his secretary to take us to lunch and see us to the station.

There are several business matters which we are to take up in correspondence, but neither of us is committed to anything, for as a matter of fact, we neither of us yet know exactly what we want.

P. and I got back to Amiens about four, and went all over the wonderful Cathedral.

It is raining hard now, as it has a great deal of the time since we left Berlin. P. is at the Reading Room of the British Museum making researches concerning the aborigines of Mexico. He has finished his Bernal Diaz, which has awakened in him a deep interest in the subject.

Clarke (Engineer), is coming here at three to report what he has done in my absence. To judge from his letters, I think he has been doing well.

I am expecting in a few days to hear from Ronacher that the German apparatus is ready. I shall not go back to Berlin unless he sends for me, and I hardly see why he should.

I have enough here to keep me very busy in the eighteen days remaining before we sail on the tenth.

P. will take day trips to Canterbury, Cambridge, etc., etc. He said he wants to stop over at Chester the day before sailing, so that he may walk around that wall and see if the view is any better than it was the last time.

We are both very well, and we love you lots. Please give much love to Howard.

Your loving husband,
J.

Philip, who was the traveling companion and occasionally the interpreter, writes of this tour with such sensibility, humor, and affection that I shall give his letter almost in toto, deleting only a few passages of purely personal interest. As a matter of fact, Philip wrote this letter in June of 1935 at my request. I wanted to have his recollections in writing for the purposes of this memoir which even then I was trying to start. Philip said in his covering letter to me, "Herewith I send you a long letter which I have written you about Father as I promised to do. It goes to you just as it wrote itself, without any attempt to edit or improve it. If it is of any use to you in 'James Means and the Problem of Manflight,' I shall be very glad." At least I had the title chosen as early as 1935, but only a few scattered passages otherwise.

And here is what Philip wrote to me:

Pomfret, Sun., 2 June 1935

Dear Howard,

Ever since last Sunday, when you told me that you are planning to write a Life of our Father (I mean James Means—not God!) I have been delighted, and I have been trying to remember things that might help you. Here, without any attempt at chronological or logical arrangement, are the results:

In the summer of 1912, Father and I went to Europe, and he made an attempt to sell or otherwise dispose of his various patents connected with flying in England, Germany, and France.

We went first to England, and lived for a while in the lugubrious grandeur of the Hotel Metropole in Northumberland Avenue. At that time the late Major George Squier was the U.S. Military Attache in London, and we saw a great deal of him as he went out of his way to help Father. Through him we went to some very interesting places, especially a big factory at a place called Surbiton, near London. There they were making aeroplanes which, today, would look terribly rickety and home-made, but which were then considered marvelous. The Big Boy at that plant—I forget his name, but he was either a big Army officer or something else more or less impressive—was very much interested in Father's patents, especially the Signaller and the Control. A deal of some kind—which I cannot remember at all—was made between Father and him.

At that same time we met various interesting and famous people. General Baden-Powell, head of the Boy Scouts (I think, but it *may* have been his Brother, also a General) was very polite to us and took us to see a number of sights, including some big military museum away from London (I never could identify it afterwards, when I lived in London, 1922-24), and also he took us all over Greenwich and Chelsea Hospital. We also met, in some Club, I think it was the Athenaeum or maybe the Royal Institution, the Duke of Norfolk, whose family-name was Howard (or rather, Fitzalan-Howard). He was the first Dook I had ever met, and I was much disappointed in him as he looked a great deal more like a shabby cabby than like a Duke. However, he was very affable, and when Father, as a joke, remarked that Howard was one of our family names, and that his grandmother had been Joanna Howard, the Duke said, 'We are distantly related then, because that lady was a great-grand-daughter of one of my predecessors.' They looked at some books, etc. and it turned out to be so. The D. of N. was very polite and kind, and showed us about a bit, inviting us to visit him in St. James's Square, and showing us other courtesies. I soon saw that, in spite of his rumpled appearance, he was very much a great gentleman, and a very kind, intelligent one.

It was at this period that we went to have tea and dinner with Sir Hiram and Lady Maxim. Sir Hiram had a lot of big albums filled with an amazing array of quaint and fascinating pictures of men's machines for flying, from Icarus down to that year. He put me down at a table and left me perfectly happy with the albums for hours while my elders talked. Lady Maxim told Father that I seemed very much interested and I was. At the end of the collection was a picture of a big condor flying over the Andes, and, written beside it, the words: "We haven't caught up with him yet!" As we were going away, Sir Hiram drew me to one side and said, 'My boy, I hope that you realize that your father has a very fine mind.' A stately, handsome and very gracious old gentleman, Sir Hiram. He contributed to the 1896 "Annual." (That was before, disgusted with the stupidity which he encountered in this country (U.S.), he became a British subject and a Knight.) Sir Hiram also appears in the Epitome.

A digression: All this was in July, 1912, as I can tell by the fact that the very first serious book about Ancient America that I ever bought was the copy of Bernal Diaz del Castillo's, *The True History of the Conquest of New Spain,* which I got at Quaritch's with some money given me by Aunt Alice Farnsworth. It is the Hakluyt Society's splendid edition. Father was very pleased that I wanted it, and gave me some other books on kindred subjects. I have the Diaz del Castillo and the other books still. Sometimes I wonder if it was not Sir Hiram's condor picture that first drew my attention to Peru. My copy of Diaz' is dated as bought on 2 August 1912, and I remember that I got it just a day or two before we went to Germany.

The trip to Germany was something of a scream. We planned to go from London to Plymouth, to take there the *Imperator* for Hamburg, and then go on to Berlin. Father expected to meet some of our Boston friends on board the *Imperator.* Well, we sent our traps ahead of us to Paddington and I was given the railway tickets to hold, and also the steamer ticket. After an early lunch we started to go to the station ourselves, walking along Northumberland Avenue in quest of a cab. Pop suddenly saw some aeroplane- or glider-models in a shop window, which he had to investigate. He told me to go on to Paddington, get our stuff from the checkroom (or whatever they call it in England) and nobble two good seats in the train. So I went ahead. Father didn't come and didn't come. I got into a fantod about it, and a kind lady, only other person in my 1st class compartment (Father always went First, as it gave him more room for his feet, books, etc.) saw that I was worrying about something. So I told her all about it, and she advised me to go on to Plymouth and let my father follow by the next train and look for me in the best hotel in Plymouth. So, as Father did not show up, I did so. As the train pulled out of Paddington, I, with my head out the window, heard a great deal of roaring and excitement outside the gate to the platform. It was Papa! They would not let him on, as the train had started.

He came on, however, by the next train, and I met him in the station in Plymouth. I expected all kinds of a wigging, but he said that it was all his own fault and that I had done just right. We spent the evening selling back the unused ticket that I had been holding for him.

Our hotel in Plymouth overlooked the Hoe, and Father gave me a vivid word picture of the Armada business. It was very exciting. Father specialised in historical word-pictures for me, and I am deeply grateful for them.

Next morning we packed up to go on board the *Imperator,* which was expected from America about noon. It was a glorious summer morning, and Plymouth harbor was all sparkling with jolly waves which lapped the pretty green shores. We found the tender and went on board of it. Another of Father's specialties was using incredibly decrepit suitcases, especially when Mother was not around to object. On this occasion he had all his soiled clothes stuffed into a suitcase that had come over on the *Mayflower.* When the tender began to dance a little the wretched suitcase rolled into something or other and completely discombobulated itself, letting all its contents out all over the deck. Just then the gigantic steamer came bounding in with every swank person I had ever heard of in Boston craning his or her neck over the rail at us. Pop, meanwhile, very calmly made two bundles of his soiled clothes, one in a bright pink pajama top, the other in a bright blue one, each done up by tying its sleeves. At that time I was all for absolute "correctness" in all particulars, especially with Boston's bluest and best looking on. But Father didn't give a continental and serenely marched up the gang-plank carrying his shameless and gaudy bundles, while I followed trying to look as if I did not belong to him. At the top of the gang-plank we met dozens of people we knew, but Pop was not in the least fazed, although *I* wanted to die of mortification. (Of course, nowadays I would just as soon do the same thing myself.)

Well, in Berlin we put up at the sublime Hotel Bristol on Unter den Linden, where we had a bathroom with a lovely sunken bath-tub big enough to swim in, or almost. We used to eat at a wonderful restaurant called Fischer's, across the way, and every day we lapped up quantities of a lovely soup called "Consommé fumée a l'estragon" the like of which I have never tasted since. Father had letters to various important Germans, named von Stumm, von Falkenhayn, von Beckteuschof, etc., who asked us to their houses and nearly killed us with heavenly food. Also, we used to go and have business talks with the fattest man I ever saw, except two, who was a merchant in Kriegsmateriall. I forget his name, but he and Father were discussing the sale in Germany of Father's patents. Things went along rosily for a while, and we also spent endless happy hours seeing sights—at Charlottenberg and Potsdam, as well as in Berlin. More word pictures—lots of them! We particularly loved the sweet little Monbijoupalast, tucked away in a quiet corner of Berlin, where the Hohenzollern Museum was. We also visited the Berlin Fine Arts Museum and other things. Our Ambassador (David Jayne Hill, I think it was) was very polite to us, and showed us about.

Then, one day, some of our friends took us to a tremendous military review at Wilhelmshaven, outside Berlin. We were in a box almost next to the Kaiser's. It was a thrilling sight. Many thousands of faultlessly drilled soldiers goose-stepping with clockwork precision as they went by the Emperor. I was wild with excitement, but Father was curiously thoughtful, and when we got back to the Bristol he suddenly remarked: "My son, these people are looking for trouble. I won't sell my patents here." We left for Paris that night.

Father's German was excellent, but his French was terrible. Mine was reasonably good, however, and I served him as an interpreter. (He used to say plaintively, "They understand my French in Cairo and in Quebec, but not in Paris.") Well, we got into touch with Louis Breguet, and some sort of a deal was made with him about the signaller, the control, and the launcher. But I don't at all remember what it was although I had to translate all the documents about it for Father. I have always suspected that Breguet rather gypped Father about the control, if not also about the other two, but probably this could not be proved. At this time we began to get increasingly abusive letters from the Kriegsmateriall man in Berlin, who was furious about our sudden departure to France. Father told him that he would do no business in Germany and then made no more rejoinders.

A very high officer in the French Army, the Marquis de Quelquechose (I can't remember his real name) was very nice to us, and took us all over the Invalides and also Saint-Cyr. Also we saw many sights. We lived in the Hotel Continental, and one night we there met in the dining-room Dean Rousmanière and his family, who joined us for dinner. Pop, although by no means pious, was delighted to see people from home, and we had a jovial evening. Soon after that we left for London, *en route* for home, and we then stopped at the Hotel Cecil, where we lived chiefly on pilafs and curries, which Father loved, and I did, too. Father and I made a trip to Boston, Lincs., and climbed the St. Botolph tower, of which he bought a large photograph which, I believe he afterwards gave to the St. Botolph Club at home.

History was one of Father's chief delights, and he had an unusual grasp upon it as well as a great gift for reconstructing scenes and events. To visit Waterloo with him, as I did at one time (I forgot when) was a great experience, and, in like manner I vividly remember his informal and quite *ex tempore* discourses to me in sundry historic places. One was the castle of Chinon, where Saint Jeanne d'Arc had her epochal audience with the King of France, picking him out by instinct from a crowd of courtiers. The castle is a picturesque ruin now, and the fireplace before which the interview took place is open to the sky. Nevertheless, Father's description of the event was so vivid that, to my imagination, the shattered walls reconstituted themselves into a lordly Gothic hall, the fireplace regained its quondam shape and function, and all around us was a throng of gaily-clad nobles and knights, with the poor King hiding among them and a false king sitting in the huge high-backed chair beside the fire, to test our Jeanne's power of penetration. Father, with that beautiful voice of his and his keen, fine features and bright eyes all alight with the enthusiasm of what he was doing, portrayed the whole incident with such sureness and precision that it came alive before me. And it is alive still, at this moment, quarter of a century later.

Yet, aside from certain parts of the "Annuals," I do not know of Father's ever having *written* any history; instead, he helped, very much *so,* to *make* it. Sometimes I have thought that he would have liked to write history, but he never found time for it. Instead, he, with such exquisite fatherly kindness, used to go out of his way to foster my fondness for it. In Rome, for instance, in the winter of 1904-05, when I was a mere lad, he used to spend hours working up his knowledge of events and places in Roman history, from Etruscan times down through the classic period and on into the papal period, and then he would take Mother and me, or me alone, to the proper place and would thrill us with a glowing account of the matter. Once, I remember, when we were standing before the great fountain in the Piazza di San Pietro, he said to me, "This city is the place of all places on earth where the human mind and human passions of all kinds, good and bad, have displayed themselves most continuously, and in the most intense degree."

Father, more than anyone I ever knew, had a truly patrician mind. He hated sham and pretense and snobbery with all his soul, and ardently loved all that was noblest, wherever they were found. Aside from rare bursts of temper, usually caused by some form or other of stupidity or of malice, he had the most perfect manners imaginable, utterly simple, dignified and kind. Their perfection came from a gracious and generous heart and from a deep-seated belief that people in all walks of life were worthy of respect, consideration, and esteem. In short, he valued people for what they *were,* not for what they *had.* I know that you, and I hope that I, have inherited this magnanimous attitude.

Your affectionate brother,

Philip

Chapter X

APPRAISAL

W ITH THE journey described in the preceding chapter, my father's activities in aeronautics came to an end. During his remaining years he was in declining health and did no more writing or inventing. He retained his interest in manflight, however, and during the four years of World War I he watched with amazement and sometimes with horror the explosive development of aviation under the compelling necessities of war. It was gratifying, however, to see at least some of his predictions come true. That man would attain great skill in flying he had always thoroughly believed. Progressive improvement in motors, in the design of aircraft, and in the skill of pilots he had fully anticipated, but as the result of peaceful evolution. He had not really expected that the chief impetus would be that of war. Of course, he had done some thinking about military flying. This is disclosed in his dealings with General Allen and in his advocacy of his signal for military purposes. He had sensed the possibility of aerial combat, etc., but believed that man having attained the blessing of flight would have the wisdom to refrain from using it for self-destruction. That this was not so saddened him.

I have, as the pages of this book will testify, raked the past and combed my memory, and now it is appropriate to attempt some appraisal of my father and his work. Certainly it can be said that he was of a scholarly and inquiring frame of mind, and whatever he may have accomplished in the field of aeronautics followed from these traits. My brother has given a perceptive word portrait of him as a human being.

His type of scholarship was more acquisitive than creative, but nonetheless it had some driving force. He was a voracious reader in many aspects of science and the humanities, especially in the study of history. When he could not by reading find the answers he desired, he was prepared to indulge in experiment to discover them. Yet he had not had the opportunity to develop a clear under-

131

standing of the nature of research and of its exactions. He had a deep love of truth and integrity and despised hypocrisy. As I view the various peregrinations of his thinking, forty years after his death, there become perceptible a certain continuity and relevance. In this perspective some salient points seem evident, and difficult questions emerge. For example, his high-school oration, quoted in Chapter I, discloses the type of interest which probably led him to M.I.T. But the question that has always troubled me is, Why did he remain there for but a single year? It seems to me that had he completed his education at the college level, and perhaps beyond, and had thus, presumably, trained his mind to some degree, and learned more of the nature and requirements of research, he could have contributed to science more effectively. Why his father, who had had the advantage of higher education himself, did not insist on his gifted son's having the benefit of it also, I have never understood. Here I am probably reflecting the opinion of my mother because I know this is how she felt about the matter, and very strongly so. My father behaved in quite the opposite way. He introduced me to biology, Darwin, Huxley, etc., at a tender age, which led me finally, through a series of permutations, to medicine. All along the line he gave me every encouragement. Similarly he gave my brother Philip encouragement in his progress to archeology.

My father's short business career (15 years only) is somewhat of a strange interlude, but I am sure it crystallized attitudes which affected his thinking in later life. For one thing he was rapidly successful. He learned how new ideas and special privileges can force the growth of a business enterprise. His special privilege was conferred by his trademark, which made it possible for him to sell his produce direct to retailers at a fixed price, cutting out the middlemen. Through this he came to the concept of mass production.

His thinking about the modus operandi of his business led him to perceive the economic fallacies inherent in protective tariffs. And this led him to labor relations, and from that to politics. He campaigned for free trade on the grounds that it would give a better break to labor. I am sure these ideas which he promulgated in 1888 were in many respects very like those expressed by President Kennedy in his State of the Union message in January 1962.

But business was not his proper dish, and, as we have seen, the Pacific gulls snatched him away from it. To withdraw suddenly from a lucrative and expanding business which bid fair to be an enduring moneymaker indicates a point of view which must be excessively rare in our society. He wanted to experiment with flying models. And this is what he did—experiment. He never referred to himself as a researcher or his work as research. It was experimenting, a process of practical self-education in a restricted field, and he was therefore, so he considered himself, the experimenter, later the inventor. Zahm and Langley he properly regarded as research men, but the rest, like himself, he thought of as experimenters. The trial and error method was their approach. My father was thoroughly convinced that a great deal could be learned from flying models. He certainly would have been elated if he could have seen his great-grandson flying a model not very different from his own but equipped with a tiny gasoline motor which could take it off the ground into free and beautiful flight. He was utterly opposed to the risking of human life in the air until perfect flight had been attained with models. The early gliding and power pilots disagreed with him thoroughly on this point. They insisted that there were many things about flying that could only be learned by getting into the air themselves and experiencing the feel of it. Now it seems to me that he should have been eager to do this, but the fact is that I have no knowledge of his ever being off the ground himself. Perhaps he was mindful of the admonition of his father's gardener that life is sweet (Chapter I), and that there is nothing to be gained by throwing it away needlessly.

Experimenting with gliding models led him to do the same with kites, and he quickly sensed the relation of these to one another and of both to the powered aircraft. That the same machine can be flown as a kite, a motorless glider, or a powered aeroplane was the connecting link. All it needs is air speed, which can be provided by a string, a motor, or by gravity. Because of his great concern for safety, he was profoundly interested in stability. Lateral stability he knew could be provided by wings with a dihedral angle, but with some loss of lift and increased swerving effect from side gusts.

The Hargrave box kite had great inherent stability and certainly was the evolutionary prototype of the subsequent motorized biplane. The perpendicular airfoils between the wings at their tips prevented side slipping and there was no dihedral angle. The Santos-Dumont, Voisin, and Farman biplanes of the early 1900's all showed a clear Hargrave ancestry. In these machines the Hargrave principle was carried out in the tail assembly as well as in the supporting wings. With the later general adoption of monoplane aircraft in commercial and military flying, the Hargrave principle became extinct, unless the present-day tail fin and rigid stabilizer can be considered remnants of it. My father referred to the Hargrave as "the wonderful Hargrave kite." Its stability attracted him greatly.

His work with kites brought the experimental period of his life to an end. It gave way, as we have seen, to his period as an editor. After completing this memoir and the studies made in its preparation, I remain convinced that the Aeronautical Annual was my father's most important contribution. It is what he will be remembered for longest in aeronautical circles. In retrospect it seems unfortunate that he did not continue it longer. I really think he "missed the bus" in giving it up. But this was rather the somewhat tragic pattern of his life. He started too many good things and dropped them before reaching their fulfillment. The Annual was a medium through which as editor he could have exercised a continuing influence on the progress of aviation. It might have become a quarterly or even a monthly, and the leading aeronautical journal in the United States. But alas it did not.

The period of invention was the last phase. It was somewhat of a throwback to the business period. Instead of a trademark, he took out patents and then tried to sell them as he had his shoes. But it did not work out that way, and none of his inventions really made the grade. None have influenced the evolution of flying. The signal, which was simple and ingenious, was quickly superseded when radio communication was perfected. The launching devices were made obsolete when aircraft became fully able to take off under their own power. It is harder to understand why the control, which seemed extraordinarily well conceived, never was taken up and made operational. The notion that the guiding of an aeroplane could be made as physiologically automatic as the riding of a bicycle, and the design of a mechanism for accomplishing it, seems to me to be both original and enlightened. The Heinrich brothers said it worked very satisfactorily in their airplanes. Why it was not used in other aircraft I am at a loss to understand. My pilot friend Mr. Wight thinks the device might have been too clumsy to operate. One might think that the pilot would have to swing his body and arms about too much, with the possible danger of hitting the copilot in the ribs or something of that sort. But actually, except when performing aerobatics or in extreme turbulence, a pilot does not have to manipulate his controls in wide movements. Also it seems to me the movement of the column could be conveyed through levers and gears in such manner that the desired action of the control surfaces could be effected without the need for excessive movement of the control column itself.

In his autobiographical sketch of 1913 (unpublished), my father had this to say about himself and his inventions:

In 1908 he made many inventions; controls, launchers, aerial signal, etc., upon which he is still working.

Mr. Means paramount idea at the present time (1913) is to bring about the standardization of flying machine control. He says that in the military use of the aeroplane there is room for only one control. If an aviator is disabled, any military aviator must be able to take his place unhampered by familiarity with some other control. He also says that the control which will be the standard will be the *best* control, whoever may be the inventor, and the best will be determined by the survival of the fittest. He does not assert that his is the best but, being the inventor, he thinks it is.

His control is constantly in use and may be seen by military men in this country at any time by appointment. It has been fully demonstrated in Europe. It is based upon the principle of mental automatism. It depends upon making the shortest cut between the brain and the machine.

My father's active mind occasionally led him to make digressions into other fields of exploration than those of flight. Concerning these I will quote from my unpublished biographical sketch of him of 1920.

Before closing it will be well to mention certain scientific works and writings in other fields than flying. In 1896 Mr. Means printed privately a short paper in pamphlet form, entitled "Twentieth Century Energy." In this he discussed the wastefulness of the steam engine and predicted that there were better ways of getting energy out of coal than by burning it to boil water. The gas engine he felt had a great future and he said that cheap gas would be a great boon to mankind. He also for a time was interested in the utilization of wind power and during the late nineties he made a series of experiments on the practicability of using wind power to produce electric current, at a small laboratory, equipped with windmill, dynamo, and storage battery, which he built on a vacant lot in Boston, Mass.

In 1899 he wrote a paper which was published by the Brockton Board of Trade in which he suggested legislation to secure lower-priced freights for Massachusetts by means of electric street railways. [Was he perceiving a function which the trucking industry is now fulfilling?] He was unsuccessful at the time but this dream like many of his flying dreams has now become fact, and it is not impossible that as coal and oil become scarcer, we shall have to fall back, as he suggested, on the ever present power of the wind as a source of energy.

My father died on December 3, 1920, and I had intended to end this memoir with these words which I have just written on January 15, 1962, when *mirabile dictu,* through my letter slot came a letter from Philip S. Hopkins, Director of the National Air Museum, Smithsonian Institution, Washington, D. C., which contains the following paragraph constituting a most fitting finale to this memoir.

We are very pleased to learn that you are preparing a memoir of your esteemed father's work in aeronautics. His "Aeronautical Annuals" were compiled at a critical period in aviation history. They made available to experimenters a selective record of much that was necessary to know, so that your father and others could further advance the art and science of human flight. His enterprising work with the Boston Aeronautical Society provided a focal point for the increase and diffusion of aeronautical knowledge. We of the National Air Museum join with the entire flying fraternity in admiration and gratitude to him, with added appreciation for his gifts to the national collections here.

LITERATURE CITED

CHANUTE, OCTAVE.

1894. Progress in flying machines. New York Engineer and Railroad Journal.

1911. Recent progress in aviation. Ann. Rep. Smithsonian Institution for 1910, pp. 145–167.

CRAVEN, THOMAS.

1931. Men of art. New York: Simon & Schuster.

GIBBS-SMITH, C. H.

1960. The aeroplane. London: H. M. Stationery Office.

HOWARD, L. O.

1905. The insect book. New York: Doubleday, Page & Co.

JAMESON, W.

1961. The wandering albatross. New York: Doubleday & Co.

LANGLEY, S. P.

1891. Experiments in aerodynamics. Smithsonian Contr. Knowledge, vol. 27, art. 1.

1893. The internal work of the wind. Smithsonian Contr. Knowledge, vol. 27, art. 2.

LILIENTHAL, OTTO.

1889. Der Vogelflug als Grundlage der Fliegekunst. Berlin.

MEANS, JAMES.

1891. Manflight. Boston Transcript.

1891. The same. Privately printed, Boston: W. B. Clarke Co.

1893. (Under pseudonym of John Meade.) The scientific value of flying models. Frank Leslie's Weekly.

1893. (Under pseudonym of John Meade.) Manflight, the last mechanical problem of the century. Boston Transcript.

1894. Problem of manflight. Privately printed; Boston: W. B. Clarke Co.

1895. (Editor.) Aeronautical Annual No. 1. Boston: W. B. Clarke Co.

1896. (Editor.) Aeronautical Annual No. 2. Boston: W. B. Clarke Co.

1897. (Editor.) Aeronautical Annual No. 3. Boston: W. B. Clarke Co.

1910. The Epitome of the Aeronautical Annual. Boston: W. B. Clarke Co.

MOUILLARD, L. F.

1881. L'empire de l'air; Essai d'ornithologie appliquée a l'aviation. Paris. (Extracted and translated version under title "The Empire of the Air" reprinted in Ann. Rep. Smithsonian Inst. for 1892, pp. 397–463.)

TINBERGEN, N.

1953. The herring gull's world. London: Collins.

INDEX

Redefining
the
American Dream

Redefining
the
American Dream

The Novels of Willa Cather

Sally Peltier Harvey

Rutherford • Madison • Teaneck
Fairleigh Dickinson University
London and Toronto: Associated University Presses

Associated University Presses
440 Forsgate Drive
Cranbury, NJ 08512

Associated University Presses
25 Sicilian Avenue
London WC1A 2QH, England

Associated University Presses
P.O.Box 338, Port Credit
Mississauga, Ontario
Canada L5G 4L8

The paper used in this publication meets the requirements
of the American National Standard for Permanence of Paper
for Printed Library Materials Z39.48–1984.

Library of Congress Cataloging-in-Publication Data

Harvey, Sally Peltier, 1948–
    Redefining the American dream: the novels of Willa Cather / Sally
    Peltier Harvey.
            p.   cm.
    Includes bibliographical references and index.
    ISBN 0-8386-3557-1 (alk. paper)
    1. Cather, Willa 1873–1947--Criticism and interpretation.
    2. National characteristics, American, in literature   3. Success in
    literature.   I Title.
    PS3505.A87Z66   1995
    813'.52--dc20   93-44678
                                                                           CIP

PRINTED IN THE UNITED STATES OF AMERICA

For my mother, Do-Be Melcon Peltier
and in memory of my father, Clinton Peltier
who taught their nine children
to cherish traditions and
to reach for dreams.

Contents

Preface

I first became acquainted with Willa Cather over thirty years ago, when, as a restless adolescent looking for summer reading in our public library, I picked up *My Ántonia*. Attracted by the interesting drawings and by the "exotic" title (I had never heard of anyone with that name—and the "my" hinted at a possible love story), I checked the book out. I finished the story feeling a bit disappointed that things had not worked out better for the Ántonia-Jim romance that I had been anticipating. In my mind, I began to formulate questions for Willa Cather, as if I might someday have the chance, actually, to ask her: Why didn't you let Jim marry Ántonia? Why did Ántonia have to lose most of her teeth by the end of the story?

Fortunately, I have become a more perceptive reader over the years, but I still find myself finishing one of Cather's novels with a head full of questions for Willa Cather. Some time ago I began to notice that the same questions kept popping into my mind as I finished various Cather novels, all having to do with Cather's view of success. Why did she find struggle more "interesting" than success, as she put it in a preface that she wrote in 1932—or did she, really? This book began as an attempt to answer such questions. As I explored Cather's views on struggle and success, I kept noticing how much our national culture—in Cather's day and even now—has been shaped by various notions of success. Everybody wants success, but not everybody agrees on what exactly it is, or what path to take toward it. I also began to notice that Cather was continually weaving subtle cultural reflections into her fiction, many of them directly confronting the success ethic in America.

In this study I examine Cather's novels in the context of the ongoing debate about success that has so occupied our nation. I see Cather sometimes reflecting prevailing attitudes about success and sometimes challenging those attitudes as she works out in her fiction her own definition of success: her redefined American Dream.

I owe much to the cultural historians cited in this study, whose research and insights have helped me to understand the intellectual climate in which Cather wrote. They have given me much to think about as I read Cather's novels, and have often pointed me in the right direction for further, fruitful research. Many Cather scholars have also helped me through their research and insights; my references to them throughout the book testify to that. I especially want to thank Susan J. Rosowski for her genuine interest in my work on Cather, and for her helpful advice on portions of the manuscript.

Karl Zender, James Woodress, and Peter Hays all read an earlier version of this book, which began as my doctoral dissertation. Each has offered invaluable assistance to me. I thank Karl especially for his careful reading and for his solid advice when I first considered approaching Cather from a cultural/historical perspective. I thank Peter for encouraging me to have greater confidence in my own assumptions. James Woodress was generous enough to agree to work with me even when he knew very little about my background in Cather studies or my abilities as a writer; he has kindly and good-naturedly seen me through this project, from prewriting stage to finished book manuscript, offering timely advice and consistent encouragement which has brought me safely through the "publishing minefield." His biography of Cather has served as a model of scholarship for me; his enthusiasm for my work has kept me going.

My thanks to Thomas Yoseloff of Fairleigh Dickinson University Press, for his helpful suggestions and for his patience with someone new to the world of book publishing. I also wish to thank the Graduate School at the University of California, Davis, for a fellowship that gave me the time to get my manuscript well underway.

Willa Cather often stressed the role of friends and family in prodding us toward our potential. I have certainly been helped in that respect by many friends and family members during my work on this book. My sister, Sue Peltier, deserves special mention here, for her constant interest in my project; the exorbitant telephone bills that she has paid testify to her loyalty. My husband, Brian, has given me valuable insights on American history. I thank him for that; but more than that, I thank him for graciously tolerating my notes and books scattered across the dining table, for pretending that he didn't mind my constant preoccupation with my work, and for continually overestimating my talent. I thank my son and daughter, Arran and Darcie, for understanding that writing is hard work, and for believing that it is worthwhile work.

Redefining
the
American Dream

1
Self, Community, and Success

During the summer of 1945, less than two years before her death, Willa Cather wrote her final short story, "The Best Years." In it, she returns to a Nebraska setting, recalling her happy relationship with her brothers, the support of family and caring teachers, the warm feelings of home. Set in 1899, the plot centers on sixteen-year-old Lesley Ferguesson, Webster County's youngest schoolteacher. Evangeline Knightly, Lesley's understanding superintendent, arranges for the homesick girl to spend an unplanned weekend with her family. Then, a few months later, tragedy strikes: Lesley dies from pneumonia after getting caught in a blizzard. The final scene takes place twenty years later, when Miss Knightly returns to Lesley's hometown to visit Lesley's grave and to see the girl's mother. Together, the two women reminisce about Lesley and the happy times of years past. "Our best years," Mrs. Ferguesson reflects, "are when we're working hardest and going right ahead when we can hardly see our way out." But the story does not end with that nostalgic remark. Mrs. Ferguesson quickly shifts from the philosophical to the lighthearted, and from the past to the future. Remarking to her old friend that the local cows have not yet learned to watch out for automobiles, she speculates optimistically: "Maybe their grandchildren calves will be more modern-minded."[1]

Thus, this final story displays a characteristic Cather dual perspective: one eye lovingly, almost elegiacally, on the past, and the other—usually a hopeful eye—on the future. Critics have always noted Cather's more obvious stance toward the past, which she herself describes—and perhaps even makes fun of—in the preface to her 1936 book of essays, *Not Under Forty:* "It is for the backward, and by one of their number, that these sketches were written."[2] But a number of critics have been less apt to notice either Cather's foothold in the present or her orientation toward the future.[3]

3

Cather seems to have consciously and consistently used the past to comment on her own times. Narrative comments in Cather's novels occasionally call our attention to this. In *The Professor's House,* the narrator, describing Godfrey St. Peter's monumental history-writing project, which took place in his upstairs study during the years of busy activity downstairs as his daughters were growing up, compares these upstairs and downstairs "dramas" to the two stories one sees in the Bayeux Tapestry. The narrator notes that while Queen Mathilde was busy creating "the big pattern of dramatic action" on the tapestry, she and her women were also creating alongside it "the little playful pattern of birds and beasts that are a story in themselves."[4] This comment on artists who tell important stories even when those stories are not "the big pattern of dramatic action" signals Cather's own attention to such a project in her fiction, as does her narrative remark about Euclide Auclair in *Shadows on the Rock,* who "often talked to his daughter of the past," but was nevertheless well aware that much was "happening in the present."[5] Here again Cather seems to be gently reminding her readers that she, too, is aware of what is happening in the present, even though, like Auclair, she often talks of the past. "Life goes on and we live in the present,"[6] observes the narrator in the opening paragraph of *Lucy Gayheart,* before moving backward in time to relate Lucy's story— again reminding us of Cather's past/present dual perspective.

Those critics who do acknowledge Cather's dual perspective primarily focus on her negative stance toward the present—especially her criticism of the shallowness and materialism so prevalent in the America of the 1920s, with its predilection for "judging success in terms of dollars," as Cather said in one interview.[7] Leon Edel's assessment of Cather's views on success has held a prominent position in Cather studies since his 1959 address on the subject, in which he noted a "paradox" in Cather's criticism of the success ethic, since she devoted so much of her fiction to celebrating that dream: "In Nebraska, amid the pioneers, she was caught up in the very heart of the 'American dream': opportunity, equality, competition for achievement, above all the idea of 'success.'" Observing in Cather's early fiction "a fascination essentially with success," Edel saw this gradually yielding to "disillusion" in her novels of the 1920s—to a realization that the "the present seemed drab" in comparison to the heroic American past of the pioneers, and that her own present as a successful novelist seemed also drab in comparison to her years of struggle. Cather "would certainly have been happier," Edel concluded, if she could have understood that the "new is not always a destruction of the old."[8]

But Cather, despite remarks in her fiction such as Auclair's—that "change is not always progress"[9]—did understand that the "new is not always a destruction of the old." She may not have celebrated the new *over* the old, but as Bernice Slote notes, nostalgia was "a tone rather than a theme" in Cather's writing.[10] Cather certainly valued the past in true antiprogressive spirit. Historians have recently recognized the strong undercurrent of antiprogressive thought running through American culture since our nation's beginnings, and are noting that this undercurrent served as a counterweight to the more obvious progressive character of our nation's development.[11] Cather would certainly have agreed with many of the critics of progress from her own era as well as from earlier times. Yet she did not sink into despair or disillusionment about the American Dream, with its focus on progress and material success, nor did she refuse to find in her present day some of the enduring values from earlier days that she celebrates in her fiction. Unlike many antiprogressives, Cather seems to have remained hopeful that these values would continue to endure for future generations. Speaking of those values, embodied in Nebraska's pioneers, she wrote in 1923: "I have always the hope that something went into the ground with those pioneers that will one day come out again."[12] In fact, it apparently became part of Cather's agenda—if an unconscious part— through her writing to transmit what she saw as enduring values rather than simply to mourn their loss.[13]

Such traditions, Cather implies in much of her fiction, provide individuals with a meaningful sense of community. In a recent study of American attitudes about individualism and commitment, Robert Bellah and his coauthors state: "We are interested in those cultural traditions and practices that . . . serve to limit and restrain the destructive side of individualism and provide alternative models for how Americans might live."[14] Cather, too, seems to have held such an interest. Through her fiction, she was able to provide positive "alternative models" to "the destructive side of individualism," models shaped from the store of traditions that she so cherished in America's past as well as in the past of new Americans, the immigrants whose traditions she so often celebrates in her fiction. "Our past becomes a part of us," she wrote in 1897 at age twenty-three. "It is in our blood."[15] This view became an ongoing theme in Cather's fiction, providing her with a means for redefining positively that American Dream which Edel finds Cather both critical of and—paradoxically—caught up in.

To understand Cather's more positive purpose in using the past to shape a usable American Dream, we might find Christopher Lasch's distinction between nostalgia and memory helpful. Lasch explains that nostalgia "undermines the ability to make intelligent use of the past" because it idealizes that past while disparaging the present. Nostalgia thus mires one in the past, while memory uses the past productively, drawing "hope and comfort from the past in order to enrich the present and to face what comes with good cheer. It sees past, present, and future as continuous."[16] Writing of Cather's constructive use of memory, Bernice Slote brings to mind Lasch's assessment of it as a tool for bringing past, present, and future together when she observes that "in the 1920s [Cather] was actually writing for, and of, the future." "Perhaps," Slote continues, "we can understand her concerns better now than we could fifty years ago."[17]

I want to look closely at one of those concerns, that same one which Edel addressed over thirty years ago: Willa Cather's preoccupation in her writing with individual accomplishment as embodied in the American Dream of success. As Edel noted, Cather does continually grapple with the concept of success that has always been so basic to American culture, a concept that pervaded the atmosphere of the late nineteenth-century America in which Cather grew up. It is time to reconsider Edel's assessment. During Cather's formative years, success in America was certainly equated with fame and fortune, a dream that Cather realized for herself in the 1920s. But that dream, with its glorification of the individual, had by the 1920s disillusioned many Americans. Many, including Cather, began to reject such a competitive, shallow view of success as they searched desperately for meaning and value in a world where individual autonomy as well as traditional goals and values were more and more frequently being called into question.

Cather, however, in her fiction moves past disillusionment, beyond mere criticism of the American Dream, and thus out of the trap of nostalgia. We can trace in Willa Cather's fiction a continuing debate with herself[18] over what constitutes success in her culture, how an individual achieves it, and how such individual accomplishment is both nurtured and hindered by community. I use the term *community* in both the narrow sense of that word, defining specific communities, and in the broader sense of a human community that transcends local and even national borders, for Cather in her fiction looks at community from both of these perspectives. In tracing Cather's inner struggles with the concepts of individualism and community as they relate to the dream of success, we can perhaps come closer to understanding how Cather was able to move past condemnation to a clear though guarded affirmation of the American Dream by redefining that dream. As she explores success, Cather's perspective shifts gradually: her view of self-fulfillment moves away from its traditional alignment with a material success that valorizes individualism and sees competition as a natural law of society. In her fiction Cather seems to work toward a redefinition of success that sees a fulfilled self *grounded in* community, although still wrestling with the problem of balancing community needs and self needs. Thus Cather moves from a troubled ambivalence about success and self-fulfillment, an uncertainty about the survival of the individual as well as an uncertainty about balancing self goals with responsibility to others, toward an eventual celebration of the *tension* between individual and community that underlies the struggle toward success, making the struggle itself more interesting than the end result, as Cather once remarked.[19] Cather, in redefining the American Dream, celebrates this tension as she continues to explore the individual's opportunities for self-fulfillment, even in an America of limited avenues to material success. Willa Cather works out in her fiction the problems inherent in the myth of success, but never totally abandons the dream.[20] A young Cather, writing an 1898 review of some of George Bernard Shaw's more satiric plays, remarked:

> Why not leave us our illusions, since this is a short journey and cold, and most-ly in the dark, and we believe, at least, that they comfort us. . . . They are worth all they cost us, and all the tears we shed for them and all the wisdom we forgo.[21]

In 1898 one of those illusions for Cather and for many Americans was the American Dream, an illusion that Cather confronted and reshaped to fit changing times as she wrote her novels.

"The American Dream" is by now certainly a cliché. Dictionary def-initions vary only slightly, usually listing social mobility, material gain, and individual accomplishment as the principal facets of the American Dream.[22] In his classic study of changing views of success in America, John Cawelti examines the image of the self-made man, that individualistic exemplar of the American Dream. Cawelti de-scribes three principal "traditions" about the self-made individual and the "ideal of success" in America: first, the Protestant work ethic, based on the belief that piety, honesty, hard work, and frugality bring a person both success in this life and salvation in the next; second, the vision of the self-made man as an economic success, with initiative, competitiveness, and aggressiveness replacing the old virtues in a late nineteenth-century atmosphere of increased industrial development; third, a tradition of success "tied to individual fulfillment and social progress rather than to wealth or status." Cawelti notes that this third "strand" of thought has existed in America from the time of Benjamin Franklin and Thomas Jefferson, both of whom saw self–improvement as a means also of improving society. In fact, as Cawelti's study makes evident, all three "strands of thought and feeling" about success have competed throughout our history.[23] The definition of success in Amer-

ica has vacillated between material accomplishment and inner fulfillment, between a valorization of individual achievement and of social
commitment.

As we view it from these various angles, then, the "American Dream"
is a cultural artifact, a unique arena in which the concepts of individualism and commitment to community stage an ongoing tug-of-war.
Robert Bellah and his coauthors note that "myths often tell important
truths about the tensions people experience and their hopes for resolv-
ing those tensions or somehow turning them to constructive use."[24] In
exploring the myth/tradition of the American Dream, Cather never
resolves the tensions between individual and community or between
material and spiritual fulfillment that are inherent in the concept of
success, but she does turn those tensions to "constructive use."

By the time Cather published her earliest anthology of stories (*The
Troll Garden*, 1905), the American Dream was already being called into
question by some of its earliest proponents, who came to realize that
only a few could go from rags to riches and that material success did
not guarantee happiness or peace of mind. Historian Daniel Rogers
notes a general disillusionment with the Horatio Alger brand of success
in the late nineteenth century: "A generation after 1870, in fact, it took
a dull reader of the rags-to-riches literature to miss the accumulating
signs of strain. . . . The publicists of mobility increasingly put their arguments in terms of the room available at the top"—a far cry from the
opportunity-for-all idea that the American Dream supposedly embodied. Rogers notes that the reality of "widespread wage earning" stood
out in stark contrast to that rags-to-riches dream.[25]

William James in 1906 identified success as a "bitch-goddess" whose
worship had created in Americans a "moral flabbiness." James went
so far as to call it "our national disease," decrying "the squalid cash
interpretation put on the word success."[26] The young Cather was certainly not unaffected by the lure of the "bitch-goddess." Cather admitted her excitement about seeing her first piece of published writing, suggesting that this moment may have helped her refocus her career goals
away from the field of medicine and toward writing as a profession:
"What youthful vanity can be unaffected by the sight of itself in print!
It had a kind of hypnotic effect."[27] The lure of fame and fortune can
inspire, but it can also cripple, as it does to Myra Henshawe in *My Mortal Enemy*, and even to Godfrey St. Peter in *The Professor's House*. It is
St. Peter who speaks of the "trap of worldly success" being sprung on
a person.[28] Much of Cather's fiction, then, is a facing up to the powerful pull of the American Dream—its ability to inspire great accomplishments as well as its damaging effects, both for society in general
and for the individual.

Lawrence Chenoweth calls the American Dream in the twentieth century "the search for the self,"[29] but in struggling toward self-definition and fulfillment, how does one balance the societal commitments that most people have come to accept as an integral part of the American Dream? "The history of the United States," writes Page Smith, "can be seen as a prolonged contest between the values of community and the code of individualism."[30] At the center of that "contest" is the perception of fulfillment in America—how to achieve it and who can achieve it. By 1909, Herbert Croly in *The Promise of American Life* was already reminding Americans that they must look beyond individual needs and desires if they hoped to find self-fulfillment: "The promise of American life is to be fulfilled . . . not merely by the abundant satisfaction of individual desires but by a large measure of individual subordination and self-denial."[31] Was either self-fulfillment or self-denial the choice Americans had to make? Croly's dictum presented a dilemma, not an answer or a promise, making all too clear the moral implications of individual accomplishment. By 1931, the idea of such individual achievement had taken on an even darker tone in historian Charles Beard's assessment of "rugged individualism." Beard voiced a conclusion that many Americans had long before reached: "In the minds of most people who shout for individualism vociferously, the creed, stripped of all flashy rhetoric, means getting money, simply that and nothing more."[32] "Getting money"—or as Cather put it in 1924, "judging success in terms of dollars"—became for many an ugly synonym for individualism. If the American Dream of individual achievement was reduced to this less-than-admirable, less-than-lofty measure, to what, then, could Americans aspire?[33]

Cather grew up during the heyday of the American Dream, as this concept gained its most materialistic interpretation and received its most enthusiastic reception. In the twenty-eight-year span during which she wrote her twelve novels, Americans in general radically altered their perceptions of and opinions about the American Dream. In reading through the Cather canon, we can trace her wrestling with her own shifting perception of success, and her attempt to refashion an American Dream without the "ugly crest of materialism" stamped on it.[34] The self-made successes in her early novels become the self-made but self-tortured "successful" individuals in her novels of the 1920s, far less certain—as Cather herself seems to have become at this time—of the road to fulfillment. But Cather, unlike many of her contemporaries, seems persistently determined to find a way to rescue rather than to reject the American Dream, especially to rescue that longstanding "tradition" which Cawelti describes—of success "tied to individual fulfillment and social progress rather than to wealth or status."[35] Her later fiction celebrates not the standard success stories of fame and fortune, but instead the spiritual and emotional fulfillment experienced by an archbishop in a new diocese or a humble apothecary and his young daughter as they nurture their traditions in a new land.

Cather, while capturing in her fiction the changing view of the American Dream, certainly reflects, too, changing cultural perceptions concerning the individual and his or her relationship to community. Cather grew up and wrote during a time span in America that saw various factors eroding the concept of an autonomous self as these same factors eroded the concept of the American Dream. Her life, as Blanche Gelfant notes, bridged the years of "confusedly rapid transition from Victorian to modern times."[36] Of this time period, Robert Wiebe observes: "Americans in a basic sense no longer knew who or where they were. The setting had altered beyond their power to understand it, and within an alien context they had lost themselves."[37] That "alien context" included Darwin's and Freud's theories, both of which left people questioning their ability to control their own actions and destinies. The pervasiveness of Darwin's ideas is evident even in Cather's earliest writing. Her first published essay, a student theme on Carlyle, describes the aging Carlyle in strong Darwinian overtones:

> Like the lone survivor of some extinct species, the last of the mammoths, tortured and harassed beyond all endurance by the smaller, though perhaps more perfectly organized offspring of the world's maturer years, this great Titan . . . rushed off into the desert to suffer alone.[38]

Edith Lewis remarks that Cather, in her teens in Red Cloud, had "long talks with Mr. Ducker [an Englishman with whom she read Greek and Latin classics] about evolution,"[39] so we can be sure that she had pondered the new position that the self now occupied in light of such scientific theories and discoveries.

Freud's theories also threatened to undermine the concept of a unified self. Increasingly uncertain about just how much control a person had over his or her behavior, many found it more difficult to support individualism enthusiastically. The concept of an ordered self, as Miles Orvell points out in his study of this transition period in America, was eroding just at the time that increased corporate control was strengthening the concept of an ordered, organized society.[40] Jackson Lears sums up this new sense of intellectual instability: "By the end of the nineteenth century, the self seemed neither independent, nor unified, nor fully conscious, but rather interdependent, discontinuous, divided. . . shaped by forces out of its conscious control." Thus, as Lears observes, "the internalized morality of self-control and autonomous achievement, the basis of modern culture, seemed at the end of its tether." A new ambivalence, Lears says, replaced the old self-confidence of rugged individualism: "Afflicted by a fragment-ing sense of autonomous selfhood, late Victorians yearned increas-ingly for oceanic dependence."[41] We see such conflict in some of Cather's troubled protagonists, such as Godfrey St. Peter, who suffers from the sort of "self–indulgent passivity"[42] characteristic of his own troubled turn-of-the-century era. In general, as Page Smith describes it, Americans at the dawn of the twentieth century were increasingly "asking self questions"[43]—and getting disturbing answers.[44] "One must know the world so well before one can know the parish," Sarah Orne Jewett had told Cather.[45] But as Cather demonstrates over and over through her fictional characters, one must know oneself so well, before one can establish a secure, defined relationship with either the world or the parish.

If the general concept of self became highly problematic during Cather's formative years, that problem was certainly exacerbated for women. In a restrictive, postfrontier society, as Sandra Gilbert and Susan Gubar point out, women faced even more limits than they had during earlier times, and saw their possibilities for self-fulfillment fur-ther diminishing.[46] Cather, who between the ages of nine and sixteen lived in the less restricted frontier society of Nebraska, may have been more sensitive than most young women of her day to the fewer options available to women—and more determined than ever to break free of such restrictions, to retain autonomy in a world that expected females to play a dependent role. Lewis recounts one of Cather's favorite sto-ries about her childhood: "I remember her telling once, when someone offered to help her, how when she was a very little child, and her par-ents would try to assist her in something, she would protest passion-ately: 'Self-alone, self-alone!'"[47] Sharon O'Brien describes the young Cather's identification with "male heroes who possessed the power and autonomy she wanted for herself."[48]

Cather, "imbued with the nineteenth-century faith in individualism," cherished that tradition as intensely as she grated against societal restrictions on women. O'Brien notes that, throughout her career, Cather was continually "creating rather than discovering a self by draw-ing on the cultural fictions available to her: the romantic story of self-discovery and the American story of self-transformation."[49] Among the "cultural fictions" available to Cather were both Emerson's and Whit-man's celebrations of the individual. Although older and more cynical about America by the time he wrote *Democratic Vistas* (1871), Whitman still identified individualism as a key concept in American society, thriving "even in the midst of immense tendencies toward aggregation."

"This idea of perfect individualism it is indeed that deepest tinges and gives character to the idea of the aggregate," he insisted.[50]

That principle of individualism and its corollary of self-fulfillment were deeply ingrained in Cather. She lived the typical American Dream of struggle toward material success and individual fulfillment, and lived it in a society that was only beginning, somewhat reluctantly, to open that dream to women. But as she struggled toward artistic achievement, Cather was also taking a closer look at that "faith in individualism" which had so early in life been instilled in her. Did such faith allow room for an equally strong faith in community? In responding to this question, Cather looked at community in general—in the sense of one's responsibilities to and need for other human beings—and at specific communities: her family, her hometown of Red Cloud, her reading public, various groups of friends, fellow artists, literary critics, and in later years, the Catholic church.

Cather was not the only one taking a second look at the individual's relationship to community during these early decades of the twentieth century. Across America the idea of community was changing, too, rocked by the same forces that were problematizing the dream of success and the view of self. Burton Bledstein explains this change in attitude toward community: "Mid-Victorians cultivated a new vision, a vertical vision [of upward mobility, both economic and social] that compelled persons to look upward, forever reaching toward their potential and their becoming, the fulfillment of their true nature." But as Bledstein makes clear, such individual striving for success negatively impacted the traditional sense of community in America—of working together for the common good of all: "Looking vertically, middle-class Americans lacked a corporate sense of community."[51] If one were to "get ahead," one might have to ignore responsibilities to others, might have to leave behind former friends and commitments—for there was limited room at the top, especially as Americans' lives became more and more directed by impersonal, giant corporations. As Cawelti points out, "the concept of the republican community gave way to the image of a loose association of individuals, each making his own way in the world."[52]

An editorial in the July 1890 *Century* magazine, a magazine that the Cather family read regularly during Cather's years at home,[53] reflects the dilemma that the struggle for material success created for many, as they struggled also with a moral commitment to community. The editors distinguish between "worldly success under the present conditions" and "the true and high success, the conduct of one's life in all honesty." They describe two types of businessmen: those "who are trying to live up to an ideal," and those who, because they are "less scrupulous," manage to outdo the morally responsible businessmen "in the mere race for wealth." Reluctantly, the editors conclude that "in the present constitution of society a lack of conscience may be an important, even a deciding, element of worldly success." Recognizing this frustrating fact, they nevertheless refuse to advocate such amoral behavior. Instead, they merely reassure readers that "the conscienceless man who reaches enormous wealth or high worldly position is not nearly so clever a fellow as his admirers think he is"; he is merely "a successful rogue."[54] As Richard Weiss makes clear in his study of what he calls the myth of success, "the association of personal virtue and material prosperity was breaking down" in the second half of the nineteenth century.[55]

A complex set of forces, then, combined to reshape cultural perceptions as Cather reached young adulthood—forces that shook the moral underpinnings on which many felt America had originally been established. A rural, small-town America—the America of Cather's Red Cloud—was rapidly becoming a mechanized, urban-centered one, like the busy city of Pittsburgh to which Cather moved in 1896. Across the nation, the image of the yeoman farmer was being supplanted by that of either the wage-earner or the industrial giant. Robert Wiebe observes: "The great casualty of America's turmoil late in the [nineteenth] century was the island of community"; he identifies "a feeling suddenly acute across the land that local America stood at bay, besieged by giant forces abroad and beset by subversion at home."[56] Thomas Bender does not view the community as a "casualty," but emphasizes, rather, its evolution. During this era, Bender points out, people were having

> to learn to live in two distinct worlds, [community and society], each with its own rules and expectations. They were involved in small communities, including family and friends, and at the same time, they identified with larger and more abstract social units: profession, class, and citizenship.... [Thus,] the whole configuration of social experience—and with it, community—was transformed.[57]

Some trauma certainly accompanied such changes in community. We can imagine how keenly Cather experienced the tension between "two distinct worlds" during this period, moving first from tiny Red Cloud to the university community at Lincoln, and then to larger and larger urban areas (Pittsburgh and New York), and to her place in the competitive, male-dominated profession of journalism.

Despite people's awareness of their immersion, for better or worse, in various communities and in those "larger and more abstract social units" which Bender defines, most—Cather included—clung to the idea of autonomy and of individual achievement in this competitive turn-of-the-century setting. The American Dream that Horatio Alger had depicted in his stories of the late nineteenth century seemed to offer hope for such continued individual achievement, despite the obviously dwindling opportunities for advancement in a society that saw wealth concentrated more and more in the hands of a few. Alger's heroes succeed through "character"—a term which encompassed those virtues of honesty and moral uprightness that were so important in nineteenth-century success literature. Such a hero, Alger insisted, no matter what his economic or social background, could achieve material success and—perhaps just as important—the respect that society affords to leaders and role models.[58] As Kenneth Lynn points out in his study of the American Dream, conditions in the decades following the Civil War, during which Horatio Alger wrote his stories, including the increased social mobility that urbanization and industrialization made possible, seemed to offer a resolution of the "contest" between individual and community. Perhaps one could have it all—virtue, a sense of responsibility to community, material success, and inner fulfillment. The Horatio Alger stories perpetuated just such a myth. As Lynn observes, "the Alger hero fired the American imagination at the instant of his maximum credibility."[59]

That hero, recast time and again in different settings, is typified in Walter Conrad, protagonist of Alger's *Strive and Succeed* (1871). Walter, from the start a virtuous though poor young man, not only betters himself but also shows his sense of responsibility to community, taking on a position as a teacher in a small town; later, when he does achieve financial success, he shares his wealth with a less fortunate (and less virtuous) cousin, whom Walter helps to reform. The strong moral overtones that the American Dream still embodied in 1870 are clear in Alger's summation of Walter Conrad's adventure: "He had striven under difficult circumstances, and he had succeeded. He felt proud and happy and grateful to God for having so ordered events as to lead to this fortune."[60]

Self-made Alger heroes such as Walter Conrad embodied Americans' hopes that one could succeed materially and still remain morally upright. But as the era of small industries and independent businessmen gave way to the era of robber barons and giant corporations, it became more and more difficult to combine the four components that had so briefly come together in the standard version of the American Dream: self-fulfillment, responsibility to community, material success, and social advancement. "Between the mythology of success and the reality of American life there now yawned a palpable and an ever-widening gulf," Lynn remarks.[61] Self-made men such as Andrew Carnegie still found ways to justify their acquisition of wealth. Carnegie stressed stewardship: the idea that one's responsibility to others increases as one gains the material means to do more for others. Opening his "Gospel of Wealth" (1889) with the noble hope that, through "the proper administration of wealth, the ties of brotherhood may still bind together the rich and poor in harmonious relationship," Carnegie still echoed the tenets of Social Darwinism: "While the law [of competition] may be sometimes hard for the individual, it is best for the race" (16).[62] In "The Gospel of Wealth," he praised "Individualism . . . the Law of Accumulation of Wealth, and the Law of Competition" as "the highest results of human experience," although he carefully reminded the millionaire that he is to be "a trustee for the poor, [entrusted] for a season with a great part of the increased wealth of the community, but administering it for the community far better than it could or would have done for itself."[63] But labor unrest over low wages and poor working conditions, culminating in national traumas such as the Haymarket Riot (1886) and the Homestead Strike (1891–92), made clear to most Americans by the late nineteenth century how little responsibility for others such "stewards" of a nation's wealth and resources were really assuming.

Cather herself visited Homestead in 1898, and although never given to preaching about reform, she wrote an editorial on "The Real Homestead" in August 1901. In it, she obliquely criticizes the idea of stewardship, first describing the Carnegie Library at Homestead, and then remarking that it is "full of good things that no one has leisure to enjoy": "Twelve-hour shifts are doubtless good economy, but they do not tend to make a literary or music-loving community." She closes her editorial with what may seem an expression of pity for the new owner of the steel mill, Mr. J. Pierpont Morgan, whose "life is given not to the enjoyment of wealth, but to the solving of problems and the amassing of power." But in her closing remark, she implies that Morgan is shirking his moral responsibility to community. Observing that civilization "has not been able to expand the individual's capacity for enjoyment," Cather adds: "Mr. Morgan could gratify the tastes of a thousand men, but it is only an infinitesimal part of his fortune that he can use upon himself."[64]

Others were noting inconsistencies in the American Dream, too, including the difficulties one faced in trying to balance community needs with individual social advancement and the quest for wealth. William Dean Howells explored those difficulties in works such as *The Rise of Silas Lapham* (1885) and *A Hazard of New Fortunes* (1890). But although the myth of easy material success accompanied by inner fulfillment was colliding head-on with reality, few were ready to abandon this attractive version of the American Dream. Despite questioning the myth in his novels, Howells in 1891 could still boast that the American "breathes a rarefied and nimble air full of shining possibilities and radiant promises," reassuring his readers that most of our ills could be averted by "honest work and unselfish behavior"[65]—those keys to success which Alger had emphasized. Theodore Dreiser certainly criticized the dream of success in his 1912 portrait of the ruthless Frank Cowperwood, "prince of a world of dreams whose reality was disillusion"; but it is impossible to miss Dreiser's admiration, too, for this rugged representative of the American Dream: "He was strong, and he knew it, and somehow he always believed in his star."[66]

Even in Cather's small western community of Red Cloud, where residents were more apt to retain a sense of community long after that sense had eroded in overpopulated urban areas, the tensions of an individualism that was becoming more competitive were evident in the late nineteenth century. A fellow student in Cather's senior class, John Tulleys, made "Self-Advertising" the topic of his speech at the 1890 graduation ceremony, proclaiming that "a man should blow his own trumpet." Displaying what Maxwell Geismar calls "the predatory thinking of the period,"[67] this young speaker reminded his audience: "Taking *by any means* as his motto, a shrewd man will succeed in any business"—recommending here that same conscience-absent approach which the *Century* editors would decry in their editorial the following month.[68]

What factors served to temper this "predatory" attitude in Willa Cather? Bernice Slote mentions two of Jacob Abbott's histories found in Cather's personal library.[69] This information gives us an important insight into the version of the American Dream that the young Cather formulated.[70] John Cawelti identifies Abbott as Alger's "most important predecessor," one even more heavily moralistic than Alger. Cawelti observes that in Abbott's histories of self-made heroes, "a strong emphasis on evangelical Protestantism remained the central element. . . . A firm believer in the ethic of industry, frugality, integrity, and piety, Abbott rarely made ambition itself a significant element in his stories."[71]

We can certainly see this in Jacob Abbott's history of Cyrus the Great (1878). Abbott praises "the nobleness and generosity" of the young Cyrus, noting that he "applied himself with great diligence" as a youth. But the story of Cyrus ends with a moral about the damaging effects of too much ambition: "We wonder that so amiable, and gentle, and generous a boy should become so selfish, and unfeeling, and overbearing a man. But such are the natural and inevitable effects of ambition and an inordinate love of power." To further drive home the lesson that such success did not guarantee self-fulfillment, Abbott concludes: "His ambition has been gratified but the gratification has brought with it no substantial peace or happiness." Similar reminders of the need for virtue and the dangers of ambition are sprinkled through Abbott's history of Alexander the Great (1876). Abbott praises Alexander for his "noble character," but adds regretfully that "he devoted its energies unfortunately to conquest and war."[72]

If this is the particular version of the Alger myth that Cather imbibed as a child, it is no wonder that she would be neither easily enticed by the materialistic trappings of the American Dream nor devastatingly disillusioned by the rude awakening that writers such as Dreiser and Fitzgerald experienced in the 1920s when they realized that material success was neither open to all nor a guarantee of happiness. Between the early influence of Abbott and of John Bunyan, whose *Pilgrim's Progress* Cather "absorbed" as a child,[73] Cather's literary upbringing was such that she might certainly have experienced tension later in her life between the desire for individual achievement and the moral imperative of commitment to community.[74] In an 1897 article on memorable characters in Dickens, she singles out Sidney Carton from *A Tale of Two Cities* because of his high moral code: "He cared for himself so little and for others so much."[75]

Cather's reading during her childhood and adolescence, then, served to reinforce community-oriented values akin to the "gift of sympathy" that she later viewed as indispensable for writing fiction.[76] A young Cather observed in 1895: "After people have ceased to seek for love there is one thing that they seem to go on seeking for, and that is sympathy."[77] Perhaps living in the isolated frontier community of Red Cloud, where people naturally banded together for emotional as well as physical survival, Cather became more sensitive to the crucial role of sympathy. Here, Cather formed strong family and community ties that would stay with her all her life, and certainly must have intensified the tension between her desire for individual achievement in a competitive world and her need for, as well as her sense of responsibility to, others. Which "communities" most markedly exerted such a dual pull on Cather while she was growing up? Certainly, her family; then, the immigrants whose farmhouses she visited to listen to the women's stories and watch them cooking; her unofficial and official teachers in that culturally diverse frontier community of Red Cloud that Mildred Bennett calls an "intellectual melting pot,"[78] teachers who introduced her to the classics in Greek and Latin, and who instilled in her an appreciation of "Old World" art and values; the local doctors whom Cather accompanied on their rounds, and who impressed her with the wider opportunities open to a male, as well as with their own concern for community. In addition to these smaller, select communities toward which Cather gravitated, was the "larger" community of Red Cloud, toward which she remained ambivalent.[79]

Such groups from Cather's formative years added depth and complexity to her definition of success, taking it far beyond the standard equation of material accomplishment with individual fulfillment so typical of late nineteenth-century American thought. The wide-ranging experiences that family and early acquaintances shared with Cather certainly added a universality to her sense of community, perhaps making Cather more sensitive to the larger implications of that term, to one's membership in the broader community of humankind. Bernice Slote and Virginia Faulkner remark: "Even though she grew up in a period of intense nationalism, Willa Cather had the view of 'one world' long before the phrase was widely used."[80] The various communities of Cather's Red Cloud years so influenced her that she later claimed that the years between ages eight and fifteen are the most important in forming one's values.[81] But Cather's Red Cloud experience gave her also a sense of community as a restrictive force. Throughout her novels, we see characters whose love-hate relationships with family, home town, or other selected and defined communities affect their own capacity for self-fulfillment and their ability to achieve individual success.

Despite such entangling relationships, Cather's community interests and loyalties did not diminish her own competitiveness. The young Cather's career story resembles that of the typical self-made man in the late nineteenth century. From humble beginnings, she competed successfully in the male-dominated world of journalism, gaining by age twenty-two a position as managing editor of a Pittsburgh-based magazine, *Home Monthly*. Not satisfied with this major accomplishment, especially notable for a woman in 1896, Cather only ten years later had moved to New York to work on the staff of one of the most influential magazines in the nation, *McClure's;* by 1908 she had become managing editor there, a position that most men of her day would have envied and few women would have considered within their reach. This early career reveals, as Woodress points out, "a very eager young woman from the provinces determined to make good"[82]—the embodiment of the late nineteenth-century American Dream. Yet Cather was already questioning that dream as she lived it. In a revealing eight-page letter to her mentor, Sarah Orne Jewett, Cather in December 1908 admitted feeling unsure of the worth of her achievement as well as personally unfulfilled.[83] O'Brien observes that "success at *McClure's* meant success according to the rules American society laid out for men."[84] Those "rules" assumed a self-reliant individualism and a competitive drive. Even as Cather realized success, then, the American Dream was taking its toll emotionally, as Cather's confession to Jewett suggests. Cather also told her friend, Elizabeth Sergeant, that she worried about "the lure of big money rewards"[85]—that dangerous material component of the American Dream.

In tracing Cather's repeated confrontation with the American Dream of success, we uncover her strategies for redefining that dream. Unlike F. Scott Fitzgerald's cynical, world-wise Jordan Baker in *The Great Gatsby,* who "was too wise ever to carry well-forgotten dreams from age to age,"[86] Cather not only carried the American Dream from one age to another, but managed to reshape it to reflect the "shining possibilities" that Howells still saw in the America of 1891 but that F. Scott Fitzgerald mourned as lost by the twenties. Cather worked to redefine that dream so that it would offer not a "well-forgotten" myth but the possibility of self-fulfillment within, sometimes even through, community—in both its nurturing and its demanding aspects. Which communities did Cather see as positive, enriching, validating? And even within such supportive communities, with what tensions did the individual wrestle? What factors did Cather see that might make self-fulfillment still possible in an America obsessed with material success? Cather offers tentative answers to these questions in her fiction, especially in her novels, but she never fully resolves the tension between self and community inherent in the American Dream. While her fiction mirrors her own struggle to succeed and to define herself within various communities, it reflects, too, the general efforts of many Americans in these early decades of the twentieth century to understand and to negotiate a path through the pressures that the American Dream exerted on the individual and on the ever-growing network of communities that comprised American society.

In his acceptance speech on receiving the Nobel Prize for Literature in 1930, Sinclair Lewis characterized the tensions that we see so often in Cather's writing: "It is my fate in this paper to swing constantly from optimism to pessimism and back, but so is it the fate of anyone who writes or speaks of anything in America—the most contradictory, the most depressing, the most stirring of any land in the world today."[87] In Cather's vision of success in America, she, too, makes constant swings from optimism to pessimism; but she seems always to conclude with some sense of affirmation.[88] I hope in this study to uncover possible reasons for that.

In Lewis's same speech, he highlighted a particular problem for the American artist, a problem to which Cather's increasing focus on community may be an unconscious, or perhaps at times a carefully crafted, response. The writer in America, Lewis noted, "has no institution, no group, to which he can turn for inspiration."[89] We see this, of course, in the exodus of writers from the United States after World War I, but Cather did not expatriate.[90] Cather in her novels, however, does seem intent—whether consciously so or not—on finding and defining her artistic "group," not particularly within America but within a tradition of artists, past, present, and future, representative of the broader Western traditions that she learned to revere early in her life, but not excluding earlier Native American traditions, to which Cather became strongly attracted when she visited the Southwest.[91] We see in her later novels an increasing concern with defining, and then aligning herself to, such an artistic community, as many of her characters become actively involved in securing a place for themselves within the larger community that Archibald MacLeish described as "riders on the earth together, brothers on that bright loveliness in the eternal cold."[92]

2
Charting a New Path to Fulfillment

Cather's first four novels, published between 1912 and 1918, demonstrate her wide swings from pessimism to optimism about the American Dream. In these novels we see guarded attempts to move beyond either rejection of or enthusiastic commitment to the American Dream, as Cather attempts to formulate a definition of success that emphasizes fulfillment rather than fame or fortune. In his 1915 commentary on American culture, *America's Coming of Age,* Van Wyck Brooks noted: "Economic self-assertion still remains to most Americans a sort of moral obligation; while self-fulfillment still looks like a pretty word for selfishness."[1] This is precisely the situation that Cather's first four protagonists confront. Their stories recount their struggles to put into perspective the standard American Dream of success, with its emphasis on "economic self-assertion"; these protagonists attempt to define clearly what they need for self-fulfillment while they also take its meaning beyond selfishness. All four are successful, self-made individuals, but each suffers the stresses and anxieties that accompany the struggle to achieve such success.

For Bartley Alexander, the hero of *Alexander's Bridge* (1912), success brings no sense of self-fulfillment. *Alexander's Bridge* instead chronicles the failure of the American Dream, its detrimental effect on the individual struggling toward self-definition. But Cather does not let go of the dream so quickly or summarily. In *O Pioneers!* (1913) and *The Song of the Lark* (1915), she celebrates success that brings with it self-fulfillment. Still, Cather's reservations about the American Dream remain evident in both of these novels. Thus, by the time she portrays the dream of success in *My Ántonia* (1918), it is a dream quite removed from either fame or fortune. Ántonia Shimerda's definition of success is a humbler one than either Alexandra Bergson's or Thea Kronborg's, yet still Ántonia appears completely fulfilled.

All four of Cather's early protagonists struggle primarily to understand self so that they can grasp what they need for fulfillment. Bartley Alexander fails in that quest; but Cather's three female heroines succeed. To varying degrees, they establish their own identities, take advantage of the opportunities for individual advancement available in turn-of-the-century America, and find their own paths to fulfillment.

In these early novels, it is as if Cather is looking closely at the factors in America that provide opportunities for success, and examining how such factors might both help and hinder the individual in his or her quest for self-fulfillment. As a woman, Cather was perhaps more sensitive to the ironies of the American Dream, which in its standard version was hardly open to women in the late nineteenth century. Lears describes "the typical Victorian female image" that Americans generally accepted. A woman was supposed to fill a variety of roles, all primarily for the purpose of helping a man achieve his American Dream. She was considered "helpmate, pillar, moral and cultural authority, self-effacing, and self-reliant."[2] Cather manipulates this accepted image, thus opening the male-dominated dream of individual success in a competitive world to women in *O Pioneers!* and *The Song of the Lark.* In *My Ántonia,* it may seem that Cather reverts to the image of women that Lears describes, at the same time that she moves away from the standard American Dream of material success. But Cather is in this novel actually clarifying the direction that her revised version of the American Dream is to take, as she reflects a national yearning for the type of inner fulfillment that the dream had promised but seldom brought.

In all four of these early novels, Cather also examines the tension between a strong sense of individualism and a commitment to community. It becomes evident that, even in this early stage of her career as a novelist, Cather was beginning to confront these tensions that strained the American Dream, and to confront the dream itself, alternately condemning and celebrating the standard components of success.

Alexander's Bridge

Literary historian Wendy Steiner, in her examination of early twentieth-century fiction, notes both a preoccupation with success and a growing disillusionment with the American Dream in the early 1900s. Steiner comments: "Perhaps the most typical story line is the subverted Horatio Alger plot, where success fails to provide satisfaction."[3] This is the case for Howells's 1885 portrait of successful paint manufacturer Silas Lapham, who experiences the darker side of success but ultimately manages to escape moral destruction. In the early 1900s, more and more subscribers to the American Dream were becoming aware of that darker side, and at the same time feeling less capable of escaping it. As Warner Berthoff remarks, "a new civilization seemed to be generating a new order, or new aggravation, of human uncertainty and discontent";[4] in *Alexander's Bridge,* Cather memorializes that aggravating "new order." The Bartley Alexander whom we meet in the opening pages of *Alexander's Bridge,* the successful, admired bridge designer and engineer described as a "tamer of rivers,"[5] is the storybook picture of success; yet he feels emotionally and spiritually impoverished. His newest undertaking, the Moorlock Bridge in Canada—to be the longest of its kind—is "the least satisfactory thing he ha[s] ever done" (37).

As a critique of the late nineteenth-century American Dream, *Alexander's Bridge* is both an inverted and a subverted Horatio Alger story. When the story opens, Bartley Alexander has already achieved the material success and respectability that Alger's young heroes gain only as their stories conclude. Alexander does not rise to success in Cather's story; instead, he plummets to moral and emotional disaster while his career remains at its height. In the opening pages of the novel, Bartley's philosophy teacher of some twenty years earlier, Lucius Wilson, reflects on this self-made man's rise to success from humble circumstances. Here we see the first subversion of the Horatio Alger plot. The typical Alger story focuses on the upright moral character of its hero from the start, even in his presuccess days. Alger's "Ragged Dick" may be only a boot-black, but he is "above doing anything mean or dishonorable. He would not steal, or cheat . . . but [is] frank and straight-forward, manly, and self-reliant. His nature [is] a noble one."[6] Yet Professor Wilson admits his former doubts about the young Bartley Alexander: "I used to feel that there was a weak spot where some day strain would tell. . . . The more dazzling the front [Bartley] presented, the higher [his] façade rose, the more I expected to see a big crack zigzagging from top to bottom" (12). Professor Wilson insists that he no longer feels such doubt; in fact, he assures Bartley's wife, Winifred: "I was always confident that [Bartley would] do something extraordinary" (7). But perhaps he protests too much; the theme of flawed character threads its way through the novel, from Wilson's early reflection that Bartley "wouldn't square" (15), to the tragically flawed design and construction of Alexander's long-awaited, grand project, the Moorlock Bridge.

At one point Bartley Alexander admits his awareness of his flaw. Speaking of his relationship with his wife, he reflects: "Two people, when they love each other, grow alike in their tastes and habits and pride, but their moral natures . . . are never welded. The base one goes on being base, and the noble one noble, to the end" (101). Many interpret Bartley Alexander's flaw in the same way that he explains it here— as a moral one. This appraisal is understandable, since he betrays his wife by his illicit sexual involvement with actress Hilda Burgoyne, and he betrays his public by allowing construction of a bridge whose stability he questions. But perhaps the real "crack" in Bartley Alexander's character, as Wilson's term, "zig-zagging," suggests, is his constant indecision about which self he wants to be—his inability to define clearly a self. Because he cannot do so, Alexander can never achieve a success accompanied by a sense of fulfillment.

In Alexander's account of his rise to success, Cather subverts Horatio Alger's typical treatment of "luck" in his plots. Alger's heroes, although they may deserve success because of their high moral character, almost always gain that success partly through a lucky twist of fate. Young Walter Conrad in *Strive and Succeed* has the good fortune to overhear an important conversation about the value of his father's mining stock. Thus, he knows that he should not sell the stock for the low price that an unscrupulous buyer has offered. Ragged Dick exhibits his bravery by saving a drowning boy. How lucky, however, that he saves not some impoverished fellow orphan but the son of a wealthy businessman, who shows his gratitude by offering Dick a "respectable" position in his counting-house. "My lucky stars are shinin' pretty bright now," Dick remarks in the conclusion of the book.[7] Similar strokes of luck lead other Alger heroes to their well-deserved successes. Bartley Alexander's success, whether well deserved or not, seems in part due to the same kind of luck. We learn that Bartley's initial opportunity came by mere chance. His first bridge contract was awarded to him when his boss developed a terminal illness and turned the job over to Bartley. "Otherwise I'd never have got anything so early," he tells Wilson (11). Cather seems determined to draw our attention to the factor of luck or chance in the Alger myth, but not to demonstrate that luck leads to happiness, as it did in Alger's stories: Bartley Alexander is a successful but not a happy man.

Beginning with a portrait of empty success, Cather traces Alexander's moral and emotional downward spiral, as he battles the "second man" (102), the "resolute offshoot of himself" (114) whom he at first sees as only a "pleasure-loving simpleton," but who becomes, as Bartley later observes, "strong and sullen . . . fighting for his life at the cost of mine" (102). Cather's divided Bartley Alexander, engaged in an inner struggle, typifies "psychological man," a personality type that Freud identified, according to cultural historian Philip Rieff, around the turn of the century: "The psychological man has withdrawn into a world always at war, where the ego is an armed force capable of achieving armistices but not peace."[8] This struggle between the two sides of oneself is depicted in *Alexander's Bridge* as the protagonist's continuing struggle against the primal youth-man within him: "No creature ever wanted so much to live," Bartley tells Hilda as he describes this other self (102). The unrest within Bartley is mirrored, too, by the "general industrial unrest" in the novel (37): the labor strikes in New York that delay his bridge projects there and that are also inadvertently responsible for the tragic collapse of the Moorlock Bridge, since Bartley leaves that project to attend to this problem, and becomes involved with Hilda again while he is in New York.[9]

The twisted Alger storyline in *Alexander's Bridge* highlights the emptiness and confusion that Cather saw so frequently accompanying success, as well as the self-division and eventual self-destruction. Echoing William James's description of success as the "national disease," Cather creates in Bartley Alexander a diseased, mentally tortured man. Bartley tells Wilson:

> After all, life doesn't offer a man much. You work like the devil and think you're getting on, and suddenly you discover that you've only been getting yourself tied up. A million details drink you dry. Your life keeps going for things you don't want, and all the while you are being built alive into a social structure you don't care a rap about. (12–13)

A decade before Sinclair Lewis's *Babbitt,* Willa Cather explores in *Alexander's Bridge* the anxieties that the worship of the "bitch-goddess" were creating in striving Americans.[10] The success-weary hero of Lewis's novel reflects:

> Better hustle. . . . Men who had made five thousand, year before last, and ten thousand last year, were urging on nerve-yelping bodies and parched brains so that they might make twenty thousand this year; and the men who had broken down immediately after making their twenty thousand dollars were hustling to catch trains, to hustle through the vacations which the hustling doctors had ordered.[11]

Bartley Alexander, too, is seeking a "vacation" that might cure his disease. He thinks that he can find—or recapture from the past—another Bartley Alexander who has the potential for personal fulfillment: "I sometimes wonder what sort of chap I'd have been if I hadn't been this sort," he tells Professor Wilson. "I want to go and live out his potentialities, too" (13).

Bartley Alexander's uncertainty and discontent lead him on a quest to reclaim this lost youth, a quest that reflects a national longing for the innocence and security that a simpler, earlier world seemed to offer, before the drive for success threatened to absorb Americans' lives, before the certainties of a rational world gave way to the relativities of a newer age. Rieff describes the "therapeutic" approach to self-fulfillment, which many success-weary Americans desperately sought during the late nineteenth century. It is an approach "with nothing at stake beyond a manipulatable sense of well-being."[12] This is exactly what Bartley Alexander seeks in his search for self: the sense of well-being that material success has not brought him. Bartley tries to recapture his lost youth through a rekindled romance with former lover Hilda Burgoyne, now a successful actress in England. Through Hilda, he hopes to bring energy, passion, excitement, and freedom into his life, but his affair causes only self-division, inner chaos, indecision, and emotional pain.

Lears notes of turn-of-the-century America that "personal identity itself came to seem problematic. For many, individual identities began to seem fragmented, diffuse."[13] Bartley's flight from one identity into another, seemingly more energetic and thus more attractive, leaves him only fragmented and uncertain. He fails to find his own lost youth; he fails to define a whole, healthy, fulfilled self. In *The Great Gatsby* (published thirteen years after Cather's novel), Fitzgerald's hero, also a victim of the American Dream, feels certain that one can repeat the past;[14] likewise, Alexander flees to the past, only to find, as does Jay Gatsby, that "he had paid a high price for living too long with a single dream."[15] But Bartley Alexander is not content even with a single dream.

When Bartley tells Wilson that he wants to live out the other Alexander's "potentialities, too," perhaps the word "too" offers a clue to his failure, for more than being unable to *define* a self, he seems unable to *choose* a single identity—energetic youth, successful engineer, devoted husband, carefree lover. He cannot make a decision that requires giving up something. He tries "to feel his own continuous identity," but he senses that unified person "fading and dying" as indecision plagues him (39). On his voyage across the Atlantic to a third rendezvous with Hilda, "he intend[s] . . . to decide upon a course of action" (73), but Alexander never makes that clear decision: "His resolution was weakening and strengthening, ebbing and flowing" (94). Alexander thus exhibits what many identify as a common reaction to abundance in nineteenth-century America, a reaction spurred by a belief in limitless human potential, limitless consumerism, and limitless opportunities for success.[16] He seems unable to establish any limits in his life. Echoing this theme, Hilda at one point admits to him: "My mistake was in wanting you to have everything. I wanted you to eat all the cakes and have them, too" (84).

Among the books that Bartley's old friend in England, Maurice Mainhall, has written is "a study of 'The Poetry of Ernest Dowson'" (21). Although Cather makes only that brief mention of this poet, a few lines from one of Dowson's more popular poems illuminate Bartley Alexander's dilemma: "I was desolate and sick of an old passion . . . I cried for madder music and for stronger wine."[17] Alexander is desolate and sick of his passion for material success and worldly fame; he seeks "madder music" and "stronger wine"—limitless pleasure and excitement. This, as Lears notes, was a typical response to the personal fragmentation that many were experiencing at this time. Lears describes the emergence of a "vitalist cult of energy and process . . . [accompanied by] a parallel recovery of the primal irrational forces in the human psyche."[18]

We see such a reaction in Bartley's affair with Hilda. Through this rekindled romance, he awakens the energetic "something unconquered" within him (38), which he envisions as a youth. He recognizes that "this youth was the most dangerous of companions" (41), and it is perhaps for this reason that he finds "a seductive excitement in renewing old experiences in imagination" (40). Cather in an 1895 journalistic piece had cited "youth and audacity" as "two qualities that the American people love."[19] Bartley Alexander, in his restless search for identity, exemplifies the national attraction to those traits, as well as the attraction to "energy and process" that Lears notes. Images of a vitalist force pervade the descriptions of this youthful being who takes hold of Bartley: "Something had broken loose in him of which he knew nothing except that it was sullen and powerful. . . . Always, now, it brought with it a sense of quickened life, of stimulating danger" (68).[20]

In an America focused on "having it all" but at the same time less certain of the individual's ability to control the forces within and around oneself, force and energy would indeed be seductive, as they are to Bartley. Unwilling to accept even the limits of temporal grounding, Bartley finds energy in "renewing old experiences," but he wants to relive those old experiences only selectively. He wants to recapture the excitement of his youthful love affair with Hilda, but certainly not his youthful poverty. Because Bartley refuses to accept any limits or to make any firm choices in his quest for self-fulfillment, time in general—the longed-for past, the momentary present, the looming future—remains continually problematic for him. Bartley thinks that he is securing a foothold in the future with his bridge-building. He sees himself as the type of man "whose dreams always took the form of definite ideas, reaching into the future" (40). Professor Wilson praises Bartley's force as the quality that "builds the bridges into the future" (17), but such a future remains out of his grasp, as the collapse of the Moorlock Bridge symbolizes, because Bartley Alexander is unable either to accept limits or to act decisively. The more Bartley projects himself into the future or tries to recapture selective portions of his past, the more clearly we see that he is trapped in the here and now, in the momentary, just as kinetic energy is of the moment. Professor Wilson early in the novel reflects that "[Bartley] was a natural force, certainly, but beyond that . . . he was not anything very really or for very long at a time" (15). In fact, when Wilson is first reunited with Bartley, the professor remarks insightfully: "No past, no future for Bartley; just the fiery moment" (8).

The past to which Bartley returns nostalgically becomes only a painful reminder of his inability, despite his successful and important societal position, to find fulfillment. The British Museum, a monument to the past, serves as a symbol of his failed quest. He and Hilda had years earlier loved to explore the museum, lingering there "to ponder by Lord Elgin's marbles upon the lastingness of some things, or, in the mummy room, upon the awful brevity of others" (33). Alexander finds in his attempt to return to the past and to live out another potentiality of his young self that he cannot live more than one life and that human life—like the mummy's and even Lord Elgin's—is brief and limited in its scope of achievement. Cather again employs the mummy image at the end of the story, as a shared memory between Hilda and Bartley, one that becomes a painful reminder of human limits: "Why did you remind me of the mummy?" Hilda asks, for it has reminded her that as "powerful" as she feels, she, like all humans, must die, just as their momentary happiness is about to die. Hilda, aware as Wilson is that Bartley represents "just the fiery moment," refuses throughout their affair to let Bartley give her any gifts other than flowers, which, of course, do not last (95). She wants no monuments to or memories of her rekindled relationship with Bartley, perhaps recognizing it as short-lived.

In contrast to Bartley's refusal to accept limits, Hilda seems acutely aware of the necessity of limits. "We make the most of our moment," she proudly asserts of herself and her fellow Londoners, but she immediately qualifies that statement: "It doesn't take pluck to fight for one's moment, but it takes pluck to go without—a lot" (93). This telling reminder of each individual's need to make choices, to set limits, perhaps even to sacrifice some things for a greater good, becomes a subtext in *Alexander's Bridge,* stressing membership in and responsibility to community. Cather seems repeatedly to criticize what Bellah and coauthors call "the destructive side of individualism"[21] as she looks at what happens when one follows either the path toward individual achievement or the equally self-focused "therapeutic" path to which

Bartley Alexander turns when success fails to bring either contentment or excitement. The "destructive side of individualism" refuses ever to subordinate the individual to community. Bartley Alexander, although he builds the bridges "over which the feet of every one of us will go" (17), shuns any sense of larger commitment: "He happened to be engaged in a work of public utility, but he was not willing to become what is called a public man" (38). To Bartley, success has robbed him of personal freedom: "He was paying for success. . . . He had expected that success would bring him freedom and power; but it had brought only power that was in itself another kind of restraint" (37). He detests "the demands made on his time by boards of civic enterprise and committees of public welfare. . . . He found himself living exactly the kind of life he had determined to escape" (37–38). Bartley's affair with Hilda, then, is in part a desperate flight from the responsibilities that accompany success—a flight that fails.

Richard Huber remarks that even during the late nineteenth century, "true success" involved commitment to and alignment with a community:

> "True success" was happiness, the joy of living, developing yourself by doing your best with the faculties that God has given you, leading a self respecting life with a noble character, peace of mind, service to others, or the love and respect of family, friends, and community.[22]

In like manner, Cather suggests that partly because Alexander feels no commitment to a public who depends on his abilities, and because he is ambivalent even about his commitment to his marriage, he can never grasp happiness or self-respect for very long. Late in the novel, he writes to Hilda: "I am never at peace. I am always on the edge of danger and change" (101).

Despite the community-conscious undercurrent in the novel, however, Cather appears less than fully committed to the nineteenth-century ideal of "true success" that Huber notes. She seems, rather, to sympathize with a protagonist plagued by community demands, perhaps reflecting in her portrait of Bartley Alexander her own personal dilemma, the demands and constraints that her commitments as managing editor at *McClure's* had put on her.[23] Cather wrote her December 1908 letter to Sarah Orne Jewett, complaining about the pressures of her job, probably around the time that she was formulating her ideas for *Alexander's Bridge;* in that letter, Cather—sounding a bit like Bartley Alexander—confesses that she does not despise journalism but gets no satisfaction out of it, that she feels like a split personality, torn between dedication to her own writing and to McClure's high expectations for her in journalism.[24] Worries about infringements upon her personal freedom resonate, too, in a confession to Elizabeth Sergeant that she feared "all the people who wanted to steal [her] energy and time."[25] James Woodress remarks that there is "a good bit of Willa Cather in Bartley Alexander";[26] we certainly see in her portrayal of Bartley Alexander Cather's own personal struggle to define her needs and at the same time to meet the demands of her various "communities," as we see, too, her confrontation with the temptations of success and with the emptiness that could accompany it.

The search for a self that had seemed dangerously thrilling to the Bartley Alexander whom we encounter at the beginning of *Alexander's Bridge* becomes at last enervating. In a broader sense, Alexander's problem suggests the "new," incapacitating disease that afflicted so many Americans involved in the scramble for success—"neurasthenia."[27] Lears identifies at the root of this societal nervousness "a longing for psychic harmony," which he calls "the profoundest symptom of late-nineteenth-century cultural crisis." Such longing left the fragmented individual vacillating between a desire for autonomy and a desire for "oceanic dependence."[28]

In Bartley's drowning, Cather gives us a final metaphor for the struggle between individual autonomy and such "oceanic dependence." When Bartley is plunged into the river as his half-built bridge collapses, he has the physical strength to survive, since he is "a strong swimmer" (126). But when several panic-stricken men surround him and cling to him for survival, he drowns. Bartley Alexander has tried, in his impulsive affair and accompanying flight into the past, to escape his responsibilities to his wife as well as to the larger community of people who depend on his skills as an engineer. But, as Cather suggests almost didactically in the bridge disaster scene, he cannot escape his commitment to others. Cather makes clear that Bartley knew before construction began on this bridge that he was making ethical compromises by allowing the building to proceed when the bridge commission had "crowded [him] too much on the cost," so that he was "having to build pretty much to the strain limit" (65). She presents the collapse of the bridge as a tragic price to pay for this earlier compromise; likewise, she depicts Bartley in his final hours realizing that the collapse of his relationship with Winifred is a tragic price to pay for refusing to accept limits, for seeking ever another "potentiality" of self. On his way to the bridge site, Bartley, who had planned to leave Winifred (even carrying in his coat pocket a letter to inform her of this), hopes that he will instead live to reconcile with her—"to recover all he had lost." The relationship has suddenly come to represent the self-fulfillment that he was unable to find in escaping it. But when he is plunged into the water, forces impair Bartley's physical autonomy, just as forces have previously impaired his psychic autonomy. The drowning workmen, emblematic both of the other self that has been fighting to live at Bartley's expense and of the other selves who depend on his skills for their physical safety, pull Bartley down in their struggle to live: "One caught him about the neck, another gripped him about the middle, and they went down together" (126).

In this image of the clinging men, Cather suggests again that one cannot escape the by-product of success: community ties. Bartley Alexander's commitment to community, to those who have made him a success, is underscored in this death scene by the phrase, "they went down together" (126). The last lines of this chapter, emphasizing "service," again suggest such commitment; the image of sickness that we noted earlier in connection with the struggle to succeed also resonates in these lines: "The mind that society had come to regard as a powerful and reliable machine, dedicated to its service, may for a long time have been sick within itself and bent upon its own destruction" (131). Both the "Gospel of Wealth" notion that material success brings with it the obligation of stewardship, and the moral imperative that true happiness comes with service to others, resurface at the end of *Alexander's Bridge,* but with a modern, Catherian twist that reveals her ambivalence toward such commitment: for Bartley Alexander, the pull of community is inescapable—and lethal. Yet, ironically, Alexander is remembered as a community-oriented man despite his quest for freedom from such responsibility. The epilogue closes with a larger-than-life portrait of the Bartley Alexander whose life touched so many others, even "the stupid and vulgar people," as Hilda Burgoyne says. "He left an echo," Professor Wilson adds. "The ripples go on in all of us" (138).

Bartley Alexander's story in one sense focuses on the consequences of ignoring one's responsibilities to others in the quest for self-fulfillment, but in another sense it celebrates the attempt—even though it is a futile one—to break free of others, to achieve autonomy in an era during which the possibility of doing so was continually being called into question. Cather's novel thus memorializes individual achievement, that crucial component of the American Dream. But our final picture of Bartley Alexander still has the same lack of clarity that his own self-definition had, as the narrator attests: "When a great man dies in his prime there is no surgeon who can say whether he did well; whether or not the future was his, as it seemed to be" (131). The final image is not of a protagonist who has found fulfillment, or of one who has been able even to identify what he needs for fulfillment, but of one who has struggled unsuccessfully to achieve autonomy and to gain any clear perception of his needs or goals. Earlier in the novel, Alexander is enveloped in fog, a metaphor for such lack of clarity. Perhaps also foreshadowing his death, Cather describes him on the deck of the ocean liner, "submerged in the vast impersonal grayness around him." Only in such a fog of escape does he feel "released from everything that troubled and perplexed him" (73).

Bartley Alexander thinks that he has found his real self in his final moments of physical struggle: "Now at last, he felt sure of himself" (159); but one cannot help feeling that this certainty is only a temporary condition—his habit of living for the moment, without a past or a future. It seems likely that, had he survived, he would again "zig-zag," at one moment choosing energy over substance—"the vibration of an unnatural excitement" (68) over the peace of a defined, limited self—only to reconsider at the next moment. Professor Wilson once had commended Bartley for "deciding to leave some birds in the bushes" (12), for not wanting them all. But Bartley Alexander has always wanted them all—which is the real "crack" in his character.

On the last night of Bartley's life, as he stares out the train window during his trip to the bridge site, he takes a mental journey into his past. He recalls his boyhood adventures around a campfire, his first bridge, his meeting with Winifred—all the times that he thought himself happy, sure of his identity and his direction in life, eager to face new challenges. These times contrast sharply with his present, a life that seems a "disaster." He wonders how it "could come about. He [feels] that he himself [is] unchanged" (114). This is perhaps the essence of Alexander's problem. He has not changed. He is still trapped in an American Dream of unlimited happiness and supreme individual achievement, still "hustling for hustling's sake," in Sinclair Lewis's words, hustling to define himself through career, through his past glories, and through projected future achievements. Thus, *Alexander's Bridge* represents not only Cather's perception that material success does not necessarily bring fulfillment, but perhaps, too, her realization that a limitless grasping had come to characterize most attempts to achieve the American Dream.

The drowning Bartley senses that Winifred is "in the water beside him, telling him to keep his head," but at the moment of death, it is as if she "let him go" (127). Perhaps she has not so much abandoned him as released him—from the burden of autonomy and into the comforting state of oceanic dependence. Perhaps she has released him, too, from the agony of perpetually striving for new heights of achievement, which was the trap built into the American Dream, leaving its victims neither satisfied nor sure of who they were.

O Pioneers!

The quest to define self that fails in *Alexander's Bridge* proves decidedly more successful in Cather's next three novels, *O Pioneers!, The Song of the Lark,* and *My Ántonia,* all of which depict the American Dream in a more positive light. It is as if, after exploring what was not fulfilling in the American Dream, Cather, unwilling to reject it totally, manages a swing toward optimism. In these novels, she seems to seek out ways in which success might be fulfilling. Her protagonists all achieve some version of the standard dream, but they also gain a sense of self-fulfillment; in doing so, they seem to confirm Cather's belief (or hope), at this stage of her life, that material success was available to most people in America, and—more importantly—that happiness could accompany it. Starting from humble beginnings, Alexandra Bergson, Thea Kronborg, and Ántonia Shimerda, through their own strength of will and resourcefulness, do find fulfillment: Alexandra develops a prosperous farm and ultimately marries her lifelong friend, Carl Linstrum; Thea achieves fame and the satisfaction of artistic accomplishment as an opera singer; Ántonia acquires the farm she had always wanted as well as a family who is devoted to her.

Gender seems a key factor in these heroines' ability to balance a desire for material success with a clear understanding of what they need for self-fulfillment.[29] Lears describes the late nineteenth-century belief in a "feminine principle," a mystical "female vitality." Such a view, he says, "joined maternal nurturance, emotional spontaneity, aesthetic responsiveness, and mythopoeic creativity."[30] Cather in these novels seems to be responding to that belief. Her heroines have the vitality, the imagination, and the self-awareness to shape for themselves a form of success that foregrounds self-fulfillment.[31] Gender may keep them on the margins of the male-dominated, aggressive, competitive scramble for success, but gender proves an asset in their efforts to achieve self-fulfillment, helping them turn inward to explore self in a way that Bartley Alexander never could.

Perhaps the key to these women's emotional as well as their material success, however, is their double marginality—as women and as immigrants (or a child of immigrants, in Thea Kronborg's case). Cather repeatedly suggests that because all three have been instilled with and retain "Old World" values, they can keep that typically "American" drive for material success from erasing or replacing their own identities. All three seem to understand that there must be something more to life than "getting on"; they define and reach for that something with a certainty that Bartley Alexander never exhibits. In these three novels, Cather depicts the special meaning that she saw the American Dream holding for immigrants: having come to America precisely because they believed that here they could succeed, most held dearly to their faith in that dream while they also held dearly to their own traditions.

Cather often commented on the values and traditions that immigrants brought to America. She had a special attachment to and appreciation for this transplanted "community," with whom she first came into contact at age nine, when her family moved from Virginia to Nebraska. In a 1926 "Biographical Sketch" that she wrote about herself (though in third person) she comments:

> Had she been born in that community [Red Cloud, Nebraska], she doubtless would have taken these things [the fascinating speech and customs of the immigrants] for granted. . . . An imaginative child, taken out of the definitely arranged background, and dropped down among struggling immigrants from all over the world, naturally found something to think about.[32]

That "something to think about" perhaps created in Cather a heightened sensitivity to the differences between the standard version of the American Dream and the immigrant version, which she interpreted as a richer, fuller definition of success, a definition that balanced an eagerness for material improvement with a deeper moral and cultural purpose for such striving.

Cather, of course, was most familiar with frontier immigrants' version of the American Dream, a drama played out on the bleak, expansive prairies, where banding together became a protection against both the loneliness and physical harshness of the environment. Perhaps she would have found less "to think about," or less that she cared to think about, if she had grown up among discontented, "struggling immigrants" in the crowded ghettos of the nation's urban areas. When in 1928, she wrote the story of a city immigrant, Anton Rosicky, it is the story of his escape to a rural world, his realization that living and working in the cutthroat urban world could quickly turn anyone into a thief or a degenerate. But in the Nebraska of Cather's childhood, the "Old World" values and the struggle to adapt to a strange environment that Cather observed in her immigrant neighbors touched her heart:

> No child with a spark of generosity could have kept from throwing herself heart and soul into the fight these people were making to master the language, to master the soil, and to hold their land and to get ahead in the world.[33]

In the American Dream envisioned by these people, "getting ahead" counted, but Cather seemed to feel that it counted for deeper, more worthwhile reasons than it did for most Americans in the early twentieth century, enslaved by the "bitch-goddess." As Cather commented in her 1923 essay on Nebraska's immigrant pioneers: "With these old men and women the attainment of material prosperity was a moral victory, because it was wrung from hard conditions, was the result of a struggle that tested character."[34] In 1924, criticizing the Americanization process for turning immigrants "into stupid replicas of American citizens," she asserted: "They have come here to live in the sense that they lived in the Old World, and if they were let alone their lives might turn into the beautiful ways of their homeland."[35] Certainly, Cather did not mean that immigrants could not claim a piece of the American Dream; rather, they could enrich the meaning of that dream.

Cather was one of the few writers to depict the "community" of new immigrants in a positive manner at a time when most Americans viewed these newcomers, especially those from southern and eastern Europe—such as the Shabatas in *O Pioneers!* and Ántonia's family—with both fear and suspicion.[36] In the years between her fictional portrayals of Alexandra Bergson in 1913 and of Ántonia Shimerda in 1918, cultural critic Randolph Bourne published his essay, "Trans-National America," in the *Atlantic* (July 1916). Bourne's essay can be read almost as a gloss on Cather's two novels about immigrants. "America shall be what the immigrant will have a hand in making it," Bourne insists, demanding "a clear and general readjustment of our attitude and our ideal." Perhaps Cather hoped through her fiction to effect such a "general readjustment." Bourne continues: "We have needed the new peoples . . . to save us from our own stagnation"[37]—a point that Jim Burden makes when he contrasts the vitality of the immigrant girls to the stagnant life in Black Hawk.

Like Cather, Bourne worried also about the stagnating effect of the Americanization process on immigrants:

> What we emphatically do not want is that these distinctive qualities [of the immigrant's cultural background] should be washed out into a tasteless, colorless fluid of uniformity. . . . [It is precisely] because the foreign-born retains this expressiveness [that he is] likely to be a better citizen of the American community.[38]

In her three immigrant novels of this period, Cather shows the qualities that immigrants bring to America from what Bourne calls "the deep cultural heart of Europe." Bourne's plea, that "we must give new edges to our pride," is certainly part of her agenda here. Thus, the American Dream, as Cather depicts it in these novels, is an expansive as well as a spiritually fulfilling dream. Cather opens it up to women and to new ethnic groups, just as Bourne insists on expanding the definition of "American": "In this category I include the migratory alien who has lived with us and caught the pioneer spirit and a sense of new social vistas." Bourne asserts the need in America for "a vivid consciousness of the new [cosmopolitan] ideal";[39] Cather, in her fiction, provides that new ideal. Her immigrants keep their own traditions, their own cultural identities, alive as they adapt, survive, and even prosper in a competitive, success-oriented America.

In each of these novels, however, Cather continues to address, as she did in *Alexander's Bridge,* the destructive elements of the dream of success. *O Pioneers!* is the story of Alexandra Bergson and her family as they struggle to succeed on the harsh Nebraska prairie. But that struggle is virtually finished by the end of Part I; then Cather contrasts Alexandra's reaction to material success with her brothers' reactions. In doing so, Cather shows the corrupting potential of the American Dream and the corrective that, in her view, Old World values could provide. For Cather, "Old World" signifies tradition, respect for the past, a clear sense of identity; in contrast are "New World" values, which emphasize rejection of the past and a pressure to conform. Herbert Croly in 1909 reminded Americans: "The better future, whatever else it may bring, must bring at any rate a continuation of the good things of the past."[40] Cather, in her portraits of immigrants who adapt to American ways while they insist upon "a continuation of the good things of the past" offers the same view. She represents that worthwhile "past," in the Old World customs that immigrants such as Alexandra continue to nurture. It becomes clear in Cather's contrast of Alexandra to her brothers that material success, if based only on a drive for modernism and conformity, hampers self-definition, as success had hampered Bartley Alexander in his efforts to define self.

Late in *O Pioneers!,* Alexandra reminds her younger brother Emil that their father "had better opportunities" than did Emil's older brothers, Lou and Oscar—"not to make money, but to make something of himself."[41] Lou and Oscar have by this time become prosperous, but since they had no motives beyond a desire for modern comforts and a fear of other people laughing at them if their actions deviated from the norm, their success appears empty to Alexandra. When the Bergson family is struggling during the early years on the prairie, Lou and Oscar would rather flee to Chicago and become bakers with their uncle, who leads a comfortable life, or move to a river farm where crop yield is consistently predictable if not abundant. They reluctantly decide to stay, only because they have neither the nerve nor the self-confidence to challenge Alexandra when she reminds them of their father's deathbed wish that they keep the farm; nor do they have the initiative to make any move on their own—even a move backwards, to a laborer's job in Chicago.

Clearly, Cather portrays the Bergson brothers as lacking a strong sense of individuality. They define themselves in terms of others, and thus, when prosperity comes, they become in Cather's eyes conforming, shallow "Americans." "The way here is for all to do alike," the old Norwegian Ivar says regretfully to Alexandra, fearful of those who might institutionalize him for his eccentric ways (92). Lou and Oscar are those unappealing "replicas of American citizens" whom Cather identifies in her Nebraska essay. Oscar marries an American woman who is embarrassed to have a foreigner for a husband; they raise their children to speak English only. Lou and his wife, Annie, although both Swedish, sometimes speak their native language at home, but are embarrassed to be " 'caught' at it." Lou has learned to speak English "like anybody from Iowa" (99). He and Annie boast that their home has all the modern conveniences. Cather describes this "type" in her Nebraska essay. The children of the immigrant farmers, she says, as if referring specifically to Lou and Oscar, "were reared amid hardships, and it is perhaps natural that they should be very much interested in material comfort, in buying whatever is expensive and ugly. . . . They want to buy everything ready-made."[42] These are the "conspicuous consumers" that Veblen identified in his 1899 *Theory of the Leisure Class.*

In the same Nebraska essay, Cather expresses her hope that the "third generation" will not be fooled into believing "that to live easily is to live happily."[43] Similarly, Alexandra Bergson puts her faith in Lou's daughter, Milly, who reminds Alexandra so much of her own mother. Alexandra is eager to buy her niece a piano because the girl has already learned the "old Swedish songs" that Alexandra's father used to sing (103). Just as Milly reminds Alexandra of her own mother, Alexandra, too, had reminded her father of his father. She had her grandfather's initiative, as John Bergson notes, recalling that his father "had built up a proud little business [in Sweden] with no capital but his own skill and foresight" (24).

Cather suggests that primarily because Alexandra retains Old World values and morals, she does not respond as Lou and Oscar do, either to material success or to the hardships that precede it. Guided by a strong sense of duty to parent, she holds onto the farm in hard times. Possessing the "foresight" of her grandfather, Alexandra knows that new ways are important in the struggle to succeed. She thus looks around the little community of Hanover and notices who is successful; she studies how they achieved that success and urges her brothers to learn from the lessons of others. Her remarks echo the rhetoric of nineteenth-century success manuals: "If only poor people could learn a little from rich people!" (58). Referring to the real estate brokers who are buying tracts of land from discouraged farmers, she tells Lou and Oscar: "They are the men to watch. . . . Let's try to do like the shrewd ones" (68).

John Bergson had noted that although "Lou and Oscar were industrious"—citing that old Horatio Alger virtue which was once seen as the key to success—they did not "use their heads" as Alexandra does (23). Alexandra's father knew that it takes more than hard work and steadiness to achieve the American Dream of success in a new, harsh land. "A pioneer should have imagination" (48), Cather's narrator remarks. And this is the trait that fits Alexandra for the new country far better than does her brothers' "industry." Alexandra observes that in Lou, "the love of routine amounted to a vice" (55): industry taken to extremes can be self-limiting. With her imaginative pioneer spirit, Alexandra is willing to take big risks. She refuses to trade their seemingly worthless high land for the river land where one can "scrape along" but "never do anything big" (64). She takes risks with new crops such as alfalfa and wheat, with new methods such as a pig corral in the sorghum field, with new equipment such as a silo. She braves the criticism of neighbors, whom Lou and Oscar always fear will be laughing at them for Alexandra's unconventional ways. There is "something individual" (83) about Alexandra's farm: she is a strange mix of new entrepreneur and Old World artisan, which, Cather suggests, is the key to her combined material success and apparent peace of mind.

Alexandra's foresight, faith in the land, and financial shrewdness give the Bergsons their American Dream by the time Book II of *O Pioneers!* opens. But just as *Alexander's Bridge* exposes the problems that come once one has grasped the American Dream, Cather's second novel, too, shows the tension between material success and self-fulfillment. Alexandra's struggle toward self-definition is certainly more focused and more rewarding than Bartley's, but it is nevertheless a struggle. At first she identifies solely with the land, defining herself through it. Once she has established her "new relation to it" (71), she almost loses herself in the land: "She [feels] as if her heart were hiding down there, somewhere, with the quail and the plover and all the little wild things that crooned or buzzed in the sun" (71). But although "it is in the soil that she best expresses herself" (84), Alexandra, having achieved her version of the American Dream, finds that neither a rich farm nor fulfilling her father's wishes allows her to define herself. Tellingly, when she looks back on her success, "well satisfied" that all the struggle "had been worth while" (213), what makes it seem so for her is the opportunity to "escape" the land—an opportunity that she has made possible for Emil: "Out of her father's children there was one who . . . had not been tied to the plow, and who had a personality apart from the soil" (213). Alexandra, who has not had "a personality apart from the soil," understands the limitations of such a self-definition.

Despite the assured sense of self that Alexandra displays through-out Book I, such autonomy grates against a desire for dependence: "There is often a good deal of the child left in people who have had to grow up too soon" (17). Although Alexandra remembers, admires, and certainly identifies with the solitary wild duck that she and Emil had seen on their river trip, "swimming and diving all by herself in the sun-light" (205), she does not want to be "all by herself." She desires secret-ly to be the one who is carried instead of the one doing all the carrying. In a recurring dream, she sees herself "being lifted up bodily and car-ried lightly by some one very strong." Still identifying with the land, she envisions herself being carried "as easily as if she were a sheaf of wheat" (206). This secret longing for dependence embarrasses and angers her. Only in the final pages of the novel is she able to voice her desire openly when she leans on Carl's shoulder and confesses: "I am tired . . . I have been very lonely" (308). What Lears would call a "long-ing for dependent passivity" struggles in Alexandra against the "drive toward autonomous action," as it did for so many caught up in the turn-of-the-century scramble for success.[44]

In Alexandra's struggle to gain or to relinquish autonomy we see her shifting relationship to community. Alexandra experiences the pull of community as both a positive and a negative force in her life. The fam-ily community gives purpose to her own struggle, but ties to family cre-ate more and more tension for Alexandra as the Bergsons achieve pros-perity. Alexandra explains to Carl that her brothers "do not altogether like my way. . . . Perhaps they think me too independent" (118). When she finally quarrels openly with them over her right to marry Carl (whom Lou and Oscar see as a fortune hunter, interested only in Alexan-dra's property), she says, "I think I would rather not have lived to find out what I have to-day" (172).

Experiencing such tension within her family, Alexandra not sur-prisingly finds more satisfaction in her own hand-picked community, one that reinforces the Old World ways that she so values. Her favorite brother, Emil, is, she tells Carl, "more Swedish than any of us" (117), despite the fact that he is the only Bergson to have attend-ed an American university. Alexandra treats her European hired hands, Barney Flinn and Nelse Jensen, as trusted family members. Her farm is "not unlike a tiny village" (83)—a village with distinc-tive Old World flavor. Three Swedish girls help her in her kitchen, and Alexandra admits that she employs them not because she needs that much help, but "to hear them giggle" (85). When the eccentric recluse, Ivar, loses his land, Alexandra adds him to her community, despite loud and continued protests from her embarrassed brothers. Alexandra Bergson is an important force in her neighbors' lives, and draws them into her community: she depends on young Marie Shabata's companionship; she invites old Mrs. Lee for a long visit each winter; she attends Sunday services with Marie in the neighboring French Catholic community.

Although Alexandra fashions her own responsive community, her relationship to her original community—her immediate family—remains burdensome. Far more crushing than her quarrel with Otto and Lou is her tragic loss of Emil. A mother figure for Emil, Alexandra has nevertheless been blind to his most pressing needs and problems. She feels that by sending him to the state university, she has given him the opportunity he needs to find fulfillment—"a chance, a whole chance" (117). But she never recognizes his emotional needs. Emil's and Marie's deaths at the hands of Frank Shabata, Marie's husband, is for Alexandra a double loss—of a brother whom she regarded as a son and of her closest friend, Marie. The loss awakens her to her inability to control all destinies, despite her strength of will and good intentions. Determined to mend her community, Alexandra later visits Frank Shabata in prison and promises to make every effort to have him pardoned.

Cather stresses the importance of community to the individual in all three of the novels written between 1913 and 1918. Gardens often symbolize for Cather such a healthy community—ordered, productive, nourishing.[45] Cather's characters cultivate gardens to provide nutrients for the body as well as nourishment for the soul. Cather uses this image only once in *Alexander's Bridge,* in a letter that Bartley writes to Hilda Burgoyne admitting that he can no longer find peace of mind. He describes the garden outside his study:

> There is a garden out there, with stars overhead, where I used to walk at night when I had a single purpose and a single heart. I can remember how I used to feel there, how beautiful everything about me was, and what life and power and freedom I felt in myself. . . . But that garden is closed to me.[46]

Bartley Alexander, no longer in control of his life, cannot feel a part of the healthy, productive community that is humankind. That world of ordered growth is closed to him.

In subsequent novels, Cather continues to suggest in her garden imagery the security, the sense of belonging, and the sense of ordered growth that humans need and that a healthy community provides: "Alexandra often said that if her mother were cast upon a desert island, she would thank God for her deliverance, make a garden, and find something to preserve" (29). The narrator in *O Pioneers!* later describes the garden behind Alexandra's new home in similarly positive terms: "When you go out of the house into the flower garden, there you feel again the order and fine arrangement manifest all over the great farm" (84). Significantly, both Lou and Oscar do not have "the patience to grow an orchard of their own" (104); but Marie Shabata's vitality and nurturing concern for others is imaged in her lush orchard as well as her indoor garden of flowering plants that bloom all winter long under her nurturing care.[47]

In *The Song of the Lark,* we see a similar reflection of a healthy, caring community in the German immigrant Mrs. Kohler's garden: "Her plants and shrubs were her companions. She lived for her men and her garden." When Mrs. Kohler takes in the old music teacher, Wunsch, she "went at him as she did at her garden," caring for him unselfishly.[48] In *My Ántonia,* young Jim Burden, newly arrived in Nebraska, settles against a "warm yellow pumpkin" in his grandmother's garden and feels "entirely happy"; later, when he moves to town, he describes one of his happiest experiences—helping the neighboring Harlings "break the ground and plant the garden". When Jim visits Ántonia after she has married, she proudly shows him her orchard, explaining that she loves the trees "as if they were people," and that her husband's expertise at grafting has made their orchard the most productive in the region.[49] As this imagery suggests, the Cuzak family is a caring, thriving community; for them, this healthy community is an important aspect of success.

Cather depicts community in a positive sense in her garden imagery, but in her repeated depictions of small towns, we find an often negative perspective on community. In *O Pioneers!* we briefly glimpse this. The young Emil sees the town of Hanover as "a very strange and perplexing place, where people wore fine clothes and had hard hearts," a place where "people might laugh at him" (5–6). Years before, in an editorial (1901), Cather gave a similar appraisal of people in small towns: "Social endeavors become discouraged in small towns," she remarked. In analyzing why this is so, she highlights a negative characteristic of competition—jealousy over others' success:

> If the people in the villages all over the western states took more interest in each other and could manufacture a smile when their neighbors had a stroke of good luck or could find a sympathetic word to say when they were in trouble . . . the corn itself would take heart o' grace and see some use in growing.[50]

Cather concluded with a despairing question: "Why is it that the common courtesies of life . . . come harder than blood in the small towns?"[51] The Cather who as a young journalist indicted small towns presents a softened, though still critical, look at such a community in both *The Song of the Lark* and *My Ántonia.*

The Song of the Lark

In *The Song of the Lark,* Cather fully explores Thea Kronborg's relationship to a small town community as she charts her own path to success and struggles to define herself. Much of the conflict in the early chapters of the novel centers on the tension that Thea feels in her relationship with her own family and with her hometown of Moonstone, modeled after Cather's own Red Cloud, as are all of the small western towns in Cather's fiction.

Thea, from her early childhood, has a strong, clear sense of self, even before she can specifically identify her needs: "She knew, of course, that there was something about her that was different. But it was more like a friendly spirit than like anything that was a part of herself. . . . The something came and went, she never knew how."[52] Over and over in *The Song of the Lark*, Cather presents images of Thea's sense of self. Both Thea's room and her voice serve as symbols of a distinct self. "Her mind worked better" when she was alone in her room; in it she felt like "a different person" (73).[53] Later, she comes to recognize her uniqueness in her voice: "Her voice, more than any other part of her, had to do with that confidence, that sense of wholeness and inner well-being that she had felt at moments ever since she could remember" (272).

Having such a clear sense of separateness, Thea does not settle for being molded or shaped by family or community pressure. Her mother recalls that "from the time she was a little thing, [she] had her own routine." Mrs. Kronborg, realizing this, often admonishes her other children to "let Thea alone" (82–83). As a nonconforming individual, Thea has "natural enemies" (75) in her small community of competitive, jealous, judgmental people. Thinking about one of her rivals, the inept singer, Lily Fisher, Thea reflects bitterly: "Lily Fisher was pretty, and she was willing to be just as big a fool as people wanted her to be. Very well; Thea Kronborg wasn't. She would rather be hated than be stupid, any day" (81).

Because the community of Moonstone and even her own family offer so little that is gratifying to Thea, she seeks out and selects her own community, as Alexandra Bergson had. Its members include her Mexican friends at the edge of town, who share her love of music; the Kohlers with their sheltering garden; her piano teacher, Wunsch, who gives Thea her start in learning to appreciate music; and the other nurturing teachers in her life—her faithful railroad friend, Ray Kennedy, and the devoted Dr. Archie. These people form a meaningful community for Thea that contrasts sharply with Moonstone in general.

Yet that larger community continues to tug at Thea. Moonstone residents consider Thea's voice, that metaphor for self, to be community property. She is expected to sing at funerals and other occasions, as if this responsibility comes with community membership. When Thea grates against this appropriation of self, she makes more "natural enemies" in Moonstone. Despite the negative pressure that Moonstone exerts on her, Thea still feels emotional ties to the town itself. Cather reveals Thea's ambivalence toward Moonstone when "a particularly disgusting sort of tramp" comes to town. The strange, "wretched-looking" outsider is understandably shunned by the entire community, including Thea, who "hoped he would not stop at their gate." When the town authorities imprison him for giving a show without a license, and then—appalled by his filthiness—release him and demand that he "get out of town, and quick," the tramp takes his revenge by lowering himself and his few belongings into the town's water standpipe (171-73). Thus drowning, he makes a statement about his own alienation as he indicts Moonstone for its unwillingness to accept an outsider. His body pollutes Moonstone's water supply, causing a typhoid epidemic.

Thea is troubled by the tramp incident, not so much because some of her schoolmates are among the typhoid victims, but because, surprisingly, she takes on the burden of guilt for the whole community. "It seems to me," she tells Dr. Archie, "that the whole town's to blame. I'm to blame, myself" (174). Archie reassures her that this was just one of those "ugly accidents," and that "people who forge ahead and do something," not this failed individual, are the ones who "really count" (176), here reflecting the typical aggressive individualism of his day.

Against this negative look at small town heartlessness, however, Cather juxtaposes Thea's almost sentimental reverie on her attachment to her hometown: "She loved the familiar trees, and the people in those little houses." But even in this moment, Thea continues to feel the tension between loyalty to community and her desire to "forge ahead and do something," for she reflects that she also "loved the unknown world beyond Denver. She felt as if she were being pulled in two, between the desire to go away forever and the desire to stay forever" (177). Revolt from the village is for Cather evidently not a clearcut issue.[54] The tension that she depicts in *The Song of the Lark* confirms this, and perhaps mirrors a general tension in small towns during this era, since the desire and opportunity for vertical mobility meant for many making choices between community loyalties and their own progress up the ladder of success.

When Ray Kennedy dies in a railroad accident, leaving Thea his life insurance, she is financially able to escape to that "unknown world beyond Denver" to study music in Chicago. Here she encounters a new, much larger community, but as she had selected a community that suited her in Moonstone, Thea again does so in Chicago, finding refuge from the impersonal city in Mrs. Lorch's comfortable home and at the home of her music teacher, Harsanyi. Ray Kennedy had told Thea: "There are a lot of halfway people in this world who help the winners win, and the failers fail. . . . It's a natural law" (156).[55] Thea finds those helpers in Chicago as she had in Moonstone.

But in Chicago, as in Moonstone, Thea experiences a negative community of petty, materialistic people, especially when she becomes both student and employee of a mercenary voice teacher, Madison Bowers, most of whose clients represent the new middle class, people with less talent than money, who want instant culture as a sign of social status. Part III of the novel, recounting Thea's frustrations with this antagonistic community, is appropriately titled, "Stupid Faces." In this atmosphere of struggling, competitive people, Thea herself begins to become harsher, a success-motivated individual who wants no ties, no encumbrances. She cannot make friends with the other girls in her boarding house: "I can't work with a lot of girls around," she tells Bowers. "They're too familiar. . . . Gets on my nerves" (317).

In the stifling atmosphere of Bowers's Chicago world, Thea at last gains a clear awareness of her need for a meaningful community and for a different purpose in life. "She believed that what she felt was despair, but it was only one of the forms of hope" (332), the narrator observes. At this point, Cather clearly differentiates between Thea Kronborg's slowly emerging drive for artistic success and self-fulfillment and a shallow, materialistic American Dream: "[In the city,] money and office and success are the consolations of impotence" (333). While fortune lets such people "suck their bone in peace," she does not let imaginative, creative youth—the Thea Kronborgs—rest: "She flicks her whip . . . upon that stream of hungry boys and girls who tramp the streets of every city, recognizable by their pride and discontent, who are the Future, and who possess the treasure of creative power" (333). It is clear that any standard definition of success will not be enough to provide fulfillment for Thea.

As Thea defines her own desires, she aligns herself with a creative community: the time-spanning community of female artists with whom she finds kinship during her visit to the ancient cliff dwellings in the Southwest.[56] Here Thea finally determines what she wants to do at the same moment that she recognizes these women's efforts to find a place for art in their lives while they struggled simply to survive. Thea's newly discovered community suggests the type of community that Cather herself found nurturing and inspiring, and suggests, too, Cather's reverence for the artistic traditions that she saw as nurturing the imaginative life of a community.

Bathing in the quiet stream, Thea finds there "a continuity of life that

reached back into the old time" (378). Taking on the role of appreciative observer and vicarious participant, she envisions the stream as a
backdrop to an earlier drama: "[It was] the only living thing left of the
drama that had been played out in the [canyon] centuries ago" (378).
Thea comes to appreciate the artistic endeavors of this ancient community during the days that she spends in Panther Canyon. Henry Bilt-
mer, having lived all his life near these cliff dwellings, explains to Thea
the importance of pottery as a medium of artistic expression for the
ancient people: "The strongest Indian need was expressed in those
graceful jars, fashioned slowly by hand, without the aid of a wheel"
(378). Thea herself discovers some fragments of pottery in the ancient
dwellings, heightening her sense of a tie between herself and these earlier artists.

Walt Whitman in the Preface to *Leaves of Grass* praises "all the
grandeur and good of the few ancient nations whose fragments of
annals we inherit";[57] Thea Kronborg recognizes in the fragments of
pottery that she finds the same "grandeur and good." She recognizes,
too, her privileges and obligations as inheritor of those fragments:
"These potsherds were like fetters that bound one to a long chain of
human endeavor." She is grateful to these ancient people for their early
contribution to art: "In their own way, those people had felt the beginnings of what was to come" (380).

As Ray Kennedy had once observed about the ancient ruins, "All
these things made one feel that one ought to do one's best, and help to
fulfil some desire of the dust that slept there." Feeling a part of this
community, Thea finds purpose and meaning for her own individual
endeavors; she suddenly feels "united and strong" (380). For the rest
of the novel, it is Thea's sense of membership in this art-focused community, extending from these ancient artists to her present-day fellow
artists and audiences, that inspires her, helping her to define herself and
giving meaning to her life. She fulfills herself through a sense of duty
to these other lovers of art—"an obligation to do one's best" (375).
When Thea leaves Panther Canyon, she is ready for the long struggle
that becoming an opera singer entails, including years of study in the
enriching Old World atmosphere of Germany.

At the same moment that Thea finds her real community in Panther
Canyon, she recognizes that, up to this time, a standardized version of
the American Dream had directed much of her life; her parents had a
lucrative future "mapped out" for her as a piano teacher in Moonstone,
not as the singer that she now knows she must become. In the quiet
atmosphere of the cliff dwellings, steeped in a meaningful past of artistic endeavor and removed from the negative influences of Moonstone
and Chicago—of both rural and urban America infected by the "nation-

al disease," the drive for success—Thea realizes that she has unwittingly let herself get caught up in that same hustling for hustling's sake
to which Babbitt later falls victim: "All her life she had been hurrying
and sputtering, as if she had been born behind time and had been trying to catch up" (372).

Thea finally takes control of her own life, as Dr. Archie had once told
her she must someday do. At that time, still a believer in the standard
American Dream, she had told him that money was "the only thing that
counts" because "to do any of the things one wants to do, one has to
have lots and lots of money" (304–5). But when Dr. Archie responded
that, yes, she could make money, "if you care about that more than anything else," Thea had replied: "I only want impossible things. . . . The
others don't interest me" (305). Archie's answer to that—"If you decide
what it is you want most, *you can get it*" (306)—recalls Wunsch's earlier advice: "There is only one big thing—desire" (95).

Once Thea identifies her real desire and attaches herself to that "long
chain of human endeavor" centered around art, she is on her way to a
different American Dream, one that sees fame and fortune as mere by-
products of an inner fulfillment, just as Cather had seen the material
success of the early pioneers as merely an outward sign of "a moral victory."[58] Thea rejects the shallow goals that clouded her vision and hid
her real self from her. Like Alexandra Bergson, she makes the decision
to take risks in order to fulfill her dreams:

> There was certainly no kindly Providence that directed one's life; and one's
> parents did not in the least care what became of one so long as one did not
> misbehave and endanger their comfort. One's life was at the mercy of blind
> chance. She had better take it in her own hands and lose everything than meek-
> ly draw the plough under the rod of parental guidance. (382)

If Cather in *The Song of the Lark* begins to clarify her redefinition of
the American Dream, shifting the focus away from fame and fortune,
she is not yet ready to leave that standardized version completely
behind. Just before Cather began to write this novel, she spent several months interviewing journalist S. S. McClure and then writing his
autobiography, which was published in *McClure's* between October
1913 and May 1914. McClure's autobiography certainly fits into the
category of the self-made success story, focusing mostly on McClure's
early years of struggle. Vestiges of that typical success story remain
in *The Song of the Lark*. Thea's drive to achieve, for example, still exemplifies that old nineteenth-century spirit of competition which pits the
individual against the common herd. Thea knows that she is part of the
"general scramble of American life where everyone comes to grab and

take his chance" (231), but she also knows that she will not become a victim. She has the competitive spirit characteristic of the most ruthless captains of industry, a spirit even more evident in Cather's 1915 edition of *The Song of the Lark* than in her revised 1937 edition,[59] although the later edition still highlights this competitive drive. On her train ride back to Moonstone after her first year in Chicago, she sits near a sick girl about her age, whose coughing keeps her awake all night. Although Thea sympathizes with this girl and even has a flower and a cup of coffee delivered to her, Thea also "smiled—though she was ashamed of it—with the natural contempt of strength for weakness, with the sense of physical security that makes the savage merciless" (274). It is this combination of desire and determination that gives Thea Kronborg the potential for self-fulfillment:

> Along with the yearning that came from some deep part of her, that was selfless and exalted, Thea had a hard kind of cockiness, a determination to get ahead. Well, there are passages in life when that fierce, stubborn self-assertion will stand its ground after the nobler feeling is overwhelmed and beaten under. (274)

Thea Kronborg does succeed; Part VI of *The Song of the Lark* and the Epilogue chronicle her life as a successful performing artist. But Cather apologized for these final sections in a 1932 Preface to her new edition of *The Song of the Lark*:

> The chief fault of the book is that it describes a descending curve; the life of a successful artist in the full tide of achievement is not so interesting as the life of a talented young girl "fighting her way," as we say. Success is never so interesting as struggle—not even to the successful, not even to the most mercenary forms of ambition. (v)

Cather's equation of success with "the most mercenary forms of ambition" recalls her negative portrait of the ambitious Madison Bowers and even of minor characters such as Moonstone's Lily Fisher. This prefatory remark may also reflect Cather's discomfort with her own secure financial position during the Depression, when this preface was written, for many of her friends and certainly a large portion of her general readership were suffering financially at this time. But although Cather notes in her 1932 preface that she should have been content to tell only the story of Thea Kronborg's struggle, the younger Willa Cather who wrote *The Song of the Lark* in 1914 and 1915 seems almost as interested in the struggle that persists after one achieves success as in the struggle up the ladder.[60]

In her portrayal of a successful Thea Kronborg, Cather depicts the continuing struggle toward creative accomplishment that drives any artist. The Thea Kronborg whom we meet in Part VI of *The Song of the Lark* is certainly an accomplished opera singer; but she seems capable of remaining excited about her career only by never allowing herself to feel satisfied: "It's the thing I want to do that I can never do. Any other effects I can get easily enough" (515). Cather in her preface may insist that the successful Thea Kronborg portrayed in the final part of the novel has ceased to struggle; but Thea struggles as intensely in her postsuccess days as she did when she was merely an aspiring singer. Thea is constantly aware of "the struggle that [makes] up her actual life" as artist (515); in fact, she welcomes and perpetuates it. One incident makes this especially clear. When a fellow opera singer falls ill during a performance, Thea agrees to fill in for her. The audience reacts with overwhelming enthusiasm to Thea's impromptu performance—their response is "something like a popular uprising" (530). Dining with Thea afterward, her friend Fred observes:

> She was much handsomer than she had been early in the evening. Excitement of this sort enriched her. It was only under such excitement . . . that she was entirely illuminated, or wholly present. At other times there was something a little cold and empty, like a big room with no people in it. (533)

Fred's simile, "like a big room with no people in it," draws our attention to Thea's and any artist's need—if often an unconscious need—for an audience. Fred, praising her dedication to her art, stresses as he does so the relationship of artist to audience: "I'm grateful to you for what you demand from yourself, when you might get off so easily. You demand more and more all the time, and you'll do more and more. One is grateful to anybody for that; it makes life in general a little less sordid" (556). To an extent, Cather suggests here that what keeps Thea's desire fresh is her relationship with a diverse, "grateful" community, whose members appreciate her talent and her efforts. Dr. Archie remarks to Fred after one of Thea's performances: "Seems to me you get a good deal for your five bucks. . . . And that, after all, is what she cares about—what people get" (510). Thus, a successful Thea Kronborg continues to struggle, certainly primarily because she loves her art, but perhaps also because of "what people get."

The final portrait of Thea Kronborg, then, is not a portrait of a smug, complacent success; it does not really describe "a descending curve," as Cather claims in her preface, but instead depicts an artist still struggling. Thea Kronborg struggles for the continued creative vitality that is in part made possible by her relationship with her audience, even if she does not openly admit the importance of that relationship. In the final scene, Cather focuses on Thea's old friend from Mexican Town in Moonstone, Spanish Johnny, who has come to see her performance. Although Thea does not see him in the crowd that gathers to catch a glimpse of the famous Kronborg as she leaves the opera hall, Johnny's approving smile, the narrator remarks, is "the only commensurate answer" to the exhausted singer's probable question, "What was the good of it all" (573).

This final focus on audience as meaningful community carries through to the epilogue, which takes place in Thea's home town of Moonstone, "nearly twenty years after Thea Kronborg left it for the last time" (575). As the epilogue opens, Cather places her readers in the role of audience at a drama. The first six paragraphs are written in present tense, in the style of stage directions: "It is a warm summer night of full moon. . . . To the east the sand hills shine white as of old" (575). The scene focuses at last on Aunt Tillie, Thea's loyal supporter from years earlier, who is bragging about her famous niece. Here we see a double emphasis on audience, for Tillie in the epilogue plays two roles—that of performer and that of audience. We see her as storyteller, performing for an audience of sometimes eager, sometimes annoyed listeners. As the epilogue opens, she is "surrounded by a crowd of boys," telling them proudly that her niece receives "a thousand dollars a night" for her singing (575). In the final paragraph of the epilogue, we again see Tillie in the important role of storyteller: "Her stories give [the townspeople] something to talk about and to conjecture about" (581). But between these two scenes we get a glimpse of Tillie in the reverse role of audience. She recalls the thrilling week when the Metropolitan Opera Company traveled to Kansas City, and Tillie was invited by Thea to see all of her performances: "[Fred] took [Tillie] every night to the performance and left her in a box to go through her raptures unobserved" (578). Thus, Cather reminds us in her epilogue that the relationship between artist and audience is mutually beneficial.

Just as Cather closes Part VI with an emphasis on the important role that audience response plays for the performer, answering the question, "What was the good of it all," she stresses in the epilogue the important role that artist plays for the audience: "Thea Kronborg has given much noble pleasure to a world that needs all it can get" (578). The older residents of Moonstone take great interest in their children who have achieved the American Dream of fortune and fame: "A boy grew up in one of those streets who went to Omaha and built up a great business, and is now very rich. Moonstone people always speak of him and Thea together, as examples of Moonstone enterprise" (580). Cather in this commentary on small-town values, a commentary far gentler in its satire than some of her earlier remarks about small towns, reminds us that the people of Moonstone are neither artists nor "refined" lovers of art—in Thea's or most artists' sense of art appreciation. But Moonstone's residents consider Thea a part of their community, as they always have, and they interpret her success in the way that is meaningful to them. Although the Moonstone residents link Thea with the boy who "built up a great business," Cather suggests that even these people have more appreciation for the artist, who gives what no successful business tycoon ever could: "They do, however, talk oftener of Thea. A voice has even a wider appeal than a fortune" (581).

Cather's focus on audience in these final sections of *The Song of the Lark* suggests a responsive community as a key factor in the quest for self-fulfillment. Such a final focus actually confirms Cather's prefatory remark about success. Certainly, "success is never so interesting as struggle"; but in Cather's early move toward a redefinition of the American Dream, Thea Kronborg's success implies a continuing struggle, both as an artist intent on reaching new levels of creative achievement and as a performer responding to a demanding but appreciative audience. For Thea, as perhaps for Cather in her artistic endeavors, there is really no such thing as a "descending curve."

Although Cather returns to Moonstone at the end of *The Song of the Lark*, we are not in the isolated, smugly provincial Moonstone of Thea's childhood. This community needs "tidings of what their boys and girls are doing in the world," Cather says in the epilogue, to "bring to the old, memories, and to the young, dreams" (581). She uses the analogy of the water around Venice, which would become stagnant and uninhabitable if the tide from the sea did not come into it every night. Those who help a community most are the ones who bring something from the larger world to that community, just as Alexandra Bergson explains to Carl Linstrum the dangers of isolated rural life: "our minds get stiff. If the world were no wider than my cornfields, if there were not something beside this, I wouldn't feel that it was much worth while to work. . . . It's what goes on in the world that reconciles me."[61] Cather underscores this idea at the end of *O Pioneers!* when Alexandra goes out into that larger world to seek a pardon for Frank Shabata, and when Carl returns from that wider world to marry Alexandra, bringing a part of it to her farm and promising her future sojourns into that larger world. Both novels end with the idea that an isolated community is not a healthy community, that one must have a continual sense of belonging to a larger world.

Cather's justification for her own escape from Red Cloud resonates in such endings. Perhaps, too, she is here reflecting on the dramatic changes in small-town life at the turn of the century. America with its vast network of railroads was by the 1890s no longer "a nation of loosely connected islands," of self-sufficient, self-contained small towns; it had become an "integrated country."[62] Small-town residents, from farmers to storekeepers, were now aware "that someone in a distant center was pulling the strings that moved their affairs."[63] Cather confronts that change optimistically in Alexandra's positive attitude about the outside world and in the image of a fresh tide from the sea with which *The Song of the Lark* concludes.[64]

My Ántonia

When Jim Burden in *My Ántonia* experiences a sense of warmth and security in his grandmother's garden, we see once more Cather's emphasis on the importance of a larger community that shapes one's traditions, as Jim envisions his place within a continuum: "I was entirely happy. Perhaps we feel like that when we die and become a part of something entire, whether it is sun and air, or goodness and knowledge. At any rate, that is happiness; to be dissolved into something complete and great."[65] Repeatedly in her fiction, Cather emphasizes the importance of this broader community as she celebrates tradition and past human endeavor, but she also stresses the impact that a lone individual can have on that larger community of humankind: "The history of every country begins in the heart of a man or a woman."[66] In *My Ántonia*, Jim Burden ponders the passage from Virgil's Georgics: "For I shall be the first, if I live, to bring the Muse into my country" (264). Here we see the artist's special perception of responsibility to community.

But in this statement there is also the subtle reminder that one can feel restricted by this, tied to a specific, narrower community. Jim's teacher, Gaston Cleric, emphasizes for his students that " 'patria' here meant, not a nation or even a province, but the little rural neighbourhood on the Mincio where the poet was born" (264). Just as Thea Kronborg felt the pull—both positive and negative—of her "little rural neighborhood" while she made her individual way toward success and self-fulfillment, Jim Burden, on his own road toward a less fulfilling success, ponders his continuing need to belong to a community. He realizes that people from his past in Black Hawk, the immigrant girls in particular, have the special qualities that inspire artists: "If there were no girls like them in the world, there would be no poetry" (270). Cather herself felt the pull of Red Cloud as she struggled toward success as a novelist. A favorable response to *O Pioneers!* from "the home folks" in Nebraska was important to her. She told her friend Zoe Akins that, in writing this novel, "she wanted to shine a little" for that community.[67] Not only did she hope to bring the muse to her own country, but to be a muse of sorts herself, inspiring the rest of America to see the beauty in Nebraska and its people. This link to specific community was important for Cather all her life. Cather's personal commentary on the pull of community is evident in Jim Burden's remark:

> I knew that I should never be a scholar. I could never lose myself for long among impersonal things. Mental excitement was apt to send me with a rush back to my own naked land and the figures scattered upon it. . . . I suddenly found myself thinking of the places and people of my own infinitesimal past. . . . in some strange way they accompanied me through all my new experiences. (262)

The pull of community exerts a constant force on a person, as Cather well knew, both inspiring and hindering one's development as an autonomous individual and one's struggle to achieve fulfillment.

In *My Ántonia*, Ántonia Shimerda is involved in an intense project of self-development; she is shaped by the positive as well as negative pull of family, her Bohemian traditions, and the community of Black Hawk. In this respect, Ántonia is not unlike Alexandra Bergson and Thea Kronborg. But in one respect, *My Ántonia* differs markedly from these earlier "success stories." Here Cather seems far more cautious about associating material success with self-fulfillment. Ántonia is Cather's first protagonist who is not, by the standards of her era, a material success. When Ántonia's childhood friend, Lena Lingard, years later talks to Jim Burden about Ántonia, Lena laments that Ántonia had not "done very well" (327). Ántonia does not achieve fame or fortune, and only briefly leaves her little corner of Nebraska to experience—negatively—the larger world. But as a Bohemian immigrant who comes to Nebraska at the age of fourteen, she brings the traditions and values of her native country to her new corner of the world, and in the end, Ántonia achieves a happy balance between what Cather sees as "American" and "Old World" values.[68] Ántonia shapes a new American Dream that does not rely on material success yet celebrates the wealth of opportunity in America for each individual to achieve personal goals.

In the final lines of the novel, narrator Jim Burden reflects on "those early accidents of fortune which predetermined for us [Ántonia and himself] all that we can ever be" (371). But Jim, certainly not a reliable narrator in his appraisals of Ántonia, fails here to understand that Ántonia's life has been a journey of self-discovery, not a predetermined course. Undoubtedly, Ántonia's situation restricts her options: she is a poor immigrant and a woman in a world of narrowly defined roles for women. But throughout the novel, she still "tries on" various selves, and makes choices that extend her limits. She establishes more control over her own destiny than one might think possible in turn-of-the-century Nebraska. Ántonia is a realist. Even as a young girl, she faces the uncertainties of her future with her eyes open. She tells Jim: "Things will be easy for you. But they will be hard for us" (140). Despite the difficulties that Ántonia faces, when we view her at the end of the novel, she apparently has found what she needs for fulfillment.

Throughout the novel, Ántonia defines her needs, responds to opportunities, and decides how to use to her advantage the situations into which "accidents of fortune" cast her. When Widow Steavens recounts to Jim Ántonia's disastrous experience with railroad man Larry Donovan, who lured her to Denver with a promise of marriage and then abandoned her, Mrs. Steavens recalls Ántonia's initial doubts about living in Denver: " 'I'm a country girl,' she said. . . . I was counting on keeping chickens, and maybe a cow'" (309). Ántonia's doubts display her awareness of her own needs. When Jim, makes a visit to Ántonia, now living and working on her family's farm where she is raising her child, he finds her still just as sure of her needs: "I'd always be miserable in a city. I'd die of lonesomeness. I like to be where I know every stack and tree, and where all the ground is friendly. I want to live and die here" (320). Ántonia defines for Jim everything that she needs for fulfillment, adding: "I know what I've got to do. I'm going to see that my little girl has a better chance than I ever had" (320–21). The Ántonia whom Jim encounters twenty years after that conversation has found that place "where all the ground is friendly" and has, with her husband Anton's help, provided her children with the American Dream of "a better chance."

Jim sees Anton Cuzak as "the instrument of Ántonia's special mission" (367), but Cuzak is also involved in a project of self-definition. Like Ántonia, Cuzak seeks a new version of the American Dream—one in which happiness and material success do not necessarily go hand–in–hand. As Cuzak tells his story, we see that he, like Ántonia, has tried on various selves to find the one that fulfills him: a journeyman furrier in his homeland; a city-dweller in Vienna, enjoying the night life; a simple wage-earner in New York; an orange farmer in Florida; and finally, a hard-working but happy Nebraska farmer. Cuzak's story is a testimonial to the American Dream of opportunity for all. Sharing a common set of Old World traditions, he and Ántonia have weathered hard times to make a modest American Dream come true: "We got this place clear now. . . . She is a good wife for a poor man" (365), he tells Jim, unembarrassed to call himself poor, and seemingly satisfied to have given up the glamor of city life for the simple life on a farm. "His sociability was stronger than his acquisitive instinct" (366), Jim notes—Cather's sad reminder that the standard American Dream, grounded in competition and materialism, had by 1918 degenerated to little more than an "acquisitive instinct."

Throughout *My Ántonia*, Cather sets up contrasts between those characters who achieve the American Dream of material success, and those such as Ántonia and her husband, whose sense of fulfillment relies neither on fame, fortune, nor even on the competitive drive that pushed Thea Kronborg. The characters in *My Ántonia* who have the strongest sense of self and find the deepest satisfaction are, not surprisingly, the ones whose material success seems only modest. Cather most fully explores this idea in the contrast between Ántonia and Jim Burden. In the introduction, we meet Jim Burden, a successful lawyer who lives in New York and has married well by society's standards. The narrator, who "grew up" with Jim in Black Hawk, notes that Jim's wife "is handsome, energetic, executive," a patron of the arts, a woman with "her own fortune." But Jim Burden's apparent success has left him empty, as Cather suggests by juxtaposing the description of Jim's wife to this statement: "As for Jim, disappointments have not changed him." Thus, before *My Ántonia* even begins, we see Jim Burden—much like Bartley Alexander—as a success in the world's eyes, but as an unhappy vagabond of the soul, who has found no fulfillment in either his career or his personal life. Jim comes home to himself only when he experiences with Ántonia and her family a sense of belonging that success has not brought: "My mind was full of pleasant things; trips I meant to take with the Cuzak boys. . . . There were enough Cuzaks to play with for a long while yet" (370–71).

Throughout the story, Ántonia's strong sense of self contrasts sharply with Jim's passivity and indecision, his inability to define self. An orphan, Jim has only a vaguely remembered past to help him define himself when the story opens, in marked contrast to the rich past that Ántonia brings with her to Nebraska and in contrast to the exciting, colorful past of the hired man, Otto Fuchs, who at first meeting "looked lively and ferocious . . . as if he had a history" (6). When Jim arrives in Nebraska, he feels "erased, blotted out," as if he has "left even [his parents'] spirits behind" him (8). But erasure can provide an opportunity for a new self-definition, if one takes that opportunity. Jim never seems to do so. When Ántonia calls him a hero after he kills a huge rattlesnake, Jim is reticent to take on such an identity: "In reality it was a mock adventure; the game was fixed for me by chance" (49–50).

Ántonia is an active participant in her destiny, shaping her own self–image as she takes on the various roles that her circumstances force upon her. "I can work like mans now. . . . I help make this land one good farm" (123), she boasts after her father dies and she must help her brother Ambrosch plow the fields. She cheerfully assumes the role of hired hand on others' farms; later she assumes the role of hired girl in Black Hawk at the Harling house. "Not too old to learn new ways" (153), Ántonia as a hired girl learns the refinements of household life, but she also learns more about what she needs for happiness. When Mr. Harling tries to limit her outings to local dances, Ántonia moves out, risking the dangers of a housekeeping position at the residence of the ruthless Wick Cutter rather than restrict her own freedom to socialize and to enjoy the night life of Black Hawk.

Jim is a spectator more than a participant, defining himself through others' expectations or assessments; in contrast to Ántonia, he acquiesces to his grandparents' wish that he stop going to the firemen's dances. Even at the university in Lincoln, Jim cannot make his own decisions. He leaves Lincoln for Harvard, despite his happy relationship with his old friend from Black Hawk, Lena Lingard, because his professor, Gaston Cleric, tells him: "You won't do anything here now. . . . You won't recover yourself while you are playing about with this handsome Norwegian" (289). Both Cleric and Jim's grandfather decide that Jim will go to Harvard, and he passively agrees, telling Lena: "I'll never settle down and grind if I stay here" (292).

Jim's recurring dream about Lena serves to highlight his continual refusal to direct his own life and to establish his own goals.[69] In the dream he is passively "lying against" a harvested wheat shock; Lena moves toward him, carrying a curved reaping-hook, thus appearing as a goddess of the harvest (225). Lena does the talking in the dream and assumes the active role: "Now they are all gone, and I can kiss you as much as I like," she tells a passive Jim. Reflecting on this dream, Jim comments: "I used to wish I could have this flattering dream about Ántonia, but I never did" (226). The irony is that, although Jim never does have such a *dream* about Ántonia, a similar scene actually takes place between Ántonia and Jim, serving to remind the reader that Jim cannot even define what or whom he wants, much less act to realize his dreams. When Jim visits Ántonia after she has returned home with her baby, the similarities between the scene and Jim's dreamscape are striking:

> The next afternoon I walked over to the Shimerdas'. Yulka . . . told me that Ántonia was shocking wheat on the southwest quarter. I went down across the field, and Tony saw me from a long way off. She stood still by her shocks, leaning on her pitchfork, watching me as I came. (319)

Ántonia, who is harvesting shocks of wheat as Lena was in the dream, is, like Lena, the one to speak—in bold, aggressive words: "I thought you'd come, Jim. . . . I've been looking for you all day." Jim had wished that the woman who spoke invitingly to him in his recurring dream were Ántonia; but when the woman speaking invitingly to him among the harvested shocks is Ántonia, Jim remains passive and indecisive about his feelings toward her. He knows that his own sense of self is closely linked to Ántonia: "The idea of you is a part of my mind; you influence my likes and dislikes, all my tastes, hundreds of times when I don't realize it. You really are a part of me." But he cannot get any more precise than that. "I'd have liked you for a sweetheart, or a wife, or my mother or my sister" (321), he tells Ántonia. It is safer for him to want her to be "anything that a woman can be to a man" than it is to choose a specific relationship with her. Childhood becomes his preferred refuge in this wheat-field scene: "I wished I could be a little boy again, and that my way could end there" (322). In the last lines of the novel, we see the same retreat to the past, as Jim explains that what he shares with Ántonia is the "incommunicable past" (372). For all the material success that Jim Burden has been able to grasp, he cannot grasp any sense of fulfillment in the present, only in a vaguely envisioned past.

If we look at other standard success stories besides Jim's in *My Ántonia*, we see Cather continually questioning the American Dream of material success as the road to self-fulfillment. Wick Cutter is a ruthless businessman who becomes so corrupted by the drive for money that he kills his wife moments before he kills himself, making sure that he has witnesses to verify that she has died first so that her family cannot inherit his estate, which is worth, ironically, a mere one thousand dollars. Cather seems to be purposely mocking Horatio Alger's morally upright model for success by including this background on Cutter: "Cutter boasted that he never drank anything stronger than sherry, and he said he got his start in life by saving the money that other young men spent for cigars. He was full of moral maxims for boys" (209).

Lena Lingard is not the standard model of success although she becomes a successful dressmaker in Lincoln and later in San Francisco. Jim notes that she "had none of the push and self-assertiveness that get people ahead in business" (278). Still, Jim admires Lena's "self-possession" (279), the trait that he lacks. Although an immigrant, Lena is Emerson's self-reliant American. She has found success and self-fulfillment although she possesses none of the standard nineteenth-century "push and self-assertiveness," nor the standard maternal or domestic instincts attributed to women. Lena chooses not to marry, preferring, she says, "to be accountable to nobody" (291–92). "She remembered home as a place where there were always too many children, a cross man and work piling up around a sick woman" (291). Her companion when Jim meets her later in San Francisco is another former "hired girl" from Black Hawk, Tiny Soderball. Jim relates Tiny's success story, remarking that "of all the girls and boys who grew up together in Black Hawk, Tiny Soderball was to lead the most adventurous life and to achieve the most solid worldly success" (299). But although Tiny has experienced high adventure in the Klondike gold fields and has acquired great wealth through luck and hard work, she is an emotional victim of the American Dream, not its beneficiary as Lena is: "She said frankly that nothing interested her much now but making money. . . . She was satisfied with her success, but not elated. She was like someone in whom the faculty of becoming interested is worn out" (301–2). Jim's remark recalls that earlier portrait of the successful Bartley Alexander as well as Cather's portrait seven years later of a successful but disillusioned Professor Godfrey St. Peter.

Pianist Blind d'Arnault, who visits Black Hawk, represents another version of the American Dream. As Cather does with other minor characters, she gives us here the whole story of Blind d'Arnault's encounters with opportunity and hardship. A black man born in "the Far South . . . where the spirit if not the fact of slavery persisted," Samson d'Arnault was left blind by an illness during infancy. As a young child, d'Arnault became aware of what he needed for fulfillment when he heard the housemistress practicing the piano. After that, nothing could keep him from his desires. One day, at the age of six, he sneaked into the parlor and approached the piano, "as if he knew it was to piece him out and make a whole creature of him" (188). Through his desire and talent, Blind d'Arnault asserts his individuality and makes a career for himself.

Other cameo appearances in the novel highlight various versions of the American Dream: the Danish laundry girls who "were not so ambitious as Tony or Lena [but were] kind, simple girls and they were always happy" (222); Mrs. Gardener, who owned Black Hawk's hotel and opera house, but "seemed indifferent to her possessions" (182); the successful grain merchant and cattle buyer, Mr. Harling, a second-generation immigrant with a large, happy family; his daughter, Frances, who "was her father's chief clerk and virtually managed [her father's] Black Hawk office during his frequent absences" (149), sharing that prestigious managerial position with her husband after she marries; the loyal hired hands Jake and Otto who "were the sort of men who never get on somehow" (68), but who continued to seek their dream, going West together to work in the Yankee Girl Mine once the Burdens had moved to town; the Italians, Mr. and Mrs. Vanni, who take their "dance school" from town to town (194); even the unscrupulous Larry Donovan, who, after getting fired from his railroad job for "knocking down fares," goes to Mexico where "conductors get rich . . . collecting half-fares off the natives and robbing the company" (312–13).

Opportunities for material success abound in the world of *My Ántonia*, as Cather's portraits make clear. But some opportunities are already diminishing. When Jim, Ántonia, Lena, and Tiny picnic together at the river before Jim leaves for Lincoln, they see against the setting sun the image of a plow: "There it was, heroic in size, a picture writing on the sun" (245). But the plow quickly diminishes from its "heroic" size as the sun sets: "That forgotten plough had sunk back to its own littleness somewhere on the prairie" (245). Cather suggests in this image the rapidly disappearing opportunities that a vast frontier had provided.[70] The sturdy pioneer who could carve a dream for himself with a plow and a determined will was already becoming a figure of the distant past, just as the "magnified" image of the plow against the sun so quickly faded to littleness before Jim's eyes. Cather saw in that pioneering era, as she notes in her Nebraska essay, the equation of material success with moral victory; but in the world that surrounded Cather as she wrote *My Ántonia* in 1916 and 1917, material success seemed too often an obstacle to either moral victory or self-fulfillment, as Cather's portrait of Jim Burden suggests.

Jim Burden, the most detailed portrait of the unfulfilled though successful individual in *My Ántonia*, does finally achieve a belated self-fulfillment among the Cuzaks. Thus Cather focuses in the final scenes, as she had in *The Song of the Lark*, on the importance of attachment to a community. The pull of community remains a subtext throughout *My Ántonia*. Antonia is a loyal family member who supports the actions of her rough brother and her grasping mother. Jim, in fact, comments that "one result of [immigrants'] family solidarity was that the foreign farmers in our county were the first to become prosperous" (200). As a hired girl in Black Hawk, Ántonia and the other hired girls form their own tight-knit community, sometimes at odds with the closed-minded citizens of Black Hawk, who, not unlike the shallow, judgmental citizens of Moonstone in *The Song of the Lark*, view the independent, energetic "country girls . . . [as] a menace to the social order" (201). Jim Burden, walking the streets of Black Hawk late at night, reflects that in the little, flimsy houses, where people "lived like mice," life was "made up of evasions and negations" (219). He views the community of Black Hawk as a negative counterpart to the lively, supportive community that the hired girls form.

Although Black Hawk is in many respects a negatively portrayed community, Cather emphasizes in her other portrayals of the individual's relationship to community both the obligations and the rewards of community membership. The tale of the Russian immigrants, Pavel and Peter, provides a striking example of this. As members of a wedding party in Russia, entrusted with the responsibility of driving the groom's sled through the snow-covered forest, Pavel and Peter panic when a pack of wolves overtakes one-by-one the other sleds in the party. Desperate to make it safely to their village before the advancing wolves attack the exhausted horses, Pavel throws both bride and groom over the side of the sled to lighten the load. After this barbarous act against their community, the two are, of course, banished. The Bohemian, Krajiek, serves as another example of a person's refusal to act as a responsible member of a community. Krajiek deals unethically with the Shimerdas, his own fellow countrymen, when he sells his farm to them. In contrast to Krajiek is Anton Jelenik, a fellow Bohemian who comes to the aid of the Shimerdas when Mr. Shimerda commits suicide. "He came to us like a miracle in the midst of that grim business," Jim recalls (104).

Mr. Shimerda's funeral presents a positive picture of a community facing tragedy. The neighboring farmers gather for the funeral, despite the harsh winter weather, displaying a strong sense of community support that continues long after Mr. Shimerda's death, as Cather makes clear in the account of Shimerda's "grave at the crossroads." The superstitious Mrs. Shimerda insists that the grave be located there so that wagons will drive over it. But Jim points out that years afterward, when the roads were built, "the road from the north curved a little to the east just there, and the road from the west swung out a little to the south." Jim's remark stresses the sense of shared humanity and community membership that extends even to a dead foreigner, Mr. Shimerda: "I loved the spirit that could not carry out the sentence—the error from the surveyed lines, the clemency of the soft earth roads. . . . Never a tired driver passed the wooden cross, I am sure, without wishing well to the sleeper" (119).

Ántonia retains a sense of community, too, about Bohemia. "I ain't never forgot my own country," she tells Jim (238). When he visits Ántonia's farm years later, her cultural ties are stronger than ever. She and her family speak Bohemian at home; the hollyhocks add a Bohemian touch to the farm ("the Bohemians, I remembered, always planted hollyhocks"), as the *kolaches* do to the dinner table. "Americans don't have those," one of the boys boasts of the spiced plums that they have preserved, and another remarks in Bohemian that their American visitor probably does not even know what *kolaches* are (338). Ántonia's son, Leo, plays Bohemian airs on his grandfather's violin; pictures from the Old Country hang on the Cuzaks' parlor walls. But the American community that so shaped Ántonia's early years in Nebraska also holds an important place among the traditions that she has passed on to her children: "These children know all about you and Charley and Sally, like as if they'd grown up with you," she tells Jim (334). Ántonia has thus created her own community through a healthy balance of old and new.

Cather's heroine in *My Ántonia* does not need wealth to fulfill her American Dream, but, ironically, she still sees wealth as part of the dream for her children: "They have a Ford car now," she boasts of her eldest daughter, Martha, and her husband. "He's a handsome boy, and he'll be rich some day." But Ántonia seems to realize, too, that such a drive for success has its dark side: "Her husband's crazy about his farm and about having everything just right, and they almost never get away except on Sundays" (355). Success for Ántonia means having provided her children with "a better chance" (321). "I'm thankful none of my daughters will ever have to work out," she adds (344). And of her Bohemian friend, Mary, she says: "Her children will have a grand chance" (349).

Alexander's Bridge ends with a picture of the American Dream in ruins. Pursued by a dream of self-fulfillment that he cannot clarify and thus cannot attain, Bartley Alexander is at last "released" to an almost merciful death. But Cather does not simply walk away from those ruins, nor does she become trapped in them. Instead, she salvages from the ruined dream the tools to reshape it: the acknowledgement of limits that makes self-definition possible; the drive to define one's own needs and goals; the support that a caring community offers. John Cawelti observes that for many novelists of this era,

> the traditional ideal of success meant despair and disillusion with America, and to an extent, with human society itself.... The pursuit of success [became] an all-encompassing end which further separate[d] the individual from his initial goals.[71]

Cather in these early novels moves past such "despair and disillusion" by focusing on heroines who creatively shape and courageously realize their own unique dreams. But in the four novels that follow, Cather again makes a swing toward pessimism, questioning the possibility of fulfillment—of even identifying one's needs—in a society mired in materialism.

3
Crises of Self and a Glimmer of Hope

By the time Cather finished *My Ántonia*, she had begun both to question and to redefine the American Dream, minimizing the material aspect but still affirming individual achievement. The optimistic Ántonia, in her final conversation with Jim Burden, envisions a "grand chance" for her children to be materially successful as well as happy, but that "grand chance" turns sour in Cather's next four novels, all of which criticize even more harshly and more directly the drive for material success, finding it clearly at odds with both self-actualization and integrity of spirit. In Cather's first four novels, the corrupting aspects of materialism strike only the few individuals who let their values become distorted in the drive for success, but in *One of Ours* (1922), *A Lost Lady* (1923), *The Professor's House* (1925), and *My Mortal Enemy* (1926), the "national disease" seems to have taken hold of the very heart of America, leaving little room for hope—although Cather certainly makes a glimmer of hope evident.

The four protagonists in the novels written between 1922 and 1926 struggle to rescue some clear idea of self and then to hack a path toward self-fulfillment through the jungle of materialism.[1] In all four novels of this period, Cather's despairing tone strongly resembles that of her contemporaries, as many critics have noted. Typical is Bernard Baum's observation. Categorizing Cather with Eliot, Huxley, and Fitzgerald, he remarks: "All had in common a profoundly disturbing sense of modern civilization as bankrupt morally and intellectually—a desert of the spirit inhabited by hollow men."[2] Cather, however, does not end in total despair—even in *My Mortal Enemy*, her most bitter novel. She negotiates a path toward affirmation by shaping an idealistic, if somewhat vague, definition of community that recalls Thea Kronborg's inspirational "long chain of human endeavor." The four novels of this period depict troubled souls searching for a "family" to give meaning to their lives and through whom they will be able to define themselves; but what emerges as the family of choice is neither one's biological family nor one's national or ethnic family. Cather's protagonists instead find hope in various romantic notions of community when their familiar communities prove unresponsive or detrimental to their self-development. Claude Wheeler in *One of Ours* finds the prairie life that had stimulated earlier Cather characters stifling, as does Marian Forrester in *A Lost Lady*. Both die on foreign ground, but not before they find a degree of fulfillment: Claude because he feels that he is dying for people who share his ideals; Marian because she feels that she is performing for a responsive, if artificially contrived, audience. Godfrey St. Peter in *The Professor's House* sees an America that is becoming more materialistic; he desires so strongly to remove himself from such a world that he flees mentally to the pure world of Tom Outland's Blue Mesa and flees physically to his study, almost convincing himself that death offers the only real escape. St. Peter is rescued by a realization similar to Claude's: that there exists a vaguely defined but meaningful "world" of people to claim as his community. Myra Henshawe finds herself caught in the very drive for material gain that she had tried to turn her back on; her refusal to live for anyone but herself contrasts sharply with the self-sacrificing efforts of her husband, Oswald, and her young companion, Nellie, who form a caring community and thus enrich their own lives.[3]

In these four novels, then, we briefly glimpse a fairly abstract community, its members embracing ideals of brotherhood and mutual responsibility as they seek to nurture and transmit what Cather saw as enduring values. In this loosely defined community, Cather apparently saw a richness that the shallow, competitive society of a changing America could not provide. Still, Cather seems ambivalent in these four novels about the importance of one's commitment to community, just as she seems ambivalent about letting go completely of the competitive drive for success. Instead, she struggles in these works to define the place that commitment to community can have in helping the individual not only survive but find fulfillment.

In her interviews of the 1920s, we see Cather also struggling with the special problems of community involvement, especially as they concern the artist. Having written three critically acclaimed novels, Cather at this time was coming to terms with her relationship to several communities—her reading public and critics; the media, who wanted more interviews, more access to her thoughts and opinions; and her own childhood community of Red Cloud, which she both fictionalized and memorialized in her three most recent novels. A May 1921 article on Cather notes one aspect of the tension that an acclaimed writer experiences: "Of the two paths of art—give the public what it wants, or make your work so fine that the public will want it—[Willa Cather] has consistently chosen the path of fine work. She is moving unhurriedly toward a richer self-expression."[4] Self-expression and devotion to her art for Willa Cather certainly outweighed the need for public acclaim; but Cather herself, in another interview that same year, acknowledged that a writer who wants to do justice to his or her art cannot be totally self-absorbed: "If a person is wide awake and not self-centered he can see those interesting things [which make good stories] in the life of those about him."[5]

At the same time, however, Cather seemed defensive during these years about the key role that Red Cloud was playing in her success as a writer. She seemed anxious that she might appear to be exploiting for her own success the Annie Pavelkas (model for Ántonia) or Lyra Garbers (model for Marian Forrester) who so often served as the "interesting" subjects of her stories. In an October 1921 interview she stated emphatically: "I have never ceased to be thankful that I loved those people out in Republican Valley for themselves first, not because I could get 'copy' out of them."[6] That she was experiencing inner conflicts over her place in her home community is evident, too, in a November 1921 interview, in which she again made a pointed reference to the emotional pull of her own childhood community, which she by all appearances had deserted for the livelier life of Pittsburgh and then New York:

> There I was on the Atlantic coast among dear and helpful friends and surrounded by the great masters and teachers with all their tradition of learning and culture, and yet I was always being pulled back into Nebraska. . . . I could not decide which was the real and which the fake "me." . . . My deepest feelings were rooted in [Nebraska].[7]

As Cather continued during the 1920s to resolve the problem of which "me" she was, her novels of this period reflect her struggle to decide which communities she most pictured herself a part of—or wanted to be a part of. It is easy to see why a reporter in 1925 commented about her: "One feels almost a constant antagonism between Miss Cather and the world." The interviewer defends this attitude as merely "the mantle of self-defense against the probings of a curious world";[8] but Cather's "mantle of self-defense" suggests a tension that surfaces in her novels of this period as a fear of the care-laden world with its demands and pressures, its false values and petty judgments that overpower the individual until he or she can neither define self apart from that world nor see a place for an autonomous self within that world.

One of Ours

Cather seems in the 1920s to be trying to break free of the restrictive communities in her life. Despite her emotional investment in Nebraska, in *One of Ours* she takes a hard, critical look at what has happened there since Alexandra's and Ántonia's triumphs, and at what has happened to values in America in general. It is almost as though Cather expatriates emotionally in this novel—from Nebraska and from America—even though she did not physically expatriate, as others of the Lost Generation did.[9] In both *One of Ours* and *The Professor's House* we sense no attachment either to the prairie or the nation; instead, Cather suggests a letting go of anything but loyalty to the larger family of humanity, a community that for Cather's purposes transcended those problematic though more tangible national or political boundaries. This "human family" seems to embody for Cather the traditions and values that endure even as "bad governments come and go."[10] Such a community allows Cather a degree of evasiveness: in a thus broadly defined community, one need not take aggressive stands on political issues such as women's rights, social reform, or international affairs. Nevertheless, for Cather, allegiance to and celebration of this community seemed to offer survival in a troubled era, without the need to retreat to the past; she could instead bring the past forward—in a Claude Wheeler who cherishes "Old World" ideals or in a Marian Forrester whose pioneer spirit is suited to a postfrontier era. Thus, even in a period during which her novels seem more clearly and critically focused on the spiritual emptiness of early twentieth-century America, Cather's determination to identify with those who find spiritual and emotional nourishment in shared traditions and ideals allows her to maintain a sense of hope.

Early in her journalistic career (1895), Cather made a sweeping pronouncement about the human race, characteristic of the optimism that threads its way through her later writing:

> Humanity cannot utterly blast itself, even when it tries. . . . Humanity is always so much of a child, its digressions and sins are always more pitiful than terrible.[11]

But in the America of *One of Ours*, humanity is in both a pitiful and a terrible state of digression. Claude Wheeler comes to recognize this as he tries to find a place for himself in a world of materialism and waste on a prosperous farm in the Nebraska of the early 1900s. Only when he goes away to France to fight in World War I does he find his "golden chance,"[12] a sense of belonging to the larger community of people—past and present—who are willing to "die for an idea" (357).

Cather's disillusionment with the material prosperity that had once seemed to her only an innocent, outward sign of moral victory is evident from the opening pages of *One of Ours*. Claude's home is a world of waste, the result of the carelessness and shallowness that prosperity has bred in the Wheelers and even in their hired hands. Five steers have died needlessly in a blizzard the winter before, victims of the hired hands' "wanton carelessness" (6); the same disregard for life has left the mare, Molly, crippled. This is a far cry from Alexandra's faithful, caring hired hand, Ivar, who treats the horses as if they were family members. The image of Claude kicking the carcass of a chicken as he walks to the barn adds to this picture of waste.

The Wheelers have achieved the American Dream of material success on their farm, but waste seems to be the legacy of such a dream. Claude's father, as a practical joke in response to his wife's complaint that she cannot reach the cherries on the tree in their orchard, cuts down the heavily laden tree. All of these incidents foreshadow the human waste that the war will bring. These physical signs of waste also mirror the inner waste on the Wheeler farm—the emptiness of their lives, which Claude alone seems to recognize. Historian Alan Trachtenberg's comment on this era in America accurately reflects Claude's own feelings: "In its very success, middle class culture had come to seem stifling, enervating, devoid of opportunities for heroism."[13] Claude never dreams that he will have the chance to be a hero. At age nineteen, he knows that he does not fit in this stifling world where things are always measured by money and by what others think. He is not pleased with what he sees when he looks into the mirror, or looks into himself, and confronts there "exactly the sort of boy he didn't want to be" (17). He feels "pulled in two or three ways at once," and envies his Bohemian friend, Ernest Havel, who seems to "live in an atmosphere of mental liberty" (12).

Even college has not helped Claude to define himself, but has only made him feel more restricted, since his parents have sent him to a small denominational college that fosters only narrow-mindedness and obedience. For over half of *One of Ours*, we see Claude imprisoned in the complacency that Cather undoubtedly saw sweeping the country. Claude fears that he, too, will fall victim to such complacency, that he will settle for "cheap substitutes" and "easy compromises" (31).

The only people who in Claude's estimation have escaped the national sickness of waste and shallowness are his immigrant friends, Ernest Havel and the Erlichs. Again, Cather turns to immigrants, who in her view retain "Old World" values—respect for tradition, reverence for family, desire for intellectual growth—despite the pressures of their new environment. Like these immigrants, Claude cannot "make himself believe in the importance of making money or spending it" (34).

Such an attitude puts him constantly at odds with his money-minded father, his success-motivated brother, Bayliss, and his younger brother, Ralph, so fond of collecting every new piece of machinery that he sees or hears about.

But this very "American" world of Mr. Wheeler, Bayliss, and Ralph, is unfortunately the only world in which Claude can envision himself.[14] He does not see a place for himself in the richer, more meaningful world of the Erlichs: "What was the use if you were always with the wrong crowd?" (35). Claude knows that one person can make a difference in the world; he admires Joan of Arc because she had done so.[15] He envies, too, her ability to have perpetuated herself in stories. Through such characterization, Claude realizes, a person could "be born over and over again in the minds of children" (56). To Claude, that sort of existence, which extends beyond physical and temporal limits, would be more meaningful than the life that he feels doomed to live.

As if enacting a self-fulfilling prophecy, Claude stumbles into the very sort of easy compromise and meaningless existence that he dreads: he pursues for a wife the unresponsive Enid Royce, who is so tied to her political and missionary "causes" that she shuts Claude out of her life. Claude represents simply one more missionary endeavor to Enid, whose path to self-fulfillment involves spiritual conquest: she decides that she will marry Claude only after her spiritual counselor, Brother Weldon, reminds her that bringing a "promising" soul into the faith is a highly "important service" (154).

Claude is a prisoner of war in Enid's battle to save souls, just as Joan of Arc was a prisoner in an earlier world of spiritual and political unrest. Images of imprisonment abound in *One of Ours*, as Cather portrays an American Dream that has become imprisoning. Just at the time that Claude matriculates at last to the state university with its promise of mental freedom, he is forced to quit college so that he can run the Wheeler farm while his father and Ralph embark on a new quest for success: a farming venture out West. Shortly after Claude's return to the Wheeler farm, he sits one evening listening to his mother read from *Paradise Lost:* "A dungeon horrible, on all sides round." Claude's life in Nebraska is such a dungeon; his marriage places him in yet another prison. On a hot summer evening a few months after his wedding, Claude stares at the moon, envisioning himself as part of an exclusive community—a long tradition of prisoners to whom the moon has special meaning. "These children of the moon, with their unappeased longings and futile dreams, were a finer race than the children of the sun" (179), Claude concludes, here defining his community of choice. He considers other "children of the moon" with whom he feels a sense of kinship, including his passive and sensitive mother, trapped in an unrewarding marriage and in the religion that she blindly follows, and the faithful, protective, mentally deficient housekeeper, Mahailey. Another fellow prisoner is Claude's childhood friend, Gladys Farmer, who now teaches in their hometown of Frankfort, and who has always admired Claude because he is so different. Gladys, like Claude, sees the destructive aspects of the success ethic. She understands that "successful men like Bayliss Wheeler held the keys" to the prison in which "the generous ones" such as Claude remained (134).

The war liberates Claude from the prison of a complacent, successful, self-serving America. As he sails to France, Claude reflects on his life at home, envisioning himself as a criminal who had been "planted upright in the earth" and now was finally free (259). Claude's voyage across the Atlantic on a troop ship, the *Anchises*—appropriately named for the father of the mythical questing hero, Aeneas—is a symbolic journey toward rebirth and self-discovery. Like Thea Kronborg, Claude thus "makes himself born"[16] in a new career.

Earlier, when Claude had wanted a brief escape from his restrictive life, he walked to the secluded timber claim near his home to meet an imaginary Claude "who had not tied himself up with compromises" (183). When Claude becomes a lieutenant in the army and travels to France, he has the opportunity actually to become that young man. Bartley Alexander had wanted to live out the potentialities of the other self that he remembered from his youth; Claude wants only to get away from the Claude of his youth. In France he dreams of his young self plowing a field and fears for this dream-figure, who "would never, never get away" from that field or that world (350).

But Claude in France must struggle to develop the strong sense of self that he has always lacked. When he meets David Gerhardt, the accomplished violinist and self-assured lieutenant who becomes his companion, Claude is both inspired and uncomfortably prodded to redefine himself. Claude's father–in–law had once said to him, "A man hasn't got much control over his own life" (187), a view that Claude shared; but in David Gerhardt, Claude discovers someone who has taken control of his own life. For Claude, such autonomy represents success. Gerhardt represents "a finished product" (295). Despite having grown up in the same materialistic America as did Claude, David has managed to fulfill his dream of becoming a violinist, and then to make the clear choice to put that dream aside for what he perceives as a grander one: "to bring a new ideal into the world" (348).

David finds a community of like-minded individuals in France, and in doing so makes Claude feel even further marginalized from any community that might be meaningful for him. Observing Gerhardt, Claude sees clearly all that he himself has missed: "He felt that a man might have been made of him but nobody had taken the trouble to do it" (355). Claude likens himself to a clumsy bear cub or bull calf. Such images of animal clumsiness are repeatedly associated with Americans and American values in *One of Ours*. Cather depicts in these images, as well as in the French people's responses to American soldiers, her disgust with a shallow American culture that equates success with power and size, a culture that finds no place for "civilized" values—the love of art and tradition—that Cather saw as integral to self-realization. When American troops arrive in Paris, the soldiers compare the city to American cities on terms of "immensity" and "vastness," "hugeness and heaviness—the only attributes they had been taught to admire" (291). A French shopkeeper likens the American soldiers to "wolves" and "dirty pigs." She clearly recognizes "the legend of waste and prodigality" that surrounds these Americans (278).

The legacy of a debased American Dream goes everywhere with the Americans in France. Even the hotel boy who directs Claude to his friend Victor's room for dinner sees Americans in dollar terms: "Plenty money in New York, I guess! In France, no money" (280). The "lost American"—a wounded soldier who does not want to return to the United States or even to remember his life there—exemplifies the need to escape shallow American values. Although the young soldier hears from a home-town sweetheart who is "very ambitious for him to make the most of himself" (287), he has no desire to return home, having found refuge with a French family. In addition to their debased values, Americans, Cather implies, have lumbered clumsily and too slowly into the war itself. Claude, speaking to Mlle de Courcy at the Red Cross, tries to express the concern that Nebraskans felt when they read of the Battle of the Marne, but her reply carries with it a bitter indictment of American neutrality: "You were so safe. . . . Nothing could touch you, nothing!" Claude responds with a clumsy, inadequate apology: "Shame could" (331–32).

Claude does, however, find in his position as military leader an escape from America's unadmirable legacy as well as from his own lack of purpose. Before the war, the world had seemed merely "a business proposition" (356)—a fitting assessment for one raised in the business-oriented America of the early 1900s. But Claude discovers while fighting in France "that there were a great many people left who cared about something else" (356), just as he does. The war shows Claude—as it perhaps showed a hopeful Cather—that the Bayliss Wheelers do not control the future, as Gladys Farmer had feared. The "great many people who cared about something else" represent for Claude the community in which he wants to claim membership. The desire to join that community becomes most intense in the final battle scene, during which Claude realizes that "it was worth having lived in this world to have known such men" (383). The Claude Wheeler who dies heroically, leading his loyal soldiers, has truly "found his place" (389), as his mother reflects, recalling his letters, full of an enthusiasm and sureness that she had felt she would never see in one "so afraid of being fooled" (390). The irony is that Claude has been "fooled," as Cather's dark conclusion emphasizes. The ideals that for him become reality in the war effort, are, Cather indicates, alien to America.[17]

Mrs. Wheeler, mourning her son's death, reflects on the soldier–idealists returning to an America in which "the flood of meanness and greed . . . swept down and engulfed everything that was left" (389). She can understand why many of these disillusioned veterans eventually take their own lives. Cather suggests that it is emotional suicide to return to America, to recognize at last what one has fought for, after "[hoping] extravagantly and [believing] passionately" (390). Cather's disillusionment with the materialism of postwar America, a major theme in her next novel, *The Professor's House*, is direct and relentless in the epilogue of *One of Ours*. The book concludes with this negative picture, not with the more uplifting scene that precedes it, in which we see Claude perpetuated in story, like Joan of Arc.

Jim Burden "comes home" at the end of *My Ántonia*, to discover "what a little circle man's experience is."[18] Claude's story may end in similar circular fashion, on Lovely Creek "where it began" (389); but, as Cather comments at the beginning of this final chapter, "The world has changed," and the men who return to postwar America "are not the same men who went away" (387). The only positive tone in the final pages of *One of Ours* is the relief that Mrs. Wheeler feels for her son, who "died believing his own country better than it is," which, she reflects, was [a] beautiful [belief] to die with" (390)—or at least a beautiful myth.

A Lost Lady

The America about which one could still hold "beautiful beliefs" is eulogized in *A Lost Lady* (1923), Cather's next novel, which dramatizes the final days of the pioneer era, that brief period when the American Dream flourished.[19] In *A Lost Lady*, Cather depicts the aging Captain Forrester, a railroad-builder in the West, and his charming, self-possessed young wife, Marian Forrester, who in her successful efforts to meet the new challenges of a changing world, shows the dreamer's spirit of the pioneer in action, just as her husband represented that spirit for an earlier era. Marian's admirer, young Niel Herbert, does not, however, recognize that pioneer spirit in her persistent striving for "life on any terms"[20]—a "life" that includes sexual gratification outside of her marriage.

A Lost Lady is Cather's elegy to the heroic age of pioneers, but Cather still maintains her foothold in the present. Thus, this novel holds that earlier transition period up to her own changing times as a model, and perhaps as a reminder of the adjustments that the present times demanded, just as that past period had. Harold Bloom sees Cather in A Lost Lady paying tribute to "a peculiarly American dream of innocence, grace, hope." Like many critics, Bloom focuses on Cather's negative engagement with her own era and her nostalgia for a simpler past.[21] I want to focus on Cather's more hope-filled look at her own era of change in A Lost Lady, as she continues to redefine the American Dream. In describing how Captain and Marian Forrester adjust—or fail to adjust—to the closing of America's opportunity-rich period of Westward expansion and to their own change of fortune, Cather reflects on the changing view of self during her own era of uncertainty, examining how that changing view affected one's ability to achieve a form of success grounded in self-fulfillment.

Warren Susman, in his study of early twentieth-century America, sheds light on the shifting cultural perceptions about the individual that characterized these years. Using Susman's analysis as a lens through which to view A Lost Lady, Cather's forward-looking and optimistic subtext on her own era of transition becomes clear: self-fulfillment is not selfishness, but survival; adjustment and adaptation are keys to such survival. Susman notes a change in the way the self was perceived during the early decades of the twentieth century. Whereas in the nineteenth century, "a popular vision of the self defined by the word *character* became fundamental in sustaining and even in shaping the significant forms of the culture,"[22] by the twentieth century, this perspective had changed dramatically.[23] In the nineteenth-century culture of character, says Susman, "interest was almost always in some sort of higher moral law,"[24] as we have already noted in the stories of Horatio Alger and in the histories of Jacob Abbott (chapter 1). By the early 1900s, however, Susman notes a marked shift of emphasis in "the presentation of self in society," triggered by an "increasing interest in self-development . . . with somewhat less interest in moral imperatives." A new "culture of personality" was emerging, which emphasized "individual idiosyncrasies, personal needs and interests."[25]

Susman observes, too, a "growing awareness on the part of those living through the change that it was in fact occurring and that it was fundamental."[26] In A Lost Lady, Cather shows her awareness of this important cultural shift. While never denying the worth of the old culture of character, she seems heartily to endorse the new culture of personality as a friendly climate in which an American Dream of self-fulfillment can flourish. Cather's earlier heroines, Alexandra Bergson, Thea Kronborg, and Ántonia Shimerda, had managed to identify and fulfill their own "personal needs and interests"; but in *A Lost Lady*, Marian Forrester is even more fully invested in meeting her own needs.

By using two strong, memorable personalities in *A Lost Lady*, Captain Forrester to represent the waning culture of character and Marian Forrester to represent the new culture of personality, Cather comments extensively in this novel on one's ability to adapt to changing times—an ongoing Cather concern evidenced by her continued efforts to redefine the American Dream.[27] Matthew Arnold, whom Cather read extensively in her childhood, focuses on the trauma of change in his poem, "Stanzas from the Grande Chartreuse": "How should we grow in other ground? / How can we flower in foreign air?" ask the "children rear'd in shade."[28] These are questions that both Captain and Marian Forrester confront; but while the ill and aging Captain, gazing at his garden sundial, does not find an answer, the resilient, forward-looking Marian does.[29]

Captain Forrester, representative of the disappearing culture of character, embodies all of the traits that Susman finds indicative of that nineteenth-century culture. Susman notes several "key words" associated with character during the late nineteenth century, including: *"citizenship, duty . . . building, golden deeds, outdoor life, conquest, honor, reputation, morals, manners, integrity."*[30] All of these words describe Captain Forrester. He is one of the builders of the West, whose conquest of that frontier exemplifies the golden deeds of the pioneers—the American Dream in its most romantic phase.[31] He begins his decline when he can no longer live the outdoor life that has always so invigorated him. Forrester, characteristic of all builders, has always looked toward the future. His familiar toast, "Happy days!" shows the sense of bright vision and faith in tomorrow that characterized the pioneer, who—as Cather had stated in *O Pioneers!*—"should have imagination."[32] Captain Forrester has the imagination to envision a dream as "an accomplished fact" (55). Forrester has been able to conquer and to build because he clung to the belief that "what you think of and plan for day by day . . . you will get" (54), echoing Dr. Archie's advice to Thea in *The Song of the Lark*, and also sounding like many of the self-help writers of the late nineteenth century, who encouraged readers to take control of their own destiny through the power of the mind.

Susman's other descriptive terms for "character"—reputation, morals, and manners—are also prominent traits in Captain Forrester. An exemplar of his patriarchal society, he wants both a house and a wife that are showpieces. He is "gratified" (12) both by Marian's appearance and by her charming behavior toward his visitors. The expensive jewels that he buys his wife serve several purposes beyond showing his affection, indicating to all that he "[is] able to buy them, and that she [is] worthy to wear them" (52). "Worth," to Captain Forrester, is tied to reputation, manners, and morals; it stands for far more than monetary worth. Even when Niel realizes that Forrester is probably well aware of his wife's sexual transgressions, Niel observes that the Captain still "valued her" (143).

In a culture of character, citizenship, duty, and integrity are inextricably bound up with morals. Forrester embodies these traits, even when holding to them means his own financial ruin and little or no future security for his much-"valued" wife. When the bank for which he serves as president fails, he is the only one of the directors who vows to make good on the losses of his depositors. A community-minded individual, he feels a personal sense of loyalty to his investors. When Forrester suffers a stroke, Marian is left with an invalid husband and only their home and his modest pension for financial security. But for a man of character such as Captain Forrester, as their friend Judge Pomeroy tries to explain to Marian, there was no other response to the bank failure. Judge Pomeroy admits to Marian that a less old-fashioned, "smooth" lawyer such as the young, unscrupulous Ivy Peters, "might have saved something" for her, but the judge insists that neither he nor Captain Forrester, both raised to believe that one's civic responsibilities come first, could do so if it meant such a compromise. Reflecting on the changing values accompanying the changing times, Pomeroy laments that he sees no "honourable career for a lawyer, in this new business world" (93). He, like Forrester, belongs in the old culture of character, and does not feel equipped to confront the changing face of America.

But Marian Forrester, who in Niel's critical estimation refuses to "die with the pioneer period to which she belonged" (169), effectively moves from the old to the new culture. Her dynamic personality allows her to survive past the pioneer era, to adapt to a world of changing values and still to remain "valued" (143), both by her husband and by the younger community of admirers who assemble around her.

In describing the new twentieth-century fascination with personality, Susman could be referring specifically to the magnetic Marian Forrester, as well as to Cather's fascination with her:[33] "The vision of self-sacrifice began to yield to that of self-realization. . . . Literature was interested increasingly in probing personality."[34] Cather's novel not only probes the personality of this new type of pioneer, but celebrates it. Any moral judgments against Marian Forrester, who certainly has her own flexible system of ethics, are made only by the traditional, naïve Niel. Santayana's 1920 description of the "new American," which Cather quoted in an essay on Sarah Orne Jewett (1925), would fit Marian aptly: "cocksure in manner but none too sure in [her] morality."[35] Thus, "the vision of self-sacrifice" so evident in Captain Forrester yields in *A Lost Lady* to the vision of self-realization so evident in Marian Forrester, who gratifies her own personal needs and interests despite the adjustments in morality that doing so entails, but at the same time overpowers us so with her entrancing personality that we—and Cather—applaud, rather than pity or chastise, her manipulations and indiscretions.

Marian Forrester's personality captivates, mystifies, and even frustrates Niel Herbert during his boyhood in Sweet Water. Years later, a mature Niel realizes what the worshiping young Niel could not—the full impact of that magnetic personality. He reflects that Marian Forrester was herself not larger than life, but that "she had always the power of suggesting things much lovelier than herself" (172). Marian's personality is her power. Warren Susman's list of words "associated with personality" in the early twentieth century describe this exemplar of the new culture accurately: *"fascinating, stunning, attractive, magnetic, glowing, masterful, creative, dominant, forceful."*[36]

For Marian Forrester, community is still an important factor in self-fulfillment; but she redefines its role. Community is important not so much because of one's moral responsibility to others, but rather, because one needs others' responses in a culture of personality. Marian's arresting personality enables her to shape her own community—a cult of loyal followers, not unlike performer Thea Kronborg's admirers, who represent a wide cross-section of society, including railroad barons and the "common" boys from town. The narrator constantly notes Marian's "bewitching" effect on people (35). Her charm is innate and undefinable: "Something about her took hold of you in one flash" (35); and that "something" could "call up the whole sweetness of spring" (172), in the same manner that Ántonia could "leave images in the mind."[37]

Marian Forrester is a local celebrity, one of the success stories of Sweet Water just as Thea Kronborg is one of Moonstone's success stories. Thea, even after leaving her home town, gives something back to Moonstone in her success; so Marian, despite the self-focus of her actions, gives something back to her admirers, as Cather suggests in her portrait of the young immigrant boy, Adolph Blum, who spies Marian and her secret lover, Frank Ellinger, embracing in a snow-covered grove of cedars. The narrator tells us that Marian's secrets are "safe" with Adolph, and suggests that it is more than wealth and privilege that inspire such loyalty; it is what Marian, with her endearing personality, has given to him: "She treated him like a human being" (68).

But the success of any well-loved celebrity inspires envy as well as admiration. Another of the "common" town boys, bold and irreverent Ivy Peters, who comes to have such apparent control over Marian Forrester after her husband's financial failure, refuses from the start to place her in a class above him. To prove that craftiness and force are the important traits in this new era, Peters catches and blinds a female woodpecker in the grove, then lets her go to watch her flail about.[38] But the maimed bird, who is certainly symbolic of a Marian Forrester crippled by circumstances—including the limits of gender in the 1880s—manages to find its way back to its nest, "as if it had learned something by its bruises" (25).

Marian Forrester learns from her bruises, too. No matter what difficulties she encounters, she consistently finds new ways to use her captivating personality, thus not only surviving but thriving in a changing world. She defines what she needs for fulfillment, and gets it by determination and by her subtle, sparkling way of manipulating people. She marries the older Captain Forrester, who provides for her and who—in a tacitly understood exchange for her "services" as an attractive, caring wife and a hostess to his friends and associates—not only overlooks her sexual indiscretions but even provides the environment that permits them. When he is financially capable, Captain Forrester takes her to Denver and Colorado Springs every winter, where she has her fill of parties, dancing, and young men who adore her—all under her husband's admiring gaze. Later, when Forrester's health and financial situation force the couple to remain in Sweet Water, Captain Forrester invites friends to visit them, including Frank Ellinger, whom the Captain apparently knows is Marian's lover.

Even when Marian appears to be hopelessly trapped in Sweet Water—financially restricted, physically drained from caring for an invalid husband, deserted by Ellinger—she remains intent on finding ways to fulfill her needs. Although she is too loyal to consider leaving her ill husband, she tells Niel that she is continually trying to find a way "to get out of this hole" (125). If her efforts to do so include certain ethical concessions and compromises, she is willing to make them. Niel criticizes her for allowing Ivy Peters to make unethical investments for her, reminding her that "rascality isn't the only thing that succeeds in business." Her reply shows her choice of the expedient over the ethical: "It succeeds faster than anything else, though" (124).[39]

Marian's instinct for survival is stronger than what she views as an outmoded moral sense, just as it is stronger than her sense of loyalty to Judge Pomeroy. When he refuses to sell her house for the price that she wants, Marian transfers all of her legal business to Ivy Peters. "Times have changed," she tells Niel. If the changing times require an increased respect for money, Marian Forrester is ready to accept that: "Money is a very important thing. Realize that in the beginning," she advises (114). Money is a tool that Marian Forrester uses, just as she uses Ivy Peters. The supposed villain may embrace an apparently trapped and submissive Marian Forrester, but she is neither in the clutches of this man nor in the clutches of a changing economy.

A nationwide panic creates a "shrinking in values" (90), but Marian Forrester's values, as unrepresentative of the culture of character as they may be, remain constant, helping her to make the transition to a new age. She values herself and she values her loyalty to her husband, as Niel accurately notes: "Her loyalty to him stamped her more than anything else" (78). To make sure that we do not misinterpret this as a naïve Niel's inaccurate assessment, Cather at the end of the novel adds an important detail concerning Marian Forrester's continued loyalty to her husband: she sends flowers "every year" to his grave (174).[40]

Such loyalty, however, does not keep Marian Forrester from seeking out ways to save herself. Niel mistakenly perceives that she needs "the right man" to "save her" (166), just as he had seen a need to put the blinded woodpecker "out of its misery" (25). When Niel visits Marian after her husband's stroke, we are reminded of that earlier incident, for he envisions her as "a bird caught in a net." Niel wants to "rescue her and carry her . . . off the earth of sad, inevitable periods, away from age, weariness, adverse fortune!" (110). But Marian is a victim of neither age, weariness, adverse fortune, nor changing eras. Never passive, she persistently directs her own fate. Even Niel comes to realize that the life she is living is "the one she had chosen to live" (79); what he does not seem to grasp, however, is that she often *chooses* to appear in need of rescue, thus allowing herself to get what she needs for survival in a world where women's autonomy and their avenues toward self-fulfillment had certainly diminished with the restrictions imposed by a post-frontier society, as Sandra Gilbert and Susan Gubar point out.[41]

Marian knows how to adapt to changes without letting changes cripple her, as they have her husband. "She mocked outrageously at the proprieties she observed," Niel notes (79), and one of the proprieties that she often observes while she mocks it is that of the weak, submissive woman, who needs a man's protection—financial as well as physical. Marian's self-possession disarms and frightens Niel, who has typical nineteenth-century notions of women,[42] and must learn to adapt his distorted mental picture to fit the real picture that Marian Forrester represents—of a woman who survives and succeeds, both materially and emotionally, and does so often by manipulating the men who think that they are rescuing her, just as she does with Ivy Peters and even with Niel.

Marian Forrester, then, represents the American Dream boldly focused on self, almost fully disengaged from the morals and ethics to which it had been tied in the nineteenth century. For Cather's heroine of *A Lost Lady*, the American Dream is best defined as "delight." Years later, Niel recalls that Marian's "eyes . . . seemed to promise a wild delight that he has not found in life" (171). Marian is continually engaged in finding the "wild delight" in life, and in shaping a community that will help her do so. She makes every experience suit her needs, and every person "useful." Through her shrewd connection with Ivy Peters, who eventually buys her home and thus makes possible her escape to California, she meets the next man who will "save her." He is a wealthy Englishman who takes Marian to the new frontier of South America, a fitting place for a pioneer who has run out of West, as Cather suggests in her previous novel, when Claude Wheeler observes that although the West (in the pioneering sense) no longer existed, "there was still South America."[43]

Thus, Marian Forrester does literally and figuratively learn to "grow in other ground," to "flower in foreign air," as her husband does not. Her last message to Niel—"Tell him things have turned out well for me" (174)—is an assurance, perhaps even a goading reminder, that she has once again found the "wild delight" in life that Niel never seems to find. Niel, who still views her in the role of ornamental flower, which trapped such late nineteenth-century heroines as Lily Bart in Wharton's *The House of Mirth*, can only breathe a sigh of relief that Marian "was well cared for," even in her final years (174). But the self-reliant Marian Forrester has been "well cared for" all of her life, because she herself has engineered it. She is not unlike Alexandra Bergson in her achievement of autonomy, but she uses that autonomy for self-gratification much more obviously than does that earlier heroine. She is even more self-focused than a Thea Kronborg enmeshed in her art and her community of art-lovers, ancient and contemporary. Marian continually uses "all her exquisiteness" (100) to captivate and charm the people who can in any way help her find that "wild delight"—whether it be the sexual delight of an affair or the performer's delight that we see as a weary but "indomitable" (167) Marian tells the story of her first meeting with Captain Forrester to an enthralled audience, her circle of young admirers.

Marian's life is a series of such captivating performances, a fitting life for a representative of the culture of personality. Susman notes the new emphasis on performance during this time period: "Every American was to become a performing self."[44] Thus, during her final years in Sweet Water, her new community of town boys serves as audience for her "performing self," even if a disgruntled Niel sees them as mere "stage-hands . . . left to listen to her" (167). That scene of storytelling, placed strategically as our last glimpse of the entertaining, captivating Marian before her "escape" to California and South America, emphasizes Cather's awareness of this new, important role of performer in the culture of personality and of her own artistic responsibility as storyteller.[45]

Interestingly, Marian begins her story with the phrase, "Once upon a time" (164). Susman notes during the 1920s in American a "new interest in fairies, magic, dreams, fantasy"—part of the new culture of personality.[46] In this scene, as well as in her general frame for *A Lost Lady*, Cather seems attuned to such interest, perhaps playing lightheartedly with this approach, and perhaps also relegating to the realm of fairy tale the standard American Dream, as she attempted to redefine it for a changing world.[47] Cather brings the opening scene into focus on the Forrester house, which stands on a hill at the edge of town. With its entrance by way of a "stout wooden bridge," here is the castle, complete with moat. Waiting at the entrance to greet the visiting "lords and ladies" of the railroad aristocracy, is the queen herself—Marian. Continuing the fairy-tale motif, the narrator later remarks that the spirit of the pioneers was a "princely carelessness" (106), and still later describes Captain Forrester's look, which says to Niel: "A man's house is his castle" (73).

Cather, well grounded in her own era, then—its playful fascinations as well as its anxieties—reaches back into memory in *A Lost Lady* to paint a portrait that also serves as a model for her present day. Marian Forrester is suited to any new era, not by reason of her manipulations or her ethical concessions, but by her ability to move enthusiastically forward even during a period, like Cather's own postwar twenties, in which "the world did not seem over-bright to young people" (33)—as the engraving of *The House of the Poet on the Last Day of Pompeii*, hanging in the Forrester parlor, implies. "It does no good to be glum" (39), Marian Forrester tells Niel, later repeating this same optimistic view: "I expect we can manage, can't we?" (88). Through all that happens to Marian Forrester, she does "manage."

During the same year that Willa Cather wrote *A Lost Lady*, she also wrote her Nebraska essay for the "These United States" Series in *The Nation*. Like her novel of that year, the essay celebrates the state's "first cycle" of hardy pioneers. In it, Cather does not merely mourn the "end of the first cycle,"[48] but instead uses memory—as she does in *A Lost Lady*—to bring "hope and comfort"[49] to an era in which the American Dream, like Nebraska, was "stamped with the ugly crest of materialism."[50] Through looking back, she is able to look forward with affirmation, with that "hope that something went into the ground with those pioneers that will one day come out again." Her trust in the future is embodied in the "crowds of happy looking children . . . elastic and vigorous in their movements," which she describes in this essay.[51]

Elasticity—the flexibility that enables one to adapt to a changing culture—is a key trait here.[52] It is a trait that an "unyielding" Claude Wheeler lacks, as we see when Mrs. Wheeler observes him standing beside his "adaptable" friend, Ernest.[53] Certainly this trait, which Cather is encouraged to find in the newest generation of Nebraskans, is one that she had in mind, too, when she created her portrait—her "thin miniature painted on ivory"[54]—of Marian Forrester, whose elasticity is evident with every change in her circumstances.

The ending lines of Cather's essay give a current appraisal of the people of Nebraska that is far more hopeful, far less harsh, than earlier comments. In fact, that final appraisal could serve as a concise description, too, of Marian Forrester: "The people are warm, mercurial, impressionable, restless, overfond of novelty and change. These are not the qualities which make the dull chapters of history."[55] But is Marian Forrester's self-gratifying approach, with its similarities to "the new pleasure ethic"[56] of Cather's own era, the only way to achieve self-fulfillment—or even the most certain way to do so? In her next novel, Cather seems herself to pose such a question, and to offer an answer of sorts, one that centers on a different relationship with community than the self-centered one that Marian establishes.

The Professor's House

Published two years after *A Lost Lady*, *The Professor's House* focuses on a personality neither as self-assured nor as certain that he wants to survive in a changing world as Marian Forrester. Professor Godfrey St. Peter is not an old man, but he is acting old, as his wife, Lillian, complains.[57] Godfrey St. Peter's frame of mind resembles the narrator's in T. S. Eliot's poem, "Gerontion" (1920). Although, as Bernice Slote notes, we have no indication that Cather read Eliot's poetry, both authors reflect in these works similar anxieties about their era.[58] The epigraph of "Gerontion," taken from Shakespeare's *Measure for Measure*, describes Godfrey St. Peter's dilemma with uncanny accuracy: "Thou has nor youth nor age / But as it were an after dinner sleep / Dreaming of both."[59] The professor is not young, but dreams of his youth. He is not old but feels old, and might echo the narrator in "Gerontion" who laments, "I have lost my passion." Godfrey St. Peter has certainly lost the passionate love he once had for his wife. He has lost the passionate energy that kept him striving for twelve years to finish his multivolume history of the Spanish adventurers in North America, those early explorers driven like a younger Godfrey St. Peter by passion and desire. "After such knowledge, what forgiveness?" asks the narrator of "Gerontion."[60] St. Peter's world-weariness may be due in part to his immersion in the world of knowledge, as his wife suspects: "Is it merely that you know too much . . . to be happy?" (163).

Godfrey St. Peter knows too much and yet not enough, for he is unable to envision a place for himself in the changing world that his new house represents. His journey toward self-definition takes him through a dark night of the soul, during which he learns to make choices about which communities can help him find self-fulfillment. The one community from which he, like many of Cather's protagonists, turns away emphatically, is the materialistic America of his own era.

The war took away Godfrey St. Peter's brightest student, Tom Outland, leaving St. Peter with no source of inspiration. Postwar materialism and ethical shoddiness have poisoned both his family and his university. His son–in-law, Louie Marsellus, has turned Tom Outland's ideas into profit, thus "translating" Tom into "dollars and cents" (62, 132). This has divided Godfrey's family: his elder daughter Rosamond, Louie's wife, has become selfish and hardened by the loss of Tom, whom she was to marry; St. Peter's younger daughter, Kitty, and her husband, Scott, are equally poisoned by their envy of Rosamond and Louie. Godfrey St. Peter's university is also being undermined by materialism, on both an individual and an institutional level. His colleague, Dr. Crane, who altruistically helped Tom Outland with his experiments, never expecting any personal gain, now wants a share of the profits from Outland's invention; the university as a whole is caught up in the "new commercialism . . . that was undermining and vulgarizing education."[61]

The Professor, who should be glorying in the American Dream as a successful writer, teacher, and family man, instead sees himself and his world victimized by the drive for success. His "house"—if we think of that word as a metonym for his autonomous self, his family, and his university—is divided, just as American society was a house divided in the twenties, an observation that his son-in-law Scott makes: "This country's split in two, socially" (108). The old man in "Gerontion," who says, "My house is a decayed house," seems to speak for Godfrey St. Peter. Like Eliot's other casualty of modernism, J. Alfred Prufrock, St. Peter has "seen the moment of [his] greatness flicker"—his greatness both as historian and as husband and father.[62] Thus, when his financial success is translated into a new house, he holds onto the attic room of his old house where his greatness had flourished, refusing to make the transition to the new, just as he refuses to make a transition to a new phase of his life—for he feels he cannot. He becomes passive, almost helpless. He admires his wife, who can "adapt . . . so readily" (95), for that is exactly what he cannot do—and what Cather seems herself concerned about doing, as her focus on this theme in both this novel and *A Lost Lady* suggests.

Godfrey St. Peter has fulfilled his dream by writing his book, but now finds himself dissatisfied, spiritually sick. This is the same condition in which Bartley Alexander found himself after having achieved success, but in *The Professor's House*, Cather depicts the special problem that the American Dream posed for the intellectual. A few years earlier than the fictional setting of *The Professor's House*, Harvard professor, Josiah Royce, experienced a similar dissatisfaction and accompanying spiritual malaise. In a letter to his friend and fellow faculty member, William James, Royce sounds amazingly like the St. Peter who tells his doctor that he feels "tired all the time" (269) and tells himself that "he now wanted to run away from everything he had intensely cared for" (275). Royce, in his letter, remarks that he has "joined the too great army of scholarly blunderers who break down when they ought to be at their best"; he describes the feelings that led him to take a leave of absence from his position:

> There was indeed a long period of depression . . . not exactly a longing for anything good or evil, but simply the dullness that Tolstoi describes in his Confession, or the 'grief without a pang, voiceless and drear,' that Coleridge so well portrays. It was a diabolically interesting nervous state.[63]

Godfrey St. Peter is experiencing just such a "nervous state." Thus he seeks the "isolation, insulation" (26) of his old study, where he had in earlier times managed to avoid "the engaging drama" (26) taking place downstairs as his daughters were growing up.

St. Peter feels that he has been fully engaged in both his own "big pattern of dramatic action" and this "playful pattern" of family life; but Cather suggests that he has not (101). Just as the dressmaker's form in St. Peter's study (which has doubled for all these years as the seamstress Augusta's workroom) is deceptive in appearance—although it looks soft and inviting to lay one's head upon, it is not—so St. Peter's lovely memory of interwoven dramas is a self-deception. Seldom an active participant in his family's dramas, even fearing the "perilous journey" downstairs because it might prove distracting, Godfrey St. Peter scheduled some evenings with his wife and children, just as he scheduled his university duties; but his writing had been the real activity that motivated him. Although St. Peter remembers the happy days when there was the bustle of family below him, the writing of his history, the "creation" of his "splendid Spanish-adventurer sons," as Louie Marsellus calls them (165), is the one pleasure that the Professor wishes he "could have bought back" (33) with his new wealth. Cather suggests that he has been always more interested in "the big pattern of dramatic action," which his writing represented.

Cather's analogy of the Bayeux tapestry with its minor story alongside the main story (discussed in chapter 1), has a special purpose in *The Professor's House* beyond calling our attention to St. Peter's withdrawal from "the drama of domestic life" (26). It also serves to remind the reader of the special importance of sideline narratives in *The Professor's House*, which contains many stories-within-a-story, including the most obvious one in all Cather's fiction, "Tom Outland's Story," comprising the entire second book of the novel.[64] These stories, whether they take up a generous portion of the novel as the Outland story does or only a few pages, always carry home Cather's larger theme, and often provide the subtle social commentary that enriches that theme. In *The Professor's House*, we find sideline stories of struggle toward a more meaningful American Dream, as well as stories that testify to the debased values and emotional emptiness that fully characterized that dream by the twenties. Lillian St. Peter tries to understand her changed husband at the same time that she works out a delicate balance of her affections between her two emotionally needy sons-in-law. Louie, who never had the opportunity to attend college, tries to enter that academic world by joining the Arts and Letters Club and by buying the affections of both his father-in-law and college-educated Scott, just as he buys furnishings that reflect cultured tastes. Kitty struggles emotionally, feeling always incapable of competing successfully with her sister—for wealth or for love; her husband, Scott, is reduced by the new practice of journalistic syndication to the role of "writing machine" in his career life, and reduced by that unfulfilling career and its accompanying financial limitations to the role of cynic in his personal life. Roddy Blake, a laborer caught in the trap of materialism that he despises, tries to provide a better future for his friend, Tom; and in Washington, the heart of the nation, corrupt bureaucrats "do almost anything for a good lunch" (229) and harried clerks struggle to achieve a devalued American Dream. Stories of the victims and veterans of the struggle for success contrast with stories of the few who find a way out of the quicksand of materialism: Augusta, whose presence has always meant stability for St. Peter, and who becomes at last a role model for him through her "bloomless" but spiritually meaningful life; and Tom Outland, whose unwavering integrity in a materialistic world provides another role model for St. Peter, and whose journey toward self-discovery on the Blue Mesa inspires the Professor to make a similar inner journey.

These "stories in themselves," enrich *The Professor's House*, just as "the little playful pattern" on the tapestry enriches the scene of "knights and heroes" (101). Through these subplots, we see repeatedly how the American Dream of success had by 1925 become for Cather an "insupportable" dream, just as St. Peter thinks of his present life as "insupportable" (156). "Restlessness such as ours, success such as ours, striving such as ours, do not make for beauty," Cather said in a December 1924 interview.[65] This is the world that Godfrey St. Peter seeks to escape: a restless, striving, success-oriented, money-motivated world—what F. Scott Fitzgerald described that same year as a world populated by "only the pursued, the pursuing, the busy, and the tired."[66] It is a world more worried about production, cost, and appearance than about beauty, quality, or substance, as St. Peter's appraisal of the university's physics building suggests: "The architect had had a good idea. . . . [But] the State Legislature had defeated him by grinding down the contractor to cheap execution" (143).

Even the now-materialistic Rosamond St. Peter had been raised in a different world from this, and still retains some of those values. "She doesn't like anything showy," Louie comments. He remembers that when he first met her, she was wearing a simple bracelet—"a turquoise set in dull silver"—emblematic of Tom Outland, who had given the turquoise to her, and who never fell prey to the lust for shiny silver so characteristic of his era. "To me, her name spells emeralds," Louie remarks innocently, in the only rhetoric he knows to express his wife's beauty and worth. But his remark also indicates the values by which Rosamond now measures fulfillment. Tainted by her era, Rosamond surrounds herself with showy signs of success: a limousine, an expansive new home, furs, and jewels. She has lost concern for others, as we see in her treatment of Professor Crane and Augusta. Rosamond refuses her father's request to help Augusta financially when she loses a large sum of money through an unwise investment; Rosamond also ignores St. Peter's suggestion that she make some financial settlement with Professor Crane.

Ironically, Louie Marsellus, although he has converted Tom Outland's "bones into a personal asset" (47) has "not damaged himself." He may know only the world of trade, but he is still "generous and public spirited" (72). Louie has the gift of sympathy to balance the gift of technical know-how that has made him a financial success. When he hears that an embittered Scott has blackballed him so that he is denied membership in the Arts and Letters Club, Louie predicts optimistically that Scott "will come around" (170). Louie, as St. Peter tells him, is "magnanimous and magnificent" (170).[67] Like Marian Forrester, Louie has developed his own brand of integrity, and because it is not as all-consuming as Tom Outland's, he can survive in the world of the 1920s. As romantic in nature as Tom, although more subtly so, Louie is "always hoping for a period of utter, of fantastic unreasonableness, which will be the beginning of a great happiness for us all" (170). Tom "idealized the people he loved" (172), as Godfrey St. Peter eventually realizes; Louie understands the people he loves, accepts them on realistic terms—and still manages to love them. He is an opportunist with a heart, the old type of civic humanist who takes joy in his position and feels the sense of responsibility that comes with it. The Professor knows that when Rosamond refuses to take any financial responsibility either for the Cranes or for Augusta, he can count on Louie to do so. Louie finds happiness in believing that his actions can make an important, positive difference for others.

Augusta has found a similar happiness. Her religion and her service to others add mystery and importance to her life. St. Peter stresses to his students the role of art and religion in bringing people happiness. Augusta lives her art in making dresses for others; and she lives her religion in her service to those in need—she sits with sick people and helps out whenever there is a death in someone's family. When she rescues St. Peter after he is nearly asphyxiated by the faulty gas stove in his study, the recovering Godfrey has time to ponder the unique combination of art and religion in Augusta.

In this woman, Godfrey St. Peter finds the community to which he wants to belong. He envisions "a world full of Augustas, with whom one was outward bound" (281). The Professor, not unlike Bartley Alexander, had been fleeing to the past. Immersing himself in his project of editing Outland's diary, he escaped mentally to Tom Outland's Blue Mesa, perhaps hoping in so doing to get that sense of wholeness which Tom experienced there. Commenting on that experience, Tom had written: "I had my happiness unalloyed" (251). St. Peter thinks that he has found a similar "unalloyed" happiness when he makes his inner journey to recover the Kansas boy of his youth. Unalloyed happiness, however, although it may be possible in an isolated "world above the world" (240) such as the Blue Mesa, is—as St. Peter at last realizes—not an option in his world. It is as illusory as is an American Dream of equal opportunity for all, or of wealth that automatically brings with it inner peace. Thus, after his near-death experience, St. Peter makes the active choice to live in a real world; he also makes the active choice to "let something go"—that unrealistic longing for unalloyed happiness in a solitary, mental "world above the world." In place of that, he chooses community—not the communities of family or university that have so directed and so troubled his existence, but a new, rather vaguely defined community—"a world full of Augustas." For Marian Forrester, fulfillment meant finding the "wild delight" in life. For Godfrey St. Peter, learning "to live without delight" promises fulfillment (282).

Recovering on the couch in his study, with Augusta reading beside him, St. Peter sees in her "humankind" (279), someone "on the solid earth" (281). Having always unconsciously regarded her as "a corrective" (280), he at last owns up to her powerful influence and even feels "a sense of obligation toward her" (281). At the same time, he becomes aware that he no longer feels such a sense of obligation toward his family. Thus he selects the new community that will give meaning to his life and will provide a fulfillment that he has not yet gained. It is a community whose members are less success-motivated than they are other-directed, less concerned with momentary gratifications—"delight"—than they are with enduring values.

Tom Outland had found a similar sense of community on the Blue Mesa, where he discovered the remains of an ancient civilization to whom he felt an attachment similar to what Thea Kronborg feels in *The Song of the Lark*.[68] Cather sets up a shocking contrast between this community and the one Tom encounters when he travels to Washington to enlist the support of experts in studying the ruins on the mesa. In Washington, instead of interested scientists and experts, Tom meets politicians and bureaucrats who are interested only in parties, free lunches, and meeting the right people. He meets clerks who are slaves to a success ethic. On his return to the mesa Tom is further disillusioned and alienated from what he had once considered a meaningful community. His friend and fellow adventurer, Roddy Blake, caught up in a debased, competitive era, has sold the artifacts, hoping with the money to send Tom to college, so that Tom will not have to be just a "day-labourer."

It is no wonder that Tom, like Godfrey St. Peter, immerses himself in insulated worlds—the *Aeneid*, which he reads all summer on the Blue Mesa; the childhood world of young Rosamond and Kathleen, whom he entertains with his stories; the isolated university physics laboratory, where he works long into the night on his invention, the Outland engine, which will later be exploited by wartime manufacturers. The Professor wonders "what would have happened to [Tom, after the war], once the trap of worldly success had been sprung on him" (260). St. Peter seems envious that Tom has "escaped all that" (261).

But despite his temporary love affair with easeful death, Godfrey St. Peter, though less aware of it than Marian Forrester, is a survivor, who finds a way to adapt, to move ahead instead of backwards. Godfrey—

unlike the earlier Bartley Alexander—realizes at last that he "wouldn't choose to live his life over" (258). Lillian had once told him that his "ideas were best" when he was his "most human self" (162); at the end of the novel, Godfrey St. Peter seems to have found that self, and thus can recognize "humankind" in Augusta (279).

Godfrey St. Peter recovers his early self, but at the same time lets go of that naïve desire which Tom Outland never really relinquished, that desire for "happiness unalloyed," for the sort of "possession" which is as flawed in its retreat from reality as the American Dream was flawed in casting money and fame as the only reality. Willa Cather, in giving a copy of *The Professor's House* to Robert Frost, wrote that it was a story of "letting go with the heart."[69] Godfrey St. Peter lets go with the heart and then engages with the heart—finding a new community with which he can be "outward bound."

My Mortal Enemy

In *The Professor's House*, Cather moves away both from a materialistic definition of the American Dream, and from a vision of success as self-gratification. However, in offering community awareness and other-directedness as factors in achieving self-fulfillment, Cather in *The Professor's House* offers almost as abstract a community as the one that inspires Claude Wheeler in *One of Ours*. In *My Mortal Enemy*, published only a year after *The Professor's House*, Cather juxtaposes the greed and frustration that a debased American Dream engenders with the other-centeredness of a specific community of two. Myra Henshawe, the protagonist of *My Mortal Enemy*, tries like Godfrey St. Peter to let go with the heart, but she cannot. Instead, she is poisoned and fragmented by her struggle for material success; but her husband Oswald and her friend Nellie, who both take care of the dying Myra, find through that act an escape from the corrupting force of the American Dream.

Like the young Tom Outland who turns his back on Roddy's money, the young Myra turns her back on her substantial inheritance and on a life of wealth and luxury that she had lived with her great uncle since early childhood. A bigoted, ruthless businessman, Myra's great uncle warns her that he will disinherit her if she marries Protestant Oswald Henshawe, a young man of modest means, from immigrant stock; but Myra chooses to do so anyway, eloping in dramatic fashion. The fairy tale does not, however, end with "they lived happily ever after." Nellie Birdseye's Aunt Lydia, a girlhood friend of Myra, tells her niece that Myra and Oswald have been "as happy as most people"; but Nellie observes that she had expected such fairy-tale lovers to be "much happier than other people."[70]

Myra and Oswald, in fact, seem less happy than most people. As Professor St. Peter might put it, "the trap of worldly success" has been sprung on Myra, though in a different way than he envisioned it springing on Tom: Myra finds that she can neither achieve success nor ignore it. Myra is a victim of her times, so caught up in the struggle to keep up that she becomes a divided person—her own "mortal enemy."[71] Cather continually shows the two natures in Myra struggling—the "mortal" nature of worldly grasping, and an altruistic nature that rejects materialism. Like Bartley Alexander, Myra Henshawe experiences a struggle within herself, but she seems far less aware than was Bartley of what is happening to her. Consequently, she can neither mend nor forgive herself. Forgiveness is a powerful theme in *My Mortal Enemy*, and the outlook for it is grim in a world that ensnares a person in materialism.

Myra's story takes place prior to World War I, yet the "bitch-goddess" success already has a firm hold on America, and Myra contracts the national disease despite her romantic girlhood notions of defiance. Why, we might ask, does Myra become its victim while Tom Outland manages to escape such a fate? Does he escape only because he dies before the trap can be sprung? Although Cather suggests that this is partly the case, the answer perhaps lies, too, in Myra's and Tom's contrasting backgrounds. Myra has been raised in wealth and luxury by her great uncle, John Driscoll, a self-made man who exploited others to his own financial gain, making his fortune by contracting laborers. Driscoll thinks that his money can buy him everything, from his niece's loyalty to his soul's salvation. He tells Myra: "It's better to be a stray dog in this world than a man without money" (15). When Tom Outland arrives at the university, Professor St. Peter notes that Tom's background has shaped his values—very different values from those with which Myra was instilled. Tom has acquired a "dream of self-sacrificing friendship and disinterested love" that contrasts sharply with the world he enters at the university, "where advancement through personal influence was considered honourable."[72] Tom's background perhaps helps him escape Myra's fate, but the Professor realizes that Tom might have become a very different person if he had lived long enough to be trapped by "worldly success." Myra Henshawe does live long enough to become its victim.

In choosing marriage to Oswald, Myra perhaps hopes to demonstrate emphatically that one does not need wealth or position to find happiness and fulfillment—and perhaps she wants to believe that. But when she elopes, she is also acting out a dramatic, thrilling role, behaving like the "performing self" that Susman describes.[73] With her girlhood friends as audience, she plays the part of the princess who trades her kingdom for true love. "Love went out the gates and gave the dare to Fate," Nellie reflects, imagining the Driscoll mansion "as being under a spell, like the Sleeping Beauty's palace" (17). The Myra whom Nellie Birdseye finally meets some years later, however, is not the fairy-tale princess whom Aunt Lydia described, but an embittered, wicked queen. Myra Henshawe's biting sarcasm and artificial friendliness unnerve Nellie at this first meeting and at every subsequent encounter. After having embarrassed Nellie, who has been unconsciously staring with wonder at Myra's necklace of carved amethysts, Myra commands: "Tell me about the things you like best; that's the short cut to friendship" (7).

For Myra, human relationships are measured in terms of their potential for bringing one closer to fame and fortune. Thus, Myra continually seeks "short cut[s] to friendship." She has learned the standard formula for grooming friendships with both artistic and "moneyed" people, as Nellie observes when she later visits Myra in New York (39). Myra "cultivates" friendships with the German businessmen and their wives who might be able to guarantee Oswald's advancement, and with poets and theater performers who bolster her view of herself as patron of the arts (39). She buys extravagant gifts, such as an expensive holly bush for Madame Modjeska; she involves herself in her friends' romances and dramas, as her attention to the glamorous rake, Ewan Gray, suggests. The naïve Nellie observes that Myra cares "so much" for people (43), but Nellie has of course been taken in by the theatrical Myra's staged performances. The role of performer that Cather celebrates in her portraits of both Thea Kronborg and Marian Forrester is cast in a negative light in *My Mortal Enemy*. Cather suggests that this role has become too debased to remain a part of her definition of success.

Myra continually impresses Nellie in her role as gracious queen. But Nellie also sees Myra's other nature, her "insane ambition" and jealousy. Remarking on the change in Myra's features when this other Myra takes over, Nellie describes the "curl about the corners of her mouth" (40). Myra may be unable to control her bitterness and grasping drive for wealth, but she also seems to take very real pleasure in her performance as angry queen. She stages what appears to be a purposeful fit of jealous rage for Nellie one day after inviting her to lunch with Oswald. When Nellie arrives at their apartment, she hears Myra's "angry laugh" (49) through the door as Myra loudly accuses Oswald of having a mistress. Myra finally acknowledges Nellie's knock, but quickly informs Nellie that Oswald alone will take her to lunch; she makes no attempt either to apologize or to cover up for the embarrassing situation. One feels certain that Myra, ever the actress, has staged this little drama of high emotion, especially when we consider Oswald's reassuring words to Nellie as they walk away: "Myra isn't half so furious with me as she pretends" (51).

Ten years later, Nellie encounters Myra and Oswald living in poverty in a West Coast city, and again becomes an audience for Myra's performances. The setting, a shabby hotel, implies a debased West, no longer the West of a romanticized American Dream.[74] Myra, confined to a wheelchair and dying of cancer, now has both Nellie and Oswald to minister to her and to serve as an audience for her performances. She is Marian Forrester's unappealing counterpart, desperate to change her life and willing to use anyone who might help her do so, but more bitter than resilient about the changing world and her own change of fortune. Always capable of cultivating friendships that would work to her benefit, Myra welcomes Nellie as a "beloved friend coming out of the past" (62). Nellie is delighted that Myra is still "herself" (62), despite age and illness. Ironically, Nellie is right. Myra has changed very little; she is still playing roles and is dominated more than ever by an acquisitive nature that she still does not understand. Myra acts out her parts: the tortured princess "at the mercy" of her noisy upstairs neighbors (68); the wise adviser, "ambitious for [Nellie]" (64); Shakespeare's despairing Gloucester on the barren headland overlooking the sea (72); Heine's troubled romantic who yearns for death; the devout penitent who finds "solace" in the church (85).

Myra Henshawe, through years of practice, is an expert at theatrical show; as Stephen Tanner points out, her conversion at the end of the story is "self-dramatization rather than repentance."[75] Myra's "deathbed confession" is more accurately a melodramatic indictment—of God's injustice and of Oswald's devotion—as melodramatic as that earlier staged indictment of her materialistic society, her girlhood elopement with Oswald. Lying in the candlelight, with Nellie and Oswald as audience, Myra whispers, "Why must I die like this, alone with my mortal enemy?" (95). Nellie observes: "I seemed to hear her soul talking." The real and the staged have become so blurred for Myra that Nellie's observation is probably accurate.

Myra does not succeed materially, but she does at least succeed as actress, performing a convincing scene of repentance for Nellie and Oswald. Myra earlier sets up the scene for her final performance. When Nellie one afternoon takes Myra to a barren headland overlooking the sea, Myra tells her that she would be especially pleased to see it "at dawn," because dawn "is always such a forgiving time" (73). Having planned that drama and cued her audience, Myra flees to the headland a few hours before her death, after leaving a note of final rejection for Oswald. When Nellie and Oswald find Myra there, she appears almost to be posing for a portrait. She is seated regally beneath a tree, facing the sea and the "forgiving" dawn, wrapped in her furs and blankets, a crucifix in her hands. From Nellie's comment, we see that Myra has created the effect that she hoped for: "There was every reason to believe she had lived to see the dawn" (101). Myra has staged her forgiveness, just as her uncle staged his elaborate church funeral as a sign of his salvation. Not to be outdone by her uncle, Myra dictates in her will her own romantic, eccentric funeral. She will be cremated and her ashes buried "in some lonely and unfrequented place in the mountains, or in the sea" (102).

But Myra Henshawe, who resents Oswald more for his devotion to her than for anything else (92), does not want to appear weak, divided, or ambivalent in her own self-appraisal. She would rather indict herself than have others know that she is at war with herself. In her final days, she tells Nellie twice: "I am a greedy, selfish, worldly woman; I wanted success and a place in the world" (75); "I was always a grasping, worldly woman; and I was never satisfied" (88). Nellie may be taken in by Myra's theatrics, but she recognizes that this woman is self-divided, even if Myra herself refuses to admit that. When Myra makes her final plea about dying with her mortal enemy, Nellie provides a perceptive gloss: "Violent natures like hers sometimes turn against themselves . . . and all their idolatries" (96).

Not only does Myra fail to achieve the dream of a unified self; she also fails to find a community to which she can belong, aside from her responsive, caring "audience" of two, Oswald and Nellie, whom she is too proud to accept as her community. "Among my own kind I'd still have a circle" (75) Myra insists, but Cather makes it evident throughout the book that Myra's circle has always been bought and paid for. Cather in 1901 remarked, "Most of us don't try to love our friends after we are eighteen, unless we are fools or geniuses."[76] Myra, afraid of being a fool but always aspiring to genius status, consistently tries to purchase both love and friends as she struggles to achieve a dream of success that she does not recognize as debased.

But while Myra is moving further and further away from any sense of membership in the human community, she is unwittingly creating for Nellie and for Oswald an increased sense of meaningful membership in that community. Godfrey St. Peter finds a glimmer of hope when he attaches himself to the "world full of Augustas," of caring, dedicated, other-centered people who are "outward bound." When Nellie Birdseye arrives in the coastal city where she encounters the Henshawes, she is anchorless, suffering her own "temporary eclipse" (64). She envisions her neighbor in the adjacent hotel room, before she knows that he is Oswald, and in doing so, her other-centeredness begins to emerge:

"I was young, and it didn't matter so much about me; for youth there is always the hope. . . . But an old man, a gentleman, living in this shabby, comfortless place . . . it depressed me unreasonably" (58–59). On encountering Oswald and learning of Myra's condition, Nellie is challenged to move past depression and a distanced sense of pity to other-centered action. She becomes "outward bound" when she commits herself to helping Oswald. "I hope for her sake you are staying some time," Oswald says, offering an invitation for Nellie to form with him a caring community—and making clear their desperate need: "She has no one else" (60).[77]

Thus Cather's dark novel still offers a glimmer of hope for humanity—through community, a community more clearly defined if more limited in scope than either Claude Wheeler's people "who cared about something else"[78] or St. Peter's "world full of Augustas."[79] Cather once more implies that one can escape "the trap of worldly success," one can "[feel] the ground under [one's] feet,"[80] by gaining a foothold in community.

Cather's four novels of 1922–26 all suggest that such a foothold may bring one closer to self-fulfillment than can a competitive, individualistic dream of success. In her next two novels, Cather examines more closely such a new perception of success. As she does so, she confronts more directly the troubling aspects of such a community-oriented outlook, and specifies more concretely the communities that in her view offer the best opportunity for self-fulfillment: tradition and family.

4
Fulfillment through
Tradition and Family

The protagonists in the novels that Cather wrote between 1920 and 1926 experience crises of self and desperately seek new avenues to personal fulfillment. In such portrayals, Cather moves farther away from any notion of success that centers on acquisitive individualism, toward an understanding of success that is community-oriented and fundamentally at odds with wealth and position. But such an attempt at redefinition produces its own tensions, as Claude Wheeler's and Marian Forrester's contrasting ideas of community illustrate, and as is also illustrated by the sharp contrast between Godfrey St. Peter's ultimate, bittersweet affirmation of the world and the dying Myra Henshawe's harsh indictment of both her world and herself.

Willa Cather herself must certainly have experienced tension during this time period as she attempted to come to terms with her own success and the degree of fulfillment it had brought. She had received the Pulitzer Prize in 1923 for *One of Ours*. But Cather was experiencing that other by-product of success: the increased community pressure that accompanies public acclaim. Godfrey St. Peter selects and rejects certain communities at the end of *The Professor's House*; Cather, too, was having to select and reject, and was feeling the strain of making those choices. When asked in a 1926 interview what she considered "the greatest obstacle American writers have to overcome," her reply reflects the tension of increased commitment to her public: "I should say it was the lecture bug. In this country a writer has to hide and lie and almost steal in order to get time to work in—and peace of mind to work with."[1] Cather was finding herself caught in the trap of fame and fortune that she examined in her novels.

In defense of American attitudes about money and success in the twenties, philosopher and cultural critic George Santayana observed:

"The American talks about money because that is the symbol and measure he has at hand for success, intelligence, and power; but, as to money itself, he makes, loses, spends, and gives it away with a very light heart."[2] But for Cather and for many Americans, the symbol and all its trappings were becoming "insupportable," to use one of Godfrey St. Peter's terms—impossible to justify even in Santayana's sense of money as mere symbol. Further, was there a place in modern, postwar America for an individualism nurtured by and responsive to community, or did self-aggrandizement necessarily entail ignoring others' needs? Rugged individualism was certainly becoming a less likely avenue to fulfillment for many Americans at this time, while group membership was becoming the more acceptable, more possible route. Historians identify the Depression Era as a time during which people were trying to find "a way to belong, to identify with, the human community."[3]

Cather's fiction just previous to and during the Depression reflects such a move toward community. The hint of self-fulfillment through community that struggles to the surface—usually briefly and in a broad, undefined manner—in *One of Ours*, *A Lost Lady*, *The Professor's House*, and *My Mortal Enemy*, becomes a strong, overriding theme in *Death Comes for the Archbishop* (1927) and *Shadows on the Rock* (1931); that it was becoming an overriding preoccupation for Cather is evidenced also by two important short stories that she wrote during this time, "Neighbour Rosicky" (1928), and "Old Mrs. Harris" (1931).[4] In his 1929 commentary on this era, *The Rediscovery of America*, Waldo Frank observes: "With tragic need, America needs groups. . . . Having accepted mortal loneliness, [each] will grow aware of other men in the American chaos . . . others, in their way, living the same life. . . . They will create a group."[5] Cather's writings of the late twenties and early thirties express this growing awareness of membership in a group with more certainty of, and hope for, such membership providing fulfillment than we see in her earlier novels. But as if Cather is still debating this issue with herself, we sense a tension between self and other even in this very community-oriented phase of her writing, a tension that is not resolved but instead becomes more pronounced in her later novels, *Lucy Gayheart* and *Sapphira and the Slave Girl*.

In both *Death Comes for the Archbishop* and *Shadows on the Rock*, Cather clearly defines the community that more and more came to hold importance for her: the tradition-bearers who transmit values from past to present, preserving them for future generations. Lewis Mumford in 1930 stated: "Cultures cannot be isolated; they grow by perpetual intercourse across the boundaries of time and space."[6] Cather depicts such growth in these two novels. Art and religion intermingle as important components of tradition in both novels, recalling Godfrey

St. Peter's lecture remarks on these two media of human expression.[7] Not only is religion a vehicle for the transmission of tradition, but it provides for those who cherish, practice, and spread it a sense of community and of belonging—whether that religion is the firm Catholicism of French immigrants living in seventeenth-century Quebec or a more flexible Catholicism that attempts to incorporate native religions, as Cather depicts in *Death Comes for the Archbishop*. For Cather, religion connects one to a past community and bonds one to a present community that builds for the future. In a 1933 speech, Cather paraphrased a Latin inscription that she recalled seeing in a Paris art gallery: "Because of the past, we have hope for the future."[8] Religion, it seems, provided in Cather's view a means of hope by carrying that past to the future.

Like religion, family gains importance as a symbol of community in this phase of Cather's writing. As David Stouck observes, "The family, that primal experience of wholeness, was one of the moral absolutes to which [Cather] clung."[9] The family tensions that Alexandra Bergson and Thea Kronborg experience are still present in Cather's fiction of the late 1920s, but they are softened. The beauty and sacredness of family depicted in these works perhaps reflects Cather's own growing awareness of how much her family meant to her, a realization that must certainly have intensified with the death of her father in 1928 and with her mother's prolonged illness, beginning in 1928 and continuing until 1931 when she died. Cather became more and more devoted to her siblings and their children during these years, and to the three Menuhin children, whom she "adopted" as family after meeting them in 1930. Noting their importance to Cather, Elizabeth Sergeant observes: "She made a story of this prodigy [Yehudi Menuhin] and his fascinating and gifted little sisters, and parents, as if she had at last by proxy, a family exactly to her taste."[10]

In validating religion and family as two avenues to a tradition-based, self-affirming sense of community, Cather reflects a general cultural shift, as America itself moved toward an era of economic upheaval and widespread disillusionment with the American Dream. Historian David Peeler observes that American intellectuals seemed especially concerned with finding "some continuum that remained unmarred. . . . But the continuum that they sought was more of a universal *human* entity rather than a peculiarly *American* one."[11] Cather, who in Thea Kronborg's recognition of "a long chain of human endeavor" had years earlier identified such a broad, time-spanning community, continues in this period to define the dimensions of that "human entity," dimensions that include both religious and family traditions and that extend beyond America to include French missionaries and Canadian colonists.

Death Comes for the Archbishop

Where *My Mortal Enemy* shows little hope for those such as Myra Henshawe, caught up in the drive for material gain, *Death Comes for the Archbishop* celebrates a way out of that empty, unfulfilling world. Although that path appears to lead into the past, Cather's purpose in using the earlier setting of the New Mexico Territory between 1851 and 1888 seems not so much retreat, but rather, a desire to express her forward-looking belief that "because of the past we have hope for the future."

Indeed the novel—which Cather preferred to call a legend[12]—is set in an earlier era than the success-oriented worlds of *My Mortal Enemy* and *One of Ours*, even earlier than the acquisitive, competitive world of *A Lost Lady*. In deciding upon this subject for her next novel, Cather seems to be groping for an answer to an overriding question that plagued Americans in the waning days of the Roaring Twenties: What could save a nation whose great potential, so clearly seen by optimistic pioneers such as Alexandra Bergson and Captain Forrester, was being channeled more and more narrowly toward material ends and channeled into the hands of the few? Cather finds her answer in a celebration of earlier heroes and their values, heroes who would remind people of what must remain worthwhile for the present generation and what must be transmitted to the next. Claude Wheeler had marveled that, by word and phrase, "a character could perpetuate itself . . . could renew itself in every generation and be born over and over again in the minds of children."[13] Cather's legend of Archbishop Jean Latour perpetuates such a hero, Jean Baptiste Lamy, Latour's real-life model, as well as the spirit of that earlier age in America, with all its potential and hope for the future.

The novel focuses on traditions carried from one generation to the next, which is what Bishop Latour does, and what Cather shows Mexicans and Indians of the Southwest doing. For Cather, such traditions are the surest way to be "born over and over again," as Claude says, to extend self into the future while at the same time placing self securely within a present community. Waldo Frank had added to his observations about America in 1929: "I am sure, if [each person in America] comes together with his kind, that there will be strength to transform the pliant American wilderness."[14] Cather's novel shows "his kind," for Americans, as not a narrow group but an all-encompassing community of mixed backgrounds and practices. As she had in *O Pioneers!* and *My Ántonia*, in *Death Comes for the Archbishop*, Cather again celebrates the synthesis of Old World and New World values, the values of French missionaries and Indian and Mexican peasants. She thus provides a clear model for the restless generation of the twenties, shaken by the moral and physical devastation of war and by a frenzied postwar atmosphere of modernity in which many were turning away from tradition.

Jean Latour is a questing hero whose physical journey parallels his inner one. Signaling this quest motif, Cather in the prologue likens another missionary priest to Odysseus. *Death Comes for the Archbishop* is both a journey toward self-understanding and an epic adventure of religious devotion. Bishop Latour finds what he needs for personal fulfillment as he defines his community in New Mexico. He must, in fact, secure a place for himself in several communities: the community of fellow religious—some hostile, some cautious, some enthusiastic; the community of Indians with their strange superstitions and pagan ways; the community of Mexicans with their unique expressions of fervor and devotion to their faith.

But despite his important role in each of these groups, Jean Latour does not become fully absorbed by any of them. He attaches himself to these communities and finds varying degrees of fulfillment in doing so, but he asserts his individuality, too. He is the epic hero who will clean "the Augean stable,"[15] the allusion that a visiting missionary uses to suggest the corrupted state of the church in the Southwest. From the opening scene, we are reminded of Bishop Latour's uniqueness as such an epic hero. He is "a priest in a thousand" (19). The description places the bishop on a legendary level, like a knight of old, "a man of gentle birth—brave, sensitive, courteous" (19).

Latour's efforts to bring both his religion and his cultural traditions to a new land culminate in his building of a cathedral. Suggesting her theme of self-fulfillment through community, Cather makes this particular structure, built for God and for community, the most obvious mark of Bishop Latour's individuality, a symbol of a defined self tied to, but distinct from, group. When Latour first shows his companion, Father Vaillant, the hillside of yellow rock that he will use to build his cathedral, Latour makes clear the personal nature of this endeavor: "That hill . . . is my Cathedral" (240). Vaillant cannot fully comprehend Latour's burning desire to build his unique cathedral, and attempts subtly to remind the bishop of the worldliness of such a wish, "when everything about us is so poor" (241). The bishop defends his ambition by insisting that "the Cathedral is not for us. . . . We build for the future" (244).

In this statement Cather suggests not only her hero's other-centeredness, but her own agenda. Just as the bishop's cathedral, built in Old World style, brings to the New World the artistic traditions of the past, so Cather's celebration of this era in American history made it live again for the readers of the 1920s. In the bishop's defense of his actions, Cather thus defends her own project of historical fiction: transmitting that heroic spirit to a generation hungering for heroes. Cather, in her portrayal of Bishop Latour, offers her readers both saint and hero. And while Bishop Latour might be of "gentle birth," the novel abounds with examples of "common" saints and heroes, too: Father Joseph Vaillant, a baker's son, who wins the hearts of the hostile natives of Albuquerque and later moves on to do the same in Colorado during the gold rush there; the peasant, Magdalena, who risks her own life to warn the two priests that their lives are in danger; Eusabio, the Navajo leader who serves as mediator between his tribe and the Hopis; Padre Jesus de Baca, the humble priest who through his life of poverty and devotion wins the loyalty of the Indians among whom he works; Sada, the Mexican slave who holds onto her faith despite the suffering that she experiences. All of these characters from various cultures and classes share membership in "a long chain of human endeavor,"[16] each struggling to preserve and to pass on traditions.

This is what Latour means to do by building his cathedral, and why he can say, "We build for the future." Although a writer such as Mary Austin, keenly interested in the preservation of distinctive, regional native culture, disapproved of such a European style for a cathedral in New Mexico,[17] Cather seems to see in such a structure the unique blend of Old World and New World cultures in America that had fired her imagination from her early days in Nebraska and that, for her, continued to represent the strength and hope of America. "Art is made out of the love of old and intimate things," she said in an interview in 1921.[18] For Bishop Latour, the unique yellow rock from which he builds his cathedral reminds him of the papal palace at Avignon. It recalls the best of the past, as the finished structure of the cathedral will also do. In building the cathedral, he is also carrying on a family tradition, since his own ancestors in France had been instrumental in the construction of a cathedral there, as Vaillant reminds him. The bishop realizes the worldliness of his desire for such a unique, impressive cathedral, but he senses God's approval of this desire: "I could hardly have hoped that God would gratify my personal taste, my vanity, if you will, in this way" (245). As if to underscore God's approval of this "vain" project, Cather describes in a later chapter how perfectly the cathedral fits its setting, against the hills. "Either a building is a part of a place, or it is not. Once that kinship is there, time will only make it stronger," Latour's French architect tells him (272). When we see the cathedral years later, as death truly does come for the archbishop, that kinship between building and place appears stronger, just as the archbishop's kinship with his community has grown strong over the years.

Latour and Vaillant both establish a strong spirit of kinship with their people by respecting the traditions of the distinct communities within their diocese. The Southwest that they encounter on their arrival in 1851 is both culturally and geographically fragmented, as Cather makes clear in the prologue. A visiting missionary who describes the region to the cardinals in Rome emphasizes its fragmentation: the cracks and fissures, canyons and arroyos that divide the desert floor. This description is certainly a trope for the other kind of fragmentation that the two missionaries encounter in a region that encompasses Mexicans as well as numerous Indian tribes, each with its own distinct customs and language. Latour and Vaillant attempt to unite these groups spiritually in the broader community of the Church while keeping in mind that each still needs to retain its cultural uniqueness. The missionary who can succeed in the new territory, one of the cardinals in the prologue tells his companions, must "have a sense of proportion and rational adjustment" (9). It is just this sense, this "elasticity," as Cather had earlier termed "rational adjustment," that allows the two French missionaries to adapt and to succeed.

Cather seems especially eager to convey through her protagonist her own views on cultural diversity, for although Latour's life is based on that of Archbishop Lamy, Cather's fictional bishop is much more open-minded about the cultures that he encounters than was his real-life model.[19] Latour accepts the Indian converts who live on the isolated rock at Acoma, and whose church is actually decorated with paintings of their own gods of wind, rain, sun, and moon. He even accepts the Penitential Brotherhood at Abiquiu with their extravagant Holy Week reenactments of Christ's sufferings. Latour realizes that oneness of belief need not mean oneness of practice, that cultural individuality is not only an inescapable fact, but also makes for a healthy community. At one point, traveling with his Indian guide, Jacinto, Bishop Latour reflects that he cannot "transfer his own memories of European civilization into the Indian mind" any more than Jacinto can "translate" to Latour his own "long tradition" of "Indian ways" (92). Latour respects the Indians' cultural uniqueness, even the parts of it that he knows he can never comprehend, while at the same time he appreciates the similarities between his own perspective and theirs. When a white trader, Zeb Orchard, tells Latour, "the things [Indians] value most are worth nothing to us," the bishop disagrees, explaining to Zeb that he shares "their veneration for old customs" (135).

Through several metaphors, Cather emphasizes her view that groups of diverse background and belief can form a community and still maintain their distinct cultural identities. Describing the bishop's first look at the mountains around Santa Fe, the narrator notes that the green of

the aspens and evergreens remains distinct. In such a portrayal of the
landscape, Cather suggests (perhaps naïvely) that the Mexicans and
Indians of the Southwest manage to retain their cultural distinctiveness
even when the bishop brings them into his broader community of church.
We see a similar suggestion of cultural intermingling in Bishop Latour's
observation of a herd of goats at a Mexican settlement. The frolicking
animals remind him both of a Bible reference to Christ, the "Lamb of
God," and of the pagan use of the goat to symbolize "lewdness." Latour
smiles at this "mixed theology" (31); his awareness of it, however, highlights his own ability to adapt his faith to various environments and to
respect others' traditions as he preserves and transmits his.

When Father Vaillant explains that the mission bell installed at Santa
Fe was cast in 1356 and contains Spanish silver along with the other
metals, Bishop Latour reflects that the silver is more accurately Moor-
ish, since the Spanish learned all their silver techniques from the
Moors. Vaillant jokingly accuses Latour of making his bell an "infidel," but the bishop, reminds his fellow priest that the practice of ringing the Angelus bell was itself adapted from the Moslems. The bell thus
represents a cultural synthesis. The church bell also reminds Latour of
the skill of silversmithing that the Spaniards learned from the Moors
and later passed on to the Mexicans, who in turn taught the Navajos.
Cather here again focuses on the importance of traditions and of cultural indebtedness. "The passion for Americanizing everything and
everybody is a deadly disease with us," she remarked in a 1924 interview.[20] Latour understands the necessity as well as the evil of Americanization. He writes to his brother that the Church will make "these
poor Mexicans 'good Americans'" better than civil government can,
adding that he hopes in this way to "better their condition" (36). But
Bishop Latour, who strongly values his own French culture, puts quotation marks around "good Americans," for he does not intend to erase
the cultural distinctiveness of the people he serves.

At Latour's death, Cather once again highlights his respect for the
cultural distinctiveness of his people by enumerating the various communities who mourn his loss, just as she notes at Father Vaillant's
death how he had won the love and loyalty of "red men and yellow men
and white" (289). The last paragraph of *Death Comes for the Archbishop* depicts the diverse responses to the archbishop's death. Mexican and American Catholics who hear the cathedral bell tolling fall
to their knees, and Indians from several tribes go "quietly away to tell
their people" (299).

The archbishop nurtures the distinct cultural communities in his diocese while at the same time nurturing the spiritual community of the
church. As Cather in previous novels used garden imagery to symbol-

ize a healthy community, she again does so in *Death Comes for the Archbishop*. Bishop Latour sees himself as a "husbandman" who will nurture "the Faith planted by the Spanish friars" (32). The priests' own garden at Santa Fe is their personal joy as well as a symbol of the healthy spiritual community they build. It is also a symbol of hope in the future. When Latour and his helper, Tranquilino, lay out the garden and orchard, they "boldly [plan] for the future" (201). Father Vaillant, who later goes to Colorado as a missionary, laments that "nobody in Colorado planted gardens" (260)—a reminder of the spiritual unhealthiness and instability of this gold-rush community, with its material basis and uncertain future. The dead garden at Acoma serves as a contrast to Latour's and Vaillant's garden, a testimony to the unhealthy community of slave labor that Fray Baltazar had created there centuries earlier, eventually provoking the Acoma Indians so much that they killed him.

Even in old age, the archbishop still works diligently in his garden and encourages the new priests "to plant fruit trees wherever they went," quoting Pascal, "that Man was lost and saved in a garden" (267). Cather thus emphasizes the planting of traditions as a means not only of fulfilling self but of extending self, of gaining that immortality which Claude noted as he thought of the legendary Joan of Arc. Like Claude, Latour knows the importance of stories in preserving traditions. He recounts to his young priests stories and legends of the earlier missionaries (279); he tells these young men everything that he can remember about traditions in various pueblos. As he dictates local history to these new keepers of tradition, Latour worries about the disappearance of the old customs and stories of local tribes, since he never had the time to record what he observed.

While he has that regret, however, the archbishop, nearing death, feels that his life has been a success, that many of his dreams have been fulfilled. He recalls the terrible exile of the Navajos from the verdant Canyon de Chelly, and is grateful that he has lived to see that wrong righted, to see them once again thriving there. Again, Cather uses garden imagery, depicting the restored community as "an Indian Garden of Eden" (297). Perhaps we can view this reflection on exiled Navajos, placed so strategically near the end of Cather's narrative, as her own reflection on the America of the twenties, a generation in exile, cut off from the values and traditions of the past. Latour notes that the Navajos had survived and had returned to make their canyon flourish. He tells a young priest: "I do not believe, as I once did, that the Indian will perish" (297). Perhaps Cather was here considering her own troubled land, hoping that it, too, could survive the emotional trauma of the twenties.[21]

An interviewer in 1927 remarked that Willa Cather "seems in no fear that the world will come crashing around her feet."[22] Cather—despite her famous remark that "the world broke in two in 1922 or thereabouts"[23]—implies in her conclusion to *Death Comes for the Archbishop* the same faith in the future that this interviewer noticed. The Willa Cather of 1927 seems already to be looking at the purported cataclysm of "1922 or thereabouts" as the archbishop calmly looks at and says goodbye to the past, confident that "the future would take care of itself" (289).[24]

Near the end of the novel, Father Vaillant reflects on the meaning of success: "To fulfill the dreams of one's youth; that is the best that can happen to a man. No worldly success can take the place of that" (261). Thus, Cather in *Death Comes for the Archbishop* offers a new view of success, a view that seems at odds with a "worldly success" that is measured by material gain. Vaillant's remark implies that "the dreams of one's youth" are unworldly or of higher value than mere "worldly success." The standard Horatio Alger youth's dream of fame and fortune has been replaced, it would seem, by something less tangible. But exactly what has replaced it is problematic. Humans need physical signs, just as Santayana reminded readers that material gain was, to many Americans, merely a physical sign of success, or as Cather pointed out that material success for the early pioneers was a sign of moral victory. When Bishop Latour and Father Vaillant discuss the definition of a miracle, Vaillant reminds Latour that while doctrine is important, perhaps even more important is "something we can hold in our hands and love"—his definition of a miracle (50). What is the measure of success that we "can hold in our hands" if one can measure it neither by fame nor fortune?

Ironically, the two missionaries who renounce worldly wealth and measure success by those better-than-worldly dreams of their youth still manage to attain to some degree the standard physical measures of success—both fame and fortune. Devoted followers come from far and near to Father Vaillant's funeral in Colorado as they do to honor the archbishop when he dies. Both priests find fulfillment by immersing themselves in the communities that they serve; but both attain a stature and fame that mark them as unique personalities, thus placing them above those communities. Vaillant at one point remarks that in Latour, God had graced the new diocese with "a fine personality" (254).

Father Vaillant, as unworldly as he is where his own personal needs are concerned, accumulates material wealth in the name of the Church and becomes caught up in the same late nineteenth-century grab for land that brings material success to Alexandra Bergson and her brothers—although Vaillant experiences more difficulties in his venture

than did Alexandra. He borrows money to buy land for the church, later
floating bonds in France to pay off his loans; eventually, "dishonest
brokers [bring] reproach upon his name" (287). The archbishop leaves
a more gratifying physical measure of his success in the form of his
cathedral, as we have noted. Cather identifies his desire to build the
cathedral as a "very keen worldly ambition." It is clear, too, that Latour
sees the cathedral as an extension of himself, a way to place himself
permanently in the community that he has served. He envisions the
cathedral as "a continuation of himself and his purpose, a physical body
full of his aspirations" that would remain long past his own life" (175).
Just as an author leaves "a physical body" of writing as "a continuation
of himself and his purpose," so the archbishop, in Cather's characteristic manner, fuses religion and art in his cathedral, leaving for future
generations an artifact that reflects his "fine personality."

Thus, although Cather in *Death Comes for the Archbishop* redefines
self-fulfillment in terms of service to and identification with community, that fulfillment still bears many marks of the standard American
Dream of success. But those marks, to use Santayana's words, are "the
symbol and measure" that Cather has at hand to suggest self-fulfillment. As Richard Weiss notes, "On the level of symbol, the pursuit of
the material and the pursuit of the ideal have a symbiotic relationship
in the American mind that is one of the most distinctive and enduring
marks of our culture."[25] For the heroes of *Death Comes for the Archbishop*, two priests dedicated to a community of souls, the road to self-
fulfillment is the same road that leads to spiritual community and "the
pursuit of the ideal." While creating a healthy spiritual community,
Latour and Vaillant fulfill their need for group as well as their desire
for success; they accomplish "the dreams of [their] youth." Apparently, Cather would have us understand that, despite the hardships that
both men endure, along the way they establish a happy balance between
self needs and others' needs.

Shadows on the Rock

In *Shadows on the Rock*, twelve-year-old Cécile Auclair and her father,
Euclide, leave no legacy of land or cathedrals; they find no more fame
than did Ántonia, but they do find fulfillment through community—
their own tiny community of French immigrants in seventeenth-century Quebec as well as a larger community to which they are linked by
cultural and religious traditions. An interviewer in 1928, at the time
that Cather was writing *Shadows on the Rock*, remarked that Willa
Cather's personal charm was "augmented by her democracy, and her

easy and gracious commonness."26 One might say that the same qualities make the young Cécile and her father so appealing; they are portraits of a success that, even more clearly than the success of Jean Latour and Joseph Vaillant, has freed itself from all vestiges of fame and fortune. Published in 1931, *Shadows on the Rock* seems an appropriate Depression-era novel, with its poor-but-happy, Shirley Temple heroine, who teaches readers that they can find personal happiness without money or fame. And in the spirit of the Depression-era intellectual, more interested in a universal human community than in a specifically American community,27 Cather "un-Americanizes" her setting by moving it beyond the United States to Canada.

In *Shadows on the Rock*, Cather seems intent, as she also seemed in *Death Comes for the Archbishop*, on bringing forward from the past the values and traditions that she found lacking in her world. Perhaps to remind her readers that she herself was neither mired in the past nor out of touch with reality, Cather included two footnotes that give factual information about structures that are part of her setting. The first also serves as a commentary on the madness for modernizing things. Referring to the Church of Notre Dame de la Victoire, Cather notes that its "charm . . . was greatly spoiled" by alterations made in 1929. Cather, who visited Quebec for the first time in 1928 and made four subsequent visits before completing her novel at the end of 1930, experienced the "unfortunate alterations" firsthand. The second footnote, concerning the reformed Bishop Saint-Vallier's humble residence after his return to Quebec, again brings readers into the present. Cather informs readers that the hospital founded by the bishop in 1700 "still stands today," with the bishop's own two rooms left "unchanged". Her epigraph, like these statements, takes readers out of fiction into history. It is an excerpt from a letter written in 1653 by Mother Marie de l'Incarnation to another member of her religious order living in France.

In these factual references, Cather perhaps reflects a growing defensiveness about being labeled nostalgic or escapist.28 Such accusations certainly presented problems for someone who valued tradition as Cather did. Cather seems to be trying especially in *Shadows on the Rock* to define her need for tradition and at the same time to assert that one must keep a balanced perspective on the past. "Change is not always progress,"29 Auclair reminds the modern-minded, negatively portrayed Bishop Saint-Vallier, who, as Auclair observes, seemed to enjoy changing things "for the sake of change . . . [destroying] the old before he had clearly thought out the new" (122).

Nevertheless, the old ways, as Cather demonstrates time and again in this novel, are not always best. In fact, Saint-Vallier's destructive changes are actually a reinstatement of the old, traditional policy of placing priests permanently in parishes, in place of Laval's newer, more flexible "system of a moveable clergy" (120). Euclide Auclair on several occasions tells stories about atrocities that he observed in France under the long-established laws. The narrator notes that "though [Auclair] was a creature of habit . . . his mind was free" (31). Thus, although Auclair treasures many Old World customs and perpetuates them in his new home in Quebec, he has no admiration for some Old World conditions—such as the "poverty and hunger" that he recalls in France during the days of Court "extravagances" (32). Just as he does with politics, in his scientific world, Euclide decides which of the "old ways" he will revere and which he will reject. He opposes the new practice of blood-letting; he looks back to the thirteenth century as one of the "golden ages of medicine" (29). But when Cécile asks him about giving a person ground human bone to cure an illness, after she hears just such a tale of a miraculous recovery, he remarks that this long-standing practice is detrimental.

Auclair's mind is definitely free to select from new ways and old ways as he sees fit, underscoring a major theme in *Shadows on the Rock*. Indeed, tradition is important, for it gives one membership in that time-spanning community which preserves and transmits culture to future generations. But one must not preserve or transmit blindly; instead, one must select carefully from that storehouse of tradition to create a healthy community in the present. In an editorial about Cather's speaking tour of the Midwest in 1921, Harvey Newbranch, her former classmate at the University of Nebraska and at that time the editor of the *Omaha World-Herald*, caught in Cather's remarks a similar message:

> When the race, the community, or the individual becomes more interested in discovering principles that are eternal, many old customs will be reverenced more highly; many will be abandoned and viewed as moss-grown ruins of the medieval age.[30]

As she implies in her characterization of Euclide Auclair, Cather is selective in what she feels should be valued and transmitted, just as she is selective in considering what a new era, including her own, had to offer.

But how does one decide which "principles" are "eternal," which should be "reverenced more highly" and which should be "abandoned and viewed as moss-grown ruins"? Cather at the end of the twenties seems especially to reverence communal values—represented by religion and family—and perhaps to abandon in her fiction, or at least to temper, the bolder individualism that early heroines such as Thea Kronborg and Marian Forrester display. Respect for community and culture pervade her two novels of this period, with religion serving as a bind-

ing force. Both novels elevate Catholicism, specificially, to a position
of importance, focusing on its use of ritual and its focus on the unex-
plainable—miracles.[31] Bishop Latour calls miracles "human vision
corrected by divine love"[32]—a synthesis of the human and the supernatural, Cather implies, echoing her theme of culture as synthesis.
Catholicism appears to represent for Cather not only a specific, unified
community but a community that both safeguards and transmits culture. Signs and symbols are more than mere trappings of a culture,
Cather suggests. They, like the simple pots and pans that Cécile cherishes, are what make for shared experience.

Robert Bellah and coauthors observe that "the cultural traditions of
a people—its symbols, ideals, and ways of feeling—is always an argument about the meaning of the destiny its members share."[33] In *Shadows on the Rock*, we see the members of the Quebec community involved
in such an "argument" about their shared destiny. The result is a synthesis of French traditions and new ways to fit a strange new world. The
most admirable characters in *Shadows on the Rock* are those who
accomplish such a synthesis.[34] They identify themselves as Canadians
although they feel tied by religious and cultural tradition to France. We
see an enthusiasm for Canada in minor characters such as the shoe-
maker's mother, old Madame Pommier, who is pleased that in Canada
there is a special veneration for the Holy Family that she had not
observed in France. But in Cather's major characters, she stresses synthesis. Cécile displays an ideal synthesis of New World youthful energy and hope with Old World reverence for culture, as does her future
husband, Canadian-born Pierre Charron, who "ha[s] the good manners
of the Old World, the dash and daring of the New" (172). Charron is a
perfect transition figure between the two worlds. His name brings to
mind the transition figure from Greek mythology, Charon, who ferries
people between the world of the living and the world of the dead.[35] Like
the ancient Charon, Pierre Charron, too, spends much of his time in his
small boat, traveling the rivers of Canada with his furs. Charron scoffs
at Old World tradition, telling Cécile that both she and he are "Canadians"; but his "old ideals of clan-loyalty" mark him as a synthesis,
like Cécile, of new and old (172, 174).

Cécile comes more and more to identify with Canada as the novel
progresses. We are given a hint of this near the beginning of the novel,
when her mother notices in the eyes of her daughter "the blue of Canadian blueberries" (25); later, when Madame Pommier tells Cécile about
Canadian devotion to the Holy Family, Cécile feels pleased that Canadians have "things of their own" (101). In Quebec, she feels that she is
in her "own place" (104); by the end of the novel, when her father is
considering returning to France, she desperately wants to stay in Que-

bec (228). But despite her strong allegiance to Quebec, Cécile treasures the French ways that structure much of her day-to-day existence. Tradition, preserved selectively and valued not for itself but for the ideals that it embodies, is an important "rock" to which one can cling, Cather suggests.

At one point in the novel, Cather especially emphasizes this theme of traditions carried to a new land, highlighting religion as a specific vehicle for the transmission of culture. The narrator observes that a person who "carries his gods with him" founds a colony that has

> graces, traditions, riches of the mind and spirit. Its history will shine with bright incidents, slight, perhaps, but precious as in life itself, where the great matters are often as worthless as astronomical distances, and the trifles dear as the heart's blood. (98)

This commentary follows immediately a description of the happy communities of nuns, who have brought with them to the New World their "family," in the form of their fellow religious as well as in the form of their spiritual family—the saints, the apostles, the Holy Family. Religion for Cather is an important means of preserving and transmitting traditions, as this novel repeatedly shows.[36]

Religion is equally important in *Shadows on the Rock* for its power to bind a community and to help forge a Canadian identity. The stories of Canadian martyrs and saints, including the story of the beloved recluse, Jean le Ber, inspire the people of Quebec. Jean le Ber has given up all worldly comforts to live in her tiny cell behind the church altar in Montreal, where she prays and makes clothing for the poor as well as altar-cloths and vestments for poor parishes in Canada. Her story is "told and re-told with loving exaggeration" in Canadian homes, bringing pleasure wherever it is told. The need for concrete expressions of Canadian as well as French traditions is repeated often in *Shadows on the Rock*, just as the title image, a shadow, serves as evidence of someone's presence. Father Vaillant calls a miracle "something we can hold in our hands and love,"[37] emphasizing the human need for something tangible to represent what is incomprehensible. This same idea surfaces in *Shadows on the Rock*. The people of Canada want to know that Christ is near them even in this remote colony. They delight to hear of the "miracle at Montreal"—the recluse being visited by angels— because such a miracle captures "the experience of a moment, which might have been lost in ecstasy, [making that experience] an actual possession [that] can be bequeathed to another" (137).

Cather, whom Harold Bloom identifies as "a belated Aesthete," linking her to Walter Pater,[38] here provides a solution to Pater's problem with the "awful brevity" of ecstasy. "We have an interval and then our place knows us no more," Pater says. "Our one chance lies in expanding that interval."[39] Tradition, Cather suggests, expressed concretely in stories, rituals, and everyday customs, lets us expand that interval as it lets us capture in concrete form "the experience of the moment."[40] It lets us make of an ecstatic experience "an actual possession" that can be *bequeathed*. A similar thought occurs to Cécile's young friend, Jacques, when he sees Cécile's silver cup with her name engraved on it and realizes that such a "possession," with its engraved name, will remain after a person's death, keeping his or her memory alive in future generations.

Besides offering religion as a vehicle for transmitting traditions, Cather's narrative remark on adventurers who carry their gods with them also underscores her theme of tradition as an extension of self into the future. Cather in this commentary expresses an overriding hope that the best of the old can adapt itself to fit a new setting, to enrich that environment and to secure a place among future generations. Her remark ends with an emphasis on the "slight . . . but precious"—"the trifles" that are as "dear as the heart's blood," as vital to tradition as one's gods. Cécile's mother, who has been dead for several years when *Shadows on the Rock* opens, trained her daughter to carry on the traditions of the Old World. In Madame Auclair's attitude toward tradition, Cather conveys her own reverence. Madame Auclair knows that she is entrusting to Cécile "a feeling about life that had come down to her through so many centuries. . . . The sense of 'our way'" (25). Cécile's dramatic realization of what her mother has entrusted to her and its importance in her life is the climactic scene in the novel, suggesting how much value Cather placed on the nonspectacular incidents of daily life that carry on traditions. There is no monumental undertaking in *Shadows on the Rock*, as was the case in earlier novels: Bartley Alexander's world-renowned building projects, Alexandra Bergson's impressive farming venture, Thea Kronborg's opera career, Claude Wheeler's wartime heroism, Captain Forrester's railroads across Western America, Godfrey St. Peter's multivolume history, or Archbishop Latour's magnificent and unique cathedral. Little things and minor events are the undertakings that matter in *Shadows on the Rock*, as Cécile comes to understand—the dinner ritual at the Auclairs that makes Euclide feel like "a civilized man and a Frenchman" (17); market day and the meticulous preparations for the long winter; feast days and holy days that bring the community together; fireside stories of French and Canadian saints and martyrs.

These everyday events are the "orderly procession of activities [that hold] life together on the rock" (105). Cécile comes truly to understand her commitment to tradition after she is briefly deprived of the "slight but precious" rituals of daily living that she has always performed. She accompanies Pierre only four miles down the river to visit a man named Harnois, who lives with his wife and three small daughters on the Ile d'Orleans. Pierre and Cécile remain at the Harnois house for two days and nights; Cécile during this time tries to accustom herself to their rough way of living, but she is so miserable away from her household customs and rituals that she asks Pierre to take her home a day before he had planned to leave. Later analyzing her reaction to this strange environment, she reflects that the Harnois family's "kind ways" were "not enough; one had to have kind things about one, too" (197). This epiphany marks Cécile's rite of passage to adulthood, as she claims the values that will be hers. At home, surrounded by the "kind things" of her own household, performing her daily chores, Cécile realizes that she does these tasks not merely to be a dutiful daughter: "She did them for herself, quite as much" (198).

In presenting a heroine who prefers domestic chores and her humble, cozy kitchen to a world only a few miles away in which one is confronted with new ways and a new environment, is Cather losing faith in the "elasticity" of a Marian Forrester or a Jean Latour, the risk-taking of an Alexandra Bergson or an Ántonia Shimerda? Is Cather instead recommending stasis in her portrait of Cécile Auclair? In this novel, written in a period of social and political unrest in America, Cather may be reflecting a conservative fear of the changes during her own era, intensified by her awareness of the growing number of fellow artists who, disgusted with a capitalistic, class-defined America, were turning to socialism and communism to find both solace and the sense of community that seemed absent from the competitive, materialistic America of the past decade.[41]

But if Cather's emphasis in *Shadows on the Rock* reflects such political conservatism, her other writing from this same period suggests some discomfort with membership in such a conservatively defined community. Was she, in remaining conservative politically, fearful of being marginalized by her own community of fellow artists, beyond the marginalization that she perhaps already experienced in a male-dominated world of literary greats such as Hemingway, Lewis, and Fitzgerald? In a letter published in *The Saturday Review of Literature* in October of 1931, Cather seems purposely to distance herself and her own views from what she portrays and celebrates in *Shadows on the Rock*:

> [In Quebec] is the curious endurance of a kind of culture, narrow but definite. There another age persists. There . . . I caught something new to me; a kind of feeling about life and human fate that I could not accept, wholly, but which I could not but admire.[42]

She seems intent on separating herself from Cécile's protected, devout, "narrow" world. While Cather admires the "curious endurance" of traditions, she seems concerned at the same time about being judged too strictly conservative, either in her social views or in her literary opinions. In her only speech ever to be broadcast (1933), a tribute to the novel, she recognized the value of traditional literary forms (Greek and Elizabethan drama) but she praised, too, the nineteenth-century Russian novelists "who flashed out in the north like a new constellation" and "did more for the future than they knew"—emphasizing that "they had no benumbing literary traditions behind them." Traditions are valuable, Cather suggests, but they can also be "benumbing," hampering one's artistic potential. "We cling to our old formulae," she laments in her speech, adding that a formula can be "pernicious." Cather emphasizes, however, the "eternal principles" that always served as a driving force for her art: "[The Russian novelists] had a glorious language, new to literature, but old in human feeling and wisdom and suffering, and they were themselves men singularly direct and powerful, with sympathies as wide as humanity."[43] Cather admires these artists for their individuality ("singularly direct and powerful") and their gift of sympathy ("sympathies as wide as humanity").

In this revealing speech, then, we see Cather's own inner debate about holding onto the past and moving boldly into the future, and her continuing debate with herself about the importance of individualism in a changing world. Cather both comes to the defense of and indicts her own artistic community in this speech, when she comments on "the American novelist [who] has been confined, or has confined himself," to shallow themes that reflect a debased American Dream: "how the young man got his girl . . . and how he succeeded in business." Her judgment on such subjects in American literature is clear and harsh: "Of course only a people with very little background and very childish tastes could have any patience with such a shallow conception."[44] Thus Cather in the early 1930s, when she wrote *Shadows on the Rock*, was still negotiating a position for herself on the American Dream—one that would remove her from any "shallow conception" of success while still allowing her to retain a respect for the individualism so vital to any artist, and a position that would also let her feel a part of a community with "sympathies as wide as humanity."

In her portraits of Cécile and Euclide Auclair, both of whom also struggle to define a place for themselves in a community and to define their own individual needs, Cather thus images her own similar inner struggle. Their synthesis of old ways and new mirrors Cather's attempt at such a synthesis, which perhaps became more difficult to achieve as she aged and as she experienced the social and political turmoil of the thirties. Cécile Auclair slowly discovers her community in *Shadows on the Rock*, realizing at last that she belongs in Canada. Auclair and Cécile need their community—family, village, church, traditions—for fulfillment. The idea of personal fulfillment through community so pervades *Shadows on the Rock* that it would appear in this novel that the individual becomes happily dissolved in community, as Jim Burden felt "dissolved into something complete and great."[45] At one point, Cécile, lying in bed recovering from an illness, envisions the town, the river, and the forest as "layers and layers of shelter" (158), echoing the theme of community as shelter.

The people on the rock of Quebec depend upon one another for help, as Auclair so aptly illustrates, since all villagers avail themselves of his services. His house and shop are appropriately situated between the upper and lower sections of the village, accessible to all. Auclair also symbolizes commitment to community in his role as analyst/listener for both the highest and the lowest of Quebec's citizens: the governor, Count Fontenac, and the outcast, Blinker. Auclair is the Count's physician, but, the narrator notes that his main function is "to listen occasionally, when the Governor felt lonely" (240). Earlier in the novel, we see Auclair performing this same service for the unfortunate Blinker. Auclair and Cécile have taken Blinker in, almost as a member of the family, giving him food, a warm place, and a friendly atmosphere in return for his help with minor household chores. When Blinker asks Auclair for sleeping medicine, the apothecary encourages Blinker instead to talk to him. Blinker confesses that he was formerly an executioner in France, and is troubled about the innocent people that he put to death. By listening to and empathizing with Blinker, Auclair solves the troubled man's sleeping problems. Just as Auclair takes responsibility for others in the community, Cécile helps the unfortunate in Quebec, actively seeking the Count's help for young Jacques, the neglected son of a local prostitute, and herself serving as surrogate mother and teacher for the boy. Even the recluse, Jean le Ber, although she is shut away from the world, shows her commitment to community by her prayers for others and her production of garments for the poor.

In one scene of the epilogue, Cather changes to first person plural, as if to pull readers closer toward an identity with this tightly knit community. The scene depicts a humble, other-centered Bishop Saint-Vallier returning after a thirteen-year absence from Quebec. "Suffering teaches us compassion" (162), Auclair had told Blinker earlier. Saint-Vallier, deprived of his community in Quebec, has at last, through suffering, learned compassion. Cather extends the invitation to exercise compassion directly to her readers here in an analogy that she uses to explain Auclair's surprise at his feelings of affection for the returned bishop. The narrator observes that once in awhile, a boastful person whom we may have always found irritating "shows us another side, another man, really; a man uncertain, and puzzled, and in the dark like

ourselves" (279). Auclair has seen this other man in the bishop;
Cather's analogy brings to mind Waldo Frank's comment about Americans' "tragic need" for groups, a need that involves Cather's famous
"gift of sympathy"—an awareness of "others, in their way, living the
same life," as Waldo Frank terms it.[46]

Perhaps such a need seems so strong in *Shadows on the Rock* because
it was at this time so strong for Cather herself. It is likely that a desire
to belong had overshadowed the competitive desire for individual
accomplishment that certainly was ingrained in Cather, growing up in
an era of cutthroat competition in America. Woodress points out that
in the half-decade between 1928 and 1932 during which Cather wrote
Shadows on the Rock, "she was a ship without moorings,"[47] having lost
her parents and also having been forced to leave the apartment that had
been her New York home for years and now was scheduled to be torn
down. As a woman writer, she may have been feeling "without moorings," too. Although she had received critical acclaim for *Death Comes
for the Archbishop*, she expressed in a letter written in January 1931 the
disadvantages of being a woman writer.[48] Also, as we have already
observed, social and political tensions most likely created for Cather
an inner tension about the social and political communities to which
she felt most closely allied.

Despite such an intensified need for community, Cather, however,
remained selective in her choices. In 1926 she built an isolated cottage
on Grand Manan, off the coast of New Brunswick. She cherished her
peaceful, secluded visits to the island, selecting as her only real friend
there the local doctor. Yet, more eager than ever at this stage of her life
to strengthen ties with her own siblings, Cather organized a family
reunion at Christmas in Red Cloud, after her mother's death in 1931.

Cather's need for family reflects not only a growing personal awareness of the importance of this community, but a growing national
reawakening to "the strength and power of the family as a unit."[49] In
her two highly acclaimed short stories written during this period,
Cather narrows her community of choice to family, celebrating such
"strength and power."

"Neighbour Rosicky" and "Old Mrs. Harris"

In both "Neighbour Rosicky" and "Old Mrs. Harris," Cather demonstrates through her two protagonists, as she had through the Auclairs
and through most of the other characters in *Shadows on the Rock*, that
dedication to others can be an avenue to self-fulfillment, bringing one
a surer, more meaningful sense of success than that which the standard

American Dream represented, with its ethos of acquisitive individualism. Immersion in family can as well provide a way to survive beyond death, as the protagonists of these two stories demonstrate. Family becomes an extension of self, survival in the form of a new generation who will carry on specific family values and traditions. Cather in these stories foregrounds the grandparent-grandchild connection: Old Mrs. Harris and granddaughter, Vickie; Anton Rosicky and the expected grandchild that Rosicky does not live to see. Hope lies in that third generation, Cather suggests. As she had noted in her Nebraska essay, grandchildren may "go back to the old sources of culture and wisdom—not as a duty, but with burning desire."[50] Rosicky tries to keep an appreciation of rural life and values alive in his sons, so that his grandchild can experience a world free from the cruelty that he encountered in the city; Mrs. Harris secretly intervenes to make it possible for Vickie to "go back to the old sources of culture and wisdom" that she will be able to encounter by attending college. In both stories, youth symbolizes hope in the future, and grandparents serve as nurturers who "boldly [plan] for the future," as Cather had said in *Death Comes for the Archbishop*.

We see this eye on the future in a crucial scene of "Neighbour Rosicky," when Rosicky rakes the thistles out of the alfalfa field that lies between his farm and Rudolph's, to encourage his disheartened son. Rosicky's oldest son, Rudolph, is not weathering hard times well, and has become restless and discontented with farm life. Rosicky preaches mildly to him, "You got plenty to eat an' keep warm an' plenty water to keep clean. When you got them you can't have it very hard." But Rudolph counters: "I've got to have a good deal more than that."[51] Standard notions of success are taking root in Rudolph's mind, just as the thistles are invading his alfalfa field. In Cather's Nebraska essay, she had complained: "The belief that snug success and easy money are the real aims of human life has settled down over our prairies."[52] Before it takes root in Rudolph, Rosicky acts to eradicate that view by winning over Rudolph's American wife, Polly, who especially represents the future, since she is expecting Rosicky's grandchild. He knows that if Polly does not become discouraged with the hard, uncertain life of the farmer—if she comes to realize that "snug success and easy money" are not "the real aims of human life"— Rudolph will be more apt to stay on the farm.

The hard work of guaranteeing such a happier future for his family proves fatal to Rosicky, for it is work of the heart, and Dr. Burleigh has warned him that his heart cannot take any more "heavy work" (4). When Rosicky rakes the thistle, he suffers a heart attack, but his act of love touches Polly: she sees his "special gift for loving people" (66) in the hours during which she cares for him after his heart attack. Throughout the story, Rosicky's body serves as a text that tells the story of his caring and his endurance. As she cares for her stricken father–in–law, Polly reads that text. Holding Rosicky's hand, she reads in it the character of Rosicky himself—"cleverness . . . generosity" (67). This act of reading awakens Polly to the importance of life lived on a farm, where one can nurture such traits. Thus Rosicky, who always "liked tailoring" (26), mends by his actions and by his very being the relationship between Rudolph and Polly, as well as each one's self-division.

Besides planting seeds of love by his action, Rosicky does so by his storytelling. Through stories of his own earlier struggles, he gives his children, including Polly, a feeling for the very horror that he wants neither his children nor their children ever to experience—the horror of human pitted against human that he experienced in the city. As the family gathers on Christmas Eve, Rosicky tells a story of his London days. Earlier, the narrator had noted that Rosicky's London experience was "a sore spot in his mind that wouldn't bear touching" (27). But on Christmas Eve, Rosicky decides to touch that sore spot, and the narrator notes that although Rosicky usually spoke Czech to his sons, he tells his story in English this time, so that Polly, too, will hear it.

Surprisingly, his tale does not focus so much on the cruelties of a life without money as on the horrible moral transformation that took place within Rosicky as he lived such an existence. The "sore spot," we discover, is Rosicky's shame, for hunger had one Christmas Eve driven him to steal from his impoverished landlady the roast goose that she had made for her family and her boarders. Rosicky wants his children never to be driven to such desperation that they ignore community, as he had done in his impulsive act of thievery: "In the city all the foulness and misery and brutality of your neighbours was a part of your life" (59). If his children can only remain on the land, Rosicky feels they will never be so morally threatened. To demonstrate that even in hard times, living on the land is better than any other way of life, Mary Rosicky tells another story—of a year that the entire corn crop was ruined by heat and drought. She recounts how her husband decided to find a shady spot for a family picnic on the very day that they had witnessed their corn withering in the hot wind. Mary finishes the story: "An' we enjoyed ourselves that year, poor as we was" (49).

Rosicky's conscious, desperate effort to keep his children on the land does wear out his heart, but only physically. When the doctor admonishes Rosicky to take care of his heart, Rosicky replies, "Maybe I don't know how" (5). But of course, he does know how. He knows that by nurturing the little community of family—including the extended family that Polly represents—he is guaranteeing the survival of his own self, in the form of traditions and values that will be carried on after he is gone. The word "neighbour" in the title of the story signals Cather's focus on community, the healthy community that the extended family of Rosickys represents, figured not only in the healthy Rosicky children but in the geraniums that bloom in the middle of winter in the Rosicky home and in the lush alfalfa field where the destructive thistle will not take root.

Throughout the story, Cather juxtaposes Rosicky's definition of success with the standard American definition. Tom Marshall, a neighboring rancher, represents the standard version of the American Dream. He owns a large, efficient farm and plenty of new machinery, but on Marshall's farm there is "no comfort whatever" (8). To Mary Rosicky, who is more concerned with people than with production, the Marshalls' failure to provide Dr. Ed with a good breakfast after he had delivered a baby there shows their poverty of spirit. She does not understand that sort of action any more than she can understand the local creamery agent's attempt to persuade her to sell the cream from her cows: "I'd rather put some colour into my children's faces than put money into the bank" (25). Rosicky and his wife live by a different definition of success than do their neighbors. As Dr. Burleigh reflects, "people as generous and warm-hearted and affectionate as the Rosickys never got ahead much" (15).

When Rosicky dreams of success, it is a dream not of fame and fortune, but of freedom and family.[53] As a young man working in a New York factory, he had realized the emptiness and loneliness of a life based only on the pursuit of wealth. Significantly, he had come to such a realization on Independence Day, and had from that day begun "to save a little money to buy his liberty" (32). Rosicky escapes from a competitive, lonely world that focuses only on getting and spending. Cather uses the image of a tree with "but one tap-root that goes down deep" to describe this man who chooses to plant his tap-root in Nebraska (32). Images of healthy, enduring, growing things in "Neighbour Rosicky" remind us of the healthy community that he nurtures and eventually gives his life for: his family. This is not a tragic sacrifice, however; it is a life-affirming effort, expressing the same hope that Cather expressed in her Nebraska essay, as well as in the closing lines of *O Pioneers!*: "Fortunate country, that is one day to receive hearts like Alexandra's into its bosom, to give them out again in the yellow wheat, in the rustling corn, in the shining eyes of youth."[54] This idea was still with her in 1928, when she wrote "Neighbour Rosicky"—hope in a future community built on the values of an earlier one.

That idea carries over to "Old Mrs. Harris," although in this story we see a greater tension between the dreams of the old and the dreams of the young—somewhat less certainty that the struggle of the older generation to nurture a community embodied in family can either succeed or serve as a form of self-extension. The three women in the story—Old Mrs. Harris, her daughter Victoria, and her granddaughter, Vickie—represent three generations. Cather portrays the struggle of each one in her own way to find a form of emotional survival and self-fulfillment in the late nineteenth-century world of limited opportunities for women. Grandma Harris, raised in the South with its traditional definition of a woman's role, is trying to adjust to her new life with her daughter's family in Skyline, a small, Western town as full of judgmental neighbors as Thea Kronborg's Moonstone. She cannot understand this competitive society where the customs that she feels give dignity to one's life seem valued by so few. She is used to a world in which old people were "tied to the chariot of young life,"[55] a fate with which Mrs. Harris seems comfortable, although Cather's image suggests her own ambivalence about such a life. Mrs. Harris is satisfied with her position in the family, perhaps because it is the only role that she knows; at any rate, she does not want the good–intentioned pity of her neighbor Mrs. Rosen or the critical pseudoconcern of another neighbor, Mrs. Jackson.

Mrs. Harris's definition of success fits neither her daughter's, her granddaughter's, nor that of the people of Skyline. In Mrs. Harris's world, older women accept "unprotestingly, almost gratefully," their role as housekeeper for a younger generation (134). Mrs. Harris has a clear idea of what fulfillment is for a woman, but her daughter Victoria does not share her mother's views. Mrs. Harris sees having children as "the most important thing in the world" for a woman (120); yet Victoria, who certainly loves her children in an easy, natural manner, still feels trapped in this limiting role. Near the end of the story, she finds out that she is expecting her sixth child, and suffers extreme depression: "Life hadn't used her right" (178), she reflects, wishing that she could run away to Tennessee, back to her carefree girlhood. But while her husband can temporarily run away from the problem of too many children and a depressed wife, Victoria is trapped. She locks herself in her bedroom, signifying her inner feeling of imprisonment. Mr. Templeton can easily forget one piece of "property," his wife, and escape to another piece of property, his farm on the North Platte. But Victoria feels chained: "She was sick of it all; sick of dragging this chain of life that never let her rest" (178).

The image of the chain reveals a great deal about Cather's persistent ambivalence toward community, whether that community is family, town, a select group, or even the community that one's traditions represent. Is one chained in a negative, restrictive manner to others—having responsibility for them that limits one's freedom, one's potential for self-actualization? In Victoria's predicament, we see such negative implications (and even in her mother's view of being "tied to the chariot of young life"). In *O Pioneers!*, Marie Shabata feels chained to an unhappy marriage: "Always the same yearning, the same pulling at the chain—until the instinct to live had torn itself . . . until the chain secured a dead woman, who might cautiously be released."[56] But the chain image can connote a sense of belonging, an awareness of responsibility to a community that inspires a person, as it does for Thea Kronborg. The feeling that she is bound to "a long chain of human endeavor" liberates as well as obliges Thea to fulfill her own artistic potential: "The Cliff-Dwellers had lengthened her past. She had older and higher obligations."[57]

Cather also uses the chain image in describing Mrs. Rosen's relationship to the Templeton family in "Old Mrs. Harris." Mrs. Rosen opens her home to the Templetons, especially to young Vickie who loves to borrow books and to read in the quiet parlor, but Mrs. Rosen is not so sure that she wants to accept the responsibility that Vickie subtly places on her. When Vickie displays admiration for Mrs. Rosen's knowledge, the narrator remarks that Vickie "added another link to the chain of responsibility Mrs. Rosen unwillingly bore and tried to shake off—the irritating sense of being somehow responsible for Vickie" (108–9). But Mrs. Rosen is really more willing to take on such a burden than she lets herself believe; she obviously experiences some sense of fulfillment from this "chain of responsibility." Later, when Mrs. Harris overcomes her pride and goes to Mrs. Rosen with the news that Vickie will not be able to attend college, despite having won a highly competitive scholarship, because she still needs three hundred dollars that her parents cannot provide, Mrs. Rosen enthusiastically assumes the responsibility, assuring Mrs. Harris that she and Mr. Rosen will lend Vickie the money.

In using the chain image sometimes to express a restrictive force and at other times a positively binding force, Cather shows her vacillation between optimism and pessimism about community—her recognition of both its burdensome aspects and its self–validating aspects. In her own life, especially in 1931 when she wrote this story, she probably had an even stronger sense of the "chains" that bound her to friends and relatives. She certainly sought out and shaped a community to which she could continue to belong—in maintaining and nurturing old friendships in Nebraska and new ones such as hers with the Menuhin family. But her responsibilities to friends and family must also have weighed on her. She spent a great deal of money helping out members of her Nebraska community who were hard hit by the Depression, even going so far as to suggest selling the movie rights to *The Song of the Lark*. Knowing Cather's aversion to the movie industry, one realizes that even considering such an idea involved sacrifice, evidencing the weight of responsibility that she must have felt to her community. She also serialized *Lucy Gayheart* to raise money for friends who needed help.[58]

Belonging to a tradition and to specific communities whose loyalties and affections she could depend on were important matters for Cather. And yet one senses that she never felt wholly immersed in any of these groups, even her own family, keeping that characteristic distance of the artist which she described in an early essay.[59] Perhaps, just as Louie Marsellus suggests that the professor's literary creations were his own "splendid Spanish-adventurer sons,"[60] Cather held a similar view of her literary creations. Anton Rosicky and Mrs. Harris see in their children and their grandchildren the possibility of their own survival; Cather may have looked forward to a form of survival in her literary "children." Storytelling is a crucial factor in Rosicky's success with convincing Polly and Rudolph to stay on the farm, to continue the tradition that he and Mary have begun. Cather as storyteller was perhaps hoping for the same sort of foothold in the future.

Four years after the publication of these two stories in *Obscure Destinies*, Cather in her famous introduction to her collection of essays, *Not Under Forty*, seems even more narrowly to define her community of choice. She says that her collection is "for the backward, and by one of their number." This might lead one to believe that she was closing herself off from the idea of community in any sense that might connect her with her present world or with future generations. But Cather's title and her preface to that book of essays actually offer a challenging invitation to those under forty to make themselves part of her tradition-reverencing community by finding in the experiences of an older generation—the general topic of these essays—the significance that Cather certainly saw there for young and old. Thus in the preface, Cather perhaps employs reverse psychology, enticing younger readers to discover the broader appeal of her themes for both the "backward" and the "forward-goers." She singles out Thomas Mann for his dual perspective, his "forwardness" as well as his "backwardness." In her essay on Mann, "Joseph and His Brothers," she again suggests her own hopeful purpose as she comments on the Bible characters: "Tradition held them together."[61] Calling the Old Testament the "greatest record of the orphan soul trying to find its kin somewhere in the universe,"[62] Cather stresses her focus on kinship and community.

By celebrating literary and artistic tradition as Cather does in the essays, novels, and stories of these years, she thus continues her project of holding a community together. Cather, when she wrote "Neighbour Rosicky" and "Old Mrs. Harris," was looking both backward and forward, as she did so often—looking backward with reverence and love for her own parents and her own traditions, but looking forward, too, with characteristic hope in the next generation, in those "under forty"—a hope to which an older generation clings. Through the faith in youth that her protagonists display, she proclaims her own membership in that future community. Moments before his death, Rosicky notes optimistically that "Polly would make a fine woman after the foolishness wore off" (69); Mrs. Harris, shortly before her death, reflects that she is "perfectly happy" in the company of her twin grandsons: "They had in common all the realest and truest things" (184). A 1931 photograph of Willa Cather, taken a few days after Christmas, shows her in Red Cloud among a group of children, for whom she had given a party.[63] Looking at this photograph, one feels a similar sense of kinship between Willa Cather and these children, who represent that future in which she certainly must have hoped to have a place. The Willa Cather of the later 1930s, who wrote *Lucy Gayheart* and *Sapphira and the Slave Girl*, seems less certain of that place, yet just as determined, like the "orphan soul," to find her "kin."

5

Facing America's Failed Dream

Recalling the atmosphere in America following the 1929 stock-market crash, Carey Williams, who was practicing law in 1929, remarked: "It was a mood of great bewilderment. No one had anticipated it."[1] For a great number of Americans, a sense of personal failure accompanied those feelings of bewilderment. Sherwood Anderson, like many writers of fiction, turned to documentary writing. Touring the nation to interview Depression victims in 1935, he commented: "The amazing thing to observe is that there is so very little bitterness."[2] People, Anderson noted, assumed personal responsibility for their situation. Studs Terkel interviewed two psychologists who treated patients during the Depression. Their observations echo Anderson's:

> In those days everybody accepted his role, responsibility for his own fate. Everybody, more or less, blamed himself. . . . There was an acceptance that it was your own fault, your own indolence, your lack of ability. . . . People felt burdened by an excess of conscience, an excess of guilt and wrongdoing.[3]

Much of the fiction of the thirties that did not directly address the problems facing a Depression-wracked America still reflected the sense of failure and guilt that pervaded society. Charles Hearn notes: "The great story of the Depression era was the story of failure, not the story of success, and a consistent pattern in the literature of the decade is a searching and many-angled anatomy of failure, hardship, and loss."[4] It should not surprise us, then, that Cather in 1935 published her own "many-angled anatomy of failure, hardship, and loss"—*Lucy Gayheart*—followed in 1940 by *Sapphira and the Slave Girl*, which also explores the darker side of life in America—an earlier America where slavery existed. In *Sapphira*, Cather reflects, besides the mood of failure that is so evident in *Lucy Gayheart*, an added sense of guilt and fear, suggesting a darkening national mood in the latter half of the thirties, when, besides dealing with their domestic crisis, Americans also found it impossible to ignore the international crisis brought on by the rise of fascism.

But just as Cather's earlier optimism had brought her past repudiation of material success to a reshaping of the American Dream, her optimism even during this dark period of American history kept her from presenting in either *Lucy Gayheart* or *Sapphira and the Slave Girl* merely an anatomy of failure, fear, or guilt. She continues in this late fiction to look for meaningful ways to redefine the American Dream, toward a self-fulfillment that goes deeper than what the standard version of that dream, now in ruins in America, had ever been capable of bringing. David Stouck observes that Cather in her fiction of this period seems "no longer driven by the Faustian urge to power through her writing."[5] Cather depicts, too, an America no longer driven by such an urge, realizing more fully than ever the emptiness of that once-revered dream of success.

As historian Robert McElvaine notes in his study of this era, American society was "quickly reject[ing] the acquisitive individualism associated with the business ethic of the twenties." "But," he adds, "[Americans] were slower to see just what they might replace [that ethic] with." Certainly, many looked to "community-oriented values simply because so many were in need."[6] Page Smith writes that the hardship of the Depression produced "a new sense of what we might call national community."[7] Richard Pells concurs: "At no point was there such a distaste for [the concept of a competitive society composed of separate individuals] as in the opening years of the depression."[8]

But despite such apparently eager, unquestioning renunciation of individualism, many clung to that earlier concept, fearful of what its loss might mean. Warren Susman finds "a deep current of pessimism in the Thirties about the possible survival of individualism . . . [because of] the drive for unity and conformity."[9] In Cather's novels of this period, we certainly see such concern for the survival of individualism, as well as a critique of conformity; but we also see the other side of the dilemma, as Susman observes about the nation as a whole: "A sense of some need for a kind of commitment in a world somehow between eras." He points to a "redefinition of the role of the individual" in response to this dilemma, a "search for involvement" exemplified in Dale Carnegie's bestseller, *How to Win Friends and Influence People*, and in psychologist Alfred Adler's popular theories about "fitting in."[10]

The sense of such a changed national outlook resonates in Cather's fiction, as does a certain discomfort with that change. As always, Cather grates against having to "fit in," but her fiction nevertheless reflects an increasing preoccupation with membership in and commitment to a community. Thus, the debate that seemed to resolve itself so smoothly in *Death Comes for the Archbishop* and *Shadows on the Rock*, with their clear message of fulfillment through community, becomes once more a heated exchange in Cather's final two novels.

During the Depression, "events had destroyed much of the [American] dream's basis in reality, but they had not destroyed the extravagant expectations and the habit of dreaming which lay behind the quest for material success."[11] Some writers of this era tried to keep the illusion alive, to encourage self-deception, while others staged a "direct frontal attack on the myth of success."[12] Cather did neither. Staging a frontal attack on the myth of success had never been her strategy, despite her rejection of that myth; nor had she ever valorized self-deception, as Eugene O'Neill does in *The Iceman Cometh* (1940), portraying a group of failures who share "pipe dreams" at Harry Hope's bar. Cather in her fiction does, however, continue to question Americans' "extravagant expectations."

We see this in *Lucy Gayheart*. Cather criticizes the "habit of dreaming" in her portrayal of the indecisive, sentimental Lucy. Yet as much as Cather attacks the dreamer who does not act, she also celebrates, especially in her characterizations of Harry Gordon in *Lucy Gayheart* and Sapphira Colbert in *Sapphira and the Slave Girl*, the individual's strength to endure and to shape his or her own existence under restrictive conditions. Cather still finds it possible for the individual to exercise a marked degree of autonomy, even in the world of crumbling institutions that Americans faced in the thirties, a world that is figured in *Sapphira and the Slave Girl* by an earlier world of crumbling institutions—the world of Southern slavery.

In Cather's last two novels, however, even autonomous individuals seem troubled about their place within a group—whether it be the family, their local community, or in a broader sense, the human community. They seem more certain than ever that, for their own personal fulfillment, they need to secure that place. Such concern in Cather's fiction perhaps reflects the aging artist's need to find a secure place for herself as a literary figure: Cather turned sixty while she was writing *Lucy Gayheart*. But the concern for community in Cather's fiction of the thirties also suggests her awareness of the changing atmosphere in America, although she never goes as far as some of her contemporaries in encouraging a spirit of collectivism or sacrifice to community. Writers such as Steinbeck in *Of Mice and Men* (1937) depict characters who reject "personal ambition and individual self-aggrandizement in favor of companionship and cooperation"[13]. Cather, although interested in the role of companionship and cooperation in her characters' life-decisions, never completely rejects individual ambition. Perhaps she is too much "a child of the nineties"[14]—or too realistic about human nature—to do so.

Lucy Gayheart

Lucy Gayheart aptly reflects the "cult of failure"[15] that existed in Depression America, even though the setting for most of the novel is three decades earlier.[16] Lucy fails at love; she fails, too, in her attempt to break away from her home town of Haverford and to become a professional accompanist. When Clement Sebastian, a famous singer who has taken her under his wing, drowns during a European concert tour, Lucy loses a lover (although it is doubtful that he ever saw Lucy as such) as well as the person who could have provided her the opportunity to achieve her career goals. After Sebastian's death, Lucy returns to Haverford, feeling empty and without a goal or a direction, as many certainly felt after their material failures during the thirties.

Adding to Lucy's emotional hardship at home is the presence of her former lover, Harry Gordon, a successful banker who married out of anger after Lucy refused his marriage proposal and misleadingly intimated that she and Sebastian were lovers. Lucy wants to rekindle a friendship with Harry, but he wants only to punish her. Harry unwittingly has a hand in her accidental death when he encounters Lucy on her way to ice skate at the river, and—despite the bitter cold and her entreaty—refuses to give her a ride. The rejected Lucy, blinded by rage, does not notice that the river has changed its course; thus, she skates in an unsafe location, breaks through the ice, and drowns. Harry Gordon's story comprises Book III of the novel. He must live with his momentary act of disregard and with his painful memories of Lucy.

Although the setting for most of *Lucy Gayheart* is 1902 (with Book III taking place twenty-five years later, on the eve of the Depression), Cather continually comments in this novel on the diminished opportunities that she certainly must have noticed in the America of the 1930s, with its "cramped possibilities and limited rewards,"[17] an America in which "the fundamental unreality of the American Dream" had become glaringly evident.[18] Lucy's observation of "so many sad and discouraged people" as she walks through the streets of Chicago in 1902 could apply equally to Cather's own time.[19] In such a dismal world, what opportunities for self-fulfillment exist? Lucy's inability or unwillingness to shape her own future, even from the limited possibilities available to her, provides an answer. Cather suggests that what Lucy does not do—i.e., define her needs and then exercise some degree of control over her life—is exactly what one must do, despite the "cramped possibilities and limited rewards."[20]

In *Lucy Gayheart*, individual responses to disillusion and defeat reflect each character's degree of success in defining self. Lucy is one of the weakest, least defined of the selves that Cather portrays. Harry Gordon, Clement Sebastian, and even minor characters such as Mrs.

Ramsay have a stronger sense of self than we ever see in Lucy. This does not mean that the stronger characters do not, to some degree, define themselves through others. At one point in the novel, Harry Gordon reflects that, through Lucy, he can "live" the sentimental "part of himself" that otherwise does not emerge (107). The comment is revealing in a general sense for all the characters in *Lucy Gayheart*. Each discovers a part of self that he or she can live, or fulfill, only through another person. For Harry, it is this important sentimental side. Even Sebastian, who so aptly fits the Byronic-hero mold of the lone individual, realizes his emotional dependency on others. He needs the enthusiasm that his audiences provide and the freshness of youth that Lucy represents. Mrs. Ramsay, too, needs others, as we see when she asks Lucy to come play the piano for her.

But Lucy's problem is that she *always* tries to live through other persons; she never develops any degree of autonomy, perhaps partly because, unlike Thea Kronborg, Lucy had no strong, supportive, maternal role model since her mother died when she was young and her older sister, Pauline, is a less-than-nurturing influence.[21] Susan Rosowski sees Lucy losing self when she becomes involved with Sebastian—a Dracula-type, who "grows stronger, fresher, younger, while [Lucy] becomes increasingly passive and dependent."[22] But Lucy's identity problem starts long before she meets Sebastian, and continues long after his death. In Lucy's last conversation with Pauline, only a few hours before Lucy drowns, she reveals an important fact about how she shaped her life goals. Arguing with Pauline, who resents how little concern Lucy shows for the family's financial circumstances as she pursues her studies, Lucy reminds her sister that it was their father's idea that Lucy prepare for a career in music. Unlike Thea Kronborg, Cather's earlier artist who began as a pianist but discovered her real desire—to sing—and struggled to attain that goal even if it meant going against her parents' plans for her, Lucy has been molded by parental expectations, and has remained in that mold. Lucy became the musician "self" that her father decided she should be; she then became the accompanist that both her teacher, Auerbach, and Clement Sebastian decided she should be. When she returns to Haverford, she spends her days in the orchard, avoiding decisions. Her only real act is her half-hearted pursuit of Harry, from which she is fairly easily discouraged. Others continue to make her decisions for her. It is really Mrs. Ramsay who makes the decision for Lucy to "go right on living" (165), encouraging her to return to Chicago. But if Harry Gordon had reconciled with Lucy, she probably would have become whatever self he suggested, completely forgetting about the "sweetheart Life" that awaited her in Chicago (184).

Lucy feels as if she is about to make a monumental decision, "as if she were standing on the edge of something, about to take some plunge or departure" (182); but the only plunge we actually see her take is her fatal, accidental fall through the ice into the river where she drowns. Even though she writes to Auerbach to find out if she can once again work for him in Chicago, that decision is only a vague move forward, with very little clear intent beyond getting away from the "frozen people" of Haverford (198), and "back to a world that strove after excellence" (181). Lucy writes: "The only way for me, is to do the things I used to do and to do them harder" (185). Both her vagueness and her sense of resignation in this statement indicate that she has not really identified her desires.

Lucy's passivity is evident even in the opening scene, as she gazes at the first stars coming out in the night sky while Harry drives her home from a day of ice skating. Here, Lucy gets a brief glimpse of a time-spanning world similar to the one that fired Thea Kronborg's desire in *The Song of the Lark*. Lucy observes one of the stars as "a signal" from another time and place. For Thea Kronborg, such a "signal" from a distant world (the ancient pottery that she finds in Panther Canyon) inspires, offering her a sense of her place in a larger, meaningful community, but Lucy's "signal" serves only to frighten her, making her feel "small and lost" (11–12).[23] Lucy turns away, here and throughout the novel, from any opportunity to define her own needs or desires, preferring to let others direct her life. It is revealing that her death results from her failure to notice that the river has changed its course, for Lucy is never fully aware of her own course. She feels that she is "in pursuit of something . . . [that she can] never catch up with." She thinks that, through Sebastian, she can at last realize the "flashes of promise" that she glimpses (183–84), but since she never defines the promise for herself, she cannot realize her goals, even with the powerful Sebastian's apparent desire to help her. Alfred Kazin observed that many young intellectuals in the thirties "lived between dread and a wild new hope."[24] *Lucy Gayheart*, too, lives such a life of vacillation.

In this state, the only needs that Lucy is able to define for herself are generalized, and ridiculously sentimental: "She wanted flowers and music and enchantment and love" (184). Lucy wants to remain in the isolated, insulated studio world where she works with Sebastian—above the world, like Tom Outland's isolated Blue Mesa—but defeatism engulfs her even at her most hopeful moments. She sees her chance for happiness constantly "threatened": "the way of the world was against it." Lucy has a "fear of falling back into forever" (102), not the longing to be a part of something complete and great that we see in *My Ántonia*, or the desire of Thea Kronborg to be a link in a long chain of human endeavor.25 Lucy wants to become "nothing but one's desire": a vague, unspecified goal that tellingly follows a perhaps unconscious wish to escape self-definition—"to lose one's life and one's body" (102).

Why is the desire to escape or flee so strong in Lucy, when such similar circumstances—a restrictive small town and family life, an opportunity to become part of a different world—fire Thea Kronborg's imagination and drive her to success?26 Is the perspective from which Willa Cather viewed the world in 1933 so much bleaker than it was when she wrote *The Song of the Lark*, some twenty years earlier, that there is no hope for an individual to achieve her desires? Perhaps in this portrait of a nonsurvivor, Cather is expressing a degree of anxiety over "the survival of individualism"—the worry that Susman sees as an undercurrent in the thirties. In 1932, less than a year before she began writing *Lucy Gayheart*, Cather wrote a preface to a new edition of *The Song of the Lark*. In it, we see that the issue of individual struggle and achievement held a key position in her thoughts at this time. She writes that Thea's story "set out to tell of an artist's awakening and struggle; her floundering escape from a smug, domestic, self-satisfied provincial world of utter ignorance."27 Thea Kronborg escapes and defines herself; in *Lucy Gayheart*, Cather tells the other side of Thea's story, the story that she found perhaps more realistic, or at least more threatening, in the atmosphere of "constant dread"28 that characterized the 1930s.

"I gave up my illusions [during the Depression]," one man remarked. "No more Horatio Alger."29 But *Lucy Gayheart* prefers to run away rather than face disillusion. Throughout the book, Lucy is "running away" (231), as the footprints that the young Lucy left in the wet cement in front of her home signify, and as does the aria that Lucy plays at her first audition, *Vision fugitive*.30 Lucy continually flees from any real vision of herself, just as she hides behind a pillar while she watches Sebastian perform at the music hall (38). She is "not ambitious," as Auerbach tells Sebastian; this trait is here a sign of Lucy's fear, not an indication of a strong individual making clear choices, as it is in Cather's earlier portrayal of Lena Lingard in *My Ántonia*.

Lucy seems always out of control of her life, just as she is when the ice begins to crack under her feet. Even when a young Lucy, in love with Sebastian, asserts herself enough to avoid marriage to Harry, her choice of words shows the passive role into which she repeatedly places herself. She tells Harry that her "life is tied up with someone else" (110). Because she feels so out of control, Lucy continually gives up. When Sebastian asks the auditioning Lucy to play *Die Winterreise*, which she has already heard his accompanist, Mockford, play skillfully, she prefaces her performance with a discouraged remark about her inability to match Mockford's skill. When Sebastian must leave her to go to Europe, even though he provides the opportunity for her to continue working in his studio and to meet him in New York later that year, she feels already that her opportunities are over ("slipping away") and that she has "no power to struggle" (118). Once she has lied to Harry about her relationship with Sebastian, she gives up on ever righting that wrong, resigning herself to the fact that she has lost Harry's friendship. Lucy does not have the spirit of an Alexandra Bergson, an Ántonia Shimerda, or a Marian Forrester—for "life on any terms." Perhaps this is Cather's reflection on a prevalent attitude among Americans, many of whom had lost their drive for "life on any terms" in such a dismal world. Many, like Lucy, seemed resigned to the fact that "some people got very little" (117).

Cather implies that, to a large extent, it is Lucy's inability to use the past in the positive way that Lasch suggests—"to enrich the present and to face what comes with good cheer"[31]—that traps her in failure. This is the same problem that Cather perhaps saw crippling many Americans during the Depression. Lucy does not seem capable of learning from her past. She feels that "she snatched what she could, from the present and the past" (61), but she does not do so with any purpose toward the future—only with a fear that it would all certainly end soon, as it does for Lucy even before her death, leaving her unfulfilled, feeling that "an enormous emptiness had opened on all sides of her" (116). Noting the tendency in the thirties to forget the past, Kazin recalls that writers often found liberation in having "nothing to go back to"—"no tradition to hold them down."[32] For a traditionalist such as Cather, however, it became more important to find a place for the past, for enduring values and traditions, in one's present life, as that present became a more unstable, threatening place. Pells notes that for many writers of this era such respect for the past meant more specifically a "return to the older, more traditional values of individualism."[33] Although Cather focuses more fully on such a return in *Sapphira and the Slave Girl*, her concerns about the survival of the individual surface repeatedly in *Lucy Gayheart*.

In Lucy's sister, Pauline, Cather comments both compassionately and critically on the need to conform or "fit in," which she saw being taken to neurotic extremes in the America of the 1930s, thus threatening the survival of the individual. Pauline is completely immersed in community, but feels just as empty as her passive sister. Where Lucy is too weak ever to develop an autonomous self, Pauline is submerged in community, struggling constantly to be everything that Haverford expects her to be. She is other-centered in an all-consuming way. Left with the responsibility of raising young Lucy when their mother dies, Pauline lives through Lucy, but continually finds herself competing with Lucy for community praise. She is torn between her motherly love and loyalty to what is "Gayheart" in Lucy (167), and her own need for a fulfilling, individual existence. What she resents about Lucy is what she sees as "most individual," perhaps because she herself has trouble being "individual." Pauline is a divided person like so many of Cather's characters— "always walking behind herself" (168). She tries to "fit in" in Haverford, which is no easy task with an eccentric father and a sister who has returned from Chicago under mysterious circumstances. Pauline's last verbal exchange is an argument with Lucy over responsibility, ending with Pauline's good–intentioned though half-hearted effort to follow her angered sister down the street in order to give her a shawl to protect her from the cold weather. This scene characterizes the two forces struggling within Pauline: sisterly resentment and maternal love—both hinging on her relationship to Lucy. Pauline so defines herself through Lucy that after Lucy's death, Pauline disappears from the narrative, except for brief, distanced references to her death.[34]

Reflecting a Depression atmosphere where too many barriers to fulfillment exist, Cather gives us no person in *Lucy Gayheart* who achieves the self-realization that so many of her earlier characters do; but the characters in *Lucy Gayheart* who do attain a degree of fulfillment manage to do so because they are able either to break free of the need to conform, or are able to learn from the past—as neither Lucy nor Pauline can do—and as Cather seems to have been continually trying to do in formulating her new definition of the American Dream. Clement Sebastian, in Lucy's mind, is a troubled artist. She perceives that he is sad, but he corrects her appraisal, explaining that all people have "disappointments" (85). Like Harry Gordon at the end of the novel, Sebastian apparently has learned to bear disappointments instead of running from them; he finds the strength to bear them in supportive communities. Sebastian manages always to find loyal people to serve as a counterweight to his disappointments. When he is touring across the United States, he enjoys the friendly people from choral societies with whom he works (68). In Lucy, he finds emotional support; he is especially attracted to her because of her "chivalrous loyalty" (80). Sebastian finds solace, too, in the larger community of humankind to which he feels connected through time by religion and tradition: "He had unclouded faith in the old and lovely dreams of man" (87).

Although Lucy does not recognize it, Sebastian has a realistic attitude about his own success as an artist. Lucy thinks that he lacks regard for his fame and fortune: "You don't value it enough, truly you don't!" (85). But Sebastian's perspective on success has been shaped by his ability to learn from his experience, and to adjust his attitude accordingly. When he reads of an old friend's death, he gives up his childish desire to recapture his youth and finally faces himself truthfully and courageously. Realizing that he has few friends, no real home, no family, and not even a country to call his own, Sebastian observes: "Surely a man couldn't congratulate himself upon a career which had led to such results" (77–78).[35] Coming to terms with what has happened to his life in his struggle for personal achievement, he begins actively to seek Lucy's companionship, and becomes other-centered enough to take part in her career development. When he leaves Lucy, his talk is of their future together, of the "many things he would like to show her" on his return (127).

Sebastian learns to redefine success. He changes, although his abrupt death does not allow us to see fully his development. Harry Gordon, whose story this novel is as much as it is Lucy's, learns the most from experience.[36] Harry learns that he lives in a world of chance, random accident, a world that he cannot control—a lesson that more and more Americans were learning after a world war and a nationwide economic depression. Harry had thought that he could control time, that he could "punish" Lucy for awhile, yet eventually reconcile with her. When she drowns accidentally, he realizes how foolish such an idea was. He was too patient in putting off his reconciliation with her, just as he was too impatient in rushing into marriage with another woman when Lucy angered him.

But Harry, as haunted as he is by Lucy's death, does not wallow in despair. By becoming an active, community-focused man, he brings meaning to his life. Harry is, of course, community-oriented by nature of his job as town banker; but he does not really let himself become a concerned community member until after Lucy's death. Harry realizes that he is serving a "life sentence" (221) of guilt for his unintentional part in Lucy's death, but her death forces him to look squarely at himself, as Sebastian does after his friend's death. In doing so, Harry begins "to understand [his life] a little better" (214).

In fact, we are assured that Harry understands "a little better" both himself and his responsibilities to his community. We see this in his generous gift of the Gayheart house (ownership of which has gone to Harry's bank after Mr. Gayheart's death) to his employee, Milton Chase (228); we see it, too, in his humane treatment of a local farmer, Nick Wakefield, when the bank has to foreclose on his farm (212–13). Instead of living through Lucy, as he had once hoped in a rather shallow sense to do, or through community, as Pauline tries too diligently to do, Harry has learned to accept himself and his life—a life in which suffering is a reality, but is balanced by a degree of gratification. In the final lines, Cather makes this clear and at the same time strikes a note of affirmation for the small town, a community with which she displays a continuing love-hate relationship in her fiction. Harry accepts the fact that he will remain in Haverford, and that his home town is simply "the place where he had disappointments and had learned to bear them" (231).[37]

Learning to bear disappointments is an inescapable—even a constructive—part of life, Cather reminds us, especially in a world where "the old beliefs of men had been shattered" (221). This is Harry Gordon's world of 1927 and Willa Cather's world of the thirties. But bearing disappointments with the help of others is better, as Harry also realizes. He ponders how much "easier" things would have been after Lucy's death if he had been able to share with someone the story of his last encounter with her. Cather thus continues to move away from romantic notions of the lone individual. Blanche Gelfant notes that "kindness is the single value that Willa Cather did not blot out" in *Lucy Gayheart*, seeing in the novel a "plea for compassion" and an "insistence upon the characters' need for mutual support."[38] In analyzing the effects of the Depression on American society, Robert McElvaine sees this crisis "as having effected a 'feminization' of American society. The self-centered, aggressive, competitive, 'male' ethic of the 1920's was discredited," replaced by what he terms "female" values: "cooperation and compassion."[39] These are the values that Harry Gordon adopts and the values that Willa Cather stresses in *Lucy Gayheart*.

Perhaps reflecting her own sense of such values as "female," Cather foregrounds them in her portrayal of Mrs. Ramsay in the novel. As the widow of one of Haverford's founders, Mrs. Ramsay holds a key position among the townspeople. Despite her minor role in the novel, her importance is suggested by Cather's strategic introduction of this character at the beginning of Book II, immediately following the crisis of Sebastian's death which concludes Book I. Mrs. Ramsay is instrumental in shaking Lucy out of her grief and in pointing her toward some goal, if only a vague, generalized one. But beyond that role in the plot, Mrs. Ramsay holds a crucial thematic role in *Lucy Gayheart*. She, like the other characters who achieve some degree of personal success, has changed. Through her daughter's observations, we learn that Mrs. Ramsay has not always been the concerned person whom we meet in Book II, but has "softened with time" (144). Even more telling is the remark that she has become "more interested in other people" (144).[40] Mrs. Ramsay's daughter, observing her mother's sympathy for Lucy, reflects that it is not the "quick, passionate sympathy" that she used to see in her mother, but is "more like the Divine compassion" (146–47). Cather may be coming face to face here with her own aging process, both her fears about it and her optimistic appraisal of the changes she saw (or hoped for) in her own attitudes. Mrs. Ramsay, with "divine compassion," takes responsibility for Lucy. She insists that Lucy come to visit, and she then advises her to "go right on living," despite the fact that "sometimes people disappoint us, and sometimes we disappoint ourselves" (165).

Cather here uses the same word that she uses when Sebastian reassures Lucy that he is not really a sad person ("everyone has disappointments"), and that she again uses at the end of the novel, when Harry Gordon decides that one's home town is a good place to be ("the place where he had disappointments and learned to bear them"). Clement Sebastian's death is certainly more than a disappointment, but Lucy has redefined her whole life through that event. Not aware of this larger tragedy in Lucy's life, Mrs. Ramsay encourages her to rescue the happiness that she can from her year in Chicago. She reminds Lucy to put the sadness of that year—whatever it might be—in a temporal perspective: "Don't let a backward spring discourage you" (165). This may also be Cather's optimistic advice to America, suffering its own "backward spring." Cather seems unwilling to turn her face away from that possibility of fulfillment which she always sees on the horizon—even in an era when such possibility, once magnified like her famous image of the plow in *My Ántonia*, "heroic in size" against the sun, had (like that image) suddenly diminished.

"Nobody ever recognizes a period until it has gone by," a character remarks in Cather's story, "The Old Beauty," written a few years after she wrote *Lucy Gayheart*.[41] But just as Cather recognized and addressed in her earlier fiction the problems of a society focused on a dream of success that had become synonymous with acquisitive individualism, she recognizes in this later fiction the needs and anxieties of a society that saw that dream shatter. Cather had earlier redefined success to include a sense of community as both gratifying and fulfilling to the individual. She tries in her later fiction to express continued faith in that revised dream, a faith now reinforced by a national focus on community.

But Cather tries at the same time in this later fiction to highlight the individual. It is an eventual awareness of each person's uniqueness that makes characters such as Mrs. Ramsay and Harry Gordon capable of responding to others in ways that will both create and perpetuate a strong, healthy community. Cather closes *Lucy Gayheart* with an appropriate symbol and recognition of individual uniqueness: Harry notices Lucy's three footprints, made years ago in the wet cement of the sidewalk. They serve as a vivid reminder of this unique person. Harry Gordon, in fact, has a stronger sense of Lucy as individual than she herself ever has. As a young man, he admits to himself that there is "nobody like her" (21). After her death, he reflects that she is the "one face, one figure" in his past that stands out (223). When Harry, having learned to bear disappointments and to become an involved, caring member of his community, sees again these footprints in the final pages of the novel, they serve as a source of pleasant reflection on the past, not a source of regret or remorse. The narrator remarks, in fact, that Harry is "not a man haunted by remorse" (224).

Cather is no more interested in remorse than she is in counterproductive nostalgia. Remorse, like nostalgia, only mires one in the past, as it does for "The Old Beauty," who "broods on the things she might have done for her friends and didn't."[42] Harry Gordon does not brood, but does change (as Mrs. Ramsay did), becoming more "interested" in others. Thus, a novel that reflects the sense of failure so prevalent in Depression America is still, in typical Cather manner, a novel of hope. "We do not want cynicism," Sherwood Anderson insists in the introduction to *Puzzled America*. "We want belief. Can we find it in one another . . . ? There is a willingness to believe, a hunger for belief, a determination to believe."[43] Cather throughout *Lucy Gayheart* exhibits that determination to believe which still survived in an America suffering both economically and emotionally. Her novel asks, as Anderson asks, "Can we find [belief] in one another?" But the novel stops short of affirming community wholeheartedly; instead, it displays a persistent preoccupation with "one another" as a possible source of belief, coupled with a shaky but insistent focus on self apart from that community.

Sapphira and the Slave Girl

The same preoccupation with commitment to community that we see in *Lucy Gayheart* continues in Cather's final novel, but her move toward community is still a guarded one, as if the idea is nagging at her more than settling in. Always, Cather remains much more cautious in her approach to community than most writers of the thirties, who turned with enthusiasm (short-lived for some) toward more radical political doctrines—especially socialism and Marxism—in their commitment to and fascination with the idea of community, and whose fiction became a vehicle for such political expressions.[44] For Cather, living in an America gone fanatic on collectivism, individual achievement and self-fulfillment remain important themes. Harry Gordon learns to consider others, but he is not ascetic; he "enjoys his prosperity."[45] Sapphira Colbert, the heroine of Cather's last novel, provides even stronger proof of Cather's continued celebration of individual achievement. In this novel, Cather continues to highlight the tension between dedication to community and self-gratification, a tension that she seems, at last, to prefer to any resolution.

In one respect, Cather in *Sapphira* is still conducting her own "many-angled anatomy of failure, hardship, and loss." But in this novel, Cather depicts, too, what Warren Susman identifies as "an overwhelming sense of shame" during the Depression. He notes in popular radio programs of this time period "a kind of ritual humiliation of the hero . . . from which the hero ultimately emerges with some kind of triumph, even though it be a minor one."[46] This is the sort of hero that Cather creates in Sapphira Colbert, one who suffers loss, shame, and humiliation but "ultimately emerges with some kind of triumph." In *Sapphira*, Willa Cather thus not only reflects obliquely upon the darker issues of her own era, but moves past that darkness in what might seem a surprising swing toward optimism at the end of a "disturbing" novel.[47] But such a final note of affirmation is, as we have seen, more characteristic than it is surprising in Willa Cather's novels.

The shame of slavery provides the focal point for the theme of shame and guilt in *Sapphira and the Slave Girl*. Sapphira's daughter, Rachel Blake, openly denounces slavery. People in Back Creek generally do not own slaves and disapprove of slavery. But Henry Colbert, although he feels guilty about owning slaves (which he has acquired through his marriage to Sapphira), is too passive to do anything about the situation, even though he has the legal right to free his wife's slaves. Henry tries to assuage his guilt by rationalizing that all humans are "in bonds."[48] Cather's portrait of a troubled Henry Colbert, not sure of his moral stand on slavery, suggests not only the general shame of the Depression era but perhaps her own anxieties about her racial views.[49] Such anxieties may have intensified as Cather became aware of increased racial tensions in America during the Depression. "Black people suffered a disproportionate share of the burden [of unemployment]" at this time. Many white Americans, now out of work, resented blacks who did hold jobs; thus, racial violence increased:

> The number of lynchings in the United States rose from eight in 1932 to twenty-eight, fifteen, and twenty in the three succeeding years. A Depression-era study showed a positive correlation between the number of lynchings in the Deep South and economic distress.[50]

Writer Nathan Asch, in his account of a bus trip across America in 1936, recalls his disturbing encounter with a racist America that he, not unlike many other Americans, would have preferred to deny the existence of—or at least to ignore: "What I wanted to see were Southern whites and negroes organized together." Instead, Asch found racial violence: "They were hanging negroes"; "a negro preacher had disappeared and . . . his body had been found by the side of a creek, filled with bullets and the testicles cut off."[51]

Henry is not the only character who suffers guilt pangs in *Sapphira and the Slave Girl*. Sapphira, the real "master" of the Colbert household, as her husband happily confirms (50), makes a concerted effort always to show that she is confident about her attitudes and in control of every situation. Still, she is plagued by guilt, humiliation, and even self-doubt. Cather highlights this by sharply contrasting the image of the strong, self-possessed Sapphira with that of the crippled, frustrated Sapphira. When the book opens, we first see the mistress of the house at the breakfast table, smoothly orchestrating the serving of the meal and cheerfully but persistently countering Henry's unwillingness to sell the slave Nancy, a suggestion that Sapphira has made because she is beginning to feel out of control of that situation: she is growing increasingly jealous of her husband's attention to Nancy. When Henry insists that he will never sign to sell Nancy, Sapphira only remarks to herself: "Then we must find some other way" (9). Seemingly unruffled by her confrontation with her husband, Sapphira, having finished her breakfast and her conversation, rings for her servant. Only at this point do we realize that Sapphira is crippled, confined to a wheelchair because her feet and ankles are swollen and deformed by dropsy. Later, we discover a further humiliation that she has suffered: she has married a man who is socially "no match" for her, and has therefore exiled herself to Back Creek (the name itself suggests a social move backwards)—a far enough distance from her family that she can return "without embarrassment" for visits (25, 27). In addition, Sapphira suffers the humiliation of her husband's physical separation from her, for Henry actually lives and sleeps at the mill house, joining his wife only for visits and for some meals.

Sapphira's humiliation and embarrassment perhaps reflect the mood of many Depression victims, but she does not fall into the role of passive victim as *Lucy Gayheart* does. Sapphira is so determined to keep her husband away from Nancy, who faithfully attends him at the mill house, that she desperately conceives a plan: she invites her nephew, Martin Colbert, a known rake, for an extended visit, providing him with many opportunities to rape Nancy. But even in this ingenious, devious plan, Sapphira is frustrated and humiliated. Rachel hears of Nancy's danger and arranges for the girl's escape to Canada. As Rachel works out this plan, she regrets what such an outwitting of her mother will mean. Reflecting on her mother's loss of physical beauty and ability, Rachel feels "sorry to have brought another humiliation to one who had already lost so much" (246).

Sapphira is greatly mortified by her daughter's act of rebellion as well as her husband's passive assistance (Henry leaves his coat, with money in the pocket, hanging where Rachel can reach it). But Sapphira soon realizes how minimal is the pain of hurt pride when she suffers the loss of her grandchild, a loss for which she partly blames herself. Not long after an angry Sapphira banishes Rachel and her two daughters from the Colbert home, one of the girls, Betty, dies from diphtheria. Rachel had once told the frightened Nancy that everyone experiences fear and depression, "but we come right again, and bear our lot" (216). Sapphira, through the loss of her grandchild, comes "right again," realizing that false pride has clouded her judgment. A reformed Sapphira extends her love and kindness once more to her daughter and her surviving granddaughter; by mending her familial community, she thus experiences final triumph.

Besides the national shame of slavery in *Sapphira and the Slave Girl*, the situation of the poor whites in the hills near Back Creek serves in the novel as a source of American shame, a negative reflection on the American Dream, underscoring the inequality of opportunity that has been a more typical part of our tradition than the rags-to-riches story. The cheerful but impoverished Mrs. Ringer, who embodies the desire for "life on any terms" that Cather depicted in Marian Forrester, reminds us in her conversation with Rachel Blake that the American Dream was never equally open to all—neither in the 1856 setting of the novel nor certainly during the 1930s when Cather was writing *Sapphira and the Slave Girl*. Although Mrs. Ringer resolutely tells Rachel, "I kin bear anything," she also tells her: "I wisht I could a-had your chance" (118, 126), for Rachel has had, through her privileged birth, the opportunity for education that was denied a poverty-stricken, lower-class Mrs. Ringer. Mrs. Ringer may live in America, the land of opportunity, but she is in many ways as incapable of exercising control over her life as are the slaves in this novel.

The Depression, perhaps more than any period in American history, made people aware of the economic inequities that had existed in America. McElvaine points out that during this period, "many in the middle class [began] to identify with those below them." He notes that one man wrote to President Roosevelt in 1934, expressing a view that more and more people were sharing: "I realize that in the United States, there is enough for all, but on account of selfishness and greed, some are getting, while others are not."[52] While this is a more embittered approach than Mrs. Ringer's to Rachel Blake, both statements express a similar awareness of inequality; both point a finger of shame at a nation that professes to offer an equal dream to all. That shame was part of the general spirit of the thirties.

In Cather's epilogue, we find perhaps her most obvious reflections on the defeat and disillusionment so prevalent in Depression America, but we also find here her characteristic note of final affirmation. She describes attitudes in Back Creek after the Civil War: "The Rebel soldiers who came back were tired, discouraged, but not humiliated or embittered by failure" (276). In this commentary, placed strategically before Nancy's triumphant return to the Colbert estate, Cather implies that, just as the "Back Creek boys" now look forward to a life of rebuilding ("Now they could mend the barn roof where it leaked, help the old woman with her garden, and keep the wood-pile high" [276]), Americans in 1938 should start thinking about the future in a positive manner. This seems perhaps too optimistic an outlook, since the Nazi threat loomed larger in Europe—a situation of which Cather was well aware, and one that greatly troubled her[53]—and since the national economy, which had begun to show signs of recovery under the New Deal in 1935 and 1936, experienced another recession between 1937 and 1938, when Cather began writing *Sapphira*.

But in her optimism at the end of *Sapphira and the Slave Girl*, we again see Cather expressing what Lasch sees as a long-standing tradition in America (and what he prescribes for America today): a "vigorous form of hope, which trusts life without denying its tragic character."[54] It is the same hope that Till expresses in her description of Sapphira's last hours. The weak but cheerful Sapphira gazes out across the snow-covered fields; seeing the reflection of the candlelit tea table in the window, Till imagines another tea table outside, with "fine folks" from Sapphira's girlhood at Chestnut Hill, waiting for Sapphira to go away with them (294). This death scene of forgiveness and membership in a community contrasts sharply with Myra Henshawe's staged scene of forgiveness as she gazes out at the ocean. Like Till, we sense that Sapphira has truly attained forgiveness, and in mending her own family has found fulfillment through community, as her imagined reunion with her Chestnut Hill community, the people from whom she has so long been exiled, signifies.[55] Also suggesting a "vigorous form of hope" is Henry Colbert's final observation about his wife's tenacity, which could serve equally well to express Cather's respect for a nation that was struggling admirably to overcome the physical and psychological hardships of the Depression: "He had always been proud of her. When she was young, she was fearless and independent. . . . After she was old and ill, she never lowered her flag" (268).

Interestingly, Cather turns to a sense of fulfillment through community at the end of a novel that has alternately celebrated and criticized the self-possessed, solitary individual, in the person of Sapphira Colbert. It is as if Cather is continuing her ongoing debate with herself about the value of such a spirit of individualism in a changing America, unsure that such self-reliance and self-focus is possible or even desirable anymore, yet unwilling to let go completely of the individualism that she had always prized so highly. In her earliest description of Sapphira Colbert, Cather implies that Sapphira's "placid self-esteem" is a negative trait (15); Cather later remarks in a tone of mild but more definite condemnation, that Sapphira "though often generous . . . thought of other people only in their relation to herself" (220). But Cather does not place a completely negative value judgment on such self-centeredness, for she ultimately represents Sapphira's autonomy of spirit as admirable. Henry at length realizes that Sapphira's self-possession, her "composure, which he had sometimes called heart-lessness" was really "strength." He admires her ability always to be "mistress of the situation and of herself" (268).

Still, Cather recognizes in this novel the need to have a place, to feel connected to others in the bonds of friendship and community. Repeated references to that need appear in *Sapphira and the Slave Girl*. Sapphira, aging and lonely, regrets her earlier coldness toward her own father when he was in a similar condition: "She wished she had been kinder to him. . . . There was something he wanted more than he wanted clean linen" (104 –5). Mrs. Ringer sends for Rachel Blake, ostensibly to have her injured foot treated, but Rachel understands that the old woman is really lonely (118). With the postmistress, Mrs. Bywaters, Rachel is "drawn together by deep convictions they had in common" (145). The Colbert slaves value the community to which they belong, and fear anything that might disrupt it. Samson begs Henry Colbert not to give him his freedom; Till, who had been taught by her mistress to "value her place," feels more loyalty to that original community than she does to her daughter, Nancy: "Till had been a Dodderidge [Sapphira's maiden name] before ever she was Nancy's mother" (219). Nancy's greatest fear when she escapes is the loss of her community: "I can't go off amongst strangers. . . . I can't bear to belong nowheres!" (237). Even the immoral, unseemly Martin Colbert understands and respects the value of friends, of membership in a validating, supportive community. When he tells his cousin Rachel about a visit that he made to Washington, D.C., where he had met some of her husband's former acquaintances, he remarks with sincerity that few people "will leave friends who'll be missing us after six or seven years" (173).

The epilogue underscores this theme, with its perspective from the eyes of a five-year-old child, looking back with love and appreciation on the community to which she felt such nurturing ties. Recalling the day of Nancy's reunion with her mother, the child-narrator notes her own confinement to bed with a cold, but also notes that she "was not alone in the room. Two others were there to keep me company" (280). Till even arranges for the reunion to take place upstairs, in the child's sickroom, so that the child can feel wholly included in this community event. In the pages that follow, the child observes and participates in a close-knit community of women, of whom Till is the principal bearer of traditions. The narrator recalls the time spent at Till's cabin, hearing "the old stories" and viewing "Till's keepsakes and treasures" (291)—those tangible and intangible things which bind a community.

Although *Sapphira and the Slave Girl* closes with a picture of a child securely enclosed within a caring, tradition-reverencing community,[56] and with a picture of the strong-willed Sapphira enclosed within an imaginary but believable community, Cather by no means fully resolves the issue of self-fulfillment in favor of community by the conclusion of this novel. She does, however, in writing such a novel at this time, perhaps acknowledge her own commitment to her American community. *Sapphira and the Slave Girl* furnished Depression-weary, war-threatened Americans with what many reviewers saw as a gift: a story that let Americans purge themselves of guilt and shame to emerge "with some kind of triumph."[57] Dorothy Canfield Fisher, in a December 1940 review of *Sapphira and the Slave Girl*, wrote of the "consoling values" that Cather offered to "readers aching with shame."[58] In another review, Morton Zabel praised her for "defining the spiritual forces that have gone into the making of our culture," and doing so "at a moment when our spiritual riches, at best not too plentiful, are put to every possible test of confusion and debasement."[59] For Cather, it would seem that those spiritual riches included both a highly valued sense of individuality and a perhaps more reluctantly acknowledged but just as evident sense of community.

6
"Creative Tension"

In the last few years of her life, Willa Cather looked back, both in her letters and in her fiction, on her accomplishments as well as on the persistent frustrations and anxieties in her life. As she did so, she continued to clarify the unique version of the American Dream that she had lived and had explored in her fiction. Critic Fanny Butcher, who knew Cather for thirty-five years, remarked that Cather seemed "wholly fulfilled within herself";[1] Cather by age seventy would have probably agreed. Only two years before her death, she wrote to her long-time friend Zoe Akins that she had gotten from life much of what she wanted and had also been able to escape, for the most part, what she strongly did not want—too much money, too much publicity, too many people to meet.[2] In this comment, Cather seems to repudiate more emphatically than ever the standard American Dream of fame and fortune, yet she continued in her final writing to cling to its basic philosophical valorization of individual achievement while rejecting its material trappings.

Recognition from a community and membership in a community seem also to have mattered more than ever to Cather in her final years.[3] But at the same time, she seems even more acutely aware of, and more intent on expressing, the need for separateness from group if one's individuality is to survive. This is, of course, the dilemma that Cather addressed over and over again, from various angles, throughout her life. How could one achieve that happiness which Jim Burden describes, of being "dissolved into something complete and great," without dissolving one's unique, autonomous self? It is the same problem that Cather addresses directly in her essay on Katherine Mansfield (1925), discussing the "double life" that people lead—"the group life . . . and, underneath, another—secret and passionate and intense—which is the real life." Referring in that essay to the individual's place in the family, Cather is also referring, certainly, to the individual's place in the broader family of humanity: "Every individual . . . is clinging passionately to his individual soul, is in terror of losing it in the general family flavour."[4]

As we have seen, a version of this dilemma continued to trouble many Americans through the first half of the twentieth century. In *America Now*, a collection of essays published in 1938, John Chamberlain identified as "the central problem of the thirties," "the relation of the individual to the mass."[5] At the same time that Cather was exploring in her Mansfield essay the "terror" of losing one's individual soul, John Dewey was encouraging Americans to break down the boundaries that individualism can create: "To gain an integrated individuality, each of us needs to cultivate his own garden. But there is no fence about this garden. . . . Our garden is the world." Citing Emerson, Dewey reminded Americans that interaction with "the society of your contemporaries" was "the only means by which the possibilities of individuality can be realized."[6] A decade later, Dewey reiterated even more strongly the role of community for individualistic Americans: "Cooperation . . . is as much a part of the democratic ideal as is personal initiative."[7] But could individualism and a sense of community realistically coexist in a nation so accustomed to viewing competition rather than cooperation as the road to success? Most writers of the 1930s felt hopeful about "a new American dream [shaped] out of a synthesis of the new sense of communalism and the traditional American belief in personal freedom, equality, and the dignity of the individual."[8]

Cather, as we have seen, was feeling her way toward such a definition long before the thirties, but always with a keen awareness of the realistic, perhaps necessary, tension between community and individual. Thus, she did not seem as determined as many of her contemporaries to find a balance or a synthesis between those two poles. Hemingway in *For Whom the Bell Tolls* (1941) almost submerges the individual in community. His hero, Robert Jordan, dies for the cause through which he comes to define himself, helping Republican forces in the Spanish Civil War. Steinbeck's Jim Nolan (*In Dubious Battle*, 1936) also submerges himself in a group cause for which he gives his life, fighting for the rights of migrant farm workers in California. Sherwood Anderson, self-conscious about his responsibility to community, remarked in 1932: "If [in order to have a healthy society] . . . we of the so-called artist class have to be submerged, let us be submerged."[9] But, as Richard Pells notes, such enthusiasm for community often ended, not in a balance or a synthesis of self and community, but in the death of individuality. For many of those who "inexorably moved from rebellion to 'responsibility'" in the 1930s, Pells observes, "the search for community slowly became a celebration of conformity." In the process, the "necessary and creative tension between . . . self and society was irrevocably shattered."[10]

For Cather, that tension was never shattered. It resonates even in her later fiction, suggesting that she recognized this tension between self and community as both "necessary and creative." Creative tension seems to have become the key to Cather's redefined American Dream, making possible a sense of individual fulfillment that hinges on community—not in the nineteenth-century view of stewardship or a moral imperative, but in a symbiotic manner. Robert Bellah and coauthors see in present-day American society the same pull of two forces that Cather's fiction acknowledges: "However much Americans extol the autonomy and self-reliance of the individual, they do not imagine that a good life can be lived alone." In interviewing people across America, Bellah and his colleagues found a "deep desire for autonomy and self-realization combined with an equally deep conviction that life has no meaning unless shared with others in the context of community." While Bellah and coauthors examine the aspects of our culture that enable "the individual to think of commitments . . . as enhancements of the sense of individual well-being rather than moral imperatives," they also admit that a synthesis of self and community is not so easy, that "inner tensions" between self and community take a toll, adding up to "a classic case of ambivalence."[11] Cather would most likely see such ambivalence as healthy—a necessary component of her redefined American Dream.

Keeping in mind Cather's recognition of the healthy tension that exists between self and community, I want to look closely at her two final short stories, "Before Breakfast," written during the summer of 1944, and "The Best Years," written during the summer of 1945.[12] If we view them as companion pieces, they offer a fitting final statement from Cather on the balance between self and community that remains, happily, a tug-of-war.[13] We have already looked briefly at Cather's celebration of familial love in "The Best Years" (see chap. 1). The story, written as a gift for her brother Roscoe, focuses on other-centeredness and on feeling "complete and absolute"[14] as part of a group—whether that group is family or merely others to whom one feels a sense of responsibility, as it is for Superintendent Evangeline Knightly. The other-centered Miss Knightly goes out of her way to give young, homesick Lesley Ferguesson a weekend visit with her family. Lesley, too, is other-centered, both in her role as older sister and in her role as teacher. She spends her hard-earned money to buy her brother a winter coat, even though doing so means that she cannot afford to live as comfort-

ably; she guides her class to safety when a blizzard strikes, despite the
fatal risk that she takes in doing so.

Lesley is, in fact, perhaps too other-centered, as her premature death
suggests. Cather does not, then, yield in this final story to a view of
self-sacrifice as the preferred route to personal fulfillment. To see her
redefined American Dream in "The Best Years," we need to look
beyond Lesley, to her father. James Ferguesson is a nonconformist, too
"unconventional" to be readily accepted in the small community of
MacAlpin (101). He is sincerely dedicated to Populism as a political
belief, to "experimental" farming as a career, and to "an idea" as the
most important "crop" on his farm (103–4).[15] His neighbors good-
naturedly poke fun at him for his strange ways, but James Ferguesson
achieves a rich American Dream, guarding and nurturing his own individuality while still managing to provide adequately for his family's
physical needs—and to provide more than adequately, by his example,
for their inner growth. Ferguesson spends time alone every day, thinking. Future-oriented, he sees "the great change that was coming for the
benefit of all mankind" (103), just as the equally optimistic and equally misunderstood Louie Marsellus in *The Professor's House* looks forward to "a period of utter, of fantastic unreasonableness, which will be
the beginning of a great happiness for us all."[16] Ferguesson, like Louie,
is an "idealist"—"never afraid of ridicule" (103–4). Robert Cherney
sees in this characterization Cather's criticism of Populism, but while
that may be Cather's lighthearted purpose here, the attention that she
gives to James Ferguesson in this story, along with her overriding affirmation of family solidarity, suggest a more serious purpose.[17] James
Ferguesson, as much as he may puzzle and sometimes even frustrate
his wife and children, serves as Cather's testimonial to a healthy sense
of individuality that strains against a commitment to community. He
represents the "creative tension" between self and community that
Cather apparently comes to accept as fundamental to a meaningful
American Dream. Ferguesson's family "ha[s] a deep respect for him"
(100). That the narrow-minded residents of MacAlpin do not share the
family's opinion is an even stronger signal of Cather's own admiration
for this character.

For the Ferguesson children, their father is an inspiration in a con-
voluted way that underscores Cather's alternative approach to the
struggle for success. Bound together by the "conviction" that their
father is "misunderstood" by his neighbors, the children, in a seemingly typical American spirit of competition, feel that they must "do better than other children"—not so much to get ahead for themselves, but
to vindicate their father from community ridicule (104). The Ferguessons are a success-motivated and a future-oriented family, embodying

Cather's own optimism about the future, which she clung to even after witnessing the devastation of two world wars.

The Ferguesson children respect the individuality of their father, and of each other: "Each child had his own dream-adventure. They did not exchange confidences; every 'fellow' had a right to his own" (109). This strong individualism exists alongside an equally strong "clan feeling" that the Ferguesson children share (113). Mrs. Ferguesson is assured her individuality through "clan" efforts: the boys contribute money from their own part-time jobs to pay for having the family laundry done at the local steam laundry so that their mother, freed from that chore, has time for the community activities that interest her.

Despite the tragedy of Lesley's death, which family members carry in their hearts, the Ferguessons whom Evangeline Knightly visits twenty years later have prospered, their lives and careers reflecting Cather's view of the many kinds of success possible in an America that encourages individual achievement, but not at the expense of community. The forward-looking James Ferguesson's "thinking" has paid off. He has a government position that has enabled him to build a fine, new home. The boys are each living a version of the American Dream—two as sheep ranchers in Wyoming, one as a chemist, one holding a position with Marshall Field.

In this late-life story, Cather celebrates, then, the self-realization that community can promote and the individuality that group can nurture, as she on a larger scale celebrates the grand and varied possibilities for self-fulfillment that she still saw in America.[18] But Cather nevertheless makes clear in the words of Lesley's mother her own persistent ambivalence about material success: "Our best years are when we're working hardest and going right ahead when we can hardly see our way out" (136). As is the case with many of Cather's characters, Mrs. Ferguesson experienced a greater sense of fulfillment when struggle fired her life. For Mrs. Ferguesson, the American Dream in its *potential* for individual success is, as Cather had once said about struggle, far more "interesting."[19]

For James Ferguesson, however, the early as well as the later years are all "best years." He is successful from the start in asserting and maintaining his individuality through his own strength of will and through his family's support. His political community plays an important role in his self-development, too, not only in eventually securing him a job, but earlier, in providing him with a means of self-expression. In fact, we never actually see Ferguesson experience the tension inherent in the balance between self and community, although such tension is implied throughout the story. That is not, however, the case for Henry Grenfell, the middle-aged protagonist of Cather's other late-life story,

"Before Breakfast." Grenfell is involved in a philosophical struggle to define his place in the human community and at the same time to retain his individuality. A successful businessman, he escapes each summer to the privacy and separation that he craves, and that his deserted island off the coast of Canada affords him. But such an escape involves risk, as Grenfell comes to realize. "He wanted all this glorious loneliness for himself. He had paid dearly for it," the narrator remarks, referring specifically to the expense of Grenfell's vacation, but ironically to the emotional price Grenfell pays for his separation from the human community (159).[20] That price, as Grenfell awakes to discover, is the dread of feeling "unrelated to anything" (149).

The story opens after Grenfell has spent a night of "revelation, revaluation," looking back over his life, trying to fix a place for himself in the present and to foresee a meaningful future. Like Cather's earlier hero, Bartley Alexander, Henry Grenfell is an unaware and weary casualty of the struggle for material success. We meet him at the crucial moment when he will either redefine the American Dream for himself or will succumb to the emptiness of that standard dream. A self-made man, Grenfell's personal glories are in the past. He recalls with pride his hard childhood, spent working as a telegraph boy, helping to support his mother and sisters after his father's death. He describes these times as "the years . . . that make character" (150), regretting that his sons have not had that experience, even though they have had the opportunity for education that he never had.[21]

But as much as Grenfell takes pleasure in his hard-won success, his years of character-building, and his rugged individualism, he wakes up on his lonely island to realize: "He had got ahead wonderfully . . . but, somehow, ahead on the wrong road" (158). He has no meaningful relationship with either his wife or his sons. He thinks that he craves solitude, but it becomes apparent that unconsciously he craves the fellowship with other humans that makes one's individuality apparent—that sense of human companionship without which a person feels "unrelated to anything." As he admires the morning star, he thinks to himself that it is beautiful "only when somebody *saw* it" (158). His realization is the beginning of a series of encounters in which we see Henry Grenfell's hunger for a human response.

This hunger drives Grenfell to conjure up companions. He attaches human emotions to the snowshoe hare outside his cabin window, seeing it as "puzzled and furtive" (143). Wanting to feel some connection to that hare, Grenfell naïvely assumes that it is the same hare that had frequented his garden two years earlier and interprets its present actions as a sort of greeting. When Grenfell catches a glimpse of the morning star, he thinks of it as showing "impersonal splendour"; yet he addresses it personally, as an old friend, and manages to find a connecting link between it and himself. Thinking of an unpleasant conversation he had had the day before with his neighbor on the island, a geologist whose scientific calculation of the island's age has intruded upon Grenfell's romantic notions about "his" island (159), Grenfell addresses the star: "What's a hundred and thirty-six million years to you, Madam? . . . Let's leave that to the professors, Madam, you and me" (144).

Later, when his anxieties plague him so much that he needs to run away from self-contemplation, he escapes for an early-morning walk, still thinking that he craves only solitude. But even at this point, he continues to seek companionship. He addresses a familiar tree as "Grandfather," complimenting it for having endured in such a harsh climate. He anthropomorphizes the birches, imagining them hugging the earth, which also bears human qualities, seeming "kinder than the stormy air" (162). The piece of land on which he sits to gaze out to sea is personified, too: an "elbow of land" (163).

Grenfell unconsciously creates a community of sorts, but he still refuses to admit any desire for a connection with the human community. Then, as he sits gazing at the beach below him, he notices his neighbor-geologist's daughter, about to take an early morning swim in the cold waters of the North Atlantic. At first he is shocked and concerned—almost annoyed, for he feels somehow responsible for her safety, as Mrs. Rosen in "Old Mrs. Harris" had felt an irritating sense of responsibility for young Vickie. But as Grenfell observes the young woman, he begins to feel that he understands her, and begins to forge a link between the two of them. He interprets her act of braving the cold water as the same type of commitment to self that has so often motivated him: "She didn't have to keep face—except to herself. . . . He knew just how she felt" (165–66).

This is an understandable observation for an aging author such as Cather to make, reassuring herself that her endeavors had been inspired not by public pressure but by her own demands on herself. Grenfell, in observing the young swimmer and all the other struggling, surviving living things on the island, at last defines his community. He claims his place among all those, like himself and the young swimmer, whose integrity to self pushes them toward high accomplishment. Grenfell's is a rather exclusive community, composed of those with "the ginger to care hard and work hard" (157). He recalls that, as a boy, "he knew he could get on if he tried hard, since most lads emphatically did not try hard" (150). In that same community Grenfell places those weather-beaten trees who survive in such an "unkind" climate (162), and even "that first amphibious frog-toad" who managed to find another water-hole when its own had dried up millions of years ago.[22] Henry Grenfell realizes, with much joy, that his "relationship" with his island and with humanity, represented by the brave girl whose actions show her kinship to him, is "unchanged" (162)—although, ironically, for Grenfell it is changed, since he now feels connected to the human community in a way that he did not recognize earlier.

In this story, written after years of artistic endeavor, Willa Cather may be reasserting her own relationship as artist to a "long chain of human endeavour"[23]—to the community that helped to make her efforts worthwhile. In "Willa Cather's Aristocrats," Patricia Yongue suggests that Cather was all her life "enamored of people of great wealth and aesthetic sensibility who had come by their money either through artistic accomplishments or through inheritance."[24] The community that Yongue describes is in some ways similar to the community of artists and lovers of art with whom I see Cather continually wanting to align herself; but Yongue sees a conflict that I suggest Cather resolves in her later fiction. Yongue finds Cather's antimaterialistic values in conflict with her desire to be part of such an exclusive and necessarily wealth-based aesthetic community. I suggest that Cather's belief in and continued emphasis on the importance of struggle provides a resolution of this potential source of conflict. Whether that struggle is toward achieving the material success that enables one to enter a world of aesthetic appreciation or toward perfecting one's own artistic ability, the struggle itself establishes one's place in a broader community that includes aesthetically oriented aristocrats and "commoners," both of whom Cather seemed to believe could belong to the same community—especially in America's atmosphere of at least potential equality.

Yongue, specifically in examining the conflict between privilege and democracy in *A Lost Lady*, notes that the American Dream was an "aesthetically and aristocratically founded democratic ideal," and as such, inevitably created tension, a tension that, Yongue says, Cather experienced in defining her own relationship to such an "aesthetic/aristocratic" community. Yongue notices Cather's concern with "the seeming contradiction between her aristocratic and more democratic impulses."[25] But Cather's later fiction shows her acceptance, with little discomfort, of that "seeming contradiction." Cather seems to accept the tension between the aristocratic and democratic impulses as inevitable (just as she seems to have eventually accepted the tension between individual and community as inevitable). She thus can attach herself to both communities—that of a hard-working, uneducated Ántonia Shimerda and of an aristocratic Sapphira Colbert. Henry Grenfell, after all, manages to make a place for himself in both communities, as Cather emphasizes by stressing his love of Shakespeare,

Scott, Dickens, and Fielding—despite the fact that he grew up with no formal education and thus claims a very unaristocratic, unaesthetic background.

Many of Cather's later writings suggest her increased need to feel a part of such a wide-ranging community of artists and art lovers who share similar values, despite their differing economic or class backgrounds. When Bernard de Voto, the editor of the *Saturday Review of Literature*, published in 1937 a defense of his editorial policy in response to the accusation that he lacked commitment to social causes, Cather enthusiastically wrote to thank him for so clearly stating her own beliefs, as if she felt the need to claim membership in the same community of thought as de Voto. In that letter, she identifies herself with a community whose members find a meaning in life that goes deeper than economics, and she specifically includes in that community both taxi drivers and elevator boys. She emphasizes that she is well acquainted with these people, as if to clarify that her community crosses class lines and income levels.[26]

De Voto had in his editorial, among other things, given his own definition of worthwhile literature: "The literature that most interests me is the literature of man's loneliness and hope."[27] In "Before Breakfast," Cather shows her own interest in both of those aspects of the human condition, represented (as she had also done in "Old Mrs. Harris") by old age (Grenfell) and youth (the young swimmer). Returning to his cabin, ready for breakfast, Grenfell reflects: "Plucky youth is more bracing than enduring age" (166). Yet it is clear that one needs both the pluck of youth and the endurance of age to fulfill one's dreams. Even more importantly, one needs a sense of connection to others, the feeling of belonging. Grenfell is sure that he knows just how the young swimmer felt; similarly, Cather wanted to assure de Voto that he had expressed exactly what she felt, that they belonged to the same like-minded community. Thus, in "Before Breakfast," Cather explores once more the tension between an isolated, autonomous selfhood and the need for community. Significantly, Grenfell returns, not to an empty cabin, but to one in which he will share a meal with another human being, even if it is only the person hired to prepare his breakfast.

Cather's feeling of belonging to a group who shared the same values about art and humanity was challenged more than ever in her later years by the changing intellectual atmosphere in America and the increasing pressure on artists to reflect social concerns in their own work. Richard Pells observes that "a growing number of writers were eagerly lining up to repent their prodigal past and swear allegiance to the new gospel of social commitment."[28] Writers such as Malcolm Cowley urged fellow artists to "deal in one way or another with the problems of the day."[29]

Such a view is reminiscent of the demands that Progressives had earlier tried to place on artists—and that Cather deplored then, too, when she worked at *McClure's*.[30] Lionel Trilling, in his famous condemnation of Cather (1933), accused her of making "the wrong choice," preferring "the calm security of her dreams" to active involvement in "the movement to destroy and rebuild" the present world with its many faults.[31] Under such attack, Cather looked beyond America and beyond her own era, to the broader community of artists with whom she had always felt a deep kinship —reaching back to the English and European Romantics and even to the ancient Greeks and the Hebrews, all part of what Slote calls Cather's "secret web of connections and relationships."[32]

This is exactly what Cather does in her defense of escapism, first published as a letter to the editor of *The Commonweal* (17 April 1936). Not only does Cather justify in this essay her refusal to use her fiction as a vehicle for social reform, but she establishes once more her membership in a time-spanning community of artists who, through their art, pour out a balm upon the world, as Keats might say. Cather in her letter links herself to the ancient Indian artists whom she had earlier celebrated in the Panther Canyon scene of *The Song of the Lark*; to poets such as Shelley, who were "useful" to society not as revolutionaries, but "only . . . because they refresh[ed] and recharge[d] the spirit"; to the Hebrew prophets and Greek dramatists who understood that the world would always have its "hatreds and jealousies and treacheries," just as individual families do. All of these, Cather writes, helped the world not by becoming socially or politically involved in solving its problems, but—as she herself had tried to do—by creating art that would "gratify something that had no concern with food or shelter."[33]

In her essay on escapism, Cather not only aligns herself with this broad and prestigious community, but explains why artists are especially sensitive to the tension between self and community: They can be useful to a community only by being "*left out* of the social and industrial routine."[34] The artist's connection to humanity is his or her separateness from it—a view from which she did not waver throughout her life. In an 1894 newspaper column, she had explained that the artist "is not made to live like other men; his soul is strung differently. . . . The fewer friends he has the better; every friend means one more manager. Friends demand weekly dividends on the interest they invest in one."[35] Recognizing "the revolt against individuality" in her present-day society, Cather in her essay on escapism admits that in such an atmosphere, artists are of course singled out for blame, since "the artist is of all men the most individual."[36] But her admission is not made defensively. Rather, Cather insists on the necessity of this trait: it is a constant in a world that "has a habit of being in a bad way from time to time." The "art of escape" is as important to that troubled world as is the very different "art" of the pamphleteer. Having defined her community in its broadest sense in this essay—and with the calmness of someone who feels certain she has the support of others who share her values—Cather closes her essay by describing the community to which she most certainly does not belong, using Mary Colum's remark from the *Yale Review*: "The people who talk about the art of escape simply know nothing about art at all." Cather adds emphatically: "At *all*, I echo!"[37]

Just as Henry Grenfell in "Before Breakfast" discovers with relief that his relationship to his island and to humanity is "unchanged," Cather in her essay on escapism seems to be reassuring herself, and perhaps the world, that the artist's relationship to the world remains unchanged. The artist continues to provide escape from the "bad way" into which the world continually gets itself. The artist, while exhibiting this commitment to community, still continually reasserts the individuality that is a hallmark of artistic creation. To Cather, that the artist has a responsibility to community seems almost too obvious to mention, just as the loyalty that the Ferguesson children feel toward family is "a consciousness they shared," but an unspoken one: "They never spoke of that covenant to each other."[38] Cather views the relationship between artist/individual and community as a more fundamental one than the artificial, strained one that the politically committed were trying so hard to forge. Bernard de Voto had stated it this way: "What interests me is primarily the human emotions and experiences that have only a secondary connection with social movements."[39] Cather in an unpublished essay fragment made a similar statement: "[Every artist must be] more interested in his own little story and his foolish little people than in the Preservation of the Indian or Sex or Tuberculosis."[40]

But even one who only obliquely commits herself to humanity by providing that much-needed escape, as Cather did, still feels, certainly, the need for a "connectedness to others,"[41] as Cather must have felt even more intensely in her old age. As independent and socially uncommitted as she was, Cather still held membership in the Episcopal church (which she joined at age forty-eight), in the National Institute of Arts and Letters (which she joined at age fifty-five), and in the American Academy (which she joined at age sixty-five). She expressed to friends in her later years her gratification at being recognized by fellow artists; one of the last friendships that she made and cultivated was with the Norwegian novelist Sigrid Undset—a fellow artist.[42]

She continued, too, to admire and to consider as dear to her as family that group of artists from a younger generation who had so impressed her, the Menuhins. But the Willa Cather whom Yehudi Menuhin recalls in his autobiography remained selective about her community and committed to individual achievement: "She had a contempt for anything too much owned or determined by mobs, reserving admiration for high individual endeavor, withdrawing more and more from society even as she drew closer to us."[43] Still, Willa Cather understood her need—any artist's need—for the community from which he or she must also remain separate. Menuhin recalls a letter that she wrote to him in 1936, responding to his concerns about whether he should make Europe or America his home. Her response shows her own preoccupation with belonging to a place or to a people, for she stresses the importance of a "sense of belonging" for any artist. She tells Menuhin that America is his home, although she admits that artists who choose to remain in America confront a problem: they "miss the companionship of seasoned and disciplined minds."[44] Here again Cather reaches toward that broader community of artists, a community that bridges national boundaries; but she seems to realize, too, that one needs a physical sense of place: "the earth, the sky, the slang in the streets." She speaks of American artists who had gone abroad, deciding that "they would be French," and had "never amounted to anything": "They can't be *really* French, you see, so they are just unconscious impostors." Cather seems in this letter, to be working out her own relationship to the American community: "The things his own country makes him feel . . . are about the best capital a writer has to draw upon," she states, in the practical vocabulary of corporate America.[45]

That need to belong seems to have been a key theme in her unfinished novel, which Cather had tentatively planned to title, "Hard Punishments." The story was set in fourteenth-century Avignon, during the period of papal residency in France. The main characters were two boys, André and Pierre, one of noble birth, the other the son of a peasant—both apparent outcasts from their communities, having been physically maimed as punishments for minor crimes. Another key character was an aging, blind priest, Father Ambrose, who comforted André after he had had his tongue torn out as a punishment for blasphemy. Although we can only speculate from the information that Edith Lewis was willing to give and from the notes that Cather had made in a history of Avignon that she was reading as she worked on the manuscript, Cather's focus, at least in part, seems to be the "community" that this trio of unique individuals comprised. The one extant scene describes the three, a newly forged family of sorts, attending together a midnight Christmas Mass—a communal celebration.[46]

Cather at the end of her life turned to the past in her Avignon story, but like the rest of her historical fiction, this novel would have certainly been just as clearly focused on her own times. The repressive society of "Hard Punishments," with its severe punishments for those such as André and Pierre who do not conform to prescribed ways, may be suggestive of a postwar America where a fear of communism was creating a more restrictive society, one that celebrated conformity more than individuality.[47] But even in exploring the harsh world of fourteenth-century France, Cather seems interested in highlighting the fellowship that unites persons from diverse backgrounds and that nurtures the individual.

Elizabeth Sergeant, speculating on Cather's reaction to the people from diverse backgrounds who might visit her grave, suggests Cather's world sense of community:

> If a young veteran of the Korean War . . . stopped by [her grave]—a man with an Asian outlook, one of those constrained to hail and accept (as Thornton Wilder said in his Alumni Day address to Harvard students in 1951) "that painfully emerging unity of those who live on the one inhabited star"—she would surely receive him as a new Tom Outland.[48]

An awareness of that "painfully emerging unity" comes to Godfrey St. Peter when he recognizes the existence of "a world full of Augustas"—a meaningful community to which he can belong and can commit himself. Repeatedly in Cather's fiction we glimpse such recognition of the self-affirming aspects of community that balance the "dissolving" aspects, straining in a positive manner against what Bellah and associates call "the destructive side of individualism."[49]

Although we do not know how Cather's Avignon story might have ended, it is a fairly safe guess that it would have been on a note of affirmation, one that recognized the human need for fellowship but did not deny the equally important need for a sense of separateness and individual achievement. This was Cather's revised American Dream of self-fulfillment achieved through a healthy tension between self and community. In a 1923 interview, at the height of her fame and also at the height of her supposed disgust with a materialistic America, Willa Cather made a characteristic swing toward optimism in her assessment of her present world, and of its future possibilities: "Bad governments come and go without altering the direction of a people's progress. The sanity of people always brings things right."[50] This is the same sort of optimistic turn that Cather makes time and again in her novels, just when she seems to be taking the most critical look at humanity in general and at America in particular. Keeping this attitude in mind, we might say about Willa Cather's view of America what she once said about Sarah Orne Jewett's view of New England: "She early learned to love her country for what it was. What is quite as important, she saw it as it was."[51] For Cather, that vision of America never ceased to recognize an imperfect but evolving dream of personal fulfillment, and "the sanity of people" to bring things right.

Notes

Chapter 1. Self, Community, and Success

1. Willa Cather, "The Best Years," in *The Old Beauty and Others* (New York: Vintage Books, 1976), 136, 138.

2. Willa Cather, preface to *Not Under Forty* (New York: Alfred A. Knopf, 1954).

3. Dorothy Van Ghent has questioned the use of the word "elegist" to describe Cather, arguing that her fictions are "characterized by a sense of the past . . . as persistent human truth *repossessed*—salvaged, redeemed—by virtue of memory and art" ("Willa Cather," in *Willa Cather*, ed. Harold Bloom [New York: Chelsea House Publishers, 1985], 71—my italics). Historian Marcus Cunliffe also recognizes that Cather is grounded in her own era: "Each of us is, after all, a prisoner of the *Zeitgeist*. . . . [Thus,] Willa Cather does . . . help to shed light on her own age" ("The Two or More Worlds of Willa Cather," in *The Art of Willa Cather*, ed. Bernice Slote and Virginia Faulkner [Lincoln: University of Nebraska Press, 1974], 24). While I explore here the cultural tensions created by the success ethic, Cunliffe focuses on the "tensions between West and East" that run through Cather's fiction, mirroring cultural tensions. Phyllis Rose theorizes that Cather "herself encouraged the flattening of her work into a glorification of the past, a lament for the shabbiness of the present." Rose proposes that Cather did so "perhaps in order to mask the radically unacceptable nature of her private life" ("The Case of Willa Cather," in *Modernism Reconsidered*, ed. Robert Kiely [Cambridge: Harvard University Press, 1983], 124). I do not think that Cather consciously encouraged the "flattening of her work"; I do feel that she recognized the narrow vision with which many readers and critics regarded her fiction, and that she even occasionally poked fun at their limiting viewpoint, as she does in the statement quoted above from her preface to *Not Under Forty*.

4. Willa Cather, *The Professor's House* (New York: Vintage Books, 1973), 101.

5. Willa Cather, *Shadows on the Rock* (New York: Vintage Books, 1971), 20.

6. Willa Cather, *Lucy Gayheart* (New York: Vintage Books, 1976), 3.

7. Willa Cather, interview with Rose C. Feld, "Restlessness Such as Ours Does Not Make for Beauty," *New York Times*, 21 December 1924, in *Willa Cather in Person*, ed. L. Brent Bohlke (Lincoln: University of Nebraska Press, 1986), 70. See Philip Gerber, *Willa Cather* (Boston: Twayne Publishers, 1975), chap. 2, "The Reign of Mammon," for a thorough discussion of Cather's preoccupation with the materialism of her own era. See also Edward and Lillian Bloom, *Willa Cather's Gift of Sympathy* (Carbondale: Southern Illinois University Press, 1962), chap. 2, "Hard Molds of Provincialism."

8. Leon Edel, *Willa Cather: The Paradox of Success* (Washington, D.C.: Library of Congress, 1960), 5, 7, 16. Edel maintained this view in later studies. In a 1971 essay on Cather, he described the "profoundly American subject" of Cather's novels: "the drive of strong-willed persons to achievement and their discovery of how illusory success can be. . . . It is the conquest, the achievement, the success that interests her" ("Willa Cather," in *Notable American Women, 1607–1950: A Biographical Dictionary*, ed. Edward T. James [Cambridge: Harvard Univesity Press, 1971], 307–8). In 1974 Edel made a similar appraisal, calling Cather "a creature of old and fixed habits" who "always was a writer of 'success' stories" ("Homage to Willa Cather," in Slote and Faulkner, *Art,* 202).

9. Cather, *Shadows*, 119.

10. Bernice Slote, ed. *The Kingdom of Art: Willa Cather's First Principles and Critical Statements* (Lincoln: University of Nebraska Press, 1967), 34.

11. Christopher Lasch explores antiprogressive thought in America in *The True and Only Heaven: Progress and Its Critics* (New York: W. W. Norton and Co., 1991). In his preface, he notes an increasing interest among "historians and social critics [in investigating] the Atlantic tradition of republicanism or civic humanism, historically an important competitor of the liberal [i.e., progressive] tradition." Lasch briefly mentions Cather in his study, categorizing her as one of the "civilized minority" in the 1920s who criticized backwardness and provincialism in America while retaining a faith in popular self-government, whereas most alienated liberals at that time saw self-government as "incompatible with progress" (Lasch, *Heaven*, 14–15, 421). I am indebted to Lasch's explanation of antiprogressive attitudes in the late nineteenth and early twentieth centuries. I do not, however, see Cather fitting neatly into the antiprogressive category, as Lasch suggests. Her respect for tradition and her denunciation of materialism align her more closely with antiprogressives than with advocates of progress, but Cather seems more optimistic than do Lasch's critics of progress, with their tragic, resigned perspective on the future. Nevertheless, Lasch's analysis is extremely helpful in understanding some of Cather's attitudes and possible influences on her.

Casey Blake's book, *Beloved Community: The Cultural Criticism of Randolph Bourne, Van Wyck Brooks, Waldo Frank, and Lewis Mumford* (Chapel Hill: University of North Carolina Press, 1990), has also informed my study, offering a helpful analysis of late nineteenth-century and early twentieth-century cultural criticism that I see resonating in Cather's fiction.

12. Willa Cather, "Nebraska: The End of the First Cycle," *Nation* 117 (5 September 1923): 235.

13. David Stouck voices a similar opinion: "Cather never reviews the past for purely antiquarian reasons or ancestor worship; instead she looks to see if in its thought and art there are things lost that we need here today" ("*The Professor's House* and the Issues of History," in *Willa Cather: Family, Community, and History*, ed. John Murphy [Provo, Utah: The Brigham Young University Humanities Publications Center, 1990], 210). Eudora Welty makes a similar point: "Willa Cather's history . . . did not imprison the present, but instructed it, passed on a meaning. . . . She opened her mind to the past as she would to a wise teacher. When she saw the connections, the natural channels opening, she let the past come flooding into the present" ("The House of Willa Cather," in Slote and Faulkner, *Art,* 7–8). See also Lois Zamora's assessment: "[Cather] clearly wished to avoid romanticizing the past by separating it from the present, a tendency of popular historical romance which she recognized and self-consciously rejected" ("The Usable Past: The Idea of History in Modern U.S. and Latin American Fiction," in *Do the Americas Have a Common Literature?*, ed. Gustavo Perez Firmat [Durham, N.C.: Duke University Press, 1990], 19).

14. Robert N. Bellah et al., *Habits of the Heart: Individualism and Commitment in American Life* (Berkeley: University of California Press, 1985), viii.

15. Willa Cather, "Old Books and New," *Home Monthly*, October 1897, in *The World and the Parish: Willa Cather's Articles and Reviews, 1893–1902*, 2 vols., ed. William Curtin (Lincoln: University of Nebraska Press, 1970), 1:359.

16. Lasch, *Heaven*, 83.

17. Bernice Slote, "An Appointment with the Future: Willa Cather," in *The Twenties: Fiction, Poetry, Drama*, ed. Warren French (Deland, Fla.: Everett/Edwards, Inc., 1975), 47. Slote here echoes Henry Steele Commager's positive assessment of certain traditionalist writers of the 1920s, including Willa Cather: "It is a safe prophecy that they will speak to the twenty-first [century] more directly than most of their more vociferous and sensational contemporaries" (*The American Mind* [New Haven: Yale University Press, 1950], 142).

18. I am indebted to Merrill Skaggs for this phrase, which she uses to describe much of the tension in Cather's late fiction: "We can trace her debates with herself and the questions with which she wrestled through her stunning fictions" (*After the World Broke in Two: The Later Novels of Willa Cather* [Charlottesville: University Press of Virginia, 1990], 184). Skaggs focuses on Cather's post-1922 fiction, whereas I trace Cather's "wrestling"—specifically with the issue of success—through all of her novels.

19. "Success is never so interesting as struggle," Cather stated in her 1932 preface to a revised edition of *The Song of the Lark* (Boston: Houghton Mifflin Co., 1943), v.

20. Richard Weiss states: "The 'dream' and the 'myth' represent two separate and distinct threads in the fabric of American culture, and the use of them as synonyms assumes an identity where none exists." He sees the "dream" as an outgrowth of the "new possibilities for wealth and power that industrialization brought in its wake"; the "myth," on the other hand, he associates with "the values of a merchant-agrarian society, religious, moderate, and simple in tone," which was already on its way out in America (*The American Myth of Success* [New York: Basic Books, Inc., 1969], 91). I propose that Cather, however, tried to apply those values of the older society to the later industrial era with its "new possibilities." Thus, she often viewed wealth and power as mere outward signs of less tangible values that she hoped could still survive in her society. I discuss this view of wealth at greater length in chap. 4. When I describe the American Dream as myth, I refer more specifically to the popular, though certainly misleading, late nineteenth-century belief that all in America had an equal opportunity to achieve material success, and that material success brings with it a sense of self-fulfillment.

21. Willa Cather, review of Shaw's *Plays, Pleasant and Unpleasant, Pittsburgh Leader*, 2 December 1898, in Curtin, *Parish*, 2:596.

22. The "American Dream" is defined as "the U.S. ideal according to which equality of opportunity permits any American to aspire to high attainment and material success" in *Webster's New World Dictionary of American English*, Third College Edition, 1988. *The Random House Dictionary of the English Language*, Second Edition, 1987, gives a similar definition: "1. The ideals of freedom, equality, and opportunity traditionally held to be available to every American. 2. A life of personal happiness and material comfort as traditionally sought by individuals in the United States." It identifies 1930–35 as the years during which the term first came into widespread use. *The American Heritage Dictionary*, Second College Edition, 1982, defines the American Dream as "an American ideal of social equality and especially material success."

23. John G. Cawelti, *Apostles of the Self-Made Man* (Chicago: The University of Chicago Press, 1965), 5, 9. See pp. 9–35 for a full description of these various "strands." I find Cawelti's analysis of the interplay between the various "traditions" of success more illuminating than the oversimplified conclusion that Richard Huber reaches about the concept of success in America: "In America success has meant money making and translating it into status . . . [which is] not the same thing as happiness" (*The American Idea of Success* [New York: McGraw-Hill Publishers, 1971], 1).

24. Bellah et al., *Habits*, 40.

25. Daniel Rogers, *The Work Ethic in Industrial America, 1850–1920* (Chicago: The University of Chicago Press, 1978), 37.

26. William James to H. G. Wells, 11 September 1906, *The Letters of William James*, ed. Henry James, Jr. (Boston: Little, Brown and Co., 1926), 260. Kenneth Lynn notes that James's statement "has been for half a century the keynote . . . of literary and social historians of American civilization . . . [who] have adopted [it] as a weapon with which to belabor American businessmen, but have refused to concede that our writers as well as our industrialists have exalted the bitch-goddess" (*The Dream of Success: A Study of the Modern American Imagination* [Boston: Little, Brown and Co., 1955], 248). In the very term, "bitch-goddess," James suggests the approach-avoidance stance that has for so long characterized attitudes toward success in America, including Cather's own attitude.

27. Willa Cather to Will Owen Jones, letter to the editor, *Nebraska State Journal*, 24 July 1927, in Bohlke, *Person*, 180–81.

28. Cather, *Professor's*, 260.

29. Lawrence Chenoweth, *The American Dream of Success: The Search for the Self in the Twentieth Century* (North Scituate, Mass: Duxbury Press, 1974).

30. Page Smith, *Redeeming the Time: A People's History of the 1920's and the New Deal* (New York: McGraw-Hill, 1987), 849. For a similar analysis, see J. R. Pole, "Individualism and Conformity," in *Encyclopedia of American Political History*, ed. Jack P. Greene (New York: Scribner's, 1984), 633–34. Pole traces the history of this "contest," making it clear that "individualism . . . as a concept . . . is categorically inconceivable without the alternative concept of community and of conformity to community values." He concludes didactically that "the American way . . . is at its most valuable when the individually creative impulse revives the hopes of the community." Cather seems in her fiction of the late 1920s to have reached a similar conclusion (see chap. 4, below), although she later moves beyond such a facile resolution of the success dilemma.

31. Herbert Croly, *The Promise of American Life* (New York: MacMillan, 1909), 217.

32. Charles Beard, "The Myth of Rugged Individualism," *Harper's* 164 (December 1931): 21.

33. In my study, I often use the term "American" to refer to the general population of the United States or to a general set of attitudes and opinions prevalent in America during the period in which Cather was writing; and I suggest throughout this study that Cather's own debate about the American Dream, a recurring subtext in her fiction, represents a tension that many Americans of her era were experiencing. I recognize that my use of the term "American" in such a generalized manner does not fully account for the diverse experiences and opinions of the many Americans from various economic, ethnic, and cultural backgrounds. In fact, this is part of the problem that Cather herself encountered as she tried to redefine such a broad concept as the American Dream for a society that was becoming more and more diverse; her ultimate decision (whether conscious or unconscious) to leave the issue unresolved may to some degree suggest a sensitivity to such diversity. Bernice Slote notes that Cather in her writing celebrated cultural diversity more than most of her contemporaries did ("Appointment," 47–48). Christopher Lasch also notes this (*Heaven*, 421).

I find George Santayana's qualification of the term, "American," helpful in explaining my own use of it, as well as Cather's probable understanding of it: "I speak of the American in the singular, as if there were not millions of them, north and south, east and west, of both sexes, of all ages, and of various races, professions, and religions. Of course the one American I speak of is mythical; but to speak in parables is inevitable in such a subject, and it is perhaps as well to do so frankly" (*Character and Opinion in the United States* [New York: Charles Scribner's Sons, 1920], 167).

34. Cather, "First Cycle," 238.

35. Cawelti, *Apostles*, 5.

36. Blanche Gelfant, *Women Writing in America: Voices in Collage* (Hanover, N.H.: University Press of New England, 1984), 239. See also Ellen Moers, "The Survivors: Into the Twentieth Century," *Twentieth Century Literature* 20 (January 1974): 1–10, for a discussion of Cather and other literary figures who "survived" the transition from a Victorian to a modern culture.

37. Robert H. Wiebe, *The Search for Order, 1877–1920* (New York: Hill and Wang, 1967), 42–43.

38. Willa Cather, "Concerning Thomas Carlyle," in Slote, *Kingdom*, 424–25.

39. Edith Lewis, *Willa Cather Living* (New York: Alfred A. Knopf, 1976), 22. James Woodress calls Ducker "perhaps the most important influence of all her 'friends of childhood'" (*Willa Cather: A Literary Life* [Lincoln: University of Nebraska Press, 1987], 53).

40. Miles Orvell, *The Real Thing: Imitation and Authenticity in American Culture, 1889–1940* (Chapel Hill: The University of North Carolina Press, 1980), xviii.

41. Jackson Lears, *No Place of Grace: Antimodernism and the Transformation of American Culture, 1889–1920* (New York: Pantheon Books, 1981), 38–39, 6, 219.

42. Ibid., 222.

43. Page Smith, *America Enters the World: A People's History of the Progressive Era and World War I* (New York: McGraw-Hill, 1985), 911.

44. Lears is especially illuminating on the crisis of autonomy in this era. See in particular chap. 6: "From Patriarchy to Nirvana: Patterns of Ambivalence" (*Grace*, 218–60), in which he discusses the strong appeal of "mind cure" and mysticism, both of which many turned to in their struggle with the autonomy/dependence dilemma (*Grace*, 218–60). See also Richard Weiss, *Myth*, chap. 5–7 (especially 164–72). Weiss examines in detail the New Thought movement as a "new success cult" that sought to restore people's faith in an autonomous self (133). Perhaps Cather's early journalistic work on Mary Baker Eddy, whose religion of Christian Science incorporated many of the attitudes of the New Thought movement, made Cather even more aware of the general interest in restoring the autonomous self that pervaded American culture during this time period.

45. Sarah Orne Jewett to Willa Cather, 13 December 1908, *Letters of Sarah Orne Jewett*, ed. Annie Fields (Boston: Houghton Mifflin Co., 1911), 249.

46. Sandra Gilbert and Susan Gubar, *No Man's Land: The Place of the Woman Writer in the Twentieth Century* (New Haven: Yale University Press, 1988), 173–74.

47. Lewis, *Cather Living*, 175.

48. Sharon O'Brien, *Willa Cather: The Emerging Voice* (New York: Oxford University Press, 1987), 83. O'Brien further suggests that the restrictions on individual autonomy that women experienced during this era may have played a role in Cather's choice to remain unmarried and to seek women as her closest friends:

Such women [who, like Cather, wanted to pursue professional careers] could not accommodate desires for independent achievement with the selflessness demanded by marriage and motherhood or accept a heterosexual relationship structured by male dominance and feminine subordination.

Thus, like Cather, they chose as their closest friends women "who encouraged or shared their ambition" (*Emerging Voice*, 139). These women, among them Sarah Orne Jewett, Edith Lewis, and Elizabeth Sergeant, formed an important support community for Cather. Similarly, James Woodress notes that "Cather derived her greatest comfort, pleasure, moral support, and satisfaction from friendships with members of her own sex" ("Cather and her Friends," in *Critical Essays on Willa Cather*, ed. John Murphy [Boston: G. K. Hall and Co., 1984], 94).

A number of scholars have made insightful, exhaustive studies of gender resonances in Cather's work, and of the forces in her life that may have influenced her own sexual preferences. I am especially indebted to the following for their helpful analyses; specific references throughout this study testify to their influence: Sharon O'Brien, Susan Rosowski, Ellen Moers, Blanche Gelfant, Hermione Lee, Sandra Gilbert, and Susan Gubar. See also Patrick W. Shaw, *Willa Cather and the Art of Conflict: Re–visioning Her Creative Imagination* (Troy, N.Y.: Whitson Publishing Co., 1992). Shaw asserts that Cather's "conflicts—especially the homoerotic tensions—were the energy source for her creativity" (3). I, too, see tension as a positive force for Cather's creativity, but I focus on the cultural tensions that the success ethic created for her.

49. O'Brien, *Emerging Voice*, 7.

50. Walt Whitman, *Democratic Vistas, and Other Papers* (1871; reprint, St. Clair Shores, Mich.: Scholarly Press, 1970), 17–18.

51. Burton Bledstein, *The Culture of Professionalism: The Middle Class and the Development of Higher Education in America* (New York: W. W. Norton and Co., 1976), 105, 108.

52. Cawelti, *Apostles*, 43.

53. Slote confirms this (*Kingdom*, 39).

54. "On Lack of Conscience As a Means of Success," *Century* 40 (July 1890): 474. Cather most likely would have read this editorial, which was published a short time after her graduation from high school in June 1890, and shortly before her departure for the larger, more competitive community of scholars at the University of Nebraska. This was also just a short time before her first endeavors in the competitive world of journalism, which is interesting in light of the fact that the editors of the *Century* single out journalism as a career in which it is highly difficult to "reap worldly success . . . scrupulously" (474).

55. Weiss, *Myth*, 112.

56. Wiebe, *Order*, 44–45.

57. Thomas Bender, *Community and Social Change in America* (New Brunswick, N.J.: Rutgers University Press, 1978), 136.

58. I use "his" here since, on the whole, the success literature of the nineteenth century, including Alger's stories, was directed toward and focused on males.

59. Lynn, *Dream of Success*, 253.

60. Horatio Alger, *Strive and Success, or the Progress of Walter Conrad* (New York: Street and Smith Publishers, 1872) 301. Despite Alger's care to link success to virtue, Gary Scharnhorst points out that American publishers in later years adapted the Alger stories to fit the popular ideologies of their particular era. More than once, writes Scharnhorst, "[the stories] were editorially reinvented to appeal to a new generation of readers": "Whereas in his own time Alger was credited with inventing a moral hero who becomes modestly successful, during the early years of this century he seemed to have invented a successful hero who is modestly moral" (*The Lost Life of Horatio Alger, Jr.* [Bloomington: Indiana University Press, 1985], 151–52). Weiss also notes that Alger's heroes do not exhibit "the aggressive acquisitiveness of the time" (*Myth*, 59).

61. Lynn, *Dream of Success*, 9–10. Cawelti contrasts this new "overriding emphasis on the pursuit and use of wealth" with the earlier nineteenth-century view "that individual economic advancement and productivity was the best way of assuring both the individual and the general welfare" (*Apostles*, 169, 46).

62. Andrew Carnegie, "The Gospel of Wealth," in *The Gospel of Wealth and Other Timely Essays*, ed. Edward C. Kirkland (Cambridge: The Belknap Press of Harvard University Press, 1962), 14, 16. A young Cather—certainly influenced by Herbert Spencer, whose theories gained popularity in America—made a remarkably similar appraisal in an 1895 editorial: "Nature is pretty rough on the individual at times, but to the type she is wonderfully kind" (Willa Cather, "On Nature and Romance," *Courier*, 25 November 1895, in Slote, *Kingdom*, 232).

63. Carnegie, "Gospel," 19, 28.

64. Willa Cather, "The Real Homestead," *Courier*, 24 August 1901, in Curtin, *Parish*, 2:854–59.

65. William Dean Howells, *Criticism and Fiction and Other Essays*, ed. Clara Marburg Kirk and Rudolf Kirk (New York: New York University Press, 1959), 61–62.

66. Theodore Dreiser, *The Financier* (1912; reprint, Cleveland: World Publishing Co., 1946), 503, 271. For assessments of Dreiser's stance toward success, see Lynn, *Dream of Success*, 13–74, Cawelti, *Apostles*, 217, 228–30, and Charles Hearn, *The American Dream in the Great Depression* (Westport, Conn.: The Greenwood Press, 1977), 35–39. All three authors point out Dreiser's ambivalence toward success—his continued attraction to the dream as he criticized it. Richard Lingeman, in his biography of Dreiser, sees Dreiser's message about the American dream as ultimately negative: "We need dreams to lure us into achievement, Dreiser says, but once we attain them we inevitably find disillusionment—or death" (*Theodore Dreiser: An American Journey, 1908–1945*, 2 vols. [New York: G. P. Putnam's Sons, 1990], 2:72). This view of Dreiser closely resembles Leon Edel's assessment of Cather's "problem" with success.

67. Maxwell Geismar, *Rebels and Ancestors* (Boston: Houghton, Mifflin Co., 1953), 388.

68. I take my account of this speech from Woodress, *Life*, 60.

69. Slote, *Kingdom*, 39.

70. Although Cather certainly was aware of Alger's stories (perhaps even parodying his stock hero, as I note later in my discussion of Wick Cutter), I see no evidence that she read these works; it is likely that someone raised on the classics, as Cather was, would not view Alger's stories as particularly worthwhile reading material. Among the books that she recommends for children in her 1896 and 1897 newspaper columns are *Swiss Family Robinson, Treasure Island, The Mill on the Floss*, and *The Prince and the Pauper*. "Things were much better in the old days when a boy read only *Pilgrim's Progress* and *The Holy War* and Foxe's *Book of Martyrs*, and was pounded through a dozen books of *The Aeneid*," Cather observes ("Books Old and New," *Home Monthly*, 12 April 1896, in Curtin, *Parish*, 334).

71. Cawelti, *Apostles*, 103–4.

72. Jacob Abbott, *Histories of Cyrus the Great and Alexander the Great* (New York: Harper and Brothers, 1880), 85–86, 288–89, 14.

73. Slote, *Kingdom*, 35.

74. Both David Stouck and John Murphy note such tension. Stouck sees in Cather's fiction "a strong undercurrent of thought and feeling which turns away from the romantic dreams of selfhood . . . and which views art . . . as a process of sympathy for people, places, and events" ("Willa Cather and the Indian Heritage," *Twentieth Century Literature* 22 [December 1976]: 433). Murphy notes "two conflicting strains woven through Willa Cather's fiction: one leads toward and the other away from home and family" ("Willa Cather and Catholic Themes," *Western American Literature* 17 [Spring 1982]: 53).

75. Willa Cather, "Old Books and New," *Home Monthly*, September 1897, in Curtin, *Parish*, 1:354.

76. "This gift of sympathy is [the writer's] great gift," Cather observed in a 1925 essay on Sarah Orne Jewett ("The Best Stories of Sarah Orne Jewett," in *Willa Cather On Writing* [Lincoln: University of Nebraska Press, 1976], 51).

77. Willa Cather, review of *The Green Carnation*, by Robert Hichins, *Nebraska State Journal*, 12 May 1895, in Curtin, *Parish*, 1:153.

78. Mildred R. Bennett, *The World of Willa Cather* (Lincoln: University of Nebraska Press, 1961), xiii.

79. See Bennett, *World*, for a thorough discussion of Cather's "love-hate relation-

ship" with Red Cloud. See also Woodress, *Life*, chap. 3 (44–63). In an assessment based on recently discovered letters, Marilyn Arnold finds Cather much more positively inclined toward "the provinces," as she once called Red Cloud: "In spite of the satire . . . the overwhelming message of hundreds of letters from and about the provinces is a message of love" ("Poses of the Mind, Paeans of the Heart: Cather's Letters of Life in the Provinces," in Murphy, *Family, Community, and History*, 13).

80. Slote and Faulkner, *Art*, viii.

81. Willa Cather, "To Live Intensely Is Creed Of Willa S. Cather, Authoress," *Omaha Daily News*, 29 October 1921, in Bohlke, *Person*, 30.

82. Woodress, *Life*, xvi.

83. Willa Cather to Sarah Orne Jewett, 19 December 1908, Willa Cather Collection, Houghton Library, Harvard University, Cambridge. Hereafter cited as Cather letter to Jewett. Cather stipulated in her will that her letters were not to be published, perhaps because she realized how revealing such spontaneous writing can be. In a 1926 essay on Stephen Crane, she comments on a piece of Crane's spontaneous writing, his "bundle of impressions called 'War Memories'": "Sometimes when a man is writing carelessly, without the restraint he puts upon himself when he is in good form, one can surprise some of his secrets and read rather more than he perhaps intended" ("Stephen Crane's *Wounds in the Rain and Other Impressions of War*," in *On Writing*, 72). I find Cather's letters revealing in just this way; thus, although paraphrasing is always clumsy and leaves one open to the dangers of misrepresentation, I refer occasionally to her letters.

84. O'Brien, *Emerging Voice*, 345.

85. Elizabeth Shepley Sergeant, *Willa Cather, A Memoir* (1953; reprint, Philadelphia: J. B. Lippincott, 1963), 62.

86. F. Scott Fitzgerald, *The Great Gatsby* (New York: Charles Scribner's Sons, 1925), 136.

87. Sinclair Lewis, "The American Fear of Literature," in *The Man from Main Street: A Sinclair Lewis Reader*," ed. Harry E. Maule and Melville H. Cane (New York: Random House, 1953), 13.

88. Susan J. Rosowski makes a similar assessment, noting a "process of denial and reaffirmation" in Cather's fiction (*The Voyage Perilous: Willa Cather's Romanticism* [Lincoln: University of Nebraska Press, 1986], 12). Rosowski explores this process as a romantic trait.

89. Sinclair Lewis, "American Fear," in Maule and Cane, *Man from Main Street*, 14.

90. "I cannot produce my kind of work away from the American idiom," Cather explained to one interviewer in July 1925 (interview with Walter Tittle, *Century Magazine*, in Bohlke, *Person*, 84).

91. For recent studies of Cather's treatment of Native American traditions in her fiction, see Bernice Slote, "Willa Cather and Plains Culture," *Vision and Refuge: Essays on the Literature of the Great Plains*, ed. Virginia Faulkner with Frederick C. Luebke (Lincoln: University of Nebraska Press, 1982), 93–105; and Stouck, "Willa Cather and the Indian Heritage." Both Slote and Stouck see Cather celebrating these traditions, especially in *The Song of the Lark*, *A Lost Lady*, and *The Professor's House*. In contrast, these recent essays offer a revisionist stance: Joseph Urgo, "How Context Determines Fact: Historicism in Willa Cather's *A Lost Lady*," *Studies in American Fiction* 17 (Autumn 1989): 183–92; Walter Michaels, "The Vanishing American," *American Literary History* 2 (Summer 1990): 220–41; and Mike Fischer, "Pastoralism and its Discontents: Willa Cather and the Burden of Imperialism," *Mosaic* 23 (Winter 1990): 31–44. All three authors see Cather's treatment of Native American traditions as problematic, revealing both Cather's and the nation's efforts (whether conscious or unconscious) to rewrite the conquest and attempted extermination of the Native American population in America. I confront these views at greater length in my specific discus-

sions of the three novels mentioned here; in general, I find their essays helpful in understanding other cultural tensions, besides that created by the success ethic, which Cather and many of her contemporaries experienced, and which she perhaps tried to work out in her fiction.

92. Archibald MacLeish, "Bubble of Blue Air," *Riders on the Earth: Essays and Recollections* (Boston: Houghton Mifflin Co., 1978), xiv.

Chapter 2. Charting a New Path to Fulfillment

1. Van Wyck Brooks, *America's Coming of Age* (1915; reprint, New York: Octagon Books, 1975), 32.

2. Lears, *Grace*, 16.

3. Wendy Steiner, "The Diversity of American Fiction," in *Columbia Literary History of the United States*, ed. Emory Elliott (New York: Columbia University Press, 1988), 860.

4. Warner Berthoff, "Culture and Consciousness," in Elliott, *Columbia*, 482.

5. Willa Cather, *Alexander's Bridge* (Lincoln: University of Nebraska Press, 1977), 9. Subsequent citations are noted parenthetically in the text.

6. Alger, Jr., Horatio. *Ragged Dick and Mark, the Match Boy* (1867; reprint, New York: Macmillan, 1962), 43.

7. Alger, *Ragged Dick*, 213.

8. Philip Rieff, "The Emergence of Psychological Man," in *Freud: The Mind of the Moralist* (New York: Viking Press, 1959), 356.

9. Cather presents the strikes through Bartley's perspective: they are a frustration in his attempts to accomplish his goals. But by bringing the reality of "general industrial unrest" even briefly into the spotlight in this novel, she underscores, too, the disillusionment with the American Dream that was beginning to pervade society, especially the working class, who saw their socioeconomic mobility blocked.

10. Bernice Slote observes: "[Cather's] short stories before 1905 and her journalistic comment in her early years anticipated much of the social criticism later developed by Sinclair Lewis and others" ("Appointment," in French, *The Twenties*, 47).

11. Sinclair Lewis, *Babbitt* (1992; reprint, New York: The New American Library, 1963), 128.

12. Philip Rieff, *The Triumph of the Therapeutic: Uses of Faith after Freud* (New York: Harper and Row, 1966), 13.

13. Lears, *Grace*, 32.

14. Fitzgerald, *Gatsby*, 111.

15. Ibid., 162.

16. Warren Susman discusses Americans' refusal to accept limits (*Culture as History: The Transformation of American Society in the Twentieth Century*, [New York: Pantheon Books, 1984], 112), as does Lears (*Grace*, xiv); Lasch calls "a sense of limits" the "unifying thread" in his study of antiprogressive thought in America (*Heaven*, 17). Cawelti, commenting on writers who were beginning to question the American Dream in the early twentieth century, also points to the issue of limits: "It is time, these writers seem to say, to reopen the question of man's nature, to rediscover its limits, and to learn once more how to live within those limits" (*Apostles*, 236).

17. Ernest Dowson, "Non Sum Qualis Eram Bonae Sub Regno Cynarae," in *The Poetry of Ernest Dowson*, ed. Desmond Flower (Rutherford, N.J.: Fairleigh Dickinson University Press, 1970), 52.

18. Lears, *Grace*, 57.

19. Willa Cather, "An Heir Apparent," *Pittsburgh Leader*, 3 June 1899, in Curtin, *Parish*, 2:705.

20. In her introduction to the 1977 edition of *Alexander's Bridge*, Bernice Slote makes a similar suggestion concerning the focus on energy in the novel, linking this theme to the dynamo image that Henry Adams used.

21. Bellah et al., *Habits*, viii.

22. Richard Huber, *The American Idea of Success* (New York: McGraw-Hill, 1971), 96–97. He adds an interesting remark: "Whether true success and material success were a contradiction or simply a natural tension between opposites depended on the individual success writer" (98). Cather, it seems, came increasingly to see the two in a state of natural tension.

23. Rosowski also notes this connection (*Voyage*, 39).

24. Cather letter to Jewett. Slote describes Cather's conflict at this time in much the same way that Cather describes Bartley Alexander's struggle with his other self: "[Cather's] success [at *McClure's*] had a life of its own; it was a twin destiny not wholly joined to that of the artist. Like two selves, within her world they jostled and were not one" (introduction to *"Uncle Valentine" and Other Stories* [Lincoln: University of Nebraska Press, 1973], xiii–iv).

25. Sergeant, *Memoir*, 62.

26. Woodress, *Life*, 217.

27. Lears offers an illuminating discussion of this culturally triggered malady (*Grace*, 47–58).

28. Ibid., 55, 29.

29. Perhaps Cather is calling our attention to gender as a key factor in achieving a fulfillment-based success by giving Alexandra the feminine form of Cather's previous hero's name.

30. Lears, *Grace*, 248, 250.

31. Sharon O'Brien stresses gender as a key factor in the three protagonists' triumphs ("Mothers, Daughters, and the 'Art Necessity': Willa Cather and the Creative Process," in *American Novelists Revisited: Essays in Feminist Criticism*, ed. Fritz Fleischmann [Boston: G. K. Hall, 1982], 281, 284, 287).

32. Willa Cather, "A Biographical Sketch," in *A Biographical Sketch, an English Opinion, Reviews and Articles Concerning her Later Books and an Abridged Bibliography* (1933; reprint, Folcroft, Pa.: The Folcroft Press, Inc., 1975), 1.

33. Ibid., 2. See Woodress, "Writing Cather's Biography," *Cather Studies*, ed. Susan J. Rosowski (Lincoln: University of Nebraska Press, 1990), 1:108–9, for a discussion of the fiction about herself that Cather wove into this biographical sketch.

34. Cather, "First Cycle," 238.

35. Cather, "Restlessness," in Bohlke, *Person*, 71.

36. Books such as Rena M. Atchison's *Un-American Immigration: Its Present Effects and Future Perils. A Study from the Census of 1890*, (Chicago: C. H. Kerr and Co., 1894), warned of the threat posed by the new, non-Anglo-Saxon immigrants from southern and eastern Europe. Anti–immigration organizations such as the Immigration Restriction League, founded in 1894, called for a literacy test for immigrants; by 1917 such a test became law, shortly before quota systems were established in the National Origins Act of 1924.

37. Randolph Bourne, "Trans-National America," *The Atlantic Monthly* 118 (July 1916): 87. Lasch notes that Cather and Bourne were two of the few voices in favor of cultural pluralism in the early 1900s (*Heaven*, 421).

38. Bourne, "Trans-National," 90.

39. Ibid., 91, 92, 96, 97.

40. Croly, *Promise*, 16.

41. Willa Cather, *O Pioneers!* (1913; reprint, Boston: Houghton Mifflin Company, 1941), 237. Subsequent citations are noted parenthetically in the text.

42. Cather, "First Cycle," 238.

43. Ibid.

44. Lears, *Grace*, 119.

45. Interestingly, Van Wyck Brooks, in *America's Coming of Age* (1915), uses similar growth/garden imagery to outline his plan for a healthy nation, urging Americans to "build that garden in the cosmic wilderness . . . fertilizing the soil, cultivating and protecting the most beautiful and the greatest variety of plants" (154). He saw everywhere in America "an unchecked, uncharted, unorganized vitality" that needed to be "worked into an organism, into fruitful values" (164).

46. Cather, *Alexander's Bridge*, 101.

47. Cather uses this same image of indoor plants that bloom all winter in "Neighbour Rosicky," where we again see a caring, nurturing family.

48. Cather, *Lark*, 28–29.

49. Willa Cather, *My Ántonia* (1918; reprint, Boston: Houghton, Mifflin Company, 1954), 18, 193, 340.

50. Willa Cather, "Small Town Life," *Courier*, 24 August 1901, in Curtin, *Parish*, 2:849.

51. Ibid., 850.

52. Cather, *Lark*, 100. Subsequent citations are noted parenthetically in the text.

53. O'Brien generalizes this point, calling Cather's own attic bedroom her "private space to construct a real self." O'Brien observes that this bedroom "appears in [Cather's] fiction as an architectural metaphor of the female protagonist's search for creativity, identity, autonomy" (*Emerging Voice*, 104, 85).

54. Edward and Lillian Bloom also note Cather's "attack upon smug provincialism" (*Gift of Sympathy*, 249). I find Cather's attitude ambivalent rather than firmly committed. Thus I prefer Marilyn Arnold's appraisal: "In Cather's view conflicts and tensions were a natural part of community and family life" ("Poses," 5). Similarly, Elizabeth Sergeant reports that Cather criticized Sinclair Lewis for his cynical view of small towns: "When Sinclair Lewis looked at a small town he found only commonness, cheapness, ignorance" (*Memoir*, 167).

55. Cather echoes in Ray's statement a line from one of her favorite childhood poems, Matthew Arnold's "Sohrab and Rustum": "Some are born to do great deeds, and live, / As some are born to be obscur'd and die" (in *Matthew Arnold*, ed. Miriam Allott and Robert H. Super [Oxford: Oxford University Press, 1986], 204).

56. O'Brien similarly observes that Thea identifies with these ancient women artists (*Emerging Voice*, 416). I agree with Zamora, who notes that this scene dramatizes "a concept of American history as unconscious racial and cultural memory. . . . [Because Thea has] gone back to the rich communal and mythic roots of America, she is able to rejoin and enrich contemporary culture" ("Usable Past," 22–23).

57. Walt Whitman, *Leaves of Grass*, preface to 1855 edition, x, in *The American Tradition in Literature*, ed. George Perkins et al., 6th ed. (New York: Random House, 1985), 2:24.

58. Cather, "First Cycle," 238.

59. Robin Heyeck and James Woodress note that in Cather's 1937 revision of *The Song of the Lark*, "character revisions of Thea make her less self-centered or aggressive, eliminate passages which emphasize how much she used other people" ("Willa Cather's Cuts and Revisions in *The Song of the Lark*," *Modern Fiction Studies* 25 [Winter 1979–80]: 656). Willa Cather in 1937 was probably far less comfortable with traits such as these that would have been acceptable and even praised in the early decades of the twentieth century when the competitive success ethic permeated American thought.

60. Cather's greater interest in 1915 in exploring what happens *after* one succeeds is evidenced by the greater length of the last two sections in the 1915 version *The Song of the Lark*. Heyeck and Woodress note that when Cather revised in 1937, she removed "from the last two parts and the Epilogue all but 153 of the 6,900 words she cut." In fact, Cather trimmed "by more than one-third" part VI, which particularly focuses on Thea as a successful opera singer ("Cather's Cuts and Revisions," 653, 655).

61. Cather, *O Pioneers!*, 124.

62. Wiebe, *Order*, 4, 11.

63. Ibid., 14–15.

64. Such insistence on a community's need for the outside world may also be Cather's comment, on the verge of World War I, that Americans should not ignore the "wider world."

65. Cather, *My Ántonia*, 18. Subsequent citiations are noted parenthetically in the text. The last sentence of this quotation is inscribed on Cather's tombstone, suggesting the importance that such a sense of belonging had for Cather.

66. Cather, *O Pioneers!*, 65.

67. Woodress, *Life*, 239.

68. I disagree with Mike Fischer, who sees in Cather's use of Bohemian immigrants, both in *O Pioneers!* and in *My Ántonia*, either a conscious or an unconscious championing of this ethnic group because they were the "most Western and consequently least threatening of the Eastern European peoples." Fischer points out that American propagandists also used the Bohemian Czechs, ostensibly for this same reason. He claims that "in this context, Cather's portrait of Ántonia can be read as a text that romanticizes the United States's relationship to non-Anglo-Saxon peoples." It seems far more likely that Cather wrote about Bohemians because many of her most vivid childhood experiences revolved around her Bohemian neighbor in Red Cloud, Annie Pavelka, the Miner family's "hired girl," after whom Cather modeled Ántonia. More convincing is Fischer's argument that Cather's "conception of western history as the story of immigrant settlers blinded her to the effects of such immigration on the West's native populations" ("Pastoralism," 41).

69. See Blanche Gelfant (*Women Writing*) for a discussion of this dream as a reflection of Jim's (and Cather's) sexual anxieties. Along those lines, we can perhaps view Jim's sexual anxieties as a further manifestation of his general inability to define himself clearly.

70. "Suddenly we have found that there is no longer any Frontier," Frank Norris commented in 1902 ("The Frontier Gone at Last," in *The Call of the Wild: 1900–1916*, ed. Roderick Nash, The American Culture Series, no. 6 [New York: George Braziller, 1970], 69). Cather explores this theme again in *A Lost Lady*.

71. Cawelti, *Apostles*, 229, 233.

Chapter 3. Crises of Self and a Glimmer of Hope

1. Perhaps to better depict her darker vision of a materialistic America, Cather in these novels makes a slight shift in setting to more recent eras. Cather celebrated the pioneer past of the 1880s and 1890s in *O Pioneers!* and *My Ántonia*, whereas *A Lost Lady* is set in a somewhat later West; *Alexander's Bridge*, like *My Mortal Enemy*, is set in an urban America during the first decade of the twentieth century, but Cather moves to a World War I setting for *One of Ours*, and to a postwar setting for *The Professor's House*.

2. Bernard Baum, "Willa Cather's Waste Land," *South Atlantic Quarterly* 48 (1949): 590. See also Harold Bloom and Phyllis Rose, who note connections between Cather and other modernists.

3. Although Cather's female protagonists, Marian Forrester and Myra Henshawe, seem more self-serving than Claude Wheeler and Godfrey St. Peter, Cather moves back and forth across gender lines in her portrayal of community-responsive characters in the novels of this period. Claude's mother, the endearing housekeeper Mahailey, and the other-centered Gladys Farmer in *One of Ours* are other-centered women; Captain Forrester in *A Lost Lady* faces his own financial ruin rather than jeopardize those who invested in his bank; the sewing woman, Augusta, in *The Professor's House*, and even St. Peter's wife, Lillian, exhibit concern for others; both Nellie Birdseye and Oswald Henshawe in *My Mortal Enemy* focus on others.

4. Latrobe Carroll, "Willa Sibert Cather," *Bookman*, 3 May 1921, in Bohlke, *Person*, 24.

5. "A Talk with Miss Cather," *Webster County Argus*, 29 September 1921, in Bohlke, *Person*, 27.

6. "To Live Intensely Is Creed of Willa S. Cather, Authoress," *Omaha Daily News*, 29 October 1921, in Bohlke, *Person*, 30.

7. Eva Mahoney, "How Willa Cather Found Herself," *Omaha World-Herald*, 27 November 1921, in Bohlke, *Person*, 37.

8. Alleen Sumner, "Prize Novelist Finds Writing and Eating Kin," *Cleveland Press*, 20 November 1925, in Bohlke, *Person*, 87.

9. A 1931 profile of Cather characterizes her as "scornful of expatriate writers" (Louise Bogan, "Profiles: American Classic," *New Yorker*, 8 August 1931, in Bohlke, *Person*, 114).

10. "Today's Novels Give Much Hope to Miss Cather," *New York World*, 21 May 1923, in Bohlke, *Person*, 59.

11. Willa Cather, "On Nature and Romance," in Slote, *Kingdom*, 232.

12. Willa Cather, *One of Ours* (New York: Vintage Books, 1971), 272. Subsequent citations are noted parenthetically in the text.

13. Alan Trachtenberg, *The Incorporation of America: Culture and Society in the Gilded Age* (New York: Hill and Wang, 1982), 141.

14. Lisa Steinman, in *Made in America: Science, Technology, and American Modernist Poets* (New Haven: Yale University Press, 1987), illuminates this "American" setting, with its special allegiance to technology, business, and commerce (1910–45), especially as that setting was perceived by modernist poets. See chap. 1 and 2 for an insightful analysis of the general forces at work on American artists in this era.

15. Cather's use of Joan of Arc suggests a celebration of women who break free from restrictive societal roles, as it also suggests Cather's affinity for the nonconforming individual, apart from society yet contributing to it. Another factor, however, may have guided Cather in her choice of this heroine as she wrote *One of Ours*: Joan of Arc was canonized in 1921.

16. Cather, *Lark*, 221.

17. Sharon O'Brien argues that the novel contains a "submerged narrative" that associates war "not with male heroism but with mutilation, infantilization, and emasculation," thus revealing "Cather's antiromantic vision of the realities of war" as well as "the woman writer's survivor guilt" ("Combat Envy and Survivor Guilt: Willa Cather's 'Manly Battle Yarn,'" in *Arms and the Woman: War, Gender, and Literary Representation*, ed. Helen M. Cooper, Adrienne Munich, and Susan Merrill Squier [Chapel Hill: University of North Carolina Press, 1989], 188). I agree with O'Brien's appraisal, and see that submerged narrative intensifying the final irony—Claude's belief that he died for a worthwhile cause.

18. Cather, *My Ántonia*, 372.

19. Susan Rosowski, in "Willa Cather's *A Lost Lady*: Art Versus the Closing Frontier" (*Great Plains Quarterly* 2 [Fall 1982]: 239), similarly describes the era portrayed

in *A Lost Lady* as "an American frontier that promised a pioneer experience of boundless opportunity at the same time it restricted that experience to a strikingly brief period." In another essay, Rosowski sees the West of *A Lost Lady* as a victim, suffering "beneath the very race it had given rise to" ("Willa Cather and the Fatality of Place: O *Pioneers!*, *My Ántonia*, and *A Lost Lady*," in *Geography and Literature: A Meeting of the Disciplines*, ed. William E. Mallory and Paul Simpson-Housley [Syracuse, N.Y.: Syracuse University Press, 1987], 92). Although I find this reading illuminating, I see Cather focusing purposefully on survival rather than on victimization in this novel—even though Marian Forrester ultimately must move to South America to find a place that still lends itself to her adaptable pioneering spirit.

20. Willa Cather, *A Lost Lady* (New York: Vintage Books, 1972), 169. Subsequent citations are noted parenthetically in the text.

21. Harold Bloom, ed., *Willa Cather*, Modern Critical Views Series (New York: Chelsea House Publishers, 1985), 1. Cather, Bloom claims, reflects in her fiction "the era's malaise." I see Cather focusing, however, on a way to cure "the era's malaise." As O'Brien notes, Cather's fiction of the twenties, despite its tone of "disaffection with modern American society," makes "commitments to continuing and to accepting change, process and life's inevitable disappointments" ("Mothers, Daughters," 287–88).

22. *Warren Susman, Culture as History: The Transformation of American Society in the Twentieth Century* (New York: Pantheon Books, 1984), 273.

23. See Bledstein, *Culture of Professionalism*, chap. 4 ("Character"), 129–58, for a discussion of the wide-ranging applications and implications of this term in nineteenth-century America.

24. Susman, *Culture*, 273.

25. Ibid., 274–77.

26. Ibid., 275.

27. James Folsom stresses Cather's theme of adjusting to change. Success for Cather's characters, he says, "depends primarily upon a willingness to put aside the past and to face the future with hope" ("Willa Cather," in *Twentieth-Century Western Writers*, ed. James Vinson [New York: Macmillan Publishing Company, Inc., 1982], 152). We see this concern with adaptation as early as her 1891 Carlyle essay, mentioned in chap. 1, in which she describes the aging Carlyle trying to survive in a world of changing values. The same preoccupation is evident in Cather's epigraph to *The Troll Garden* (1905): she quotes from Charles Kingsley's 1891 lecture, "The Roman and the Teuton," an allegorical account of another time of change and upheaval—the overthrow of the Roman Empire by Teutonic tribes.

28. Arnold, "Stanzas from the Grande Chartreuse," in Allott and Super, *Matthew Arnold*, 164–65.

29. Agreeing with Niel, Edward and Lillian Bloom see Marian Forrester as a failure because she *does* adapt (*Gift of Sympathy*, 70). I agree with Susan Rosowski, who in "Willa Cather's *A Lost Lady*: The Paradoxes of Change" (*Novel* 11 [Fall 1977]: 52), provides a contrasting appraisal of Marian Forrester, and a particularly enlightening analysis of Cather's focus "on human adaptation to change." Rosowski sees Marian and Niel struggling to maintain "the constancy of a moral-aesthetic order amidst the disorder of cultural and economic change" (62). My analysis, although indebted to hers, looks at cultural concerns that resonate in the novel, rather than aesthetic ones. Also moving past the view of Marian Forrester as a failure is Ellen Moers, who views Cather's "lost lady" as "a great teacher," a key figure in transmitting "civilized standards" to a new generation (*Literary Women: The Great Writers* [Garden City, N.Y.: Doubleday, 1976], 239).

30. Susman, *Culture*, 273.

31. Joseph Urgo, in his analysis of *A Lost Lady*, makes clear that this was neither an "American Dream" nor a "romantic phase" of our history for Native Americans, the vic-

tims of the pioneer era. Referring to Captain Forrester, Urgo observes: "His historic stature is the result of what is *unsaid*, or left out, of his history, and what is selected as significant, worthy of narration" ("How Context," 185). I agree that Cather paints a romantic portrait of Captain Forrester and of the pioneer era in *A Lost Lady*, evading or quickly moving past any discussion of the Indian problem, a dilemma that she must certainly have found uncomfortable—she briefly mentions Ivy Peters's exploitation of Indians and Marian Forrester's distaste for such behavior, although Marian nevertheless permits it. Perhaps Cather's selective omission of Native Americans' plight as victims of the pioneer era also reflects her strong belief that fiction should not be used for social protest. See her famous letter (1936) on art as escape ("Escapism," in *On Writing*, 18–29), which I discuss more fully in chap. 5.

32. Cather, *O Pioneers!*, 48.

33. Explaining that she had not tried to make a "character study" of Lyra Garber, the real-life model for Marian Forrester, but rather a "portrait," Cather in 1925 told an interviewer: "There was no fun in it unless I could get her just as I remembered her and produce *the effect she had on me* and the many others who knew her" (interview with Flora Merrill, *New York World*, 19 April 1925, in Bohlke, *Person*, 77—my italics).

34. Susman, *Culture*, 276.

35. Willa Cather, "Miss Jewett," in *Forty*, 94.

36. Susman, *Culture*, 276.

37. Cather, *My Ántonia*, 352. Cather used this phrase even in her earliest writing to note the powerful, indelible imprint of an arresting personality. In an 1895 article on Robert Louis Stevenson, she remarks: "One would like to leave an image for a few years upon men's minds," as Marian Forrester does on Niel's mind and as Ántonia does on Jim's (Willa Cather, *Courier*, 2 November 1895, in Slote, *Kingdom*, 313).

38. Emphasizing the gender of the woodpecker, Ivy addresses the bird as "Miss Female" (23), although the narrator refers to the woodpecker as "it."

39. One is reminded, in observing Marian Forrester's "ethics," of William James's pragmatic definition of truth: "The true is only the expedient in the way of our thinking, just as the right is only the expedient in the way of behaving" (William James, *The Moral Philosophy of William James*, ed. John K. Roth [New York: Apollo Editions, 1969], 304). Cather, as her friend George Seibel remarked, was "a devoted disciple" of William James (noted in Curtin, *Parish*, 850).

40. Loyalty, an important issue in the self/community dialogue of the early 1900s in America, was the focus of Josiah Royce's *The Philosophy of Loyalty* and *The Philosophy of Josiah Royce*, ed. John K. Roth [New York: Apollo Editions, 1908]). Marian Forrester seems to demonstrate a happy balance between what Royce saw as one extreme, thoughtless individualism, and the other extreme, loyalty to the *idea* of loyalty.

41. Sandra Gilbert and Susan Gubar, however, see Marian Forrester as "desperate," like the bird after Ivy Peters blinds it. For Gilbert and Gubar, she is one of Cather's representatives of the "fall into gender from the sexual frontier"—the world of Alexandra Bergson and Ántonia Shimerda, both of whom had more freedom because they lived in an earlier era when "women were economically productive and socially central" (*No Man's Land*, 260, 173–74). I see Cather focusing more positively on the bird's ability to "learn" and thus to survive, and likewise on Marian's ability to find ways to survive even in a world of narrowing opportunities for women.

42. We are given a clue to this early in the novel, when the young Niel and his friends are conversing with Mrs. Forrester. His friend George remarks that "most women can't [swim]"; Marian Forrester, who throughout the novel forces Niel to adjust his stereotypical nineteenth-century view of women as frail and in need of rescue, corrects George, insisting that "everybody" swims in California (18).

43. Cather, *One of Ours*, 104.

44. Susman, *Culture*, 220.

45. Cather scholars have commented on Cather's own affinity for the role of performer: "Willa Cather was always something of an actress," writes Mildred Bennett (*World*, 170). Slote remarks that Cather "became an actress" through her fiction, "creating and recreating for herself and in her writing new landscapes, voices, rooms" (Bernice Slote, "Willa Cather: The Secret Web," *Five Essays on Willa Cather: The Merrimack Symposium*, ed. John J. Murphy [North Andover, Mass.: Merrimack College, 1974], 1).

46. Susman, *Culture*, xxvi.

47. See Marilyn Berg Callander's book for an examination of fairy-tale allusions throughout the Cather canon, although Callendar does not examine *A Lost Lady* in much detail (*Willa Cather and the Fairy Tale* [Ann Arbor, Mich.: UMI Research Press, 1989]). Woodress, in his discussion of *A Lost Lady*, notes: "The omniscient narrator begins like the teller of a fairy tale" (*Life*, 343).

48. Robert Cherney suggests that Cather may have been influenced in her choice of title for this essay by Oswald Spengler's view of history as cyclical. Although I see much evidence in Cather's writing that she did share Spengler's cyclical view of history, I do not find Cather's work in the early 1920s echoing the drastically negative "themes of cultural decline and imminent destruction" that Cherney claims it does ("Nebraska, 1883–1925: Cather's Version and History's," in Murphy, *Family, Community, and History,* 238). Cather faces up to those possibilities and moves past despair, finding new reasons to hope that the next "cycle" might have something positive to offer. Lasch, in reviewing all of the essays in the "These United States" series, notes that Cather's is one of the least cynical in its outlook for America (*Heaven*, 421).

49. Lasch, *Heaven*, 83.

50. Cather, "First Cycle," 238. Patricia Yongue compares Cather's essay to *A Lost Lady* ("*A Lost Lady*: The End of the First Cycle," *Western American Literature* 7 [1972]: 3–12). Although she notes that the Nebraska essay ends with Cather expressing hope, Yongue feels that *A Lost Lady*, along with Cather's other fiction of the early twenties, "bypasses this optimistic posture for the most part, because it reflects . . . the temporary defeat of the pioneer nobility at the hands of the machine" (4). Yongue sees Marian Forrester as representative of an "aesthetic decline" (11) in America. I contend that Cather, in her depiction of Marian Forrester, is less interested in aesthetics than in pragmatism and adaptation.

51. Cather, "First Cycle," 237–38.

52. Her perspective here, as well as her wording, is similar to Santayana's 1920 observation: "Civilisation is perhaps approaching one of those long winters that overtake it from time to time. . . . Such a catastrophe would be no reason for despair. Nothing lasts forever; but the elasticity of life is wonderful" (Santayana, *Character*, v). Cather's fondness for "elasticity" is evident in a remark that she made in 1933 about the novel genre: "Looking back over its short history, perhaps the most arresting thing one notices about the novel is its amazing elasticity and variety" (Willa Cather, "On the Novel," speech, 4 May 1933, in Bohlke, *Person*, 169).

53. Cather, *One of Ours*, 48.

54. Flora Merrill, "A Short Story Course Can Only Delay," interview of Willa Cather, *New York World*, 19 April 1925, in Bohlke, *Person*, 77.

55. Cather, "First Cycle," 238.

56. Susman, *Culture*, 111.

57. Cather, *Professor's*, 162. Subsequent citations are noted parenthetically in the text.

58. Slote, "Appointment," 39. For other comparisons of Cather to Eliot, see Baum ("Cather's Waste Land"), David Stouck (*Willa Cather's Imagination* [Lincoln: Univer-

sity of Nebraska Press, 1975], 88–89 and 93–95), and John Holland, "Willa Cather," in Harold Bloom, *Cather*, 171. Both Susman (*Culture*, 121) and Orvell (*Real Thing*, 148) see "Gerontion" as especially representative of the anxieties of this era.

59. T. S. Eliot, "Gerontion," *Collected Poems, 1909–1962* (New York: Harcourt, Brace, and World, Inc., 1963), 29.

60. Ibid., 30.

61. In this political subtext, Cather's novel reflects the concerns of many writers and thinkers of her day. Randolph Bourne, whom Cather admired as a critic, wrote in 1915 of a growing public suspicion that "self-perpetuating boards" of university trustees were consulting "their own interests and the interests of the donors of the vested wealth . . . as faithful corporation directors," thus hampering the academic freedom of faculty members. "The newer state universities are controlled in exactly the same spirit," Bourne notes, sounding as if he is observing first-hand the situation at Cather's fictional university in *The Professor's House* (Randolph Bourne, "Who Owns the Universities?" *The New Republic*, 17 July 1915, 269–70).

62. Eliot, "Gerontion," 7.

63. Josiah Royce to William James, 1888, *The Letters of Josiah Royce*, ed. John Clendenning (Chicago: University of Chicago Press, 1970), 215, cited in Bledstein, *Culture of Professionalism*, 103–4.

64. Cather signals her special preoccupation with sideline narratives in *The Professor's House* by her dedication of the novel to Jan Hambourg, "because he likes narrative."

65. Cather, "Restlessness," in Bohlke, *Person*, 71.

66. Fitzgerald, *Great Gatsby*, 81.

67. Loretta Wasserman agrees that Cather portrays Louie Marsellus positively ("The Music of Time," 237). Louie's remark here resembles a statement by Robert Louis Stevenson that Cather highlights in an 1895 essay on that author: "I believe in the ultimate decency of things; ay, and if I woke in hell, should still believe it!" About Stevenson's remark, the young Cather comments: "Stevenson never wrote a greater sentence. . . . There's optimism for you, the kind of optimism that produces and creates and brings into being, that is the source of all life in art and all art in life" (Willa Cather, "The Passing Show," *Courier*, 2 November 1895, in Slote, *Kingdom*, 314). In Cather's portrayal of Louie Marsellus, this same high regard for the individual who has faith in "the ultimate decency of things" is evident.

68. See David Stouck, "Willa Cather and the Indian Heritage," 435, for a discussion of the "close-knit communal nature" of the tribe on the Blue Mesa. For a more negative but thought-provoking appraisal of the Blue Mesa story, see Walter Michaels's examination of Tom Outland's experience in light of changing immigration laws in the 1920s, and the nativism and "preoccupation with ancestors" in America at this time. Michaels sees this episode reflecting an attitude of American racial superiority: "If the Indians had not been perceived as vanishing, they could not have become the exemplary instance of what it meant to have a culture" ("The Vanishing American," 221, 232).

69. I agree with David Stouck's remarks in "Willa Cather and *The Professor's House*: 'Letting Go with the Heart,'" *Western American Literature* 7 (1972): 20, 24. He finds that St. Peter "has let go of . . . the will to power . . . the instinct to possess and dominate"; he argues, too, that Cather "could no longer endorse the pursuits of a materialistic and competitive society," as this novel demonstrates. But I find Cather at this point still uncomfortable with completely "letting go" of the individualism inherent in the competitive, materialistic American Dream, as her nebulous "outward bound" solution implies.

70. Willa Cather, *My Mortal Enemy* (New York: Vintage Books, 1954), 17. Subsequent citations are noted parenthetically in the text.

71. Cather supposedly intended that phrase to describe Myra's feelings about her

husband, whom she comes to hate; but as James Woodress notes, the text "easily accommodates" the alternate reading of Myra as her own "mortal enemy" (Woodress, *Life*, 384).

72. Cather, *Professor's*, 172.

73. Susman, *Culture*, 220.

74. Glen Love makes a similar observation, seeing this particular setting as symbolic of "the emptiness of westering devoid of a dream" (Glen Love, *The New Americans: The Westerner and the Modern Experience in the American Novel*, [Lewisburg, Pa.: Bucknell University Press, 1982], 160).

75. StephenL. Tanner, "Seeking and Finding in Cather's *My Mortal Enemy*," *Literature and Belief* 8 (1988): 35.

76. Cather, "Small Town Life," in Curtin, *Parish*, 850.

77. In contrast to this newly forged community whose members feel a responsibility to Myra, even when she shuts them out physically and emotionally, is the uncaring community of upstairs neighbors, the Poindexters, who take no responsibility for the emotional anguish that they cause by their noise–intrusions.

78. Cather, *One of Ours*, 357.

79. Cather, *Professor's*, 281.

80. Ibid., 283.

Chapter 4. Fulfillment Through Tradition and Family

1. Willa Cather, interview, *Nebraska State Journal*, 5 September 1926, in Bohlke, *Person*, 90.

2. Santayana, *Character and Opinion*, 170.

3. Hearn, *American Dream*, 139. Susman, makes a similar point. See chap. 10, "Culture and Commitment," in *Culture*, 184–210. See also Orvell, *Real Thing*, 155, and Richard Pells, section III, "The Search for Community," in *Radical Vision and American Dreams: Social Thought in the Depression Years* (New York: Harper and Row, 1973), 96–150.

4. These stories were serialized before being published in *Obscure Destinies* (1932).

5. Waldo Frank, *The Re-discovery of America: An Introduction to a Philosophy of American Life* (New York: Charles Scribner's Sons, 1929), 279, 309.

6. Lewis Mumford, "What I Believe," *Forum* 84 (November 1930): 264.

7. Cather, *Professor's*, 69.

8. Cather, "On the Novel," speech, in Bohlke, *Person*, 170.

9. Stouck, "Issues of History," in Murphy, *Family, Community, and History*, 210.

10. Sergeant, *Memoir*, 253.

11. David Peeler, *Hope Among Us Yet: Social Criticism and Social Solace in Depression America* (Athens: University of Georgia Press, 1987), 7.

12. Willa Cather, "On *Death Comes for the Archbishop*," in *On Writing*, 9.

13. Cather, *One of Ours*, 56.

14. Frank, *Re-discovery*, 309.

15. Willa Cather, *Death Comes for the Archbishop* (New York: Vintage Books, 1971), 7. Subsequent citations are noted parenthetically in the text.

16. Cather, *Lark*, 380.

17. Woodress, *Life*, 405.

18. Myrtle Mason, "Nebraska Scored for Its Many Laws by Willa Cather," *Omaha Bee*, 30 and 31 October 1921, in Bohlke, *Person*, 149.

19. Woodress (*Life*, 401) discusses the differences between Latour and Lamy.

20. Cather, "Restlessness," in Bohlke, *Person*, 72.

21. Ann Fisher-Wirth finds Cather's story of the Canyon de Chelly too "complete," obfuscating the "irrevocable losses" that the Navajos suffered: "Cather seems to offer the Navajo story, against her own bitter knowledge, as assurance to the heart's deepest longing that all which has been lost will be restored" ("Dispossession and Redemption in the Novels of Willa Cather," *Cather Studies* (1990), 1:50. I agree that Cather's purpose here is to keep a hopeful stance even when she sees in her own era little reason for hope, and even if she must be selective in her recounting of the Navajo experience in the Canyon de Chelly.

22. "Literature Leads to High Place," *Hastings Daily Tribune*, 27 April 1927, in Bohlke, *Person*, 99.

23. Cather, *Forty*, preface.

24. Also recognizing Willa Cather's optimistic engagement with her own world, Ellen Moers comments on Cather's famous remark: "Willa Cather should have said . . . 'the world broke in two, but I did not'" ("The Survivors," 9).

25. Weiss, *Myth*, 149.

26. "Famous Nebraska Authoress Visits New Superior Hospital," *Superior Express*, 12 January 1928, in Bohlke, *Person*, 102–3.

27. Peeler, *Hope Among Us*, 7.

28. Cather in 1936 wrote a defense of escapism, which I discuss in chap. 6. In a 1937 letter to friend and critic, Carl Van Vechten, Cather expressed her frustration with being labeled nostalgic.

29. Cather, *Shadows*, 63, 274, 119. Subsequent citations are noted parenthetically in the text.

30. Harvey Newbranch, "Every Man a King," *Omaha World-Herald*, November 1921, in Bohlke, *Person*, 151.

31. Although Cather joined the Episcopal church in December 1922, she apparently saw the Catholic church as an attractive community. John Murphy in "Willa Cather and Catholic Themes" (*Western American Literature* 17 [1982]:53–60), observes that Catholicism, with its "concept of the Church as family" provided for Cather a sense of family security without the "fear of drowning in the home context" (55, 56). Catholicism instead "made family a romantic and mysterious adventure" (57) for Cather. I share Murphy's views, but feel that Catholicism particularly appealed to Cather because it represented long-standing tradition, made concrete in ritual and symbol. Perhaps she never felt the need to convert to Catholicism because such similar ritual, symbol, and long-standing tradition were also part of her own Episcopal religion.

32. Cather, *Death Comes*, 50.

33. Bellah et al., *Habits*, 27.

34. In "American Experience and European Tradition," James Woodress notes that Cather's fiction is itself such a synthesis, "a subtle blend" of two kinds of experience: "a successful graft of her native experience onto the roots and trunk of European culture" (James Woodress, "Willa Cather: American Experience and European Tradition," in Slote and Faulkner, *Art*, 47).

35. Woodress (*Life*, 361) emphasizes that Cather's use of allusion is, as a rule, "unobtrusive," as is certainly the case here.

36. Woodress makes a similar point (*Life*, 429).

37. Cather, *Death Comes*, 50.

38. Bloom, *Willa Cather*, 2.

39. Walter Pater, *The Renaissance: Studies in Art and Poetry*, ed. Donald L. Hill (Berkeley: University of California Press, 1980), 189–90.

40. Cather's views on tradition here resemble closely Lewis Mumford's remarks on "The Emergence of a Past," published in 1925: "The past is . . . a reservoir from which

we can replenish our own emptiness, [and] so far from being the ever–vanishing moment, it is the abiding heritage in a community's life" (Lewis Mumford, "The Emergence of a Past," *New Republic*, 25 November 1925, 19).

41. In his history of the Depression, Robert McElvaine remarks: "Marxism seemed to many in the American intelligentsia of the thirties to support their own moral condemnations of the marketplace economy and to uphold the values of community, justice, and cooperation that so many writers of the period favored" (Robert McElvaine, *The Great Depression: America, 1929–41* [New York: Times Books, 1984], 205).

42. Willa Cather, "On *Shadows on the Rock*," in *On Writing*, 15.

43. Cather, "On the Novel," speech, in Bohlke, *Person,* 170.

44. Ibid., 169.

45. Cather, *My Ántonia*, 18.

46. Frank, *Re-discovery*, 309.

47. Woodress, *Life*, 413.

48. Willa Cather to Mr. Bain, 14 January 1931 (University of Michigan Collection). This is noted in Woodress, *Life*, 423.

49. Susman, *Culture*, 171.

50. Cather, "First Cycle," 238.

51. Willa Cather, "Neighbour Rosicky," in *Obscure Destinies* (New York: Vintage Books, 1974), 45. Subsequent citations are noted parenthetically in the text.

52. Cather, "First Cycle," 238.

53. Commenting on "Neighbour Rosicky," Merrill Skaggs notes Cather's "courage to affirm a new route to, or definition of, the American dream of success" ("Cather's Complex Tale of a Simple Man, 'Neighbour Rosicky,'" in Murphy, *Family, Community, and History*, 83). I share her view, and extend it: Cather was involved in an ongoing project of redefining the American dream in her fiction.

54. Cather, *O Pioneers!*, 308.

55. Willa Cather, "Old Mrs. Harris," in *Obscure Destinies* (New York: Vintage Books, 1974), 97. Subsequent citations are noted parenthetically in the text.

56. Cather, *O Pioneers!*, 248.

57. Cather, *Lark*, 383.

58. See Bohlke, *Person*, 157, for Cather's aversion to motion pictures. Woodress (*Life*, 437) notes that serializing, too, was "something she hated to do."

59. Cather remarks: "The artist, poor fellow, has but one care, one purpose, one hope—his work. That is all God gave him; in place of love, of happiness, of popularity, only that" (Willa Cather, "The Rights of Genius," *Nebraska State Journal*, 21 October, 1894, in Slote, *Kingdom*, 142). I discuss this view at greater length in chap. 6.

60. Cather, *Professor's*, 165.

61. Cather, *Forty*, 106.

62. Ibid., 97.

63. This photograph is reproduced in Bennett, *World*. Woodress explains that the party, which Cather gave for the children of friends, was a celebration of Holy Innocents Day (*Life*, 436).

Chapter 5. Facing America's Failed Dream

1. Studs Terkel, *Hard Times: An Oral History of the Great Depression* (New York: Washington Square Press, 1970), 277.

2. Sherwood Anderson, *Puzzled America* (New York: Charles Scribner's Sons, 1935), ix.

3. Terkel, *Hard Times*, 102, 229.

4. Hearn, *American Dream*, 134.

5. Stouck, *Imagination*, 291.

6. McElvaine, *Great Depression*, 338, 33.

7. Smith, *Redeeming*, 848.

8. Pells, *Radical Vision*, 365–66.

9. Susman, *Culture*, 168.

10. Ibid., 191, 200.

11. Hearn, *American Dream*, 106.

12. Ibid., 165. Alfred Kazin describes fellow disillusioned young college graduates who turned to such "direct frontal attack[s]": "They had broken with the studious patterns we had all been raised in; they had given up solemnly trying to inch their way up the ladder. They had broken with the bourgeois world and its false ambitions" (Alfred Kazin, *Starting Out in the Thirties* [New York: Vintage Books, 1980], 88).

13. Hearn, *American Dream*, 90.

14. I am indebted to John Randall for this phrase, although he uses it to classify Cather as a disciple of Pater, which he sees evident in her dedication to art (4–6). I am referring instead to the possible influence that late nineteenth-century attitudes about rugged individualism and the self-made individual continued to have on Cather throughout her life.

15. Hearn, *American Dream*, 131.

16. Rosowski sees in this novel Cather's view of "the destiny incurred upon a person by being female": "In dying as in living, Lucy is caught by forces of which she is ignorant and over which she has no control" ("Female Landscapes," 241). I see Cather here representing in a more general way the "forces" over which so many Americans, male and female, had no control at this time.

17. Hearn, *American Dream*, 190.

18. Pells, *Radical Vision*, 366. Most critics see in the darker tone of *Lucy Gayheart* either Cather's reflection on aging, her changing attitude toward art, or her anxiety about impending world war. See, for example, section V, "Dark Romanticism" in Rosowski, *Voyage Perilous* (207–45). My principal focus is the Depression–induced cultural resonances that add to Cather's dark tone in *Lucy Gayheart*—and the sense of hope that Cather nevertheless manages to retain.

19. Cather, *Lucy Gayheart*, 62. Subsequent citations are noted parenthetically in the text.

20. Lucy's passivity mirrors the nation's. McElvaine cites a commentary in *The New Republic* (January 1933): "What is surprising is the passive resignation with which the blow [i.e., the Depression] has been accepted" (in McElvaine, *Great Depression*, 81).

21. Susan Hallgarth compares Thea and Lucy, also noting that "Lucy has neither mother nor mentor" (Susan Hallgarth, "The Woman Who Would Be Artist in *The Song of the Lark* and *Lucy Gayheart*," in Murphy, *Family, Community, and History*, 171).

22. Rosowski, *Voyage*, 225.

23. Several critics see this as a key scene. Susan Rosowski notes Lucy's fear of this "overpowering" force ("Willa Cather's Female Landscapes: *The Song of the Lark* and *Lucy Gayheart*," *Women's Studies* 11 [1984]: 240). Merrill Skaggs remarks: "Any reader of Cather should know that Lucy will come to no good end when she decides that the star 'was too bright and too sharp'" (*After the World*, 156). Blanche Gelfant, on the other hand, writes that "Cather was attempting to make Lucy soar out of the mundane world into her dream," in a celebration of the romantic imagination. She sees Lucy attempting to "disembody" herself, to become "like music." Gelfant asserts that "throughout the novel, Lucy yearns to renew her communion with the gleaming stars of the sky," i.e., this higher life of the imagination (*Women Writing*, 126–27, 119). Although I disagree with the view that Lucy has "the strength of her desire," Gelfant provides an illuminating reading of *Lucy Gayheart* as Cather's own statement of doubt about language.

24. Kazin, *Starting Out*, 57.

25. Sharon O'Brien notes that the "characters [in Cather's fiction] who find fulfill-ment most often do so by connecting to 'something complete and great' that enriches, extends, and defines the self even as it dissolves it." Yet, notes O'Brien, Cather "simul-taneously . . . dreaded self-annihilation and obliteration" (*Emerging Voice*, 48). Cather's characterization of a fearful *Lucy Gayheart* may reflect that dread.

26. Although I agree with Hallgarth's analysis of the contrasts between Thea Kron-borg and Lucy Gayheart, I find it difficult to envision Lucy as ultimately "victorious"—a conclusion that Hallgarth reaches on the grounds that Lucy "discover[s] the female in art and then affirm[s] Life and her own autonomous self" ("Woman Who Would Be," 173). I see Lucy as too dependent on others' shaping views of her to triumph either as artist or as autonomous self.

27. Cather, *Lark*, vi.

28. Terkel, *Hard Times*, 485.

29. Ibid., 527.

30. Skaggs sees Lucy's activity throughout the novel as "movement that goes nowhere" (*After the World*, 157), while I see it as erratic, but purposeful: a flight *away* from any type of self-confrontation. The last sentence of the novel seems to stress that aspect of *Lucy Gayheart*'s personality, when it describes her "three light footprints, *run-ning away*" (231—my italics). It is interesting to view Lucy's habit of "running away" in light of a comment that Cather made to friends in 1933. She remarked that she had been "running away from herself all her life and was happiest when she was running the fastest" (Woodress, *Life*, 452). Perhaps in her characterization of *Lucy Gayheart*, whom Cather found somewhat unappealing as a protagonist, Cather is facing up to an aspect of her own personality that she also found unappealing.

31. Lasch, *Heaven*, 83.

32. Kazin, *Starting Out*, 14.

33. Pells, *Radical Vision*, 227.

34. See Mary Ryder's essay for a discussion of this and other portrayals of the "sis-ter-sister bond" in Cather's fiction. Ryder sees in this novel, as in *The Song of the Lark* and *The Professor's House*, Cather's examination of "the failure of sisters to accept their dependence and similarity while acknowledging their need for independence and differ-ence" ("Loosing the Tie That Binds: Sisterhood in Cather," in Murphy, *Family, Com-munity, and History*, 41, 46–47). This seems to me to highlight one aspect of Cather's concern with self-definition.

35. David Stouck sees this as a key passage in understanding Cather's late-life per-spective on artistic accomplishment (*Imagination*, 298). The passage certainly reflects Cather's preoccupation with what "community" an artist might be able to claim as his or her own.

36. Merrill Skaggs sees Harry as the character with whom Cather identifies: "The emotional energy she invests in this story, does not derive from either of the lovers [Lucy, Sebastian] but from Harry Gordon. It is Harry Gordon's predicament that justifies the effort of writing—or reading the book" (*After the World*, 161–62). Skaggs, however, focuses on Cather's own personal struggle, imaged in Harry Gordon's, suggesting that Cather's "most important and sustaining reason" for writing *Lucy Gayheart* was "to come to terms with the lifetime of pain that survivors—such as she was—can suffer from their betrayals" (*After the World*, 163). I focus not on the betrayals that Gordon (or Cather) survived, but on the self-disappointment that Harry confronts and moves beyond, as it reflects a nation's self-disappointment.

37. This idea seems to have been ingrained in Cather from childhood. One of her favorite poems, "Lines," by Thomas Campbell, ends: "To bear is to conquer our fate" (*The Complete Poetical Works of Thomas Campbell* [Boston: Crosby and Nichols, 1865], 161).

38. Gelfant, *Women Writing*, 142.

39. McElvaine, *Great Depression*, 340–41.

40. In *A Lost Lady*, Niel Herbert makes a similar remark about Marian Forrester: "She couldn't help being interested in people, even very commonplace people" (70); but Cather's connotation is different in *Lucy Gayheart*, suggesting no longer an interest of curious delight but rather, one of humanitarian concern. Marian Forrester, Niel continues, is interested in people's stories or their amusing mannerisms; Mrs. Ramsay's interest is in people's well-being. Perhaps this merely reflects the varying "interests" of young and old; but it might also serve as an indication of the older Cather's changing perspective.

41. Willa Cather, "The Old Beauty," in *The Old Beauty and Others* (New York: Vintage Books, 1976), 36.

42. Ibid., 43.

43. Anderson, *Puzzled*, xv–xvi.

44. See Pells, *Radical Vision*, and Blake, *Beloved Community*, for thorough, insightful discussions of the sense of community that pervaded American thought during this era, and of its more radical political ramifications. Pells presents an illuminating and thorough analysis of the cautious, highly ambivalent adoption of collectivist values by Depression authors in chap. 5, "Documentaries, Fiction, and the Depression," 195–251. See also Kazin's account of his personal experience with such writers during the thirties (*Starting Out*). Although Willa Cather did not fit readily into the "Beloved Community" (Randolph Bourne's term, from which Blake takes his title) of more radical, politically oriented writers described in these studies, in some respects she seems to locate herself on the fringes of that community, despite her apolitical stance. Pells notes, too, that many writers, despite their "fashionable collectivism," retained an underlying belief in the importance of individual achievement (*Radical Vision*, 249, 246–49).

45. Cather, *Lucy Gayheart*, 224.

46. Susman, *Culture*, 195–96.

47. Rosowski, *Voyage*, 234.

48. Willa Cather, *Sapphira and the Slave Girl* (New York: Vintage Books, 1975), 110. Subsequent citations are noted parenthetically in the text.

49. Hermione Lee notes that "Cather's treatment of her black characters is problematic" in this novel. Lee calls Cather's "version of black slavery . . . a dated historical curiosity," but cites evidence from Cather's letters indicating that she was "unaware" that she was caricaturing blacks, and unaware of her sentimentalized picture of slavery (*Willa Cather: Double Lives* [New York: Pantheon Books, 1989], 365). I agree, although I see in her presentation of Henry Colbert's guilt and anxiety perhaps an unconscious self-revelation.

50. McElvaine, *Great Depression*, 187.

51. Nathan Asch, *The Road: In Search of America* (New York: W. W. Norton and Co., 1937), 57, 49.

52. McElvaine, *Great Depression*, 223, 206.

53. See Woodress, *Life*, 479–80, for Cather's reaction to Hitler's aggression in 1938. Edith Lewis also discusses Cather's attitude toward the impending war: "Many people thought [Cather] was 'not interested' in the war; but, indeed, she felt it too much to make it the subject of casual conversation. When the French army surrendered [22 June 1940], she wrote in her 'Line-a-day', 'There seems to be no future at all for people of my generation'" (*Cather Living*, 184)—a bleak perspective against which she seems to struggle in her late fiction.

Several critics see Cather's feelings about the impending war behind her darkening vision in *Sapphira*. Susan Rosowski writes that this "may well be the most directly political of all her writing," noting that "the fall of 1937, during which Cather began work on *Sapphira and the Slave Girl*, was a time of increasingly ominous tensions pointing to the war that Cather felt would be 'the end of all'" (*Voyage*, 244). Merrill Skaggs makes a connection between Cather's feelings of horror and helplessness "as a teetering world prepared to tumble and smash" and her book, which "depicts lives lived in a time when a way of life begins to crumble" (*After the World*, 168). Alfred Kazin sympathetically indicts fellow intellectuals in the thirties as "sick, deluded ex-utopians, so long victims of their easy credulity"; he identifies September 1938 as an especially disillusioning period for many socialists and Marxists in America who could not believe that Stalin would sign a nonaggression pact with Hitler: "Everyone was guilty, and in a way, everything was too" (*Starting Out*, 156, 142). In the guilt that pervades *Sapphira and the Slave Girl*, Cather may be reflecting this general mood of "intellectual guilt" that Kazin notes (*Starting Out*, 111).

While I agree that Willa Cather's concern over the world situation certainly resonates in the novel, I am here primarily interested in examining how *Sapphira* reflects Cather's years of living in a society suffering from the psychological effects of economic depression and domestic crisis.

54. Lasch, *Heaven*, 530.

55. Susan Rosowski also notes the focus on community at the end of what she sees as an otherwise darkly gothic novel; she calls Sapphira's change of heart about her daughter "a rejoining with the human community," noting that "Cather completes the return to the human community" with the reunion of Nancy and Till (*Voyage*, 242–43). David Stouck stresses the mending in the novel when he calls this "a romance of forgiveness" (*Imagination*, 230).

56. This is reminiscent of the child Cécile, in *Shadows on the Rock*, who feels so securely enveloped within her little community (*Shadows*, 158).

57. Susman, *Culture*, 196.

58. Dorothy Canfield Fisher, Review of *Sapphira and the Slave Girl*, by Willa Cather, *Book-of-the-Month Club News,* December 1940, in *Critical Essays on Willa Cather*, ed. John Murphy (Boston: G.K. Hall, 1984) 284–86.

59. Morton Zabel, "The Tone of the Time," review of *Sapphira and the Slave Girl*, by Willa Cather, *Nation* 151 (7 December 1940): 575–76.

Chapter 6. "Creative Tension"

1. Fanny Butcher, *Many Lives—One Love (*New York: Harper and Row Publishers, Inc., 1972], 354.

2. Willa Cather to Zoe Akins, 5 January 1945, Henry E. Huntington Library, San Marino, Calif.

3. See Woodress, *Life*, 497–503, for details on the "sort of communal life" that Cather was living in her late years.

4. Willa Cather, "Katherine Mansfield," in *Forty*, 135–36.

5. John Chamberlain, "Literature," in *America Now*: *An Inquiry into Civilization in the United States*, ed. Harold E. Stearns (New York: Charles Scribner's Sons, 1938), 44.

6. John Dewey, *Individualism Old and New* (New York: Minton, Balch and Co., 1929), 170–71.

7. John Dewey, *Freedom and Culture* (New York: G. P. Putnam's Sons, 1939), 22.

8. Hearn, *American Dream*, 197.

9. *New Masses* 8 (August 1932): 10. Quoted in Pells, *Radical Vision*, 167. Pells's discussion of artists who turned toward community emphasizes the strong current of individualism that continues to run through their writing (*Radical Vision*, 202–39).

10. Pells, *Radical Vision*, 367. Casey Blake refers to a similar "creative tension" in his appraisal of cultural critics, Randolph Bourne, Van Wyck Brooks, Waldo Frank, and Lewis Mumford—the "Young Americans": "[They] sought to foster a creative tension between the claims of spirit and society, culture and practice, self and community" (*Beloved Community*, 300). Although Cather did not address political or cultural issues in the same direct manner that the Young Americans did, through her fiction she enters into the Young Americans' intellectual discussion and seems to share their desire "to foster a creative tension."

11. Bellah et al., *Habits*, 84, 150, 47.

12. Unable to go to her cottage at Grand Manan, Cather spent both of these summers at an isolated retreat off the coast of northeastern Maine, Mt. Desert Island. In this peaceful, secluded spot, she wrote these two final stories, both of which appear in *The Old Beauty and Others*, published in 1948.

13. Sharon O'Brien observes that Cather "strove for a precarious balance between self and other," although O'Brien uses these terms in a slightly different manner, primarily to discuss Cather's psychological state—"her desire simultaneously to possess a demarcated ego and to lose herself in something larger than the self" (*Emerging Voice*, 48).

14. Cather, "Best Years," in *The Old Beauty*, 112. Subsequent citations are noted parenthetically in the text.

15. The characterization of James Ferguesson brings to mind Susan Rosowski's assessment of Cather's purpose throughout her career: "Willa Cather early took up the romantic challenge to vindicate imaginative thought in a world threatened by materialism and pursued it with remarkable consistency throughout her career" (*Voyage Perilous*, x). In Cather's last story, she continues "to vindicate imaginative thought" in her portrait of James Ferguesson.

16. Cather, *Professor's*, 170.

17. Cherney, "Nebraska," in Murphy, *Family, Community, and History*. I agree with Cherney that Cather probably disliked Populism, but politics never really held Cather's attention, and I think it unlikely, especially at the close of her life, that Cather would devote a significant portion of a story meant to celebrate her own family to criticism of a long-dead political movement. Although she probably wanted to depict, in a kindly, retrospective fashion, the political confusion in Webster County, Nebraska, during her adolescence, her portrait of James Ferguesson, and of his family's admiration and love for him, seems much more purposeful—and more positive—than Cherney suggests. See Lasch, *Heaven*, 221–25, for a revisionist appraisal of Populist politics that makes clear the political chaos which a young Cather must have observed in Red Cloud during the 1880s. Besides Cherney's essay, see Evelyn Hinz's "Willa Cather's Technique and the Ideology of Populism" for a discussion of Populist resonances in Cather's fiction (*Western American Literature* 7 [1972]: 47–61). These authors also examine Populist influences in Cather's writing: John Randall, *Landscape*; David Daiches, *Willa Cather: A Critical Introduction* (Ithaca: Cornell University Press, 1951); Edward and Lillian Bloom, *Gift of Sympathy*.

18. Cather's vision of an America of grand and varied possibilities evades, of course, some of the more uncomfortable realities of which she was certainly aware, and which she must have seen as testing the openness of the American Dream. She seems determined throughout her fiction, however, to depict pathways to personal fulfillment that are open to all—to immigrants such as Alexandra, Ántonia, and Anton Rosicky; to women such as Marian Forrester and Thea Kronborg; to blacks such as Nancy and Blind d'Arnault. Distancing herself historically from these representatives of marginalized groups, she perhaps found it easier to depict an America that offered them opportunities for success equal to, or even more fulfilling in the long run than, the opportunities that it offered to white males such as Bartley Alexander, Jim Burden, or Godfrey St. Peter. It

is possible that she was also attempting in her characterizations of minorities to bring history forward as an encouraging, positive model for her present-day readers. Lois Zamora points out that Cather "still believed in the possibility of finding a historical center that would hold, a possibility which most European and U. S. modernists had, at the time Cather was writing, largely dismissed" ("Usable Past," 24). This belief, as we have seen, constantly provided her with a way to redefine rather than abandon the American Dream. Noting Cather's typical western setting, Bernice Slote also draws a connection between Cather's use of history and her optimism about "the better future that was always in the Western dream" ("Plains Culture," 97).

19. Cather, *Lark*, v.

20. Willa Cather, "Before Breakfast," in *The Old Beauty and Others* (New York: Vintage Books, 1976), 159. Subsequent citations are noted parenthetically in the text. Cather was perhaps using the name Grenfell ironically. Sir Wilfred Grenfell (1865–1940), a British physician and medical missionary to Labrador (famous enough that Cather would have certainly known of him), seems a very other-centered "namesake" for her self–involved protagonist who tries so hard to get away from people. I thank Peter Hays for pointing out the possible connection between Cather's fictional Grenfell and this historical figure.

21. Cather seems in this late story still to be poking fun at the Alger myth, especially its characteristic ingredient of luck or chance. The poor but hard-working young Grenfell, on a rare vacation, is bicycling in the mountains when he collides with a young woman. He runs two miles to her hotel to tell her family that she has been injured. Her father, as fate would have it, is "a legend" (151)—a highly successful businessman who chooses Henry to marry their daughter. The suggestion is that Henry's material success is as much due to this fortunate accident, so typical in Alger stories, as to his hard work.

22. See Marilyn Arnold's essay, "Cather's Last Three Stories: A Testament of Life and Endurance," for a full treatment of the theme of survival and adaptation in "Before Breakfast," "The Best Years," and "The Old Beauty" (*Great Plains Quarterly* 4 [Fall 1984]: 238–44). In another essay, Arnold notes Cather's optimism about the future in these final stories, observing that even the most pessimistic of her characters, Henry Grenfell, "never succumbs to the temptation of lasting despair" (in Wasserman, *Short Fiction*, 167).

23. Cather, *Lark*, 380.

24. Patricia Yongue, "Willa Cather's Aristocrats," in two parts, *Southern Humanities Review* 14 (Winter and Spring 1980): 47.

25. Ibid., 119–24.

26. Willa Cather to Bernard de Voto, 10 March 1937, Stanford University, Calif.

27. Bernard de Voto, editorial, *Saturday Review of Literature*, 13 February 1937, 20.

28. *Radical Vision*, 160.

29. Malcolm Cowley, *Exile's Return* (1934; reprint, New York: Viking Press, 1951), 305.

30. For a discussion of Cather's reluctant but inevitable involvement in "the polemics of the thirties," see Woodress, *Life*, 468–69.

31. Lionel Trilling, "The Case Against Willa Cather," in *Willa Cather and Her Critics*, ed. James Schroeter (Ithaca: Cornell University Press, 1967), 146–47.

32. Slote, "Web," in *Five Essays*, 2. Many writers in the 1930s and 1940s were looking with enthusiasm to the broader community of humankind as America itself became more conscious of its international ties. Harold Stearns reminded readers in *America Now*: "The republic of letters is an international republic. It rests in the faith that humanity is more than a nation, a race, a religious creed, or a system of economics" ("The Intellectual Life," in Stearns, *America Now*, 378). Commenting on the valiant efforts of Leftist forces during the Spanish Civil War, H. G. Wells in his 1940 edition of *The Outline*

of History praised "the human thrust towards that better order of freedom and brother-hood," noting "the common purpose" that is moving us "*towards* a world unification" (*The Outline of History* [1940; reprint, 1949, Garden City, N.Y.: Garden City Books], 1165).

33. Willa Cather, "Escapism," in *On Writing*, 19–22.

34. Ibid., 21 (my italics).

35. Cather, "Rights of Genius," in Slote, *Kingdom*, 142. Compare this assessment of artists by Cather to Blanche Gelfant's remarks on Cather's "clear and clearheaded intention to create a design for living which would allow her solitude in which to write and yet not leave her isolated and lonely." To accomplish this, Gelfant writes, Cather "chose friends who furthered or fitted into this design" (*Women Writing*, 241).

36. Cather, "Escapism," in *On Writing*, 26.

37. Ibid., 19, 29.

38. Cather, "The Best Years," in *Old Beauty and Others*, 104.

39. de Voto, editorial, 20.

40. Willa Cather, "Light on Adobe Walls," in *On Writing*, 125.

41. Bellah et al., *Habits*, 84.

42. See Woodress, *Life*, 502, for a discussion of Cather's feelings about fellow artists in her final years.

43. Yehudi Menuhin, *Unfinished Journey* (New York: Alfred A. Knopf, Inc., 1977), 129. Although I agree that Cather was selective about her community, I find James Schroeter too limited in his view of Cather's selectivity: "Her fraternity of heroes was cosmopolitan and democratic, but it was also terribly exclusive, and you were admitted only if you had shared the early years together." He sees this as the reason for the "faint hostility to the Jew in [Cather's] major literature of the 1920's" (*Willa Cather and Her Critics*, 381). I see her portrayal of Jewish people (Louie Marsellus in *The Professor's House* and Mrs. Rosen in "Old Mrs. Harris") as generally positive (see my discussion of these characters in chaps. 3 and 4, above). I do not find her excluding this group from her community.

44. Willa Cather to Yehudi Menuhin, in *Unfinished Journey*, by Yehudi Menuhin, 130. Despite Cather's restriction in her will against printing her letters, an excerpt from this letter appears in Menuhin's autobiography (Menuhin gives the date of the letter as "early in 1936"); page citations refer to that book.

45. Ibid., 130.

46. See Woodress, *Life*, 493–94, for a helpful description of this extant passage from the destroyed manuscript.

47. The proposed title alone, "Hard Punishments," suggests Cather's preoccupation with governmental or institutional control over the individual. George Kates notes, too, that Cather, inside the back cover of Okey's *The Story of Avignon*, made seven "notations of what became of special importance for her in planning this tale." Two of the words listed are "Law" and "Prisons" ("Willa Cather's Unfinished Avignon Story," in *Five Stories*, by Willa Cather [New York: Vintage Books, 1956], 201–2). In Edith Lewis's account to Kates of Cather's work on this novel, Lewis states:

> Willa Cather was greatly interested in the subject of blasphemy, [which was regarded in the fourteenth century as] . . . not only a sin, but a crime, and was punished by the civil law. . . . Why was it held in such special reprobation? And why, in spite of the risk, did people so often succumb to the temptation to blaspheme? (in Kates, "Avignon Story," 201)

This focus on an individual's refusal to bow to speech restrictions perhaps reflects Cather's concern or preoccupation with restrictions being placed on individual artistic expression in the late 1940s.

48. Sergeant, *Memoir*, 283.

49. Bellah et al., *Habits*, viii.

50. "Today's Novels Give Much Hope to Miss Cather," *New York World*, 21 May 1923, in Bohlke, *Person*, 59. Bernice Slote notes that in Cather's Bible, Cather marked Psalm 30:5: "Weeping may endure for a night, but joy cometh in the morning"—an optimistic sentiment similar to the one Cather expressed in this interview.

51. Cather, "Jewett," in *On Writing*, 56.

Works Cited

Abbott, Jacob. *Histories of Cyrus the Great and Alexander the Great*. Chatauqua Edition. New York: Harper and Brothers, 1880.

Alger, Horatio, Jr. *Ragged Dick and Mark, the Match Boy*. 1867. Reprint. Collier Books Edition. New York: Macmillan Publishing Co., Inc., 1962.

———. *Strive and Succeed, or the Progress of Walter Conrad*. New York: Street and Smith Publishers, 1872.

"American Dream." *The American Heritage Dictionary*. Second College Edition, 1982.

———. *The Random House Dictionary of the English Language*. Second Edition, 1987.

———. *Webster's New World Dictionary of American English*. Third College Edition, 1988.

Anderson, Sherwood. *Puzzled America*. New York: Charles Scribner's Sons, 1935.

Arnold, Marilyn. "Cather's Last Three Stories: A Testament of Life and Endurance." *Great Plains Quarterly* 4 (Fall 1984): 238–44.

Arnold, Matthew. "Stanzas from the Grande Chartreuse." In *Matthew Arnold*, edited by Miriam Allott and Robert H. Super, Oxford Authors Series. Oxford: Oxford University Press, 1986. 159–65.

Asch, Nathan. *The Road: In Search of America*. New York: W. W. Norton and Company, Inc., 1937.

Baum, Bernard. "Willa Cather's Waste Land." *South Atlantic Quarterly* 48 (1949): 589–601.

Beard, Charles. "The Myth of Rugged American Individualism" *Harper's* 164 (December 1931): 13–22.

Bellah, Robert N., Richard Madsen, William M. Sullivan, Ann Swidler, and Steven M. Tipton. *Habits of the Heart: Individualism and Commitment in American Life*. Berkeley: University of California Press, 1985.

Bender, Thomas. *Community and Social Change in America*. New Brunswick, N.J.: Rutgers University Press, 1978.

Bennett, Mildred R. *The World of Willa Cather*. Lincoln: University of Nebraska Press, 1961.

Blake, Casey Nelson. *Beloved Community: The Cultural Criticism of Randolph Bourne, Van Wyck Brooks, Waldo Frank, and Lewis Mumford*. Cultural Studies of the United States. Chapel Hill: The University of North Carolina Press, 1990.

Bledstein, Burton. *The Culture of Professionalism: The Middle Class and the Development of Higher Education in America.* New York: W. W. Norton and Company, Inc., 1976.

Bloom, Edward A. and Lillian D. *Willa Cather's Gift of Sympathy.* Crosscurrents: Modern Critiques. Carbondale: Southern Illinois University Press, 1962.

Bloom, Harold, ed. *Willa Cather.* Modern Critical Views. New York: Chelsea House Publishers, 1985.

Bohlke, L. Brent, ed. *Willa Cather in Person: Interviews, Speeches, and Letters.* Lincoln: University of Nebraska Press, 1986.

Bourne, Randolph. "Trans-National America." *The Atlantic Monthly* 118 (July 1916): 86–97.

———. "Who Owns the Universities?" *New Republic,* 17 July 1915, 269–70.

Brooks, Van Wyck. *America's Coming of Age.* 1915. Reprint. New York: Octagon Books, 1975.

Butcher, Fanny. *Many Lives—One Love.* New York: Harper and Row Publishers, Inc., 1972.

Callander, Marilyn Berg. *Willa Cather and the Fairy Tale.* Ann Arbor, Mich.: UMI Research Press, 1989.

Campbell, Thomas. *The Complete Poetical Works of Thomas Campbell.* Boston: Crosby and Nichols, 1865.

Carnegie, Andrew. "The Gospel of Wealth." In *The Gospel of Wealth and Other Timely Essays,* edited by Edward C. Kirkland, 14–29. Cambridge: The Belknap Press of Harvard University Press, 1962.

Cather, Willa. *Alexander's Bridge.* Introduction by Bernice Slote. Lincoln: University of Nebraska Press, 1977.

———. *Death Comes for the Archbishop.* New York: Vintage Books, 1971.

———. Letter to Zoe Akins, 5 January 1945. Henry E. Huntington Library, San Marino, Calif.

———. Letter to Bernard de Voto, 10 March 1937. Stanford University, Calif.

———. Letter to Sarah Orne Jewett, 19 December 1908. Houghton Library, Harvard University, Mass.

———. *A Lost Lady.* New York: Vintage Books, 1972.

———. *Lucy Gayheart.* New York: Vintage Books, 1976.

———. *My Ántonia.* Boston: Houghton Mifflin Company, Sentry Edition, 1954.

———. *My Mortal Enemy.* New York: Vintage Books, 1954.

———. "Nebraska: The End of the First Cycle." *Nation* 117 (5 September 1923): 236–38.

———. *Not Under Forty.* New York: Alfred A. Knopf, Inc., 1964.

———. *O Pioneers!* Boston: Houghton Mifflin Company, Sentry Edition, 1941.

———. *Obscure Destinies.* New York: Vintage Books, 1974.

———. *The Old Beauty and Others.* New York: Vintage Books, 1976.

———. *On Writing.* Lincoln: University of Nebraska Press, 1976.

———. *One of Ours.* New York: Vintage Books, 1971.

———. *The Professor's House.* New York: Vintage Books, 1973.

———. *Sapphira and the Slave Girl.* New York: Vintage Books, 1977.

————. *Shadows on the Rock*. New York: Vintage Books, 1971.

————. *The Song of the Lark*. Boston: Houghton Mifflin Company, Sentry Edition, 1943.

————. *The Troll Garden*. Edited by James Woodress. Lincoln: University of Nebraska Press, 1983.

————. *A Biographical Sketch, an English Opinion, Reviews and Articles Concerning her Later Books and an Abridged Bibliography*. 1933. Reprint. Folcroft, Pa.: The Folcroft Press, Inc., 1975.

Cawelti, John G. *Apostles of the Self-Made Man*. Chicago: The University of Chicago Press, 1965.

Chamberlain, John. "Literature." In *America Now: An Inquiry into Civilization in the United States*, edited by Harold E. Stearns, 36–47. New York: Charles Scribner's Sons, 1938.

Chenoweth, Lawrence. *The American Dream of Success: The Search for the Self in the Twentieth Century*. North Scituate, Mass.: Duxbury Press, 1974.

————. "Willa Cather and the Populists." *Great Plains Quarterly* 3 (1983): 206–18.

Commager, Henry Steele. *The American Mind: An Interpretation of American Thought and Character Since the 1880's*. New Haven: Yale University Press, 1950.

Cowley, Malcolm. *Exile's Return*. 1934. Reprint. New York: The Viking Press, Inc., 1951.

Croly, Herbert. *The Promise of American Life*. New York: MacMillan Publishing Company, Inc., 1909.

Curtin, William, ed. *The World and the Parish: Willa Cather's Articles and Reviews, 1893–1902*. 2 vols. Lincoln: University of Nebraska Press, 1970.

Daiches, David. *Willa Cather: A Critical Introduction*. Ithaca: Cornell University Press, 1951.

de Voto, Bernard. Editorial. *Saturday Review of Literature* 13 February 1937, 8, 20.

Dewey, John. *Freedom and Culture*. New York: G. P. Putnam's Sons, 1939.

————. *Individualism Old and New*. New York: Minton, Balch & Company, 1929.

Dowson, Ernest. "Non Sum Qualis Eram Bonae Sub Regno Cynarae." In *The Poetry of Ernest Dowson*, edited by Desmond Flower, 52. Rutherford, N.J.: Farleigh Dickinson University Press, 1970.

Dreiser, Theodore. *The Financier*. 1912. Reprint. Cleveland: World Publishing Company, 1946.

Edel, Leon. "Willa Cather." In *Notable American Women, 1607–1950: A Biographical Dictionary*, edited by Edward T. James. Vol. 1. Cambridge: Harvard University Press, 1971.

————. *Willa Cather: The Paradox of Success*. Washington, D. C.: Library of Congress, 1960.

Eliot, T. S. *Collected Poems, 1909–1962*. New York: Harcourt, Brace, and World, Inc., 1963.

Elliott, Emory, ed. *Columbia Literary History of the United States*. New York: Columbia University Press, 1988.

Fischer, Mike. "Pastoralism and its Discontents: Willa Cather and the Burden of Imperialism." *Mosaic* 23 (Winter 1990): 31–44.

Fisher-Wirth, Ann W. "Dispossession and Redemption in the Novels of Willa Cather."

In *Cather Studies*, edited by Susan J. Rosowski, 1:36–54. Lincoln: University of Nebraska Press, 1990.

Fitzgerald, F. Scott. *The Great Gatsby*. New York: Charles Scribner's Sons, 1925.

Folsom, James. "Willa Cather." In *Twentieth-Century Western Writers*, edited by James Vinson, 150–53. New York: MacMillan, 1982.

Frank, Waldo. *The Re-discovery of America: An Introduction to a Philosophy of American Life*. New York: Charles Scribner's Sons, 1929.

Geismar, Maxwell. *Rebels and Ancestors*. Boston: Houghton Mifflin Company, 1953.

Gelfant, Blanche. *Women Writing in America: Voices in Collage*. Hanover, N.H.: University Press of New England, 1984.

Gerber, Philip L. *Willa Cather*. Boston: Twayne Publishers, 1975.

Gilbert, Sandra, and Susan Gubar. *No Man's Land: The Place of the Woman Writer in the Twentieth Century*. Vol. 2: "Sexchanges." New Haven: Yale University Press, 1988.

Hearn, Charles. *The American Dream in the Great Depression*. Contributions in American Studies, No. 28. Westport, Conn.: Greenwood Press, 1977.

Heyeck, Robin and James Woodress. "Willa Cather's Cuts and Revisions in *The Song of the Lark*." *Modern Fiction Studies* 25 (Winter 1979–80): 651–58.

Hinz, Evelyn J. "Willa Cather's Technique and the Ideology of Populism." *Western American Literature* 7 (1972): 47–61.

Howells, William Dean. *Criticism and Fiction and Other Essays*. Edited by Clara Marburg Kirk and Rudolf Kirk. New York: New York University Press, 1959.

Huber, Richard M. *The American Idea of Success*. New York: McGraw-Hill, Inc., 1971.

James, William. *The Letters of William James*. Edited by Henry James, Jr. Boston: Little, Brown, and Company, 1926.

———. *The Moral Philosophy of William James*. Edited by John K. Roth. New York: Apollo Editions, 1969.

Jewett, Sarah Orne. *Letters of Sarah Orne Jewett*. Edited by Annie Fields. Boston: Houghton Mifflin Company, 1911.

Kates, George. "Willa Cather's Unfinished Avignon Story." In *Five Stories*, by Willa Cather, 177–214. New York: Vintage Books, 1956.

Kazin, Alfred. *Starting Out in the Thirties*. New York: Vintage Books, 1980.

Kronenberger, Louis. "In Dubious Battle." Review of *Not Under Forty*, by Willa Cather. *Nation* 143 (19 December 1936): 738.

Lasch, Christopher. *The True and Only Heaven: Progress and Its Critics*. New York: W. W. Norton and Company, Inc., 1991.

Lears, Jackson. *No Place of Grace: Antimodernism and the Transformation of American Culture, 1880–1920*. New York: Pantheon Books, 1981.

Lee, Hermione. *Will Cather: Double Lives*. New York: Pantheon Books, 1989.

Lewis, Edith. *Willa Cather Living*. 1953. Reprint. New York: Alfred A. Knopf, Inc., 1976.

Lewis, Sinclair. *Babbitt*. Signet Classics Edition. New York: The New American Library, 1963.

———. "The American Fear of Literature." In *The Man From Main Street: A Sinclair Lewis Reader*, edited by Harry E. Maule and Melville H. Cane, 3–17. New York: Random House, 1953.

Lingeman, Richard. *Theodore Dreiser: An American Journey*. 2 vols. New York: G. P. Putnam's Sons, 1990.

Love, Glen A. *The New Americans: The Westerner and the Modern Experience in the American Novel.* Lewisburg, Pa.: Bucknell University Press, 1982.

Lynn, Kenneth S. *The Dream of Success: A Study of the Modern American Imagination.* Boston: Little, Brown, and Company, 1955.

McElvaine, Robert S. *The Great Depression: America, 1929–41.* New York: Times Books, 1984.

MacLeish, Archibald. "Bubble of Blue Air." In *Riders on the Earth: Essays and Recollections*, xiii–xiv. Boston: Houghton Mifflin Company, 1978.

Marchand, Roland. *Advertising the American Dream: Making Way for Modernity, 1920–1940.* Berkeley: University of California Press, 1985.

Menuhin, Yehudi. *Unfinished Journey.* New York: Alfred A. Knopf, Inc., 1977.

Michaels, Walter Benn. "The Vanishing American." *American Literary History* 2 (Summer 1990): 220–41.

Moers, Ellen. *Literary Women: The Great Writers.* Garden City, N.Y.: Doubleday and Company, Inc., 1976.

———. "The Survivors: Into the Twentieth Century." *Twentieth Century Literature* 20 (January 1974): 1–10.

Mumford, Lewis. "The Emergence of a Past." *New Republic,* 25 November 1925, 18–19.

———. "What I Believe." *Forum* 84 (November 1930): 263–68.

Murphy, John J. "Willa Cather and Catholic Themes." *Western American Literature* 17 (Spring 1982): 53–60.

———, ed. *Critical Essays on Willa Cather.* Boston: G. K. Hall & Company, 1984.

———, ed. *Willa Cather: Family, Community, and History.* The BYU Symposium. Provo, Utah: The Brigham Young University Humanities Publications Center, 1990.

Norris, Frank. "The Frontier Gone at Last." In *The Call of the Wild: 1900–1916*, edited by Roderick Nash. 69–78. The American Culture VI.1902. Reprint. New York: George Braziller, 1970.

O'Brien, Sharon. "Combat Envy and Survivor Guilt: Willa Cather's 'Manly Battle Yarn.'" In *Arms and the Woman: War, Gender, and Literary Representation*, edited by Helen M. Cooper, Adrienne Auslander Munich, and Susan Merrill Squier, 184–204. Chapel Hill: University of North Carolina Press, 1989.

———. "Mothers, Daughters, and the 'Art Necessity': Willa Cather and the Creative Process." In *American Novelists Revisited: Essays in Feminist Criticism,* edited by Fritz Fleischmann, 265–98. Boston: G. K. Hall, 1982.

———. *Willa Cather: The Emerging Voice.* New York: Oxford University Press, 1987.

"On Lack of Conscience As a Means of Success." Editorial. *Century* 40 (July 1890): 474.

Orvell, Miles. *The Real Thing: Imitation and Authenticity in American Culture, 1880–1940.* Cultural Studies of the United States. Chapel Hill: The University of North Carolina Press, 1989.

Pater, Walter. *The Renaissance: Studies in Art and Poetry.* Edited by Donald L. Hill. Berkeley: University of California Press, 1980.

Peeler, David P. *Hope Among Us Yet: Social Criticism and Social Solace in Depression America.* Athens: University of Georgia Press, 1987.

Pells, Richard. *Radical Vision and American Dreams: Culture and Social Thought in the Depression Years.* New York: Harper and Row Publishers, Inc., 1973.

Pole, J. R. "Individualism and Conformity." In *Encyclopedia of American Political His-*

tory: Studies of the Principal Movements and Ideas. Vol. 2, edited by Jack P. Greene, 622–635. New York: Charles Scribner's Sons, 1984.

Quirk, Tom. *Bergson and American Culture: The Worlds of Willa Cather and Wallace Stevens*. Chapel Hill: University of North Carolina Press, 1990.

Randall, John. *The Landscape and the Looking Glass: Willa Cather's Search for Value*. Boston: Houghton Mifflin Company, 1960.

Rieff, Philip. "The Emergence of Psychological Man." In *Freud: The Mind of the Moralist*, 329–57. New York: The Viking Press, Inc., 1959.

————. *The Triumph of the Therapeutic: Uses of Faith after Freud*. New York: Harper and Row Publishers, Inc., 1966.

Rogers, Daniel. *The Work Ethic in Industrial America, 1850–1920*. Chicago: The University of Chicago Press, 1978.

Rose, Phyllis. "The Case of Willa Cather." In *Modernism Reconsidered*, edited by Robert Kiely, 123–45. English Studies 11. Cambridge: Harvard University Press, 1983.

Rosowski, Susan J. *The Voyage Perilous: Willa Cather's Romanticism*. Lincoln: University of Nebraska Press, 1986.

————. "Willa Cather and the Fatality of Place: *O Pioneers!*, *My Ántonia*, and *A Lost Lady*." In *Geography and Literature: A Meeting of the Disciplines*, edited by William E. Mallory and Paul Simpson-Housley, 81–94. Syracuse: Syracuse University Press, 1987.

————. "Willa Cather's *A Lost Lady*: Art Versus the Closing Frontier." *Great Plains Quarterly* 2 (Fall 1982): 239–48.

————. "Willa Cather's *A Lost Lady*: The Paradoxes of Change." *Novel* 11 (Fall 1977): 51–62.

————. "Willa Cather's Female Landscapes: *The Song of the Lark* and *Lucy Gayheart*." *Women's Studies* 11 (1984): 233–46.

Roth, John K. *American Dreams: Meditations on Life in the United States*. San Francisco: Chandler & Sharp Publishers, 1976.

Royce, Josiah. *The Letters of Josiah Royce*. Edited by John Clendenning. Chicago: University of Chicago Press, 1970.

————. *The Philosophy of Loyalty*. *The Philosophy of Josiah Royce*. Edited by John K. Roth. New York: Apollo Editions, 1971.

Santayana, George. *Character and Opinion in the United States*. New York: Charles Scribner's Sons, 1920.

Scharnhorst, Gary, with Jack Bates. *The Lost Life of Horatio Alger, Jr.* Bloomington: Indiana University Press, 1985.

Schroeter, James, ed. *Willa Cather and Her Critics*. Ithaca: Cornell University Press, 1967.

Sergeant, Elizabeth Shepley. *Willa Cather, A Memoir*. 1953. Reprint. Philadelphia: J. B. Lippincott, 1963.

Skaggs, Merrill Maguire. *After the World Broke in Two: The Later Novels of Willa Cather*. Charlottesville: University Press of Virginia, 1990.

Slote, Bernice. "An Appointment with the Future: Willa Cather." In *The Twenties: Fiction, Poetry, Drama*, edited by Warren French, 39–40. Deland, Fla.: Everett/Edwards, Inc., 1975.

————. Introduction. *"Uncle Valentine" and Other Stories: Willa Cather's Uncollected Short Fiction, 1915–29*. Lincoln: University of Nebraska Press, 1973.

————. "Willa Cather and Plains Culture." In *Vision and Refuge: Essays on the Literature of the Great Plains*, edited by Virginia Faulkner with Frederick C. Luebke, 93–105. Lincoln: University of Nebraska Press, 1982.

————. "Willa Cather: The Secret Web." In *Five Essays on Willa Cather: The Merrimack Symposium*, edited by John J. Murphy, 1–19. North Andover, Mass.: Merrimack College, 1974.

————, ed. *The Kingdom of Art: Willa Cather's First Principles and Critical Statements*. Lincoln: University of Nebraska Press, 1967.

————, and Virginia Faulkner, eds. *The Art of Willa Cather*. Lincoln: University of Nebraska Press, 1974.

Smith, Page. *America Enters the World: A People's History of the Progressive Era and World War I*. Vol. 7. New York: McGraw-Hill, Inc., 1985.

————. *Redeeming the Time: A People's History of the 1920's and the New Deal*. Vol. 8. New York: McGraw-Hill, Inc., 1987.

Stauffer, Helen Winter and Susan J. Rosowski. *Women and Western American Literature*. Troy, N.Y.: The Whitson Publishing Co., 1982.

Stearns, Harold. "The Intellectual Life." In *America Now: An Inquiry into Civilization in the United States*, edited by Harold E. Stearns, 373–82. New York: Charles Scribner's Sons, 1938.

Steinman, Lisa M. *Made in America: Science, Technology, and American Modernist Poets*. New Haven: Yale University Press, 1987.

Stouck, David. "Willa Cather and the Indian Heritage." *Twentieth Century Literature* 22 (December 1976): 433–43.

————. "Willa Cather and *The Professor's House*: 'Letting Go with the Heart.'" *Western American Literature* 7 (1972): 13–24.

————. *Willa Cather's Imagination*. Lincoln: University of Nebraska Press, 1975.

Susman, Warren I. *Culture as History: The Transformation of American Society in the Twentieth Century*. New York: Pantheon Books, 1984.

Tanner, Stephen L. "Seeking and Finding in Cather's *My Mortal Enemy*." *Literature and Belief* 8 (1988): 27–38.

Terkel, Studs. *Hard Times: An Oral History of the Great Depression*. New York: Washington Square Press, 1970.

Thacker, Robert. *The Great Prairie Fact and the Literary Imagination*. Albuquerque: University of New Mexico Press, 1989.

Trachtenberg, Alan. *The Incorporation of America: Culture and Society in the Gilded Age*. American Century Series. New York: Hill and Wang, 1982.

Urgo, Joseph R. "How Context Determines Fact: Historicism in Willa Cather's *A Lost Lady*." *Studies in American Fiction* 17 (Autumn 1989): 183–92.

Wasserman, Loretta. *Willa Cather: A Study of the Short Fiction*. Twayne's Studies in Short Fiction 19. Boston: Twayne Publishers, 1991.

————. "The Music of Time: Henri Bergson and Willa Cather." *American Literature* 57 (May 1985): 226–39.

Weiss, Richard. *The American Myth of Success: From Horatio Alger to Norman Vincent Peale*. New York: Basic Books, Inc., 1969.

Wells, H. G. *The Outline of History*. Garden City, N.Y.: Garden City Books, 1949.

Whitman, Walt. *Democratic Vistas, and Other Papers*. 1871. Reprint. St. Clair Shores, Mich.: Scholarly Press, 1970.

————. Preface to 1855 Edition of *Leaves of Grass*. In *The American Tradition in Literature*, edited by George Perkins et al. 14–27. 6th ed. New York: Random House, 1985.

Wiebe, Robert H. *The Search for Order, 1877–1920*. The Making of America. America Century Series. New York: Hill and Wang, 1967.

————. *Willa Cather: A Literary Life*. Lincoln: University of Nebraska Press, 1987.

————. "Writing Cather's Biography." In *Cather Studies*, edited by Susan J. Rosowski, 1:103–14. Lincoln: University of Nebraska Press, 1990.

Yongue, Patricia Lee. *"A Lost Lady*: The End of the First Cycle." *Western American Literature* 7 (1972): 3–12.

————. "Willa Cather's Aristocrats" (Parts I and II). *Southern Humanities Review* 14 (Winter, Spring 1980): 43–56, 111–25.

Zabel, Morton. "The Tone of the Time." Review of *Sapphira and the Slave Girl*, by Willa Cather. *Nation* 151 (7 December 1940): 574–76.

Zamora, Lois Parkinson. "The Usable Past: The Idea of History in Modern U. S. and Latin American Fiction." In *Do the Americas Have a Common Literature?*, edited by Gustavo Perez Firmat, 7–38. Durham, N.C.: Duke University Press, 1990.

Index